THE *PAST & PRESENT* BO

General Editor
ALICE RIO

The Society of Prisoners

The Society of Prisoners

*Anglo-French Wars and Incarceration
in the Eighteenth Century*

RENAUD MORIEUX

OXFORD
UNIVERSITY PRESS

OXFORD
UNIVERSITY PRESS

Great Clarendon Street, Oxford, OX2 6DP,
United Kingdom

Oxford University Press is a department of the University of Oxford.
It furthers the University's objective of excellence in research, scholarship,
and education by publishing worldwide. Oxford is a registered trade mark of
Oxford University Press in the UK and in certain other countries

First published 2019
First published in paperback 2022

Published in the United States of America by Oxford University Press
198 Madison Avenue, New York, NY 10016, United States of America

British Library Cataloguing in Publication Data
Data available

Library of Congress Cataloging in Publication Data
Data available

ISBN 978–0–19–872358–5 (Hbk.)
ISBN 978–0–19–286803–9 (Pbk.)

DOI: 10.1093/oso/9780198723585.001.0001

Acknowledgements

The process of preparing this book has been lengthy, tortuous, and uneven. The project has been with me, more or less, for over a decade. I would like to think that I took my time because I was maturing, like an old whisky, but the reality is that many things (mostly good things!) got in the way, on the personal and professional fronts.

In my experience, the history of a book is necessarily also the history of the people one encounters. In this sense, this book has been a hugely rewarding endeavour. I owe a great debt to countless friends and colleagues.

First of all there are those who have read the whole manuscript, whose comments and suggestions have been invaluable: Quentin Deluermoz, Joanna Innes, Jean-Pierre Jessenne, Antoine Lilti, and the three anonymous readers from OUP and the *Past & Present* series. I also want to thank the series editor Alice Rio and OUP editor Cathryn Steele, who have been a pleasure to work with.

I am grateful too to those who have read and commented on substantial parts of the book: Catherine Arnold, Andrew Arsan, Gareth Atkins, David Bell, Christopher Burlinson, Ben Crewe, Peter Garnsey, Paul Halliday, Julian Hoppit, Margaret Hunt, Pieter Judson, Mary Laven, Peter Mandler, Natividad Planas, Surabhi Ranganathan, and Charles Walton. Over the years, I have discussed my project with many, including (and there were others): John Arnold, Eyal Benvenisti, Maxine Berg, John Brewer, Vincent Brown, Alain Cabantous, Erica Charters, Chris Clark, Linda Colley, Stephen Conway, Michael Edwards, Catherine Evans, Bronwen Everill, Joel Felix, Joel Isaac, Sam James, Colin Jones, Sara Johnson, Duncan Kelly, Larry Klein, Isaac Nakhimovsky, Surabhi Ranganathan, Nick Ray, Jake Richards, John Robertson, Emma Rothschild, Hamish Scott, Simon Schaffer, Sujit Sivasundaram, Leigh Shaw-Taylor, Hillary Taylor, Frank Trentmann, Richard Tuck, Michael Waibel, Alex Walsham, Daniel Widener, Nuala Zahedieh, and Jean-Paul Zuniga. I also want to express my gratitude to the researchers who have generously shared sources or references with me: Callum Easton, Linda and Marsha Frey, Ben Gilding, Aaron Graham, Julian Hoppit, Simon McDonald, Annika Raapke, Nick Ray, Michael Roberts, John Shovlin, and Andrew Thompson. Colleagues and friends at the Cambridge Faculty of History and at Jesus College have provided me with constant support.

I have presented papers on the topic at the Modern British History and the Modern Cultural History seminars in Cambridge, the Diaspora Studies seminar in Edinburgh, the European University Institute in Florence, the Centre for History and Economics seminar in Harvard, the Economic and Social History and the French History seminars at the Institute of Historical Research in London, the Graduate Seminar in History in Oxford, the 'Histoire transnationale et globale de la France' seminar at the Ecole Normale Supérieure in Paris, the Eighteenth-Century seminar at Princeton, the Reformation and Early Modern seminar at St Andrews, and the Global History seminar at Warwick. I would like to thank the organizers and the audiences whose insightful comments have helped me refine my arguments.

I was fortunate to have been awarded a Philip Leverhulme Prize in 2014, which allowed me to take a research sabbatical for two years. I am very grateful to the Leverhulme Trust for this opportunity to conduct my research in privileged conditions. I have been able to use the expertise of research assistants Baptiste Bonnefoy, Sara Caputo, Philip Loft, Drishti Ramdewa, and Hanna Woods: I give them my warm thanks. I spent two very productive months at the Centre for History and Economics at Harvard, where I was a Visiting Fellow in the spring of 2017, thanks to the support of Emma Rothschild. I also benefited from an early-career fellowship at CRASSH in Cambridge in 2014.

Finally, I want to thank my son Oscar, whose tireless curiosity for prisoners' escapes would worry any other parent, and Philippine, who gently and lovingly nudged me across the finishing line.

Parts of chapters 2, 5, and 6 have previously appeared in print, in the *Historical Journal*, 56 (2013), in Laurent Bourquin et al. (eds.), *Le patriotisme par les armes* (2014), and in John Arnold et al. (eds.), *History after Hobsbawm* (2017).

Contents

List of illustrations

Book cover

Gueydon, Henry de, *Vue de l'intérieure de Mill-Prison de Plymouth et de ses environs en 1798* (1798). Anne S.K. Brown Military Collection, Brown University Library.

Charts

List of Abbreviations

BFBS   British and Foreign Bible Society
CTP   Council of Trade and Plantations
LCA   Lords of the Admiralty
S&W   Office of the Commissioners for the Sick & Wounded Seamen and Prisoners of War (Sick & Wounded Board)
SSM   Secrétaire d'Etat de la Marine
TB   Transport Board
TO   Transport Office

Note on Text

Emphasis and punctuation as in original unless otherwise stated.
All translations from the French are mine unless otherwise stated.

Introduction

A few days after war was declared between France and Britain, in February 1793, the inhabitants of the Devon town of Ashburton decided to reward those of their parishioners who would voluntarily enlist in the navy or the army by giving them a bounty. The money, which was to be raised by subscription, would be divided among the widows and children of the men who might be killed during the war. The inhabitants proclaimed their patriotism, expressing their desire 'to avenge in a signal manner the Cause of Justice and humanity which has been so cruelly insulted' by France, and hoped that other British cities would emulate Ashburton's example. Seventy-one individuals, including seven women, signed the resolution, which was sent to the British government and published in local and national papers.[1] Four years later, when the war was still raging, a petition from the 'Principal Inhabitants' of Ashburton, dated 4 September 1797, was addressed to the Commissioners of the Transport Board, the administration in charge of prisoners of war.[2] The twenty-seven individuals who signed this document, including many who had written the 1793 resolution, objected to the government's decision to remove the prisoners on parole in Ashburton to Tiverton. They outlined a variety of reasons to justify keeping these foreigners in the local community. In particular, the petitioners praised the behaviour of the Frenchmen:

> Notwithstanding the very great number of French prisoners here on parole the majority of whom, are men of the lowest Class perfectly illiterate, such has been there general Demeanour that so far from having had reason to complain of them, that on a late occasion in consequence of a dreadfull fire taking place here in the course of the night, such were their active Exertions and such their Services, that we convey'd to them our public Thanks for their Conduct, as the only recompences we could with propriety make them.

These prisoners also represented a valuable resource in a time of scarcity. Ashburton, it was argued, had experienced 'considerable diminution of its Trade' due to the war. Should the prisoners be removed, 'a large Class of People', who were

---

[1] 'Bounties to Seamen At Ashburton', 16 February 1793, *Devon Notes*, pp. 197–8.
[2] Because this book argues that the form this institution took in the eighteenth century is original, and to avoid implicit analogies with the twentieth century, I avoid the contemporary acronym 'POW' throughout.

The Society of Prisoners: Anglo-French Wars and Incarceration in the Eighteenth Century. Renaud Morieux, Oxford University Press (2019). © Renaud Morieux. DOI: 10.1093/oso/9780198723585.001.0001

not receiving parochial assistance, would be deprived of the supplementary income they made by hiring their lodgings to the Frenchmen.[3] The Transport Board replied that its decision had been motivated by security issues, as the town was judged to be too close to Plymouth, one of the two main ports and shipyards in the country. The other reason put forward by the Board was 'to remove entirely all further Ground of those Disputes and Complaints, which have of late unpleasantly existed relative to the Prisoners & their Situation'.[4] The inhabitants asked the Board to reconsider its decision. They pointed out that Ashburton had accommodated prisoners on parole in previous conflicts and defended themselves against the accusation that they had 'any private attachment to Frenchmen or French Principles', arguing that the public good was their only preoccupation, underlining the success of the subscription for sailors started in 1793.[5]

As this example illustrates, the prisoner of war inhabits a third space between friendship and enmity, a twilight zone between two worlds.[6] Philosopher Michael Walzer writes about 'the limbo of statelessness', a metaphor which suggests a state of in-betweenness.[7] This book aims at understanding this peculiar social institution, and the specific form it took in the eighteenth century.

I. War Captivity: A 'Fragile' Social Institution

Defining the social boundaries of war captivity depended on how one defined both war and the enemy. For this reason, deciding which groups were legitimate prisoners of war was always contested. War captivity, as a social institution, was thus inherently 'fragile'[8]—not because it was imperfect, but because these structural tensions ran within it.

The perspective chosen here echoes, without strictly replicating, a historiographical change that has been described as the move from military history to the history of war. These labels designate a general shift in scholarship, with the focus turning to the impact of war on societies, and not simply the (much-maligned) study of grand strategy, battles, and the armed forces. The scholarly attention given to the experience of civilians has, for instance, led to a reconsideration of the relations between the home front and the combat zone, with a focus on veterans or women, deserters, and the wounded.[9] Captivity is a particularly fruitful domain of

---

[3] Copy of petition from the 'Principal Inhabitants' of Ashburton to Transport Office (TO), 4 September 1797, The National Archives, Kew (TNA), ADM1/5125.

[4] TO, 7 September 1797, ibid. An anonymous letter was apparently the cause of these allegations.

[5] Henry Gervis (one of the petitioners), to Transport Board, 19 September 1797, ibid. See also 'A Memorial of the Clergy Chief Magistrates, and other principal Inhabitants of the Town of Ashburton in the County of Devon' to Lords of the Admiralty (LCA), 19 September 1797, ibid.

[6] Calloway, 'Indian captivities', p. 208.   [7] Walzer, 'Prisoners of war', APSR, p. 777.

[8] Douglas, How Institutions, p. 49.

[9] Kroener, 'Modern state'; Charters, Rosenhaft, and Smith, Civilians.

research that has been opened up by this new socio-cultural approach to the history of war in the twentieth century.[10]

By comparison, the study of prisoners of war in the eighteenth century has long been dominated by 'traditional' military history. The rules of exchange of prisoners that were institutionalized in bilateral meetings have been studied from the perspective of their impact on strategy, while the administrative history of specific state institutions dealing with prisoners of war has also been undertaken.[11] The 'French Wars' of 1793–1815 predominate histories of warfare over this timespan,[12] with a never-ending fascination for the sinister hulks (the prison-ships which held the French prisoners) and Napoleon's cruelty towards his captives.[13] More recently, the American War of Independence has also attracted the attention of historians, who have used war imprisonment as a lens through which to study the rise of a patriotic consciousness among the insurgents.[14] The field is undoubtedly changing, with new and exciting work being conducted on literacy, cultures of honour, the history of medicine, and confinement.[15]

Sociologist Siniša Malešević defines warfare as a 'social institution that involves organisation, ritualism, group mobilisation, social hierarchy and many other social prerequisites'.[16] Applying this label to war captivity in the eighteenth century makes sense. While this book focuses on Franco-British wars, it has, I hope, broader implications. War captivity is an ideal observatory to address three interrelated questions. First, is it so clear what a prisoner of war was in the eighteenth century, from a legal viewpoint? Second, war captivity is a state institution: what does it tell us about what the eighteenth-century state was, how it transformed itself, and why it endured? The third approach could be termed a social history of international relations. The aim here is to understand how eighteenth-century societies were affected by war: how the detention of foreign enemies on home soil revealed and challenged social values, representations, hierarchies, and practices.

II. What Was a Prisoner of War? The Normative Framework and Its Limitations

The perspective chosen in this book involves focusing on the murky background *before* modern understandings of international law. I do not propose a basic

---

[10] Becker, *Oubliés*; Cochet, *Soldats*; Fishman, *We Will Wait*; Jones, *Violence*; Rachamimov, *POWs*; MacKenzie, 'Treatment'.

[11] Anderson, 'Establishment'; Charters, 'Administration'; Wilson, 'Prisoners'; Lagadec, Le Prat, and Perréon, 'Un aspect'.

[12] See, for example, Chamberlain, *Hell*; Daly, 'Lost legions'; Le Carvèse, 'Prisonniers'; Marquis, 'Convention'. Francis Abell's book covers a longer period, but he does not indicate its sources: *Prisoners of War*.

[13] Lewis, *Napoleon*; Masson, *Sépulcres*.

[14] See, for example, Knight, 'Prisoner exchange'; Miller, *Dangerous Guests*; Burrows, *Forgotten Patriots*.

[15] Charters, *Disease*; Duché, 'Passage'; Leunig, van Lottum, and Poulsen, 'Surprisingly gentle'.

[16] Malešević, *Sociology of War*, p. 92.

diachronic account of the development of that 'law'—documenting the 'birth' of the 'POW', from Grotius through Vattel and the Lieber Code on the proper treatment of civilians and prisoners of war (1860), all the way to the Hague (1907) and Geneva Conventions (1864 and 1906).[17] In other words, rather than an implied modern telos, which sees the modern international law with respect to prisoners of war unfold from the eighteenth century onwards, this is an account that assumes that the state, and especially the state-at-war, remains full of contradictions, reversals, and hybrid arrangements, even up to the present day.[18] This approach is influenced by the work of legal historians such as Lauren Benton and Paul Halliday, who emphasize the need to guard ourselves against triumphalist and purely normative legal histories.[19]

The history of the laws of war and the laws of nation in the eighteenth century is well-trodden ground. This is not the place to rewrite this history; my purpose is rather to shed light on a process beginning in the sixteenth century, which shaped the figure of the prisoner of war as it came to be understood in the eighteenth century, as a protected status. This period has been described as the heyday of the humanization or taming of war, illustrating the Enlightenment 'consensus' on cosmopolitanism.[20] The intellectual origins of this process are linked to the laws of war, as they were formulated by scholastic jurists in the sixteenth and seventeenth centuries. These men displayed new sensibilities about cruelty to the enemy and, more generally, to unarmed persons such as women, travellers, or clergymen—those whom Alberico Gentili called *innocentes*.[21] The decline of just war theory, which was sidelined by the emerging law of nations, gave rise to the belief that civilized nations should fight 'humane' or 'moderate' warfare. By the eighteenth century, this idea had become consensual among legal writers and philosophers.[22] The concept of the prisoner of war, as it emerged in this period, meant that once defeated enemy combatants had laid down their weapons, they should normally not be killed or enslaved; they must be kept in custody (in prison or not), and should be exchanged during the war or released at the end of war.[23] As Emer de Vattel put it in 1760, 'prisoners may be put into confinement, and even fettered if there be reason to apprehend that they will rise on their captors, or make their escape. But they are not to be treated harshly', because 'they are men, and unfortunate'.[24] The life of the prisoner was placed, as it were, in the hands of the captor state, which entered into a contractual agreement with the enemy state, based on reciprocal obligations to treat prisoners 'humanely'.

---

[17] Witt, *Lincoln's Code*.   [18] Rosas, *Legal Status*.
[19] Benton, *Search*; Halliday, *Habeas Corpus*.
[20] Best, *Humanity*, p. 46; Howard, *Laws of War*.   [21] Duchhardt, 'War', pp. 286–8.
[22] Zurbuchen, 'Vattel's *law of nations*'; Tuck, *Rights of War*, pp. 67, 171–2.
[23] The idea that a captive taken in a just war was a legitimate slave prevailed for centuries: Witt, *Lincoln's Code*, pp. 29–31; Drescher, *Abolition*, pp. 10–14, 16–17, 19.
[24] Vattel, *Law of Nations*, book III, ch. 8, par. 150.

The only legitimate agents, in the law of nations, were sovereign states. By contrast with the Middle Ages, when war was an extension of private feuds, it was now described as a relationship between states and professional armies.[25] Monarchical states had managed to monopolize violence.[26] The consequences for prisoners of war were manifold. They were not to be held responsible for decisions made by their sovereigns: they were neither 'guilty' nor 'criminals'. And they were no longer the private property of their captors.[27] It was the state's duty to protect the life of 'their' prisoners and care for them. It is often considered that these ideas, despite some initial uncertainties, began to be implemented at the start of the early-modern era, when armies became more professional, disciplined, and respectful of civilian populations.[28]

This account is problematic, firstly, because the coherence of the law of nations should not be overemphasized. Not all legal writers agreed with regard to the actual rights that should be granted to prisoners of war. Grotius' writings on the topic were 'full of contradictions and logical inconsistencies', arguing on the one hand that 'a considerable degree of arbitrary action' towards prisoners was allowable, while also calling for 'tempered warfare' and restraints.[29] In our period, the laws of war belonged to the realm of customary law, rather than the law codified in treaties between states, and they were arguably a mess of contingencies and exceptions. Hersch Lauterpacht thus wrote that 'if international law is, in some ways, at the vanishing point of law, the law of war is, perhaps even more conspicuously, at the vanishing point of international law'.[30] The law of the sea, which was a strand of the law of nations, was notoriously complex and difficult to understand. In the end, more than the writings of legal writers, the codes of conduct adopted by soldiers and sailors themselves may have been the main driver behind the limitation of violence.[31]

There is a strong case, then, for re-examining the legal norms that governed the treatment of captives. Emphasis must be placed on how war captivity actually worked, and not only how it was legitimized.[32] The categorization of captives was a very practical issue; from this perspective, was there a distinctive nature of war imprisonment vis-à-vis other forms of captivity? I argue that prisoners of war need to be placed alongside other, cognate categories. We must also question the specificity of a European or perhaps Franco-British culture of warfare and captivity—instead of assuming its existence at the outset—by examining the spaces and scales of captivity. When one looks at actual situations of detention, the definitions of war and peace themselves can be questioned.

---

[25] Duchhardt, 'War', p. 280; Neff, *War*, p. 101; Whitman, *Verdict*.
[26] Whitman, *Verdict*, pp. 133–71.   [27] Neff, *War*, pp. 114–15.
[28] Duffy, *Military Experience*.   [29] Duchhardt, 'War', pp. 288, 291.
[30] Lauterpacht, 'Problem', p. 382.   [31] Donagan, 'Codes'.
[32] This is not to say that legal theory and legal practices and customs are necessarily antithetical: Benton, *Search*, pp. 121, 157–60; Halliday, 'Law's histories'.

A. Categorizing the Prisoner of War

Who was, effectively, made a prisoner of war, according to what criteria, and did these definitions evolve over the course of the century? While the distinctions between foreigner and national and between combatant and non-combatant are central, in contemporary definitions, in determining who can be labelled as a prisoner of war, in the eighteenth century this very vocabulary was emerging and changing. For example, the parole of honour, one of the privileges awarded to some prisoners, was not a pure replication of a medieval practice: beyond officers, many groups aspired to this privilege, and its social perimeters fluctuated depending on the period.

At any given time, the prisoner of war could signify different things for different people. The rich historiography of Mediterranean contacts between Christians and Muslims in the sixteenth and the seventeenth centuries, focusing on the exchange of captives, has demonstrated that the meaning of statuses such as 'slave', 'captive', or 'pirate' changed with the context.[33] In the same way, historians of slavery have long emphasized that rather than opposing 'freedom' and 'unfree-dom', it often makes more sense to think in terms of a spectrum: legal statuses were porous, and social practices rarely mirrored legal norms.[34] Following this premise, we must scrutinize the contexts in which the category of the prisoner of war and those of the penal prisoner, the slave, and the traitor were not compartmentalized.

Categorization was a social as well as an intellectual and political problem. The first assignment of a label to a captive was made on the spot, for instance, by the captain of a privateer, who decided that a ship was his legitimate prize, and that the captured crew were lawful prisoners of war who would be brought to shore to be delivered to the state administration and detained. In this sense, despite his lack of legal training, a ship's captain, just like a colonial governor or an admiral, played a part in implementing the laws of war.[35] Was an Irish Jacobite sailor serving in the French navy to be treated like a rebel or like a prisoner of war once he was captured by the British? The answer to this question depended on how legitimate the choice to fight for a foreign prince was considered to be, and this was widely debated throughout the eighteenth century. While there was a nor-mative consensus about the existence of the category of the prisoner of war, the exact content of the category, and its boundaries with other categories, were impossible to determine in principle.

The narrative, with regard to the category, is therefore one of continuity. As I will show, when the British and French stories differed, it was largely due to political factors. When international wars intersected with 'civil wars', this blurred

---

[33] Tarruell, 'Prisoners'; Hershenzon, 'Political economy'; Fontenay, 'Esclaves'; Weiss, *Captives*.
[34] Drescher, *Abolition*, pp. 4–5, 20–21.   [35] For this argument, see Benton, *Search*, p. 24.

allegiances and complicated the assignation of categories and their comparability. This was the case between the 1690s and the 1740s, when religious minorities, the Jacobites and the Huguenots, waged war against their sovereign states. This was a period of intense reflection on the status of the prisoner of war. The American War of Independence, on the British side, and the French Wars, on the French side, were also turning-points, for political and ideological reasons.

B. Spaces and Scales

Is this a specifically Franco-British and 'European' story? On the one hand, the idea was deeply ingrained in European thought that western Europe shared a set of legal institutions and political and cultural values, such as civility, the rule of law, and the law of nations, which were embodied in what Vattel called 'the humanity of the Europeans'.[36] As already mentioned, Europeans also shared a similar culture of warfare, based on the same 'grammar of violence'.[37] What happened when these conflicts took place outside Europe, on the high seas or in the colonies? As pointed out by Eliga Gould, the customary law of nations regarding the capture and treatment of prisoners of war could simply be overlooked in territories considered to be beyond the pale of civilization.[38] Similarly, Lauren Benton states that 'the whole of the imperial world represented a zone of legal anomaly vis-à-vis the metropole'. This is not to say, she argues, that the extra-European world and oceanic spaces were zones of lawlessness, but rather that they were spaces of legal innovation and creativity.[39] 'Distinct legal regions' could thus coexist within a single empire.[40] The same individuals could be categorized as prisoners of war if captured in European waters, and as pirates or slaves if captured in the West Indies.[41] Legal status was therefore partly linked to geography. The captives themselves tried to manipulate the labels that were ascribed to them, actively engaging in the game of classification.

We must pay close attention to these legal asymmetries. Whether a capture took place in Europe or in the colonies, on the high seas or on land, the line between legality and illegality could be blurred, as the laws of war, or the law of the sea, or the common law, could variously be activated, involving different actors. In this book, we will focus on liminal spaces: spaces where legal regimes could overlap and collide, affecting the forms of the social institution. At the global-regional scale, the Atlantic Ocean, as a key zone of predation, will provide us with such an observatory. Adopting a maritime focus is all the more important because sovereignties at sea were entangled and legal spaces many-layered, a fact which is

---

[36] Vattel, *Law of Nations*, book III, ch. 8, par. 150.   [37] Lee, *Barbarians*, p. 8.
[38] Gould, 'Zones', p. 483.   [39] Benton, *Search*, p. 28.   [40] Ibid., p. 137.
[41] Gould, 'Zones', p. 506.

often ignored in narratives about eighteenth-century wars.[42] But legal geography is not just an issue of colony versus metropole, nor is it solely an oceanic problem. The territories of European states were also characterized by multiple legalities.[43] Border-crossing affected legal status. For example, an enemy privateer could be labelled a pirate if captured while navigating up a river.[44] The occupants of prison-ships and parole zones were subjected to multiple kinds of law, which could conflict with one another. Knowing exactly by what rights the prisoners of war should be recognized was always debated. Focusing on such liminal zones thus raises the question of the geographical reach of the law.

These spatial and legal heterogeneities also meant that it was possible for two European countries to be officially at peace while being engaged in disguised, indirect, and quasi-permanent hostilities far away from Europe.[45] Peace treaties divided up the world's oceans into zones of cessation of hostilities at sea and determined whether a prize was legal or not.[46] Deciding when war had begun and peace had ended could be controversial, and it created the conditions for disputes over the spatial and temporal coordinates of a specific capture, and, by implication, its legality.[47] The fact that the temporalities of war and peace varied across space also means that the dichotomy between war and peace cannot be taken for granted.

C. Peace and War, Peace in War

The study of war captivity leads us to reflect on the meaning of war. While conceding that there is no universal definition of war, Stephen Neff proposes four key criteria that seem to apply everywhere.[48] First, by contrast with interpersonal violence, war opposes collectivities, such as states. The concept of the prisoner of war does not make sense in a conflict with so-called pirates or bandits. We saw, however, that the use of these labels depends a great deal on context. Second, a war is waged against foreigners, not domestic enemies. Does this mean that subjects of a king who serve in foreign armies and navies, or subjects rebelling against their legitimate sovereigns, are refused the status of prisoners of war? While the answer to these questions seems to be straightforward today, in the eighteenth century this was not the case, because subjecthood, nationhood, and allegiance did not always overlap. Third, war is a rule-governed activity. This relies

---

[42] War at sea was and is fundamentally different from war on land: Benvenisti and Cohen, 'War', pp. 1384–5. For these reasons, David Bell leaves it outside the remit of his study: *First Total War*, p. 17.
[43] Benton, *Search*, p. 9.
[44] Commissaire Lempereur to Secrétaire d'Etat de la *Marine* (SSM), 20 August 1695: Archives Nationales, Paris (AN), MAR/B3/88, fo. 90.
[45] Gould, 'Zones', pp. 479–82.
[46] Morieux, *Channel*, pp. 160–7; Steele, *English Atlantic*, pp. 189–98.
[47] Neff, *War*, p. 178.   [48] Ibid., p. 15.

on the notion that 'there was a substantial set of shared values...between the opposing sides'.[49] The question here is to know what happens when there is a breakdown in this shared culture. When the enemy stops abiding by the rules of war, what happens to its prisoners? And what happens when there is a disagreement about the meaning of these norms?

Fourth, the concept of war relies on a 'more or less definite boundary between times of war and times of peace'.[50] This must also be unpacked. Grotius's famous statement, '*inter bellum et pacem nihil est medium*',[51] was only true on a normative level. Many wars, especially after the middle of the eighteenth century, were fought without a preliminary declaration.[52]

In turn, these uneasy conceptual and temporal distinctions between war and peace could complicate the categorization of the enemy. The prisoner of war was theoretically released when the war ended. But if the war was described as permanent and endemic, because it was waged against *hostes humani generis*, peace with them was impossible. In other words, depending on whether an armed confrontation was characterized as a 'war' or not, this would modify the status of the prisoners. As we know, in the post-9/11 world, talking about a permanent war against 'barbarism' or essentialized enemies opens the possibility of detaining 'unlawful enemy combatants' *sine die*.[53] Refusing to grant the enemy the status of prisoners of war is another way to deny the legitimacy of their struggle, and potentially to extend their detention after the war ends.

This discussion chimes in with the analysis of sociologists of war and political scientists, who have emphasized, especially with reference to the so-called 'new wars' that have emerged after 1945, that the distinction between the state of war and the state of peace has lost its significance. As argued by Dominique Linhardt and Cédric Moreau de Bellaing, it is imperative to

> Break with a priori definitions, according to which war and peace refer to ideal and absolute conceptions—all the more ideal and absolute in that they define clearly separate and opposed states—to adopt instead an approach by degrees, the only one capable of determining how, according to which modalities and processes, there can be war in peace and peace in war.[54]

The length of any war is always highly unpredictable, which has consequences for the prisoners as well as the states. One of the pains of imprisonment is the loss of temporal points of reference, and particularly the uncertainty regarding one's

---

[49] Ibid., p. 23.   [50] Ibid., pp. 15–23.
[51] *De Iure Belli ac Pacis*, cited in Greenwood, 'Concept', p. 285.
[52] Maurice, *Hostilities*; Neff, *War*, pp. 110, 120, 121, 179.
[53] Gross and Ni Aolain, *Law*, p. 179.
[54] Linhardt and Moreau de Bellaing, 'Ni guerre', pp. 19–20. See also Marchal, 'Frontières'. Similarly, jurists disagree over the definition of war: Greenwood, 'Concept'.

moment of liberation.[55] This torment was even more acute for prisoners of war who could, in principle, remain in detention until the end of the war, a *terminus ad quem* which was by definition unknown.[56] Some prisoners went mad, and others committed suicide.[57]

While war captivity exemplifies the extension of Franco-British rivalry to the world in the eighteenth century, it also shows the persistence of non-conflictual relations within war. After they are captured, the prisoners of war enter into a moral contract not to continue the fight.[58] War captivity puts antagonistic groups—not in the sense of a quasi-atavistic religious or national hostility, but because their sovereigns are engaged in a war—in peaceful contact with each other, suspending violence as it were. This statement does not entail an irenic view of the eighteenth century, which would ignore the violence of war. This is not a book about human nature, either, such as might argue that human beings are inherently 'peaceful'. But if war captivity is considered as a social phenomenon, then prisoners of war and their treatment provide us with a window into the diverse ways in which societies in the eighteenth century dealt with armed conflict. The aim is ultimately to reconceptualize the far-too-neat dividing line often drawn between war and peace, by paying attention to situations in which the status of the enemy was undecided, unclear, or ever-changing. This seems to turn the logic of what is conventionally understood as 'war' on its head.

III. The State at War

The study of war captivity, then, can tell us something important about the developmental history of international legal ideas and practices. Such a focus, and this is the second argument, provides a vantage point from which we can re-examine the history of the state at war in the long eighteenth century. The forms and functions of war captivity reflect social and political structures at a given time. In seventeenth- and eighteenth-century Europe, the role played by war in the building or formation of the modern state was crucial.[59] If European war captivity was significantly different, this is probably to be traced to distinctive features of European states and the European state system. That system was structured around substantially autonomous states, many of which were prone to engage in

---

[55] Goffman, *Asylums*, p. 67. On the psychological consequences of detention without bounds, see Bosworth, *Inside Immigration*, pp. 165–9.

[56] For example, in 1711, two English prisoners detained in Dinan asked to be freed, after nine years of detention: Lempereur to SSM, 19 July 1711, AN, MAR/B3/195, fos. 192–v. Out of pity, Lempereur allowed them to reside in the town on their parole: ibid., 18 August 1711, fo. 238. They escaped: 11 October 1711, fo. 303v.

[57] Crowhurst, *French War*, p. 191.   [58] Walzer, 'Prisoners', p. 779.

[59] See, for example, Stone, *Imperial State*; Asch, 'War'; Rommelse, 'Early modern naval revolution'. Specifically on prisoners of war: Rommelse and Downing, 'State formation'.

hostile fashion with other states. War in turn shaped these states, setting them on what has been termed a fiscal-military path of development.[60] But if European states were affected and transformed by war, different states produced different types of war and war captivity.

A moral ambiguity lay at the heart of eighteenth-century conceptions of war: it was described both as despicable and as a necessary evil in order to attain peace.[61] What was the aim of making prisoners of war? From the state's perspective, the life of combatants had to be preserved because they were too valuable to be slaughtered on the battlefield. They had to be exchanged and sent back to wage war. War captivity was in this sense a social mechanism invented by European states to control the modes of relations between combatants, allowing for the conservation of this fighting force. As noted by Stephen Neff, the treaties for the exchanges of prisoners of war, which became customary from the late seventeenth century onwards, partly resulted from calls for 'greater humanity in warfare', but they were also linked to sheer demographic factors, namely the state's constant thirst for manpower.[62] The European practice of the exchange of prisoners during or after the war seemed particularly strange to Amerindians.[63] In fact, the exchange of prisoners during the war, which was normal in eighteenth-century European wars, had become obsolete by the early twentieth century.[64] This reminds us that the meaning and function of prisoners of war vary with the cultures and societies; within a given society, or in the context of a long conflict with the same enemy, it could also shift over time.

How quantitatively significant was prisoner-taking in the wars between Britain and France? How many people are we talking about? The scale and cost of eighteenth-century wars was unprecedented.[65] After 1650, the size of the armies rose.[66] Naval warfare was also fought on a larger scale, involving on average bigger armies and heavier fleets of battleships, which needed to be manned by more sailors. A seventy-four-gun ship carried up to 750 men, and a hundred-gun ship more than 1,000. Besides petty officers and trained seamen, who constituted more than half of the crews, on board were also marines, gunners, soldiers, and other landsmen.[67] When one of these huge naval superstructures was captured, the number of prisoners of war who had to be found accommodation was very significant. These are some of the reasons behind the greater numbers of prisoners that were taken in

---

[60] Brewer, *Sinews*; Storrs, *Fiscal-Military State*.
[61] Malešević, *Sociology*, pp. 267–73; Bell, *Total War*, ch. 1; Kroener, 'Modern state', pp. 217–19.
[62] Neff, *War*, p. 295.
[63] Lee, *Barbarians*, pp. 156–7; Starkey, *War*, pp. 191–4; Steele, 'Surrendering rites', pp. 155–6; Richter, 'War', p. 535.
[64] Jones, *Violence*, p. 14.
[65] Between 3,000 and 4,000 prisoners of war were perhaps detained in England at the end of the first Anglo-Dutch war: Rommelse and Downing, 'State formation', p. 156.
[66] Parker, *Military Revolution*; Rodger, *Military Revolution*.
[67] Baugh, *British Naval Administration*, pp. 188–9.

Franco-British wars. But number-counting is a tricky business—it was then and it is now. In 1758, the Maréchal de Belleisle, the French secretary of state for War, candidly confessed that he had no idea of 'the number of prisoners [France] has [in Britain], nor about their names, qualities, or since when they had been there, the conditions of their capture, or the places of their detention'.[68] This should serve as a warning for us: our own figures are necessarily estimations.

When we compare the numbers of prisoners taken on each side, the first thing to note is that Britain always captured and detained many more prisoners than France.[69] While accurate figures about the number of British prisoners of war in France are often lacking, and while that number will have fluctuated from year to year, as shown in Chart 1.1, it is clear that, with the exception of the War of the Spanish Succession, it was always much lower. Thus, between 1744 and 1746, there were 3.5 times more French prisoners in Britain than British prisoners in France (26,220/6,974).[70] In 1758, the ratio was 6.5 (19,632/3,000), and in 1814, it was 4.3 (70,000/16,000).[71] As the scale of warfare was expanding, and although Britain's population and territory were much smaller than those of France, Britain made the choice to commit ever more resources to detain prisoners of war: this phenomenon must be explained.

This striking difference in numbers was the outcome of a deliberate strategy, which aimed at incapacitating French manpower at sea. According to James Pritchard, the capture of French sailors by the British 'may have been the most

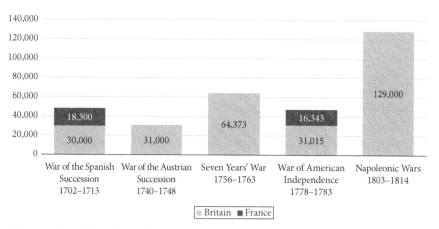

Chart 1.1. Total number of prisoners of war detained per war.

---

[68] Copy of instructions to Duc d'Aiguillon, 22 September 1758, AN, MAR/B4/97, fo. 167.
[69] Sources: Le Goff, 'L'impact', p. 106; *HCJ*, vol. 15, 16 January 1707, pp. 498–9; Sick & Wounded Board (S&W) to LCA, 27 October 1762, TNA, ADM98/9, fos. 110v–111; S&W to LCA, 13 March 1783, ADM98/14, fo. 162v; Le Carvèse, 'Prisonniers'.
[70] S&W to LCA, 13 March 1746, ADM98/4, fo. 73v.
[71] Copy of Aiguillon to Belleisle, 22 September 1758, AN, MAR/B4/97, fo. 166; Daly, 'Lost legions', p. 363; Lewis, *Napoleon*, p. 264.

serious drain on the [French] navy's resources'.[72] Throughout the eighteenth century, the British government resorted to war captivity as a weapon against the French Marine Royale, which was suffering from an endemic shortage of seamen.[73] The detention of prisoners of war was intrinsically linked to the challenges of recruitment in the armed and naval forces in that period, a manning problem that all states faced, but which was dealt with more successfully by Britain than France.[74] The French navy, from 1660 to 1815, could rely on a relatively stable number of sailors, on average 50,000 men, who were raised through the *classes* system. If seafaring men in the broad sense are included, such as carpenters, the number reaches 80,000. In addition, there were between 10,000 and 15,000 naval officers. But invalidity, injury, diseases, desertion, and various exemptions considerably reduced the number of men available for service in the navy.[75] These problems were not specific to France,[76] but the recourse to impressment allowed the British navy to increase the number of its sailors in a more flexible way, as shown in Chart 1.2.[77] Since France's overall pool of sailors was limited, it suffered disproportionally more from their detention.[78] As the wars went on, its stock of sailors inevitably decreased.[79] The success of this British strategy of targeting French seamen was demonstrated during the Seven Years' War: in 1758, out of 60,137 French sailors, a third (19,632) were detained in Britain.[80] From 1757 onwards, the British monarchy selectively released the 'least useful' prisoners, such as landsmen, soldiers, and passengers, while imprisoning sailors for longer periods.[81] The capture of prisoners of war was therefore a vital element in the struggle for naval supremacy in the eighteenth century.

This imbalance in the number of prisoners captured by Britain and France raises important questions. Did it have any consequences for the treatment of prisoners in both countries? Were conditions and places of detention influenced by this fact? I argue that we must think in terms of a symbiotic logic, according to which the treatment of prisoners by one side was primarily determined by how the other side dealt with theirs. While the balance of the comparison tilts frankly to the British side, the transnational perspective allows us to understand when, and

---

[72] Pritchard, *Louis XV's Navy*, p. 81.   [73] Anderson, 'Establishment'; Le Goff, 'Impact'.

[74] On population as resource: Lindegren, 'Men'. On recruitment, see Bruijn, 'States', pp. 97–8. On manning the navy, see Rodger, *Wooden World*, pp. 145–204.

[75] Pritchard, *Louis XV's Navy*, pp. 61–80; Meyer and Acerra, *Histoire*, pp. 68–9; Meyer, 'Problèmes', pp. 119–22; Acerra and Meyer, *Marines*, pp. 31, 54.

[76] The challenges facing the British navy were very similar: Baugh, *British Naval Administration*, pp. 147–240.

[77] Sources: for Britain, Rodger, *Command*, Appendix 6. For France: Acerra and Meyer, *Marines*, p. 28, and Part 3; Le Goff, 'Impact', pp. 116–17; Pritchard, *Louis XV's Navy*, pp. 73–4.

[78] On desertions, see Morriss, *Foundations*, pp. 249–62.

[79] Acerra and Meyer, *Marines*, pp. 31–3.

[80] Pritchard, *Louis XV's Navy*, table 4 p. 74; 'Account of Charge of Maintaining and supporting prisoners of war from 14 october 1755 to 11 november 1762', 12 March 1763, TNA, ADM98/9, fo. 159.

[81] Le Goff, 'L'impact', pp. 108–9; Anderson, 'Establishment'; Le Goff, 'Problèmes', pp. 219–22; Cabantous, *Dix-mille*, pp. 196–7.

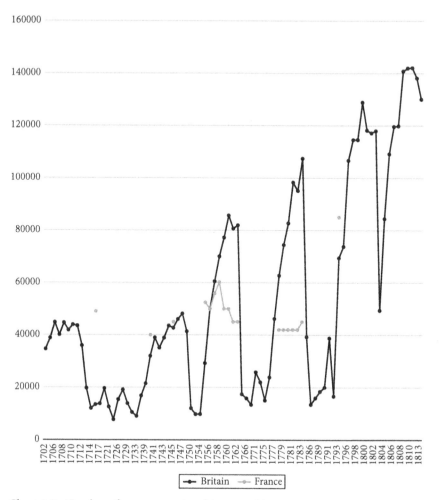

Chart 1.2. Number of seamen mustered in navy ships.

why, British policies and practices were similar to the French, and when and why they differed. Approaches to war captivity in Britain can, in part, be traced back to a distinctly British context, such as the loss of the American colonies and the debates about prison reform. At the same time, it is relevant to understand that notions of retaliation and emulation were premised on the gathering of knowledge about how British prisoners were treated in France.

The British state officials in charge of prisoners of war observed in 1762 that they had no idea about 'the real number of prisoners' who had been taken and 'sent into His Majesty's Dominions abroad', or died there, because 'no regular returns are sent to us'.[82] The detention and exchange of prisoners outside Europe

---

[82] S&W to LCA, 27 October 1762, TNA, ADM98/9, fo. 110v.

were indeed administered by governors or naval commanders, who often exchanged them locally and never entered their numbers in central accounts.[83] But we know that eighteenth-century wars between France and Britain were global; the total number of prisoners was larger than the figures mentioned above, if one includes those taken and detained in Pondicherry, Quebec, and Jamaica. The relatively low figure for prisoners of war detained during the American War of Independence finds its explanation here: for the first time, the British supremacy at sea was contested by a Franco-Spanish, and later Dutch, alliance. Thousands of British and French prisoners were detained in colonial prisons, in New York and Spanish Town (Kingston), as well as in Plymouth or Dunkirk. This conflict constituted a turning-point in the history of war imprisonment in Britain, paving the way to the new forms of incarceration during the French Wars. In the metropole, the overflow of detention spaces caused by the blockade of the Atlantic made it near-impossible to transport convicts to America. In this period, war imprisonment in Britain overlapped with debates about prison reform.

How do the figures discussed above compare with numbers of prisoners captured on land, and by other European powers? The numbers of prisoners captured and detained after major land battles were even more considerable than those captured at sea, due to the superior size of the armies.[84] For example, at the Battle of Blenheim (1704), the French armies lost 14,000 prisoners to the Allies, and another 6,000 at Ramillies (1706).[85] More than 45,000 Austrians and Saxons were captured by Prussia during the Second Silesian War (1744–5).[86] Over the course of the Seven Years' War, Austria might have lost more than 78,000 prisoners in Europe.[87] During the Napoleonic Wars, the number of prisoners captured in battles increased, proportionally to the size of the armies. At this point, the reader might legitimately wonder why one should focus on the Franco-British case at all.

The fact that Franco-British wars were waged at sea, as well as on land, was one of their distinctive features. In addition, different rules applied on land and at sea.[88] This does not mean that only seamen were imprisoned—far from it: many landsmen served on board ships. But even prisoners captured on land were often transferred to Britain by sea or repatriated from France to Britain by sea. For example, 5,000 of the 11,000 prisoners taken at Blenheim in 1704 were brought to Britain.[89] During the Seven Years' War, prisoners from Nouvelle-France and India were transported to France and Britain. During the Peninsular Wars, Wellington sent 20,000 French captives from Spain to England in 1810–11, due to the lack of

---

[83] Anderson, 'Impact', pp. 245–6.   [84] A point made by Wilson, 'Prisoners', p. 39.
[85] Chandler, *Art of Warfare*, pp. 302–4.   [86] Wilson, 'Prisoners', p. 40.
[87] Ibid., 54n10.
[88] Savory, 'Convention'; 'Notice sur les cartels d'échange' [March 1810], AMAE, MDA48, fos. 248–63.
[89] Scouller, *Armies*, p. 314.

facilities in the Iberian Peninsula.[90] These conflicts were always much more than just *Franco-British* wars. Spanish, Dutch, Irish, and 'American' individuals also appear in naval archives, and the crews of privateers were even more cosmopolitan than those on navy ships, composed as they were of foreign sailors and deserters.[91] A constant subject of discussion was whether the flag under which the prisoners served when they were captured, or their subjecthood, should be the main factor in determining their fate.

The ability of the British and French states to capture, move, detain, and feed large numbers of enemies, sometimes for many years, was a historical novelty. Doing this while avoiding major epidemics was a major achievement.[92] Running a prisoner of war regime on the scale practised in the eighteenth century was a formidable challenge, involving planning (a predicament since the length of a war was unforeseeable), logistics, transportation, storage capacity, and information networks spanning vast geographical spaces. Marching hundreds of prisoners on land, from a port to a detention facility, overcoming bad weather, bad-quality roads, and the prisoners' passive resistance, was no mean feat. The interconnection between the component parts of the operation was key. A ship captain needed to know in which port he should unload his cargo of prisoners; the prison administration needed to make sure that enough room would be available for the newcomers; a prison governor needed to order a sufficient quantity of food rations, and so on. In England, a specialized state bureaucracy was invented at the end of the seventeenth century to deal with the detention of enemies, which would remain fundamentally the same in the eighteenth century. It was centralized under the aegis of Commissioners for the Sick and Wounded Seamen and Exchange of Prisoners of War (also called the Sick and Hurt Board), a branch of the Admiralty.[93] From the Seven Years' War onwards, the administration of prisoners of war in the West Indies was also increasingly centralized. In France, the administration of warfare was also bureaucratized, and the system was nominally placed in the hands of the ministers of the 'Marine' and the 'Guerre'.[94]

This brings us to the Napoleonic Wars. The challenges faced by the two countries during this long conflict were different, as were the solutions that were developed to address them. Napoleonic France captured a very large number of prisoners from its European enemies, but they were taken on the Continent, not at sea, and consequently there was a relatively small proportion of British prisoners

---

[90] Lewis, *Napoleon*, p. 58. The majority of the prisoners captured by Spain and Portugal followed the same route: Chamberlain, *Hell*, pp. 14–15, 21–4.

[91] Pritchard, *Louis XV's Navy*, p. 81.   [92] Leunig, van Lottum and Poulsen, 'Surprisingly gentle'.

[93] The commissioners, whose number varied between two and five, were also in charge of the care and exchange of naval prisoners of war, under the direction of the Lords of the Admiralty: Baugh, *British Naval Administration*, pp. 48–61; Watson, 'Commission', pp. 184–224; Charters, *Disease*, pp. 130–5.

[94] Acerra and Zysberg, *Essor*; Pritchard, *Louis XV's Navy*; Bruijn, 'States', pp. 92–3.

among them.[95] France largely relied on its existing infrastructure of military fortresses, dating back to the late seventeenth century, to accommodate its captive enemies. In this respect, there was no radical departure from the eighteenth century: the places of detention used for prisoners of war remained multipurpose and catch-all institutions.

Britain took a very different path, and the challenges it faced were more novel that those faced by France. In order to explain this we must consider the whole period between 1780 and 1815. The British 'fiscal-military' state became increasingly capable of addressing successfully the numerous problems presented by the ever-larger numbers of prisoners of war it held. Several developments took place from the 1780s onwards, which allowed the processing of larger numbers of prisoners. The naval bureaucracy grew and was streamlined according to principles of efficiency, morality, and accountability, in line with the more general campaign for reforming the government in this period.[96] From 1796, the Transport Board, created in 1794, centralized the hiring of ships to serve as transports, notably to bring back or repatriate prisoners of war, in addition to taking care of their detention.[97] The staff employed in the Prisoner of War department increased steadily, from ten clerks in 1796 to fourteen in 1809 and twenty-seven in 1814, to deal with the rising number of prisoners, who had to be fed, clothed, and transported, while the custodial staff had to be paid and detention spaces hired and repaired.[98] A total of 70,000 prisoners of war were detained in Britain in 1801, five times more than the total for the War of the Spanish Succession as a whole. The French Wars saw annual expenditures for the war effort shoot up and taxes were raised.[99] This allowed Britain to sustain a war that lasted longer than any in the eighteenth century, by mobilizing a larger proportion of its male population in its armed forces than any other European country, including France.[100] The first purpose-built war prisons, which appeared during the Revolutionary and Napoleonic Wars, were in some ways the product of the coalescence between 'economical', moral, and political concerns that had been taking shape in Britain since the 1780s. To make economies of scale, war prisons were bigger than ever before, and their disposition was adapted to the people they accommodated, who were strictly separated from normal detainees.

---

[95] A total of 70,000 Austrians were thus detained by the French in 1805, and 70,000 Prussians in 1806–7, while 65,000 Spanish prisoners were detained over the course of the Napoleonic Wars: Marquis, 'Convention', 66n1.

[96] Harling, *Waning*; Morriss, *Foundations*; Knight, *Britain*.

[97] Sutcliffe, *British Expeditionary Warfare*. In 1796, the Transport Board took over the care of prisoners of war in health, while the Sick & Hurt Office looked after ill prisoners. In 1806, the whole business was placed under the responsibility of the Transport Board.

[98] *Seventh Report*, Appendix, p. 624; *Eighteenth Report*, p. 344; *Ninth Report*, p. 8; *Transport Office: Estimates*, pp. 3–4.

[99] O'Brien, 'Nature'.   [100] Knight, *Britain*, pp. 155, 260; Morriss, *Foundations*, pp. 223–8.

Although there is no doubt that the state grew and changed in the eighteenth century, it is problematic to describe it as the prefiguration of the modern bureaucratic state, as a (supposedly) rational and efficient administrative machine.[101] The eighteenth-century state was no leviathan. War captivity tested the limits of the state, stretching its capacities as much as it contributed to 'building' it.[102] Furthermore, different arms of the state competed with each other: admirals and colonial governors tried to oversee the detention of prisoners, press gangs tried to seize returned prisoners from the Agents for Prisoners of War, the army fought with the navy to control prison depots, and counties resisted against the central state's attempts at dumping prisoners on them. At times, especially when they were overburdened with a large influx of prisoners, states struggled to detain and maintain them safely and at a reasonable cost. To address these problems, the 'contractor-state' relied on and collaborated with 'private' and civilian actors, to detain, to feed and clothe, to monitor and transport the prisoners, from the seventeenth to the early nineteenth century.[103] Non-state forms of war captivity, which predated the eighteenth century, survived in this period. Privateering, a private war on trade sponsored by the state, was the most obvious manifestation of this, and the privateers, as predators and as prisoners, are central actors in our story. But this was a more general phenomenon. Prisoners on parole were accommodated in private houses, and ordinary prisoners were frequently put in county houses or farms rented out by the state. Prisoners were fed by private contractors, while capital outlays relied on private bankers. The transportation of prisoners between Caribbean islands, across the Channel or across the Atlantic was commonly contracted to private merchants. More surprisingly perhaps, prisoners themselves were asked to play an active role in these transfers. Because sailors were a precious commodity, in the Atlantic Ocean prisoners were, for instance, asked to help man the merchant ships that would transport them back to Europe.

Does it follow that states detained more prisoners because they could? Should the fact that so many prisoners survived in captivity, or at least do not appear to have died in larger numbers than soldiers or hospital inmates, rather be explained by ideological factors? The two dimensions need not be presented as contradictory: as pointed out by Warren E. Lee, since the end of the seventeenth century, in Europe, 'cultural values stressing restraint had been joined to a new bureaucratic capacity to wage war according to those values'.[104] States at war also had to take

---

[101] For criticisms of this claim, see Baugh, *British Naval Administration*, pp. 32, 83–92; Innes, 'Central government'; Hoppit, 'Checking'; Graham, 'British fiscal-military states'.

[102] Gunn, 'War', p. 382; Lindegren, 'Men'; Gunn, 'War', p. 382.

[103] On the contractor-state: Parrott, 'From military enterprise'; Graham and Walsh, *British Fiscal-Military States*; Bowen, 'Contractor state'; Knight, *Britain*. On prisoners in the seventeenth century: Rommelse and Downing, 'State formation'.

[104] Lee, *Barbarians*, p. 186.

into account issues of reciprocity in the treatment of their enemies, and to conform to moral, 'civilized', and 'humanitarian' norms that they had helped to define in the course of the eighteenth century. These ideas usually contributed to limiting violence towards captive enemies.

On the other hand, moral imperatives and notions of state necessity sometimes pulled in opposite directions, and there were moments when the discourse opposing barbarism and civilization could justify forms of retaliation against the enemy. Such ideological changes are a plausible explanation for the differences in the treatment of prisoners in Britain and France that emerged during the Napoleonic Wars.[105] The regular exchange of individual prisoners according to rank slowed down in the 1790s, and 'after 1810 the exchange system collapsed irrevocably' between Britain and France.[106] The protections awarded to prisoners on parole were also significantly weakened. Release on parole, especially on the French side, decreased as well.[107] In France, the new idea of the nations-at-arms and the proclaimed break from Ancien Regime warfare affected the very concept of the prisoner of war. The turning point was the decree of 26 May 1794 (7 Prairial Year II) refusing to 'make any English or Hanoverian prisoners', which was extended to Spaniards by the Decree of 24 Thermidor.[108] This had consequences on the ground, and some massacres of prisoners of war, which were a rarity in the eighteenth century, took place in this period.[109] However, these laws were not applied indiscriminately, and many soldiers probably refused to implement them.[110] In any case, the decrees were repealed on 30 December 1794 (10 Nivôse Year II) because, as stated by French representatives, they were 'contrary to all the laws; they upset the law of nations and the laws of war', and were 'insulting humanity', in addition to the fact that they exposed French soldiers to reprisals.[111] The real novelty of the decree of 23 May 1803 (2 Prairial Year XI), following which 700–800 British male civilians between the ages of eighteen and sixty present on the French soil were captured, was not so much (as is often contended) that it broke with the eighteenth-century tradition of exempting non-combatants from war imprisonment. As I show in this book, many civilians were labelled as prisoners of war throughout the period. What was new was the *official* stretching of the category of prisoner of war to include non-combatants, who Napoleon

---

[105] Crowhurst, *French War*; Crimmin, 'Prisoners'; Daly, 'Lost legions'.

[106] Crowhurst, *French War*, p. 173; Lewis, *Napoleon*, pp. 66–82; Crimmin, 'Prisoners', p. 18 (quotation). The number of French prisoners released from Britain during the Napoleonic Wars was not negligible, however: around 40,000 individuals (Le Carvèse, 'Prisonniers', table 5).

[107] Daly, 'Lost legions', p. 368; Lewis, *Napoleon*, pp. 61–5. Although it is often argued that the repeated failures to conclude a general cartel of exchange illustrate the rise of new ideas about war, only one such cartel was successfully negotiated in the eighteenth century, in 1780: Anderson, 'Establishment', p. 79.

[108] See Jones and McDonald, 'Robespierre', pp. 5–8.

[109] Bell, *First Total War*, pp. 174, 181, 213; Dwyer, 'Memories'.

[110] Best, *Humanity*, p. 81; Jones and McDonald, 'Robespierre', pp. 7–8.

[111] Brival and Bréard, *Gazette Nationale*, 1 January 1795, p. 422.

insisted should be exchanged against French soldiers and sailors. At the same time, the measure was presented in a traditional legal language, as retaliation against the British capture of French vessels, including merchant ships and fishing boats, before the declaration of war. Such dilemmas, the consideration as to whether economic, military, political, or moral issues should be prioritized in the treatment of prisoners of war, were always in the minds of decision-makers. Delineating their debate is crucial to understanding whether a paradigmatic change affected the treatment of prisoners of war at the end of the eighteenth century, in theory and in practice.

In sum, the book argues that, in the same way that the history of international law can fruitfully be re-examined by testing general and normative accounts against a detailed examination of how legal ideas worked in different contexts, enacting a similar displacement for the history of the modern state can be productive. *The Society of Prisoners* offers a historical and pragmatic sociology of the modern state: rather than a political theory of the state, or an economic and material history of the state, this is a social history. The emphasis is placed on state/society relations, and on the creativity and resilience of societies in the face of war.

IV. The War Prison

I have argued that the methodological disjunction between war and peace is questionable. The impact of war did not simply vanish once hostilities stopped. With these continuities in mind, it is not that surprising that war imprisonment and 'penal' imprisonment (the term is anachronistic for most of the eighteenth century) had much in common.

It is a thesis of this book that war imprisonment overlapped with other forms of imprisonment. While this has been pointed out in passing, for instance with reference to the use of prison hulks for convicts as well as prisoners of war, these relationships have never been addressed explicitly. First, as we have seen, discussions about prisoners of war, among politicians, lawyers, or philosophers, often invoked other categories of detainees. The whole logic of John Howard's plea for separating detainees according to their crimes was influenced by his direct observations of prisoners of war in France and Britain. Howard himself had experienced captivity: on his return from Portugal in 1756, his ship was captured by a French privateer; he was detained in Brittany, and he complained about the 'barbarity' with which his compatriots were treated. It is often alleged that this imprisonment aroused his interest in the prison question, which would occupy him until his death.[112] His famous *State of the Prisons* (1780 ed.) dealt with

---

[112] *State of the Prison* (1777), p. 22.

prisoners of war, alongside felons and debtors. Second, the links between war imprisonment and normal imprisonment ran deeper than these analogies and comparisons. In practice, these populations of inmates might be looked after by the same groups, such as the turnkeys, and sometimes were cohabitating in the same buildings. What does this detention in prison-like places tell us about the expectations of guards and the self-perceptions and lived experiences of prisoners of war? What kind of power dynamics were created by the complex institutional structure of these places of detention?

Focusing on these parallels and overlaps leads us to identify some false assumptions. For instance, while it is true that, unlike the penal detainee, the prisoner of war was not supposed to be punished for his deeds, and his loss of liberty was not the result of a penalty or a sentence, the fact that both groups were subjected to a similar disciplinary apparatus means that their experiences of incarceration might be more similar than has hitherto been assumed. Similar techniques for policing these carceral spaces were used, such as the reliance on written and customary disciplinary rules that might have originated in the same source. Max Weber wrote that 'the discipline of the army is...the womb of all discipline'.[113] The fact that the detention of these men was administered by the Admiralty or the army facilitated the circulation of these military models, but ideas flowed in multiple directions. For example, if, as is often alleged, the purpose of the incarceration of prisoners of war was not their 'reformation', since they had not committed any offence, then the sending of missionaries into British prisons and hulks to convert them, in the 1800s, becomes problematic. These regulations were also the product of the transfer of ideas across borders.

Given these continuities and overlaps, the historiography of prisons, which has developed in France and Britain since the 1970s and has centred on justice, crime and social reform, is useful for the analysis of war captivity.[114] Also relevant from our perspective is penal sociology, which has remained a vibrant field of research since the 1950s. Prison sociologists favour the term 'institution' to designate these social-political-spatial structures. To mention only the pioneers of the discipline, Gresham Sykes has written about the 'custodial institution' and the prison itself as a 'social system' or as 'a social organization'.[115] Erving Goffman proposed the concept of 'total institutions', which, he held, could be applied to prisons, as well as schools, psychiatric hospitals, nursing homes, concentration camps, or convents, in particular because of their shared formal features.[116] The idea that different forms of imprisonment should be placed on an intellectual continuum was also advanced by Michel Foucault, for whom the criminal, the insane, and the poor, for instance, were detained within the same institutional framework and

[113] Quoted in Kroener, 'Modern state', p. 195.
[114] See, for example, Foucault, *Discipline*; Petit, *Peines*; Innes, 'King's Bench Prison'; Finn, *Character*.
[115] Sykes, *Society*, pp. 6, 38.   [116] Goffman, *Asylums*.

subjected to the same kind of disciplinary regime. It is, however, striking that, apart from passing mentions, prisoners of war are rarely mentioned in these discussions, even among historians of the prison influenced by Goffman.[117] In fact, although Goffman did not study prisoners of war per se, they were integral to his argument. Goffman used psychiatric work on the brainwashing of prisoners of war by both sides during the Korean War to help him define the process of 'conversion' taking place in a total institution.[118] One implication we could draw from Goffman's work is that the social structures and adaptations in prisoners of war camps are likely to be the same as in other contemporary institutions. By contrast, the 'importation' perspective, which contends that a pre-existing culture is imported within the prison, would lead us to believe that the kind of social system we would find among prisoners of war—'aliens' within the state that has captured them—might be very different from what we would expect to find in a prison.[119] Other questions follow from this. How far do sociological debates on coercion, domination and resistance, soft power and legitimacy in contemporary prisons, apply to war imprisonment in the eighteenth century?[120] Can these ideas be transplanted to a period when imprisonment took place on different scales, often took different forms, and involved very different communities?

Sociologists of prisons have reached the important conclusion that the prison can be studied both as an autonomous space and as an observatory of the society that creates it.[121] These two perspectives, the prison-as-society and the prison-in-society, are taken up in the book. Furthermore, the focus on war prisons can enrich the history of imprisonment more generally.

A. The War Prison as Society

Gresham Sykes wrote: 'we must see prison life as something more than a matter of walls and bars, of cells and locks. We must see the prison as a society within a society.'[122] According to Sykes, 'prison society' encompasses the guards, the prisoners, and most importantly their interactions behind walls. What he calls the 'corruption' of the boundary between guards and prisoners is consubstantial to that world. Social order cannot be maintained by written rules alone, but also requires informal relations. Consequently, the custodians have to rely on some

---

[117] See, for example, Ignatieff, *Just Measure*, pp. 11, 14.

[118] Goffman, *Asylums*, pp. 60–5. Goffman drew on Schein, 'Chinese indoctrination'. On this dimension of Goffman's work, see Staub, *Madness*.

[119] Crewe, 'Sociology'.

[120] See, in a very large literature, Bosworth, *Encyclopedia*; Crewe, 'Soft power'; Liebling, 'Distinctions'; Rubin, 'Resistance or friction'; Sparks, Bottoms, and Hay, *Prisons*.

[121] Combessie, *Sociologie*; Wacquant, 'Curious eclipse', pp. 384–6.

[122] Sykes, *Society*, introduction, p. xxx.

cooperation on the part of the inmates, a cooperation that has to be constantly negotiated, because this relationship is fundamentally unstable. Sykes uses Weber's concept of the *Gebietsverband* to describe the prison society: 'a territorial group living under a regime imposed by a ruling few. Like a province which has been conquered by force of arms, the community of prisoners has come to accept the validity of the regime constructed by their rulers, but the subjugation is not complete.' Indeed, continues Sykes, while prisoners usually do not deny 'the legitimacy of confinement', they do not always feel an obligation to obey: 'the prisoner thus accepts the fact of his captivity at one level and rejects it at another.'[123] This analogy, it seems, works better for prisoners of war, as defeated enemies, than for penal detainees.[124] It is important, therefore, to emphasize that the war prison was a space of constraint and violence, but coercion was not unlimited.

There seems to be one salient difference between prisoners of war and 'normal' prisoners: because the former were normally foreigners, they came under the law of nations, and could appeal to different authorities. Their extraneity sets them apart from the host society, and seems to challenge the applicability of Sykes' framework to our own. According to the prison sociologist, a fundamental link exists between the captors and their captives, who are 'drawn from the same culture and ... hold many of the same values and beliefs. They share a common language and a common historical experience.'[125] Without presupposing that a shared background necessarily leads to mutual sympathy, the foreignness of the prisoners raises specific issues, such as linguistic misunderstandings and miscommunication, as shown by recent sociological work on immigration detention centres.[126]

But this does not mean that the 'boundary' was not crossed, to use Goffman's phrasing.[127] Even in 'supermax' prisons or in Guantanamo, economic, religious, or cultural exchanges between guards and prisoners happen all the time.[128] The state of enmity is never static. In France as in Britain, a variety of social groups were asked to look after prisoners of war, such as soldiers, militiamen, invalids, or civilians. There is no reason to suppose that these people all behaved in the same way towards their captives. Some might see their prisoners as poor fellows deserving pity and help, or alternatively as partners in crime or potential sources of income; others might see them as dangerous enemies who needed to be tamed.

---

[123] Ibid., p. 48.
[124] Recent scholarship on the prison has emphasized, implicitly criticizing Sykes, the importance of normative consent in accomplishing penal order. See, for instance, Sparks and Bottoms, 'Legitimacy'.
[125] Ibid., p. 33.
[126] Foreign nationals are still a minority in contemporary French and British prisons, respectively 17.6 per cent (2010) and 13 per cent (England and Wales, 2013): Fischer, 'Detention', p. 696; Bosworth, *Inside Immigration*, p. 3.
[127] Goffman, *Asylum*, p. 19.
[128] For the former, see Western, 'Introduction', in Sykes, *Society*, pp. xx–xxi.

Instances of fraternization between guards and inmates were frequent, but violence was rife too. The relevance of national affiliations in terms of explaining the nature of the social interactions between prisoners of war and their captors must thus be questioned from the outset. The presence of prisoners of war sometimes provoked, and sometimes revealed, latent tensions within host societies, just as often as it enhanced local solidarities.[129] Did imprisonment abroad create new bonds? Did it untie older solidarities? Did it create new opportunities for settling old grudges?

B. The War Prison in Society

Although the Foucauldian paradigm, according to which the birth of the modern prison contributed to the development of a 'new technology of power' exercised by the state over individuals, has been challenged, it remains highly suggestive; certainly, its contention that a focus on prison helps explain the society that gives birth to it remains the starting point of any research on prisons.[130] Unlike penal prisoners, who might hope to be visited by family and kin, prisoners of war faced the double penalty of imprisonment abroad, away from home in a foreign country.[131] That said, war imprisonment did not simply involve seclusion from the outside world. One of the aims of the book is to 'open' the prison, because the concept of confinement does not accurately describe the world of most early-modern prisons, which were not enclosed spaces.[132] In eighteenth-century Britain and France, lawyers, traders, or families could penetrate prisons with relative ease. One might suggest a parallel with convents in early-modern Europe, which have been traditionally studied as institutions of confinement, until a more recent historiography has shown that they were structurally connected to the outside.[133]

The supposed purpose of war imprisonment was to neutralize enemies, to prevent them from escaping, fraternizing with local populations, or causing public disorder. Instead, I propose to consider war captivity as a window offering multiple opportunities for social interaction, within and across prison walls, emphasizing what Goffman calls the 'permeability' of total institutions.[134] The logic of the demonstration hinges on the experience of prisoners of war as the pivot of social relations within and outside the prison. War is conceived as a social experience that does not simply destroy societies, but also creates new social ties

---

[129] Malešević, *Sociology*, p. 47.
[130] Foucault, *Dits et Ecrits*, vol. III, p. 153. For the criticism of Foucault, see Garland, *Punishment*.
[131] Trombik, 'Incarceration'.   [132] Innes, 'King's Bench Prison'; Paton, *No Bond*.
[133] Heullant-Donat, Claustre, and Lusset, *Enfermements*.
[134] Goffman, *Asylums*, p. 111. Goffman had a much more sophisticated understanding of the relationship between the prison and the exterior than is often recognized: see Crewe et al., 'Emotional geography'.

and redefines existing ones, which often transcended the nation-state order. The notion of the prisoner of war as mediator is influenced by the secondary literature on Amerindian captivity.[135] Prisoners of the Powhatan Amerindians were conceived as and given the role of go-betweens, which reveals a belief in the notion that assimilation or cultural 'conversion' was possible—a process which has been described as a sort of 'Stockholm syndrome'.[136] They could be incorporated into the society of their captors through marriage or adoption, as living proofs of mutual goodwill.[137] Acculturation worked in both directions,[138] and the persisting presence of these outsiders in a foreign community contributed to limiting the intensity of violence in warfare, by facilitating the transmission of information about the other's way of thinking.[139] Many French, Spanish, or English captives in the hands of Amerindians 'went native',[140] refusing to return to their families at the close of the wars, even when treaties were concluded between Amerindians and Europeans to this effect.[141] While this also happened in the Franco-British case—many prisoners of war married local women and stayed abroad after the war[142]—this is not the main object of interest in this book, which focuses on the first three stages of captivity: capture, detention, and release. But the fact that so many European captives made the choice to remain with their captors after the war tells us something important about the possibility to cross social and cultural boundaries.

Instead of studying these men as if they dwelt in a world apart, the book focuses on prisoners of war as social and cultural intermediaries between French and British societies. As the image on the cover of this book makes clear, captivity zones were places of intermingling, where people of different statuses would socialize, not always in a conflictual mode. In this sense, the society of prisoners is a society that not only generates imprisonment, but is also structured by its interactions with prisoners of war. Here as well, the work of prison sociologists is helpful. These studies of contemporary prisons often focus on the interface between the prison and the outside world, which they analyse in terms of social ecology, underlining the symbolic exclusions that reinforce the physical enclosure.[143] But most of the eighteenth-century war prisons were not hidden from view. They were eminently visible, and so were their occupants. These spaces accordingly provide a lens through

---

[135] Richter, 'War', pp. 529–35; Axtell, 'White Indians', pp. 72–4.
[136] Stern, 'White Indians', p. 279.   [137] Lee, 'Peace chiefs'.
[138] Axtell, 'White Indians', p. 66; Stern, 'White Indians', pp. 262–3; Vaughan and Richter, 'Crossing'.
[139] Lee, 'Peace chiefs', pp. 706–7.   [140] Stern, 'White Indians', pp. 263–4.
[141] Axtell, 'White Indians', pp. 60–1. For a different interpretation, see Vaughan and Richter, 'Crossing'.
[142] See, for example, 14 January 1762, Cumbria Archive Centre, Carlisle, DRC/7; 25 February 1800, Devon Record Office, Exeter (DRO), DEX/7/b/1808/70. In his journal, prisoner Peter Fea listed the 'English prisoners who had Wives in France', distinguishing 'English Wives' and 'French Wives': Fea's journal (1810–14), DRO, 1317M/F/1.
[143] Combessie, 'Marking'.

which to glimpse the repercussions of international conflicts at the level of local communities, small towns, and villages. In the context of war captivity, soldiers and sailors, as well as other groups, found themselves entering into contact with civilians, militiamen, administrators, and the civil society more generally. It is important to note that local communities were not necessarily opposed to receiving these prisoners.

As the encounter was extended onto a new terrain, the meaning of warfare changed. By the situation of captivity, the prisoner of war's extraneity was often lessened or toned down, as he developed interactions, links, and exchanges with the host society. Rather than being seen only as one of division between worlds that do not communicate with each other, the experience of captivity can therefore be analysed, in the words of Norbert Elias, as a social configuration, in which new social connections are forged.[144] In their unusual situation as unwilling migrants who spent weeks, months, and more commonly several years in a foreign society, prisoners of war contributed to the mutual knowledge of French and British people in this period. War, and more specifically war captivity, did not necessarily pave the way to inter-group hatred, sharpening 'group boundaries across the lines of conflict'.[145] Otherwise, it would be difficult to make sense of the testimony of Arthur Young, the famous writer on agriculture, as he was travelling in France in 1787, writing in his journal: 'Met a man employed on the roads who was prisoner at Falmouth four years; he does not seem to have any rancour against the English; nor yet was he very well pleased with his treatment.'[146]

Might the framework we just outlined apply to the period of the French Wars as well? With respect to the experience of prisoners and their interactions with civilians, it is possible to highlight long-term continuities, as well as ruptures, with the eighteenth century. Certainly, the breakdown of established practices regarding prisoners increased the length of detention, by comparison with most eighteenth-century wars.[147] Examining the interface between civilian populations and captive enemies might offer fresh perspectives on the transformation of political culture during the French Wars. One point of departure with the eighteenth century relates to the official use of prisoners of war in the war of ideas. In Britain, for the first time, attempts to convert prisoners of war were openly undertaken. Fearing the dissemination of dangerous ideas among local populations, both governments banned theatrical performances by prisoners of war, as they 'may be Dangerous in political or licentious Principles, and may

---

[144] For this approach, see Morieux, 'French prisoners'; Deluermoz, *Policiers*.
[145] Malešević, *Sociology*, p. 179, and 219–333.
[146] Young, *Travels in France*, 31 May 1787, pp. 18–19.
[147] Alain Cabantous estimates that in the eighteenth century, a privateer stayed on average three to four years in captivity, and sailors in warships two to three years: *Dix-mille*, p. 197. Farrell Mulvey, a doctor, was detained for twelve years in France, and this is rather typical: see his *Sketches* (1818).

occasionally and improperly have together some of His Majesty's Subjects to attend them'.[148] These alarmist measures were not unjustified: there was mutual curiosity and interest between the prisoners and civilian populations. The prisoners themselves proclaimed their patriotism, as those British sailors who sang 'God save the Queen' or 'Rule Britannia' in the face of their guards, or those French prisoners who defied orders and proudly wore the national cockade.[149] Commissioner Serle, sent by the Transport Board to investigate the mood of the prisoners on parole in Cornwall in 1797, reported that several French officers had made overtures of marriage to women in the neighbourhood, which local magistrates did their best to discourage and prevent.[150] This tension between state policies and social attitudes remained integral to captivity zones even at the height of the French Wars.

War captivity provides a unique vantage point from which to understand how whole societies, and not simply combatants, confronted the enemy. For civilians, interacting with prisoners of war was not a rare experience. The young Edward Gibbon, like thousands of other English men, served in the English militia, and one of his duties was to guard the 2,000 French prisoners detained at Forton, near Portsmouth.[151] He put these contacts to fruitful use, and his first book, *Essay on the Study of Literature* (1764), was 'transcribed by one of the French prisoners at Petersfield', according to his memoirs.[152] Many men and women took an interest in the welfare of prisoners of war. Oliver Goldsmith, Samuel Johnson, John Wesley, Samuel Whitbread, as well as hundreds of anonymous British men and women, were involved in philanthropic campaigns supporting the prisoners, from the Seven Years' War onwards, including during the Napoleonic Wars. The role of prisoners of war in war economics has also been overlooked. War did not completely interrupt trade circuits, but it redeployed them: prisoners of war, by their sole presence or through their direct involvement, played an essential role in this phenomenon.

War captivity as a Franco-British social institution emerged in part out of new conceptions of war and state formation; but it owed its origin in particular to one simple fact: tens of thousands of prisoners were translocated in another country, where they sojourned for years. The presence of these men, and sometimes women, in the territory of their enemies, came under scrutiny, along with other aspects of war, such as the rule of law, governance, economic matters, or health issues. Philosophers such as David Hume and Rousseau, legal writers such as Vattel, and scientists such as Joseph Banks wrote about the subject, in passing or

---

[148] TO's circular, 8 October 1811, TNA, ADM98/170, fo. 103. For France, see Marquis, 'Convention', pp. 69–70.

[149] Le Prat, 'Faire face', p. 223; Abell, *Prisoners*, pp. 442–5. See also Crimmin, 'Prisoners', p. 19.

[150] Ibid., p. 45.

[151] Gibbon to Sir Thomas Worsley, 8 July 1762, in Gibbon, *Letters*, vol. I, p. 131.

[152] Gibbon, *Miscellaneous Works*, p. 102.

more substantially.[153] But more than these famous individuals, it is the thousands of ordinary prisoners, as well as the populations they interacted and exchanged with, who are the subject of this book.

Such a topic requires varying the levels of approach and the types of sources, from small scale to large scale, depending on the object of study. To follow the prisoners' journeys from their ships to the prisons, in Europe and the colonies, an immense volume of material is available in the naval, colonial, and local archives in both France and Britain, which are saturated with cases involving prisoners of war. The rich political and juridical debates about war imprisonment fill the pages of parliamentary debates. The prisoners' experience, which has escaped the attention of historians, can be tracked thanks to 'ego-documents', such as individual petitions and memoirs. These sources are supplemented by legal treatises, pamphlets, private correspondence, and objects made by the prisoners.

Over the years that it took me to complete this project, it expanded greatly, and I had to make choices. There certainly could be more in the book about the prisoners' own perceptions; the bulk of my archives are state archives, which are read against the grain, but I decided not to study captivity narratives systematically. Furthermore, there is too little about women and gender relations—which is a topic I hope to explore in the future. Finally, a more comprehensive and definitive study of the French Wars remains to be done.

Chapter 1 considers the limits of international legal norms, which fail to encapsulate the complexity of the category. The chapter focuses on groups whose very belonging to the category of the prisoner of war was questioned. Paul Halliday warns us against teleological accounts of the history of international law, which contend that the eighteenth century saw the beginning of the triumph of liberal modernity, with the putative diminishing of legal anomalies and a greater standardization of legal categories.[154] I emphasize the contingency of the category 'prisoner of war', its lack of clarity, and the dependence on particular situations to give it specific definition.

Chapter 2 brings the societal dimension into the picture. There, the focus is on individuals and groups who were considered by everyone to be lawfully detained as prisoners of war: while they were understood by all sides to be 'alien enemies', public discussion revolved around their 'just' treatment in captivity. The study of philanthropic campaigns for improving the treatment of prisoners of war, or the sending of missionaries into prisons, demonstrates the particularity of the prisoner of war, as an enemy and a fellow human being.

---

[153] In 1765, David Hume intervened in a diplomatic dispute between Hanover and France about the expense of maintaining prisoners of war: Waldmann, *Further Letters*, Appendix IV. Joseph Banks spent much time trying to obtain the release of imprisoned scientists during the French Wars: Lipkowitz, ' "Sciences" '.

[154] Halliday, *Habeas Corpus*, pp. 35 and *passim*.

Chapter 3 defines prisoners of war as forced migrants. Although the notions of circulation and imprisonment seem antithetical, this chapter posits that spatial displacements were at the heart of the experience of war imprisonment. By comparing metropolitan, Atlantic, and Caribbean mobility, the shared features of the eighteenth-century state, at home and in the colonies, are highlighted. The prisoners' strategies to play the system are, I argue, a side-effect of the limitations of the reach of the state.

Chapter 4 changes the scale of analysis, by turning to prison buildings. These spaces of detention were, until the last quarter of the eighteenth century in Britain, and for the whole period in France, not purpose-built for prisoners of war. This absence of specialization tells us something important about the distance between the legal construction of the category of the prisoner of war and actual practices of internment. The chapter shows that war prisons must be understood in the same conceptual framework as prison 'reform' in the eighteenth century. Paying attention to the materiality of the prisons also entails looking at the multiple ways in which prisoners reconfigured these spaces, adapting or even destroying them.

Without presupposing that eighteenth-century wars changed the social fabric for good, I follow in chapter 5 Georg Simmel's hypothesis that war challenged established hierarchies and relations.[155] War is not just destruction and coercion: new 'social spaces' are invented and reproduce themselves in wartime.[156] The extreme cases of prisoners on parole on the one hand, and of the black combatants who were enslaved on the other, show that people's ability to play with labels ascribed by the state was socially differentiated.

Chapter 6 takes us back into the prison, to consider the question of order and disorder, from the perspective of everyday interactions. Rather than the laws of war, it is the laws of the prison that are the focus. While war prisons were violent spaces, the transactions between guards and prisoners varied considerably, from riots to corruption. Moreover, just like debtors' prisons, war prisons were connected to host societies, as is demonstrated by the study of escapes and prison markets.

The book closes with an epilogue, which sheds new light on a famous case. Napoleon was labelled in 1815 as a permanent prisoner of war, an individual at war against the civil society of European nations, even though France was then at peace with the rest of Europe. Around Napoleon, a miniature and inverted society of prisoners took shape on St Helena, which was structured by his presence and that of his small retinue. This status of the prisoner of the international community was a novelty. It also drew on eighteenth-century discussions, and it established a precedent. The status of Napoleon in St Helena was never settled, because the famous captive always refused the label that was assigned to him. For all prisoners of war, definitional issues were—and still are—eminently political.

---

[155] Malešević, *Sociology*, p. 44.   [156] Marchal, 'Frontières', pp. 42, 50; Neff, *War*, p. 13.

1

Defining the Prisoner of War in International Law: A Comparative Approach

I. Introduction

The present-day category of the prisoner of war, in the form that has been inherited from the international conventions of the twentieth century, needs to be deconstructed. One way of doing this is to confront official legal and administrative labels, and the ways in which they operated. Almost all of the recent scholarship on the law of war and of nations has focused on canonical writers from Gentili to Vattel. Very little has been written about how the law of nations worked. This in turn must lead us to explore sources of a different kind, which historians of legal ideas typically overlook.

Limitations of and exceptions to prisoner of war status are to be found in eighteenth-century treatises on the law of nations, but historians have often taken these for granted. In fact, historians need to ask in which cases international law did matter—and in which cases it did not. There was always a tension between legal categories and social practice. Were the distinctions between 'civilian' and 'combatant' meaningful, and how did they operate in practice? Were concepts of national belonging, ethnicity, religion, gender, or class important criteria for determining the treatment of captives?

This chapter is less a normative and intellectual history of international law than it is an examination of how state administrators tried to find ways to force the law to fit the contingencies of a situation. I will give attention not so much to the category of 'the' prisoner of war itself, as to the variety of contexts in which someone could come under this label. Instead of asking 'what is a prisoner of war?', I approach the question indirectly, by asking who is and who *isn't* a prisoner of war, depending on the situations and contexts. At times, the category expands; at others, it shrinks, with the number of exemptions rising. Ultimately, we cannot focus on the category of the prisoner of war alone, or we would miss a crucial dimension. Instead of presupposing that we are dealing with a well-defined concept in international law, we need to situate the prisoner of war in a continuum with other, 'neighbouring' categories,[1] in order to understand what the similarities

[1] Goffman, *Asylums*, p. 120.

The Society of Prisoners: Anglo-French Wars and Incarceration in the Eighteenth Century. Renaud Morieux, Oxford University Press (2019). © Renaud Morieux. DOI: 10.1093/oso/9780198723585.001.0001

and differences between them were.[2] Instead of a succession of modes of captivity, I suggest that it makes more sense to think in terms of the coexistence and even hybridization between them. Methodologically, adopting this frame of analysis requires, for now, that we do not consider that normative legal categories such as the prisoner of war exhaust all possible practical outcomes. In other words, we must forget what we think we know about what a prisoner of war is or was.

The contours of this legal category can be delineated by addressing a prior set of questions: where is a prisoner of war, i.e. how do different types of law intersect, spatially? When is a prisoner of war—that is, does war captivity always end when the peace is signed? Does it always begin when the war is declared? Who is the prisoner of war? Is the distinction between combatant and civilian always clear-cut and meaningful? And are these categories legal or political in nature? In turn, this analysis brings to the fore basic but fundamental questions such as: what is the relationship between the individual and the state? What exactly is a state?

We will proceed by breaking down three intellectual assumptions that have structured the study of the laws of war in the eighteenth century. The chapter opens with two sections that raise fundamental questions of definition, to suggest the porosity of the category of the prisoner of war. First, I explore the pertinence of the distinction between soldiers and civilians. Second, I break down the connection between state and nation, to consider the case of individuals captured while fighting against their sovereign. The third section complicates the definition further, by focusing on the practice of hostage-taking.

II. Can 'Civilians' be Prisoners of War?

Emer de Vattel was the most famous proponent of the view that wars were becoming more moderate in the eighteenth century. A sign of this civilizing process, for him, was the clearer distinction between soldiers and civilians. While 'formerly', he argued,

> every one capable of carrying arms became a soldier ... At present war is carried on by regular troops: the people, the peasants, the citizens, take no part in it, and generally have nothing to fear from the sword of the enemy. ... A laudable custom, truly worthy of those nations who value themselves on their humanity.[3]

Private wars had been replaced by public wars, and this went together with the exemption and protection of non-combatants from the evils of war.[4] However, as

---

[2] I am inspired in particular by Paul Halliday's work on the fluidity of early modern concepts of subjecthood: on prisoners of war, see *Habeas Corpus*, pp. 165–173 and 'Subjecthood'.

[3] Vattel, *Law of Nations*, book III, ch. 8, par. 147.

[4] McKeogh, 'Civilian immunity', pp. 74–5. See also Steinhoff, 'Killing civilians'; Roberts, 'Civilian'.

we will see in the following section, legal writers themselves sometimes articulated contradictory positions. And in practice, even women, who embodied the much-lauded principle of moderation in warfare, were frequently treated as prisoners of war for much of the eighteenth century. This complicates the very distinction between combatants and civilians: while the status of the prisoner of war is a protection for combatants, applying the category to civilians who do not fight appears to be a negation of their immunity. While gender and age were always presented as justifications for these legal exemptions, it is striking that most, if not all, of the secondary literature on the laws of war and civilians concerns itself only with the war on land. As the final section shows, the war at sea destabilizes this narrative even further.

A. Constraints in Warfare and Exemptions

From the Middle Ages onwards, just war theory (*jus ad bellum*) granted immunity to non-combatants, while acknowledging that they might become 'collateral damage' in extreme situations.[5] The Peace of God movement of the tenth and eleventh centuries witnessed the 'first systematic attempts to define and protect the status of non-combatants', granting immunity to clergy, women, children, the elderly, peasants, and the poor, among others.[6] In the sixteenth century, scholastic theologians placed themselves in the tradition of medieval canonists, such as Francisco de Vitoria, who considered that even in wars against infidels like the Turks, women were 'presumed innocent at least as far as the war is concerned', while in wars against Christians, peasants, children, travellers, and 'other peaceful civilians' were 'all to be presumed innocent'.[7] Although these theological traditions continued to be referred to across the Middle Ages and beyond, in practice, how far these immunities were respected is doubtful.

Another intellectual tradition, theorized by Christian thinkers from the Middle Ages and the Renaissance, defined which behaviours were acceptable and which were not. The focus was placed on the way in which war was waged on the battlefield (*jus in bello*).[8] Burlamaqui is exemplary of the increasing consensus, among eighteenth-century legal writers in Europe, that the life of non-combatants and prisoners of war should be spared. He wrote:

> In general even the laws of war require, that we should abstain from slaughter as much as possible, and not shed human blood without necessity. We ought not

---

[5] Howard, 'Constraints', p. 3; Keen, *Laws of War*, pp. 189–217.
[6] Stacey, 'The age', pp. 29, 35.   [7] *Political Writings*, quoted in Tuck, 'Democracy', p. 322.
[8] Parker, 'Early modern Europe', pp. 41–2; Best, *Humanity*, pp. 50–1; Johnson, *Just War Tradition*, ch. 3; Donagan, 'Codes and conduct', pp. 65–95; Lee, *Barbarians*, ch. 3–4; Neff, *War*, pp. 39–82.

therefore directly and deliberately to kill prisoners of war, nor those, who ask quarter, or surrender themselves, much less old men, women, and children; in general we should spare all those, whose age and profession render them unfit to carry arms, and who have no other share in the war, than being in the enemy's country.[9]

According to Jean-Matthieu Mattéi, this type of statement reveals the shift in the legal doctrine about the laws of war that took place between the end of the seventeenth century and the first half of the eighteenth. The number of exceptions increased within a 'permissive' framework, that is, with the accepting of a certain degree of violence; from the middle of the eighteenth century, the laws of war became 'prohibitive', which led to a process of normalization and codification of the principle of protection.[10] The distinction between combatants, who were seen as the enemies proper, and civilians, who now benefited from 'a sort of general immunity', whatever their status, sharpened.[11] However, in the quote above, Burlamaqui did not mention the possibility of treating civilians as prisoners of war: he distinguished the two categories. Even in the nineteenth century, the laws of international armed conflict remained silent on the question of civilians as prisoners of war: the Geneva Convention of 1864 did not define 'who was entitled to POW status'.[12]

Despite the proliferation of exceptions, in legal doctrine the definition of the enemy remained strikingly broad in the eighteenth century: Martens wrote in 1789 that 'war authorizes to consider as enemies all the subjects of the state against whom it has been declared'.[13] We must briefly return to Vattel here, since the ambiguity of his writings on the subject of non-combatants has been noted by historians.[14] Thus, Richard Tuck notes that 'the question of the status of civilian non-combatants in a legitimate war is, historically, much more contentious than many modern commentators imagine'.[15] Whereas Rousseau, for instance, considered that the only enemies were soldiers, Vattel saw all the subjects of a state as collective enemies: enmity was defined in the first case by the fact of bearing arms, and in the second by belonging to a state at war.[16] Thus, he still counted women, children, the aged, and the sick, as well as the clergy, men of letters, 'and other persons, whose callings are very remote from military affairs as *enemies* [my emphasis] who offer no resistance, and consequently the belligerent has no right to maltreat or otherwise offer violence to them'.[17]

---

[9] Burlamaqui, *Principles*, book III, part 4, ch. 6, IX.   [10] Mattéi, *Histoire*, pp. 638–41, 657, 708.
[11] Ibid., pp. 384, 402, 656.   [12] Benvenisti and Cohen, 'War', p. 1392.
[13] Martens, *Précis*, book VIII, ch. 4, par. 272, p. 231.
[14] Starkey, *War*, p. 18; Best, *Humanity*, pp. 54–5.   [15] Tuck, 'Democracy', p. 321.
[16] Senellart, 'Qualification', par. 24.   [17] Vattel, *Law of Nations*, book III, ch. 8, par. 145, 146.

Furthermore, the realities of the military situation meant that it was legitimate for a general to imprison women and children if the necessity of war dictated it.[18] There could also be cases in which it was lawful to put prisoners to death, for instance, when fighting 'a formidable nation, savage and perfidious' and when our own salvation was at stake: in such situations, 'necessity' should prevail over 'humanity'.[19] By the same token, it was also lawful to enslave those prisoners of war whom one had the right to kill.[20] Ultimately, as Michel Senellart remarks, according to Vattel,

> The respect of non-combatants does not come from the fact that they should not be considered as enemies, but from the absence of danger which they represent as non-resisting enemies. This [was a] negative qualification, defining an attitude and not a status... The immunity of non-combatants, therefore, is not guaranteed by law...
>
> Between the prohibition to take the life of enemy non-combatants and the right to imprison them for tactical reasons an indeterminate space opens up, in which the laws of war unfold. This space does not mirror the sharing out between legal and illegal, but defines the limits of acceptable humanity, or tolerable inhumanity, depending on the imperatives of military action.[21]

As Vattel's views demonstrate, the fate of non-combatants, including women and children, often depended more on local circumstances and military necessity than on legal theory.

B. Women and Children

Women and children epitomized the 'innocent civilian' in the eighteenth century as in the present day.[22] Granting a status of exemption to women and children, in time of war, was not as straightforward as legal writers tended to argue. In reality, women were frequently incarcerated with their husbands. This could be down to the woman's choice, as in 1695, when the nine men composing the crew of a small English ship captured by a privateer from Dunkirk were put in prison. 'The wife of the English captain who had desired to follow her husband in prison' was detained with them.[23] Clearly, women were not considered to be 'normal' prisoners. The

---

[18] Ibid., par. 148. See McKeogh, 'Civilian', pp. 77–82; Benvenisti and Cohen, 'War', pp. 1406–7; Luban, 'Military necessity'.

[19] Vattel, *Law of Nations*, book III, ch. 8, par. 151. On the seventeenth century, see Donagan, *War*, pp. 157–8, 161–3.

[20] Vattel, *Law of Nations*, book III, ch. 8, par. 152.   [21] Senellart, 'Qualification', par. 25–7.

[22] Charli Carpenter, '*Innocent Women*'; Zanetti, 'Women'.

[23] 27 December 1695, Archives Nationales, Paris (AN), MAR/B3/88, fo. 286v.

lists of prisoners of war composed by the naval administrators in the ports would usually mention women separately, as a subcategory alongside the captains, surgeons, passengers, sailors, and soldiers. Thus, in St Malo, the *Marine* administrator listed the names of 268 individuals who had been sent back to England on 26 June 1703, among whom were twenty-four 'Supernumeraries. Women and children.'[24] The assessment of his colleague from Dunkirk was blunter: the nine women who had been brought with other people by privateers were 'soldiers' wives and other insignificant people', who should be released without delay, since they could not be exchanged and at the same time 'clutter up the prison'.[25] However, during the War of the Spanish Succession, state administrators and officials did not agree on the treatment of these groups. For instance, whether they should be accounted for in the lists of prisoners and entered into the balance of exchange was not decided.[26] Their social status could also influence the decision to release them or not. Commissaire Chasteauneuf in Calais decided to send back home four English women who were in prison, because of their 'humble origins', by which he presumably meant that their exchange value was not great.[27]

At the beginning of the War of the Austrian Succession, the British and French stances were at odds with one another. On the British side, women passengers captured at sea, as well as children, were commonly released.[28] In the summer of 1744, the Lords of the Admiralty recommended freeing them without investigating further: 'We ... direct you to set her at liberty & to give her a passport to return to France, and to do the same by all women & girls, and all boys not exceeding twelve years of age, that have been or shall hereafter be taken.'[29] On the other hand, on the French side, there was a clear reluctance to let the British women imprisoned in France go 'for free'. Thus, at the beginning of September 1744, 633 English male prisoners were detained in Brest, and fifty-two women, among whom were '7 who deserve some consideration', according to Bigot de la Mothe, *Intendant de la Marine*. These gentlewomen requested permission to return to England, but the French authorities only consented to this on the condition that they promised that 'they would obtain the return from England of a similar number of men'.[30] The course of action chosen in France was therefore to treat women prisoners like officers, who were given their freedom on parole.

---

[24] St Sulpice to Secrétaire d'Etat de la Marine (SSM), 'Rolle des noms', 26 September 1703, MAR/F2/83.
[25] Vergier to SSM, 31 January 1703, MAR/B3/120, fos. 25v–26.
[26] See, for example, St Sulpice to SSM, 6 July 1703, MAR/B3/120, fo. 525v.
[27] Chasteauneuf to SSM, 16 January 1710, MAR/B3/178, fo. 362v.
[28] Lords of the Admiralty (LCA) to Sick & Wounded Board (S&W), 18, 25 July 1744, National Maritime Museum, Greenwich (NMM), ADM/M/388, nos. 112, 122.
[29] LCA to S&W, ibid., 8 August 1744, no. 148.
[30] SSM to Bigot de la Mothe, 3 September 1744, AN, MAR/B2/323, fo. 73. See also SSM to chevalier de Camilly, commander of Brest, 28 August 1744, and SSM to du Teillay, *commissaire de la Marine* in Rochefort, 2 December 1744, MAR/B2/323, fos. 62, 243v.

Attempts were made to clarify the question of the exemption of women. At the end of August 1744, British and French officials met at the Castle of Wattignies (northern France) to discuss the project of a cartel, and they put their arguments on the table. Different principles of justification clashed. The British listed the (bad) reasons that the French had for exchanging women as prisoners: the discrepancy between their pretentions to be a civilized nation and their attitude to the *beau sexe* ('very unbecoming the politess, which that nation is so apt to boast, for subjecting the sex to the hardships attendant on prisoners of war'); the lack of coherence of this policy, which classed women as prisoners but proposed to exempt boys under twelve; and economic rationality, based on the French assumption that English women travelled more often by water, hence more would be taken and exchanged for French men. By contrast, a high moral ground dictated the British policy: 'It is already a rule in England, to set at liberty, without any consideration, all female prisoners, as well as the boys abovementioned. It is to be hoped, the French, upon second thoughts, will not give occasion even to a bare suspension of these acts of generosity.'[31] 'As they cannot have any part in acts of hostility in the war', the British commissioner added, women were to be con-sidered not as prisoners of war but 'as neutrals'.[32] The onus for adopting such a policy was placed on France.

The French negotiators used a different set of arguments. First, in previous wars, women had been exchanged like other passengers. And, second, an unfair comparative advantage transgressed 'the principles of equality' and reciprocity.[33] Indeed, British women tended to travel by sea, whereas very few French women did so: consequently, 'there is in Brest a considerable number of imprisoned women and girls, whereas we are not aware of any French [woman] in England'.[34] The cost of the subsistence of these women, while imprisoned in France, thus had to be compensated by the British.[35] In the end, argued the French, while ship boys and boys under twelve years old might be released without ransom, 'women girls and all other passengers' had to be entered in the balance of exchanges 'on the same footing as the rest of the crews'.[36] While Hume, the British negotiator of the cartel, 'thought women ought not to be looked upon as Prisoners of War', his French counterpart, Commissaire Givry, insisted on it, which 'is owing to having above 200 of them now in France'.[37] The French officials' opposition to the release of women was evidently not one of principle. In Givry's own words, this issue

[31] 'Some observations', 4 September 1744, The National Archives, Kew (TNA), ADM98/2, fo. 10.
[32] 'Observations of the Commissioners', 27 November 1744, ibid., fo. 78.
[33] French proposal of a cartel, with English comments [December 1744], article 12, ibid., fo. 71v.
[34] SSM to Bigot de la Mothe, 14 December 1744, AN, MAR/B2/323, fo. 257.
[35] French proposal of a cartel [December 1744], article 12, TNA, ADM98/2, fos. 71v–72.
[36] Givry, 'Observations', 30 August 1744, AN, Marine F2/72, fo. 75.
[37] Meeting of De Givry and Hume, 28 August 1744, TNA, ADM98/2, fo. 8.

should not stand in the way of the conclusion of the cartel 'because it is in fact a trifling matter'.[38]

Until the end of 1744, British women were still treated as prisoners and exchanged as such by the French.[39] However, the negotiation of a general exchange cartel, in 1744–5, was a turning point. Although the negotiation ultimately failed, some basic agreement was reached regarding women.[40] Article 12 of the project, which circulated in June 1745, stated that 'women will not be included in the exchanges, but they will be maintained by the state in whose territories they will find themselves until they travel by the first packets. They will only be mentioned on the registers for the record.'[41] From then on, women were generally released without difficulties, and they were not accounted for in the exchanges of prisoners.[42] While this was not universally implemented,[43] 'all Women in general who are taken in the Enemy's Ships' were now discharged and sent home without delay.[44] The same principles were applied to young boys on both sides of the Channel.[45]

Women and children were released from captivity in the conflicts that followed. During the Seven Years' War, the precedent of the 1740s was invoked to justify these decisions.[46] Women and children under twelve were now sent home on a regular basis, as shown by an account drafted in September 1757 by the Office for the Sick and Wounded Seamen, which estimated that more than 6,000 prisoners had been exchanged between France and Britain since December 1756, adding that 'there have been 180 women and children sent to France and 27 received from thence who are not brought to account'.[47] Reasons of practicability led to this evolution. The lack of places to accommodate prisoners of war put pressure on the central and local administrations. In May 1757, for example, more than 200 French boys were prisoners of war at Portsmouth. Brushing aside potential objections to this measure, the Sick & Wounded Board advocated the release of all boys—not only those under twelve, but those between twelve and fourteen years of age as well—because this 'would be of great Benefit by the thinning the Prisons'.[48] A couple of years later, when a great number of French men, women, and children arrived at Plymouth from India, the 'considerable expense' that these people occasioned to the crown motivated the decision to send them to France, alongside the numerous officers of the French India Company also detained in Plymouth.[49]

---

[38] De Givry, 13 September 1744, AN, MAR/B2/323, fo. 536.

[39] Clairambault, *commissaire de la Marine* in Port-Louis to SSM, 2 October, 7 December 1744, ibid., fos. 187, 231.

[40] Cabantous, 'Gens de mer', p. 259.   [41] TNA, ADM98/2, fo. 161v.

[42] Guillot to S&W, 19 November, 16 December 1745, ADM97/103, fos. 62v, 73.

[43] Guillot to SSM, 1 September 1746, AN, MAR/B3/445, fos. 204–5.

[44] LCA to S&W, 24 November 1747, NMM, ADM/M/400, no. 389.

[45] Charron, Dunkirk, to SSM, 4 February 1745, AN, MAR/B3/429, fo. 46v.

[46] 28 August 1756, TNA, ADM98/5, fo. 197; Moras to S&W, 11 June 1757, ADM97/106, fo. 20.

[47] 1 September 1757, ADM98/6, fo. 227v.   [48] S&W to LCA, 19 May 1757, ibid., fo. 156.

[49] S&W to LCA, 11 May 1762, ADM98/9, fo. 72v.

However, one should note that their swift release did not mean that women and children were not prisoners of war, only that they were granted a sort of administrative exemption, based on customary agreements, by virtue of their sex or age, and because they were not worth spending scarce resources on. Hence, in 1758 Madame Quaire, who had been 'taken and carried prisoner to Bristol', where she was 'permitted to lodge in a private house' to cure a wound she had received, was allowed to return to France in a neutral ship. But when she requested to reside in London, this was refused, on the grounds that 'prisoners of war have not been permitted, though several have desired it, to reside in England, on account of the general objection, which must subsist against suffering such people to continue at large in the kingdom, whose principles and views cannot be ascertained'.[50] By definition, exemptions to the status of the prisoner of war could always be revoked by the authorities, and this happened regularly. Beyond the case of women, passengers, or civilians, this was a feature of war imprisonment more generally in the eighteenth century.

During the American War of Independence, the question of whether or not to label women and children as prisoners of war was still undecided. On the one hand, they were never released before their rights were first ascertained. A memorandum written in September 1778 detailed the prevailing practice during the earlier conflict at Dinan. Women and children were given 'preference' of release, and their treatment in the Breton town resembled that of officers on parole: 'they had the freedom of the town, like captains and officers . . . , [and] were like other prisoners collecting their food ration from [Dinan] Castle.'[51] This remained the practice towards women passengers.[52] On the other hand, their exceptional status was recognized, as in this French circular to the *Intendants* and *commissaires généraux de la Marine* of December 1778: 'Women will only be considered as passengers, and they will receive the same treatment as their husbands until they are sent back home' (article 13).[53] Article 11 of the general cartel concluded in March 1780 between France and Britain stated that:

All passengers who are not serving in the military or the navy, . . . will not be held to be Prisoners, but they will be given the freedom to return home, without being entered in the list of exchanges, as soon as they have proven, with authentic certificates, that they are really exceptional cases. All women, children, servants, under twelve years old, will not be held to be Prisoners, nor entered in the list of exchanges.[54]

[50] S&W to LCA, 4 February 1758, NMM, ADM/F/17.
[51] 'Mémoire', Dépôt de la Marine, 24 September 1778, AN, Marine F2/72, no. 21.
[52] Casamajor, Rochefort, 29 August 1778: AN, Marine F2/82, no. 013.
[53] 14 December 1778, ibid.   [54] *CTS*, vol. 47.

By implication, as stated in the article, husbands also sometimes benefited from these measures. They often requested to be set free in order to escort their wives home. This was the object of the request made in 1757 by the French captain of a merchant ship, whose wife was heavily pregnant and in a 'very bad State of Health', and therefore unable to proceed to France: he asked, with the support of the Sick & Wounded Board, to be allowed to accompany her 'upon causing Security to be given that he will procure the Release of an English Captain'.[55] The practice of releasing gentlewomen while placing them under the 'protection' or 'care' of men 'of certain Ranks' became established during the American War of Independence.[56] These women often travelled home together with returning prisoners of war, which might have explained this caution. For instance, two French ladies, one the wife of the late French governor of Chandernagore, the other of a factor in India, accompanied by gentlemen and several servants, objected to going to France on board a cartel ship, 'on Account of the American Prisoners going over in the said Ships'.[57]

With the French Wars, the exceptional status of women and children was finally recognized. This was stated in the project of a general cartel of exchange negotiated in 1798.[58] The administrative regulations adopted in Britain in 1803 testify to the same idea: the *Instructions for Agents* listed these two groups, together with surgeons, chaplains, schoolmasters, or passengers 'who are not engaged in the naval or military Service of the Enemy, nor Sea-faring Persons', among those 'considered as Non-Combatants', who were 'to be immediately released'.[59] The 1807 'Instructions for Agents' seemed to settle the question once and for all: 'You are not to receive any Women or Girls into your Custody, if you can possibly avoid it, as such Persons are not meant to be treated as Prisoners of War.'[60] In reality, these exemptions did not prevent Napoleon from detaining hundreds of women and children who had 'voluntarily' chosen to stay alongside their husbands in May 1803.[61] Likewise, British prisons and hospitals received many women, who were detained together with their husbands. The Wesleyan reverend William Toase, narrating his visit to a Kent hospital in 1811, mentioned an elderly Dutch woman, who had been captured by an English ship while fishing with her husband, leaving behind four small children.[62] This case was far from exceptional. The incarceration of women and children continued until the very end of our period, as shown by an 1812 return of prisoners of war

---

[55]   26 February 1757, TNA, ADM98/6, fo. 102.

[56]   S&W to LCA, 11 September, 6 October 1778, ADM98/11, fos. 125v, 138v. See also Mayor of Dartmouth to S&W, 28 April 1779, ADM98/12, fo. 2.

[57]   Cowdry to S&W, Mill Prison Plymouth, ADM97/127/1.

[58]   'Project of a General Cartel', presented to the Ministers of Britain, article 11, in *Report* (1798), Appendix, p. 76.

[59]   *Instructions for Agents* (1803), no. 6.   [60]   'Instructions for Agents' (1807), article V, p. 5.

[61]   Alger, *Napoléon's British Visitors*; Duché, 'Passage', ch. 2.

[62]   Toase, *Wesleyan Mission*, p. 31.

detained in Britain. At this time, the vast majority of prisoners were French. The document numbered more than 3,231 French prisoners on parole, including 211 'Passengers, and other Persons of respectability' and 115 women and children. Another 49,418 people were 'in confinement', of whom thirty-seven were women and children.[63]

Gender was a criterion, theoretically at least, for being exempted from becoming a prisoner of war. Occupation was another, and legal writers listed the categories of people, farmers, merchants, or artisans, who played no part in war and as such should be protected. But the war at sea presented specific challenges to this view: the very concept of civilians was applied imperfectly at sea.

III. Traitors and Rebels

After questioning the soldier/civilian dichotomy, this section turns towards a consideration of state and nation, in examining the categories of 'traitor' and 'rebel'. From reading the present-day literature on the laws of war, one might assume that the very status of the prisoner of war is granted only to national combatants. Tellingly, however, international treaties are silent on the issue of what happens to the people who are captured while fighting against 'their own' country. But, by international custom, these people are not entitled to the status of the prisoner of war. While the tension between legislation and custom is fundamental, this conception is a product of the late nineteenth century, an age in which the nation-state was seen as triumphant, and it should not be projected backwards into the eighteenth century. We need to break down the 'natural' connection between state and nation. There are further reasons for doing this. It is well known that European armies and navies were made up of individuals who came from various countries, and whose religious confessions and ethnicities were extremely varied, in that period and beyond.[64] At sea, this was the case in merchant ships as well as in the navy. While the presence of foreigners in the armed forces was normal, it could be problematic when people were captured while fighting for the enemy. Establishing whether these people had voluntarily enlisted or had been coerced was crucial in this context. There were indeed continuous attempts to recruit imprisoned enemy soldiers or sailors, and these attempts were widely considered to be a transgression of the law of nations. In what follows, I focus on the first half of the eighteenth century, a period which defined principles that remained valid in the following decades.

---

[63] 'A return', 26 June 1812. The return also listed thirty-six Danes on parole, and 1,832 in confinement. Many more boys under twelve were detained in hulks: Branch Johnson, *English Prison Hulks*, pp. 52–3.

[64] Conway, *Britannia's Auxiliaries*; Kiernan, 'Foreign mercenaries'; Caputo, 'Alien seamen'.

Instead of looking ahead to the nineteenth century, we should travel back in time. One major consequence of the Protestant Reformation and, in particular, of the Peace of Augsburg (1555) was the attempt by European states to fill their territory with a population whose religion was consistent with that of their sovereign. The impact of this upon European armies and navies was considerable, as became apparent during the War of the League of Augsburg and the War of the Spanish Succession. The 1690s were a period when the absolute coherence between allegiance to the monarchy and religious confession was asserted with urgency in both England and France. But these aims only increased the blurred nature of military configurations, which saw people cross state allegiances on a regular basis. Religious difference was indeed the major drive behind the wars that opposed France and Britain until 1715, and, to an extent, until 1745. The Revocation of the Edict of Nantes in France and the accession of William of Orange to the throne accelerated the movements of soldiers and sailors in both directions, who chose to fight for a sovereign who shared their confession, rather than for their 'legitimate' king.[65] After the Treaty of Limerick of 1691, perhaps 15,000 soldiers, accompanied by 4,000 women and children, left Ireland for service to France, to help prepare an invasion of England and pave the way for a return of the Stuarts to the throne.[66] There were many ways to defy the state's religion, but the most extreme one was to join the ranks of the enemy. This situation exposed the sailors captured on board enemy ships to the risk of being branded as traitors, and not as prisoners of war.[67] At the same time, the never-ending need of states for sailors meant that applying the law rigorously was not always the preferred option. This section considers what happened when the prisoner's 'nation' came into conflict with his religious confession. Could the status of a prisoner of war be granted to a 'national' fighting for the enemy? How pliable and reversible was subjecthood?

The first thing to observe is that the recruitment of prisoners of war to one's armed forces was very common throughout the eighteenth century, even though international treaties made it illegal.[68] In France, the officers serving in the Irish regiments of the French army made it their business, with the French monarchy's blessing, to comb prison depots and recruit their countrymen as well as English men into French privateers and men-of-war and, at times, into privateers fighting under the commission of King James.[69] In 1695, Louis Lebigot de Gastines, *commissaire général de la Marine* in St Malo thus gave his permission to some of these officers 'to do some levies among the Dinan prisoners', while asking them

---

[65] Cullen, 'Irish diaspora', pp. 139–40.   [66] Rowlands, *Army in Exile*, p. 5.
[67] This issue had been abundantly discussed for the English Civil War, when each side claimed that their enemies were 'traitors': Donagan, *War*, pp. 130–2.
[68] On forced enlistment, see, for example, 'Convention de l'Ecluse' between Britain and France for prisoners of war of the 'ground troops', 6 February 1759, article 24, AN, MAR/B4/97, fo. 215.
[69] For a study of these Irish privateers during the Nine Years' War, see Bromley, *Corsairs*, ch. 8.

'not to use any violence against them'.[70] During the War of the Spanish Succession, complaints about these recruitments led state authorities to try to limit this phenomenon, but keeping the Irish recruiting officers under control was difficult.[71] The reputation of insubordination of these men was already well established by then.[72] In February 1706, the *commissaire de la Marine* in St Malo, Jean-Baptiste Lempereur, wrote to the English commissioners that he had obeyed their request and prevented Irish officers 'from mingling' with their prisoners, sending them a safe distance away from the prisons.[73] In reality, this did not have much effect, and controversy over this issue rose in the following months. One Ellis Brand, lieutenant in an English man-of-war, returning from Dunkirk, declared that Irish soldiers

> [had] abducted his servant named david bryan, and forced him to serve the King of France.... Also declares that more than ten or twelve men of the crew of the *Ecureuil* were recruited in the service of the French, and believes truly that it was through the interposition of these Irish soldiers, who were authorized to come into the prison when they wanted'.[74]

In the same way, the French officially complained to their British counterparts about the fate of French prisoners in England, and the 'violence done to these poor people, by forcing them to serve on English ships', while they swore they would never recruit Irishmen in the French navy, even those who 'were often willing to stay in France'.[75] While a certain amount of duplicity was certainly present on both sides, one should not underestimate the extent to which recruiting officers disregarded the instructions they received to stop such practices, as shown by internal administrative correspondence. In the Breton towns where the Irish regiments were concentrated, Irish captains did exactly as they wished in 1707–9. In Dinan, the French Commissaire Lempereur noted that one of these Irish officers had recruited and retained English prisoners of war, 'despite everything I told him', and had beaten with a stick an English captain who was complaining about this.[76] Such behaviours irked Michel Chamillart, the secretary of state for War, who ordered in desperation, just as he had done three years before, that these Irish officers 'withdraw 6 or 7 leagues from these towns', while the most violent of them should be punished, since their behaviour exposed French prisoners in England to the risk of reprisals. But the minister's next sentence casts the whole affair in a different light: 'the encouragement I have

[70] Gastines, 22 May 1695, AN, MAR/B3/89, fo. 88.
[71] On the violence resorted to by Irish jailors to recruit English prisoners into the French service, see Scouller, *Armies*, pp. 318–20.
[72] Genet-Rouffiac, *Grand Exil*, pp. 166, 172–3.
[73] Copy of Lempereur to S&W, 9 February 1706, AN, MAR/B3/135, fo. 71.
[74] In copy of S&W to Lempereur, 26 October 1706, ibid., fo. 350.
[75] SSM to Count of Sunderland, 9 November 1707, MAR/B2/199 fo. 641.
[76] Lempereur to SSM, 10 March 1709, MAR/B3/169, fo. 77.

given in the ports to the merchants who trade in Scotland and Ireland will procure you enough goodwill, without the officers of these being obliged to recruit [prisoners] by force.'[77] In other words, the recruitment of Catholic Irishmen or Englishmen was not the issue, as long as they willingly enlisted in the French navy or had deserted from the British armed forces. On the other hand, forcefully recruiting prisoners of war was eminently problematic, not least because it exposed French prisoners recently converted to Catholicism to the same risks in Britain.[78] In reality, when given the choice between being released from prison and serving in the navy, or being confined for an indeterminate period of time while starving, it is no wonder that hundreds of French Huguenots and Irish Catholics willingly changed sides.[79]

During the War of the Austrian Succession, the French ministry was less reticent about the recruitment of Irish, as well as English, Catholic prisoners, offering them their freedom in return for enlisting in the French armed forces.[80] The successful endeavours of the recruiting officers of the Irish regiments, such as Lord Drummond's and Lord Clare's regiments, in Dunkirk, Calais or Dieppe, alarmed the Sick & Wounded Board. The problem, as these British officials were well aware, was the 'Necessities and Misery of the unhappy Men' who could easily be tempted to enlist, as their hope to be exchanged receded into a distant future.[81] The same causes produced the same effects in Britain, where Protestant prisoners volunteered to serve in the navy.[82]

The prisoners' faith thus remained a key criterion in determining whether it was legitimate to recruit them. The assumption, which was generally confirmed by practice, was that prisoners who shared the same faith as their captors would be more willing to serve a new sovereign. The Lords of the Admiralty thus gave orders to enlist Protestant prisoners only, whose confession had been ascertained by a French minister.[83] During the American War of Independence, recriminations about the forced enlistment of prisoners of war continued on both sides, with the same emphasis being placed on constraint or willingness.[84] Answering

[77] Chamillart to unknown, 13 March 1709, MAR/B2/214, fos. 749–50.
[78] Chamillart to [Lempereur], 1 May 1709, MAR/B2/215, fo. 388–90. See also petition by former British prisoners of war in France describing the 'deceitfull practices' used to decoy them 'into the French service', in S&W to Pontchartrain, 5 October 1709, British Library, London (BL), Add MS61593, fo. 1116.
[79] SSM to Lempereur, 27 November 1709, AN, MAR/B2/217, fos. 855–6. See Scouller, *Armies*, pp. 301–3.
[80] SSM to Bigot de la Mothe, 3 July 1744, MAR/B2/323, fo. 8; to Guillot, 12 August 1744, fo. 46; to Marquis de Coëtmen, 21 August 1744, fo. 58; to Bigot de la Mothe, 17 May 1745, MAR/B2/325, fos. 244; to S&W, 18 June 1745, fo. 847.
[81] S&W to LCA, 29 November 1744, TNA, ADM98/2, fo. 50, enclosing a letter from William Norton in Dunkirk, 6 November 1744, fo. 50v. See also same to same, 2 April 1747, ADM98/4, fo. 82.
[82] S&W to LCA, 17 July 1747, ADM98/4, fos. 132–v.
[83] S&W to LCA, 1 March 1747, ibid., fo. 199; S&W to LCA, 20, 22, 28 April 1758, NMM, ADM/F/17.
[84] S&W to LCA, 10 August 1779, TNA, ADM98/12, fo. 68; summary of the memorandum written on 7 August 1778 by French prisoners detained in a New York hulk, AN, MAR/4/151, fos. 119–20.

French complaints in December 1779, the Sick & Wounded Board thus remarked that the number of French prisoners entered into British service had been 'very inconsiderable, and as far as we know [these men] have voluntarily offered themselves, and not been obtained either by Stratagem, Ill Usage or Violence'.[85] The link between the religious and military dimensions was clearly highlighted in the 1780 cartel of exchange negotiated by the two countries:

> It will be expressly forbidden, & it will not be suffered in any way, that anyone should resort to scheming, seduction or force, to engage or compel any Prisoner, on either side, to change religion, or transgress the fidelity they owe to their King & their country, by entering into the service of the Power in whose domain they may be Prisoners.[86]

Whether they had been forcefully recruited or not, it was questionable whether the men who had been captured wearing enemy uniforms should be treated as prisoners of war or not. Irish Catholics captured on board French ships or under the commission of King James could be prosecuted as traitors and hanged, while the French Huguenots captured in English ships faced the prospect of being sent to the galleys. The case of the Irish is particularly interesting, as it reveals the different factors that could play a role in the state's treatment of such people. Essentially, in Britain the monarchy, backed by most lawyers, considered that the allegiance Irishmen owed to the King of England and Ireland was inalienable: serving an enemy was an act of treason. Subjects of the crown captured while on board enemy ships of war or privateers 'are not considered as prisoners of war, but as rebels', wrote the English judge Sir Michael Foster in 1762.[87] The French monarchy argued, on the other hand, that these men were prisoners of war: they were to be treated according to the law of nations, and had to be released. These clear-cut opinions, backed by referring to the common law or the law of nations, failed, once again, to describe reality accurately. There were many factors behind the decision to label a prisoner in this or that way.

The status of the Irish Catholics who migrated to France as a consequence of the Glorious Revolution should have been settled by the Treaty of Limerick. Concluded on 3 October 1691, this agreement put an end to the war in Ireland between the partisans of William of Orange and those of James II. It allowed Irish, English, and Scottish Jacobite officers and soldiers to leave freely for France, accompanied by their families, and continue to serve James II in the Irish Brigade.[88] But the Irish parliament was reluctant to implement the civil articles of the treaty, which paved the way for a long discussion in Britain about the

[85] S&W to LCA, 27 December 1779, TNA, ADM98/12, fo. 154.
[86] CTS, vol. 47.   [87] Foster, Discourse, pp. 59–61.
[88] Treaty of Limerick (3 October 1691), 'Military articles', pp. 149–54.

binding obligations of an international treaty on the Irish and English parlia-
ments.[89] The advantages normally granted to Irish soldiers by the treaty were
legally contested in Britain. The Irishmen captured on board French privateers or
men-of-war were thus convicted by English courts, and 'variously charged with
high treason, robbery, piracy and murder', despite invoking the protection of the
Treaty of Limerick for their defence.[90]

For example, one Thomas Reilly wrote from 'Plemus' [Plymouth], in June 1693,
that he was ill-treated in prison 'because I am an Irishman which surprises me
very much given that I have my wife and my children in Nantes that I am
domiciled there and that I have been captured while under the service of the
King of France in the *Prince de Galles* where I was the Cap.'''. He asked to be
exchanged as a prisoner of war, 'being presently the subjects [sic] of France'.[91] But
people like Reilly, and especially the men who were captured under King James's
commission, were prosecuted as traitors or pirates in England, and in 1694–6,
some of them were hanged.[92] This news was received with gloom across the
Channel. In August 1694, the secretary of state for the *Marine* thus informed
Commissaire Gastines that in England, 'they will hang without mercy, all the
English and Irish men they will take on our vessels'.[93] In October, the French
minister received a letter from a French captain from Honfleur, who had just
returned from London prisons, 'who told me the same,...that seven have been
hanged recently, and the others are facing the same fate'.[94] However, many more
Irish privateers were pardoned than executed in the following years; most of them
were exchanged as prisoners of war.[95]

During the War of the Spanish Succession, cases of this sort continued to be
very common, not least because the interpretation of the Treaty of Limerick
differed in Britain and in France, but also because the articulation between
municipal law and the laws of nation was not the same in both countries. The
question of multiple allegiances was also a vexed one.[96] The case of Peter Drake is
well documented, in particular thanks to the memoirs he wrote in 1753.[97] In 1707,
this Irish-born Catholic, born in 1671, was captured on board a French privateer
from Dunkirk, and put in the notorious Marshalsea prison in London. In a
petition to the Earl of Sunderland, summarized by the Sick & Wounded Board,
he explained that he had moved to France legally, 'pursuant to the Treaty of
Lymrick' of 1691. For his defence, he argued that he had been serving on the

---

[89] O'Higgins, 'Treaty'.   [90] Ibid., p. 224. See Bromley, *Corsairs*, pp. 157–65.
[91] Thomas Reilly to 'Gatinnes', June 1693, AN, MAR/B3/75, fo. 349.
[92] Lempereur to SSM, 2 June 1695, MAR/B3/88, fo. 59. On these seven men, see Bromley, *Corsairs*,
pp. 158–9, 162. On the legal debate about the status of the privateers serving James, see Rubin, *Law of
Piracy*, pp. 69–76.
[93] SSM to Gastines, 15 August 1694, MAR/B2/82, fo. 191v.   [94] Ibid., 13 October 1694, fo. 237v.
[95] Bromley, *Corsairs*, pp. 162–5; Halliday, 'Subjecthood', p. 19.
[96] John Bromley describes similar cases during the 1690s: *Corsairs*, pp. 161–2.
[97] See critical edition by S.A. Burrell: *Amiable Renegade*.

French ship in order to prepare his escape to England and 'getting home into his [own] country'. He also presented attestations written on his behalf 'from several persons... of good repute tho Roman Catholicks'. The commissioners doubted his motives, since he should have had plenty of opportunities to get away without fighting in an enemy privateer.[98] By the time of his arrest, Drake had already served in Dutch, Spanish, French, and English armies.[99]

How to categorize Drake was not straightforward. The Sick & Wounded Board asked the Attorney General for his guidance, 'whether he ought to be tried as a traytor, or whether we may exchange him as a subject of France, but if neither, that he may give good security for his peacable behavior in England'.[100] These labels were all potentially legitimate, and the decision to favour one or the other was above all political. In the end, he was transferred to Newgate and tried for treason in June 1708; despite invoking the military articles of Limerick, he was found guilty and sentenced to death. The sentence was later commuted to life imprisonment, before he was granted a royal pardon.[101] By the summer of 1709, Drake had returned to the French service, but he was soon captured and made a prisoner on parole. In the spring of 1710, he turned coat once again and joined an English regiment.[102] Not everyone managed to jump ship with such alacrity and success. An English captain in the French service 'Nightingale', Thomas Smith, was also detained with Drake; he was executed in June 1708.[103]

The echo of Smith's and Drake's treatment reverberated in France and elsewhere. Lempereur wrote on 3 November 1709 that 'the adventure of Mrs Smith and Drak is indeed a sad and gloomy omen for the Irishmen who had the bad luck to fall into the hands of the English'.[104] The French ministry also asked Lempereur to confirm 'whether it is true that the English had hanged the Irishmen captured on board French privateers'.[105] Beyond this specific case, Paul O'Higgins argues that the trial of Peter Drake probably established an important precedent: from then on, the English courts refused to extend the meaning of the Treaty of Limerick to protect Irish soldiers in the service of France: they were traitors. However, O'Higgins adds that 'the intention of the Military Articles' was implemented 'by administrative action': these same men 'were treated not as traitors but

---

[98] S&W to Earl of Sunderland, 3 May 1707, BL, Add MS61591, fos. 127-v. His memoirs do not dissipate the impression that he hid 'the real Truth of [his] Story' behind multiple smokescreens: see *Memoirs*, pp. 9 (quotation), 17–18 on faked identities.

[99] *Amiable Renegade*, introduction, pp. xx, xxxiv–xxxv.

[100] S&W to Sunderland, 3 May 1707, BL, Add MS61591, fo. 127v.

[101] Drake, *Memoirs*, pp. 150–2, 164–6. Records of the trial are in TNA, HCA1/16, fo. 168. It may very well be that the prosecution was undertaken with this outcome in mind.

[102] *Amicable Renegade*, introduction, pp. xxxvi–xxxix.

[103] Drake, *Memoirs*, p. 157. The French authorities mistakenly characterized Smith as an Irishman: Lempereur to S&W, 18 April 1708, BL, MS61592, fo. 59.

[104] Lempereur to SSM, 3 November 1709, AN, MAR/B3/169, fo. 335.

[105] SSM to Lempereur, 6 November 1709, MAR/B2/217, fo. 557.

as ordinary prisoners of war, despite the fact that in English law they were traitors'.[106]

What should take precedence when assessing the claims of these people? The law of the country in which they were born? The law of the country where they had found asylum? Or the law of nations? The answer to this determined the legal categories applied to the prisoners. Much creativity was required on the part of the state administrators in charge of dealing with the exchange of prisoners of war. For instance, in 1706–7, one Mr Murphy, an Irishman imprisoned in Guernsey, had been captured bearing arms against the British monarchy, in the French service. The release of 'Mr. Morphy' was claimed by Commissaire Lempereur in St Malo, 'because having been married above 12 years at Brest, he is by consequence become a subject of the king, and can be look'd upon as no other in England'. It was not right, added Lempereur, to regard Murphy 'only as your subject'.[107] He probably meant by this that Murphy now owed allegiance to Louis XIV. Wisely, the French commissaire chose to keep a pious silence on the preferred allegiance of Jacobites, who by definition saw James II, the Stuart Pretender, as their true monarch. Without complicating further what is already a complex case, the indelibility of one's subjecthood remained a particularly thorny legal problem in the eighteenth century.[108] Murphy, added Lempereur, was 'by right esteemed a naturalized French man', thanks to his lawful settlement in France following the Treaty of Limerick[109]—an agreement 'which ought to be regarded as sacred by the English, so that he cannot be detained without Injustice'.[110] There, Lempereur might have been carried away by his desire to win the argument, because the situation of Jacobite exiles in France was more complicated. They had certainly been granted a special status by Louis XIV, as a 'foreign nation' organized around its monarch, the Stuart Pretender.[111] But they were not systematically naturalized, even though, by royal favour, they were given the same rights as French subjects by Louis XIV.[112]

In any case, French laws as well as the laws of nation concurred that this man was a legitimate prisoner of war. But in exchange for his release, the Sick & Wounded Board demanded the release of Mr Pérault—a French Protestant

---

[106] O'Higgins, 'Treaty', p. 225, quoting J.C. O'Callaghan, *History of the Irish Brigades in the Service of France* (Glasgow, n.d.), pp. 436–7. The same 'utilitarian' principles had been at work during the English Civil War: Donagan, *War*, pp. 131–2.

[107] Extract of Lempereur to S&W, 27 July 1706, BL, Add MS61591, fo. 67.

[108] Holdsworth, *English Law*, vol. IX, pp. 86–91.

[109] Extract of Lempereur's letter, in S&W to Sunderland, 10 April 1707, BL, Add MS61591, fo. 112. The English commissioners underlined the irony of the situation, since their own requests for the release of French Huguenots sent to the galleys, despite being also naturalized and settled in England, had hit a wall in France: copy of S&W to Lempereur, 26 October 1706, AN, MAR/B3/135, fo. 345v.

[110] Extract of translation of Lempereur to S&W [25 January 1707], BL, Add MS61591, fos. 103–4v.

[111] Dubost and Sahlins, *Et si on faisait payer?*, p. 47.

[112] Genet-Rouffiac, *Grand Exil*, pp. 286–90.

merchant naturalized in England, who had been taken as a passenger and sent to the galleys.[113] Lempereur found the equivalence irrelevant:

> You must permit me to tell you, that as there is no resemblance between them, there can also be no reason for your demand, Pérault is a subject of the king, and a refugee, that can no way be reckoned a Prisoner of War, and who having been found on board a neutrall ship, was condemned according to the laws of the land as a transgressor of his prince's orders and the laws of his country.[114]

This presentation glossed over the fact that Pérault, by virtue of his naturalization, had also become a subject of England, and as such, prisoner of war or not, he benefited from the protection of Anne. In both cases, the negotiators asserted that the subjecthood of the people whom they described as 'rebels' or 'renegades'[115] was inalienable, while at the time underlining that the naturalization of these foreigners immunized them against the reach of their state of origin. The same individuals were considered under a completely different light on both sides of the Channel.

A more pragmatic approach was also possible, and the French monarchy proposed to overlook the prisoners' national origin, and to take into consideration their confession and the 'nationality' of the ship on board which they had been captured. In April 1708, Commissaire Lempereur thus wrote of the Irish soldiers and sailors who faced the death penalty in Britain for having served in France that 'it suits us perfectly that people of that nation be entered in the exchanges as French and you can also release [Huguenots] as English'.[116] This suggested that national labels were reversible—an idea that mirrored the practice of so many soldiers and sailors who served a foreign state and fought against their own sovereign. In May 1708, Lempereur came back to this issue, confessing his surprise when he had read in the 'Gazettes d'Hollande' that Thomas Smith and Peter Drake were about to be 'tried for high treason'. According to the Treaty of Limerick, he argued, 'one cannot employ against them any rigor without violating the laws of war and the Convention for the equal and reciprocal Exchange, regardless of the nation'.[117] In August, Lempereur firmed up this proposal, and sent to the Sick & Wounded Board a list of preconditions for the conclusion of a cartel between the two countries:

---

[113] Extract of letter from Lempereur, in S&W to Sunderland, 10 April 1707, BL, Add MS61591, fo. 112.
[114] Extract of translation of Lempereur [25 January 1707], ibid., fos. 103–4v.
[115] Copy of Lempereur to S&W, 9 February 1706, AN, MAR/B3/135, fo. 69.
[116] SSM to Lempereur, 11 April 1708, MAR/B2/207, fos 149–50.
[117] Lempereur to S&W, 30 May 1708, BL, Add MS61592, fo. 108.

All the prisoners captured by ships of either of the two nations will be sent back, without any distinction of birth or status, so that Englishmen or Irishmen found on French ships, will be considered as French, and Frenchmen found on English [ships] as English.[118]

The key verb here is 'passer pour', which was translated, in another English letter, as 'reputed' or 'reckon'd as': this conveys the sense that national belonging had nothing to do with an essence, and everything to do with a convention.[119] If it suited state interests, the prisoners could be labelled in various ways, and it did not really matter whether they were legally French, English, Irish, or Spanish, as the Frenchmen taken in the Spanish fleet during the American War of Independence, who 'could not be considered otherwise than as Spanish prisoners'.[120]

A case over which much ink was spilled, because it epitomized the differences of understanding between French and British positions, was that of a French seventy-gun ship, the *Salisbury*, which had been captured in February 1708 off the Firth of Forth. The ship belonged to a squadron that had sailed from France to land the Pretender James II and his troops in Scotland. The 400 mostly Irish and Scottish Jacobite soldiers on board were made prisoners, and were put in the Tower of London, in Newgate prison, and in the Marshalsea prison, where they were treated like criminals, and, they wrote, refused the 'same subsistence as officers of their rank are normally given when they are prisoners in France'.[121] Lempereur, the French commissaire at St Malo, offered to trade these men against Huguenot prisoners detained in France, and, after almost two years of negotiation, his British counterparts consented to exchange some of them.[122] In May 1709, two commissioners of the Sick & Wounded Board thus visited Newgate prison, to examine the Irish officers taken on board the *Salisbury*, and found 'that several of them were born in France, and the rest were actually in the service at the time of the capitulation of Limrick'. They concluded that these men 'may be treated as Prisoners of War, & proposed to the Comm.rs of France as a proper exchange' for the French Huguenots serving in British regiments, who were detained in France as reprisals.[123] But the French minister of the *Marine*, the

[118] Lempereur to S&W, ibid., 3 August 1708, fos. 153–v.
[119] Robert Hunter, governor of New York, to Lord [Sunderland], 28 December 1708, BL, Add MS61595, fos. 58–v.
[120] S&W to LCA, 3 July 1780, TNA, ADM98/13, fo. 5v.
[121] Petition by the Irish prisoners of the Salisbury to Sunderland, undated [October 1708?], BL, Add MS61595, fo. 55. See also Sir Charles Hedges, secretary of state and judge of Admiralty Court, to Sunderland, 18 May 1710, fo. 135.
[122] SSM to Lempereur, 2 January 1709, AN, MAR/B2/214, fo. 53; 16 February 1709, MAR/B2/217, fo. 492, fos. 847–8.
[123] S&W to Sunderland, 26 May 1709, BL, Add MS61593, fo. 58.

Comte de Pontchartrain, had been mistaken in interpreting this as an agreement, on the part of Britain,

> That the Irish and Scotts, & others in the like circonstance, should be exchanged as French, and the French protestants as if they were English; our proposal only was, ... to exchange some Irishmen having the French king's commission for some French protestants taken at sea with Her Majesty's commissions, but we never intended to make it a general rule.[124]

Pontchartrain insisted that all the people captured on board the *Salisbury*, detained in Newgate and the Tower of London, should be exchanged alongside the others, arguing that there was no reason to treat them differently.[125] The British government, however, considered that some high-profile individuals deserved special consideration. The sons of Charles Middleton, a former secretary of state of Charles II, who joined James II in exile in France and converted to Catholicism, were on board the *Salisbury*. They were labelled as 'prisoners of state' which, in the opinion of Lempereur, was a 'very bad pretext' for refusing to exchange them, given the hope France had been nurturing that all Irish prisoners in England would be 'regarded as French'.[126] An important contextual element must be brought into the picture to understand this difference. French and British war aims were asymmetrical between 1688 and 1748: while the French monarchy intended at times to overthrow the 'regime' in Britain by a Jacobite restoration, the British monarchy mainly aimed at limiting the power of France, whatever extreme rhetoric was sometimes spouted. In any case, the French monarchy chose to cast the Middletons as prisoners of war, and argued that they were detained 'against the law of nations in the tower of London', contrasting this treatment with 'that which the English and also the prisoners from other nations receive in France'.[127]

   To try to force the British to modify their stance regarding the officers of the *Salisbury*, the French monarchy adopted another strategy, by taking reprisals against French Protestant officers captured at sea in the service of Britain.[128] When some of the Irish officers were released from the 'Tour de la Neugatte' (Newgate) and put on their parole in Canterbury, the French in turn softened their position towards the Huguenots imprisoned in Brest, who were similarly sent on their parole to Rennes.[129] And because Middleton was still treated as a 'criminal of state'

---

[124] Ibid., 17 June 1709, fo. 77.
[125] Pontchartrain to Sunderland, 22 May 1709, BL, Add MS61594, fo. 50v.
[126] SSM to Lempereur, 18 September 1709, AN, MAR/B2/216, fos. 1147–8. See also Lempereur to S&W, 16 October 1709, MAR/B3/169, fo. 326v.
[127] SSM to Count of Dartmouth, 24 October 1710, MAR/B2/223, fos. 210–11. See also same to same, 17 December 1710, fos. 672–3.
[128] SSM to S. [Segent], 13 March 1709, MAR/B2/214, fos. 748v-749, fo. 748. See also Bragart to Major General Wills colonel of a regiment of Marines, 21 February 1709, BL, Add MS61595, fo. 74.
[129] SSM to Lempereur, 10 July 1709, AN, MAR/B2/216, fos. 188–9.

in Britain,[130] the order was given to imprison two high-ranking Huguenots officers on their parole in Rennes in St Malo Castle.[131] In the following years, the treatment of Huguenots prisoners in France continued to mirror that of the Irish prisoners in Britain, oscillating between the granting of extensive privileges and reprisals.[132]

In the end, how meaningful were these legal categories for the prisoners themselves? The complexity of their situation cannot be overemphasized, and it is one of the challenges faced by the historian neither to oversimplify their stories, nor to muddy the water even more. Instead of essentializing the nation, it is important to convey how arbitrary the selection of categories and their assignation by the state could be. War complicated this even more than was usual. Take the example of La Valette, a Frenchman who belonged to a company of Huguenots in the service of the United Provinces. These soldiers were voyaging on board an English ship navigating between England and Barcelona, which was captured in 1709 by the French. The men were put in prison in Dinan. Although a convention on the exchange of prisoners of war existed between France and the United Provinces, the French government argued that it did not apply there, since this treaty only regarded prisoners captured on land: what mattered in this instance was the nationality of the ship on which La Valette had been captured; accordingly, he could only be exchanged against 'the Catholic English, Irish, and Scots taken at sea in the service of the [French] King held prisoners in England'.[133] In fact, La Valette was detained by the French as a reprisal for the detention of the officers of the *Salisbury* in England.[134] Commissaire Lempereur, who had to implement this order, interceded in La Valette's favour. He wrote to the secretary of state for the *Marine* in February 1709: 'Your Grace I am asking for mercy for poor La Valette, a good and chivalrous man, who, solely because of the misfortune of his birth, has engaged to serve [our] enemies, and who, not being in the service of the English, does not come into the category of reprisals.'[135] Despite emphasizing La Valette's good reputation in France, Lempereur's pleas fell on deaf ears, and La Valette remained in prison.[136]

These highly contextual practices towards prisoners of war continued throughout the eighteenth century, and were linked to the constant problem of manpower for the navies.[137] The American War of Independence, as civil wars do, brought a

---

[130] Lempereur to SSM, 8 September 1709, MAR/B3/169, fo. 274.
[131] SSM to Lempereur, 25 August, 4 September 1709, MAR/B2/216, fos. 1106–7, 1216–17; Same to same, 27 November 1709, MAR/B2/217, fos. 848–9.
[132] For an example of the former, see Pontchartrain to Dartmouth, 30 July 1710, TNA, SP78/157, fo. 218; for the latter, SSM to Lempereur, 28 November 1711, AN, MAR/B2/226, fo. 318.
[133] SSM to Chamillart, ministre de la guerre, 9 January 1709, MAR/B2/214, fo. 115.
[134] SSM to Lempereur, 20 February 1709, ibid., fos. 535–6.
[135] Lempereur to SSM, 24 February 1709, MAR/B3/169, fo. 64v.
[136] Lempereur to SSM, 10 March, 7 April 1709, ibid., fos. 77v–78, 104v–5v.
[137] See 13 Geo. 2, c3 (1740): 'Foreign mariners having served, during the present war, or that shall, … in any future war, serve two years aboard *British* ships, are to be deemed natural-born subjects.' For specific examples, see S&W to LCA, 29 October 1746, and enclosed documents, TNA, ADM98/4, fos. 18–19.

whole new layer of complexity to the double issue of enmity and subjecthood, as
people's allegiances cut across their national affiliations. Until 1782, American
insurgents captured by the British were not granted the status of prisoners of war,
which would have been seen in Britain as a form of recognition of the legitimacy of
their movement. They were considered to be rebels to their king.[138] But these
assignations of categories were reversible, despite what the laws of war said. Thus,
in 1778, 'a deserter from a rebel unit who had then enlisted in a loyalist regiment'
was subsequently captured by the American insurgents; he should have been
hanged as a traitor if European codes of war had been strictly followed. Instead,
the British commander of a loyalist unit obtained his exchange as a prisoner of
war—even though he was normally not eligible.[139] There, the category of the
prisoner of war was recast to fit a particular situation. Just like at the beginning of
the eighteenth century, the nationality of the ship often prevailed with regard to
exchanges of prisoners: British commissioners thus contended that Frenchmen
taken in the Spanish fleet 'could not be considered otherwise than as Spanish
prisoners'.[140] Taken to extremes, this logic could lead to situations that, even to
contemporaries, were counter-intuitive: the Commissioners for the Sick &
Wounded Board thus wondered what to do with the crew of a captured American
privateer, which had 'only 3 American Prisoners on Board', while the rest of the
sailors consisted 'chiefly of French, Spanish, and Dutch' sailors. It was not clear to
these officials whether they should be considered and exchanged as Americans,
because they had been taken under an American flag, or exchanged according to
their subjecthood.[141] In general, the terminological confusion during this war was
extreme, and the administrators in charge of prisoners of war often asked for
clarifications, because words that had a clear meaning before the war, such as
'British', acquired new connotations.[142] Ascertaining these people's 'real' origins
was often impossible, because it ultimately relied on their own testimonies, as in
the case of nine prisoners confined in Edinburgh who, according to the Agent for
Prisoners there, 'are supposed to be Irish but... call themselves Americans'.[143]

Seafaring groups were particularly prone to play with multiple national affiliations, and during the American War of Independence, European states contributed to maintaining these entanglements by encouraging valuable individuals to
switch allegiances. A striking example is that of Luke Ryan, an Irish-born privateer
at the French service, who was captured and detained in Edinburgh.[144] Charles-
Alexandre de Calonne, the *Intendant* of Lille, explained to the Marquis de
Castries, the secretary of state for the *Marine*, why the French government should
claim this man. Legally speaking, he was 'reputed national, being established in

[138] Anderson, 'Treatment', pp. 66–7.   [139] Selesky, 'Colonial America', p. 77.
[140] S&W to LCA, 3 July 1780, TNA, ADM98/13, fo. 5v.
[141] 31 January 1783, ADM98/14, fo. 152v.
[142] On this terminology, see Wahrman, 'English problem'.
[143] S&W to LCA, 6 February 1782, TNA, ADM98/14, fo. 44.   [144] See Rutherford, 'The king'.

Dunkirk where he had been admitted to the bourgeoisie, where he pays the *capitation*, and where his whole fortune, which is considerable, is domiciled'. He was also a very brave man, 'who so far has proved [very] useful, and shows much affection for France'. All in all, there were 'enough reasons to consider him a national'. But for the same reasons, Ryan's profile made him particularly attractive to the British navy. The Admiralty negotiated with the captive privateer, giving him the choice between commanding a fifty-gun ship and being treated 'as a perfidious subject'.[145] In these discussions, subjecthood was a bargaining chip, alongside privileges and monetary rewards.

All these examples remind us that 'nationality' was an anachronistic notion for most of the eighteenth century, not simply because people shifted their allegiances and played with the language of the nation, but also because states themselves blurred the legal distinctions between subjecthood, foreignness, and states of enmity. Someone born within the territory of a prince could nonetheless, in practice, be reclassified and exchanged as a 'foreign' prisoner of war, just as a foreigner could be claimed as a 'national' depending on the flag one was fighting under. And it is striking that this happened even during the period that is often considered to have invented modern concepts of the nation. During the Revolutionary and Napoleonic Wars, just as before, war was waged by 'multinational' armies and navies. It also remained a common practice, although an illegal one, to recruit prisoners of war, voluntarily or not, instead of exchanging them.[146] This state of affairs was officially given recognition in the 1807 Instructions for the British Agents for the Prisoners of War: 'All Prisoners are to be considered as belonging to the Country in whose immediate Service or Employment they shall have been taken and not according to the Countries of which they may have been Natives or Subjects.'[147] The discussion was never settled for good.[148]

The importance of this cannot be overstressed: state attempts to bring order to an unruly system were not always ones that pointed in the direction of the nation state. This in turn opens up the possibility to rethink the relationship between public and private wars.

---

[145] Draft of Calonne to Marquis of Castries, 21 June 1781, Archives Départementales du Nord, Lille (ADN), C4624/1. Ryan was sentenced to death, and only released in 1784, following pressure from the French government: Anderson, 'Treatment', 69n1.

[146] Compare *Report on the Treatment* (1798) , p. 12, with 'Project of a General Cartel...between France and Great Britain' (31 August 1796), presented to the Ministers of Britain, article 16, in ibid., Appendix, p. 76.

[147] 'Instructions for Agents' (1807), article XIV, p. 11. See also Transport Office to Edwards Gibbons, 4 August 1793, TNA, ADM98/284, fo. 68; Portland to LCA, 23 June 1796, *Report* (1798), Appendix, p. 71.

[148] See, for example, the debate in 1810–11 regarding whether Hanoverians, Spanish, Portuguese, and Sicilians prisoners in French hands should be counted as in the British service or not: *Papers relating... General Exchange.*

IV. Private and Public Prisoners

A. Who Owns the Captive of War?

It has been persuasively demonstrated that the very category of the prisoner of war was a manifestation of the growth of states in Europe, from the end of the Middle Ages onwards.[149] I would like to argue, however, that not all forms of war captivity were linked to the state—or not only to the state. If this hypothesis is right, we must then broaden the question of war captivity beyond the study of 'prisoners of war', defined a priori and in the abstract. We must start by looking at the diversity of types of captivity, and examine the boundaries and overlaps between them.

To begin with, we must qualify the macro-narrative already alluded to, which draws a natural connection between the prisoner of war and the rise of public or state-led wars. There has been a tendency in the historiography of the laws of war to emphasize a kind of linear succession of historical stages, with the monarchical monopolization of violence and the demise of medieval forms of 'private' wars.[150] But the very divide between private and public wars is not helpful in understanding war captivity in the eighteenth century. Indeed, while the prisoner of war was primarily a prisoner by and of the state, there were many situations in which 'private' actors played a central part in the ways in which prisoners, as well as other war captives, were captured, detained, and exchanged in our period. The example of hostages, explored in what follows, shows that there were many more overlaps between prisoners of war and other categories than has previously been assumed.

The question of who was the rightful 'owner' of an individual captured during a war, and of the nature of the owner's rights over them, was discussed at great length by legal writers in the seventeenth and eighteenth centuries. In fact, it had been an established topic of reflection since Antiquity. In the seventeenth century, most of these authors agreed that, among Christian states, enslaving one's prisoners was no longer legitimate. This practice had been replaced by a less violent alternative: that of ransoming them. For Charles Molloy, writing in 1682, 'Prisoners taken in War do not become perfect Slaves, as of old, but only remain in the Custody of the Captor, till *Ransoms are paid*.'[151] This view was still held by Gaspard Réal de Curban, in 1764: 'the ransom that is paid for prisoners, when it is not possible to find other prisoners to exchange them against, is a living proof of the slavery they found themselves under; it is a kind of survival of the ancient custom.'[152] Eighty years apart, both authors agreed that individuals captured

---

[149] Contamine, 'Growth'; Keen, *Laws*; Ambühl, *Prisoners*.

[150] See Whitman, *Verdict*.

[151] Molloy, *De Jure Maritimo*, p. 419. Molloy's opinions on slavery are discussed in Drescher, *Abolition*, pp. 75–6.

[152] Réal, *Science*, vol. V, ch. 2, section VIII, par. 4, p. 509. Réal was also of the opinion that the rights of the victor over the prisoners of war 'followed the same rules as those he has over his enemies' properties': par. 1, p. 507.

during a war were the property of their captor. According to them, conceptually a genealogical link existed between the ransoming of the captive and the previous practice of enslaving him. They also agreed that the rights of the victor over the prisoners of war were based on the same principles as those he had over his enemies' property. In this sense, the status of the prisoner was still governed by the law of plunder, as it had been in the Middle Ages: prisoners of war were considered spoils of war, like any other commodity.

In practice, well into the seventeenth century, prisoners of war were part of the booty, shared between the combatants who had captured them.[153] The state was only one protagonist, if a powerful one, among many. As argued by Paul Vo-Ha with regard to France, the persistence of the private ransoming of captives, throughout the sixteenth and seventeenth centuries, 'nuances the alleged *étatisation* of war captivity'.[154] This was a haphazard process, impaired by the resistance of local actors, as well as the state's own limitations.[155]

In the sixteenth century, the rank of the captive still determined how much he could be redeemed for.[156] For the same reason, for Molloy a general captured by a common soldier would 'become Prisoner immediately to that Prince or State under whom the Captor served'. On the other hand, an '*inferior Soldier*' could 'become absolutely the Captors to dispose of'.[157] The cost of providing their captive with the necessaries of life usually led the captors to 'yield him up as a Prisoner of War to be disposed of by that Prince or State under whom he serves'.[158] Therefore, captors could decide to trade their captives as their private property or to transfer them to the state.[159] The answer to the question of who 'owned' the captives—the state or the individual who captured them—was not totally settled.

In the seventeenth century, the French absolutist state asserted its claim to decide upon the fortune of prisoners, while deploring the continuing practice of privately ransoming the captives.[160] Offering rewards or compensations to the captors, the king increasingly became the main redistributor of the wealth generated through capture. But 'the private economy of ransom' remained dynamic at the beginning of the eighteenth century, when individual soldiers would ransom their prisoners and release them at their convenience, independently of diplomatic conventions.[161] Moreover, hard economic realities exposed how illusory the state's ambitions to become the sole arbiter of the prisoners' fate really were. The survival of the prisoners of war was hence placed in the hands of private creditors and intermediaries, and their release depended in part on the settlement of these debts.

---

[153] Contamine, 'Ransom', pp. 173–4, 179–80.
[154] Vo-Ha, *Rendre*, p. 207.   [155] Ibid., p. 210.   [156] Ibid., p. 208.
[157] Molloy, *De Jure*, p. 419 (referring to the 1673 *Articles of War for His Majesty's Forces*).
[158] Ibid.   [159] Grotius, *Laws of War*, book III, ch. 7, par. 9.
[160] Vo-Ha, *Rendre*, p. 212; Contamine, 'Ransom', pp. 190, 192.
[161] Vo-Ha, *Rendre*, pp. 212–15.

In the eighteenth century, the view prevailed among most legal writers that in theory the 'sovereign' was the sole rightful owner of the person and property of the captive.[162] For Vattel, writing in 1758, while 'formerly prisoners of war were obliged to redeem themselves', and 'the ransom' belonged to their 'individual captors', 'the modern custom' was different.[163] Later authors, such as Robert Ward, went further, and argued that the private ransoming of war captives had become obsolete and unlawful. The selling of prisoners against ransoms was an illustration of a major flaw in '*private* hostilities', which never 'will constitute what is called a legitimate and public state of war'.[164] For centuries, the prisoner had remained 'the property of his captor', who had total latitude to free him or keep him imprisoned 'at pleasure'.[165] This ancient practice, to Ward's satisfaction, had been 'abolished', thanks to 'the mildness of modern improvements':[166] namely, the definition of the modern laws of war, which themselves proceeded from the rise of the modern state.[167] The emergence of a new status, that of the prisoner of war, was the outcome of this process. Their fate was now tied to the decisions of the state, and not to the will of their private captors, and their imprisonment depended solely on the state of international relations. The 'cartels', these general exchanges of prisoners first invented in sixteenth-century Italy, illustrate the systemic change by which the state increasingly held the key to the release of the prisoners.[168]

For Ward and most eighteenth-century legal writers, the words 'hostage' and 'ransoms' evoked a distant medieval period, where honour and private captivity ruled supreme; by contrast, the prisoner of war was a fairly recent invention. But were the two statuses mutually exclusive? Studies of medieval warfare reveal that ransoms, while they were in law private matters between the captor and the captive, did not escape the supervision of public authorities either.[169] The right of the king to put prisoners of war to death, still attested to in the sixteenth century, indicates that the monarchy's prerogative was superior to that of his subjects; monarchs also commonly confiscated prisoners, compensating the captors for their loss.[170] In the fifteenth century, argues Philippe Contamine, 'the king was clearly in a position to break contracts...made privately between prisoners and captors'.[171]

At the same time, we know that private forms of naval warfare thrived during the medieval and early modern period, and continued throughout the eighteenth century and beyond. Privateering is an obvious example. It involved private

[162] Réal, *Science*, pp. 512–13.
[163] Vattel, *Law of Nations*, book III, ch. 8, par. 153.
[164] Ward, *Enquiry*, vol. I, p. 294. On Ward, see Whitman, *Verdict*, pp. 216–19, 222.
[165] Ward, *Enquiry*, vol. I, pp. 299–301.   [166] Ibid., p. 297.
[167] Ibid., pp. 298–9.   [168] Contamine, 'Ransom', pp. 186, 191.
[169] Ibid.; Keen, *Laws*, pp. 156–85; Ambühl, *Prisoners*, ch. 2.
[170] Contamine, 'Ransom', pp. 167–70, 176, 186.   [171] Ibid., p. 170.

merchants who practised lawful plunder at sea.[172] By attacking the enemy's trade they enriched themselves, while upholding the interests of their state. The double nature of this economic activity was reflected in the ambiguity of the status of those who were captured by privateers. Three scenarios were possible. The first scenario was the following: a merchant ship was seized and brought in as a prize to the privateer's port of origin; his crew were prisoners of war, who were imprisoned and eventually exchanged. The ship and its cargo were sold for the mutual benefit of the privateer's owners and the state, who took a proportion of the profit. The second scenario was to ransom the prize. A third possibility, though strictly forbidden by the states, also occurred frequently: to release one's prisoners before landing, without declaring the capture.[173]

In the eighteenth century, state conventions differentiated the captives depending on who their captor was, as in 1712 when France and Britain agreed to free their prisoners made at sea before a certain date, 'with the exception of hostages'—which can only be explained by the belief that the fate of hostages primarily depended on the decision of their captors.[174] In what follows, I am concerned chiefly with the peculiar meanings of the terms 'ransoms' and 'hostages', which were specific to the war at sea. The laws of war identified three kinds of hostages. First, the hostage could be a juridical 'form of security' agreed between belligerents. Second, hostages were enemies captured by 'an act of war'. Third, they could be taken as reprisals.[175]

Although the three scenarios occurred in eighteenth-century wars between France and Britain, I am specifically interested in one situation: the taking of hostages as a security for the payment of the ransom of a ship captured by a privateer. This legal and (admittedly) quite technical difference between the hostages described above, and those we are dealing with here, was explained by Valin, a French *juge d'amirauté* from La Rochelle, in the 1760s. He noted that ransoms before the French Ordinance of *Marine* of 1681 referred to something very different: the individual ransoming of prisoners captured by privateers, who were forced to pay to be released; he compared this practice to 'the crime of piracy'. By contrast, ransoms, as they were understood in 1681, were a legal transaction for buying back a prize.[176] In the first case, the hostage was ransomed individually; in the second, he was a security. In reality, the ambiguity, evident in

---

[172] See Anderson and Gifford, Jr, 'Privateering'. Technically two kinds of vessels practised privateering: letters of marque, i.e. merchant vessels licensed to capture enemy prizes, and privateers proper, whose sole role was to seize enemy ships. As this distinction is not central in my argument, I use both interchangeably in this section.

[173] See, for example, 'Ordonnance du roi Louis XV règlementant le sort des prisonniers capturés en mer', Versailles, 4 October 1760, AN, MAR/A1/93, no. 27.

[174] Extract of Comte de Pontchartrain to Champigny, *Intendant de Marine* in Le Havre, 14 September 1712, MAR/B3/211, fo. 406. This was encapsulated in the 'Ordonnance du roi Louis XIV rendant la liberté aux sujets britanniques capturés en mer et détenus en prison', 21 September 1712, MAR/A1/47, no. 46.

[175] Mattéi, *Histoire*, p. 660.   [176] Valin, *Traité*, vol. I, p. 136.

the use of the same term, was never fully resolved—something that was the source of numerous problems.

The system must be briefly explained. It entailed the negotiation and signing of a written contract, called a ransom bill, between the two captains (the captor and the captured), by which the captured agreed to ransom his ship for a certain sum. In exchange for this, the prize ship would be released and would, theoretically, continue its journey safely (the bill of ransom served as a safe-conduct against attacks by other privateers or ships-of-war).[177] Thanks to this 'pragmatic device', the privateer did not have to bring its prize to a home port to have it condemned by a court, and could continue attacking enemy ships.[178] Although the ransom bill was normally sufficient to make a ransom legal, it was customary for the privateer to take one or more hostages from the captured ship, who would not be released until the agreed ransom had been paid. This practice was quite frequent: during the War of the Spanish Succession, French privateers ransomed about 30 per cent of the total number of ships they captured, and during the American War of Independence, 15 per cent of British merchantmen captured by foreign privateers were ransomed (507 out of 3,386).[179]

Apart from historians of privateering, few scholars have paid attention to this peculiar type of legal economic transaction between enemies in wartime.[180] William Senior has pointed out the peculiarity of this contract, which relied on the keeping of a promise that was legally binding.[181] Peter Leeson and Alex Nowrasteh fitted the study of ransoming into a narrative about the futility of state intervention and the virtues of economic liberalism.[182] They describe plunder contracts as a form of 'efficient' and painless redistribution of property, which is relatively costless for the parties involved: a contract that is 'enforceable' thanks in particular to hostage-taking. But they overlook the fact that very often the ransoms were never paid, and are not interested in the 'cost' of these arrangements for the hostages. By contrast, I now want to focus on the figure of the hostage. The broader story I am interested in is also about the state: focusing on hostages taken at sea provides an opportunity to approach the question of the links between prisoners of war and the state 'monopolization of warfare' in the eighteenth century from an original standpoint. Indeed, the hostage does not fit easily into the narrative of the transition between aristocratic and monarchical ways of warfare. My starting point is not that the state was irrelevant, but that it was not the only agent at work: traditional forms of war captivity survived into the

---

[177] Emerigon, *Traité*, p. 477. Being recaptured was always a possibility: SSM to Dartmouth, 24 October 1710, AN, MAR/B2/223, fo. 209; S&W to Guillot (French translation), 23 September 1745, MAR/B3/432, fos. 262-v.
[178] Oldham, *English Common Law*, p. 182.
[179] Leeson and Nowrasteh, 'Was privateering', p. 313.
[180] Oldham, *English Common Law*, pp. 181–4; Leeson, *Anarchy Unbound*, chs. 3–4; Bromley, *Corsairs*, pp. 67, 76, 281, 348, 364n47.
[181] Senior, 'Ransom bills', p. 51.   [182] Leeson and Nowrasteh, 'Was privateering'.

eighteenth century; a phenomenon which has been neglected, at least with respect to the war at sea.[183]

B. The Hostage, a War Captive Beyond the Reach of the State

The function of the hostage greatly differed for the states and for their private captors. For the French and British monarchies, these individuals deserved to be protected, according to the implicit contract which bonded a state and its subjects in wartime; they also served another purpose, namely to act as a check on the behaviour of privateers at sea. Hostages acted as witnesses for the state, ascertaining that the captain's reports about their captures at sea described what had really happened.[184] The role of the state—and of a state that we conceive far too neatly—has certainly been overplayed. But it still played an important function, in shaping the legal space in which non- or extra-space action occurred. The legality of the capture of prizes and hostages was determined by admiralty courts, which would examine the ship's papers and interrogate witnesses. For the captors, hostages were valuable possessions: this fact dictated every decision that was taken about these prisoners. Torn apart by contradictory interests and principles, hostages were well aware that their future depended on how they were labelled.

Why did states agree to ratify these contracts between their subjects and enemies? On the one hand, the practice of ransoming enemy prizes was often viewed with suspicion by the courts, and was often seen as a cover-up for collusion with the enemy.[185] On the other, the ransoms would encourage privateers to remain at sea and continue capturing enemy prizes.[186] However, while both states tried to put an end to the ransom system during the 1780s, these bans were ignored, and ransoms were officially revived during the French Wars.[187]

On the privateers' part, the decision to ransom a ship and take a hostage often depended on the problem of manpower. Privateers were usually small ships, which tended to have smaller crews than navy ships: they simply did not have enough hands to sail their prize to a friendly port.[188] If the capturing ship relied in part on the sailors from the captured ship (as they sometimes had perforce to do), they risked those sailors taking back the ship and sailing it away.[189] This was especially a problem when more than one ship was captured and explains why, if a

---

[183] With the exception of studies on Mediterranean captivity.

[184] 'Jugement de l'Amiral', 25 April 1697, in Chardon, *Code des Prises*, p. 205. See also Valin, *Traité des Prises*, vol. I, p. 147.

[185] On the adjudication of these ransom bills by the King's Bench at the time, see Oldham, *Mansfield Manuscripts*, vol. I, pp. 662–70.

[186] Oldham, *English Common Law*, pp. 182–3.   [187] Senior, 'Ransom bills', pp. 56–7, 60.

[188] On this, see Kert, *Privateering*, pp. 78–82.

[189] Ibid., pp. 102–3; Zabin, *Dangerous Economies*, p. 113.

privateer captured a convoy, they might well bring in some of the ships as prizes and ransom the rest.

The other reason why privateers kept capturing hostages was a legal one. Although the ransom bill was sufficient to attest to the legality of the prize, according to the 'usage' of 'all the nations of Europe', wrote Valin, the captors saw the hostage as a means of pressure 'for the safety of the payment', a security or 'a sort of guarantee for the payment of the ransom'.[190] Besides what the law said, ship-owners saw the hostage as a key and obligatory element in order to legalize their prize. If the hostage escaped, they feared that their ransom would evaporate. In 1702–3, a dispute opposed two French captains of privateers, one from St Malo and the other from La Rochelle, who both claimed to have lawfully captured a merchant ship from London. Ohanlon, *conseiller en l'amirauté de Paris*, wrote a factum for one of the captain, arguing that his rival's claims were void since his hostages had eloped: 'According to the law of nations, & the practice of all the admiralties in Europe, the said ransom has been nullified…, by means of… the release of [his] two hostages who were securities for said ransom.'[191] Citing the Roman law of postliminy, by which a prisoner of war who returns to his country recovers his entire freedom, Ohanlon argued that the impossibility of presenting the hostages cancelled the ransom claim itself.[192] The importance of the hostage to the captors, however correct or not from a legal viewpoint, is stated clearly here. In the same manner, in 1745, when an English hostage escaped from Calais, the French government demanded 'either the Man, or the Money which he agreed to pay for the ransom'. The Sick & Wounded Board confessed its ignorance about what to do in such a situation.[193] In the same way, if the hostage died, the law was unclear. Both governments agreed during the 1740s that in this case, the ransom would be void.[194] However, in the second half of the eighteenth century, British judges continued to debate whether the ransom bill was void or not, since an alien enemy could not bring a legal action in an English court of law, and that the hostage had to be the plaintiff.[195]

The hostage was a security, but in no way was he *himself* to be ransomed. In practice, the line was thin. The captains of privateers often saw the crews they captured as their private prisoners. At the beginning of September 1744, Mr Daubuz, a merchant from Falmouth, refused to deliver the captain of a French prize captured by the privateer he partly owned to the Agent for the Prisoners of War in the city. When the Agent requested that the French captain be handed to him, the ship-owner

---

[190] Valin, *Traité*, vol. I, p. 157.
[191] 'Factum pour le Sieur de la Vallée-Pottevin', AN, MAR/F2/72.   [192] Ibid.
[193] 24 April 1745, TNA, ADM98/2, fo. 130.
[194] See correspondence between Maurepas (SSM), the comte d'Aunay, the S&W and the LCA, October–November 1746: AN, MAR/B3/451, fos. 41–50; TNA, ADM98/4, fos. 21v–22v.
[195] Senior, 'Ransom bills', pp. 54–6.

replied, 'he's his prisoner, and he shall dispose of him as he thinks proper.'[196] Ten days later, the Agent was taunted by this 'Man of a haughty arrogant temper':

I desired Mr. Kingston to go with me when I went to execute Your Orders, in again demanding the Prisoner tho' we both treated him with all the civility in our power in endeavouring to persuade him to deliver up the Prisoner, he still absolutely refuses it, saying he is going to put him in some ship in order to send him to Guernsey or France, further says that whatever Prisoners for the future comes into the Harbour in Ships that he is concerned for, he will not put 'em in our hands, but send them to Truro or some other place. In short, he despises not only our Authority but also that of your Honours.[197]

Daubuz was charged with contempt. The commissioners were adamant that 'one example at least should be made'.[198] This case was not exceptional.[199] These tensions resulted from the state devolution of the capture of enemies to private actors. The question of the status of the sailors captured by privateers was a continual problem for the Admiralty, and the ransom system contributed to this, due to the confusion between the new conception of the hostage as bond, and the survival of the medieval idea of the captive as the private property of the captor. In September 1744, the commander of an English privateer exacted a ransom of £200 for the commander of a French ship from Calais. The Lords of the Admiralty regretted, in a letter to the Sick & Wounded Board, that the English commanders of privateers 'do not seem to think themselves obliged to observe any Rules with you, in regard to their Prisoners, but when it suits their own Convenience'.[200] The crown's Advocates were consulted on the matter, and concluded, citing a recent act of parliament,[201] that although privateers were fully 'entitled' to the ships and cargos which they had taken, this was not the case of 'the Persons taken on board such ships', who were 'his Majesty's Prisoners, subject to the King's Orders, and the Captains have no power to ransom any Person taken on board a French Ship, being a Subject of France'.[202] New instructions to the British privateers were consequently published in December 1744. Article I stated that the captains of privateers had to deliver the prisoners of war to the Sick & Wounded

[196] Extract of Agent to S&W, 3 September 1744, NMM, ADM/M/388, no. 206/2.

[197] Extract of Agent to S&W, 13 September 1744, ibid., 206/1. The LCA investigated the legal ways by which Mr Daubuz could be prosecuted 'for this Contempt': Thomas Corbett to S&W, 18 September 1744, ibid., no. 206.

[198] S&W to LCA, 5 November 1744, TNA, ADM98/2, fos. 38–v.

[199] See an example of a prison riot in Bristol caused by a similar situation: S&W to LCA, ibid., 24 September 1744, fos. 17v–18.

[200] LCA to S&W, 12 September 1744, NMM, ADM/M/388, no. 201. The investigation followed a complaint by the French *commissaire de la Marine* at Calais.

[201] *An Act for the better encouragement of seamen* (17 Geo. 2, c34) (1744).

[202] Opinions of Dr George Paul, His Majesty's Advocate General, and Dr William Strahan, Advocate for the Admiralty, College of Doctors' Commons, 5 September 1744, NMM, ADM/M/388, no. 201/1.

Board, who would then take charge of them; most importantly, it added that 'no Commander or other Officer of any Man of War, or private Ship of War, do presume upon any Pretence whatsoever to ransom any *French* or *Spanish* Prisoners'.[203]

The ransoming system was constantly abused at sea by illicit arrangements, and the creativity of privateers in inventing new ways of circumventing the legislation knew no bounds. For a merchant captain, being ransomed in exchange for their freedom, instead of being brought ashore as a prisoner of war, was the lesser of two evils—and the fact that it was forbidden by law was not a consideration. In 1746, a privateer from Guernsey ransomed two Frenchmen for £1,000, taking a hostage in exchange. The French commissioner for the exchange of prisoners of war denied the legality of the transaction, since the conventions between France and Britain stipulated that

> Nothing would be demanded from either side for the prisoners, who would be all exchanged man for man, so that captain Lauga should not have paid attention to the offer which was made to him in this regard by two young scatterbrains who were not informed, and he should not have been ignorant of the fact that crews are not ransomed, but only ships and their cargoes.[204]

Whether this was ignorance or a shrewd bypassing of the laws, the blurred distinction between the category of the hostage and that of the prisoner of war allowed for these types of negotiations. Private captors sometimes cast their prisoners as 'hostages', and sometimes as 'prisoners of war', depending on their needs. The next stage in the prisoners' experience also depended on this initial classification.

Because a hostage was so valuable, and because he was an alien enemy, he had to be secured. But just like their capture, the imprisonment and release of hostages were a source of tension between private actors and the state. Even in a state prison, the hostage remained under their captors' 'ownership'. Some argued that only the captor could decide to let him go freely; only he could decide to keep him imprisoned sine die. This view was contested by state administrators. In 1707, a French merchant took it upon himself to release 'his' English hostage, who was then detained in St Malo Castle, and allowed him to go to Rouen without so much as informing the French Commissaire Lempereur: 'The merchant who sent him away of his own authority without a passport deserves to be punished and I have

---

[203] 'Additional Instructions to such Merchant Ships and Vessels as have...Letters of Marque, or Commissions for private Men of War, against France and Spain', 27 December 1744, in Marsden, *Laws and Customs*, vol. II, pp. 430–1.
[204] Guillot to S&W, 24 September 1746, TNA, ADM97/103, fo. 119.

written . . . to have him put in jail for a few days.'[205] In this instance, the merchant's decision to release the hostage from prison was beyond the reach of the state. By the same token, it was the captors' duty to look after the hostages, by requiring someone to stand security for them, or, failing that, to keep them in custody. If they let them roam freely in town, it was, as the lieutenant general in Dunkirk noted in 1746, 'at their own risk'.[206]

The captors' interests could thus run against those of the state. For the former, the hostages were a capital to be preserved. For the latter, hostages were enemies who could present a danger, especially if allowed to circulate freely in port towns. But when negotiations for peace were undertaken, this could change, and they could turn into assets. The same individual was seen in a very different light depending on the stage of war and how he was cast: as an enemy threatening state security, or as a valuable commodity in need of preservation. In July 1709, the French *commissaire de la Marine* in Calais, La Martinière, ordered that seven hostages captured on the Irish coast by a Calais privateer be put in jail.[207] The Calais official considered that there might be spies among their number.[208] On their side, the owners of the privateer requested to keep the hostages in their houses, offering to give security for them. If the hostages died in prison, where the conditions of detention were 'very bad', they argued, 'it would be a loss for them'.[209] The secretary of state for the *Marine* did not budge, and ordered that all the hostages brought to Calais should be put in prison in the future.[210]

Once in prison, hostages were often left in the lurch for months, sometimes years. This, again, needs to be explained by the power that their captors held over them. The French legal writer Valin emphasized the contradictory pressures at work that determined the fate of a hostage, which contended between moral principles, and both state and private interests: 'It is absolutely just, and in the interest of all nations, that the hostages given as securities for the ransoms, be released as soon as possible by the effective payment of the ransom.' He continued: 'it has sometimes happened that the owners of the ransomed ships, have neglected to free the hostages.'[211] The whole business of hostage-taking was based on trust and the esteemed value, in both the monetary and the political sense, of the hostage. Bad faith was always possible, and value changed over time.

Unscrupulous ship-owners might be reluctant to pay a ransom. Once they had recovered their ships, which completed their journeys safely thanks to the ransom bill, the hostage could be left at the mercy of the merchant who detained him. The

[205] SSM to Lempereur 6 July 1707, AN, MAR/B2/198, fo. 90v. The ship-owner was put in prison for a few days, 'to set an example': SSM to M.ˢ de Thiange, 6 July 1707, fo. 92v.
[206] Comte d'Aunay to Comte de Maurepas, 20 October 1746, MAR/B3/451, fo. 37.
[207] La Martinière to SSM, 21 July 1709, MAR/B3/166, fo. 253.
[208] La Martinière to SSM, ibid., 9 August 1709, fo. 276v.
[209] La Martinière to SSM, ibid., fo. 277.
[210] La Martinière to SSM, ibid., 20 August 1709, fo. 293v.   [211] Valin, *Traité*, p. 158.

hostage might be a tolerable collateral damage as far as the owner was concerned, and a relatively harmless one at that: by comparison with imprisonment for debt, where the prison was used to force the debtor to pay, in the case of a ransom it was not the debtor who was incarcerated, but his employee, the hostage.[212] Solutions were considered by the states to nudge the ship-owners, such as making them pay a monthly sum to the families of the hostages.[213] Furthermore, as time went by, the cost of the detention of the hostage increased for the debtors, who had to reimburse the food and accommodation provided by the captor, as well as potential medical expenses incurred for the hostage, which all had to be refunded before his release.[214] In 1746, for instance, a French hostage was detained in Jersey although the ransom had been paid: 'he is denied his freedom under the pretext that it is owed 200# for his food and maintenance for 23 days.'[215]

The interests at stake often pulled in opposite directions, and sometimes, it was not the owner of the ransomed ship who was at fault, but the captor—who, in Valin's words, '[could] have interest in delaying the payment'.[216] This was because ransoms bills sometimes specified a penalty to be paid for each day that had passed beyond the deadline for paying the ransom, for food and/or lodging. In this case, it was in the captor's interest not to free the captive too early: this prisoner was a profitable investment, as in Guernsey, where these daily indemnities were a kind of extortion.[217] The hostages' freedom remained firmly in the hands of their captors.[218] Although, in general, the value of hostages did not, unlike Mediterranean captives, depend on the laws of offer and demand, this example shows that they could be turned into sources of income. Either way, a paradoxical logic was at work: when a debtor was already reluctant to pay the ransom, the creditor knew that the longer the hostage stayed in prison, the more money he could squeeze out of their detention. On the other hand, we cannot overstate the power of the captor: prolonging the detention raised the costs for the captor, captive, and ultimate payer. The hostage was caught between a rock and a hard place, and these different factors conspired to imperil his situation.

Yet hostages were neither totally helpless nor passive. In fact, they were expected by their captors actively to contribute to the payment of their ransoms. One of the ways to do this was to appeal to their state or the captor's state. Nehemiah Millit, who had sailed on board the *Flying Fame* sloop of Elizabeth Town in Virginia, had been compelled to volunteer as a hostage when the ship was captured by a privateer: 'Samull Bush and Briant Tragency and Richard Furlong of

[212] At the same time, it would impact on the 'credit' or reputation of the unscrupulous ship-owner, potentially making future business harder and more expensive.
[213] Response by Bory, Cherbourg, to a proposal by the SSM, 30 June 1710, AN, MAR/B3/180, fos. 348–v.
[214] Valin, *Traité*, p. 148; Aunay to Maurepas, 2 September 1746, AN, MAR/B3/451, fo. 28.
[215] SSM to Guillot, 17 June 1746, AN, MAR/B2/328, fo. 300.
[216] Valin, *Traité*, p. 159.   [217] Ibid.   [218] Ibid., p. 160.

the said town marchants and owners of the said sloop at whose request and whose account I parted with my dear liberty being most inhumanly and unchistanly [*unchristianly*] resolved to sacrifice my freedom to there own interest.' Unfortunately for him, these London merchants to whom the bill of £300 had been issued refused to pay the captors.[219] After five years in Brest prisons, in May 1713 Millit petitioned Matthew Prior, the British diplomat who was negotiating the Treaty of Utrecht in Paris. He interwove references to religious persecution, poverty, and slavery, to inspire compassion:

> Your Excellency most deplorable petitioner is like to remaine in bondage in a close and nauseous prison with out hopes of redemption and starving with hunger and nakedness having only 3 pence par day and no the relieve which will shortly put a period to my life.... whereby I may have my liberty out of this miserable condition in close confinement in a country where my religion is reproached and person like to be inslaved forever.[220]

While the outcome of this case is not known, petitioning statesmen could receive an echo. Prior certainly expressed his sympathy with the unfortunate hostages, writing to Lord Bolingbroke that 'the injustice of those wretches who should pay the respective ransoms is really flagrant and scandelous'.[221] In Britain, the Lords of the Admiralty could, and did, order the prosecution of the owners of the vessels who had not paid the ransom of their vessels.[222] French captors could also bring an action in justice in front of a French admiralty court.[223]

Beyond the recourse to the language of slavery, which was a very common political trope among prisoners, there is maybe something else at stake here.[224] We have seen how legal writers presented the hostage as a status that fundamentally departed from that of the slave. With this comparison, the petitioner probably had in mind the perpetuity of his detention, and his absolute dependence on his captor's will. In following wars, hostages continued to appeal to the state to intercede in their favour and obtain their release.[225] Henry Greenway, an English hostage detained in St Malo, wrote in June 1705 about the 'great unjustice don mee contrary to the good Laws of yo.ʳ Nation, and suffer my person not to be made a prize on thus as if I was Negro or that I was taken into Turkey'.[226] These requests usually fell on sympathetic ears. Lempereur, the French commissaire,

---

[219] Nehemiah Millit to Prior, 12 May 1713/4, TNA, SP78/158, fo. 25.
[220] Ibid.   [221] Ibid., fo. 22.   [222] S&W to LCA, 30 August 1758, NMM, ADM/F/18.
[223] The next stage was to bring the action in front of the High Court of Admiralty in Britain, through the intercession of the hostage: S&W to LCA, 24 February 1763, TNA, ADM98/9, fo. 302. This procedure was heavy, costly, and time-consuming, since its initiators were detained in a prison abroad.
[224] On the language of slavery used by British captives in India or North Africa, see Colley, *Captives*.
[225] See petition from Calais prison, 23 May 1745, in LCA to S&W, 5 June 1745, NMM, ADM/M/392, no. 170/1.
[226] 17 June 1705, AN, MAR/B3/128, fo. 297.

thus wrote to his English counterparts in February 1706, attaching two petitions written by English hostages in France to Queen Anne, demanding justice against the ship-owners who refused to pay their ransom. These were 'just complaints', wrote Lempereur, from men who 'are left to die in our prisons'.[227] Despite the goodwill of these state officials, the situation of hostages was sometimes intractable. Take the example of Jean Deane, an English hostage who had been taken by a Calais privateer, which had then been captured by another privateer, this time from Vlissingen. He wrote a petition to Lempereur in April 1706, explaining that the two captors refused to pay his ransom, laying the responsibility at each other's door. Lempereur in turn relayed 'this wretched man's' requests to the secretary of state for the *Marine*. The French official did not mince his words when he described the ordeal of the hostage:

> The shipowners who are holding him despair to be paid [and] don't want to release him…, they have been detaining him for an infinite amount of time in an obscure prison, and after giving him twenty sols per day for his food, they have suddenly reduced him to the *pain du Roy* like a criminal, and frankly this calls for revenge, but the Arabs are not more hard-hearted and inhuman than the people he is dealing with.

These imprecations and analogies with the treatment suffered by European captives in North Africa failed to obtain the release of the hostage, and Lempereur conceded that the man was beyond his remit: 'Lucky for them that I do not have the power to have justice done to the poor man.'[228] Throughout the eighteenth century, the problem remained the same: even when both states agreed that hostages should be freed, the key to their liberation was held jointly by their captors and the owners of their ship.

The comparisons that were made between hostages, captives, and slaves, whether they were justified or not, tell us something about the overlap between these categories of detainees in the minds of eighteenth-century observers. Hostages were captives of war, in the sense that their unhappy situation was due to the fact that they belonged to a country in a state of war. At the same time, their imprisonment, while the product of this international context, was also the outcome of a private transaction. At this juncture, we must dig deeper to understand whether any of the elements we have identified so far also applied to prisoners of war.

The most obvious characteristic of prisoners of war, at least how we understand it through the lens of the Geneva Conventions, is that their captivity should end once peace is concluded. But since the fate of hostages was only partly in the hands of the state, this raises the question of whether the negotiation of a peace treaty

---

[227] Copy of Lempereur to S&W, 9 February 1706, MAR/B3/135, fo. 73v.
[228] Lempereur to SSM, 14 April 1706, ibid., fo. 120v.

allowed them to be released or not. In fact, even after a peace was concluded, hostages remained trapped abroad, while prisoners of war were released.[229] After the Treaty of Paris was signed in 1763, numerous hostages were still imprisoned in France and Britain because ransoms had not been paid. One solution would have been to extend to hostages the benefit of the article devoted to prisoners of war— in other words, to treat the two categories as equivalent. Article 3 thus stipulated 'that the hostages carried away or given during the War shall be restored in six weeks from the day of the ratification of the treaty without ransom', which led the Sick & Wounded Board to wonder if its meaning was also meant to extend to 'Hostages for the Ransom of Ships'.[230] However, such efforts to conflate the two meanings of the term hostage—facilitated by the use, by state administrators and treaties, of the same word to designate prisoners of war who would be exchanged individually—were ignored.[231]

The example of Jean Normand Duplessis is sufficiently detailed in the archives to allow us to catch a glimpse of the Kafkaesque situation in which these hostages found themselves. Duplessis was the commander of a ship belonging to a Mr de la Fouche, who was also on board when the ship was taken during its voyage between Martinique and Grenada by a Liverpool privateer, commanded by John Taylor, on 23 December 1759. De la Fouche, according to Duplessis's memorandum, 'prevailed upon Mo.ʳ Duplessis to go as Hostage for the true Payment of the Money agreed upon, to which M.ʳ Duplessis consented in full Confidence that the same would have been punctually paid agreable to the Tenor of the Ransom Bill'.[232] In the first instance, Duplessis was detained at Montserrat in the Leeward Islands, and, after repeated appeals to de la Fouche to pay the ransom were ignored, he was brought to Liverpool in September 1760. He was still there in January 1764, more than four years later. Duplessis wrote letters, petitions, and memorandums to the French ministers, begging them to help him obtain his release.[233] But many criteria combined to make his situation even more impossible than was usual. The slowness in the circulation of information, and the loss of it, meant delays. And Duplessis was the victim of mislabelling, as must have been the case with hundreds of hostages at the time. The French minister plenipotentiary in London, the chevalier d'Eon, applied several times for the release of Duplessis, whom he referred to, without further details, as 'a French hostage... detained for several years at Liverpool'.[234] The term 'hostage', however, as we have seen, had

[229] See, for instance, the French 'Memoire d'Observations', [December] 1749: BL, Add MS32819, fo. 247.

[230] S&W to LCA, 31 March 1763, TNA, ADM98/9, p. 350.

[231] L. Guiguer, Commissioner for the S&W, to Lovell Stanhope, Esq., 15 August 1764, in Redington, *Calendar*, p. 438.

[232] 'A true State of Mr. Jean Duplessis', undated [after March 1763], TNA, SP42/64, 151/17c.

[233] See, for instance, his memorandum to the Chevalier d'Eon [before 30 September 1763], ibid., 151/17e.

[234] Memorandum to Earl of Halifax, 30 September 1763, ibid., 151/17d.

multiple meanings, and it took another three weeks after the Commissioners for the Sick and Wounded Seamen had received the instruction to investigate about Duplessis for them to discover, combing their books, that he was not in the custody of their Agent in Liverpool, and that he was the hostage of a merchant and not a prisoner of war.[235] To make an already difficult situation worse, the owner of the ransomed ship, de la Fouche, died while poor Duplessis was still being held hostage—of course before paying the debt that would have released him. De la Fouche's brother, a former governor of Martinique, inherited the debt, which had grown over the years: besides the ransom, the cost of maintenance and other expenses were also to be paid, the total amounting to above £1,224 in 1763.[236] He proved to be as bad a debtor as his late brother.[237]

Far from accelerating the release of the hostages, then, peace actually made it *more* difficult. Indeed, the signing of the peace treaty was a further incentive for the debtors not to pay the ransoms.[238] As the Earl of Halifax, President of the Board of Trade, noted in a letter to the Solicitor General, 'the owners or others concerned in British ships taken and ransomed as above refuse or delay the redemption of the hostages given to the enemy's privateers for the release of such prizes, upon presumption of those prisoners having a right to their liberty by virtue of the treaty.' Again, to add to their woes, hostages were confused with prisoners of war when it suited the debtors, while this conversion of status was an impossibility for state lawyers, who saw the payment of a debt as a quasi-sacred obligation. An impassable legal difficulty pertained to how the ransom money should be considered: if it was seen 'in the light of private property', argued the Earl of Halifax, then 'the Crown has no power to dispose of it by treaty', and it was doubtful that it could order the release of a French hostage detained in Britain without the payment of the ransom by the owner of the French prize ship.[239] Conversely, Halifax deplored that the crown seemed to lack the power 'to oblige the owners to redeem British subjects' detained in France by paying their ransoms.[240] These dramatic cases led the British government to explore alternative legal avenues, to put the hostages out of their misery. The prosecution of the owners of the prizes at the instigation of the hostages was a possibility, as we saw

---

[235] S&W to LCA, 14 October 1763, TNA, ADM98/9, fo. 219; LCA to Halifax, 1 November 1763, SP42/64, 151/17a.

[236] 'A true State of Mr. Jean Duplessis', ibid., 151/17c.

[237] Petition of John Farleton of Liverpool Merchant to the Earl of Egremont, secretary of state, undated, ibid., 151/17b.

[238] The settlement of the prisoners of war debts contracted by the state was also a running sore in international relations: see the memoranda written by the French government in 1764, in Archives du Ministère des Affaires Etrangères, La Courneuve, MDA48, fos. 136–54.

[239] Earl of Halifax to Solicitor General, 29 November 1763, in Redington, *Calendar*, p. 332. The Solicitor General and the Attorney General concurred: the ransom money was 'private property', which left the hostages at bay until the ransom was paid: Report of the Attorney General, 25 January 1764, ibid., p. 384.

[240] Halifax to Solicitor General, 29 November 1763, in ibid., p. 332.

above, but the prosecutors would have had to advance the money for carrying on the suit, which they would have recovered only if they won.[241] Another solution was to threaten ship-owners of such prosecutions, by publishing advertisements in the *London Gazette*.[242] Ultimately, there needed to be a proper collaboration between both governments to facilitate the prosecution of bad debtors.[243] Like Duplessis, many British hostages remained imprisoned in Dunkirk, Bayonne, or St Malo years after the war.

Monarchies had limited means at their disposal to obtain the release of a hostage. Consequently, these men's freedom depended above all on the involvement of civil societies—another trait of early-modern captivity. It was for the hostages themselves, through the activation of their family networks, to try to obtain their own release, by legal means or otherwise.[244] The more intermediaries that were brought into the chain of support, the greater their chance was to be freed. But this could entail years of frustrated expectations. The story of Thomas Ord, the pilot of a ship from Berwick captured by a French privateer in September 1744, exemplifies this. Ord, with other members of his crew, was ransomed and brought to Calais, where he was put in prison. The owner of his ship refused to pay his ransom, and his mother decided to write a plea to the Duke of Bedford, First Lord of the Admiralty. Eventually, the Comte d'Aunay, Lieutenant General in Dunkirk, was informed of the situation,[245] and on 19 August 1746, he gave his assent for Ord's release, bringing the price of the ransom down from 245 livres to 80 livres. The money collected in England by a subscription for this hostage was capital in this decision.[246] As this reveals, a successful liberation entailed the intercession of a plurality of actors, not only within the state, but also the involvement of local society and family.

Ord was lucky to have an educated, connected, and entrepreneurial mother. Many of his contemporaries did not have this chance, and languished in prison for even longer. The hostage's capacity for action resembles Michel Fontenay's analysis of Mediterranean captives, who were 'not a passive commodity', 'intervened in person in the transaction',[247] and spent much time finding and negotiating their exchange with intermediaries. In addition, hostages were often released privately because of long time business and sometimes family connections between merchants in an English and a foreign port. When a ship was taken, an incredible array of people were mobilized to intervene, and the same thing

[241] Opinion of Advocate General, 13 March 1764, in ibid., p. 393.

[242] Draft of advertisement, in ibid. The French government offered reciprocity: Guerchy to Halifax, 3 April 1764, TNA, SP78/261, fos. 1–2.

[243] Guiguer to Lovell Stanhope, 15 August 1764, in Redington, *Calendar*, p. 438.

[244] Valin, *Traité*, p. 158.

[245] Copy of S&W to Comte d'Aunay, undated, in Aunay to Maurepas, 31 July 1746, AN, MAR/B3/451, fos. 17–v. See also copy of the supplication of Ord's mother: fos. 17v–18.

[246] Aunay to Maurepas, 19 August, 2 September 1746, ibid., fos. 20, 28.

[247] Fontenay, 'Esclaves', p. 16.

happened with hostages. Local consuls, local business agents, former and present business partners, and relatives by blood and marriage could all get involved. No wonder it sometimes seemed as if the best course of action, at least in the eyes of merchants, was simply to let someone go.[248]

Wealthy families commonly raised money to facilitate the release of their children.[249] And knowledge of this was surely an important motivation of captors. Just as with medieval prisoners and Mediterranean captives, the social rank of the hostage was inextricably linked to his value, which in turn affected his chances to be released. In fact, rank was a key determinant in the selection of the hostage over other crew members in the first place. Legislation thus stated that the hostages had to be either the captain or officers of the crew—the assumption behind this being that these well-connected and relatively affluent people would mobilize their private networks and secure their release more efficiently. As Valin put it: 'either by himself, or through his parents and friends, he will work more promptly and efficiently at delivering himself, which will accelerate the payment' of the ransom.'[250]

At this point, the question must be raised of the differences between the prisoner of war and other types of war captives. Was there anything specific about the practice of hostage-taking by French and British privateers, by comparison with the European 'captives' taken by North African privateers in the Mediterranean at the same time? The debate between historians of Mediterranean captivity is useful from our perspective. On the one hand, Michel Fontenay argues that, although primary sources tend to use the terms 'slave' and 'captive' interchangeably, there are some fundamental differences between the two.[251] Captives always knew that their captivity would be limited in time: they were aware that they would be bought back at some point.[252] For the slaves, argues Fontenay, manumission was much rarer, and in any case the end of slavery was not structurally inscribed in their status, whereas value-exchange was the very point of taking a captive. On the other hand, these different categories were not clear-cut in practice. The very idea that captivity and slavery are 'exclusive' conditions also needs to be questioned.[253]

We must therefore be careful with normative categories, and not use them uncritically as our categories of analysis. The initial classification of someone captured at sea as a hostage for a ransom, or as a prisoner of war, was determined by the captain of the privateer who had taken him in the first place, according to criteria which varied from case to case. For instance, instead of ransoming a merchant ship and taking one or two members of its crew as hostages, the master

---

[248] The correspondence captured in the Prize Papers, mostly in TNA, HCA30 and HCA32, suggests the involvement of these various actors. Some of the interrogations of the crews of these ships have been transcribed in the *Prize Papers Online* edited by Brill.

[249] As in the case of a hostage detained in Guernsey, whose parents gave 600 livres tournois to his captors in order to facilitate his exchange: Lempereur to SSM, 31 July 1709, AN, MAR/B3/169, fo. 232.

[250] Valin, *Traité*, p. 156.

[251] Fontenay, 'Esclaves', pp. 15–24.   [252] Ibid., p. 23.

[253] Hershenzon, *Captive Sea*, p. 4.

of the privateer could decide to bring them all to port as prisoners of war, entrusting them to the naval administrators in charge of them.[254] Conversely, while soldiers and the crews of ships-of-war were entitled to be treated as prisoners of war, in practice privateers did not hesitate to take hostages among them for the safe navigation of the captured ship and the release of the men on board, who would, once home, be exchanged against prisoners.[255] In September 1745, a French privateer took an English hostage in exchange for the ransom of a ship transporting fifty-nine English prisoners who was authorized to continue its journey to England. The French secretary of state for the *Marine* objected that the ransom was owed for the ship, not its human cargo, and that these prisoners should be accounted in the general exchange of prisoners between the two states.[256] The confusion was sometimes extreme, opening the door to constant bickering about the actual status of the men imprisoned. In 1746, the opinion of Jean-Joseph Guillot, the *commissaire général de la Marine* at St Malo, regarding a request from his British counterparts to release seven men who had been detained in France for fourteen months, is exemplary: 'It appears that they want to denature this case, and that they regard these people as prisoners of war and not as hostages, which is not exact.'[257] What was also at stake here was probably the attempt, by the British officials, to reclassify the hostages as prisoners of war, since they knew that the former were beyond their reach. In general, the very legitimacy of detaining hostages as securities for other prisoners—which resembled the medieval practice of hostage-taking—was always regarded with suspicion.[258] Officials usually preferred to release these men 'as prisoners of war'.[259] The very possibility of classifying and reclassifying hostages as prisoners, and the other way round, shows the reversibility between the two statuses.

C. Fishermen

In the historical literature on the impact of war on civilians, maritime populations usually do not feature. There are many explanations for that. First, even today, the laws of sea warfare are very limited with regard to protections afforded to civilians.[260] This is all the more interesting for us because, in the eighteenth

---

[254] SSM to Gaulard and Derchigny, 29 May 1744, AN, MAR/B2/322, fo. 61.
[255] 'Petition of David Jones sergeant in Capt. William Audley's company to the queen, Coll. Luke Lillington's regiment, now ransomer in the common goale of Dinan in France' [after 1706], BL, Add MS61614, fo. 20.
[256] SSM to Guillot, 31 October 1745, AN, MAR/B2/326, fo. 186v.
[257] Guillot to SSM, 30 May 1746, MAR/B3/445, fo. 129.
[258] Guillot to SSM, 7 November 1747, MAR/B3/453, fo. 107. He sent these men back to England: 20 November 1747, fo. 114.
[259] Guillot to SSM, 26 November 1746, MAR/B3/445, fo. 261.
[260] Benvenisti and Cohen, 'War', pp. 1394–5.

century, legal writers mentioned the special status of fishermen vis-à-vis other civilians. Merlin, in his *Répertoire de Jurisprudence*, wrote that fishing boats were not to be treated like other merchant ships, and were exempted from being captured 'by a sort of tacit convention between all the European nations', owing to the 'essential pacific quality of the individuals, and the desire to contribute to the progress of civilization'.[261] The conclusion of fishing truces between Channel ports show that this belief could be translated into real actions.[262] But this exemption of fishermen was not absolute, and their safety from privateers and ships of war varied considerably, depending on the period and the state of diplomatic relations. In reality, fishermen represented an important proportion of the prisoners of war, and 'humanitarian' preoccupations were not always high on the list of priorities. The old age of Charles Roussel, a seventy-year-old fisherman detained in Sissinghurst Castle, did not give him any claim for exemption: in 1761, he told the official who questioned him that he had been in prison for almost four years.[263]

Fishermen also tended to spend years in prison as hostages. Just as for other hostages, states were hard-pressed to force the privateers to free their hostages if the ransom had not been paid.[264] The capture of ransomed fishermen by privateers raised specific issues. Fishing boats were not valuable enough to waste manpower sending their (mostly) small and worthless boats to a friendly port, and there to wait until they passed through prize courts. Consequently, pillaging was the norm rather than the exception: privateers took not only the boats but often also the nets, the clothes, and boots of the crew before releasing them. Instead of being the result of a negotiation, fishermen complained, the ransom was extorted from them with violence.[265] Given the relative poverty of fishermen, the cost of their detention systematically fell on local communities. Thus in 1703/4, the mayor and jurats of Hastings complained to the Earl of Nottingham, secretary of state, that the detention of hostages from Dieppe was too costly: 'we are at a considerable charge in keeping these men [from] under a more than ordinary guard.... we humbly desire that you would remit to us the French men letters of credit for defraying their charges during their [continuance] here.'[266] This financial dimension probably explains why fishermen who had been taken as hostages were kept on board the privateers, and forced to work there, until the ransom of their ship had been paid.[267]

---

[261] Merlin, 'Prise maritime', in *Répertoire*, par. 3, article I, pp. 798, 800.

[262] Morieux, 'Diplomacy'.

[263] Interrogation of Charles Roussel, TNA, ADM105/42, fos. 50v–51.

[264] SSM to Count of Dartmouth, 17 February 1712, AN, MAR/B2/230, fo. 290.

[265] Copy of mayor of Folkestone to Correnson *commissaire des classes* in Boulogne, 17 July 1710, AN, MAR/B3/178, fo. 412; Maurepas to Van Hoey, 17/28 April 1746, TNA, SP78/230, fos. 488–9, representing the ill-treatment of Dieppe fishermen by a Jersey privateer.

[266] Mayor and Jurats of Hastings to Earl of Nottingham, 11 March 1703/4, TNA, SP34/3, fo. 199.

[267] Same to Lord Ashburnham, 24 February 1703/4, ibid., fo. 170.

Moreover, in the case of fishermen, the taking of hostages took on a political dimension, as a bargaining tool in the negotiation of fishing truces between fishing communities of both sides of the Channel. For instance, during the War of the Spanish Succession, French privateers offered to void the ransoms of the English fishermen whom they had captured if England consented to sign a convention guaranteeing the freedom of fishing during war. As is clear here, fishing communities had to play the role of mediators in this cross-Channel negotiation, alongside the captains of French privateers.[268] In 1710, twenty-two fishing-boats from Dieppe, Bourg d'Ault, and Boulogne were captured by Dover privateers as reprisals for the privateering of English fishermen by French corsairs, which transgressed the convention for the freedom of fishing.[269] The crews of the French ships were still hostages in Dover two years later, and the monarchy urged the fishing communities to pay the indemnifications they owed to the English fishermen.[270] But this was about all that the French monarchy could do: ransoms did not depend on the law of nations, and states could only spur private interests, not force them. First, the French monarchy consented to deliver passports to the Dieppe and Boulogne fishing merchants so that they could go to London, accompanied by a king's officer, and agree on a sum with their English counterparts.[271] Once this project had failed, the fishing merchants of Picardy and Normandy 'worked on a project of compromise in order to remove their hostages from their ships which are in England', which was then sent to the governments.[272] The fishing-boat owners' active participation was thus required by the state authorities, who pressed them to release their men held hostages. Finally, in May 1713, it was decided to free the hostages, leaving it to French and English commissaries to meet in London to settle a dispute that had lasted for three years.[273] The payment of the ransoms was the key to the liberation of the hostages: all the monarchy could do was to encourage and steer the seafaring communities, but it lacked the power to compel them to do so and could not obtain the release of the hostages without their collaboration.

The same phenomenon continued during the following wars: fishermen were pawns in a wider political and naval conflict. In 1744, the French government's offer to negotiate a fishing truce, which had been prompted by requests from the fishermen of Dunkirk and Boulogne, was rejected in Britain. The Count of

---

[268] Mayor and Jurats of Hastings to Nottingham, 4 March 1703/4, TNA, SP34/3, fo. 187.

[269] Etienne de Chateauneuf, Calais to unknown, 17 July 1710, SP78/154, fos. 99–v; Pontchartrain to Dartmouth, 20 May 1711, SP78/155, fo. 137; circular letter to the admiralty officers in the main French fishing ports of the Channel, 5 August 1711, AN, MAR/B2/228, fos. 174–6; SSM to Lempereur, 2 September 1711, fos. 337–8; SSM to Le Brun in Dieppe, 7 October 1711, fos. 513–14.

[270] SSM to Champigny, *Intendant* in Le Havre, 27 January, 3, 10 February 1712, AN, MAR/B2/230, fos. 174–5, 218, 252, 254.

[271] SSM to Le Brun, 4, 11 November 1711, MAR/B2/228, fos. 652–3, 684–5.

[272] [Pontchartrain] to Dartmouth, 27 January 1712, MAR/B2/230, fo. 168.

[273] [Pontchartrain] to Dartmouth, 3 May 1713, TNA, SP78/157, fos. 145–v.

Maurepas, the secretary of state for the *Marine*, then advised the merchants who equipped privateers in these French ports to target the English fishing-boats, to make the prospect of a truce more appealing across the Channel. He thus wrote to the Chamber of Commerce of Dunkirk, on 13 September 1744: 'It would be desirable to get the merchants of your port to arm a ship that would be solely intended to intercept English fishermen, capture their ships, sink them, and make many fishermen prisoners of war.'[274] This cynical policy of a war against civilians was not exceptional, and France often dragged its fishermen into conflicts, to have a pretext for making diplomatic claims, as in Newfoundland.[275] One notes that the French government was careful to disguise its strategy, since officially it could not be seen to intervene in a matter that was beyond its jurisdiction.

Even when ship-owners consented to pay the ransoms, the financial cost was explicitly devolved to the local communities and not honoured by the state—a pattern that recurs throughout this book. In 1712, for example, the merchants of Dieppe relented, and offered to pay a proportion of the ransom.[276] But the cost of the detention of hostages weighed on fishing communities as a whole. One instrument of this could be the raising of taxes on local fishermen by the state.[277] A more original solution was a private manifestation of the same idea: merchants from Dieppe implemented a scheme by which they taxed the fishing-boats of the Dieppe parishes in order to fund the hostages' food and accommodation.[278] This forced subscription, which took the appearance of a state imposition, puzzled the French ministers.[279] In fact, the use by private actors of the financial tools of sovereign states shows that hostage-taking and ransom-paying mirrored and often overlapped with the practices of war imprisonment by the state.

In 1779, the officers of the Dunkirk Chamber of Commerce still complained of the cost of maintaining these English hostages: 'the expenses caused by the hostages of the ships whose ransoms remain to be paid, amount at least 3# per day each.'[280] Likewise, in England, the fishing-boat owners worried about the spiralling cost of the detention of their hostages in France. Francis Stephens, a Harwich merchant, wrote to Gamba, his Dunkirk correspondent, complaining that 'a poor man is not able to pay a guinea per week for the subsistence of a hostage'.[281] In order to raise the sums necessary for the ransoms, in addition to detention expenses, the mayor of Dieppe obtained from Sartine to 'make the cities

---

[274] Maurepas to Dunkirk Chamber of Commerce, 13 September 1744, AN, MAR/B2/323, fo. 580v.
[275] Morieux, 'Anglo-French fishing disputes'.
[276] SSM to Le Brun, 1, 22 June 1712, AN, MAR/B2/230, fos. 420, 557–8; Pontchartrain to Dartmouth, 24 February 1712, TNA, SP78/156, fo. 45.
[277] SSM to Champigny, 11 May 1712, AN, MAR/B2/230, fo. 281.
[278] SSM to Richebourg, 24 February 1712, ibid., fo. 342.
[279] SSM to Champigny, 2 March 1712, ibid., fo. 385.
[280] Copy of Dunkirk Chamber of Commerce to Sartine, 2 June 1779, ADN, C4609, no. 10.
[281] French translation of Stevens to Gamba, 20 May 1779, ibid., no. 18.

themselves contribute to the restitution of the prizes'.[282] Once again, the failure of the state to release these 'private' prisoners meant that the burden of war captivity weighed on local communities.

V. Conclusion

This chapter has begun to question some of the fundamental assumptions that have been made with regard to the definition of the prisoners of war: their relation to the state, the temporality of their detention, and the idea that the category was a product of modernity. The chapter also suggested that, if we want to analyse how war was understood in the eighteenth century, we need to broaden our focus beyond law of nations theory. This entails a different methodology.

The exemption of women and children, which was already advanced by classical legal writers, was not taken for granted on the ground, as shown by the practice of detaining them as or along prisoners of war, throughout the period we have considered. This continuity is also apparent if one looks at the concepts of 'civilian' and 'combatant', which remained unclear during the French Revolutionary and Napoleonic Wars.[283] Most wars challenge easy definitions of 'friendship' and 'enmity'—this was a fortiori the case when civil rebellions or wars overlapped with international conflicts, which happened with the Jacobite insurrections, the American insurgents or the French Revolution. The uncertainty regarding the categorization of Irish Jacobite or French Huguenots captured while fighting against their own state demonstrates this. The choice to treat them as prisoners of war was primarily an administrative decision, because the law of nations was unhelpful on the matter. More broadly, even at the end of our period, the armed forces of European powers were still composed of a large proportion of foreigners. The multifarious labels that could be assigned to them reveal the persisting tension between national affiliations and state belonging.

I have argued that normative legal categories fail to describe the social complexity of war captivity in the eighteenth century. By paying attention to the way in which categories worked in practice, and how they were circumvented, tactically used, or contested, one is ultimately led to question the constituting elements of the history of the laws of the war and the law of nations in the early modern period. I have emphasized how one individual could be categorized as a prisoner of war in one situation, and as a hostage in another. The consequences of being labelled under the former or the latter category are not to be underestimated: it could mean the difference between imprisonment limited in time by the

---

[282] Copy of LeMoyne, Dieppe mayor, to Dunkirk Chamber of Commerce, 12 June 1779, ibid., no. 14.
[283] This was further complicated by the development of new forms of asymmetric warfare: Bell, *First Total War*, ch. 8.

protection of the state, and freedom depending entirely on the will of a private captor. I am not saying that legal theory had no purchase on the ground, but I argue that the ways in which these categories were deployed essentially answered political, social, military, or economic preoccupations, rather than (or not only) moral ones. One of the main conclusions of this chapter, to which I will return throughout the book, is that it is profoundly misleading to see the state as the only protagonist that mattered in international conflicts and in international relations more broadly, in the eighteenth century and beyond. Non-state actors, including prisoners themselves, maintained a capacity to shake off the labels that were applied to them, and sometimes created new ones.

The example of hostages thus shows the limits of the 'legal' reach of the state, and complicates the notion of an all-encompassing statization of war. Privateers seemed to be driven completely, or virtually so, by financial considerations, by seeking to extract as much value as possible from what they captured, people or stuff, to offset the costs and risks that they ran. States by contrast sought some measure of organization, to make their war effort more effective, and to ease the way to making a peace—which had to come at some point. The state reliance on privateers points up some of the unsolvable contradictions of the war as it was waged in that period, in which the 'private' and the 'public' overlapped.[284] The case studies which structured this chapter all point to the continued relevance, in the eighteenth century, of older notions about the importance of private agents and the incomplete reach of the state. They speak about the hybrid legal context within which prisoners of war existed, somewhere between civil law, contract law, the customary 'rules' of war and plunder, treaties, and ecclesiastical attempts to moderate the pain for civilians. For the historian, the search for ways in which sailing communities 'applied' or 'adapted' the law of nations to their specific purposes overlooks the fact that the law of nations, in its various iterations, was sometimes purely and simply ignored. There were other varieties of law, to which people resorted. One thus needs to pay attention to the complexity and contradictions within 'state law' as well as within 'non-state' law.[285] In this sense, people were asserting different claims about what constituted law against the law of the state. Furthermore, the very nature of wars at sea involved a different set of legal issues and characters than did war on land. The private war at sea continued throughout the French Wars, despite early hesitations by French representatives to suppress privateering, as 'inhuman'.[286] Privateering was only prohibited in the 1856 Paris Declaration Respecting Maritime Law: in doing so, the states attempted to limit what legal scholars Eyal Benvenisti and Amichai Cohen call 'agency slack', reducing the autonomy of private actors in the waging of war.[287]

---

[284] Benton and Ross argue that the very language of 'private' and 'public' might be unhelpful: 'Empires', p. 6. See also Halliday, 'Law's histories'.

[285] Benton and Ross, 'Empires', pp. 4–5.   [286] Best, *Humanity*, p. 79.

[287] Benvenisti and Cohen, 'War', p. 1395.

2

Hate or Love Thy Enemy?
Humanitarian Patriotism

I. Introduction

In 1760, the 'Grand Association of the Laudable Order of Antigallicans' donated the sum of 50 pounds to a charitable campaign for clothing the French prisoners of war in Britain.[1] This society, founded in 1745 to promote economic manufactures and trade at the expense of France,[2] saw no contradiction between the display of patriotic virtue and support for disarmed foreign enemies. This chapter aims to unpack this apparent paradox.

In the eighteenth century, the principle of a moral universalism in time of war triumphed: war was fought on the moral ground as well as on the battlefield. I argue in this chapter that the language of humanitarian patriotism encapsulates the ambiguity of the discourse to make war more 'civilized' by treating the enemy 'humanely'.[3] This language brought together concepts that were often opposed; it merged cosmopolitan ideals, the emerging notion of human rights, and the defence of the national interest.[4] On the one hand, the foreign prisoner was to be treated as an innocent and suffering human, in accordance with the philanthropic ideas that developed across Europe from the 1760s onwards. On the other hand, this generosity was never devoid of self-interested considerations: to treat the enemy's nationals better and more humanely than one treated one's own was a way of gaining the higher moral ground, in part for getting the opposing government to reciprocate. These initiatives sometimes faced opposition, from those who declared that the Frenchmen were, first and foremost, to be understood as enemies rather than men, or those who held that the priority should be given to British prisoners in France.

The movement to support prisoners of war has to be placed within the broader trend for alleviating the evils of war, which took many forms in the eighteenth

---

[1] *Proceedings of the Committee* (1760).   [2] Allan, 'Laudable Association'.
[3] Augustin Cochin first used the term 'humanitarian patriotism', to refer to the way in which Jacobins justified the worst deeds towards their enemies in the name of humanity: Cochin, 'Patriotisme humanitaire'. On the contrary, I use 'humanitarian'—a term that only appeared at the beginning of the nineteenth century—in the sense of care for the suffering of a fellow human being. By the middle of the eighteenth century, the concepts of philanthropy, humanity, and patriotism began to overlap: Duprat, 'Temps des philanthropes', pp. xxx–xxxi.
[4] See Rosenfeld, 'Citizens of nowhere'.

The Society of Prisoners: Anglo-French Wars and Incarceration in the Eighteenth Century. Renaud Morieux, Oxford University Press (2019). © Renaud Morieux. DOI: 10.1093/oso/9780198723585.001.0001

century, such as the treatment of injured servicemen and veterans.[5] The chapter focuses on the political, moral, and practical ambiguities that were entailed by the act of bringing relief to enemies in wartime. A challenge that had to be overcome by supporters of the movement was the accusation that it was 'unpatriotic', by favouring the support of foreign enemies over that of fellow subjects in distress. The problem became even more complicated when the enemy behaved in an 'inhuman', 'cruel', or 'uncivilized' manner towards one's own soldiers and sailors. What should be the response to such behaviour? Depending on which values and criteria were seen as more important, the answer to this question would vary considerably.

The first and second sections focus on these political and moral ambiguities. The third and fourth sections move beyond theory to practice: I want to show how civil societies became involved in the support of prisoners of war through charitable endeavours. While in Britain the first half of the eighteenth century might have paved the way for such initiatives, with Anglican campaigns to support vulnerable populations, the Seven Years' War saw the first large-scale attempts by civil society to give assistance to French prisoners of war.[6] This campaign, which was distinctly British, deserves to be included in accounts of the rise and progress of subscription charity and of prison reform. These 'humanitarian' practices were tested during the Revolutionary and Napoleonic Wars, when systematic xenophobic propaganda increasingly opposed the defenders of 'humanity' to the national interest. Ultimately, the chapter examines the practical impact of these campaigns in changing the actual conditions of detention of prisoners.

II. The Duty to Treat the Enemy with 'Humanity'

In the eighteenth century, there was a widespread consensus that incarcerating defeated enemies was the more 'humane' and 'civilized' manner of treating them. This conception—that deprivation of liberty was a form of progress—was also applied to beliefs about reforming the criminal, the poor, or the insane.[7] This was framed in the language of 'humanity', itself rooted in several intellectual traditions. Two of these are especially relevant to the question of the treatment of prisoners of war: the law of nations, and the idea of the 'civilized' nature of eighteenth-century warfare.

A. The Law of Nations

Drawing on the writings of their sixteenth- and seventeenth-century predecessors, eighteenth-century jurists contended that combatants must respect a duty of

---

[5] Starkey, *War*, pp. 25–6.
[6] On Anglican charity in the early eighteenth century, see Sirota, *Christian Monitors*.
[7] Foucault, *Discipline*.

moderation and self-control towards the enemy. In the first instance, this was a rational argument, based on the idea of self-preservation. Besides these theoretical statements, the principle of reciprocity ruled (it still does) international relations and conduct in warfare.[8] This comparative horizon was ever-present in the work of state officials charged with looking after and exchanging prisoners of war.[9] In May 1744, for instance, the Commissioners for the Sick & Wounded Seamen were instructed to let their French counterparts know 'what allowance his Majesty orders to be made to the French prisoners here', adding that 'it is expected, an allowance of equal value shall be made to the English Prisoners in France'. They also pointed out that in Britain, efforts were made to hire larger prisons 'to prevent the inconvenience of [the French prisoners] being confined too close, and it is expected they should do the same'. *In fine*, 'the treatment our people find in France, will be the measure of the treatment of their people here, in England.'[10] Conversely, the French official in charge of exchanges at Dunkirk, Givry, wrote to the Lords of the Admiralty in November 1744 that he had received complaints from French prisoners just returned from Dover about their detention there, adding that, on the contrary, the British prisoners in France received 'the same care and charity' as 'the King my Master's own subjects'.[11]

This type of message could be read as an incentive for raising the standards. It could even lead to treating prisoners of war better than native inhabitants. During the Seven Years' War, British and French commissioners entertained a feisty correspondence, with each side complaining that their prisoners were not as well treated as they should have been, based on the strict equality that was supposed to govern this issue. Their knowledge of the situation originated in prisoners' complaints and administrative investigations, which will be analysed later. The British commissioners demanded in October 1757 that British prisoners in French hospitals be each given an individual bed, 'whatever might be customary in French hospitals in such cases for the sick of that nation [French], since French prisoners were so treated in England'. For the same reason, they asked that 'their prisoners be supplied with blankets as large and good as those given to French prisoners'.[12] Another bone of contention regarded the quantity and quality of food. In January 1758, the British officials reiterated their long-standing demand that their prisoners in France should benefit from the same deal as Frenchmen in Britain. But their complaint went further, adding that if the French failed to take action, the 'Lords of the Admiralty were resolved to deprive the French prisoners from the gentle treatment they had received so far, and make them experience *lex talionis*'.[13]

---

[8] Donagan, *War*, pp. 128–9, 131–2, 157–8, 166.   [9] Charters, *Disease*, p. 176.
[10] Lords of the Admiralty (LCA) to Sick & Wounded Board (S&W), 10 May 1744, National Maritime Museum, Greenwich (NMM), ADM/M/387, no. 31.
[11] Givry to LCA, 11 November 1744, Archives Nationales, Paris (AN), MAR/B3/421, fos. 380–v.
[12] October 1757, summarized in 'Memoire', [11] November 1758, MAR/B4/97, fos. 179–v.
[13] 3 January1758, summarized and translated in French, ibid., fo. 181.

Mistreating the enemy indeed exposed one's own soldiers to reprisals and retaliations, which were still understood to be legitimate in the context of the eighteenth-century law of nations, even though they were increasingly seen as 'relics of a ruder past'.[14] The right of reprisals is 'mimetic': one's violence is both legitimized by the other's violence, and modelled on it.[15] Thus, the undue imprisonment of a French officer in Plymouth in 1695, who was 'subjected to very close and rigorous confinement like the most lowly soldier or sailor', justified the adoption of a similar measure against an Englishman of a similar rank in Dinan: 'it would not be fair to treat him with any more humanity.'[16] Being 'humanely' treated was conditioned on a strict reciprocity from the enemy, not on the respect of abstract values. The use of reprisals was presented as reactive, placing the onus of the decision on the prisoners' own government. In 1695, Du Puys, a French naval administrator, wrote from St Malo, after giving the order to put in Dinan Castle a large number of English prisoners, 'as reprisal for our poor French prisoners, to whom they do not grant in England the least liberty', that 'we are sorry to go to such lengths, but [the English Prisoners] have to blame the harsh and cruel conduct of those who meddle with the French prisoners in England'.[17] The prisoners who were thus incarcerated as a measure of reprisals were informed, in writing, of the reasons for their ill-treatment.[18]

In 1704, Charles Verret de St Sulpice, *commissaire de la Marine* in St Malo, objected to the sending back of prisoners who were of no use to the war effort, 'the oldest the youngest and the puniest ones'. Accordingly, he decided that 'henceforth I will model myself on their behaviour . . . I will treat English prisoners with the same rigour as I am told ours are treated, . . . this is the best way of knocking some sense into the English Nation.'[19] The very same arguments were still used at the height of the Napoleonic Wars to prevent certain groups from being eligible to the parole of honour.[20]

But reprisals were only one option within a much wider repertoire of actions. Officials often presented their choices as a gradation. One could start by trying to encourage the enemy to improve their treatment of one's prisoners, and it was only if these efforts failed that more drastic options would be (reluctantly) opted for. The secretary of state for the *Marine* wrote in January 1747 that, although France had shown as much 'humanity' as possible for the British officers in its

---

[14] Neff, *War*, p. 125. Reprisals have been prohibited by international humanitarian law in the twentieth century: Kretzmer, 'Civilian immunity', pp. 95–6.

[15] Chamayou, *Chasses*, p. 110. Although the meaning of reprisals and retaliation is technically different (Neff, *War*, p. 123), our authors often used both terms interchangeably.

[16] Gastines, *commissaire général de la Marine*, to *Secrétaire d'Etat de la Marine* (SSM), 30 October 1695, AN, MAR/B3/95, fo. 255v.

[17] Du Puys to SSM, 4 December 1695, AN, MAR/B3/89, fo. 312v.

[18] Gastines to SSM, 5 June 1704, MAR/B3/123, fo. 28v.

[19] St Sulpice to SSM, 24 August 1704, ibid., fo. 568v.

[20] Transport Office (TO) to Parole Agents, 4 November 1811, The National Archives, Kew (TNA), ADM98/170, fos. 105–6.

hands, 'all the good treatment that we give to their people have not committed them to treat ours better'. Failing a swift change of attitude in Britain, the food rations given to British officers would be reduced.[21]

These two methods of negotiation aimed at the same thing: convincing the enemy that they should amend their ways. Moreover, they both illustrate what we could call the 'mirror' effect of war captivity, which can be formulated as follows: whatever is done to 'our' prisoners will affect 'their' prisoners, and vice versa. While reprisals were used throughout the period, they were invariably presented as problematic.[22] As the anonymous author of a 1758 tract put it, the refusal to exchange some prisoners for the fault of their government was fundamentally unjust. It violated 'the Rights of common Humanity'.[23] The state of war did not mean the breaking down of all social ties. A sort of 'commerce' or sociability must be preserved between enemies. This idea was expressed in different ways by different authors, and it is not my aim here to propose an intellectual history of these concepts, which would deserve much more than a collage of quotations.[24] The German philosopher Christian Wolff wrote in 1758 that 'every Nation should love the other Nations as it loves itself, enemies not excluded', while the Frenchman Abbé Réal considered in 1764 that belligerents owed each other a 'duty of humanity'.[25] The refusal of gratuitous violence was a cornerstone of the eighteenth-century laws of war.[26]

These ideas were also embedded in customary law, in military codes as well as international treaties. As this is relatively well known, a few select examples will suffice here. In 1739, George II's royal *Instructions* to privateers copied, word by word, a passage from Charles II's 1666 *Instructions* against France and Holland, which forbade the ill-treatment of enemies captured at sea, who should not be 'in cold blood killed, maimed, or by torture and cruelty inhumanely treated, contrary to the common usage and just provisions of warr'.[27] The cartels of exchange similarly emphasized monarchical benevolence and generosity towards their prisoners.[28] It was not sufficient to win a battle or a war. By the middle of the eighteenth century, all European powers felt the need to justify the behaviour of their armies and navies according to the notion of humane warfare. Considerations of self-interest as well as the rise of ethical principles led to this process.[29] The laws protecting prisoners of war were also aimed at preserving comparative advantages. In this logic, asking the enemy to feed your prisoners better might

---

[21] SSM to Guillot, 14 January 1747, AN, MAR/B2/331, fo. 14.
[22] McKeogh, 'Civilian immunity', p. 73.   [23] *Considerations on the Exchange* (1758), pp. 30–1.
[24] See Mattéi, *Histoire du droit*. This paragraph is based on this book.
[25] Wolff, *Principes du droit*, book IX, ch. 6, par. 3, quoted in Mattéi, *Histoire*, p. 209; Réal, *La Science du Gouvernement* (1764), in ibid., p. 411. See also Vattel, *Law of Nations*, book III, ch. 8, par. 158.
[26] Mattéi, *Histoire*, pp. 423–4.
[27] Marsden, *Laws and Customs*, vol. II, pp. 408–10 (quote on p. 410). The 1739 instructions are quoted in Leeson and Nowarteh, 'Was privateering', pp. 306–7.
[28] Cartel 1780, preamble, *CTS*, vol. 47.   [29] Witt, *Lincoln's Code*, pp. 4, 47.

have been a way to make war costlier for them. To return them more quickly allowed them to return more swiftly to the battlefield, etc.

In the laws of war, one instance of this moral obligation to show humanity towards the weak was the duty to spare the victims of shipwrecks, who were not to be captured and imprisoned—despite falling, negatively, within the remit of the category of the prisoner of war: they were not women, civilians, too young or too old, they were not neutrals, merchants, or fishermen. At least since the seventeenth century, the victims of shipwrecks, in the words of the 1670 treaty between England and Spain, had to be 'treated with humanity and kindness' and exempted from being made prisoners of war; they would instead be given safe-conducts to return home.[30]

In the eighteenth century, the idea became widespread that, by experiencing an act of God, or an unforeseeable natural phenomenon, the sailors' status had changed: they were no longer combatants who could lawfully be incarcerated, but innocent victims of war. Shipwreck victims were the archetype of the unfortunate sailors, fortune's fools, whose absolute deprivation should be deserving of everyone's sympathy. These principles were implemented by state officials. During the War of the Austrian Succession, French and British officials tried to outdo each other in generosity with respect to the treatment of shipwrecked sailors. In August 1744, Field Marshal George Wade, who held the joint command of the Anglo-Austrian armies in Flanders, decided to release two French sailors who had been wrecked on the Dutch coast and were detained in Ghent as prisoners of war. His secretary located this decision within the chivalric tradition of clemency to the disarmed enemy, proving the 'feelings of Candor and generosity which will always be the guide to his actions in war, as well as in more peaceful times'.[31] In turn, two months later, the mayor and aldermen of Boulogne came to the rescue of the crew of an English ship wrecked on the French coast a few days before. These men had been transferred from Boulogne prison to Calais prison, 'led by the maréchaussée handcuffed and tied with ropes, in rainy and stormy weather'. The French municipal officers vociferously protested that 'not a single person here has not protested against inhumanity such as would not be inflicted on the worst criminals'.[32] Such civilian proclamations of support for the unfortunate sailors were very common. In March 1760, an English sailor was found at sea by a French fishing boat, half-dying and clutching at the 'debris of a top-sail', the only survivor of a shipwreck.[33] Upon the insistence of the municipality of [Dunkirk], who requested that 'particular care' be given to the Englishman, Berryer, secretary of state for the Marine, was 'moved by this sentiment of humanity on their part' and approved to send him back to

[30] 'American Treaty', 8 July 1670, articles 10 and 11.
[31] Copy of Wade's secretary to 'Cressy Lieutenant de roy de Lille', 22 August 1744, AN, MAR/F2/72.
[32] Boulogne mayor and aldermen, 23 October 1744, MAR/B3/428, fo. 278.
[33] Bégon, Intendant de la Marine in Dunkirk, to S&W, 7 March 1760, TNA, ADM97/106, fo. 274.

England, 'without being considered a prisoner of war, nor to be counted in the exchanges'.[34] This was presented by the French as a just return of favour to the British,[35] although the fear of reprisals probably also played a part. Be that as it may, the sailors' place of birth or enmity did not matter: they were unfortunate, which was sufficient to entitle them to this mark of generosity.

In December 1744, a British transport vessel, the *Prospect*, was wrecked off St Malo. On board were 300 British prisoners returning home, who had forcibly taken the command of the ship and drove her onto the rocks. One hundred and forty of them drowned.[36] Lieutenant Hartwell, who commanded the vessel, testified to 'the humanity of the Gentlemen of St Malo in the Care they took of the Poor Prisoners, who were saved from the Wreck', and had ordered them to be shipped to England as soon as possible.[37] Such attitudes seem to have been very common. The crews of shipwrecked vessels were normally liberated, since they were 'regarded as passengers, and not as prisoners'.[38] On 8 July 1747, the *Maidstone*, an English ship whose commander was Augustus Keppel, a future admiral, was wrecked off the Island of Noirmoutiers, at the mouth of Nantes' river, on the French Atlantic coast.[39] The French king's officers posted in Noirmoutiers, as well as the French coastal population, did their best to 'save the men and come to their aid'. Keppel himself noted that 'We are extremely well treated here'.[40] The Comte de Maurepas, secretary of state for the *Marine*, ordered that shirts, stockings, shoes, and jackets be given to those in need, and ordered them to be returned to England as quickly as possible.[41] The Sick & Wounded Board suggested in response that, since the French minister was priding himself 'upon the Humanity which had been exercised by the French Officers & People towards Ours', the British government should 'return the good office in Kind, to such of the French Prisoners of War now in England as were taken some time since in the French Men of War by Lord Anson'.[42] Besides the desire to do good, what seems to have been at stake here was the desire not to be outdone in this show of generosity.

Despite the consensus that had been continually articulated in previous wars that shipwrecked sailors were victims, not combatants, these principles were enacted in a more haphazard way at the beginning of the American War of Independence. John Howard, the prison reformer, wrote a memorandum for the Sick & Wounded Board in January 1779, after visiting a number of French

---

[34] Ibid., fo. 274v.
[35] Letter subsequently forwarded by the S&W to LCA on 14 April 1760: ADM98/8, fo. 90.
[36] S&W to LCA, 24 December 1744, ADM98/2, fo. 84v; William Wilson, ship-owner, to Navy Board, 22 May, 11 June 1745, ADM106/1021, fos. 148, 163.
[37] LCA to S&W, 26 December 1744, NMM, ADM/M/389, no. 307.
[38] Charron, French commissaire for the prisoners at Dunkirk, 16 October 1746, TNA, ADM97/103, fo. 334.
[39] On this shipwreck, see http://www.wrecksite.eu/wreck.aspx?17117.
[40] Keppel to Admiral Anson, 'from the Island of Noirmontier', 8 July 1747, in Keppel, *Life*, p. 96.
[41] Maurepas to S&W, 21 July 1747, TNA, ADM98/4, fo. 134.
[42] S&W to LCA, 27 July 1747, ibid., fos. 134v–135.

prisons. Following his visit to Calais prison, he wrote that with few exceptions, shipwrecked sailors were not allowed hammocks, bedding, or blankets, but 'only Straw'. In front of this remark, the Commissioners for the Sick & Wounded Seamen commented:

> It has been practiced to consider shipwrecked Persons in a peculiarly compassionate light and to grant them their release. There have been instances of proper humanity on the part of the French in such Cases; the Circumstances of this information would be the proper object of representation.[43]

In the following months, citing the information gathered by Howard, the British government multiplied signs of goodwill towards French sailors wrecked in Britain and Ireland, 'as to set an example to the French to treat English shipwrecked Seamen there in like manner'.[44] As reciprocity was not forthcoming, the British commissioners explicitly wrote to their French counterparts in June 1779, demanding that 'the same humanity' be shewn by the French monarchy to its British prisoners.[45] Finally, an article about shipwrecked sailors was inserted in the 1780 Cartel. These people were to be 'set free immediately, & will be given the means to return to their respective countries, as well as clothing, if they have need of it'.[46] Until the end of the war, both governments would pride themselves in the 'miracles of humanity, boldness, courage & even intrepidity' that some of their countrymen showed to enemy sailors who had been wrecked on their coasts.[47] Similar regulations were adopted between Britain and the French allies, Spain, and the United Provinces, always in the name of 'humanity'.[48] In the same way, the treatment of shipwrecked victims was seen as a model that could be extended to other victims of war, including sick prisoners of war.[49]

The Revolutionary Wars constituted once again a turning point. It became harder for fishermen to be exempted from capture, and the plunder of prisoners when they landed seems to have become systematic.[50] Likewise, the privileged treatment heretofore given to shipwrecked seamen was discontinued. In 1796, the project of a general exchange cartel presented by France to Britain hence proposed that 'all persons, of whatsoever Denomination . . . , who may be shipwrecked in Merchant Vessels', should be 'immediately set at Liberty'. On the other hand, 'all Persons belonging to armed Vessels' who encountered the same misfortune would be considered as prisoners of war.[51] While the cartel was not successfully

---

[43] Memorandum by John Howard on British prisoners in France, 15 January 1779, TNA, ADM98/11, fo. 213v.
[44] S&W to LCA, 3 March 1779, ibid., fos. 236v–237.
[45] S&W to LCA, 26 June 1779, TNA, ADM98/12, fo. 38v.   [46] Article 13, CTS, vol. 47.
[47] Mistral, *Intendant de la Marine* in Le Havre, 6 April 1782, AN, MAR/B3/716, fo. 65.
[48] Cartel between Britain and Spain, article 9, 13 July 1781, TNA, ADM98/13, fo. 203v.
[49] S&W to LCA, 21 December 1781, ADM98/14, fo. 24.   [50] *Report* (1798), p. 14.
[51] Article 13, in ibid., p. 76.

concluded, it is revealing that the British negotiators did not object to this article. The survivors were invariably imprisoned, as in 1797, when HMS *Amazon*, a thirty-six-gun frigate, was wrecked off the Isle Bas after a fierce battle. The men who managed to reach the shore on rafts were marched to Quimper, where they were detained.[52] There are numerous examples of this change of attitude.[53]

B. The Civilized Nature of Eighteenth-century Wars

Eighteenth-century authors believed that their civilization had reached a higher state of advancement than in earlier and non-European societies. I am not interested in reassessing the notion that the eighteenth century was less violent, and, by implication, more 'humane' or more 'civilized' than other historical periods.[54] In other words, my perspective here is not to argue that the morality of historical actors did or did not explain their choices.[55] An ethical language was certainly used: it has a history, itself rooted in major social and cultural transformations.[56] For the same reason, it is not my concern to describe the eighteenth century as a period of the 'humanization of warfare'.[57] Terms such as 'civilized', or 'barbarian' were—and still are—comparative. What matters is the standard against which they were measured.[58] These concepts were rooted in the eighteenth-century search for universal explanations. In what follows, I argue that the treatment of prisoners of war was a key comparator that enabled the drawing up of a hierarchy of moral values. In these discourses, which aimed at presenting the European ways of warfare and the laws of war, as they had slowly been devised in Europe and reached their perfection in the eighteenth century, as superior to all others, I posit that the treatment of prisoners of war was paradigmatic.

The end of the practice of torturing and mistreating one's defeated and disarmed enemies suggested that the culmination of centuries of progress had been reached in Europe. One of Adam Smith's protectors, and a close friend of Hume, was Henry Home, the Scottish philosopher and judge, who became Lord Kames in 1752. Kames wrote in his *Essays on the Principles of Morality and Natural Religion* (1758):

> Putting an enemy to death in cold blood, is at present looked upon with distaste and horror, and therefore is immoral; though it was not always so in the same

[52] See An account of the wreck of HMS Amazon, NMM, REC/57.
[53] John Robertson was detained for five years after his ship was wrecked and sunk off Calais: 'Journal', 1806–11, NMM, JOD 202.
[54] See, for example, Whitman, *Verdict*, pp. 5, 128. Against the notion of 'limited wars', see Starkey, *War*, pp. 6–7; Witt, *Lincoln's Code*, p. 68.
[55] See Benvenisti and Cohen, 'War', pp. 1365–6.
[56] See Mennell, 'Anthropologues', pp. 53–64.   [57] Howard, 'Constraints', p. 5.
[58] Lee, *Barbarians*.

degree. It is considered as barbarous and inhuman, to fight with poisonous weapons, and therefore is more remarkably disapproved by the moral sense that it was originally.... We have enmity against France, which is our natural enemy. But this enmity is not directed against individuals; conscious, as we are, that it is the duty of subjects to serve their king and country. Therefore we treat prisoners of war with humanity. And now it is creeping in among civilized nations, that, in war, a cartel should be established for the exchange of prisoners.[59]

Kames was also arguing that the same practices would be described as 'inhuman' at some moments in history, and not in others.[60] The English physician William Falconer, writing in 1781, also contrasted the 'barbarous manner' of past attitudes towards prisoners of war with the present times. Aztecs, Arabs, Tartars, Scythians, Goths, Vandals, and Huns, as well as Greeks and Romans, devised particularly cruel ways of treating their enemy prisoners, while 'civilized nations' treated them 'as subjects'.[61] The treatment of prisoners of war was the yardstick by which degrees of civilization and humanity were to be measured.

This theme was prevalent throughout Robert Ward's *An Enquiry into the Foundation and History of the Law of Nations in Europe* (1795), through which the treatment of prisoners of war ran like a bloody thread. The author described in gruesome detail the systematic tortures which prisoners of war had been subjected to in the past, as a way to illustrate the ever-changing nature of the law of nations.[62] As has been emphasized by James Whitman, for Ward, displaying generosity towards a fallen and weak enemy was a character trait that defined the nobility. Despite the violence of former ages, medieval knights maintained honourable values in the midst of war. For instance, during the English Civil War of the eleventh century, the Earl of Gloucester treated his captive, King Stephen of England, 'with the greatest humanity', and 'kept him in safe but *gentle* confinement'.[63] Knights were forbidden to strike an unarmed enemy, did not avenge themselves against their former foes, and kept their oaths. Furthermore, for Ward, even during dark ages of European history, the English had always, comparatively, behaved better than the French.[64]

Ward is only an extreme example of the eighteenth-century texts that presented clemency to prisoners of war as an aristocratic and kingly virtue, a manifestation of 'true honour' and 'love of humanity'.[65] Generosity for the fallen enemy was, according to Burlamaqui, 'more glorious than his courage'.[66] He gave the example of the Duke of Cumberland, who ordered his own physician to look after a

[59] Kames, *Essays*, ch. 8, p. 51.   [60] See also Kames, *Sketches*, vol. I, pp. 222–3.
[61] Falconer, *Remarks*, pp. 245, 302–3, 245–6, 325–6, 339, 382–3.
[62] Ward, *Enquiry*, vol. I, pp. 178, 180, 211.
[63] Ward, *Enquiry*, vol. II, p. 163–4.   [64] Ward, *Enquiry*, vol. I, pp. 263, 265–6.
[65] Starkey, *War*, pp. 20–1, 69–131.   [66] Burlamaqui, *Principles*, p. 145.

seriously injured French officer, after the Battle of Dettingen in 1743.⁶⁷ This
exemplum was often cited in England as a model of gallant behaviour.⁶⁸ In his
Sketches of the History of Man (1774), Lord Kames evoked recent cases of
commendable behaviour displayed by officers towards their enemy, illustrating
the 'humanity [which] was carried to a greater height, in our late war [*the Seven
Years' War*] with France'.⁶⁹ But the example that Kames developed in a footnote
reveals something deeper about the mutations of the concept of glory in European
culture in this period. The French captain Francois Thurot, who died at sea in
1760 while fighting near the Isle of Man, was, for Kames, a hero to be admired and
remembered. He landed in Ireland with three vessels and took Carrickfergus near
Cork: 'The terror he at first spread, wrote Kames, soon yielded to admiration of his
humanity. He paid a full price for every thing', and he reprimanded those who
tried to cheat local sellers, even though his own men were close to mutiny.⁷⁰ For
Kames, 'such kindness in an enemy from whom nothing is expected but mischief,
is an illustrious instance of humanity'. This behaviour was universally to be
extolled: 'Common honesty to an enemy is not a common practice in war....
These incidents ought to be held up to princes as examples of true heroism.'
A Frenchman was thus heralded as a model to emulate by Britons: 'He will be kept
in remembrance by every true-hearted Briton, though he died fighting against us.
But he died in the field of honour, fighting for his country.'⁷¹ Literally hundreds of
articles about Thurot appeared in British and French newspapers in the years
1757-9. They emphasized how 'he behaved, in every respect, more like a friend
than an enemy'.⁷² While the Seven Years' War is often described as a period in
which new conceptions of the nation took shape in Britain and in France, this
example shows that another intellectual tradition survived in Britain, one that tied
patriotism with the sense of public interest.⁷³

Two elements are striking about Thurot's character, as he was portrayed in
these texts. First, his national origins were uncertain. He was a citizen of the sea,
the grandson of an Irish Jacobite who had emigrated to the north of France, a
fluent French, English, and Gaelic speaker, who journeyed back and forth between
the British Isles and the Continent. His crew was multinational and his wife
English.⁷⁴ A Freemason, Thurot was said to despise the pettiness of national
self-love, and chastised his French compatriots in London who abused the English

---

⁶⁷ Ibid., p. 146.
⁶⁸ In Scotland, Cumberland was seen not as a 'civilized' warrior, but as 'Butcher Cumberland', the
man who had put down the Jacobite rebellion at Culloden in 1746, executing wounded rebels on the
battlefield.
⁶⁹ Kames, *Sketches*, p. 223.   ⁷⁰ Ibid., 224n1.   ⁷¹ Ibid.
⁷² *Public Ledger* (March 1760). The same examples were developed in the *Gazette des Pays-Bas* of
11 March 1760. On Thurot's 'real' life, see, for instance, TNA, ADM98/8, fos. 82v–83.
⁷³ On the former, see Colley, *Britons*; Bell, *Cult*; Dziembowski, *Un nouveau*. On the latter, see
Rosenfeld, 'Citizens'.
⁷⁴ *Genuine and curious Memoirs*, pp. 7, 19–20, 22. On Thurot's national origins, see the long article
in *Whitehall Evening Post*, 2102 (6 September 1759).

and Irish.[75] All this was a source of fascination for his contemporaries. The second point that stood out, in Thurot's biography, regarded his humble social origins. He started his career as a smuggler before becoming the most fearsome French privateer in the Channel/North Sea area. His social standing was more modest than that of the illustrious examples mentioned in the preceding pages. Neither his cosmopolitanism nor his rusticity prevented him from being celebrated as a hero; in fact, they probably explain why he was hailed as such. Admittedly, Thurot was considered an exceptional individual. He was distinguished from the common people by royal favour: he was received at Versailles by Louis XV, who gave him the command of three frigates, just as the Flemish privateer Jean Bart had been rewarded by Louis XIV in the seventeenth century.[76] This elevated Thurot above the rank of a mere mortal. His courage was 'noble',[77] and he was separated from his comrades by 'super-human virtue'.[78] If his naval victories were rewarded by the French monarchy, it was his modest and very 'bourgeois' virtues which were emphasized in print in the next three decades. Thurot embodied a kind of heroism of the everyday, won by giving bread to the poor rather than slicing the heads of soldiers.

Such signs of courage and generosity transcended the boundaries of the nation and class. A new principle was emerging in the eighteenth century, which saw glory as 'a sign of charitable greatness'.[79] Sparing the enemy—or, better still, lavishing benefactions upon him—was almost as glorious as winning a bloody battle. The subversive potential of these new ideas cannot be overemphasized. Arguing that love of humanity was the supreme ethical virtue, and true heroism, might mean that enemies were not really enemies.[80] This is precisely what the category of the prisoner of war itself might signify.

III. The 'Inhuman' Treatment of Prisoners of War in Their Own Words

The Enlightenment introduced the concept of humanity, 'understood in a dual sense: as a species and as a sentiment'.[81] Its antonym, 'inhuman', was already current in the sixteenth century, and had a double meaning: referring both to that which does not belong to the human species, and to those who lack humanity or show cruelty.[82] As argued by Didier Fassin and Patrice Bourdelais, whom I follow here, accusing the enemy of being inhuman was an 'ideological slogan', which

---

[75] *Genuine and curious Memoirs*, p. 21.   [76] *Read's Weekly Journal*, 4014 (20 January 1759).
[77] *Avis de l'Editeur* (1760), in *Apologie du Capitaine Thurot*, p. 4.
[78] *Journal historique du Capitaine Thurot*, in *Apologie*, p. 21.
[79] Iverson, 'gloire humanisée', p. 218. See also Lilti, *Figures publiques*, ch. 4.
[80] See Rosenfeld, 'Citizens', p. 34.
[81] Fassin and Bourdelais, 'Introduction', in *Constructions*, p. 12.
[82] *Dictionnaire de l'Académie française* (1694).

'served to legitimize a political action'.[83] In this section, I pay attention to the prisoners' own language. The question that then needs to be addressed is whether these complaints were taken into account by state administrators, and, if so, why this was the case.

A. The Prisoners' Complaints

In their petitions to the 'authorities'—we will keep the term general for the moment—prisoners complained about the quantity and quality of the food they were given, of the exiguity of their lodging, about the violence of their jailors, or the length of their detention. These topics were staples of the prisoners' rhetoric throughout the eighteenth century and, one suspects, beyond this period. Prisoners of war petitions were cast in a language that piled up references to religion, natural law, the law of nations, and the laws of war, contrasting European, Christian, civilized, enlightened, and noble on the one hand, and barbarian, infidel, medieval, dark, Turk, pirates, tyrant, and inhumane on the other.[84] These comparisons were not chosen at random. They tell us something about the horizons of expectation of the prisoners, and what they considered to be just and unjust treatments. The language of 'barbarity' was commonly used in their petitions, to contrast the norms of civilization which European countries owed to each other with the ways of warfare of non-Christians and outlaws, i.e. those people who completely rejected the laws of war. It probably also built on older tropes, such as the sixteenth-century discourse on slavery and tyranny, and late seventeenth-century captivity narratives describing the fate of Europeans at the hands of Ottoman rulers.[85] In February 1709, a French bark laden for Poole was taken by a Guernsey privateer, and its crew was mistreated by their captors. Three of the French sailors were 'badly burnt with matches', and forced to enlist on board the privateer.[86] They complained about the 'inhumane and barbarous usage [they] received . . . we taking Capt. Shalew for no better than a Pyrate or Turk'.[87] In 1744, in the hospital at Farnham, the prisoners were 'the sad Sport of the Whim, and of the Brutality' of the surgeon, who made them suffer 'everything that the most barbarous Nations despise'.[88] Those detained in Edinburgh Castle accused in 1781 the Agent of 'mak[ing them] suffer so many torments by his inhumanity'.[89] All these comparisons tarred the prisoners' tormentors with the same brush: by

---

[83] Fassin, 'Ordre moral', p. 41.
[84] On the use of this language during the English Civil Wars, see Donagan, *War*, pp. 128–9, 135–6.
[85] Arnold, 'Affairs', p. 846.
[86] John Bressey, Marshal of prisoners of war on Guernsey, to S&W: 15 February 1709, BL, Add MS61593, fo. 31.
[87] Copy of the prisoners' declaration, forwarded by Bressey to S&W, ibid., fo. 32.
[88] Petition to the Duke of Newcastle, 17 March 1744, NMM, ADM/M/390, no. 96.
[89] 10 June 1781, TNA, ADM97/123/3.

their inhuman, barbarian and cruel behaviour, these torturers were excluding themselves from the community of humans, just as pirates transgressed the law of nations. The very same language was used by British prisoners in France.[90]

The prisoners also accused the prison staff of extortion, of blackmail, of humiliating them through brutality or torture: in short, of treating them like criminals. Such a rhetoric had every chance of hitting a nerve, and we must explain why. Because there was a remarkable stability to this language over the period studied here, from the late seventeenth to the early nineteenth century, one example will suffice: that of the prisoners detained at Kinsale Prison during the War of the Austrian Succession. The French prisoners in this Irish prison wrote two memoranda to the Lords of the Admiralty, levelling complaints against the Agent, the jailor, and the physician.[91] The signatories of the memorandum asked to be 'treated as prisoners of war and not as slaves', complaining about the 'tyranny' of the Agent, who beat up the prisoners who escaped. The Agent also stole the money that had been mailed to prisoners by their families, a 'criminal' behaviour that 'violate[d] the law of nations'. The doctors themselves were 'as ignorant as they are barbarian', through whose negligence many poor prisoners died.[92] After Kinsale Prison was burnt down, by accident or arson (an episode in which sixty prisoners died), the inmates were brought back in to the roofless building, in the middle of winter.[93]

In all these texts, the petitioners emphasized their bodily pain. They were starved, forced to beg for food, robbed, beaten up, and confined in holes. They pleaded to be relieved of their sufferings, appealing to the sympathy and compassion of their addressees. Because these principles were starting to become the subject of a wide consensus in this period, one can surmise that they were efficient in gathering the support of officials.[94] Indeed, at least as important as the content of the prisoners' letters is the question of the addressees of their complaints, and of the circuits of circulation of these petitions. By presenting themselves as helpless and innocent creatures in need of relief, prisoners tried, and often succeeded, in reaching out and convincing state authorities of the justice of their cause, as we will see in a moment.

Publicizing their complaints was, for the prisoners, a way of exposing the transgressions of the law of nations by the very people in charge of overseeing it in prisons. The first reason why these appeals often resonated is the fact that these same moral norms were part of the mental universe of state administrators. Prison inspections are particularly revealing. In theory, sheriffs or justices of the peace

---

[90] For example, petition by prisoners in Niort, 16 July 1779, NMM, ADM/M/408.

[91] LCA to S&W, 21 August 1747, ADM/M/399, no. 264, attaching the two memoranda.

[92] 'Les prisonniers de Kinsale' to LCA, 17 August 1747, ibid., no. 264/1. An investigation was ordered: LCA to S&W, 21 August 1747, ibid., no. 264.

[93] Derchigny to SSM, 2 April 1748, AN, MAR/B3/464, fos. 126–v.

[94] Arnold, 'Affairs', p. 851; Hunt, *Inventing*, pp. 97–8; Abruzzo, *Polemical Pain*, pp. 52–61.

(JPs) had the prerogative of inspecting 'normal' prisons, and they often did, even though until the end of the eighteenth century inspection routines were not routinized.[95] In the same way, by the beginning of the eighteenth century, war prisons were regularly inspected by envoys of the Sick & Wounded Board in Britain, and by representatives of the *Marine* in France.[96] On 28 January 1744, following epidemics in Plymouth prisons and hospitals, Captain John Hamilton, the commander of HMS *Augusta*, was sent to investigate.[97] Undertaking what he called 'a cursory round of the prisons and hospitals', three decades before John Howard, Hamilton wrote for the Lords of the Admiralty 'a minute diary of [his] progress', detailing the content of the interviews he conducted in Plymouth. Hamilton highlighted his personal concern for the suffering of the prisoners. 'A motive of compassion' led him to consider contributing his own money to the clothing of those who were naked. But upon further reflection, he decided that caring for the prisoners was to be considered 'in the light of publick saving and oeconomy'. The two motivations were not easily separable. Hamilton detailed the sufferings of prisoners lying 'absolutely naked' on hospital mattresses, and suggested that they should be provided with new clothes when discharged from the hospital: 'in this instance, as in most others, true Oeconomy leans to the side of Humanity, and ... the expence would be more than made up for, by the prevention of the Chargeableness attendant on sickness.'[98]

Hamilton interviewed the sick in every hospital; he walked about from bed to bed, gathering information from them about the number of sheets they were provided with; how they were treated by the physician, surgeons and nurses; if they had hospital caps; their food and drink regimen, and how satisfied they were with it, among other things. He tried to hear and encourage the complaints of the prisoners, in order to discover 'whether they were treated with gentleness and humanity by the officers set over them'.[99] In the report, when commenting on the different members of the custodial staff he examined, their 'humanity', or lack of it, was the key virtue that he emphasized.[100] He thus accused the head turnkey of Cock Side Prison in Plymouth of cruel behaviour, relaying the following anecdote:

> 30 January 1744.... Mr. Sooper ... is a man of a cruel and tyrannical disposition, is brutal in his common behaviour, and takes delight in beating them even for his diversion: one instance of which they produce in a practice of his to throw apples into the middle of the area for the common prisoners to scramble for, and beating them to advantage as they stoop down with a bended back.[101]

---

[95] Innes, 'Legislation', pp. 126–7.

[96] Lempereur to SSM, 30 January 1709, AN, MAR/B2/214, fos. 329v–330.

[97] John Hamilton, 'Diary of my visitation of, and enquiry into the state and condition of the hospitals and prisons, appointed for the reception of the French and Spanish Prisoners at the Port of Plymouth', in LCA to S&W, 11 February 1744, NMM, ADM/M/390, no. 46.

[98] Ibid., 30 January 1744, p. 20.   [99] Ibid., p. 15.   [100] Ibid., p. 18.   [101] Ibid., p. 18.

Forcing starving prisoners to fight for scraps of food, and turning them against each other for sport, was a mark of sadism. Hamilton's investigation illustrates the prevalence of the sensitivity to the pain of the prisoners, among the administrators in charge of their detention and exchange. This echoes a wider pattern: from the middle of the eighteenth century onwards, thanks in particular to the influence of Cesare Beccaria's *On Crimes and Punishments* (1764), physical violence towards criminals was increasingly condemned.[102] A new conception of punishment established itself: the sufferings inflicted upon the body of the criminal must be minimized, in the name of the universal principles of humanity and progress.[103] In the 1770s, argues Michael Ignatieff, the prison reformers' condemnation of 'institutional abuse and physical cruelty' and the growing public hostility to the infliction of bodily pain led to the erasure of infamous punishments from the judicial repertoire in Britain.[104] This sea change also affected the institution in charge of the detention of prisoners of war: the navy. From the Seven Years' War onwards, gratuitous violence was seen as unjust and immoral, and the discretionary power of captains was officially limited at the beginning of the nineteenth century.[105] Prison reformers, like antislavery activists, appealed to the growing contemporary preoccupation with compassion for the pain of others in order to enlist public support for their cause.[106]

Historians have overlooked the extent to which the reflection on the rights of prisoners of war prisons might have been a source of inspiration for the debate about penal reform, which accelerated in the 1770s–80s. The case of John Howard, the most famous of them, is a good illustration of this. Howard discussed prisoners of war at length in *The State of the Prisons*. Concluding the first section of the book, entitled 'General view of distress in prisons', he observed that the systematic comparison he made between houses of correction, town gaols, hospitals, hulks, and lazarettos led him to believe that all categories of prisoners were suffering in England. There was one exception to this grim statement, the prisoners of war, whose detention was a model to be emulated:

> Shall these irregularities, the sources of misery, disease, and wickedness, be endured in a nation celebrated for good sense and humanity; and who from these principles, do treat one sort of prisoners with tenderness and generosity? I mean prisoners of war.... It is the farthest thing in the world from my wish to deprive captives of any one of these benefits—I am only desirous of seeing the same humanity shewn to our own countrymen in distress; so that a consistent and uniform practice may prove our benevolence to be a firm and steady

[102] McConville, *History*, pp. 80–4; Beattie, *Crime*, pp. 556–7; McGowen, 'Civilizing punishment'.
[103] McGowen, 'Body'.
[104] Ignatieff, *Just Measure*, pp. 73, 90–1. See also Linebaugh, *London Hanged*.
[105] Rodger, *Command*, pp. 403, 488–93. See also Malcomson, *Order*.
[106] Halttunen, 'Humanitarianism'; Scarry, *Body*.

principle; and that those who are censorious may find no occasion for ascribing our kind usage of foreigners to a less amiable motive.[107]

Avoiding the accusation of partiality for foreigners, Howard then proposed to generalize the good treatment of prisoners of war to the whole carceral population in England. His painful captivity in France, during the Seven Years' War, was a decisive moment in his conversion to the cause that would occupy his life from then on. In a footnote to the first edition of his State of the Prisons (1777), Howard wrote: 'Perhaps what I suffered on this occasion, increased my sympathy with the unhappy people, whose case is the subject of this book.'[108] Captured in 1756 by a French privateer on board a Lisbon packet, Howard was deprived of water for forty hours, and given little food. He was then detained in Brest and Morlaix, where he observed 'how cruelly' his countrymen were used. While on his parole at Carhaix, he entered into a correspondence with the prisoners at Dinan, who were 'treated with such barbarity, that many hundreds had perished'.[109] Once he returned to England, he informed the Sick & Wounded Board of this situation: 'Remonstrance was made to the French court: our sailors had redress: and those that were in the three prisons mentioned above, were brought home in the first cartel-ships.'[110] The young Howard's attitude was thus typical of what many other returning prisoners of war did, writing to the authorities of their state to obtain a softening of the treatment of their peers. Was this outcome typical as well? How often were these requests to governments successful?

B. The Effect of the Complaints

Were the prisoners' complaints taken seriously? Then as now, they unquestionably had to overcome a great deal of reluctance on the part of the state officials.[111] The typical official answer was to downplay the complaint. After receiving a memorandum written by English prisoners freshly returned from Dunkirk, in February 1709, Lempereur, the French commissaire in St Malo, replied that they were not 'so much to be pitied' since they received six sols a day, and that it was 'an exaggeration' to say that the sick did not receive 'any relief'.[112] Conversely, officials showed far more understanding when they read letters written by their compatriots. When his British interlocutors denied the allegations of bad treatments in Kinsale Prison, Lempereur insisted upon his case, arguing that the great number of complaints he had received from French prisoners was proof of the deed: 'it would not be possible for all these prisoners to agree so perfectly to say the

---

[107] State of the Prisons, 1st ed. (1777) , pp. 21–2.   [108] Ibid., p. 23.   [109] Ibid., p. 22.
[110] State of the Prisons, p. 23.   [111] Farcy, '"Je désire"'; Durand, 'Construire'.
[112] Lempereur to SSM, 24 February 1709, AN, MAR/B3/169, fo. 64.

same thing.'[113] The representativeness of a prisoner's complaints was always at stake, and Lempereur's successor during the War of the Austrian Succession, Jean-Joseph Guillot, believed the declarations of one English prisoner, formerly detained at Brest, to be 'full of falsehoods' that would have been easy to dispute 'if [the Commissioners for the Sick & Wounded Seamen] had troubled themselves to question a few of the other prisoners who have been detained in Brest'.[114]

Guillot, who would serve as a *commissaire de la Marine* in St Malo until 1768 and was charged of the general correspondence with Britain on the issue of prisoners of war, was an expert interpreter of prisoners' petitions, alternately discarding or siding with them according to his own agenda. In his correspondence with the secretary of state for the *Marine*, he was very blunt about it, explaining in January 1745 that he had written in Britain about the 'treatments of our people, having seen several letters which I found very pitiful'. He confessed: 'one must not dwell on these sorts of letters in which evil is always made to look worse than it is, with a view to arousing compassion and to getting us to work faster on the exchanges.'[115] The Comte de Maurepas, in his reply, was eager to dismiss the British recriminations about the exiguity of and lack of personnel in Dinan hospital, where sick English prisoners were looked after. He added: 'you have received hitherto so many proofs of our good treatment of your prisoners that I am surprised you spare a thought on reports that are so exaggerated you yourself must be aware of it.'[116]

To explain these overstatements, Guillot came up with several explanations. Firstly, incarceration generated specific psychological stresses: 'it is certain that however kindly we use these prisoners, we will never succeed in preventing them from holding back their complaints, their long detention vexes and distresses them and troubles them, and in that state they only see their misery.'[117] Secondly, the statements of prisoners always contained an element of strategy: 'in general any prisoner aspiring to his freedom thinks he can get it sooner by piling up complaints.' At the same time, he recognized that the prisoners 'were certaintly to be pitied', and that the turnover of transport vessels should be increased, in order to empty the prisons more swiftly. He also indicated to his British interlocutors that whenever they sent him 'mémoires de plaintes', he forwarded them to local prison administrators, and that any abuse, however small, was 'redressed in no time'.

Thus, even the most cynical of the state officials acted on the prisoners' complaints, whatever his opinion as to their truthfulness might be. The prisoners' complaints, when they followed the diplomatic route, had to be answered. But there were different means by which to do this, and transparency was not always a requisite. A shrewd strategy was to use the prisoners as spokesmen, asking them to

---

[113] Lempereur to S&W, 16 October 1709, ibid., fo. 325.
[114] SSM to S&W, 17 March 1745, MAR/B2/325, fo. 734.
[115] Guillot to SSM, 27 January 1745, MAR/B3/432, fo. 61v.
[116] SSM to S&W, 18 June 1745, ibid., fo. 847.
[117] Guillot to S&W, 21 December 1746, MAR/B2/329, fo. 664.

vouch for their captors. Thus, in 1704, English prisoners in Dinan wrote a petition to the French prison officials, attesting that they were well treated, receiving good enough food rations and fresh straw. The English prisoners followed by 'very humbly' praying that the Sick & Wounded Board handle the French prisoners better, revealing what the real purpose of the petition was: namely, threats of reprisals.[118] They continued with a list of requests about food allowances, medical treatments, and other items, which were clearly only passed at the demand of the French commissaire, St Sulpice. This was also a means of putting pressure on the prisoners' families, who would be encouraged to write to their own governments.[119]

The use of prisoners as communication channels served diverse purposes. Naively, perhaps, it aimed at conveying the appearance of a spontaneous testimony from the prisoners themselves, who wrote to their country, not to complain, but to support their captors. But how could the real author of the petition, St Sulpice, who most probably dictated it to its signatories, have hoped that its addressees would be duped? It was almost certainly not the case. One hypothesis would be that the English prisoners themselves, by being forced to write to their own state with (we can presume) genuine elements of truth, were prepared for what would follow if England did not act upon these requests: they were implicitly being made witnesses to the abuses committed by their own country to the French prisoners. At the same time, they were also made aware that any sanction they would subsequently be forced to pay would not be the result of cruelty, but of just reprisals. In both cases, the onus was placed on their own state, not on France.

These practices of ventriloquizing the prisoners continued throughout the century. In 1758, the Sick & Wounded Board complained that French prisoners in Britain were better treated than their counterparts in France. These claims were based on a petition received from six masters of English vessels confined in the Château du Ha in Bordeaux. Moras, the French *commissaire de la Marine* in Bordeaux, answered by sending back declarations signed by the prisoners, which stated: 'we are as well as possible either for subsistence or for lodging... we are very well treated in the hospital.'[120] Upon receiving these documents, the Lords of the Admiralty confessed their puzzlement: 'the names of four of the six persons signed to the abovementioned Complaint... are also signed to the Certificate which set forth the good treatment they have received; but as the Writing is so different in Each, it is not in our power to say which is genuine.'[121]

---

[118] Petition to S&W, 26 April 1704, MAR/B3/123, fos. 504v–505.
[119] See, for example, Gastines to SSM, 8, 15 October 1695, MAR/B3/89, fos. 219, 225; St Sulpice to SSM, [21] December 1702, MAR/B3/117, fo. 358.
[120] 5 January 1758, in Moras to LCA, 13 January 1758, NMM, ADM/F/17.
[121] LCA to S&W, 25 January 1758, ibid. See also LCA, 'Prisoners of war. Proposal to apply for their better treatment, & to allow 3 a day to those in extreme want', 11 November 1756, TNA, ADM7/341, fos. 9–10.

What matters to us, though, is the prisoners' ability to reach out at the national or even the international level, first by writing to the Admiralty or the *Marine*, and then, if these state institutions failed to redress their demands, by contacting their own government. Thus, prisoners of war were not totally defenceless. According to Norwegian prison sociologist Thomas Mathiesen, despite the weakness of their situation, prisoners could contest the legitimacy of the power of their custodians, exercising what he calls 'censoriousness', placing the guards in an awkward position vis-à-vis norms of justice which they were supposed to subscribe to, and the legitimacy of which they could not deny. In fact, administrative correspondence used the very same language as the prisoners' complaints, which seems to indicate that these humanitarian principles were shared by both parties.[122] To cite Mathiesen, prisoners sometimes went over the head of the prison administrators to obtain a 'vertical consensus'.[123] In the case of war imprisonment, the use of the rhetoric of the law of nations, which saturated public and administrative discourse in the eighteenth century, was a means for the prisoners to mobilize outside help, and it often succeeded in eliciting the support of their own state.[124]

The ability to appeal to the protection of their own state was the one advantage that prisoners of war had over 'normal' prisoners. This is not to say that reaching out across the dual border of the prison walls and the territorial borders of the state was easy; moreover, diplomats were not always willing to lend a sympathetic ear to the pleas of prisoners. See, for instance, the carefully phrased reply from the English commissioners to their French counterparts, in February 1744:

> Because there are negligent and dishonest people in all nations, and there might have been some abuses committed by some of our officers, which we have however no knowledge of even though we have frequently informed ourselves about their conduct, even encouraged prisoners...to declare to us their grievances if they had any in order to remedy them....Thus if you would have the kindness to ascertain the places and time regarding the complaints mentioned in your letter, the matter will be immediately and fully examined.[125]

The very fact that prisoners of war could (and did) appeal to the Lords of the Admiralty and to their own government acted as a check on the power of

---

[122]   See Gastines to S&W, 6, 13 November 1695, AN, MAR/B3/89, fos. 270–1, 279v–280; S&W to Sunderland, 8 August 1708, BL, Add MS61592, fo. 80; petition from Mouchet, prisoner in Kinsale, to Commissaire Raoul in Le Havre, 12 February 1748, AN, MAR/B3/464, vo. 126.

[123]   Mathiesen, *Defences*, pp. 150–1, 84, 88. On Mathiesen, see the excellent analysis of Sparks, Bottoms, and Hay, *Prisons*, pp. 45–50. In Sissinghurst prison, the Agent described such accusations as 'being censored by the P.ʳˢ': Cooke's interview, 8 December 1761, TNA, ADM105/42, fo. 175v.

[124]   See, for instance, copy of Lempereur to Bracebridge, commissary for exchanges in Southampton, 10 February 1706, AN, MAR/B3/135, fo. 67v.

[125]   S&W to Charron, 19 February 1744, MAR/B3/429, fos. 26–v. See also the complaints of British prisoners in Bayonne: SSM to S&W, 5 June 1747, MAR/B2/331, fo. 626.

the custodians, which was not absolute. More often than not, complaining led to the launching of investigations, and also to an improvement of the prisoners' situations.[126] More rarely, the prison staff could be dismissed.[127]

Whenever they were threatened with administrative sanctions, the Agents did their best to prevent the prisoners from talking to the investigators. In Forton Prison, on 19 February 1779, an American prisoner thus wrote in his diary:

> Mar. 6. Saturday this day Came downe from London the [high] Inspector of all the Kings prisons in Englan for to Rigtifey our Grivences but non of us Culd get an Opportunaty to Speek to him on account of the Agent the Doctor and the Clark Keppet Close by His Side this Gentleman Delivered both the black holes of their prissoners both French and Americans.[128]

In the moments when the prison opens its gates to members of the public, everyone is on their best behaviour, presenting, in Goffman's words, 'an institutional display'.[129] During the wars, in addition to inspections by 'national' doctors and commissioners, foreign inspectors were sometimes allowed to enter the prisons and monitor the treatment of their compatriots. Evidently, these visits were staged and closely controlled, since the point was to present a positive view of the facilities to the visitors. But it does not mean that they were completely useless.[130] Furthermore, the sole fact that prisons were increasingly opened to these investigations from members of the public, including foreign diplomats, is saying something about the growing preoccupation with what the public might say about the 'humane' treatment of prisoners. As more recent examples show, however, prison visitors, animated with the best of intentions, can unwillingly help to legitimize the carceral regime by their sole presence.[131]

The key element in 'censoring' the guards and the prison authorities—again, using Mathiesen's concept—was the prisoners' ability to publicize their complaint. 'Public' is meant here in the sense of making their situation known, by appealing to state authorities, but also in the sense of informing the public more broadly. This was already happening in 1696, when Commissaire de Gastines wrote that

> With the greatest harshness and inhumanity, people are prevented from visiting the French officers who are prisoners of war in Plymouth, not even English people, for fear that all the knavish tricks of the jailor become known, [and that]

---

[126] This was not specific to Britain: see the thorough inspection conducted by Marchais, *Intendant de la Marine*, in La Rochelle and Niort prisons: 4 September 1779, AN, MAR/F2/82.

[127] Le Prat, 'Faire face', pp. 225–6.   [128] 'Diary of George Thompson', p. 226.

[129] Goffman, *Asylums*, pp. 94–8.

[130] For a nuanced account of prison inspections in Napoleonic France by an Irish doctor, himself a prisoner, see Mulvey, *Sketches*, pp. 41–5.

[131] As in Guantanamo with the Red Cross: Kurnaz, *Five Years*; Stafford Smith, *Bad Men*.

their just complaints [move] the public against the authors of all the bad treatments they endured from the jailor. They are only able to complain of this barbary [by speaking to] the governor of Plymouth.[132]

A long letter written in September 1756 by the Sick & Wounded Board to the Lords of the Admiralty reveals how these administrators interpreted the prisoners' letters. Referring to 'the several Complaints in general from France, and from some persons here, that the French Prisoners are not treated with proper Humanity and Care', the commissioners denied that 'either abuse or neglect' had been taking place in the prisons, as proven by the different inspections they had carried out there.[133] These state administrators also placed their action within the same legal framework as the prisoners in their complaints: 'Their Lordships will see therefore that not only the Laws of Nations, and the principles of Justice have been strictly observed, but that even the most imperfect rights of Humanity have been scrupulously complied with.' In other words, the prisoners' censorship of their custodians was very effective. But these accusations were so damaging because the controversy had taken on an international dimension: 'Such Representations & Complaints...are very Dishonourable to the Nation, and if causelessly made, matters ought to be set in a just light to Foreign States, to remove as much as possible the prejudices conceived upon the spreading such Complaints.' The action of the British monarchy was thus exposed to the 'Calumny of Individuals and the Censure of other States'.[134] We should not underestimate the importance that European states attached to the issue of *jus in bello* in the eighteenth century: the accusation of waging an immoral and cruel war weakened the state's authority and legitimacy. These modes of action were not specific to Britain. British prisoners in France used the very same practices, for the same outcomes, harming the reputation of local authorities. In Dinan in 1778, for instance, Commissaire Guillot warned the governor of the city about the 'disadvantageous rumours' circulating in the country on his account, the English prisoners complaining about extortions at the Castle: '[it would be] very dangerous for you if the Minister or the Commandant of the Province were to be acquainted with [these rumours]; they would order inquiries.'[135]

In Britain, the press avidly commented on these matters. The accusations of cruelty against British prisoners in France, and, conversely, praise for the generous treatment of Frenchmen in Britain, filled columns after columns in the newspapers.[136] This general context also explains the mutations of philanthropy in the eighteenth century.

[132] Gastines 'Mémoire', 4 July 1696: AN, MAR/B4/17, fo. 435v.
[133] S&W to LCA, 17 September 1756, TNA, ADM98/5, fo. 208v.
[134] Same to same, fos. 209, 209v.
[135] Copy of Guillot to Comte de La Bretonnière, 10 November 1778, AN, MAR/F2/82.
[136] See Black, *Natural*, p. 182.

IV. The 1759-60 Philanthropic Campaign

The emphasis of this section is on the role of civil societies, and their active involvement in assisting prisoners. While charitable initiatives to support prisoners of war in both countries certainly existed, these had remained relatively rare and localized throughout the first half of the eighteenth century.[137]

In the second half of the century, public interest in what was going on inside the prisons grew. This preoccupation, which explains the appeal and ultimate success of the campaigns for reforming the prisons, also affected perceptions of war imprisonment more broadly. As we have seen, prisoners tried to reach out by writing letters and petitions to the Sick & Wounded Board and other highly placed officials; but pressure was also put on jailors by charitable organizations and the wider public. The focus here is both on philanthropic practices, and on the meanings that a range of contemporary observers attached to these actions. We must first address the question of whether the 1759 campaign—which was, unprecedentedly, waged on a national scale—was consistent with the British state's own stance and actions. Secondly, this campaign, like antislavery or the moral reform programmes of the 1770s–80s, represented a coalition of different interests and motivations. What was new, and remained exceptional over the course of the eighteenth century, was the target of this philanthropic cause, which was aimed at alien enemies—a cause that we would not expect go unchallenged.[138] While patriotism and voluntarism flowed together, philanthropic alliances were forged and transformed as the concerns changed. In terms of methods, this campaign built on some well-established charitable traditions and institutions, but for more explicitly humanitarian, rather than strictly confessional, purposes.

But to start, we must go back to the beginning of the Seven Years' War. The war of propaganda between Britain and France reached new heights in this period.[139] The treatment of prisoners of war was part and parcel of this public and international discussion. An anonymous pamphlet, published in 1758, embodies the type of arguments that were used both to denounce the enemy's cruelty, and to emphasize one's own humanity. The anonymous author of *Considerations on the exchange of seamen, prisoners of war* began by explaining that he 'was led..., by a Love to Mankind in general, and an Affection to his Country in particular, to consider the subject of Prisoners of War'.[140] His demonstration echoed the thought of contemporary philosophers. In his *Essays on the Principles of Morality*,

[137] *A True and Authentick Narrative*, p. 12; Guillot to SSM, 10 June 1744, AN, MAR/B3/422, fo. 375.

[138] On the campaigns waged in England in the early eighteenth century to free French Huguenot galley slaves, see Arnold, 'Affairs'. On charitable relief for American prisoners in Britain during the American War of Independence, see Anderson, 'Treatment', p. 81; Prelinger, 'Benjamin Franklin', pp. 264, 270, 288–9. On British charity for British prisoners in France during the Napoleonic Wars, see Duché, 'Charitable connections'.

[139] Bell, *Cult*; Dziembowski, *Nouveau patriotisme*.   [140] *Considerations*, p. 1.

published in the same year, Lord Kames wrote that 'a *generous Nation* will be more inclin'd to listen to the Voice of *Humanity* than of *Retaliation*; there will ever be something horrid and repugnant to such a People to be oblig'd to act inhumanly, and to reduce the Innocent to perish miserably in a Prison'.[141]

Whereas retaliations and reprisals model one's own attitude on that of the enemy, humanitarian patriotism proudly proclaims a radically different alternative. Humanitarian patriotism is comparative, yet, rather than fuelling a vicious cycle that might lead to mutual destruction, it is emulative and optimistic: it aims at swaying the enemy by showing generosity to its subjects. But it is also the result of a rational calculation: hoping to bring about short-term economic and political gains, while demonstrating the moral superiority of a generous nation. *Considerations on the exchange of seamen* contrasted, in a systematic way, the condition of detention in the two countries. In English prisons, the 'Commodiousness of the Places' of confinement, the 'good Provision and Lodging', 'the great Precautions taken to secure them from all Abuses or Fraud', and 'the Regulations affix'd in all the Places of their Confinement' were a source of national pride, and 'must do Honour to this Country'.[142] By contrast, in France, wrote the author, there was no control of the central administration on 'inferior agents in government', no 'actual Inspection of their Superiors', and this lack of accountability led to abuses, 'Oppression', and 'Avarice and Extortion'.[143] Due to the despotic government in place in France, the prisoners' complaints had no chance to be heard.[144] Whether he was a naval administrator or not, the author publicized views that were widely shared within the Admiralty.[145] In the years that followed, the treatment of French prisoners in Britain would become a national debate.

A. The Donors

The spark that ignited the 1759 campaign was the French monarchy's defaulting on payments for the maintenance of its prisoners in Britain. The traditional practice was for each government to send money to the captor in order to pay for the clothes of their prisoners of war. On 15 December 1758, the Board wrote to the Lords of the Admiralty that they had 'heard that the bounty allow'd by the French King to his subjects prisoners in England is order'd to be stopt'. The news was confirmed to them by a letter received from their Agent at Petersfield.[146] This had almost immediate consequences for the French prisoners of war. It was to answer the needs of these prisoners that several local subscription campaigns began in Britain.

---

[141] *Considerations*, p. 30.
[142] The author claimed to have a direct knowledge of these matters: *Considerations*, p. 25.
[143] *Considerations*, pp. 34–5.   [144] *Considerations*, p. 34.   [145] *Considerations*, p. 25.
[146] S&W to LCA, 15 December 1758, NMM, ADM/F/18.

One such campaign took place in Liverpool, in October 1759. The Agent for Prisoners there set up a subscription and raised £50 for the prisoners, who 'were in great want of Cloaths'.[147] Upon receiving this letter, the Board wrote to the secretary of state for the *Marine*:

> We must inform you of the generosity of the inhabitants of Liverpool towards the prisoners; one of our agents in this town, moved by their situation has of his own initiative collected money, and the product was sufficient to procure clothes for the prisoners. They are by this means sheltered from the rigours of winter, and the harm to which they would have been exposed is prevented.[148]

The British officials conveyed their worries for the fate of French prisoners in Britain and Ireland more broadly, concerned that their situation 'becomes daily worse', due to their 'lack of clothes'. Winter was coming, and the prisoners were exposed, in their nudity, to diseases. The commissioners beseeched their French counterparts to come to the rescue of their compatriots, highlighting that 'the generosity and humanity with which we treat them brings honour to our country on all accounts'.[149] Not for the last time, the concepts of 'humanity' and patriotism were tied together.

All over Britain and Ireland, in October–November 1759, seemingly unconnected and private initiatives were taking place to relieve the French prisoners from their misery.[150] At Exeter, 'the Principal Gentlemen, Clergy, and Merchants' requested that the Agent provide them with an account of the prisoners 'in Want of necessary Cloathing'. He had then 'given them a List of several Hundreds of such People, who were in the greatest Distress whereupon a Subscription was opened and a Collection made; ... upwards of £250 had been already subscribed and collected'.[151] A similar collection had taken place in Edinburgh in October.[152] State officials also tried to alleviate the prisoners' sufferings: in Kinsale, the Duke of Bedford, Lord Lieutenant of Ireland, was informed that '256 of the Prisoners of War there were totally naked, not having Payment of any kind to cover them', and ordered the Treasurer of Ireland to advance £200 for this purpose, asking the Admiralty to repay him.[153]

These local initiatives laid the groundwork for a much more ambitious campaign, which started in London in December 1759 and quickly spread to the rest of the kingdom. An article published in the *Gentleman's Magazine*, dated 12 December, linked these different campaigns:

---

[147] S&W to LCA, 9 October 1759, ADM/F/20, fos. 33v–34.
[148] S&W to 'Minister of Marine in France', 9 October 1759, AN, MAR/B4/97, fos. 210v.
[149] Ibid., fo. 211v.   [150] Charters, *Disease*, p. 182.
[151] S&W to LCA, 19 November 1759, NMM, ADM/F/20.
[152] *Edinburgh Chronicle* (13–15 October 1759), cited in Conway, 'Religious links', p. 847.
[153] S&W to LCA, 27 November 1759, TNA, ADM98/8, fos. 52–v.

The following remarkable article appeared in the *Brussels Gazette*. 'The animosity of the English against the French decreases. They are now suffered to hate only those French that are in arms. A subscription is opened in the several towns and counties for cloathing the French prisoners detained in England, and the example has been followed in the capital.' The English feel for their captives as men, and cannot but pity enemies in distress, who are not in a capacity to hurt them.[154]

This episode has been generally passed over by the historiography.[155] To begin with, I will focus on the mechanics of public campaigning and sociability, against the background of a fine-grained social study of the committee founders and donors. The *Proceedings* of the Committee—which was set up to manage these philanthropic contributions, and first met in London on 18 December 1759—were published the following year. This is an exceptional source, which can be used in a number of ways, and is deserving of a systematic study. The *Proceedings* document how the public campaign was funded, in part through banking connections; organized, by linking private sociability with public networks; and advertised. The fault lines that developed over this philanthropic campaign also tell us something important about the meanings that were awarded by contemporaries to the support of foreign enemies in wartime Britain.

First, who were the organizers? The first page of the *Proceedings* lists the names of twenty-five 'noblemen and gentlemen', who were appointed as the General Committee at a meeting on 20 December 1759. We must not exaggerate the coherence of this group or their beliefs: like many twenty-first-century signatories of collective petitions, some did so as much out of personal ambition, friendship, or attraction to self-publicity, as well as humanitarian sympathies. Overall, however, the social worlds of all these men overlapped, at the intersection between the political (court, parliament, and the corporation of London), professions (merchants and manufacturers, lawyers, doctors), religious (non-conformism), benevolence (London's hospitals), and learned societies (Royal Society, Royal Society of Arts). The usual suspects of associational philanthropy in eighteenth-century Britain were well represented.[156]

Many of them were involved in politics. The treasurer was Sir George Nares, a judge, who at the time of the campaign had just been appointed a king's serjeant. Several courtiers and MPs were also among the Committee members. For instance, Francis Seymour Conway, Earl of Hertford, cousin of Horace Walpole, was a courtier, who became a lord of the bedchamber and Knight of the Garter in 1757, as well as Lord Lieutenant of Warwickshire. His whole family was well

---

[154] *Gentleman's Magazine* (*GM*), 29 (1759), p. 604, reprint of *Historical Chronicle*, December 1759.
[155] The only notable exception is Charters, *Disease*, pp. 181–7.
[156] Andrew, *Philanthropy*, ch. 3. The biographical information that follows comes from the Oxford *DNB*, unless otherwise stated.

his brother Henry Seymour Conway was also an important politician and army man. George Brudenell, duke of Montagu, another courtier, was elected a fellow of the Royal Society in 1749, a president of the Royal Society of Arts and St Luke's hospital, and a vice-president of St George's Hospital.[157] Despite their political functions, the campaigners justified their actions without pretensions to speak in the name of the state, financially or otherwise.[158]

Another four men, Sir Joseph Hankey, Robert Drummond, John Gwilt, and Thomas Hallifax, were London bankers with strong ties to the city, and were charged with collecting the subscribers' money.[159] Merchant and manufacturing interests were similarly well represented in the Committee, such as Jasper Mauduit, a woollen merchant and spokesman for the American dissenters in London,[160] and John Thornton, a very wealthy merchant who had inherited a fortune from his father, a former director of the Bank of England. An Evangelical Anglican, Thornton gave very large sums of money to charitable causes, contributing personally the immense sum of £100 to the subscription. These men certainly did not share the same concerns for taking part in the campaign.

The largest group, by occupation, were the scientists (five members), two of whom were already famous at the time. 'Dr Fothergill' (John Fothergill) was one of the most successful physicians in England, thanks to his pioneering work on scarlet fever. A Quaker, the physician and naturalist graduated from Edinburgh, and trained at St Thomas's Hospital in London. Quakers played a key part in the campaign, raising a third of the total amount.[161] George Macaulay, who signed 'Dr Macaulay' in the *Proceedings*, had been a renowned midwife since the early 1750s, and was one of the governors of the first English hospital devoted to obstetrics. He married his second wife, Catherine Macaulay, in June 1760, and shared radical sympathies with her.[162] The large presence of medical professions might be explained by the transfer of gaol fever from the prison to the court room of the Old Bailey in 1750, and the concern and new initiatives associated with it.[163]

Non-conformists, who would play a preeminent part in the eighteenth-century reform movement, were thus particularly well represented on the Committee.

One of the members of the committee was Thomas Hollis. A dilettante, he revolved in London intellectual circles and societies; he was a rational dissenter

---

[157] Three MPs belonged to the General Committee: George Brodrick, Lord Viscount Midleton (MP for Ashburton), Sir William Peere Williams (New Shoreham), and James Cocks (Ryegate).

[158] Charters, *Disease*, p. 184.   [159] 'General Account', Appendix No. III.

[160] Price, 'Last phase', pp. 79–80.

[161] £1,370 were raised 'By a Collection among the People called Quakers', out of a total of £4,139: *Proceedings*, Appendix III.

[162] Fothergill was also a close friend, from his Edinburgh days, of the surgeon William Hunter, presumably the 'Dr. Hunter' of the *Proceedings*.

[163] See ch. 6.

and a partisan of parliamentary reform, who gave a great deal of his time to charitable work.[164] The reason why Hollis is of particular interest to us is the diary he kept from April 1759 onwards, which is held at the Houghton Library in Harvard.[165] This invaluable document gives us an insider's view of the subscription campaign, by one of, if not its main, animators.

Himself an author, book collector, and book binder, Hollis was instrumental in collecting the lists of subscribers and in publishing and publicizing the Committee's *Proceedings*, through the intercession of an important London bookseller, Thomas Payne.[166] He spent a considerable amount of time disseminating copies of the publication, in Britain and across the world, following its printing at the beginning of August 1760.[167] But his contribution went beyond this. Hollis was a man of the world, who spent his time socializing in different circles, and spared no effort trying to entice the pre-eminent political and economic figures of the day to join the cause. For Hollis, this humanitarian cause and his deeply felt patriotism were perfectly coherent. Hollis was an enthusiastic patriot, celebrating military victories against France by designing and commissioning medals.[168] He dined at the recently established Marine Society, a charity founded in 1756 to bolster recruitment in the British Navy, and donated money to its founder, Jonas Hanway.[169] Hollis was also a member of the committee 'for better clothing of the British troops yet encamped in Germany'.[170] It is not a surprise, therefore, that he was also instrumental in convincing the Antigallican Society to subscribe to the scheme.[171] An admirer of William Pitt, Hollis also tried to enlist his support. On 27 December 1759, the entry in his journal reads: 'Within the morning, wrote a letter to Mr Pitt signed "An Englishman, Citizen of the World", to induce him for national & his proper honour, to attend the next meeting for relief of French prisoners, & to take the chair there for an instant.'[172] Once the book was published, he sent a copy, 'magnificently bound', to the *de facto* Prime Minister: 'In the title was written "To the Right honorable William Pitt, Minister of Britain, able, active, faithful, magnanimous, fortunate, this book is presented by an Englishman, a Lover of freedom & beneficence".'[173] It was also Hollis who came up with Terence's quotation, *Homo sum, humani nihil a me alienum puto*, in the incipit of the *Proceedings*, which were published in August 1760.[174]

---

[164] Robbins, 'Strenuous whig'.
[165] 'Thomas Hollis's diary', Houghton Library (Harvard University), MS Eng 1191, vol. I. All subsequent references to the diary come from this.
[166] Hollis, diary, 16, 29 May, 5, 7, 10, 12 June 1760, fos. 69–70, 72–5.
[167] Ibid., 6 August 1760, fo. 89. The Houghton Library at Harvard holds three copies of the *Proceedings*, one of which was given by Hollis to Harvard College, and another to Laurence Sterne.
[168] Ibid., 1 June 1759, fo. 17.   [169] Ibid., 1 January 1761, fo. 127.
[170] Hollis, diary, 9 January 1760, fo. 43.   [171] Ibid., 21 December 1759, fo. 41.
[172] Ibid., 27 December 1759, fo. 42.   [173] Ibid., 9 September 1760, fo. 95.
[174] Ibid., 27 December 1759, fo. 42.

Over the following months, thousands of caps, coats, waistcoats, shoes, breeches, and stockings, were distributed throughout Britain's war prisons. A total of 6,146 shirts, 3,134 pairs of stockings and 3,185 pairs of shoes were thus given to the prisoners.[175] Six hundred and ninety-seven subscribers, including the large number of anonymous ones, and the people who left only their initials, are listed in Appendix I.[176] To these must be added the 1,508 subscribers who contributed to private and public collections across Britain, that had sometimes begun before the national campaign started, whose names were also published in the *Proceedings*.[177] In total, the number of people who gave to the French prisoners would have been, at the very least, 2,205.[178] While the figure pales in comparison to the hundreds of thousands mobilized by the antislavery campaigns, it must nonetheless be remembered that this movement preceded them by two decades.[179]

A detailed social analysis of the subscribers falls beyond the scope of this study, and I will only briefly mention the most striking features of this list. The scores of 'gentlemen', 'noblemen', and clergymen are expected.[180] The second Marquess of Rockingham, for instance, the principal Whig leader, donated the very large sum of £21. The Duke of Bedford, Lord Lieutenant of Ireland and an ally of William Pitt, was also among the donors, as was Sir John Barnard (former Lord Mayor of London, Whig MP). Thomas Secker, the Archbishop of Canterbury, headed the sizeable group of clergymen. A number of women, mostly aristocrats, are also listed: fifty-one in the main list of subscribers (of whom twenty-three did not leave their names), and another 222 in the local lists. Charity was one of the few areas where public female participation was perceived to be legitimate in this period.[181] It is not particularly surprising, either, to find among the donors collective bodies such as the 'Opera Club', the 'Almack's Club', or the Freemasons.

But many other people of smaller means and humbler origins also contributed; as in Portsmouth, where several coopers, a bricklayer, a plumber, a barber or a pilot are listed among the donors. In Bristol, among the people who gave in the Exchange Coffee-House on 29 November 1759 were 'two poor women', who donated 1 s, 6 d. Many others contributed in nature, such as Francis Fanning, who gave the clothing 'for six boys compleat' in Plymouth, or the 'three small Gifts' of a value of 6 s, donated at Bristol, or the 3 s, 6 d 'and a Pair of Shoes' given by a Mr Cole at Gosport. This money was typically collected after the sermons, as in this London church,

---

[175] Appendix III, 'General Account'.

[176] They were also published in the British press: see, for instance, *London Evening Post*, 5025 (17–19 January 1760).

[177] Appendix IV.

[178] 'Many other collections have been made, of which no account has been transmitted to the Committee': Appendix IV, n.p. The private collections that took place in Penryn or Helston listed a total donation amount.

[179] Oldfield, *Popular Politics*.   [180] Andrew, *Philanthropy*, ch. 2, 3.

[181] Ibid., pp. 87–8.

where William Dodd, the philanthropist, was preaching: 'Collected at the Thursday Evening Lecture, at St Michael's Crooked-Lane, preached by the Rev. Mr. Dodd: 14 l., 9 d.'[182] Parishes also gave money as collective entities.[183]

The motivations of these donors would have varied considerably, but we know very little about them. The anonymous person who donated 10 s, 6 d in Bristol 'with these words, For the assistance of the poor French Prisoners at Knowle' might have placed himself or herself within the Christian tradition of the alms for the poor. Others were more straightforward about their intentions, while secretive about their names, such as 'The Mite of an Englishman, Citizen of the World, to Frenchmen, Prisoners of War and Naked', who gave the large sum of £10, 10 s, or 'Benevolus Ediensis', or 'Philanthropos'. In the same way, the secretary of the Society of Arts, the physician Peter Templeman (a close acquaintance of John Fothergill and of Thomas Hollis) enthusiastically wrote to the Committee to thank them for sending a copy of the *Proceedings*: 'The account of your proceedings is so humane and beneficent an Employment could not fail of giving the highest satisfaction to a Society, whose aim it is to improve Mankind by useful arts.'[184]

A combination of factors might have motivated someone to give to the campaign; perhaps a search for respectability, patronage or moral beliefs. The important question for us, though, concerns the way in which the entire enterprise was justified. Among these donors, there was no sense of a contradiction between this proclaimed cosmopolitism and their patriotism. The subscription was certainly not presented as a treacherously Francophile enterprise—and nor was it viewed as such by the numerous military and naval men who featured among its contributors, like 'the Non-Commission Officers and Dragoons of Colonel Hale's Regiment of Light Dragoons' (£19), or 'the Gentlemen of the Garrison' of Plymouth (£6). Despite its patriotic aims, however, the endeavour predictably faced a barrage of criticisms in the press, to which I now turn.

B. Giving to the Enemy: Treason or Moral Obligation?

One of the main venues in which the controversy developed was the *London Chronicle*, which published articles from both sides of the argument. In December 1759, a letter by 'Britannicus' was published, enthusiastically endorsing the charitable scheme. Using an argument that was already common at the time, the author differentiated between the French monarchy and the French prisoners:

---

[182] 'Dr Dodd' would be hanged for forgery in 1777: Howson, *Macaroni Parson*.

[183] For example, 'Cristleton Parish in the County of Chester' (£3, 5 s, 2 d).

[184] Peter Templeman to the Honourable Committee, 28 August 1760, Royal Society of Arts, AD/MA/100/10/400 A4/16. On Hollis and the RSA, see Abbott, 'General notes'.

Though I hate the French government,...yet, I can, by no means, entertain the same hatred for a Frenchman, as I do for his King and his Ministers; as a brave Frenchman fighting without cruelty, and without barbarity, in what he is obliged to believe to be the cause of his country, as no object of personal revenge or resentment.[185]

The author proceeded with a long and sustained attack on Cicero's statement, *Omnes Charitates, Patrio sola complectitur*, contrasting the selfishness and cruelty of Rome with the generosity of Britons, in a typical statement that blended patriotism and cosmopolitanism: 'A Briton...ought to expand his sentiments of benevolence and humanity to all the world, and to give no preference even to his own country, but that of enabling her to extend to the whole human species the reign of liberty, of humanity, and charity.' While Louis XV and his ministers were 'deaf to the hardships...of their unoffending subjects' prisoners in Britain, Britons would hold the torch of Christian virtue, by showing 'compassion and humanity' to these prisoners: 'tho' they are Frenchmen, they are men.' One's place of birth, the author argued, was never a justification to be ill-treated, 'entailed' as it was 'upon him by nature, fortune, and his parents'. Although this was the cosmopolitan doxa, it was nonetheless quite a radical statement in wartime. Against those bad Christians who proposed to treat the French prisoners like 'criminals'—handcuffing them, or making them work underground in coal mines—the author embraced a more noble attitude, which, by generously contributing towards the subscription, would entitle Britain to reap the rewards of its moral superiority: 'tho' we may conquer the French, we cannot triumph over them, but by exerting those virtues of humanity of which their government is destitute, and to which their King is a stranger.'[186]

On the opposing side of the argument, the article that probably had the most impact was published in the *London Chronicle* in January 1760.[187] In a lengthy tirade addressed to the editor of the journal, the anonymous author undertook to destroy methodically the philanthropic endeavour, mixing half-truths with blatant lies. The French, he wrote, 'are our most implacable and inveterate enemies, and the enemies of all the human race that are out of the pale of their Church', as papists, and 'enemies to our Religion, Liberty, and Trade'. Moreover, many among these French prisoners were privateers, who deserved to be treated harshly, because of the 'barbarous malice' towards the merchants they robbed. The assertion that enemy combatants were transgressing the law of nations was common during the Seven Years' War, and multiple reports of atrocities were published in

---

[185] *London Chronicle* (*LC*), 460 (8–11 December 1759), letter to the Printer signed 'Britannicus'.
[186] Ibid. Another supporter of the charitable campaign was 'J.F.' (John Fothergill?), whose article was published in the 5–8 January 1760 issue.
[187] *LC*, 479 (19–22 January 1760).

the press of both countries.[188] In the same vein, the author of the *London Chronicle* contended that, during their captivity, French prisoners continued to cause mayhem in Britain, robbing civilians and pulling down churches. The author turned the philanthropic campaign on its head, presenting it as a scam for extracting money from the credulous: 'We relieve such wretches, and at the same time, neglect *our household of faith*, our own brave soldiers and sailors, our plundered countrymen..., I dare to pronounce we *are worse than Infidels.*' According to the principle of proximity, charity should *'begin at home'*: 'Should it not rather be diffused among their distrest neighbours, and countrymen, than among insolent, ungrateful enemies, who are nobly provided for by the care of a humane Government, and cannot possibly want any thing either for back or belly, unless they consume their allowance in riot and debauchery?'[189]

Why should there be a moral imperative to alleviate the suffering of an enemy? And how 'close' does one need to be from that person to be obliged to come to their help?[190] The anonymous author of the *London Chronicle* distanced himself from these alien and heretical French prisoners, thus justifying his inaction. The article hit a raw nerve among the supporters of the subscription. Several responses were published. One of them was signed by 'S.G.'. He cited Matthew 5:44: 'But I say unto you, Love your enemies, bless them that curse you, do good to them that hate you, and pray for them which despitefully use you, and persecute you.' Dispelling lie after lie, he denied that French prisoners were ungrateful: 'the prisoners have,... received their cloathing with... millions of prayers for their humane benefactors.'[191]

Thomas Hollis and the Committee for clothing the French prisoners were also badly shaken by this 'scandalous libel'.[192] Hollis contacted the already famous Samuel Johnson, who had published His *Dictionary of the English Language* in 1755, and who agreed to compose an introduction to the *Proceedings*.[193] The principal merit of this short text, besides the publicity guaranteed by its author, was the way it powerfully encapsulated the arguments of the campaigners. Dr Johnson addressed one criticism in particular, implicitly referring to the anonymous author of the *London Chronicle*; namely, the idea that the money donated to French prisoners of war would be better spent on British soldiers: the notion that 'while we lavish pity on our enemies, we forget the misery of our friends'. Johnson refused to conceive of charity as a zero-sum game: 'It is far from

---

[188] See, for instance, *LC*, 475 (10–12 January 1760), denouncing the cruel behaviour of French captors towards their English captives in the West Indies. See Bell, *Cult*, pp. 83–95; Dziembowski, *Un nouveau*.

[189] *LC*, 479 (19–22 January 1760).

[190] Boltanski, *Distant Suffering*, p. 16. See also Moniz, *From Empire*, pp. 33–6.

[191] *LC*, 483 (29–31 January 1760).   [192] Hollis, diary, 28 January 1760, fo. 48v.

[193] He was paid a hefty five guineas for it: Hollis, diary, 12, 25 June 1760, fos. 75, 78. On Johnson and this text, see Spector, *Samuel Johnson*, pp. 27–8.

certain, that a single Englishman will suffer by the charity to the French.'[194] It was morally wrong to doubt the prisoners' misery and attribute to them the falsehoods of slanderers: 'we see their distress, and are certain of its cause; we know that they are poor and naked, and poor and naked without a crime.' This reference to the Book of Revelation should not surprise us, coming as it did from a High Anglican Christian moralist such as Johnson.[195] The prisoners were described as visible, within touching distance, which facilitated the spectator's empathy. This new political and emotional universe would become more familiar during the anti-slavery campaigns. As shown by Luc Boltanski, the question here is not to know if people deserve to be supported or deserve to be unhappy, or to distinguish between friends and enemies, but to establish that they suffer, which is the sole ground for deserving to be helped. Furthermore, what Hannah Arendt calls the 'politics of pity' universalizes individual suffering behind a general cause.[196] Taking a cosmopolitan and resolutely pacifist stance, Johnson stressed that charity towards enemies would 'soften the acrimony of adverse nations, and dispose them to peace and amity'.[197]

Assessing the motives of donors is a complex philosophical question. Is there such a thing as a disinterested gift? What part does self-love play in 'benevolent' acts, and how much reciprocity is expected from the recipients?[198] The discussion about the meaning of benevolence was one of the defining debates of the Scottish Enlightenment, which dealt more broadly with the question of the compatibility between self-love or public interest, on the one hand, and love of strangers on the other—a question with which Hume, Smith, Ferguson, or Kames all engaged.[199] Johnson asserted that having the greater good in mind was a sufficient motivation.[200] But many other defenders of the initiative, who might have shared these humanitarian and religious beliefs, explicitly saw this charitable mobilization as inherently political. It was part of the moral fight against France. According to this view, it was not so much despite, but *because* they were enemies that the prisoners had to be helped. In fact, the crueller and the more despicable the actions of their sovereign were, the more generous one should be towards his subjects. In this sense, philanthropy was the continuation of war by other means, showing the moral and religious superiority of those who were responding to violence with pity. There were political benefits to be derived from this. This is what humanitarian patriotism was about, and it would be misleading to equate it with pacifism.

Now, to portray the charity as unpatriotic, as some newspaper articles did, was so distressing for the Committee precisely because so many of its members conceived of

---

[194] Johnson, 'Introduction', p. 148.   [195] Chadwick, 'Religion'.
[196] Boltanski, *Distant Suffering*, ch. 1.   [197] Johnson, 'Introduction', p. 148.
[198] Benthall, 'Charity', pp. 360–5.
[199] Harris, 'Early reception'; Garrett and Hanley, 'Adam Smith'.
[200] Johnson, 'Introduction', p. 147.

this charitable campaign to clothe Frenchmen not as a cosmopolitan endeavour, but as a patriotic one. Thomas Hollis, already mentioned, was not the outlier here, as can be shown by looking at another subscription, which was announced at about the same time for the heroes who had triumphed over the French at the battles of Minden and Quebec, and their widows and children. That campaign, which began a few days after the campaign for clothing French prisoners, was modelled upon it.[201] In January 1760, it started to publish advertisements in the press:

> We ought to hope, that the charity shown to the French prisoners will meet its reward; but it is not doubted, that the same humane disposition which has engaged many to clothe our enemies, who are left deserted by their own nation and fellow-subjects, will lead many more to afford comfort to their brave and much deserving friends and countrymen.[202]

The names composing the steering Committee of the charity were also published in the same issue. Among its twenty-four members, one finds Sir Joseph Hankey, Thomas Hollis, Samuel Smith, and John Thornton, who were also on the Committee for clothing the French prisoners. Fifteen men, out of the twenty-four, chose to donate to both charities—the one for foreign prisoners, the other for 'home' soldiers and their families. Indeed, newspaper articles often presented the two schemes as two sides of the same coin.[203]

What kind of an impact, if any, did these polemical discussions have on donors? 'W. Sandys', from Helston in Cornwall, pointed out in a letter to the Committee dated 28 February 1760 that the vicious attack against the campaign, published in the *London Chronicle* on 22 January, probably discouraged some people from giving to the cause: 'The vulgar prejudices which were opposed to this charity, and the violent clamours raised against it, by the author of a letter, who threw on its promoters the accumulated reproach of Traitors, Jacobites, and Enemies to their Country, preventing me from receiving more.'[204] But Sandys was far from conceding the ground of patriotism to these critics, presenting the charitable campaign as the continuation of war by other means. For many Englishmen and women, beating the enemy on the battlefield and caring for them once they were imprisoned followed the same logic.

C. The Recipients

So far, we have only mentioned the presence of the French prisoners of war as targets of the campaign, not as actors. The recipients of charity are the other half

[201] See *LC*, 467 (25 December 1759).   [202] *LC*, 475 (10–12 January 1760).
[203] Letter by 'T.S.': *LC*, 483 (29–31 January 1760). See also *GM*, 30 (1760), p. 101.
[204] Appendix IV. In total, Sandys raised 32 pounds.

of the equation.[205] Understanding how the French prisoners of war reacted to these gifts from the British public is not an easy task. It is difficult to know whether the seventeen petitions of thanks in French that were annexed to the *Proceedings* of the Committee were selected from a bigger number. It is also possible that the prisoners were encouraged to write these texts. We must take into account that this publication was aimed at showing to the public how effectively the product of their benefactions had been spent. These texts followed the rules of the petition of thanks, a genre in itself, with its *passages obligés*: gratitude, the discourse of pathos, prayers for the salvation of the donor—what Marcel Mauss called the 'counter-gift', which is fundamental to complete the charitable gift.[206] A cosmopolitan discourse also permeated these texts: 'our thanks for the friendship and humanity of *messieurs* les Anglois, our benefactors' (from Biddeford in Devon); 'unprecedented kindness, that the English nation has shed upon us' (from Winchester). This was probably read as an acknowledgment, by foreigners, of the moral superiority of the English—but the 'spontaneity' of the prisoners is not a question that can be answered with this kind of source. It might be argued that they wrote what they (rightly) thought was expected of them.

Can we at least get a sense of what they did with the fruits of this benevolence? One petition, written from Sissinghurst Castle on 2 May 1760, departed from the others. In this Elizabethan aristocratic house, converted into a detention depot during the War of the Austrian Succession, about 2,000 prisoners of war were detained at the time, in very difficult conditions—which is hard to imagine when one visits these idyllic Kent Gardens today. The petition expressed with even more genuflections than the others the profound gratitude of the prisoners:

All those who have received [this support], and have been gratified, would believe themselves the unworthiest and the most ungrateful of all mortals, if they differed any longer...from sending you the most humble acknowledgements...and from praying to you pressingly to be persuaded that they are as grateful as it is possible to be; and that they wish to express to you by more emphatical terms than those they are using.

The prisoners prayed that their benefactors 'deign [to look] with compassion at the sad, and deplorable state in which they find themselves'. And they asked to be forgiven, using a religious vernacular, asking for the 'continuation of this grace, by the means of your good offices...; continue your charities'.[207] What was all this about? The rest of the petition made the request more explicit: several among the

---

[205] On the reception of charity: Ben-Amos, *Culture of Giving*; Cunningham and Innes, *Charity*; Jones, 'Some recent trends'. The only substantial analysis of the relief system for prisoners of war is Duché, 'Charitable connections'.

[206] For examples of petitions of thanks from prisoners who received food in 1747–9, see Lewis and Williams, *Private Charity*, p. 34.

[207] Sissinghurst, 2 May 1760, *Proceedings*, Appendix II, n.f.

recipients of the charitable subscription had sold or exchanged the clothes they had been given. These men had subsequently been punished and put on half-allowance. The problem was known to the administration. In December 1759, the Board had informed the Lords of the Admiralty that

> many of the Prisoners of War at several of the places of their confinement in England, owing to their want of cloathe, daily cut up their Bed Cases to make Shirts & wrap themselves in their Coverlids in the Day time, which is in effect making the Crown find them in Cloaths.[208]

According to the Agent's instructions, the prisoners ought to be put on half allowance, in order to repay the cost of the damage to their bedding, but the Board felt uneasy about it.[209] In the petition published in the *Proceedings*, the prisoners justified themselves: 'Urgent necessities', such as buying tobacco or paying for the stamps for their letters, had compelled them to act in this way. Indirectly, this passage underlines a structural feature of everyday life in prison: its commodification, and the insufficiency of cash or tender, which fuelled an economy of barter.[210] What was emphasized here was the inadequacy of the gift to address the real needs of the recipients.

At Sissinghurst, the problem did not disappear, as was highlighted by the thorough investigation conducted by the Board eighteen months later. One of the prisoners' main subjects of resentment regarded what had happened at the end of October 1761, when the Agent had summoned a muster, without notifying the prisoners that they had to wear the new clothes that had been donated to them. When many failed to produce them, this proved, in the eyes of the Agent, that they had sold or gambled them, confirming his expectations about the prisoners' lowly character. They were accordingly punished following an elaborate pricing of penalties, which varied depending on the missing item of clothing.[211] The tone adopted by the Agent, who had cross-examined the prisoners during the inquiry, shows the paternalistic framework within which he saw the charitable relation between donors and recipients:

Q18. What do you think induced your Benefactor to give you those Cloaths.
A. To cover & comfort them.
Q19. Do you think Y.^{r} Benefactor w.^{d} have given you Cloaths if he had thought
    You had Cloaths of Y.^{r} own.
A. ... they believe not.

---

[208] S&W to LCA, 26 December 1759, TNA, ADM98/8, fo. 119.
[209] Ibid., fo. 119.   [210] Ch. 6.
[211] Interviews of 26 November 1761, TNA, ADM105/42, fo. 79.

The semi-directed style of the interview aimed at the same thing: proving that the prisoners did not merit such generosity. They were chastised for not wearing their new clothes, proof they 'were not in want of them'.[212] In other words, to use the contemporary discourse on the poor, they were not the 'deserving poor'. The expectation was that they should wear their new clothes at all times. A somewhat paradoxical logic was at work here, by which the prisoners, once they had been cast as necessitous, could not shed this label without risk of being seen as dishonest. For Cooke the Agent, clearly the prisoners had abused the goodwill of their benefactors, confirming the fears of those who opposed the idea of donating to enemies in the first place.

But the prisoners' version of the events markedly diverged from the Agent's. Philippe Chauvin explained to Dr Maxwell, the commissioner who led the inquiry, that he had 'converted' his coat into a 'waistcoat lined throughout w.ʰ the same'.[213] And while Pierre Bally had gone to the muster with 'his 2 old waistcoats', he still held his new clothes, which he produced at the interview.[214] The prisoners had perfectly plausible explanations for their behaviour:

Q21. ... how come they not to wear then especially at a Muster.
A. As the Weather was then mild they wore their own Cloaths and saved the new ones against a more rigorous season.[215]

The accusation that the prisoners were ungrateful was also weakened by the investigation. Very few of them knew who had given them these clothes.[216] And most had ignored that if they 'sold or embezzled the Cloaths' they would be punished.[217] Maxwell concluded that Agent Cooke had misled the prisoners by failing to inform them that they must wear their new clothes, or that they were forbidden to sell them, and that they were liable to a specific punishment for it.[218] He ordered another muster, and found that only twenty-four prisoners, out of sixty-four, were really 'culpable'.[219] The problem then lay not in the immorality of the prisoners of war, but in the management of the distribution of aid. Did this campaign at least succeed in putting an end to the prisoners' needs? In actual fact, these efforts were short-lived. In March 1761, less than a year after the charity had proudly published its *Proceedings*, the Lords of the Admiralty wrote to the King that sixty prisoners in Portchester Castle and Fareham Hospitals were 'destitute of cloaths', and that the French Court, informed of this situation, did not do anything to relieve their distress.[220] Eighteen months later, 562 prisoners at

---

[212] Ibid., fos. 76–v.   [213] Philippe Chauvin, ibid., fo. 73v.
[214] Pierre Bally, ibid., fo. 75.   [215] Ibid., fo. 75v. See also fo. 74v.
[216] Clerk of the prison's testimony, ibid., fo. 76v.   [217] Ibid., fo. 76v.
[218] Ibid., 27 December 1761, fo. 185.   [219] Ibid., fo. 184v.
[220] LCA to the King, 6 March 1761, TNA, ADM7/341, fo. 135.

Winchester were reduced, with the Admiralty's consent, to exchanging their food rations for clothing to protect them against the inclement weather.[221]

While associational charity had begun to grow in Britain in the late seventeenth century, its association with high profile projects attracting genteel benefactors increased from the mid-century onwards.[222] But the ways in which the campaign for clothing the prisoners of war related to these wider movements has been completely overlooked. In 1759–60, the same language and strategies of propaganda, and the same groups of people, were mobilized in efforts for political reform, the reform of hospitals and prisons, the campaigns against slavery, and for help to the poor. Take the example of John Fothergill, already mentioned, who was a close friend of Benjamin Franklin and other Philadelphia Quakers since the 1740s. During the 1770s, he was a supporter of the American insurgents, and, with his close friend John Howard, was very much involved in prison reform.[223] He was also engaged in the antislavery movement.[224] Samuel Whitbread, the Bedford brewer, was another of Howard's friends who was similarly involved in these different causes, and was, like Fothergill, among the founding members of the 1759 Committee.[225] For this milieu of Quaker, Methodist, and Evangelical lawyers, industrialists, doctors and writers, the cause of prisoners of war could not be separated from the others. In 1776, Granville Sharp wrote that 'that all *mankind*, even our *professed enemies* ... must necessarily be esteemed our neighbours ... so that the same benevolence ... is indisputably due, *under the Gospel*, to *our brethren of the universe*'.[226] Written in the support of abolitionism, this could have applied, mutatis mutandis, to prisoners of war as well. And the supporters of prisoners of war faced the same problem as the opponents of slavery: namely, how to reconcile national interest with humanitarian or religious ideas.[227] During the American War of Independence, charitable campaigns for American prisoners of war were again organized in Britain, relying on the same groups and employing the same justifications.[228] While it is somehow less surprising to see Britons rushing in numbers to help their brothers from across the Atlantic, it must be underlined that this took place at the very same time as charges of atrocity towards British prisoners were being levelled against the Americans.

The significance of the 1759–60 moment was not lost on contemporaries. Oliver Goldsmith, a personal acquaintance of Thomas Hollis, praised in his

---

[221] LCA to the King, 30 September 1762, ibid., fo. 194.

[222] On the mid-eighteenth century as a turning point, see Langford, *Public Life*.

[223] He was, alongside Howard, one of the three appointees to supervise the building of the two national penitentiaries set up by the Penitentiary Act of 1779: Fox, *Dr John Fothergill*, pp. 223–5. On his role during the American War of Independence, see Moniz, *From Empire*, ch. 3.

[224] Brion Davis, *Problem*, p. 431.   [225] Ignatieff, *Just Measure*, pp. 49–50.

[226] Granville Sharp, *The Just Limitation of Slavery in the Laws of God* (1776), cited in Turley, *Culture*, p. 20.

[227] Turley, *Culture*, pp. 26–7; Colley, *Britons*, pp. 373–81; Brown, *Moral Capital*.

[228] Anderson, 'Treatment'.

Citizens of the World how 'national benevolence prevailed over national animosity'. He celebrated mankind as well as his countrymen: 'it was for Englishmen alone to be capable of such exalted virtue.'[229] Two decades later, using a Newtonian language of attraction and repulsion, Lord Kames explained that commerce between enemies could turn enmity into friendship. Thus, he wrote, 'two nations, originally strangers to each, may, by commerce or other favourable circumstance, become so well acquainted, as to change from aversion to affection.' This conversion, he added, could be 'instantaneous; as where a stranger becomes an object of pity or of gratitude. Many low persons in Britain contributed cheerfully for maintaining some French seamen made prisoners at the commencement of the late war.'[230] By their mere presence on foreign soil, the French prisoners had stirred the charity of the British people, breaking down national prejudices.

In France, the echo of this charitable campaign appears to have been very limited. It was not mentioned in the *Mercure de France* or the *Gazette de France*, nor in the *Encyclopédie*.[231] This may have been a testimony to the ability of the French monarchy to buy the silence of these gazetteers. The economic failure of the French state to meet the needs of its soldier captives abroad was sufficient reason for keeping quiet about it. The French monarchy's own propaganda was closely tied to its military successes—which were becoming rarer as the years went by.[232]

Why was there no similar campaign in France? Probably because, unlike in Britain, no political space was available for such a national movement, relying as it did on the participation of civil society and the middle classes. In France, this would have been perceived as interference in state affairs. In terms of public discourse, humanitarian patriotism relied on two closely related elements. On the one hand, the demonization of the enemy, through the denunciation of its barbary, was an ancient trope; but what was truly original was the attempt to beat the enemy on the moral ground, by giving relief to his soldiers and sailors. In France, only the first half of the equation could be publicly invoked.[233] Did the period of the French Wars modify this situation?

V. The Revolutionary and Napoleonic Wars

The French Wars saw the apogee of political and religious propaganda, in both Britain and France. During these two decades, the campaigns I have just analysed,

[229] Goldsmith, *Citizen of the World*, vol. I, pp. 70–1.
[230] Kames, *Sketches*, pp. 395–6.
[231] I found only two mentions of this campaign, in the *Gazette d'Utrecht*, 105 (31 December 1759), and in the *Gazette de Leyde*, 104 (24 December 1759). There does not appear to be anything in the *Gazette de La Haye*, nor in the *Gazette des Pays-Bas* or in the *Gazette de Bruxelles*.
[232] Dziembowski, *Nouveau patriotisme*.
[233] See the example of Lesuire's *Les Sauvages de l'Europe*, analysed by Charters, *Disease*, pp. 186–7.

and the interdependence between humanitarian and patriotic discourse, took on a new character: discourses 'solidified' in new social and political practices. While these discussions connected both sides of the Channel, the focus of the following section is on the British dimension.

A. Propaganda Campaigns and Parliamentary Inquiries

One of the main novelties of the period regards the forms and content of political debate. In both countries, the context of war between France and Britain, from 1793 onwards, increased the public discussion of international matters, while a growing number of people participated in political activities: taking part in clubs and associations, petitioning representative assemblies or demonstrating. At the same time, in Britain war also put to the test the culture of free political discussion, which had been rising since the 1760s.

At the end of the eighteenth century—arguably the process had started with the American War of Independence—genuine propaganda campaigns were orchestrated by the two governments against the alleged inhumane treatment of prisoners by the enemy. In this symbolic struggle, which redefined the 'frontiers of the *espace moral*',[234] the French Revolution redeployed and developed traditional themes. But the debate was generated on an unprecedented scale in order to mobilize public opinion, at home and abroad, around a 'just' cause. Sophie Wahnich argues that, during the French Revolution, the discourse of the inhumanity of 'the English' worked as the reverse of the discourse of the rights of man.[235] It is in this context that the inhuman treatment of enemy prisoners came to the fore. I am interested in understanding what the relays of these campaigns of opinion were, who the targets of these discourses were, and whether they were taken seriously by state authorities, to the extent that they led them to take action. By contrast with the Seven Years' War, during the 1790s–1800s a public conversation was indeed going on between France and Britain on this matter. And this had major repercussions for the response of local and central authorities.

Soon after the first prisoners were captured and detained across the Channel, the French press began to spread the news that French prisoners were being mistreated. In the session of 5 November 1794 of the Thermidorian Convention, a petitioner came to the assembly and described the capture of 3,000 Frenchmen from the Northern Army:

[234] Fassin and Bourdelais, 'Frontières'.   [235] Wahnich, 'Révolution française'.

Wages of 6 *liards* per day, sometimes without bread, often without straw, almost always covered with rags, with neither shoes nor clothes; dark and disease-ridden prisons as barracks, this is how the Marchiennes division has been treated. Lawmakers, my heart torn to pieces by my brothers' suffering, I have escaped the surveillance of my guards, and have come straight away to demand that you revenge such assaults against the laws of war.[236]

We see at work the politics of pity mentioned above, combining the universalization of the cause with the embodiment of suffering, allowing for the identification of the national collectivity with the prisoners of war. More importantly, this petition was given as wide an audience as possible. It was first read in session, which was not the case of all petitions. It was then published in the *Moniteur*, the organ of official propaganda of the government. Then it was printed in the *Bulletin de correspondance*, a sort of anthology of key texts discussed at the Convention, which were to be disseminated to local authorities. An 'honourable mention' was added to it, to highlight its importance. It was finally sent to the Committee of Public Safety.

Another way of publicly exposing the woes of the prisoners was to read at the *tribune* of the assembly their letters about the 'inhumanity' they 'encountered in England'.[237] By being publicly read, the status of the prisoner's letter changed, authenticating the claims of the French government. Publishing parliamentary reports could have the same function. In January 1798, Joseph Riou de Kersalaün, former representative of the Finistère département, produced a report at the Conseil des Cinq-Cents, 'on the sufferings of Frenchmen imprisoned in England'. It was immediately printed. Riou denounced the 'crimes' of the English government, the multiple 'acts of cruelty' towards the unhappy prisoners who were 'rotting away in the slime and garbage', and proposed to create a sumptuary 'humanity tax' to relieve the French prisoners.[238] Indeed, facing the repeated complaints from France that the food rations given to its prisoners were insufficient, while the French government refused to repay Britain for the clothes it had provided to French prisoners, the British government had decided in 1797 that each country would now look after its own prisoners.[239] In January–February 1798, hundreds of French citizens, men, women, and even children dashed to help their compatriots imprisoned in Britain, sending 'patriotic gifts' to their government to that effect. Many contributors concomitantly donated money to finance the French invasion of Britain.[240]

---

[236] *Gazette nationale*, 47 (7 November 1794).
[237] Brandberg, interpreter on the *Musette* privateer from Nantes, in *Gazette Nationale*, 264 (12 June 1797).
[238] Corps Législatif, *Rapport*, p. 8. See Morieux, 'Patriotisme', pp. 305–6.
[239] Extract of letter from TO to Charretié, 17 August 1797, in *Report* (1798), Appendix, pp. 107–8.
[240] Chanzy, 'Projet'.

In these years, the public debates about the treatment of prisoners reverberated across the Channel, and besides the French press, the British government also had to face criticisms at home. The controversy that started at Liverpool in January 1798 exemplifies the new means which authorities, local and central, were forced to use to respond to these public challenges. In a letter published on 20 January 1798 in the *Liverpool Courier*, 'Philanthropos' described at length the bad treatments experienced by the French prisoners in the Mersey town. The content of the letter is not unfamiliar: the Frenchmen were starving, their bread was awful and the water tepid, while their jailors were compared to 'American savages' or to 'Robespierre'. But the justification of the recourse to publication is particularly significant:

To the Editor of the Courier. Liverpool, Jan. 12.

Sir,

One of the advantages of your Daily Paper, is the early and universal communication of whatever may affect the credit or discredit of your Country: it brings a fact directly home, and is the most convenient source of information. This advantage I shall make use of, to lay before this Nation the Case of the French Prisoners now lying in Liverpool Prison.[241]

From then on, a controversy began in the press, with several papers reproducing the letter.[242] An investigation was subsequently carried out in the prison by a delegation led by the city corporation, the results of which were again published in a large number of British papers.[243] The mayor of Liverpool, Thomas Staniforth, also wrote an open letter to the editor of the *Courier*, illustrating the practical consequences of these public accusations. As soon as he had read Philanthropos' letter, he explained, he had taken the decision 'to investigate the truth or falsehood' of these allegations, which were 'calculated to cast an indelible blot and stigma of disgrace and infamy' on his town, on the Sick & Wounded Board, and beyond that, 'upon the Nation at large, for suffering...the inhumanity and general atrocity alluded to in that Letter'.[244] The magistrate also warned about the risk of reprisals against British prisoners, and insisted on the need to publish widely his refutation and the report of his inspection of Liverpool, in order to convince the 'impartial and unprejudiced people' of the malevolence of 'Philanthropos'. In fact, most of the newspapers contented themselves with reproducing this long report, *in extenso*. This inquiry explicitly followed the model of Howard's

---

[241] Reproduced in the *Sun*, 1671 (31 January 1798).

[242] See, for instance, *True Briton*, 1685 (22 January 1798).

[243] *London Chronicle*, 6073 (1 February 1798); *Lloyd's Evening Post*, 6309 (31 January 1798).

[244] The mayor of Liverpool to the editor of the *Courier*, 26 January 1798, reproduced in *Sun*, 1671 (31 January 1798).

prison inspections, interrogating prisoners and prison staff, verifying the quality and quantity of the food, and examining the beds.

What is striking, by comparison with the period of the Seven Years' War studied earlier, is not only the carrying out of an investigation following attacks in the national press, but also the publicizing of its results, again in the newspapers.[245] Furthermore, parliament entered the process of publicly refuting these accusations, perhaps due to a sense that only it could provide effective inquisitorial oversight and counter these public attacks.[246] It commissioned a very detailed enquiry into the treatment of French prisoners in Britain. Several MPs asked that the information thus collected be shown in the House of Commons, in order to convince Britain's allies, as well as its enemies, that the laws of war were respected.

A parliamentary committee was put in place—a rare practice in eighteenth-century Britain.[247] Among its members, besides military men, one notes the names of Henry Thornton, a banker and philanthropist, and the son of John Thornton, one of the founding members of the 1759 subscription, and William Wilberforce, another figure who drove philanthropic endeavours in this period.[248] One of the committee members, Edward Bootle-Wilbraham, the MP for Newcastle under Lyme, declared on 7 June 1798 that it was

> The duty of the House to make that report and these resolutions as public as possible, that all the world might see the falsity of the statement of our enemies upon the subject... and he farther hoped, that every nation acting with us would be made acquainted with the true state of the fact.[249]

The decision was accordingly taken to circulate the investigation on the French prisoners as widely as possible, nationally and in Europe—which was a rare practice.[250] This report was published *in extenso* in the House of Commons journals, as well as separately. The newspapers, especially the loyalist press, also published large extracts.[251] The very form of the report illustrates the triumph of an administrative culture founded on statistical proofs.[252] It was 167 pages long, including twenty pages of introduction, and ninety-one supporting documents.[253]

---

[245] This is partly linked to the boom of print in this period: McLeod, *War of Ideas*; Wahnich, *Impossible citoyen*.

[246] Many parliamentary enquiries focussed on metropolitan debtors' prisons, not subject to ordinary local authority control: Innes, 'Legislation', pp. 126–7.

[247] Ibid., 125n77.   [248] 22 March 1798, *HCJ*, vol. 53, col. 398.

[249] 7 June 1798, *Parliamentary Register*, vol. 6, p. 292.

[250] 7 June 1798, *HCJ*, vol. 53, col. 659.

[251] *Anti-Jacobin*, 33 (25 June 1798). The extensive investigation led by the American Congress to assess the veracity of atrocities committed by British troops, in 1770s, might have been a precedent for this: Hoock, 'Mangled bodies', pp. 129–34. However, the 1798 inquiry was a *response* to French accusations of cruelty, not an indictment against enemy practices.

[252] Innes, *Legislation*, p. 125. See also Eastwood, '"Amplifying"'.

[253] *Report on Treatment* (1798) , p. 4.

The investigation also shows the generalization and standardization, during the 1790s, of methods that we encountered earlier in the century, such as the interrogation of witnesses *in situ* in order to obtain 'first-hand' proofs and hear prisoners' complaints.[254] The report reproduced all the French and British decrees and diplomatic correspondence, as well as the letters from prisoners of war. In its conclusion, the committee of enquiry stated that the accusation of cruelty towards French prisoners of war was 'utterly void of foundation', and had been 'fabricated, and industriously supported by the enemy, for the double purpose of justifying their own ill treatment of British prisoners, and of irritating the minds of their countrymen against this nation'.[255] A former officer on parole in France hence testified that in Nantes, 'it was said, the French Prisoners in England were so rigorously confined; and Accounts to this Effect were stuck on the Walls, representing that the French Prisoners were fed on dead Dogs and Cats, and were brought out and shot en Masse for the Amusement of the Populace'.[256] The authors of the report highlighted the widely shared idea that the French were waging a war of a new kind, treating their prisoners 'with a Degree of Rigour and Inhumanity unwarranted by the Usages of War among civilized Nations'.[257] Debate proliferated from one public arena to another: beginning in the press, it resonated in parliament, which generated new newspaper articles. In both countries, governments considered limiting the freedom of speech, and tried to prosecute journalists, publishers, and booksellers, who were accused of publishing false or anti-patriotic information about the prisoners.[258] At the same time, governments contributed to this phenomenon, publicizing their rebuttal of enemy 'lies'.[259]

Prisoners also played a role in the publicization of these controversies, and were able to make themselves heard outside, appealing to representative institutions to obtain the launching of official investigations.[260] The war of ideas also took place inside the prisons. In France, antimonarchical pamphlets were translated into English, comparing their conditions to that of slaves and encouraging them to join the cause of the revolution.[261] In 1810, printed copies of the project of a convention for the exchange of prisoners were distributed among the prisoners in Britain, 'particularly those about to proceed to France, for the purpose of counteracting the gross Misrepresentations and Falsehoods of the *Moniteur* on this Subject, giving Publicity to the liberal and humane Disposition of His Majesty's

[254] Ibid., pp. 48–51, 87–8. See Innes, 'Legislation', p. 126.   [255] *Report* (1798), p. 20.
[256] Deposition of John McWhinnie, merchant of London, before the Committee on the Treatment of Prisoners of War, 20 April 1798, in *Report* (1798), p. 57.
[257] *Report* (1798), p. 20.
[258] Walton, *Policing*; Bélissa and Wahnich, 'Crimes'; Jones and McDonald, 'Robespierre'.
[259] See the official 'Correspondence with the French government relative to Prisoners of war' (1802).
[260] Such as the British prisoners in Angoulême in 1797: *Report* (1798), p. 89; or the French prisoners in Dartmoor: TO to Cotgrave, 30 April, 8 June 1813, TNA, ADM98/227, fos. 95v, 107.
[261] Le Prat, 'Faire face', pp. 222–3.

Government, to alleviate the Miseries of War'.[262] In 1813, copies of *L'Ambigu*, a royalist periodical published in London by a French émigré, Jean-Gabriel Peltier, were disseminated in the prison depots and prison hulks, 'through the Medium of the most intelligent Prisoners who may chuse to read them', and the Transport Office enquired whether this had had any effect.[263] During the French Wars, governments became more conscious than ever that the war prisons were not insulated from wider political discussions, and they tried to influence the prisoners' political allegiances before they returned home. As soon as the British government heard the news of Napoleon's abdication, a circular was sent to the prison depots to enquire 'whether any and what Number of them have declared in favour of the Bourbons, or are likely to declare themselves if separated from the other Prisoners'.[264] On the other hand, those 'of a dangerous character' were to be detained and sent home 'separately'.[265]

B. Prisoners of War and Missionaries

Political propaganda and religious campaigns were arguably two sides of the same coin. Moral reformers could see the large presence of foreigners on British territory as an opportunity to target a population that had traditionally remained outside their reach: namely, foreign sailors. In this section, I want to examine the attempts to convert prisoners of war, and more radically, to turn them into Christian missionaries.

Since the Seven Years' War at least, dissenters had been interested in war prisons. For the Methodists, being charitable to the Catholic prisoners of war and distributing religious tracts to them both aimed towards the same goal: that of propagating the Protestant faith to these lost souls. In 1759, at Knowle prison near Bristol, a charitable collection was thus made by 'the Revd Mr John Wesley the Methodist Preacher at his Tabernacle there for Cloathing some of the French Prisoners who are almost naked', and £20 worth of shirts and waistcoats were to be distributed 'amongst the most necessitous of them'.[266] Wesley repeatedly preached for these prisoners, and successfully appealed for money in the English press.[267] During the American War of Independence, the Wesleyans tried again to pursue these endeavours. Thomas Coke, the first Methodist 'bishop' and among those jostling to be John Wesley's successor, thus desired to be permitted to distribute 'some tracts by the Rev. Mr. Westley to Spanish and French prisoners of war', but the Sick & Wounded Board replied that it 'may give offence to the

[262] TO to prison depots, 10 December 1810, TNA, ADM98/170, fo. 65.
[263] TO to prison depots, 25 November, 23 December 1813, ibid., fos. 172–3, 176.
[264] TO's circular, 7 April 1814, ibid., fo. 216.   [265] TO's circular, 17 May 1814, ibid., fo. 194.
[266] S&W to LCA, 27 November 1759, TNA, ADM98/8, fos. 52v–53.
[267] Rogal, 'John Wesley', pp. 332–3. See *LC*, 460 (8–11 December 1759).

respective courts and might justly be considered a violation of the cartel'.[268] As we saw in chapter 1, such initiatives indeed transgressed international agreements, which stated that the helplessness of prisoners of war should not be exploited to convert them.[269]

But during the French Wars, the situation was quite different, with a renewed emphasis on the enemy's religion, or lack of it. This justified reaching out to prisoners on a spiritual level, officially breaking down with eighteenth-century norms. In many ways, this movement to convert prisoners of war was a natural extension of the prison philanthropy movement of the 1760s, which we have examined above, with the idea that the prisoner was a weak and innocent soul awaiting salvation. In the early eighteenth century, initiatives led by the Anglican *Society for the Propagation of Christian Knowledge* had targeted sailors, merchants, and prisoners, but not prisoners of war.[270] The Evangelicals and the dissenters' push for moral reform, from the 1780s onwards, and the general rise of interest in missionary activity in this period, provides the background to the missionary effort to proselytize to prisoners of war.[271] Their aim was to educate and 'civilize' those left outside the parish system, such as sailors and convicts. Methodists in particular, who believed that Christ had died for humanity as a whole, emphasized that everyone could be reached and saved by his message; this idea naturally extended to prisoners of war. In this sense, Catholic French and Spanish soldiers and sailors were not enemies. Prison depots and hulks were thus to become the rear base for propagating the true faith and fighting heathenism.

In practice, spaces of detention also changed in the late eighteenth century, with much higher concentrations of inmates detained in confined spaces. This made prisons ideal places for experimenting with spiritual, as well as medical, remedies. During the French Wars, the British government massively resorted to hulks, or prison ships.[272] On 6 September 1812, the French officers on board the Brunswick prison ship wrote a long petition of thanks to the 'Methodist Missionary Committee'. These prisoners emphasized that the missionaries' visits alleviated their sense of being cut off from the outside world:

> We are all sensible of the degree of courage that was necessary for men who were not constrained by any authority, to penetrate into these dungeons of sorry,— where the infected air we breathe, the multitude of unhappy victims that are crowded into them, and the various diseases to which they are subject, and by which many have been hurried to the grave,—to induce them to come and spend

---

[268] S&W to LCA, 6 July 1781, TNA, ADM98/13, fos. 194–v.
[269] Proselytism was explicitly forbidden in international regulations. See 1780 Cartel, article 21, CSP, 47.
[270] Sirota, *Christian Monitors*, pp. 112–31.   [271] See Lovegrove, *Established Church*.
[272] Ch. 4.

whole days amongst us, and expose themselves to the same diseases which affect us;—the whole proves that nothing but Christian charity could produce such an effect.[273]

The missionaries were commended for opening the prison and sharing in the prisoners' travails. They helped them forget about their sorry present and dream of a less painful future. One year later, now back in France, one of the signatories of this petition, Colonel Lebertre, published a narrative, *Aperçu du traitement qu'éprouvent les prisonniers français en Angleterre*, which denounced his captivity in England. Tellingly, he did not mention the Methodists. The work of these missionaries deserves to be analysed in more details.

The wretched conditions of detention on board hulks justified the Methodist preachers' professed aim to rescue the miserable. William Toase, the Wesleyan chairman of the Portsmouth District, began to preach to prisoners in hulks in the river Medway.[274] In 1810, ten prison ships lay there at anchor, loaded with 7,000 prisoners in total. 'Providence', as he put it in his reminiscences, published in 1835, opened the way to his first visits to the prison ships.[275] At the invitation of its captain, he started in March 1810 with the *Glory*, a ship in which 1,000 men and boys, mainly French, were held captive. On the first day, Toase was struck by the 'ignorance of all religion, depravity of heart and life, and misery, in almost all its forms, [which] appeared throughout this ship'.[276] He came back the following day, and began preaching to these men in French, holding religious conversations with prisoners individually. Thereafter, he visited them once a week, distributing copies of the New Testament as well as 'hundreds of religious tracts'.[277] He had to overcome the suspicion of the government towards Methodism, which was accused of stirring disorder among the disaffected classes in Britain;[278] the consequences of preaching to foreigners were potentially even more worrying. Public preaching to the prisoners was forbidden by the Transport Board in May 1810, and this interruption lasted for more than a year.[279] However, through the intercession of Dr Coke, the Transport Board allowed Toase to preach publicly again, 'as long as there is no impropriety in his discourses or conduct'.[280]

Subsequently, Toase was officially appointed to evangelize the prisoners of war by the Wesleyan Conference, and began this new role in September 1811. In typical Methodist fashion, Toase harangued very large numbers. At Portchester Castle, for instance, he stood in the middle of the yard, on a shaky table which a

[273] 'The Committee of the Prisoners of War, on board the Brunswick, to . . . the Methodist Missionary Committee', 6 September 1812, in Toase, *Wesleyan Mission*, p. 42. In Toase's text, the petition was signed 'Le Bertre, Colonel and Chevalier de l'Empire, Vatable, Colonel, &c'.

[274] Toase was also minister in Portsmouth and Andover: Wesley, *Minutes*, p. 16.

[275] Toase, *Wesleyan Mission*, p. 24.   [276] Ibid., p. 25.   [277] Ibid., pp. 25–6.

[278] Hole, *Pulpits*, pp. 108, 113–14; Gilbert, 'Methodism'; Hempton, *Methodism*, pp. 55–84.

[279] Toase, *Wesleyan Mission*, p. 26.

[280] Order from the Transport Office to Dr Coke, 1 June 1811, in ibid., p. 29.

prisoner held still with his back.[281] In his journal, Toase gave exempla of the faith experienced by the prisoners who had been touched by the sacred text. Hence on 22 March 1812, on board the *Trusty*: 'When it was announced that the Minister was come, numbers came up from the lower ward on crutches, to hear that word of salvation which gives life, and health, and peace to all that receive it.'[282]

The British and Foreign Bible Society (BFBS), an ecumenical and non-sectarian association founded in 1804, supported this proselytizing campaign.[283] From its inception, the BFBS tried to print as many bibles as possible as cheaply as possible and in as many languages as possible, and not just for servicemen. Confined populations were among its targets.[284] Convicts, sick soldiers, the poor, and the widows of sailors were treated in the same way, because the experience of incarceration was believed to transcend their differences.[285]

Thousands of prisoners of war, coming from the disbanded Franco-Spanish fleet at Trafalgar, as well as French, Danish, Dutch or American merchant seafarers seized as prizes, began to be brought to the hulks in December 1805: the BFBS focused on them from the beginning.[286] John Owen, a leading early member of the society, explained why the unfortunate prisoners of war, whose spiritual relief had been hitherto neglected by religious institutions, deserved special consideration with respect to other confined groups:

> Separated from their country and their natural connections, and arrested in their career of professional duty, they had to suffer all the hardships of bondage and privation in an enemy's country, and that, in many cases, for a conduct which would have entitled them to respect and remuneration in their own. The very circumstances which so honorably discriminated them from other subjects of confinement, and rendered their case more deserving of compassion, placed them at the same time at a still greater distance from the means and the prospect of relief.[287]

By mid-March 1806, Spanish and French prisoners were already supplied with 'the Protestant versions of the Scriptures' in their native languages; tens of thousands of copies were given out in the following years.[288] Between 1 April 1810 and 31 March 1811, 1,066 copies were handed out to prisoners still in depots or hulks, and 2,000 to those embarking on cartels. While the vast majority of the copies given to prisoners of war were in the French language (2,653/3,066, or 86.5

---

[281] Toase, *Wesleyan Mission*, p. 38.   [282] Ibid., p. 35.

[283] See Atkins, 'Christian heroes', p. 408.

[284] Committee of the BFBS, undated, Cambridge University Library (CUL), BFBS, BSA/D1/5/4, p. 192.

[285] George White Esq., Chatham, 7 January 1814: CUL, BFBS, BSA/D1/5/6, pp. 78–9.

[286] Kverndal, 'Sowing', pp. 329, 331; Kverndal, *Seamen's Missions*, pp. 130–8.

[287] Owen, *History*, vol. I, p. 209.

[288] *Second Report* (1806), p. 121; 'Seven thousand copies of the French Testament alone have been voted to the French Prisoners of War', *Fourth Report* (1808), in *Reports of the BFBS*, vol. I, pp. 14, 42.

per cent), bibles in Spanish, Portuguese, Dutch, German, Italian, or Danish were also distributed, which reflects the relative proportions of captives by state, as well as the cosmopolitan nature of the armies and navies of the time.[289] British prisoners in Russia or in France were not forgotten, and in early March 1813, 2,200 bibles and 3,300 Testaments 'for the use of British Prisoners of War at the eleven Depots in France', contained in twenty-two cases, were sent to the French *Ministre de la Guerre* in Paris.[290] The holy cargo never reached its destination.[291]

It is important to emphasize the political dimension of this massive distribution of bibles and testaments to prisoners of war, which was another iteration of humanitarian patriotism. John Owen wrote in his *History* of the BFBL, in 1816, that 'this commerce of pure and gratuitous benevolence' meant 'literally returning good for evil, blessing for cursing, mercy for vengeance'.[292] Missionary work was not immune from employing a patriotic and nationalist tone; it was, after all, the *British* and Foreign Bible Society, which proudly proclaimed the providential destiny of the British nation in evangelizing 'the habitable globe', including Napoleonic France.[293] In a reply to the bishop of Denmark, who had thanked the Bible Society for supplying this country's prisoners with the holy text, the Society's President, John Teignmouth, for example, wrote that 'the poor, the afflicted, and the desolate' were the chief objects of the Society's devotion, adding that none among those had 'stronger claims on its compassion and benevolence, than the unfortunate prisoners of war'. He placed this initiative in a spirit of 'Christian benevolence and love towards our brethren of every nation', which should override 'the afflictive dispensations of war'.[294] It was easy to take the next step, to present this generosity as an intrinsically British national trait. Hence, the Rochester (Kent) branch of the Bible Society prided itself in its participation in the distribution of bibles and testaments to French and American prisoners in prison ships on the Medway, congratulating 'the labours of those British Christians who have wished to alleviate the sorrows of their enemies, and to point out to them a land where enmity and captivity are alike unknown!'.[295] In the same manner, the Manchester and Salford Bible Society observed in 1811: 'Is there a poor Foreigner, whom the fate of war has brought into the prisons of this happier land, whose

---

[289] Table in 'Report from the Hon. Mrs. –', 31 March 1811, in *Reports of the BFBS*, vol. II (1811–13), Seventh Report (1811), p. 166.

[290] Joseph Tarn (assistant secretary to the Bible Society) to Mr Sylvester de Sacy at Paris, 16 June 1814, CUL, BSA/D1/5/6, pp. 189–90. On Russia, see *Ninth Report*, p. 523.

[291] William Gordon, British chaplain at Verdun to John Owen, secretary to the BFBS in London, 13 December 1813, CUL, BSA/D1/5/6, pp. 99–100.

[292] Owen, *History*, vol. I, p. 211.

[293] James Otis, Morse, Cherry Valley Otoego County State of New York, 18 September 1815, CUL, BSA/D1/5/7, p. 298. A Bible Society was founded in Paris during the wars, which Owen hoped would thrive once Napoleon had been defeated, and contribute to restoring spiritual order in France: Owen, *History*, vol. II, 573–5.

[294] To Frederick Munter, Bishop of Zealand, 12 February 1813, *Ninth Report*, p. 473.

[295] Undated extract, *Summary Account*, p. 67.

fainting soul is now tasting refreshment at the Fountain of Life?'[296] Neither the birthplace of prisoners, nor their types and places of confinement, mattered in the eyes of the BFBS: whether French, Spanish, or Danish; whether in hospital ships, prison ships, or cartel ships; in England or in Scotland, Lisbon, Malta, or Zante in the Ionian Islands, they were all entitled to this charity.[297] What mattered was their state of deprivation and helplessness, which the reading of Scripture would alleviate.

In addition to his preaching, Toase's proselyted by encouraging the forming of small circulating libraries in each ship, composed essentially of Bibles, Testaments, and religious tracts, in French, German, Italian, Dutch, and Spanish.[298] The same operation was repeated from October 1811 onwards, when Wesleyan missionaries were allowed to visit the nine other hulks on the Medway, land prisons and hulks in Portsmouth and Plymouth, as well as Dartmoor, Stapleton, and Norman Cross.[299]

At the end of the war, the distribution of bibles and other religious tracts to departing prisoners became the principal activity in which the priests were engaged. When prisoners embarked on cartels to Holland, Spain, or France, they were given copies of the Scriptures to distribute back home.[300] In February 1811, the Committee of the Bristol Auxiliary Bible Society thus stated that the purpose of these gifts was the 'conveying into the heart of France the illumination of the gospel'.[301] In his journal, on the date of 26 November 1811, Toase noted: 'Twenty-eight invalids were sent home this day. I gave them twenty-eight Testaments, six Bibles, and several religious tracts for distribution. The Surgeon who accompanied them took four Bibles, which he promised to give to four poor families in France.'[302] By this means, prisoners in turn took the role of religious missionaries who would convert their nations.[303] The belief that miscreants would be converted merely by being exposed to the sacred text reveals a high dose of optimism, and the actual impact of this campaign on the prisoners' faith remains doubtful.

Detailing his daily work on the week beginning 15 April 1814, Toase interwove his own observations with supposedly direct quotes from the prisoners who had digested the Bible, quoting Matthew 25:36–40:

[296] 'Extract from the Official Report of the Annual Meeting of the Manchester and Salford Auxiliary Bible Society', 27 March 1811, Reports of the BFBS, seventh report, vol. II, p. 143.

[297] On the distribution of bibles and new testaments to prisoners of war in Scotland, see Ninth Report, p. 394. On Danish prisoners, see Owen, History, vol. I, p. 395. On Malta and Greek islands, see letter from a correspondent at Malta, Valetta, 29 October 1814, eleventh report, Summary Account, pp. 78–9.

[298] Toase, Wesleyan Mission, pp. 31–2.

[299] Robert Peel to Dr Coke, October 1811, in ibid., pp. 32–3. Schools for prisoners were established in each ship: Toase, Wesleyan Mission, p. 36.

[300] Owen, History, vol. II, pp. 560–1.

[301] February 1811, in Reports of the BFBS, seventh report (1811), p. 127.

[302] Toase, Wesleyan Mission, p. 34.

[303] On this 'work of dispersion', see Canton, History, vol. I, pp. 127–8.

O how pleasing it was to hear the poor liberated captives say, 'We are glad to possess this Bible, we will carry it home to our families; this Bible shall always remain in my family.' One said, 'I have nine children, do give me one for them.' Others said, 'You found us naked, and you clothed us; in prison, and you visited us.' We occupied a portion of each day in preaching farewell sermons on board the respective ships. My last text was, '*La paix soit avec vous.*'[304]

By this means, Toase concluded, 'Many hundreds were taught to read the Scriptures; great numbers of copies of the word of God were sent into France, and to all parts of the continent'.[305] Converting the prisoners, and turning them into evangelists, helped disseminating the faith on a global scale.[306]

VI. Conclusion

As argued by Heather Jones, definitions of 'acceptable violent practices' against prisoners were not fixed during the First World War: there were 'shifting social, political and legal understandings of what constituted transgressive "atrocities" or acceptable "reprisals"'.[307] The dominant language, in the eighteenth century, to denote these flexible norms of violence, was that of barbarism and civilization. The distinction between the barbarian and the civilized warrior could be blurred in practice.[308] When European combatants fought together with Amerindians, as was frequently the case during the Seven Years' War and the American War of Independence, they were tarred with the same brush in propaganda as their 'savage' accomplices who butchered prisoners of war and killed women and children.[309] At different times, throughout the eighteenth century, reciprocal accusations of fighting uncivilized and inhuman wars, particularly in the manner they dealt with their captives, were hurled between France and Britain. This was not specific to these two countries, and accounts of massacres of prisoners were compiled, by the insurgents during the American War of Independence, or by the USA during the War of 1812, to demonstrate British violations of the laws of war and to assert their own moral superiority.[310]

---

[304] Toase, *Wesleyan Mission*, pp. 39–40. The Gospel of St Matthew was particularly meaningful for prisoners, and 1,000 'extra copies of the Gospel of St Matthew only' were distributed among Spanish prisoners in 1806: *Second Report* (1806), p. 121.

[305] Toase, *Wesleyan Mission*, p. 40.

[306] This movement was part of a wider crusade for moral reform: Atkins, 'Christian heroes', pp. 411–12.

[307] Jones, *Violence*, pp. 3, 4.   [308] Lee, *Barbarians*.

[309] Selesky, 'Colonial America', pp. 66–7, 70–1; Bell, *Cult*, ch. 3. See also Steele, *Betrayals*, pp. 149–85.

[310] Witt, *Lincoln's Code*, pp. 35sq, 101; Starkey, 'Paoli', pp. 20–5; Starkey, *War*, pp. 166–8; Hoock, 'Mangled bodies'. On the War of 1812, see Doyle, *Enemy*, pp. 49–68.

This raises the question of the novelty of the Revolutionary and Napoleonic Wars. Already at the end of the eighteenth century, many authors contended that the French Wars had put an end to traditional perceptions of civilized warfare, which was exemplified in the frequent massacres of prisoners of war. In Vendée, in Jaffa or in St Domingue, British authors insisted, the French were stretching humanitarian and civilized values, by slaughtering their captive prisoners. This was a deliberate state policy, not just the missteps of a couple of soldiers left alone to decide what to do on the battlefield. In his *Footsteps of Blood, or, the March of the Republicans* (1803), John Adolphus linked these different episodes into a coherent narrative of state abuse. Describing the massacre of their Ottoman prisoners by the French armies in Jaffa in 1799, the author contrasted Napoleon's attitude to that of his troops. 'In the moment of revenge, when the laws of war justified the rage', the French troops had nonetheless decided to spare the garrison of Jaffa, and refused 'to dishonour themselves'. But Bonaparte was 'determined to relieve himself from the maintenance and care of THREE THOUSAND EIGHT HUNDRED prisoners' and ordered them to be shot. The French general observed the scene 'through a telescope' and 'could not restrain his joy, but broke out into exclamations of approval'.[311]

According to Philip Dwyer, the massacre of prisoners of war was one of the three 'types of extreme violence' (with the sacking of towns and the abuse of civilians), most commonly evoked in 'accounts of the Revolutionary and Napoleonic Wars'.[312] Historians are divided, however, as to whether mass violence during this period was the norm or the exception.[313] There are plenty of examples of massacres of prisoners by all sides, which, contends Dwyer, became 'more commonplace' the longer the wars went on.[314] While there was a consensus that such cruel acts transgressed the laws of war, they were often presented as retaliations against provocations; they were also justified in the name of 'liberty', 'enlightenment', and 'civilization'.[315] However, other historians argue that it is the nature of the wars, which involved unprecedented numbers of irregular fighters, which explains these massacres, in Spain, Russia, Southern Italy, the Austrian Tyrol, or Vendée. As time went on, customary practices developed, and enemy combatants were commonly spared.[316]

In other ways, as this chapter has argued, there was also continuity between the French Wars and the eighteenth century. A variety of options were available to deal with the violence inflicted by the enemy on one's prisoners. The most traditional response was symmetrical reprisals, or *lex talionis*; but reprisals could also be gradual, depending on the type of behaviour expected or observed. While

---

[311] Adolphus, *Footsteps*, p. 67. Contemporary estimates range between 2,400 and 3,000 prisoners: Dwyer, ' "It still" ', p. 382.
[312] Dwyer, ' "It still" ', p. 383.   [313] Ibid., 383–4n11.   [314] Ibid., p. 395.
[315] Ibid., 404n131; Dwyer, 'Violence', p. 123; Bell, *First Total War*.
[316] Scheipers, 'Status', p. 400; Rothenberg, 'Age of Napoleon', pp. 90–2.

the 'struggle over the moral high ground' has become a common characteristic of contemporary wars, it took a specific form in our period.[317] A new grammar of justification emerged, which translated into political and social practices. Humanitarian patriotism did not mirror the action of the enemy. It relied instead of what Lynn Hunt has called 'imagined empathy', a discourse which, she argues, became omnipresent by the mid-eighteenth century, and was challenged during the French Revolution.[318] A comparison between two British cartoons, however, illustrates the continuity of this discourse throughout the period.

'The Contrast' (1759 or 1760) (Fig. 2.1) shows on one side 'a French Prisoner in England'. In the pocket of his long coat is a bent piece of paper, with the words 'to cloath the French Prisoners Coat Shirt'. On the floor, some remaining bits of a letter from Paris, which have been torn by a playful cat, refer to the fact that the French monarch had stopped sending money to care for 'ses Sujets en Angleter'. On the wall, one can make out the outline of an etching, representing an act of charity with the words 'Cloathing y. naked'. The Frenchman who occupies the centre of the image is enjoying a huge slice of sausage with bread, while a pretty waitress is handing him a large piece of beef. On the other side of the etching, an emaciated and sly French waiter is serving 'an English Prisoner in France' some

Fig. 2.1. *The Contrast* [1758]. Courtesy of the Lewis Walpole Library, Yale University.

[317] Lutz and Millar, 'War', p. 487.   [318] Hunt, *Inventing*, pp. 32, 75sq, 178.

Fig. 2.2. *French alias Corsican Villainy or the contrast to English humanity* (1804). Anne S.K. Brown Military Collection, Brown University Library.

frog meat. The prisoner's belt hangs loosely around his empty stomach. The message is clear: while French prisoners were treated with generosity in England, their English homologues were starving in France.

The second engraving, 'French alias Corsican Villainy or the Contrast to English Humanity' (1804) (Fig. 2.2), refers, on one side, to Napoleon's various war crimes in Jaffa, and his disdain for human lives, including 'Women & Children'. The other side is set in the West Indies; a British general is preventing a black combatant from executing his French prisoner, and says: 'We know they are our Enemies & yours & the Enemies of all Mankind, nevertheless Humanity is so strongly planted in the Breast of an Englishman, that he can become an humble beggar for the lives, even of his Enemies when they are subdued.'

These admirable attitudes towards their prisoners, it was hoped, would generate international sympathy for the captors. The Methodists, at the end of the eighteenth century, added a new layer to this moral struggle: they understood that prisoners of war were structurally destined to return home, using them to proselyte. The idea that prisoners were never fully settled is the guiding hypothesis of the next chapter.

3

The Multiple Geographies
of War Captivity

I. Introduction

In September 1782, Marc Lates, a sailor from Bayonne on the French Atlantic coast, was captured as he was serving on board a brigantine from Baltimore, on its journey between St Domingue and Havana. After a detention in 'La Vermude' (Bermudas), he was repatriated to England, and eventually landed in Calais a year after he had been captured, on 13 September 1783.[1] This example is just one among dozens of others that can be discovered by delving into a single folder held in the Archives Nationales in Paris. Throughout the eighteenth century, prisoners of war were captured, detained and exchanged all over the world, from Gorée in Senegal to the Cape of Good Hope, from Quebec to Pondicherry, and from the Caribbean to the Mediterranean.[2] The wars between France and Britain were fought on a global stage.

The links between war captivity and forced mobility are the focus of this chapter. It is often forgotten that prisoners of war, by definition, moved, and that this mobility was systemic. For anyone captured at sea, phases of detention on land alternated with internment on anchored or moving ships. The circulations of prisoners of war within, between, and across empires are all part of the same system, which can only be fully understood by bringing together two historiographies.

First, histories of prisons usually focus on specific places, without considering that these places were themselves part of a wider system of circulations. But deprivation of liberty fits within a broader circulatory logic. Confinement in a prison and modes of containment at the border can be considered within the same analytical framework: they both entail a monitoring and channelling of mobility, which was specific neither to the context of war, nor to the eighteenth century, although it increased during our period.[3] Geographers have recently begun to pay attention to these links between incarceration and mobility.[4]

---

[1] 'Etat des prisonniers français', Calais, 13 September 1783, Archives Nationales, Paris (AN), MAR/F2/101. Likewise, the British prisoners captured in the West Indies were often repatriated to Britain via Portugal: John Hort to Lord Hillsborough, 17 September 1780, The National Archives, Kew (TNA), SP89/87, fos. 302–4.
[2] Multiple examples of these global circulations are scattered in AN, MAR/F2/83.
[3] Morieux, *The Channel*, ch. 8. For a contemporary analysis of these phenomena, see Tazzioli and Garelli, 'Containment'.
[4] Moran, *Carceral Geography*; Gill, *Carceral Spaces*; Gill, Conlon, and Moran, 'Carceral'.

The Society of Prisoners: Anglo-French Wars and Incarceration in the Eighteenth Century. Renaud Morieux, Oxford University Press (2019). © Renaud Morieux. DOI: 10.1093/oso/9780198723585.001.0001

Second, the historiography of imperial circulations has focused on phenomena of interconnection, through the study of migrations, trade networks, or the transfer of information, inside and between empires.[5] For the British, Spanish, and Dutch empires, studies of merchants and trade companies have underlined the importance of networks linking the metropolis and the colonies, questioning the very notions of 'centre' and 'peripheries'.[6] Transoceanic migrations, constrained or not, have been studied by historians for some time: the journeys and experiences of indentured servants, convicts, or slaves crossing the Atlantic are well-established subjects of research.[7] But prisoners of war are absent from this picture.[8]

Conversely, studies of prisoners of war, and of incarceration more generally, have not been interested in the movements that precede or follow internment. Journeys *to* the prison meant travelling on board ships and walking dozens of miles on land; likewise, journeys *from* the prison, after being liberated or exchanged, entailed walking to the port, then embarking on a ship, landing, and again walking home, unless one was unfortunate enough to be forcefully recruited by the navy or the army. Between freedom and incarceration there existed a variety of intermediary movements and situations.

What is the right vocabulary with which to characterize their movements? The lexicon of forced migrations raises conceptual problems. Captivity was a secondary experience of displacement, following, for example, impressment in the navy. Considering prisoners of war as unwilling migrants is problematic: these men were not sent to the colonies for the purpose of working in the plantations, or because they had been sentenced to transportation. But, like other coerced migrants, prisoners of war were displaced against their will, which is one justification for treating them comparatively.

Comparing these migrations with other types of transfers of population, constrained or not, such as soldiers, slaves and convicts, raises new questions. Did states invent specific modes of monitoring migratory flows, whose form would have varied with the type of migrants; or, on the contrary, can we identify a sort of administrative routine, which accrued over time, allowing the state to apply the same techniques to various groups? While the bulk of the chapter is concerned with the structure of these regimes of circulation, it is important to examine these structures in conjunction with the displacements and uprootedness that were experienced by prisoners themselves.

While the case of Marc Lates, with whom I opened this chapter, shows that the circulations of prisoners in different parts of the world were intertwined, in the interests of clarity this chapter is organized according to broad geographical units. Instead of starting in Europe, we will begin with the Caribbean—always a site of

---

[5] Glaisyer, 'Networking'.   [6] See, for instance, Hopkins, 'Back'.
[7] Canny, *Europeans*; Ward, *Networks*; Eltis, 'Free'.
[8] See, for example, Bowen, Mancke, and Reid, *Britain's Oceanic Empire*.

conflict during European wars—in order to emphasize the importance of distance, and the autonomy of a regional regime of carceral circulation vis-à-vis the metropolis. As is well known, in the Caribbean, economic tensions increasingly pitted European states and colonial societies against one another: prisoners of war were an important element in this internal conflict. We need to vary the scale of analysis, because it is neither just a regional story, nor simply a transatlantic story either: 'hemispheric' connections with the American mainland, south and north, also mattered. Whether they were exchanged locally or sent to Europe, the prisoners captured in the Caribbean were encouraged actively to contribute to their own freedom, following a model that I will explain in the second section. In the third and final section, the scale of analysis will change: the focus will be placed on the movements of prisoners in Europe—specifically, across the Channel and within Britain and France. Ultimately, the argument that the state worked in comparable ways in Europe and in the Caribbean sides with recent work on European imperialisms in the eighteenth century.[9]

II. The Caribbean Circulatory Regime

The circulation of prisoners of war, just like that of convicts studied by Kerry Ward and Lauren Benton, reveals something about the structure of empires: it provides a way to think about them not as politically and spatially homogeneous, but as discontinuous things.[10] Limiting ourselves to a top-down style of imperial history would be unsatisfactory. Putting the detention and, crucially, the exchange of prisoners of war at the centre of the analysis allows us to underline the importance of local and regional arrangements, as well as the conflicting strategies of governors, local assemblies, admirals, and parishes.

A. The Caribbean Mediterranean: A Crossroads between Empires

Arguments have been made to defend the common geographical identity of a region that has been described, in an allusion to Braudel's masterpiece, as *a Mediterranean that includes the neighbouring American mainland*.[11] The Caribbean indigenous population had been largely wiped out by the beginning of the eighteenth century. Everywhere, slavery was omnipresent. The West Indies suffered from

---

[9] Bayly, *Imperial Meridian*; Stern, *Company-State*; Hodson and Rushforth, 'Absolutely Atlantic'.
[10] Benton, *Search*, pp. 162–221; Ward, *Networks*.
[11] There are almost as many definitions of the region as there are historians of the Caribbean and of America. See, for example, Mulcahy, *Hubs of Empire*; Bassi, 'Beyond'.

structural economic problems: the monoculture of plantations necessitated the importation of basic consumer goods from North America and Europe;[12] the region often suffered from drought, and was hit by tropical storms and hurricanes between July and October—one of the reasons why military operations took place between November and June. The Caribbean had the highest mortality rate for both colonists and slaves in British America.[13] It was also a 'death trap' for soldiers and sailors coming from Europe, who were ill-equipped to face a cocktail of heat, mosquitos, and tropical diseases.[14] Although some of these remarks also apply to the French and Spanish West Indies, these were richer than the British islands, and had more ancient and more solid productive structures.

The Caribbean was a zone of intersection between empires, with multiple overlaps of sovereignty. Frequent invasions caused displacements of populations and resulted in widespread captivity, involving blacks and Creoles as well as Europeans. Furthermore, commercial and migratory networks linked these islands.[15] All these elements make it an ideal place for writing a history of connections and crossings—an approach which has been applied, in the last two decades, to Caribbean 'inhabitants' such as smugglers, soldiers, and European ethnic minorities.[16] Prisoners of war, by contrast with these groups, were not free; but, in common with them, they were not tied to the plantation system either (unlike slaves or indentured servants). Surprisingly, the captivity of prisoners of war in the West Indies has been understudied, despite the revival of interest in mobile populations within the region.[17] While this section focuses on the British West Indies, the analysis takes on the Caribbean as a whole.

The Caribbean was situated at the intersection of important commercial routes. Its waters were, as the governor of Barbados remarked in 1702, 'infested with corsairs and pirates'.[18] In October 1704, out of the 108 ships that left Barbados and the Windward Islands for England, only sixty-one arrived at their destination: the others were captured by French privateers.[19] These predators were much more numerous in the West Indies than in the North Atlantic, illustrating the centrality of this region in imperial economies, as well as the possibilities its geography offered for raiding. For instance, British privateers from the North American colonies and the West Indies took 682 prizes during the War of the Austrian Succession, against only eighty off North American coasts.[20] They targeted Spanish fleets from Veracruz and Portobello, loaded with silver, and French merchant ships carrying sugar from Martinique and Guadeloupe. Spanish privateers from

---

[12] O'Shaughnessy, *Empire Divided*, pp. 58 sq.   [13] Mulcahy, *Hubs*, p. 5.

[14] McNeill, *Mosquito Empires*.   [15] Koot, *Empire*.   [16] Cromwell, 'More than slaves'.

[17] With the exception of Pares, 'Prisoners of war'.

[18] William Roberts to Earl of Nottingham, 10 November 1702, Colonial State Papers (*CSP*), vol. 20, p. 713.

[19] Oliver, *History*, p. lxxiv.

[20] Swanson, *Predators*, pp. 135–6. These figures are probably underestimated, since they are calculated from reports of prizes in the Anglophone colonial press.

Florida and Havana, and French privateers radiating from Martinique, prowled along North American coasts, swooping down on merchant ships from Boston. They also ambushed British ships laden with colonial goods, from Antigua, Jamaica, or Barbados.[21] Warships added a further layer of insecurity to these colonial waters.[22] A French merchant, Arnaud Cadau, wrote from Bordeaux to his Martinique correspondent in February 1745, in a letter which (fittingly) never reached its intended destination: 'the arrival of a ship is regarded here as a sort of miracle.'[23]

The uncertainty of navigation in these waters explains in part why there existed an autonomous Caribbean circulatory regime, which cannot be understood simply by reference to the so-called Atlantic economy. The traffics of prisoners of war in the Caribbean need to be envisaged in their regional economic and environmental perspectives, and not simply through their military dimension. The economic function, and not just the economic consequences, of these exchanges of prisoners of war must be underlined.[24] The Caribbean circulatory system was characterized by three enduring variables. First, this was a zone where commercial exchanges were dense. Second, this was an economy of predation. Indeed, taking part in the business of war was sometimes the only means of employment for the poorest white populations on the islands. Third, privateers also constituted a large proportion of the prisoners *taken* in the Caribbean (as was the case in Europe).

B. Who Should Pay for the Prisoners of War?

1. The Colonists

The arrival of deprived foreigners in colonies increased the pressure on fragile economies. It also exacerbated institutional and financial tensions between the islands, and between the islands and the metropolis. According to the British Crown, the cost of maintaining prisoners of war was part of the defence of the islands, which must weigh on the colonists themselves, because it was in their own interest. This was a well-known rhetoric, used throughout the century, which became a bone of contention between the North American colonies and Britain. The Council of Trade and Plantations (the future Board of Trade) wrote to the governor of Virginia, in 1713, that the colonial assembly must reimburse the sums it had received for the accommodation and sustenance of prisoners of war, 'because these services were solely for their advantage and security, . . . all prisoners of war taken in the Plantations are constantly subsisted at the charge of those

---

[21] Ibid., pp. 143, 149–50.   [22] Ibid., pp. 152, 172–7; Mulcahy, *Hubs*, p. 196.
[23] Arnaud Cadau to Mr Campas, 17 February 1745, TNA, HCA30/239.
[24] The logic of structural mobility within the Caribbean shared some traits with Mediterranean captivity: Fontenay, 'Esclaves'; Hershenzon, *Captive Sea*.

Colonies where they are taken'.[25] The question of the 'duty of protection' that central governments owed colonial populations was raised through the case of prisoners of war.[26]

The different state institutions involved typically attempted to pass this burden on to one another. The issue of prisoners of war was indeed only one of many constitutional and financial vexations that were rocking the British imperial state in the eighteenth century.[27] But it was private individuals who advanced the expenses of lodging, sustaining, clothing, or paying for the transport of the prisoners, and struggled to get their money back. In January 1703, the Council of Jamaica thus voted to reimburse the sums advanced by William Lewis, a churchwarden of Kingston, 'for the relief of French prisoners at 15d. per diem'.[28] Governors often relayed the grievances of colonists on the matter. In 1711, the governor of Antigua wrote to the Council of Trade and Plantations to ask for the monarchy's help, 'this Island bearing the whole charge' of the transport of prisoners to and from there.[29]

Another solution, adopted by the Assembly of Barbados in August 1702, was to make the privateers pay for the detention and transport of the men they had captured, while the prisoners 'taken in vessels of war, shall be maintained at the charge of the public'. The measure was not viable because it penalized the privateers. Captain Alexander Forrister, commanding the *Seaflower* privateer, petitioned the Assembly of Barbados 'praying to be eased of the charge of maintaining upwards of 60 French and Spanish prisoners', which was granted.[30] The Assembly supported the privateers' claims, stating in September 1702 that it was 'too great a charge to lye upon the captors, and would be a great discourage-ment to the fitting out privateers'.[31] Subsequently, the Assembly proposed to limit to fourteen days the period during which privateer owners should maintain their prisoners, after which time 'the country' would take over. The Assembly came up with more detailed proposals on the subject of prisoners. One of the suggestions was to deliver the Spanish prisoners captured by the islanders to consenting planters, who would employ them 'in labour for their provisions, victuals and cloathes until such time as they shall be ordered to be returned by the country in order to their sending them off'. In this way, the prisoners themselves would pay for the cost of their detention.[32] However, the Council of Barbados decided against this measure, on the basis that it was 'contrary to custom for prisoners of war to be

---

[25] Council of Trade and Plantations (CTP) to Lieutenant Governor Spotswood, 20 July 1713, *CSP*, vol. 27, p. 206.

[26] Hoppit, 'Compensating'; Hoppit, 'Compulsion'.

[27] Greene, *Negotiated Authorities*, pp. 43–77.   [28] 28 January 1703, *CSP*, vol. 21, p. 161.

[29] Governor Douglas to CTP, [August?] 1711, ibid., p. 67.

[30] Minutes of Council in Assembly of Barbados, 27 August, 1 September 1702, *CSP*, vol. 20, pp. 566, 574.

[31] Ibid. 8 September 1702, p. 584.   [32] Ibid, p. 585.

made to work'.[33] Even if this was ultimately rejected, the discussion reveals what was in the minds of those concerned: finding a way to make private actors contribute to the cost of imprisonment. The broader question of putting prisoners of war to work, in the plantations or elsewhere, was not settled either.[34]

The recriminations of governors and colonial assemblies focused on the Royal Navy, which was not contributing to the maintenance of prisoners of war.[35] In 1756, for instance, Henry Wilmot, the agent representing the interests of Antigua in London, complained that Admiral Frankland, who commanded the naval forces in the region, refused to have anything to do with prisoners of war. To prevent them from starving, the governor of the Windward Islands, George Thomas, had to supply the prisoners with water, wood, and other necessaries. At the same time, wrote Wilmot, the 'Public of Antigua' had also been 'as a considerable Expence', providing the prisoners 'with house room'. The agent representing Antigua concluded that it was unfair to ask the colonists to bear such a burden, contrasting the situation with that of the metropole:

> As I presume the French Prisoners here in England are supplied with every Necessary at the Public Expense, it seems to me almost of course that they should be so at Antigua, where (after the great expense of building of Barracks, repairing of Fortifications and the additional subsistence of the Regiment there) they are utterly unable to bear any further expense.[36]

The Sick & Wounded Board also refused to be accountable for the detention of prisoners in Antigua, arguing that during the War of the Austrian Succession their office 'had not any Concern with such Prisoners' in the Leeward.[37] This institutional uncertainty did not help matters. In February 1757, the Board thus wrote that the Lords of the Admiralty had 'not been pleased to give us any orders touching proper places for their confinement, or guards for their security; and as we are therefore at a loss to know, whether it is intended this part of the service shall be in our management, or in that of the governors of the respective places'.[38]

The expenses created by the presence of the prisoners of war were a general phenomenon, which weighed on the British imperial state as a whole, inducing specific forms of constrained mobility, both local and regional, as we will now see.

---

[33] Ibid., 9 September 1702, pp. 586–7.   [34] Ch. 4.

[35] On 9 June 1703, the minutes of the Council of Jamaica thus mentioned the '16s. paid to John Mosely, purser of HMS *Windsor*, for 1,476 days' diet of French and Spanish prisoners': *CSP*, vol. 21, p. 493.

[36] Henry Wilmot to Lords Commissioners of the Admiralty (LCA), 18 April 1757, National Maritime Museum, Greenwich (NMM), ADM/E/20. Document communicated by Cori Convertito-Farrar. On Wilmot, see Oliver, *History*, vol. II, p. 273.

[37] Sick & Wounded Board (S&W) to LCA, 1 February 1757, TNA, ADM98/6, fo. 81.

[38] Ibid., 12 February 1757, fo. 87v.

2. Bad Neighbours: The Example of Jamaican Parishes during the American War of Independence

The American War of Independence caused a severe economic crisis in the British West Indies.[39] The isles' severance from North America caused food and supplies shortages and quasi-famine in islands such as Antigua. The war disrupted trade, creating a rise in insurance and freight rates, an increase of import duties, and a decline of slave trade. The production of sugar fell, while the operating costs of plantations grew.[40] Competition with the British navy for ships and sailors, and the prohibition of trade with the North American colonies, badly hit the British Caribbean.[41] Privateering was revived during the war, with new players, North American merchants, who fitted vessels against British and West Indian merchant ships, carried goods and munitions to the rebels, and forced the British admiralty to divide its already scattered and weakened forces between North America and the protection of the West Indies.[42] Manned by a large number of Frenchmen, American privateers damaged the British West Indies to such an extent that the transatlantic trade was almost paralysed.[43] In addition to the dire economic and military situation, Jamaica was not spared by adverse weather conditions: the island was struck by three hurricanes in four years, in 1778, 1780, and 1781, and suffered from starvation in 1779.[44]

In this context, in January 1781 the arrival in Jamaica of hundreds of French and Spanish prisoners from the Leeward Islands provoked complaints. This affair deserves to be narrated in some detail, because it shows the types of burdens the prisoners imposed on the places where they were held, and how local populations attempted to deal with them.[45] On 11 January, the governor's Office ordered the Agent for Prisoners, Thomas Neville, 'to take immediate steps' for the relief of the Spanish prisoners freshly arrived at Montego Bay.[46]

Two days later, governor Edward Barry expressed his opposition to Neville's plan to march the prisoners from Montego Bay to Kingston, which was on the other side of the island (see Fig. 3.1), on the ground of the 'inconvenience & expence' it would cause, as well as the 'alarm it might give the inhabitants'. Instead, governor Barry suggested, a transport ship should send them to 'the nearest & most convenient Spanish port' in the Caribbean.[47] But it was already too late, and the Agent replied ten days later that the prisoners were probably out of reach by then:

---

[39] O'Shaughnessy, *Empire*, pp. 160–7.   [40] Carrington, *British West Indies*, pp. 59–64.
[41] Ibid., pp. 65–6. The insufficient number of soldiers and sailors was an endemic problem for all the colonial empires: Harding, *Amphibious Warfare*, pp. 154–5.
[42] Carrington, *British West Indies*, pp. 91–7.
[43] Ibid., pp. 64–5; O'Shaughnessy, *Empire*, pp. 154–8.
[44] Mulcahy, *Hurricanes*, pp. 108–9; Schwartz, *Sea of Storms*, pp. 93–8.
[45] All the references cited below come from TNA, CO137/80.
[46] Governor Barry's Office to Neville, fo. 98.   [47] Barry to Neville, 13 January 1781, fo. 100.

Fig. 3.1. Carez, *Carte géographique, statistique et historique de la Jamaïque* (1825). Wikimedia.org.

Unfurnished with any particular information where these men may be, it is impossible that I should send a number of horses and carriages from this town to hunt after a number of people, who I suppose according to custom, are paid no attention to in their journey, and are dispersed by this time all over the country.[48]

On 24 January 1781, the governor wrote to the Agent, depicting the 'sickly & miserable' state of the prisoners who had been seen marching from Montego Bay to Kingston. The poor men, he feared, faced certain death 'on the road' if they did not get help.[49] The landowners whose properties the prisoners passed through complained that they did not have the means to support them. The magistrates and vestry of the parish of Montego Bay hence petitioned the governor:

---

[48] Neville to Barry, 23 January 1781, fo. 102.   [49] Ibid., 24 January 1781, fo. 104.

The Spanish prisoners, who are thrown on our hands at a time when we daily experience the severest distress from want of provision, and we have been obliged to support them from a fund which is nearly exhausted, and which was intended for the distressed poor of this place, who are now exposed in the most poignant distress, from which we find ourselves unable to relieve them.[50]

These local officials criticized the externalization of the cost of war to colonial populations. Rather than asking for compensation, the Montego Bay parish officers took a more drastic measure. They decided to solve the problem by making it disappear: by removing the prisoners elsewhere, to the next parish, adopting a manoeuvre reminiscent of the attitude of English parishes who rejected the non-resident poor. The prisoners were escorted, by road, to Kingston, via the neighbouring parish of Trelawny. However, the *Custos* of Trelawny refused to allow the prisoners to pass through their parish, or to maintain them while there.[51] The Montego Bay people were back to square one. Another solution was considered: that of sending the prisoners to Kingston by sea, by using navy ships; but this also failed, owing to the reluctance of the Admiralty to contribute to the scheme. Despite the presence of three men-of-war in the port, none of the ship captains 'would receive a prisoner'.[52]

In the end, the assembly of the inhabitants of Montego Bay parish took the matter in its own hands, and, 'without orders from the magistrates or vestry', secretly walked 112 Spanish prisoners of war to Martha Brae, in Trelawny parish. On 17 February, the clerk of the vestry of Montego Bay exonerated himself from the disaster that would surely ensue:

God knows how the miserable wretches will reach town, or if a fourth of them will not die by the way, if they do, god forgive the person whose duty it was to see this business better conducted, in future I believe the prisoners of war will be allowed to stay here longer than possibly can be avoided, but turned a drift to go to town or get off the Island, just as opportunity offers, or it suits their own conveniency, what may be the consequences or what great evils may arise therefrom I leave you to judge.[53]

Meanwhile, the travails of the Spanish prisoners, tossed around like a wisp of straw on a rolling sea, were not over. On 20 February 1781, the JPs and vestry of St Ann's parish, contiguous and to the east of Trelawny, wrote in their turn to the governor, complaining of the presence of these prisoners, who had been 'sent from

---

[50] Magistrates and vestry of Montego Bay to Barry, 24 January 1781, fo. 106.
[51] *Custos* were high-ranking JPs, representatives of the governor in the parish.
[52] Magistrates and vestry of Montego Bay to Barry, 24 January 1781, fo. 106; Barry to Magistrates and vestry of Montego Bay, 1 February 1781, fo. 108.
[53] Fra.ˢ Mairez to Barry, 17 February 1781, fos. 114–v.

Leeward to this Parish', on their way to Kingston, deprived of all resources, while the parish was neither equipped nor willing to receive these men.[54]

Serious administrative and economic problems, which saw different organs of the state apparatus pull in different directions, resulted in the loss of human lives. The vestry clerk of Montego Bay suggested, 'for the good and safety of the Island ... that the commanders of vessels be enjoined to land no more prisoners here, or that a commissary be appointed to receive and feed them.'[55] Neither suggestion would be paid heed to, at least before the end of the eighteenth century, and thousands of prisoners of war would continue to arrive in Jamaica in the following years and decades.[56] Through their multiple journeys, they paid the price of this maladministration. The sequential displacements of the prisoners are to be explained by the inability of a parish to face on its own the financial costs they entailed.[57]

This type of incident reveals the primacy of an ad-hoc administration, which seems to be at odds with the policies adopted in the metropoles, as we will see. Within Jamaica, the example of the parishes was indicative of a broader institutional problem, which was felt across the British West Indies. Because every institution laid the responsibility of caring for the prisoners of war at each other's door, the ultimate solution was to get rid of them altogether, and exchange them with British prisoners detained in French or Spanish islands, through so-called 'cartels' of exchange.

C. Regional Cartels of Exchange

The logic we identified between Jamaican parishes was also at work, on a larger scale, between the West Indian islands: their governors tried to dispense with the financial burden incurred by accommodating the prisoners of war by passing responsibility onto one another, without ever expressing a sense of collective solidarity. This was partly the result of the institutional structure of the British Empire in America. Despite their dependence on the same sovereign, the British West Indian islands lacked political, economic, and geographical unity, and they had more links with Europe than they did with one another.[58]

This was reflected in the absence of a centralized system for the regional administration of prisoners of war, and in the practice of bilateral exchange

---

[54] William Vox, St Ann, to Governor Dalling, 20 February 1781, fo. 116.

[55] Fra.ˢ Mairez, St James, to Barry, 17 February 1781, fo. 114v.

[56] An act passed in 1801 tried to sort out these problems by placing the sole authority and financial responsibility of the treatment and return of prisoners of war on the commissioners for the prisoners on the island: 'An act for enforcing the instructions' (41 Geo. 3, c19).

[57] The attitude of these Jamaican planters probably reflected their feeling that the navy's demands on them were unfair: O'Shaughnessy, *Empire*, pp. 43–51.

[58] Ibid., pp. 100, 127.

of prisoners of war between islands. West Indian islands commonly exchanged prisoners of war with their neighbours. Between Hispaniola and Jamaica, and between the French and British West Indies, bilateral conventions for the exchange of prisoners of war, or 'cartels', were negotiated between governors.

For example, a cartel was signed in December 1702 between Martinique and Barbados. This agreement only involved these two islands, and excluded English prisoners from Antigua, Nevis, or Jamaica.[59] The practice was already well established by 1705, when the exchange of prisoners between Havana (Hispaniola) and Jamaica was already described as 'customary'.[60] The same year, an agreement was signed between Antigua and Martinique, by which French and English prisoners in the Leeward Islands could not be detained for more than ten days before being exchanged. Using a system of national equivalences we have already encountered, the agreement was extended to the Spaniards, who were to be 'treated as French', and the Dutch, 'as English' (article IV). English prisoners detained in other islands were explicitly excluded from the benefit of the convention (article VII).[61] Throughout the eighteenth century, other cartels were signed, between Florida and South Carolina (1741), Martinique and Barbados (1745), and between the governor of the Leeward Islands and Martinique (1757).[62] They were also negotiated during the American War of Independence, between Jamaica and Cuba, St Domingue, or Curaçao.[63]

The geography of the Caribbean Sea facilitated direct transimperial exchanges between neighbouring islands. There were certainly more communications between islands belonging to different empires—say, between St Kitts and Guadeloupe—than between these two islands and, respectively, Jamaica and St Domingue. Thus, in 1797, it was between the Bahamas and Havana, and not between London and Madrid, that a cartel was settled, following the model of past agreements between Jamaica and Venezuela.[64] In general, cartels built on a well-established tradition of regional conventions, locally negotiated and concluded between West Indian populations.[65]

[59] 'Copy of the cartel settled between Barbados and Martinique for restoring the prisoners on both sides', 11 December 1702, *CSP*, vol. 21, p. 46. It was interrupted in June 1703: *Journal of Assembly of Barbados*, 8 June 1703, ibid., p. 492.

[60] Dyer's report to Board of Trade, 10 August 1705, *Journal of the Board of Trade and Plantations* (*JBTP*), vol. 1, pp. 160–3.

[61] Copy of agreement between Machault, *Intendant* for the French West Indies, concluded in Martinique by Colonel Edward Byam, member of the Council of Antigua, in Lieutenant Governor Johnson to CTP, 6 February 1705, *CSP*, vol. 22, p. 373.

[62] 1 August 1711, *JBTP*, vol. 2, pp. 296–7; 17 November 1741 and 12 June 1745, *JBTP*, vol. 8, pp. 1–4, 166–71; Secrétaire d'Etat de la Marine (SSM) to S&W, 17 February 1747, AN, MAR/B2/331, fo. 543v; 21 April 1757, *JBTP*, vol. 10, p. 317; S&W to LCA, 3 August 1757, TNA, ADM98/6, fo. 204.

[63] Copy of 'Articles of Convention for the Exchange of Prisoners of War', by Dalling, governor of Jamaica to d'Argout, commander of St Domingue, 1 February 1779, NMM, ADM/M/407; Anderson, 'Impact', 247n1.

[64] AGI, Seville, Estado 1, no. 66 (1).

[65] Burns, *History*, pp. 193, 306–8, 323, 338–9, 341, 347–8.

To characterize this system of exchanges, it is possible to think in terms of a kind of regional jurisprudence, which adapted to the international balance of power, but also depended on the relations between colonial authorities and local communities. Agreements of this kind could only take place because of the density of economic exchanges linking French, English, Spanish, and Dutch islands, in peacetime as in war.[66] In 1710, an English mariner, Samuel Brise, described to the Board of Trade how widespread the smuggling trade was, and how problematic the distinction (often drawn by historians) between licit and illicit trade really was: in Curacao (United Provinces), where he had lived for four years, he saw the daily landing of Virginian tobacco; in St Thomas, a Danish free port, he witnessed the coming and going of ships from Carolina; in French Martinique, where he was detained for eighteen months as a prisoner of war, he gazed at ships from Antigua, unloading beef, pork, and flour.[67] The multipolar exchanges of prisoners that took place in the Caribbean were an integral part of these economic activities.

Colonial governors (appointed by the monarchy) were the main players in the negotiation and conclusion of cartels in the West Indies.[68] A project of a general cartel between Britain and France, in 1744, thus stated that governors in 'America' would be ordered to 'come to an agreement' with respect to the general exchange of prisoners.[69] The decision to conclude a global exchange or a man-for-man exchange was entrusted to them.[70] This was a major difference with Europe, where the administration and exchange of prisoners of war was one of the responsibilities of the Sick & Wounded Board. This devolution went so far that in 1711, the Board replied to French officials that they could not 'become acquainted with what happened in the colonies and beyond the tropics', because this fell within the governors' jurisdiction.[71] On the other hand, the prerogative of governors was increasingly contested by another branch of the imperial state, the navy, a phenomenon that exemplified the attempt of the metropole to regain control over its colonies in the last quarter of the eighteenth century. Dissensions about the cartels symbolized this competition that ran within the imperial state.

Some admirals, such as Admiral Rodney, tried to snatch the authority to administer the prisoners from the hands of governors. Diplomacy was not Rodney's strong suit, and he wrote bluntly on 30 December 1780 to Bouillé, Governor-General of the French Windward Islands:

---

[66] Zahedieh, 'Merchants'; Zahedieh, 'A frugal'.   [67] 16 January 1710, *JBTP*, vol. 2, pp. 109–21.
[68] Watson, 'Commission', pp. 252–4.
[69] Article 11, AN, MAR/F2/71. The cartel was never agreed on.
[70] Duke of Nottingham to governor Granville from Barbados, 14 September 1703, *CSP*, vol. 21, p. 685; S&W to LCA, 21 February 1757, TNA, ADM98/6, fos. 96–v.
[71] Lempereur to SSM, 22 April 1711, AN, MAR/B3/195, fo. 120.

All Prisoners of War whatever are under my Direction: No Governor has any Right or will be permitted to interfere in that Disposal. Whatever Cartel Your Excellency may think it necessary to send for the benefit of both Nations during this unhappy War must be address'd to me as Admiral and Commander in Chief of His British Majesty's Fleet in these Seas, no others will be permitted to proceed to any of His Majesty's Islands.[72]

While Rodney no doubt delighted in flexing his muscles and bickering with colonial governors, he was also repeating what two generations of admirals had been saying before him: regional cartels harmed Britain's trade. Thus, Charles Middleton wrote from HMS *Arundel* on 4 December 1759, evoking the damages caused by French privateers to British merchant trade in the West Indies. He denounced

the ill-consequences of a cartel from which all our evils spring. Had no such agreement been made, half the cruisers that are now here would have protected the trade;...the enemy's privateers would have remained in port for want of men, and we should not have had the same prisoners eight or ten times in our jails; nay, many of them returned upon their cruising station before the ship who took them.[73]

British naval commanders were hostile to local conventions of exchange, which had the effect of releasing these men in no time. Instead, they advocated the transportation of prisoners to Europe, to prevent the enemy from manning its ships or strengthening its regiments. Of course, there was a paradox here, since the navy was unwilling to pay for the upkeep of prisoners while complaining about their exchange.

The problems caused by regional exchanges were already well known at the beginning of the eighteenth century. Robert Lowther, the governor of Barbados, explained in 1711 that 'the people of Martinique are the very dregs and refuse of the French Nation, and that they intirely subsist by piracy and privateering, and that they lose nothing when they fall into our hands but some armes and ammunition'. If a cartel was signed, he argued, a privateer taken in week one would be sent back to Martinique on week two, and would be back on the English coasts by week three, 'for they have nothing wherewith to subsist themselves and families but what they take from us, and that therefore it must of necessity happen thus, unless they are sent to Europe'. On the contrary, Lowther continued, by

---

[72] Rodney, *Letter-Books*, p. 119. By contrast, the French placed the prisoners of war business in the hands of General d'Estaing (vice-admiral of the Asian and American seas) alone, which gave them a comparative 'advantage' when transacting with British governors in the West Indies: [Rodney] to Lord George Germain, 4 April 1779, NMM, ADM/M/407.

[73] Laughton, *Barham Papers*, p. 12.

expatriating them to Europe, 'there is not one in 50 can ever return to Martinique, having neither mony nor credit to accomplish it, but must be constrained into the King's service'. In this way, moreover, numerous poor families in Martinique would be ruined, forcing the French state to increase poor rates, and obliging French inhabitants to buy goods from the British themselves. That British prisoners might face retaliation for the harsh way they treated the French did not worry the governor: unlike the French, they had 'either money, credit or friends to support them under such a misfortune, and to replace them in the same way of livelihood'.[74] The Council of Trade and Plantations agreed with the governor and accepted his reasons for refusing a cartel with the French.[75] However, cartels continued to be negotiated and agreed throughout the eighteenth century and beyond.

D. The Flags of Truce System: The Prisoners as Trade Enablers

To facilitate the exchange of prisoners of war and their frictionless circulation across the Caribbean Sea, the flags of truce system, analysed by Richard Pares and Thomas Truxes, was set up.[76] It was invented in order to allow North American merchants to continue trading with French, Spanish, or Dutch Caribbean islands and circumvent parliamentary regulations which, ever since the Molasses Act of 1733, had been trying to force them to buy their colonial goods from the British West Indies.[77] Governors granted flags of truce to merchants, authorizing their ships to circulate on a given journey. It is only after 1761 that the maintaining and transport of prisoners was solely assumed by the Admiralty.[78] The scheme was justified by the transport of prisoners between Caribbean islands by these private ships: to make their voyage worthwhile, the captains of merchant ships argued, they had to be allowed to trade as well. The prisoners thus became the condition of quasi-permanent circulations: they were effectively used as living, breathing passports. This gives us another explanation for the governors' continuing support of regional cartels, despite their limitations: prisoners on the move were a vital cog in the machinery of Caribbean trade.

Ships from Rhode Island and New England smuggled with Martinique and the Dutch island of St Eustatius, where they sold construction wood and bought rum, under the pretext of transporting prisoners.[79] On 31 January 1747, the *Endeavour*, for example, left New York for Cap Français (St Domingue), with a flag of truce and twelve prisoners on board. At the height of the War of the Austrian

---

[74] Lowther to CTP, 20 August 1711, *CSP*, vol. 26, pp. 73–4.
[75] CTP to Lowther, 22 November 1711, ibid., p. 161.
[76] Pares, *War*, pp. 446–55; Truxes, *Defying Empire*, ch. 5. See also Pares, *Yankees*.
[77] O'Shaughnessy, *Empire*, pp. 62–9.   [78] Anderson, 'Impact', pp. 246–8.
[79] Board of Trade, 6 December 1750: *JBTP*, vol. 9, pp. 126–46 (https://www.british-history.ac.uk/jrnl-trade-plantations/vol9).

Succession, the ship was carrying a cargo of fish, flour, beef, and beer, which was unloaded in the French island. On its way back, it was loaded with nine British prisoners and thirty-six casks of sugar, thirty-six of molasses and 200 sugarloaves, to be sold on in New York.[80] The traffic of prisoners of war was thus deeply entwined with the smuggling trade, and just as the captains forged papers, kept false registers and false clearances, they did not much care whether the prisoners were 'really' exchanged, or even existed at all. What they cared about was to have a prisoner on board, whose presence would serve as a safe-conduct during their journey. Some captains 'imported' prisoners from neighbouring colonies when there were none on their own island.[81] Other ship-owners 'hired' prisoners for the duration of the trip, and 'during their absence [they] took care of their wives and families'.[82] In Pennsylvania, the governor issued blank flags of truce, on which 'imaginary French names were written', and then sold them to the other colonies.[83] The governor of Bermuda would provide every vessel leaving the island, whatever its destination, with a French prisoner of war, to be protected in case of an encounter with a French privateer.[84] This practice was generalized to the entirety of the West Indies during the Seven Years' War.[85]

While colonial governors were actively contributing to these traffics, it is no surprise that navy admirals objected to them. Aware that illicit trade was one of the raisons d'être of the recourse to flags of truce by North American merchants, British admirals did their best to tighten the screw on their use. Admiral Charles Knowles, who had fought a great number of battles in the West Indies during the War of Jenkins' Ear, testified before the Board of Trade, on 4 December 1750:

> [He]... said that the Northern colonies used to buy French prisoners at a great price one of another, for a pretence to go to the French Islands, that he had at length been obliged to threaten the French Governors that he would send to England all French prisoners, if they delivered any English to the Northern flags of truce.[86]

Some cartels adopted during the American War of Independence also made it obligatory for flags of truce to carry at least a certain number of prisoners to be exchanged, allocated a maximum number of prisoners per ton, and limited the length of their stay in the port of arrival.[87] This practice was probably modelled on the laws of slavery and the Royal African Company's regulations, which prevented

[80] Before arriving in New York, the ship was intercepted by a British man-of-war and brought to Boston, where the judge of the Admiralty acquitted its captain, for reasons that were not specified: Session of 7 December 1750, *JBTP*, vol. 9, pp. 126–46.

[81] Pares, *War*, p. 448.   [82] Ibid.   [83] Ibid.   [84] Ibid., p. 449.

[85] Ibid., pp. 449–51.   [86] *JBTP*, vol. 9, pp. 126–46.

[87] Copy of 'Articles of Convention for the Exchange of Prisoners of War', by governor of Jamaica to commander of St Domingue, 1 February 1779, article 8, NMM, ADM/M/407.

the use of slaves as covers for smuggling.[88] This shows the transfer of experience from one institution of forced mobility to another.

While the roots of the problem had been identified ever since the inception of flags of truce, abuses continued until the end of the century. During the American War of Independence, smuggling between West Indian planters and North American rebels thrived, again with the help of colonial governors.[89] One striking example is that of Eliphalet Fitch, a Boston merchant settled in Kingston (Jamaica), who set up from September 1781, in concert with Francisco de Miranda, the Spanish aide-de-camp of the Cuba commander-in-chief, 'a smuggling operation of war material' (linen, cotton, cordage, and sailcloth) and slaves between Jamaica and Cuba, using the exchange of fictitious Spanish prisoners of war as a cover.[90]

The system survived for so long because it was the product of a fruitful encounter between the economic advantages of the colonial populations, and the military concerns of the imperial states. British governors closed their eyes to these illicit practices because the collaboration of colonists was too important to the war effort, and the British monarchy could not afford to alienate them.[91] They were certainly aware that merchants and contractors were losing no opportunity to make money out of the business of trafficking prisoners of war: overcharging the Admiralty for hiring their ships, victualling the prisoners, or renting out detention facilities, in addition to smuggling with the enemy. But there were also very good reasons for letting this continue. Governors also used the transit of prisoners of war between Caribbean islands for strategic purposes. Transport ship captains or returned prisoners could bring back precious knowledge about the moves of enemy squadrons or the state of their fortifications, in addition to supplies in times of scarcity. This practice continued throughout the period.[92]

The flags of truce system survived for so long because the British state did not have the means of sending big armies and navies across the Atlantic; it simply could not wage a massive war overseas without relying on colonial merchants.

III. Atlantic Crossings

So far, I have not mentioned an obvious solution to these troubles caused by the circulations of prisoners of war, which would have been to detain them locally.

---

[88] O'Malley, *Final Passages*, ch. 4 and 6; Zahedieh, 'Merchants', p. 591.

[89] Carrington, *British West Indies*, pp. 67–73.

[90] Miranda was initially sent to Jamaica to agree a cartel for the exchange of Spanish prisoners of war there against the English at Havana: Parry, 'Eliphalet Fitch', pp. 87–8. On this, see also Robertson, *Francisco de Miranda*, pp. 235–9.

[91] Just like the French government encouraged English 'smogleurs' to come to Boulogne or Dunkirk: Morieux, *Channel*, pp. 259–68.

[92] See, for example, CTP to Governor Johnson (Nevis), 26 April 1705, *CSP*, vol. 22, p. 507; Extract of Governor Burt to Lord George Germain, 2 November 1778, NMM, ADM/M/407.

This was precisely the root of the matter: for reasons that I will now explain, the detention facilities in the West Indies were neither sufficient nor satisfactory. Two solutions existed to solve this problem: to exchange the prisoners locally, or to send them to Europe—whether their home was across the Atlantic or not. The two solutions were adopted concurrently for most of the century,[93] but during the American War of Independence, the idea of transporting the prisoners to Europe was increasingly seen as a more viable alternative.

A. Local Detention or Transportation to Europe?
The American War of Independence

In February 1779, the Marquis de Bouillé, governor of the French West Indies, received the worrying information that close to 400 French prisoners were detained in Antigua and St Christopher, and that several of them 'suffered greatly from their detention, and would undoubtedly perish if they were not exchanged'.[94] This assessment was soon confirmed by British officials. In May 1779, Lord George Germain, secretary of state for the American Department, stated that 'Great Inconveniencies appear to have already happened in the West India Islands from the want of places of Confinement for Prisoners taken at Sea, & brought in there'.[95] This was certainly an understatement of the crisis, as we will now see by looking at one island in particular: Jamaica.

Bearing in mind that Jamaica was the wealthiest British island, and better equipped for holding prisoners, the situation elsewhere would, if anything, have been worse. The local detention of prisoners of war presented a number of issues. Local populations resented being asked to contribute to their support. The fear of physical, moral, and political contagion of prisoners of war was particularly intense in a colonial context—especially in a tropical climate, where epidemics were a common experience. In February 1779, the governor of Jamaica, John Dalling, wrote to Germain that he had been 'at a great loss for places of security for French Prisoners' in the island. Not only had the hospital at Greenwich 'burnt down', but the 'Barracks of the Town of Kingston', which had previously been used for that purpose, were no longer an option:

> From their being situated in the heart of the Town the people considering it as a great nuisance and their fears in these climes of contagious disorders spreading in consequence of the situation of their Barracks, and late Violences, even to Murder, having been committed in the Streets for want as they suppose of

---

[93] Anderson, 'Impact', pp. 247–8.
[94] Extracts of letters to Bouillé regarding prisoners' exchange, 18 February 1779, AN, MAR/F2/71.
[95] Copy of Germain to LCA, 29 May 1779, NMM, ADM/M/407.

their usual military force, I have not been able neither could I wish to endeavour that the Prisoners should remain longer in them.[96]

By the end of 1782, as Kingston was flooded with sick soldiers and prisoners of war, the grievances of the local populations led the grand jury of the county of Surrey, where Kingston was located, to investigate on the matter of places of detention. 'The several hospital prisons, barracks, ... and the houses taken up by the commissary of prisoners of war, in the said town of Kingston' were visited. The magistrates concluded that the great number of the sick in these places, who were then about 1,500, presented a great risk of 'an epidemical disorder', especially since these places were 'situated in almost every quarter of the town'. Consequently, they advised that 'the troops and prisoners of war ought to be immediately removed from the town of Kingston; and that hospital ships ought to be provided, for the immediate reception of the sick and convalescent'.[97] Accommodating prisoners of war in the 'Gaols in this Country' was not an option either, as coexistence risked facilitating 'communication' between 'the wretched Inhabitants' of the jails and prisoners of war.[98]

On the other hand, from the perspective of the British imperial state, using existing facilities presented the advantage of dropping the financial burden of the prisoners' maintenance upon local populations. But as the war wore on, the cost of the detention of the prisoners spiralled, increasing the pressure on the state. In August–September 1780, the Sick & Wounded Board complained that the cost of maintaining French, Spanish, Dutch, and American prisoners 'on the Continent, and in the Islands [was] extremely heavy' and became 'a heavy Charge upon the Public'.[99] As Britain held many more prisoners than its enemies, an exchange was impossible.[100] It should not surprise us that the Board suggested

the sending to Europe from time to time, as often as could be, such surpluses of Prisoners, by which means though their Passage would form a very considerable Article of Expence, the saving between that, and the maintaining them for a length of time on those Islands may be considerable too.[101]

---

[96] Extract of Dalling to Germain, 27 February 1779, ibid.
[97] Presentment to the grand jury of the Surrey Assize court, 20, 29 November 1782, *Journals of the Assembly of Jamaica* (*JAJ*), vol. VII, pp. 509–10, 518–19.
[98] Extract of Dalling to Germain, 27 February 1779, NMM, ADM/M/407. In 1770, there were only three penal institutions on the island, i.e. the county goals in Spanish Town, Kingston, and Savanna La Mar. By 1780, this number had risen to at least twelve, but these buildings remained small by comparison with the reformed prisons built in Britain at the same time: Paton, *No Bond*, pp. 19, 22, 24–5.
[99] S&W to LCA, 21 August, TNA, ADM98/13, fo. 33v.
[100] S&W to LCA, 7 September 1780, ibid., fo. 37.
[101] S&W to LCA, 7 September 1780, ibid., fo. 37.

Given the Caribbean detention conundrum, transferring the prisoners to Europe made sense. These structural problems were exposed even more vividly when a combination of natural and human disasters hit the islands, laying bare the paucity of prison facilities. In normal times, building durable prisons in the Caribbean was already a challenge. The tropical climate damaged wooden fences, but building brick walls was expensive.[102] In Barbados, contemporary estimates put the number of the dead following the terrible hurricane of October 1780 at 6,500.[103] There were no shelters for prisoners of war and the standing sick in December, leading the governor to observe: 'our prisons being open it will be impossible to Guard Prisoners of War in this Island, I therefore hope they be sent to the other Islands.'[104] In January 1781, he noted with relief that thanks to the presence of British troops and militia units, order had been maintained, even though there were '70,000 negroes and 800 Prisoners of war loose in the Country during our late disaster'.[105]

In an already precarious situation, an unexpected British victory paradoxically added salt to the wounds of the islanders. The famous victory of Admiral Rodney against a large French fleet at the Battle of the Saintes, between Guadeloupe and Dominica (9–12 April 1782), is remembered because the French commander, Admiral de Grasse, was captured and triumphantly taken to Britain, and for its tactical innovations (it is then that the 'breaking of the line' tactic might have been invented). But standard accounts of the war only mention in passing that, alongside the French admiral, the British navy took five French ships of the line, and another four a week later.[106] What happened to the crews of these ships?

According to Rodney's estimate, the navy took around 6,000 French prisoners of war during these engagements.[107] While he might have slightly exaggerated the figure, there is no doubt that his success made the accommodation of this considerable number of men a matter of urgency. Rodney was immediately confronted with the crowded conditions of the scarce prison facilities in the British West Indies. Five thousand French prisoners were kept for a time on board the ships anchored in Port-Royal (Jamaica). Five weeks after the battle, with the fear of epidemics, as always, in the background, Rodney urged the administrative authorities in Jamaica to provide places for the detention of these people. At that time, the facilities for confining prisoners of war could only hold 700 men, themselves in very unsatisfactory conditions.[108]

---

[102] 'An Estimate of work necessary to be done in fitting up the present Bath House for the reception of the French Prisoners', in Mr Stephen's, 2 June 1779, NMM, ADM/M/407.

[103] Rodney to Vice Admiral Sir Peter Parker, 18 December 1780, in Rodney, *Letter-Books*, p. 101.

[104] Governor James Cunningham to Rodney, 7 December 1780, ibid., p. 88.

[105] Governor James Cunningham to Lord Germain, 22 January 1781, quoted in Mulcahy, *Hurricanes*, p. 99. The figure of 800 prisoners refers to the Spanish prisoners, whose prison in Bridgetown had been destroyed by the storm of 1780: Schwartz, *Sea of Storms*, p. 123.

[106] Dull, *French Navy*, pp. 283–4; Gardiner, *Navies*, pp. 123–7.

[107] HMS *Formidable*, at sea, 28 April 1782, in Laughton, *Barham Papers*, vol. II, p. 282.

[108] Rodney to Stephens, 18 May 1782, *Letter-Books*, vol. II, p. 413.

Rodney refused to exchange the French soldiers locally, since they were crucial to the French war effort in the region, and he preferred to send them to Europe.[109] He ordered every ship of war and every merchant ship bound for Britain to load a cargo of prisoners, 'by which means care will be taken that not one single French soldier shall remain in the island of Jamaica'.[110] The Board concurred, and they wrote to the Lords of the Admiralty on 28 June 1782 that 4,000 French prisoners of war taken by Rodney had been carried to Jamaica, that they 'were provided for in Tents that 750 were to be sent home in the Kings Ships, 500 in Merchant Ships and 1,000 in Naval Transports'.[111]

The imprisonment crisis that hit Jamaica during the American War of Independence could not be solved. While in principle all parties agreed that long-term detention in the West Indies was far from an ideal solution, in practice, financial pressures got in the way of political, sanitary, and military expediencies, forcing thousands of French prisoners of war to rot in makeshift places of detention.[112] On 6 December 1782, Admiral Joshua Rowley, commander-in-chief at Jamaica, wrote a letter to the lieutenant-governor of the island, in which he confessed his impotence:

I have used every means in my power to reduce the number of prisoners from the town of Kingston, by sending as many as possible to Europe in the transports and other vessels, which I will continue to do at every opportunity. I have long since given directions for the commissary to hire a number of vessels for the same purpose, which he has not been able to do; it is, therefore, out of my power at present to remedy the evil complained of; which I much wish to have done, as I conceive the prisoners would be better and more secure when afloat.[113]

An analysis of the detention and forced mobility of prisoners of war only through disputes over finance risks overlooking the consequences for those most directly affected—the prisoners themselves. Treated like commodities, transferred from ship to port, from a port to a hospital, and then piled under tents, the prisoners bore a heavy burden. The eighteenth-century French and British monarchies collected data as a means to exert their sovereignty over vast expanses of land and disparate collections of people. Thousands of tables and statistics were patiently gathered by state bureaucrats. 'Marine F2/94' is a register held in the Archives Nationales in Paris. Composed in 1791 to deliver death certificates to the families of deceased sailors,[114] it lists the names of the French prisoners who died

---

[109] See Anderson, 'The impact'.   [110] Ibid.

[111] S&W to LCA, 28 June 1782, TNA, ADM98/14, fo. 103v.

[112] Bills had been drawn upon the S&W for £32,176 for the subsistence of the prisoners of war in Jamaica on Michaelmas Quarter 1782, and £45,924 in Christmas Quarter 1782: S&W to LCA, 15 April 1782, ibid., fo. 175v.

[113] Rowley to Lieutenant-Governor of Jamaica, 6 December 1782: JAJ, vol. 7, 7 December 1782, p. 526.

[114] As noted by Le Goff, who also subjects the document to internal criticism: 'Impact', p. 105.

anywhere in the world between 1770 to 1791, with their rank, the name of the ship in which they were taken, the date of their death, and their place of detention.[115] In total, the register contains 3,129 names for the period between 1778 and 1783, when France was at war with Britain. Of these, 1,873 prisoners died in the West Indies; in Antigua, Barbados, Bermuda, Saint-Lucia, or Saint-Christopher. But the greatest death trap, by far, was Jamaica: 1,638 Frenchmen died there between 1778 and 1783. The number of fatalities per year steadily increased from 1781 onwards: seven men died in Jamaica in 1778, forty-five in 1780, 277 in 1781, 909 in 1782, and 353 in 1783. One can hypothesize that the peak in 1782 was correlated to the Victory of the Saintes (April 1782). As shown on chart 3.1, the monthly break-down of these fatalities for 1782 (chart 3.1) shows that they increased in propor-tion with overcrowding. The worries that the Kingston local magistrates had over the health hazard presented by the prisoners, in November–December 1782, were justified. From May to December 1782, prisoners were dying in high numbers: on average 106 per month. The Sick & Wounded letter quoted above, dated 28 June 1782, gave the figure of 4,000 Frenchmen being carried to Jamaica following the Saintes. A high estimate would assume that all the prisoners (856) who died in Jamaica between May and December 1782 had been captured at the Saintes.[116] The situation only worsened in the following months. By the end of 1782, the British navy was getting the upper hand in the Caribbean, capturing American, French, and Spanish privateers and transport vessels, making hundreds of prison-ers in the process.[117]

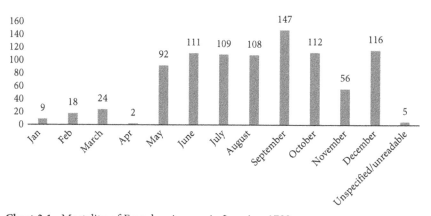

Chart 3.1. Mortality of French prisoners in Jamaica, 1782.

---

[115] 'Etat Civil. Prisonniers de Guerre décédés de 1770 à 1791. A à Z', AN, F2/94.
[116] I have also allocated the five unspecified names to the same group.
[117] See 'An Account of vessels taken and destroyed . . . , between the 14th of December, 1782, and the 2d of February, 1783', *The Remembrancer* (1783), p. 305. The peak in March 1783 was perhaps caused

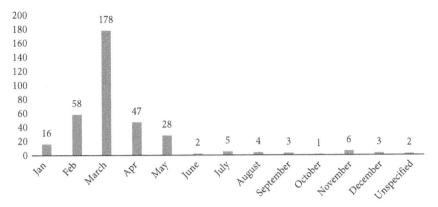

Chart 3.2. Mortality of French prisoners in Jamaica, 1783.

Let us compare these figures with those compiled after the Seven Years' War by the British Office for the Exchange of Prisoners of War, to settle reciprocal debts after the war. This document, drawn up in 1764, lists the French prisoners who died in prison in Britain and its colonies during the war. In total, 10,777 names are given.[118] The vast majority of French prisoners died in Britain during the Seven Years' War.[119] But a substantial number died outside Europe, for instance, in Canada (1,169) and in the West Indies (707). These figures are considerably smaller than during the American War of Independence. For instance, 581 died in Jamaica during the Seven Years' War, against 1,262 in 1782–3. This difference can be explained in several ways. The scale of the conflict certainly intensified in the region in the 1770s–80s, which naturally would have increased the sheer number of prisoners. But this explanation is not sufficient to account for such a difference. Prisoners of war in the West Indies died in higher numbers because they stayed for longer periods of time in the islands. In the Caribbean, the exchange of prisoners of war was paralysed during the American War of Independence, in part because regional cartels were less frequent. More prisoners of war were trapped in these islands, in worse conditions. The same cause had produced the same effect in Britain during the Seven Years' War.[120]

by the capture of a Spanish frigate, the *Santa Catalina*, on 17 February 1783: Extract of Rear-Admiral Rowley to Mr Stephens, 10 February 1783, ibid.

---

[118] AN, F2/93.
[119] For a compared analysis of the mortality of French prisoners in Britain between 1744 and 1783, see Le Goff, 'Impact'.
[120] Ibid.

This high mortality led the British government to explore alternative solutions. One of them was to kill two birds with one stone, by releasing the prisoners while putting them to good use.

B. Manning Enemy Ships

The fate of the prisoners in Jamaica who were cast from parish to parish during the American War of Independence is paradigmatic of the experience of forced migration, in the West Indies and in Europe. Being a prisoner of war implied being on the move for weeks, sometimes months. States could turn a financial burden into a resource, by recruiting the prisoners in military or commercial fleets. The prisoners were aware of this, and they often described their dreadful conditions of detention as having pressured them to face an impossible choice: either to die in hell-holes, or to serve on board the enemies' ships.

In 1703, 300 English prisoners in Martinique petitioned Queen Anne, stating that they had been incarcerated for sixteen months in the island. They stated that, out of sheer misery, the majority of the 1,500 English prisoners who had passed through the French island during that period had joined the French navy, and converted to Catholicism.[121] Although it is difficult to measure, the same phenomenon continued to take place throughout the century, in colonial waters as well as in Europe.

During the American War of Independence, Britain resorted once again to recruiting prisoners of war to serve in its navy and army, and fight off the rising tide of its enemies. On 30 June 1778, a Frenchman named Gaullier Junior sent eight densely written pages to his parents in Bordeaux, dated from Grande Terre (Guadeloupe). He narrated what had happened to him since he had last sent them news, more than a year earlier. His parents never read this letter, because the ship carrying it to Europe, the *Duc de Mouchy*, was intercepted and its papers confiscated.[122] The document is an example of the so-called 'Prize Papers', a treasure of an archive that has only recently drawn the attention of historians.[123] This huge collection, which covers the period 1592–1855, is part of the High Court of Admiralty archives, held at the National Archives in Kew. It is made up of all the documents and 'things' that the British navy and British privateers captured on board enemy ships: playing cards, parrot feathers, seaweed, and musical sheets, as well as innumerable family letters.[124] According to his epistolary account, Gaullier had left New England on 3 May 1777, presumably on board an American

---

[121] 'H.M. subjects prisoners at Martinique to the Queen', 26 June 1704, *CSP*, vol. 22, p. 185.
[122] TNA, HCA32/313.
[123] See Cullen, Shovlin, and Truxes, *Bordeaux-Dublin Letters*.
[124] *Prize Papers Online 1: American Revolutionary War and Fourth Anglo-Dutch War* (Brill, Leiden, and Boston: 2014) (http://primarysources.brillonline.com/browse/prize-papers-part-1-online).

ship, and had been captured by British vessels blocking the mouth of the River of Philadelphia' (the Lower Delaware), on 2 June 1777. He was detained in one of these vessels for fourteen days, and then sent to the 'Nouvelle Iorque' (New York), where General Admiral Howe, British Commander in Chief in North America, 'distributed us in several ships to be detained Prisoner'.[125] Deprived of everything, and fearing that he would 'starve to death' in this prison-ship, Gaullier volunteered to serve as a sailor in one of the British vessels anchored in New York. His conditions of living were not better there, and he caught lice and scabies; after four and a half months of this regime, he deserted. He was captured again and put in prison in New York. The rest of his adventures cannot be told in great detail; suffice to say that he reached Martinique on 2 March 1778. This example is typical of the choices made by prisoners who, as a last resort, would trade one form of incarceration for another. The dreadful conditions of detention in the West Indies certainly motivated the prisoners to switch sides. A French officer, Chevalier St Our, wrote in June 1781 that, in Kingston, the prison where he was held captive had been built for 400 inmates, but was inhabited by more than twice this number.[126] St Our rhetorically asked why these prisoners were left for so long 'at the charge of the colony'. Was it 'for the pleasure of making these unfortunate men suffer and die, or to force them to give up the service of their king and *patrie*'?[127]

Instead of considering imprisonment and forced mobility as two opposites, it is crucial to understand that these two phenomena were often intertwined. In the Caribbean, some prisoners were never landed: they were detained on board moving prisons. Many British sailors returning from captivity testified that they had been kept on board the French and Dutch ships of war that had captured them, and forced to work among the captor's crew. In May 1781, John Watson, an English mate of a Bristol brig, was captured and embarked on board the *Diadem*, a seventy-four-gun ship commanded by the Comte de Monteclerc; despite his ill health, he was 'seized upon the capstan and beat in the most cruel manner, with sticks, on the body and soles of the feet, till he was quite insensible; after which he was ... put into irons, without any reason but that of refusing to work'.[128] Another sailor, William Harvey, testified that he had been 'eight months a prisoner on board the Sovereign', which sailed from Martinique on 8 April 1781, and engaged in action at the Battles of Fort Royal (29 April 1781), and Saint Kitts (25–6 January 1782)—all the while, Harvey was on board, presumably to help man the vessel against his own compatriots.[129]

---

[125] TNA, HCA32/313.   [126] St Our, 10 June 1781, TNA, CO137/80, fos. 241–v.
[127] Ibid., fos. 242v.
[128] According to the testimony of another English prisoner, John Hay, late gunner of the sloop Antigua: Laughton, *Barham Papers*, vol. I, p. 186.
[129] Ibid., pp. 186–7.

The use of prisoners as sailors must be placed in the context of the competition for skilled sailors, which was even more intense in wartime than in peacetime. Military navies and privateers competed for the same people, while fishing-boats and merchant captains struggled to man their vessels. The excess death rate in the tropics and the high probability of being captured increased the challenge for merchant ships returning to Europe. Sailors and soldiers were a rare resource, too precious to be left to languish in prison. But while the forced labour and impressment of prisoners of war was forbidden, there were ways around this. Although the enlistment of prisoners on board ships of war to serve against their own sovereign was forbidden, employing them in a merchant ship was not. The needs of the merchants and those of the prisoners of war were thus perfectly compatible. The merchants were badly in need of sailors, and Caribbean jails were overcrowded with starving sailors who dreamt of returning home.

Using prisoners of war to man merchant ships had already been resorted to in the 1740s, and probably before. In November 1744, the Lords of the Admiralty wrote to the Sick & Wounded Board that

> several Masters of Merchant Ships lately come from Jamaica under Convoy of His Majesty's ship the York, that not being able to Man their Ships with His Majesty's Subjects, Governor Trelawney did, on their application to him, indulge them with a Number of French & Spanish Prisoners to compleat their Complements.

When the ships arrived in Portsmouth, the Agent for the Prisoners there disregarded the agreement negotiated in Jamaica, and put these men in prison. In contrast, the Lords of the Admiralty insisted that 'the said French & Spanish Prisoners be returned to the Masters, to enable them to Navigate their Ships to the respective Ports where they are to unload'.[130] As this exchange testifies, the status of these prisoners was uncertain: after being released from their jails and working alongside British sailors, they were back to square one. The Lords of the Admiralty contested their imprisonment because it damaged the interests of the merchants, not because the prisoners had been wronged. It was not clear either whether the prisoners had willingly taken on the merchants' offer, or whether they had been coerced.

By the beginning of the Seven Years' War, the use of prisoners by merchant captains to man their ships was normal, as explained by a captain who testified in front of the Board in September 1756, accompanied by two French prisoners he had brought to England from Antigua. The commissioners summarized the interview as follows:

[130] LCA to S&W, 29 November 1744, NMM, ADM/M/389, no. 273.

[He] acquainted Us, that being in want of hands to Navigate her to England, he applied to the Commanding Officer of the Troops there, for two of the Prisoners then on the said Island, for that purpose, who told him, that if he could agree with the People, and they would go, he would give an Order to the Officer of the Guard to deliver them, which he did accordingly.[131]

The prisoners had been tempted to join these British merchant crews by the dual attraction of being contracted for their wages, and being promised 'their Liberty' on arrival. But the Board was not sure whether such a promise made in Antigua bound the Admiralty or not. The prisoners volunteered for these voyages, full of hope that their captivity would reach its end once they had fulfilled their part of the bargain, but nothing was less certain. In the end, much depended on the decisions of the ship captain in whose hands they had placed their fate.

During the American War of Independence, the British navy, in agreement with the Admiralty, officially encouraged the captains of merchant ships convoyed across the Atlantic to take prisoners with them.[132] Consequently, the practice became more systematic, in response to the shortage of manpower that hit the British fleet more generally. The destiny that awaited these men when they landed in British or Irish ports was never straightforward. In 1779, several cases of French or Spanish prisoners released from hulks or prisons in North America and the West Indies were discussed by the Admiralty. In particular, twelve French prisoners who had been released from a prison ship in New York to help British transport ships to cross the Atlantic were, on arrival, delivered up to the Agent for Prisoners in Ireland. This struck the Board as profoundly shocking. Using a language we have encountered before, these officials insisted that a 'reasonable gratification' be given to these men 'for the Service they have rendered the Owners' of the transport ships. Moreover, these prisoners had been 'compelled to come', 'obliged to Navigate English Ships to Europe': they should 'be paid for their labour' and released forthwith, in preference. The attitude of the masters of the transports showed their 'injustice and inhumanity' towards 'many poor people of whose services they had been availed when no other Men were to be had'.[133] Similar orders were given in June 1779 to discharge French prisoners who had helped navigating merchant ships that came from Antigua or Jamaica under convoy.[134] In the following years, the practice of releasing these prisoners by preference became ingrained.[135] Enlisting in the enemy's merchant fleet had

---

[131] S&W to LCA, 1 October 1756, TNA, ADM98/5, fos. 222–v.

[132] Rodney to Campbell, 23 May 1782, *Letter-Books*, vol. I, p. 429.

[133] S&W to LCA, 15 May 1779, TNA, ADM98/12, fo. 9. The prisoners were released: LCA to S&W, 3 June 1779, NMM, ADM/M/407.

[134] LCA to S&W, 10, 23 June 1779, NMM, ADM/M/407.

[135] S&W to LCA, 9 October 1781, TNA, ADM98/13, fo. 240; S&W to LCA, 26 August 1782, ADM98/14, fos. 121v–122.

become a way to earn one's freedom, according to a logic that rewarded good behaviour on the part of the prisoners. Conversely, Admiralty officials now came to the rescue of the prisoners who had been the victims of a breach of faith on the part of shipmasters. Disrespecting a promise, even one made to a prisoner of war, became unacceptable.

It was, however, always possible for unscrupulous ship captains to abuse their position of power and make empty promises. This was shown in one classic legal decision, the 'Case of Three Spanish Sailors', discussed by William Blackstone.[136] Blackstone's interpretation remains famous because he used this case to argue that an alien enemy or a prisoner of war had no right to be set at liberty by appealing to habeas corpus; this is also the reason why this case was so hotly debated post-9/11, in the context of the discussion over the rights of 'unlawful enemy combatants' detained in Guantanamo.[137] What really happened to these sailors is never mentioned in legal history textbooks. Blackstone acknowledged that 'the story, as related by them, is not much to the credit' of the captain who had abused them, and added that the prisoners 'may find some relief from the Board of Admiralty'.[138] The three prisoners, who were in reality like the three musketeers, *four* (three Spaniards and one Frenchman), petitioned the Lords of the Admiralty in October 1779. This is the story they told. After being captured by a British man of war, they had been carried over to Jamaica:

> That whilst your Memorialists and many others were detained in prison at Kingston a scarcity of seamen prevailing in the English Fleet it was signified to them that such of them as chose to enter as Seamen on board the Fleet then bound to England might be at liberty so to do and on their arrival in England be at liberty to go to their respective homes.[139]

Alongside more than a hundred French and Spanish seamen also in prison, they 'entered on board Sundry Ships performed the Voyage and arrived therein in England'. But unlike all the other sailors in a similar situation, the petitioners had not been paid by the captain, Hannibal Lush, and on arrival in the Thames they were put on board the *Nightingale*, a hospital ship, where they were detained as prisoners of war. The prisoners further explained that they had been given the choice, back in Kingston, to board a French cartel ship that would have transported them to a French Caribbean island. But, in the hope that they would 'be nearer their Native Country if they returned with the Fleet to England', they had

[136] Blackstone, *Reports of Cases*, 1324.

[137] Hamburger, 'Beyond protection', p. 1891; Halliday, *Habeas Corpus*; Boumediene v Bush.

[138] Blackstone, *Reports of Cases*, 1324; Hamburger, 'Beyond protection', p. 1864.

[139] 'The humble Memorial and Petition of John Baptista Fouquerit Joseph Martain Antonio Joze and Blas Feron now detained as Prisoners of War on board the Nightingale Tender', in LCA to S&W, 21 October 1779, NMM, ADM/M/409.

volunteered to serve in Lush's merchant ship.[140] To the Lords of the Admiralty's request for more details,[141] the Board explained that no promise had been made to the prisoners, in Jamaica, to be released on arrival: they 'were taken out of Prison at Jamaica to assist English Merchant Ships, to proceed to England, and there to be delivered as Prisoners'. It was bad luck, concluded the Board, that the prisoners had not stayed in Jamaica: instead of being the victims of a fool's game, they would already have been free. Instead, they would have to be sent 'as Prisoners on board the Security Prison Ship in the Medway'.[142]

Offering to work under the command of an enemy merchant captain, the prisoners did their best with the bad hand they had been dealt: they got out of prison, and avoided the accusation of betrayal. The prisoners were able to seize these opportunities because they possessed skills that were rare and valuable, especially in the Caribbean context. While entrusting enemy prisoners to work alongside free subjects on board the ships might seem surprising, the early modern economy offers many comparable examples, such as the plantation, where slaves could work alongside freedmen and indentured servants. The prisoners of war we have just encountered were in a comparatively better situation than slaves: they had chosen the lesser of two evils by embarking on merchant ships, were paid to work, and worked to be freed.

Any prisoner captured at sea remained on board the ship that had captured them for days, if not weeks or months. If we look at these individual trajectories, it appears that incarceration was often just one episode in much more complex itineraries. As they moved from one place to another, prisoners switched allegiances, while their status was also updated, according to a logic that has been analysed by Rebecca Scott.[143] As these peregrinations show, a prisoner's status and occupation before captivity could affect the way in which he/she was treated. Chance encounters did also play their part in determining one's treatment. At sea, the one individual who held the power to reclassify a prisoner and modify his conditions of detention was the ship's captain.

I have so far analysed the institutional structures of the imperial state, and its inability to cope with massive arrivals of prisoners of war, which explains why it relied so heavily on private interests. We have also seen that prisoners of war were not completely helpless. While the pains of endless mobility intensified the pains of imprisonment, prisoners could try to shape their own history. But how far does this analysis characterize the West Indies only, and how far does it reveal something more profound about war captivity and the state in the long eighteenth century?

---

[140] Ibid.   [141] LCA to S&W, 21 October 1779, NMM, ADM/M/409.
[142] S&W to LCA, 27 October 1779, TNA, ADM98/12, fos. 119v–120. Similar practices continued during the French Wars: Transport Office to Edward Gibbons, 4 August 1793, ADM98/284, fo. 67.
[143] Scott, 'Paper thin'.

IV. European Mobility

Large numbers of prisoners were transported by sea across Europe, not just across the Atlantic. Even though European and Atlantic circulations were connected, the former had their own logic as well, due to the proximity of metropolitan centres of power. The figures in Europe were also much higher, as can be seen by looking at a 'General account of ransoms for the transportation of French prisoners from the commencement of hostilities to 30 June 1780'. These lists, which were broken down into different categories of prisoners (soldiers, sailors, privateers, passengers, etc.), give us the total number of 3,747 individuals who were carried across the Channel during the first two years of the American War of Independence.[144]

The first section tackles the issue of the problematic articulation between circulation on land and at sea. To exchange the prisoners and bring them back to their country of origin, the number of possible itineraries was almost infinite. A vital issue that state administrators had to confront was the very materiality of these voyages, which had a financial and human cost. The second section focuses on the mobility of prisoners on land. These massive transfers of population, involving hundreds of prisoners at a time walking on country roads, did not pass unnoticed by civilians. In fact, local populations were key actors in enabling these traffics. The third section considers a specific but common scenario, which saw returning prisoners try to hijack the ships that were carrying them home. This case study underlines, once again, that prisoners were never a passive commodity, patiently waiting in line to be brought back to the front. The chapter ends with a focus on one single prisoner, in order to get a sense of how this forced mobility was experienced by its main protagonists.

A. Moving by Land or Sea: The Problem of Distance

The history of circulations tends to draw attention to effortless flows, of men, capitals, or ideas. Analysing the materiality of voyages can help us nuance the idea that circulations are necessarily frictionless.[145] Comparative studies of transoceanic mortality, which compare the mortality of slaves with other groups, show that the figures depend on the particular moments that one focuses on within longer itineraries.[146] For a long time, historians were almost exclusively interested in the 'Middle Passage', whereas the capture of the slaves, their transportation to the coasts, and their acclimation to the plantation caused as many deaths as the crossing of the Atlantic itself. It is likewise necessary to take into account the long inland journeys between places of detention or towards ports of

---

[144] AN, MAR/F2/98.   [145] Tsing, *Friction*; Finn, '"Frictions"'.
[146] Klein, Engerman, Haines, and Shlomowitz, 'Slave trade'.

embarkation, and then the long wait in the ports themselves. Voyages on board transport ships, even across the Channel, were no pleasure cruises. For common prisoners, the comfort was minimal, and many of them, already weakened by a long captivity, only reached their homeland to die in hospitals.[147]

The itineraries followed by the prisoners thus mattered a great deal for their health, and sometimes their very survival. Clearly, this was a preoccupation for the officials who dealt with the exchanges of prisoners of war. But this was also a financial and strategic matter for the states—an object of constant discussions when cartels of exchange were negotiated. It could indeed be advantageous for the captor state to release their prisoners in dribs and drabs and to slow down their return home, thus affecting the forces at the enemy's disposal. The official ports of exchange for British and French prisoners were defined in these negotiations. Already in 1690, Dover and Plymouth on the British side, and St Malo and Calais on the French side, were the main locations.[148] The number of the ports changed little across the period. In the 1745 cartel, the following routes were added to the Dover–Calais one: Portsmouth–St Malo, Plymouth–Morlaix, Kinsale–Morlaix, Kinsale–Bayonne, and Port-Mahon–Marseille.[149] These ports were the main collecting points, the 'general rendezvous' for all prisoners of war.[150] Besides the cartels, the itineraries followed by the transport ships show that some routes retained their prevalence throughout the period, such as Morlaix–Whitehaven or Bristol–Le Havre.[151]

The selection of the ports was an important matter, and determined the distances which prisoners would have to walk or travel by sea, with its consequences on safety, health, and cost. The 1780 Cartel stated that, in the selection of 'the most convenient ports' for transporting the prisoners of war, both states should be aware of 'the inconvenience of long marches of the said prisoners from the places of their confinement to the ports of embarkation'.[152] Distance was linked to cost, since prisoners had to be fed by their captors along their journey, until reaching their homeland.[153] Walking prisoners across long distances meant recruiting and paying military escorts, as well as the prisoners' food and accommodation, for weeks.[154] These expenses could quickly snowball if the prisoners were in large numbers. The captains of transport ships, which were usually

---

[147] Cabantous, *Dix-mille*, pp. 198–204.

[148] 'Articles proposez', 7 December 1690, AN, MAR/F2/71.

[149] 'Articles du Projet de Cartel' [June 1745], article 3, TNA, ADM98/2, fo. 160v.

[150] An expression used a propos Kinsale, for all the prisoners in Ireland: LCA to S&W, 10 July 1744, NMM, ADM/M/388. In 1780, the Mediterranean route was abandoned: 1780 Cartel, articles 28–9, in *CTS*, vol. 47, p. 304.

[151] See the hundreds of lists of exchanges in AN, MAR/F2/91 (1760–2) and F2/93 (1763).

[152] 1780 Cartel, article 26, in *CTS*, vol. 47, p. 303.

[153] 'Copie. Estat des conditions' (1708), article 2, British Library, London (BL), Add MS61592, fo. 153. This was always a fraught issue. See 'Mémoire', [11] November 1758, AN, MAR/B4/97, fo. 178.

[154] See, for example, S&W to LCA, 2 July 1782, TNA, ADM98/14, fo. 105v.

privately owned, were paid a certain sum per head of prisoner, which increased with the distance. Thus, between Dover and Calais the captain was paid in 1780 '6 sous sterling' per man, between other Channel ports the sum was '10^s 6^d' per head, and for any other route between other French or British/Irish ports, 1 guinea.[155] The army and navy's consent to 'lend' military escorts or navy ships to convoy the prisoners was also key.[156]

The longer the distance there was to cover on land, the bigger were the potential troubles with the local population.[157] In December 1778, Lord Amherst, commander-in-chief of the British Army, considered that marching prisoners from the Downs to Winchester, with halts in Portsmouth and Forton Prison, presented too many problems. It would give them opportunities to escape, while 'the towns thro' which they must pass being full of troops, they would be marched only in small Parties'. The Lords of the Admiralty concurred and decided to move these prisoners by sea.[158]

Financial and strategic preoccupations did not mean that caring for the prisoners' health was completely overlooked, but sometimes satisfying all these aims was impossible. This conundrum was never solved. In 1762, the Sick & Wounded Board proposed to march French prisoners from York to Plymouth, more than 500 km to the south. They wrote to the Lords of the Admiralty that they were aware of

> the great distance of those Places, and to the inconveniences that unavoidably arise therefore; but [they imagined] the Prisoners might support the fatigue without hazarding their health by being allowed proper halting days, and that the Escorts of His Majesty's Troops are frequently changed on so long a march.

Marching the prisoners was the best way 'of saving extraordinary Expence'.[159] Governments could deliberately instruct the captains of transport ships and privateers to land their prisoners far away. This would entail more expenses for their enemies, as well as more time for the prisoners to get home, and ultimately to return to the battlefield or to warships. The *commissaire général de la Marine* in St Malo, Guillot, thus wrote to his British counterpart, in 1746, that fifty French prisoners from the south-west and south-east of France had lately been landed in Brittany, on their return from Britain. They would have to walk across the whole

[155] Cartel 1780, article 30, *CTS*, vol. 47, p. 304. See also 'Articles proposez', 7 December 1690, AN, MAR/F2/71; 'Articles du Projet de Cartel', [June 1745], article 3, TNA, ADM98/2, fo. 160v.
[156] Colonel Ellison to S&W, 30 May 1745, TNA, ADM98/2, fo. 140v; S&W to LCA, 9 May 1758, NMM, ADM/F/17.
[157] S&W to LCA, 1 April 1763, TNA, ADM98/9, fos. 173–v.
[158] LCA to S&W, 12 December 1778, NMM, ADM/M/406.
[159] S&W to LCA, 12 April 1762, TNA, ADM98/9, fo. 65.

country to get home. Instead, Guillot asked optimistically that the geographical origins of these men be taken into account:

> If, without upsetting your operations, you could advise your Agents to pay attention only to put *Bretons* and *Normands*, *Poitevins* and *Saintongeais* in the packet-boats going to St Malo and Morlaix [*in Brittany*], *Flamands*, *Picards* and even *Normands* in those going to Calais and Dunkirk, and *Gascons*, *Bearnais* and *Provençaux* in those going to Bordeaux and Bayonne, I would be much obliged to you.[160]

Conversely, prolonging the forced exile of the prisoners, even when their exchange had been agreed, could aim at obliging the captor state to continue paying for their detention—money that could otherwise have been spent elsewhere. To do this, the states could deliberately slow down the turnover of cartel ships that had been sent to collect the prisoners. For instance, in 1707 the Board complained that English transport ships sent to France with released French prisoners were detained for too long in St Malo and Calais, and took more than six weeks to complete their loop across the Channel: 'by this means the French King has the service of his seamen wch we send over for a long time, whilst Her Majesty is deprived of that of hers.'[161] But deliberately slowing down the exchanges could be a dangerous game: prisoners who had lost all hope to ever return home were easy targets for army and navy recruiters.[162] And the longer a ship was waiting for its cargo of prisoners, the higher the 'Charge of demurrage' would be, noted the Board in 1780.[163] Instructions to the captains of transport boats accordingly stated that little time should be wasted in the transfer between leaving the prisons and departing from the port.[164]

Shipping prisoners of war was a dangerous and costly business. Privateers and transport-boat owners needed deep pockets to be able to pay for the many expenses incurred during the voyage of the prisoners, and to bear the wait until the state would repay them.[165] And reimbursements did not always come.[166] The problem was similar for the private ship-owners who were hired by colonial governors to carry prisoners of war from Guadeloupe, Newfoundland or Cape Breton, and struggled to be paid once they arrived in Europe.[167] Being looted, hijacked, captured, fired at, or wrecked were some of the risks that ship-owners

---

[160] Guillot to S&W, 16 November 1746, ADM97/103, fo. 131.

[161] S&W to Sunderland, 16 December 1707, BL, Add MS61592, fo. 28.

[162] LCA to S&W, 16 March 1745, NMM, ADM/M/391, no. 146.

[163] 21 February 1780, TNA, ADM98/12, fo. 185v.

[164] Sartine, 'Instructions pour les capitaines', 18 March 1780, articles 2–3, AN, MAR/F2/98; 'Instructions for Agents' (1807), articles 40–1, pp. 26–7.

[165] S&W to Sunderland, 17 June 1709, BL, Add MS61593, fo. 77; LCA to S&W, 10 July 1744, NMM, ADM/M/388, no. 106.

[166] SSM to Des Marets, 27 February 1709, AN, MAR/B2/214, fos. 621–3.

[167] LCA to S&W, 10 October, 21 December 1745, NMM, ADM/M/393, nos. 269, 359; S&W to LCA, 7 July 1761, TNA, ADM98/8, fo. 216v.

were ready to take.[168] But they also repaid themselves by asking their human cargo to share these risks. In Europe as in the West Indies, some prisoners even paid for their passage with their own money,[169] or, as we saw, manned the ships that carried them home.

The duties of captors towards their prisoners, during their transportation, were regulated, but practice greatly differed from theory. At sea, this was partly due to the states' devolution of the transport of prisoners to British private entrepreneurs, which remained the norm until 1794, when the Transport Board was created.[170] In Europe as in the Atlantic, both states hired private ships to transport the prisoners between France and Britain (as well as troops, provisions, and guns).[171] This implied corruption, fraud, and cutting corners to save money. It also had reper-cussions on the itineraries followed by prisoners on land, which could be explained by the ship-owners' search for profit. Captain Charles Gibson, of Gibson & Eyre Company, won the market for the transport of prisoners during the years 1703–4. He had offered to transport English prisoners from Dover to Calais pro bono, while Captain Eyre would carry them between St Malo and Plymouth. The value of his cargo depending on the number of prisoners he transported, Gibson decided to have them marched from Dinan, which was only a few kilometres from St Malo, to Calais, more than 500 km away. Those prisoners who bribed him were given the choice to be exchanged without waiting for their turn.[172] The crooked captain lost his contract.[173] Knowing that such a circuit endangered the prisoners' health, the British government thereafter refused to countenance the repatriation of British prisoners from Brittany through Calais and Dunkirk.[174] Depending on one's resources and rank, the time and space of captivity could expand or shrink.

B. The Mechanics of Inland Journeys

At almost any given time, the country roads of France and Britain were criss-crossed by troops of prisoners of war, in an apparently disorganized ballet. There were inwards circulations, i.e. 'returning' prisoners, back on home land, or 'arriving' prisoners, who were marched from the ports to their prisons;

---

[168] LCA to S&W, 9 June 1783, NMM, ADM/M/414; 22 August 1749, ADM/M/403, no. 290; 21 March 1746, ADM/M/397, no. 81. Packet boats owners were indemnified by the government in advance of their voyage, in case of capture: S&W to LCA, 10, 12 August 1758, ADM/F/18.
[169] SSM to Guillot, 13 February 1745, AN, MAR/B2/325, fo. 79.
[170] Condon, 'Establishment'.
[171] On contractors at the beginning of the eighteenth century, see Watson, 'Commission', pp. 240–4.
[172] 'Memorial of the S&W to the Lords of the Privy Council', 21 June 1704, TNA, SP34/4, fos. 74–6.
[173] Order from Prince George to S&W, 6 November 1704, SP42/119, fo. 91. On this, see also Watson, 'Commission', pp. 242–4.
[174] Scouller, Armies, p. 313.

as well as outwards circulations, i.e. prisoners who marched to the ports to be sent home. There were also prisoners who were transferred internally, from one place of detention to another, because the fear of an invasion could dictate that prisoners be moved away from the coasts. This could also occur because parliamentary elections or assizes were held (in Britain) or provincial estates (in France) were gathered in towns where the presence of prisoners of war, just like that of the soldiers guarding them, was seen as disruptive.[175] While these movements were not always well coordinated, there was a rationale behind them. The same mechanisms were at work for all these groups, with some nuances in France and Britain. More strikingly, as I will now show, the logistics presiding over the movements of prisoners of war was not specific to them.

In France, French prisoners freshly arrived in their homeland, and English prisoners marched to the coast on their way to England, usually followed the same itineraries. More broadly, the same state apparatus handled different categories of moving people. Galley-slaves on their way to Brest, Marseille, or Rochefort, and soldiers on their way to the front or on leave, all walked along the same roads.[176] The same system seems to have been in place since at least the 1690s.[177] Let us look at a specific example: in April 1762, four English officers and forty-two soldiers were painstakingly trudging along the roads of Brittany. They had been captured by a privateer from Dunkirk. After landing in Brest, the little troop, which also included one chaplain, six officers' and soldiers' wives and two children, was gathered up in Dinan, 200 km to the east. Five of the soldiers were immediately sent to the hospital, and the others to the Castle (the main prison in the town).[178] These prisoners walked in the footsteps of French soldiers, whose voyages across France were closely monitored by the so-called *étape* system, used for feeding and lodging moving troops.[179] The transportation of foreign prisoners, as well as 'national' prisoners on their return from captivity, utilized the same infrastructure, followed the same routes, stopped in the same places, and

---

[175] The prisoners were evacuated from Dinan where the Estates of Brittany were to meet: Lempereur to SSM, 5 April, 7, 18 October 1711, AN, MAR/B3/195, fos. 109, 298v, 314v. The removal of the militia and troops guarding the prisoners, in times of elections and assizes, was debated: Secretary at War to attorney and solicitor general, 16 June 1747, TNA, ADM98/4, fo. 118v; Charles Jenkinson to Earl of Bute, April 1761, Bute Archives at Mount Stuart, BU/98/6/355; mayor of Winchester to Secretary at War, in S&W to LCA, 25 February 1780, TNA, ADM98/12, fos. 188–v.

[176] Joannic-Séta, *Bagne*; Rappaport, *Chaîne*.

[177] See, for example, Gastines to SSM, 23 October and 5 November 1691, AN, MAR/B3/64, fos. 279, 287.

[178] The group was enlarged by another sergeant and twelve soldiers from the British East India Company, already in Dinan: Marquis de la Chartre, 'Etat des troupes angloises', 16 April 1762, Archives Départementales d'Ille-et-Vilaine, Rennes, ADIV, C1090; Védier to Choiseul, list of names and ranks of the prisoners, 28 April 1762, ibid.

[179] Perréon, *Armée*; Biloghi, *Logistique*.

mobilized the same personnel and the same pre-printed forms as the *étapes* system.[180]

Their peregrination had been prepared well in advance. Two months before, in February 1762, the Duc de Choiseul, secretary of state in charge of *Guerre* and *Marine*, had sent a plan of march to Védier, *commissaire ordinaire des guerres* in Brittany.[181] The prisoners would travel across northern France, from Dinan to Calais, according to a precise 'feuille de route' that listed all the towns and villages in which they would stop daily.[182] The journey totalled more than 700 km, on average 20 km per day. The chief 'conductor' of the prisoners was an *exempt* or brigade commander of the *Maréchaussée*, a rural police force centrally organized by the monarchy, who was accompanied by two constables (*cavaliers*, also known as *archers*).[183] This man regularly updated the list, whether because prisoners eloped or had to stop on the road to be hospitalized. He was to prevent the prisoners from causing 'disorder', but also protect them against attempts by army recruiters to capture them.[184] This was hard work, with no certainty to be paid for it, but this income was badly needed for men who were often very poor.[185]

In each stopping place, the itinerant troop would be lodged in houses or stables prepared for that purpose. On 21 April 1762, the mayor and municipal officers of Fougères and Antrain, two small Breton towns, were informed that the troop of English prisoners, on their way from Dinan, would arrive five days later. Town officials were ordered 'to have houses and barns prepared to lodge these prisoners, to have sentries placed at the doors and other exits of these houses ... , to provide the prisoners with bread & straw on the same footing as the king's troops, by taking receipts from an officer'.[186] The mechanics was as regular as clockwork. On 26 April, just as planned, the sixty-five prisoners arrived in Antrain, where they stayed until the following day. There, they were provided with sixty-five 'rations of bread, and twenty-five bales of straw', as well as 'two carriages to transport their luggage and sick men from Antrain to Fougères, five leagues away'.[187] Charles

[180] The 'étapes' system ascertained that returning prisoners stayed on the right tracks and joined companies of soldiers: orders from Comte d'Argenson, secretary of state for *Guerre*, 22 February 1745, AN, MAR/F2/88, fo. 717. Soldiers returning from captivity were given new shoes and clothing: Choiseul to *Intendant* of Rouen, 31 December 1761, Archives Départementales de Seine-Maritime, Rouen (ADSM), C773.

[181] Choiseul to Védier, 16 February 1762, ADIV, C1090.

[182] This road map was communicated to the *Intendants* of each region they passed through: drafts of letters of 18, 21 April 1762.

[183] See, for example, Gastines, 23 October 1691, AN, MAR/B3/64, fos. 279–v; Rostan, *commissaire de la Marine* at Bordeaux and Bayonne, 16 January 1745, MAR/B2/325, fo. 357. The prisoners of war duty was one of the 'extraordinary' duties of the Maréchaussée, who was also paid extra for catching deserters or escaped Huguenots. See Cameron, 'Police'; Emsley, *Gendarmes*, pp. 13–36.

[184] Marquis de la Chartre to [Choiseul], 16 April 1762, ADIV, C1090.

[185] A year later, the exempt of the Dinan Maréchaussée, Ernault, still had not been paid for his efforts: [Védier] to Choiseul, 17 April 1763, ibid. See Cameron, 'Police', p. 59.

[186] [Védier] to mayors and inhabitants of Fougères and Antrain, 21 April 1762, ADIV, C1090.

[187] Receipt by Ernault, *exempt de la Maréchaussée* in Dinan, 27 April 1762, ibid.

Moor, an English lieutenant, certified that he had received the said goods.[188] The mayor of Antrain filled and signed the 'feuille de route' accordingly, like all his colleagues, certifying the identity and number of the prisoners and the date of their arrival and departure.[189] If they wanted to buy anything else, the prisoners could use the money advanced to them by the French monarchy at the beginning of the journey, the amount of which depended on the distance covered and their rank—a system that applied to both foreign prisoners and French returnees.[190] Despite some institutional differences, in practice the management of the transfer of sailors was very similar to that of soldiers, and it sometimes involved the same personnel.[191]

Monitoring the mobility of prisoners of war involved large sections of society. Accounting documents, listing the names of those who asked to be paid for contributing to the transfer of prisoners of war, help us get a more precise idea of who these people were. In October 1779, a seven-page long 'Extract' was drawn up in Brest by the administration of the Marine, listing seventy-seven individuals who had corralled the prisoners in Brittany, for the first six months of the year.[192] Besides army or navy men who guarded them, a variety of civilians were also involved in this mobility: carrying, feeding, or curing them. Carters carried baggage and sick men, the *Messageries royales* (the institution in charge of transporting passengers as well as mail on the French territory) carriages and the horses to pull them, mayors advanced the money for buying bread and straw, and surgeons and apothecaries looked after the prisoners who had been recaptured and wounded in the process. For many people, then, the presence of prisoners was a welcome source of revenue. The four 'Musicians of the Regiment of Poitou in garrison at Broons' (56 km inland from St Malo), who were rewarded for capturing English prisoners who had escaped on the road, probably did not see the prisoners as a burden.

In Britain as in France, the central government was able to apply more stringent control on the movement of prisoners, thanks to a greater coordination with local authorities than was the case in the West Indies. The transfer of prisoners of war was modelled on the movements of troops across the land.[193] Regiments of militia and soldiers usually escorted the prisoners, and divisions of 100 or sometimes 200 prisoners were commonly marched across the country, between different places of confinement.[194] But, even more so than in France, the collaboration of army

---

[188] Receipt acknowledging receipt of 600 livres from governor of Dinan, 12 April 1762, ibid.

[189] The final feuille de route, signed by all these mayors along the journey and finally by the *commissaire des guerres* in Dinan on 26 April 1762, is in Stanford University Library, Special Collections, M1368/2/2.

[190] SSM to Lusançay, 30 May 1708, AN, MAR/B2/207, fo. 755.

[191] See SSM to S&W, 24 October 1746, MAR/B2/329, fo. 693; 'Règlement concernant les prisonniers ennemis détenus en France', articles 1 and 2, undated, in 'Circulaire', 14 December 1778, MAR/F2/82.

[192] 'Extrait du fond à remettre au port de Brest', 20 October 1779, MAR/F2/82.

[193] Houlding, *Fit for Service*; Hayter, *Army*.

[194] S&W to LCA, 26 July, 29 September 1762, TNA, ADM98/9, fos. 83v, 106. The soldiers on prisoners of war duties were paid for their expenses (Scouller, *Armies*, p. 148), but it took them

commanders (and, ultimately of the secretary of state for *Guerre*, who held the power to allocate these men to this role) was never guaranteed.[195]

The bad state of the roads, and competition with the army for the use of temporary places of accommodation, could also complicate the transfer of prisoners, in Britain as in France.[196] And the beginnings of wars always highlighted the lack of preparation. In December 1756, the Agent at Portsmouth wrote that it was 'absolutely impracticable' to find accommodation for prisoners, whose removal had been ordered from Portchester to Sissinghurst, in the towns through which they had to pass.[197] The messenger he had dispatched in Kent to provide quarters for these 250 prisoners had returned empty-handed. At Petersfield, his very thorough inspection had been unsuccessful. The barns were 'almost all full of Grain', and 'every Place that might otherwise have served on this Occasion, is engaged as a Magazine of Storage for the Hessian Troops'. The owners of the few stables and public houses that were available rubbed their hands at the prospect of such an easy profit: 'They will ... on no condition, sign any Agreement, to quarter any certain Number, but refer their Forms to the Time of the Prisoners arrival, plainly to make an advantage of our Distress.' A maximum of 100 prisoners could be accommodated at any one time in Petersfield.[198]

Despite these obstacles, some situations, such as the prospect of an invasion, left no other choice but to transfer massive numbers of prisoners inland. In June 1759, the Lords of the Admiralty ordered the removal to Carlisle and Berwick-upon-Tweed of all the prisoners on parole in the south of England. The Board came up with an elaborate proposal. The prisoners would be marched in divisions of fifty men, 'as larger numbers would not be easily accommodated'. Each division would be accompanied by two 'Conductors'. Wagons would be provided for the baggage and for sick prisoners. The main challenge was distance: according to the source, 460 miles separated the parole towns in Cornwall and Carlisle, which could be covered in nine weeks by prisoners walking 10 miles a day, with two halting days a week. The proposal was endorsed by the Lords of the Admiralty, but it was too ambitious and it was dropped.[199] Similar measures were adopted during the other conflicts.[200]

Distance did not have the same impact on all the prisoners. Rank determined life in captivity. In transport boats, high-ranked officers and passengers were

months to be reimbursed: LCA to S&W, 19 February 1744, NMM, ADM/M/390, no. 55; same to same, 12 September, 2 October 1778, ADM/M/406.

---

[195] Orders to provide the Agents with guards were often ignored: S&W to LCA, 7 April 1763, TNA, ADM98/9, fo. 175v.

[196] S&W to LCA, 29 September 1762, ibid., fo. 106.

[197] S&W to LCA, 3 December 1756, ADM98/6, fo. 18v.

[198] Extract of Agent for Prisoners at Portsmouth, 2 December 1756, ibid., fos. 19–v.

[199] S&W to LCA, 18 June 1759, NMM, ADM/F/19.

[200] As in December 1745, when fear of a French invasion combined with the Jacobite rebellion: 6 December 1745, ADM/M/393, no. 342. The parole system was re-established a few weeks later: 28 December 1745, ibid., no. 369. See also ch. 4.

entitled to travel in a cabin, and to eat at the captain's table.[201] In the same way, on the road, prisoners on parole were entitled to 'travelling charges' when they were removed from one parole zone to another.[202] There is no reason to feel sorry for the gentlemen who travelled between Portsmouth, Winchester, and Salisbury in 1748. The Agent at Portsmouth submitted two bills for the expense of conducting and re-conducting two of these prisoners, Messieurs Jonquière and St George.[203] Between 25 and 27 July 1748, the Agent paid coachmen, horses, coaches, and chaises to bring these officers from Salisbury to Gosport, Fareham, and Fitchfield. Multiple carriages for the prisoners' baggage were also hired, and a further nine pounds were spent at Rumsey 'for Entertainement of the French Officers &c'.[204] The list is far from exhaustive. No wonder that the Sick & Wounded Board remarked that 'more good Husbandry might have been used on that Occasion'. The Lords of the Admiralty consented to pay.[205] Similar measures were in place in France. In 1778, English captains of packet boats and commissioned officers travelled between Niort and La Rochelle in carriages, 'in the sole company of the *exempt de la Prévôté de la Marine*'.[206]

While common prisoners did not travel in coaches, they were allowed to bring personal possessions on their journey. Conveying hundreds of men and their trunks was evidently dearer than a few dozen prisoners on parole. In 1781, the Board wrote that the custom to provide carriages for the prisoners' baggage was proving to be very expensive, 'owing to our having avoided to give such directions as might deprive any of them of the little property which had been left them by the Captors of the Ships in which they were taken'. Thus, the Dutch prisoners at Plymouth, who were to march to Bristol, had filled 'one hundred and twenty three large Chests' with their property, in addition to 'Beds and other Baggage'. Clearly, some rule needed to be established to keep expenses under control. At the same time, psychological considerations had to be borne in mind: 'any restrictions in this case not heretofore practised may now be considered as a hardship.' From then on, each prisoner would only be allowed twenty pounds weight, 'besides what he himself could carry'.[207]

C. Slipping Away

While governments aimed to control the movements of the men who came back from captivity, in order, eventually, to use them again on ships or in the armies,

---

[201] Captain of the *Glasgow* responding to 'a Memorial against Him, by some French Cadetts or Voluntiers', 25 September 1746, NMM, ADM/M/396, no. 226/1; Sartine, 'Instructions pour les capitaines', 18 March 1780, articles 9, 13, AN, MAR/F2/98.
[202] S&W to LCA, 26 November 1756, TNA, ADM98/6, fos. 15v–16.
[203] LCA to S&W, 21 November 1749, NMM, ADM/M/403, no. 292.
[204] 'Charge of conducting and conveying sundry French Prisoners of War', ibid., no. 293/1.
[205] LCA to S&W, 24 November 1749, ibid., no. 293.   [206] 25 August 1778, AN, MAR/F2/82.
[207] S&W to LCA, 20 April 1781, TNA, ADM98/13, fos. 162–v.

the prisoners were, understandably, eager to return home. These two aims were not in principle incompatible. Recruiting officers sometimes managed to tempt men who came back from captivity in a miserable state 'to enter themselves voluntarily' in the navy, by lavishing meat and drinks on them.[208] Being released from prison was not synonymous with being free. Prisoners were closely monitored by state administrations in both countries, from their release to their landing in their home state. And surveillance did not stop there. The captains of the cartel ships delivered paperwork to the *commissaires des classes* or Agents for Prisoners in the ports, attesting that the men who set foot on land were those they claimed to be. In France, sailors back from captivity were instructed 'as soon as they arrive to present themselves to the Bureau des Classes of their Department, failing which they will be punished as Deserters'.[209] Desertion was an obsession for the states, and the army and navy administrations resorted to 'paper identities' to track the prisoner' movements, detailing his 'signalement', where he came from, and his destination.[210] By inventing a bureaucratic apparatus that collected an ever-increasing variety of data about individuals, eighteenth-century states created the fiction that they had the power to identify people. But their real hold on the individual remained weak.

Pre-printed or manuscript safe-conducts, and passports of various shapes, were created and delivered to returning prisoners. On 7 July 1757, the *classes* administration of Dunkirk delivered a form to Cornelius Bresm, aged fifty-four years, face 'round', eyes 'blue', and nose 'long', who had just landed in Calais. He was given two days to present himself to his department.[211] On 17 July, the *Bureau Général des Classes* at St Malo delivered a certificate to Antoine Mequot, from Dunkirk, also 'returning from the English prisons', with orders to let him pass unhindered. The sailor was given fifteen days to return home, failing which he would be considered a deserter.[212] The same procedure was perfected during the Napoleonic Wars—with debatable success.[213]

There were good reasons for suspecting that these men would not conform to these road maps. Escapes tended to multiply when rumours of peace spread among the prisoners, who were losing patience and were eager to return home.[214] For instance, the Treaty of Paris was signed on 10 February 1763, but escapes of prisoners, officers, and sailors alike, increased exponentially from January onwards. Dozens of lists of names, mentioning the mode of transportation, and

---

[208] John Guy, Plymouth, to Navy Board, 30 March 1697, TNA, ADM 106/504, fo. 260.
[209] Order for Jean Vanhoute carpenter from Dunkirk, Bureau des Classes, Dunkirk, 17 March 1758, AN, MAR/F/2/88, fo. 52.
[210] Noiriel, *Etat*; Denis, *Histoire*, pp. 183–210; About and Denis, *Histoire*; Morieux, *Channel*.
[211] Bureau des Classes, Dunkirk, 7 July 1757, AN, MAR/F2/86, n. 34.
[212] Bureau Classes, St Malo, 17 July 1757, ibid., no. 35.
[213] Fouché to Prefect of Seine-Inférieure, 29 Pluviôse an 9 [18 February 1801], ADSM, 1M209. See Denis, *Histoire*, pp. 205–10; Forrest, *Conscripts*.
[214] Malo to SSM, 1, 10 August 1748, AN, MAR/B3/463, fos. 134, 152.

the origins and domiciles of prisoners of war who had escaped from Britain and landed in Boulogne, Calais, or Le Havre, were compiled in the French ports.[215] The prisoners who had escaped and those who were exchanged often travelled on board the same ships, smuggling or neutral vessels, packet-boats, or fishing-boats.[216] The demarcation between licit and illicit mobility, there as elsewhere, was murky.

The limits of identification documents, as modes of tracking down early modern mobility, are well known to historians.[217] The lists of names carefully drawn up by *Marine* administrators show that they were also aware of the prisoners' ability to slip away during their complicated journeys over land and sea. Several sailors from the Department of Agde, in southern France, who had been captured in 1777–8, were thus described by a clerk as having 'disappeared'. Two other sailors, also from Agde, had escaped from Bristol and landed at Nantes, from where, a clerk wrote, 'we have received no information regarding their whereabouts'.[218] Another administrator drew up a list containing the names of the sailors from the administrative district of Rouen who had been captured 'by the English' since the beginning of the war, but concluded that it 'cannot be absolutely exact', due to the 'diverse changes and replacements of crews about which we have no information'.[219] And the same men could be counted several times, if they had been captured more than once.[220] This inability of the state machinery to gather accurate knowledge about sailors was a constant problem.

Many prisoners profited from the confusion to vanish apparently into thin air. A favourite technique was to claim fake identities. We have seen in chapter 1 how much categorization mattered: the difference between one label and another could be that between freedom and the gallows. Such stories, and the archives are full of them, give us a sense of the strategies used by mariners to go AWOL. Bernard Borel, captain of the *Victorieux*, who was captured and detained at Bristol from March 1778, was thus released by pretending to be Spanish (Spain was not yet at war with Britain), and he obtained a passport from the Ambassador of Spain in Britain.[221] The use of false identities could work in unexpected ways. The status of a prisoner of war could be convenient for people who needed to travel across borders. In 1706, the Sick & Wounded Board wrote to the secretary of state Charles Hedges to tell the story of one such daring young man. Massey, the seventeen-year-old son from a brewer at St Malo who supplied beer to the prison, ran away from his father, who treated him 'very severely'. To get across the

---

[215] 'Liste des noms et demeures', Bureau des Classes, Calais, 5 March 1763, MAR/F2/93.
[216] Cartel proposal, article 6, TNA, ADM98/2, fo. 68v; S&W to LCA, 29 December 1744, ibid., fo. 87.
[217] See references in n. 210.
[218] 'Liste des gens de Mer…Departement d'Agde', 31 December 1778, AN, MAR/F2/95.
[219] 'Liste des noms', Bureau des Classes, Rouen, 1 February 1779, ibid.
[220] 'Liste des noms', 1 May 1779, ibid.
[221] 'Liste des gens de Mer…Agde', 31 December 1778, ibid. British privateers and fishermen often claimed to be Americans to avoid being detained as prisoners of war: Archives Départementales du Nord, Lille, L13162 (1796); ADSM, 1M208 (1807).

Channel, he had managed to join 'the crowd of English Prisoners' released from St Malo, and boarded a Transport Vessel. He then went to Bristol, where he rejoined an English merchant at which he had boarded before the war, to learn the English language. The Bristol merchant convinced him to change his mind and return to France. But he was not as lucky the second time, and his attempt to board another transport at Weymouth led him to be suspected to be a spy, and put in prison for 'a long time' before being released.[222] Cartel ships were convenient modes of transportation for deserters too, or even for compulsive turncoats, who used them as free rides.[223]

Many people completely turned the logic of the system on its head by posing as prisoners of war in order to get a free journey home.[224] In October 1783, nine passengers set for Calais, disembarking from a Dover ship. The *rôle de débarquement* illustrates the gap between the identities claimed by these passengers in their statements and the identities that were attributed to them by state agents: 'claiming to be from Corsica coming from Martinique', 'Id. from Cadix coming from the coast of Guinee', 'Id. Basque coming from Antigua', and so on. The *amirauté* official at Calais noted, as an aside, that he had refused to pay for these prisoners' expenses

> Because in the course of the interrogations to which they were submitted in this harbour, it was discovered that they had betrayed the good faith of Mr. the ambassador, and during the war had not served on any French vessel, he had simply given the order that they be returned home. Some of these sailors are Italian and Spanish.[225]

These itineraries were made possible because of the relative fluidity of social statuses and national affiliations in the context of war captivity. Identifying where these people really came from and who they were was always a challenge for state officials in the port. Their transient occupations, and the context of war, allowed them to claim a different label in each place.

For another group of people, being captured as prisoners of war was not a curse but a blessing in disguise. Privateers and men-of-war did not discriminate when they saw an enemy ship. This category included the ships carrying felons sentenced to transportation to America. In 1746, the *Plain Dealer*, a merchant ship bound to America with thirty-five felons on board, was captured on its passage

---

[222] S&W to Secretary Hedges, 28 May 1706, BL, Add MS61591, fos. 26–v.

[223] Châteauneuf to SSM, 25 May 1708, AN, MAR/B3/155, fos. 551–2v; commander of the Susannah Transport to S&W, 22 May 1747, TNA, ADM98/4, fo. 110v.

[224] French prisoners in Britain used fake identities in order to be exchanged first: S&W to Givry, 20 November 1744, AN, MAR/B3/421, fo. 415.

[225] Passengers landed in Calais on 23 October 1783 from the English packet boat *The Courier*, MAR/F2/101. See also MAR/B3/465, 1748, fos. 119–21.

across the Atlantic. These men were brought to St Malo, and then exchanged alongside other prisoners of war. When the Board realized the mistake, it was too late: 'there seems all the Reason in the World to believe those People were set at Liberty, upon the Transp.ᵗ coming to that Place as hath been usual for Prisoners of War to be.'[226] Others were less lucky: in 1748 Jacobite rebels transported to Antigua, whose ship had been captured by the French and brought to Martinique, were exchanged in a regional cartel. Their journey was completed with a few more stops than initially planned.[227] In the following conflicts, the Admiralty tried to be more careful with such passengers, and instead of returning them to Britain 'in the ordinary course of Exchanges', it sent instead convict vessels to pick them up in France.[228]

The enemy was not always to be found abroad, as returning prisoners of war found out when they touched home ground. In Britain, press gangs did not hesitate to target them; but the prisoners did not wait patiently to be picked up, and they tried to take control of the transport vessels, precisely for that reason. Mutinies on board transport ships were so common that they were expected.[229] The fear of impressment was stronger than that of being hanged for betraying one's country. In November 1744, the Lords of the Admiralty worried that too many of the British prisoners in France were enticed to join the French Navy because they were scared to be impressed, despite the instructions never to impress 'such released prisoners, in their return home to England'.[230] Clearly the message failed to hit home. In March 1745, the commander of the *Towey* transport, coming from St Malo with 217 prisoners on board, 'took possession of the ship', which they brought to Weymouth. According to the ship master, the fear of being impressed on arrival had caused the mutiny: 'I used the Uttermost of my Endeavour and assur'd them I had your Promise not a Man should be prest, which they gave no Ear to, but I beleive had it been in Writing, they might have complied.'[231] The Board accordingly suggested furnishing the masters of each transport ship with a declaration of this kind, which was accepted by the Lords of the Admiralty.[232] But this did not work either. In June 1745, the *Charming Molly*, another British transport ship bound for Plymouth from St Malo, was hijacked by

---

[226] S&W to LCA, 16 October 1746, TNA, ADM98/4, fo. 11. Upon enquiry, it was found out that these convicts 'were all gone from Plymouth': same to same, fo. 32.

[227] LCA to S&W, 30 April 1748, NMM, ADM/M/402, no. 143.

[228] S&W to LCA, 16 June, 10 August, 26 September 1757, TNA, ADM98/6, fos. 175, 210v–211, 243.

[229] On these desertions of prisoners, see Rodger, *Wooden World*, p. 201.

[230] LCA to S&W, 2 November 1744, NMM, ADM/M/389, no. 248.

[231] Extract of William Powel, Commander of the *Towey* Transport to S&W, Portsmouth, 31 March 1745, TNA, ADM98/2, fos. 125–v.

[232] S&W to LCA, 1 April 1745, ibid., fo. 124. The LCA, by their declaration of 3 April 1745, ordered this to be done in the future.

the prisoners she was carrying. Her master, William Powell, wrote to the Sick & Wounded Board:

> Although I produced and read to them Their Lordship's Certificates [*that they should not be impressed on arrival*] and used all the Arguments I was capable of, to persuade them to suffer the Ship to proceed to her designed Port, they all insisted on the Contrary, and told me they would either carry the Ship into Portland or Torbay.[233]

Two years later, the same thing happened to the same ship. This time, Captain William Powell left St Malo with 211 prisoners. The *Charming Molly* was forced by contrary winds to put in at Guernsey, where twenty-six prisoners left the ship and refused to come back on board. And when he finally managed to depart for England, the captain was compelled to put the prisoners on shore near Swanage in Dorset.[234] The prisoners certainly had good reasons for taking the Lords of the Admiralty's promises with a certain amount of salt, since these orders were disregarded by the commanders of ships-of-war. All the guarantees in the world were not sufficient to protect the prisoners against the zeal of impressment officers. In June 1746, two men-of-war came across a transport ship from St Malo, carrying 183 British prisoners of war home, and poached twenty-seven 'private Men' from her; they cared little that the transport was carrying orders from the Admiralty protecting these men from the press.[235] Whenever possible, the Lords of the Admiralty ordered to set these men at liberty.[236]

The avidity of press gangs knew no bounds, and even the crews of transport ships could be forcefully recruited in the navy, paralysing the exchanges, as happened in 1760 in Belfast and in Louisbourg in Quebec.[237] Even landing outside their intended port of destination was no guarantee that the prisoners would be safe. In October 1746, the 169 British prisoners on board a transport that had left St Malo for England forced the vessel to land at Weymouth. The prisoners then applied to the Agent there for 'Certificates', which, according to the Lords of the Admiralty's order of 4 June 1746, would protect them from impressment. As they were waiting for their documents to be completed, the Agent's house was 'beset' by an impressment crew led by Captain Arbuthnot of HMS sloop *Jamaica*—a repeat offender.[238] Using swords, cutlasses, and bludgeons, the press gang stabbed a prisoner who was trying to escape, while another jumped out of a back window. For the

---

[233] Copy of Powell to S&W, in S&W to LCA, 19 July 1745, ibid., fo. 179.
[234] S&W to LCA, 22 August 1747, TNA, ADM98/4, fos. 141v–142.
[235] LCA to S&W, 18 June 1746, NMM, ADM/M/395, no. 144.
[236] S&W to LCA, 1 April 1746, TNA, ADM98/4, fo. 208.
[237] S&W to LCA, 12 May, 5 November 1760, ADM98/8, fos. 96, 134v–136.
[238] S&W to LCA, 29 October 1746, ADM98/4, fos. 19v–20. On an earlier case involving the same man, see S&W to LCA, 25 February 1746, fo. 69; Extract of Agent at Weymouth to the S&W, 23 February 1746, fos. 69v–70.

Board, which reported the incident in great detail, such behaviour was abhorrent on many levels. Impressing prisoners of war was heartless: 'The People were the greatest objects of Charity, he ever saw from France, most of them being distempered with the Itch, and half of them quite Naked, looking as if they had been almost starved with hunger and cold.' It was also a clear challenge to the authority of the Lords of the Admiralty, as well as 'a very Injurious Insult upon our Agent'. And it risked introducing sickness in the navy.[239] Captain Arbuthnot had chosen plainly to ignore the documents presented to him, even though they were 'bearing the Seal of this Office'.[240] The commissioners obtained to be empowered to display more authority on the matter when confronted to naval commanders and press masters.[241]

During the American War of Independence, the Board reviewed the situation. Various measures had been adopted in former wars to prevent the prisoners from rerouting the transport ships, to avoid being impressed 'immediately upon their return from Captivity'. They had all failed. In the eyes of the Board, it was once again the prisoners who needed to be reassured, rather than the press gangs to be tamed. They proposed in 1780 to publish a notification from the Lords of the Admiralty in the *Gazette*, 'that Prisoners so released might depend upon their being exempted from the Press, and at liberty upon their landing in England to return to their own homes'. 'Gazettes or printed Copies of the Notification' should also be forwarded to France, to be distributed to all the places of detention for British prisoners there, as well as 'affixed . . . to the Masts of the English and French Vessels employed as Cartels'.[242] Action was urgent: the following day, two French ships carrying British prisoners were blocked in Dover by press gangs.[243] Proclamations of good faith meant little if they could not be implemented, and the prisoners were not taken in by the Admiralty's promises. As the possibility of being impressed never receded, a symptom of the ever-growing needs of the Navy for manpower, returning prisoners kept recruiting the transport vessels.[244] Such desperate and radical actions could end badly, and some of these hijacked ships wrecked.[245]

Let us pause for a moment. Naval mutinies and desertions were not rare in eighteenth-century Britain.[246] But what is striking about the mutinies of prisoners of war—and there are many others—is the clarity of the intentions of the mutineers, or so it seems. One needs to imagine the sour mixture of frustration, anxiety, and sheer pain that the prisoners had had to swallow for years. When

[239] S&W to LCA, 29 October 1746, ibid., fo. 20.   [240] Ibid., 11 November 1746, fo. 28.

[241] LCA, 14 November 1746, cited in S&W to LCA, 20 January 1780, TNA, ADM98/12, fo. 172v.

[242] S&W to LCA, 20 January 1780, ibid., fos. 172v, 173.

[243] S&W to LCA, 21 January 1780, ibid., fo. 174v.

[244] S&W to LCA, 15 January 1781, TNA, ADM98/13, fo. 99; same to same, 1 January 1782, ADM98/14, fo. 30.

[245] See the several letters from Irving, Lieutenant Governor of Guernsey, to Sir Stanier Porten, under-secretary to the Southern Department, about such incidents in April–May 1780: NMM, ADM/M/410.

[246] Frykman et al., *Mutiny*.

their return home was at last materializing, the prospect of being grabbed by press gangs, a few leagues from the English coast, must have been unbearable. Tempers were already running high before the prisoners boarded the ships.[247]

Not once does one read a condemnation of the behaviour of the prisoners on the part of naval administrators. The Admiralty blamed the press gangs and the British navy, which was unable to show the most elementary mercy to these men. The eighteenth-century British state was thus stretched by internal tensions, which constrained its actions and its ability to match goals with practices.

It would also be a mistake to assume that prisoners of war felt an uncritical urge to submit to their monarchy, at all costs. For them, the difference between enlisting voluntarily in the enemy's armed forces, to avoid dying in prison abroad, and being impressed by the navy, was neither necessarily obvious nor important. Only the consequences that were to be paid, in the short or the long term, mattered. But the same logic applied to state administrators, whose expectations regarding the behaviour of the prisoners of war varied considerably, depending on the needs of the state. The constant deficit in manpower meant that state officials preferred to close their eyes when they caught deserters. Similarly, while the prisoners were not supposed to 'take possession' of the transport ships and reroute them, we also saw that, across the Atlantic, sailors were recruited to man the ships whose crews were insufficient. In the same way, within Europe, or between India and Europe, released prisoners of war were commonly asked to man the ships bringing them home.[248] In some extreme situations, when their survival was considered to be at risk, they were given boats and encouraged to run away.[249]

The analysis so far has relied on official discourses, which have been read, whenever possible, against the grain. The prisoners' voice can also sometimes be heard.

D. The 'Trackless Wild': Prisoners on the Road

In France, the Revolutionary Wars disrupted the system used for almost a century to monitor the prisoners' travels on land. In the 1790s, the economic situation of the country meant that prisoners of all ranks were commonly plundered on landing and closely confined. Travelling allowances were often discontinued by the French government or poached by greedy guards.[250] Napoleon moved the prison depots far away from the maritime borders, which entailed long and

---

[247] LCA to S&W, 6 October 1780, NMM, ADM/M/410.
[248] LCA to S&W, 10 August 1744, NMM, ADM/M/388, no. 152; LCA to S&W, 7 October 1746, ADM/M/396, no. 238; S&W to LCA, 17 August 1762, TNA, ADM98/9, fo. 92; S&W to LCA, 26 August 1782, ADM98/14, fo. 121.
[249] As in Gibraltar: LCA to S&W, 8 March 1744, NMM, ADM/M/390, no. 77.
[250] Depositions by British prisoners, 21 April 1798, in *Report* (1798), Appendix, pp. 55–9.

troublesome walks.[251] This is the period I want to focus on briefly in this final section, to shed light on two moments: when the prisoners were brought into captivity, and when they were released.

Peter Fea, a shipmaster from Hull born in 1764, was detained as a prisoner during the Napoleonic Wars, between 1810 and 1814. During his captivity, he kept a diary in a small notebook, which covers eighty-nine pages, in which he documented his daily and often uneventful life in France. Entitled 'Remarks on the passage of the Britannia from Gibraltar to St Maloes' & there to Auyonne in France a Prisoner of War', this document, kept in the Devon Record Office at Exeter, gives us a sense of the psychological and material consequences of forced mobility.[252]

Fea had left Gibraltar under convoy, on 1 January 1810. On 28 January, as his ship, the Britannia, had been separated from the convoy by a storm, it met the St Joseph, a privateer from St Malo, which plundered it, burnt it down, and captured its crew. On 1 February, the prisoners landed in St Malo, and were sent to Solidor Tower. Peter Fea remained there for a month, during which time the captains of French merchant vessels or privateers tried to enlist the prisoners at their service, often with success.[253] Fea refused. Instead, on 28 February he began a journey that would bring him to Auxonne in Burgundy (Eastern France), where he arrived on 24 April 1810—after walking 630 km. Auxonne was a prison depot reserved for masters and mates of merchant vessels, as well as passengers and foreigners in the service of enemy countries, and their families. In January 1814, there were around 1,426 prisoners in this depot.[254] The modus operandi during the Napoleonic Wars was very similar to the Ancien Regime étapes system: the gendarmerie had succeeded the Maréchaussée, and escorted the prisoners on the road, following a predetermined route. The prisoners were allocated a sum by the French government at the beginning of each stage, with which they had to provide themselves 'with every thing'.[255] On leaving St Malo, Fea was given '50 Sols per day on the March'.[256] But prisoners, like all migrants, were easy prey for unscrupulous men, and the money soon vanished. On 2 March 1810, Fea wrote: 'March't from Hoalde to Rennes & was Rob'd ½ livre of my pay by the Gend.me.' His woes did not stop there, and he added, on the same day: 'Was Egregiously extortioned on & could find none to speak to or assist us & had no Money nor anything allowed me gave my bed away.' While his pay was a long time coming, biological needs could not wait. Starving the prisoners was a powerful way to coerce them. On 13 March 1810, he wrote: 'the sailors had no bread allowed them that refused Marching & was righted next day by the genda.mes.' In Chartres, he was 'refused Victuals without Money in hand'.[257] The

[251] Lewis, Napoleon, pp. 83–115, 169–201.   [252] DRO, Exeter, 1317M/F/1.
[253] Fea, Diary, 5, 7, 8, 21–4 February 1810.   [254] Mulvey, Sketches, pp. 1–2.
[255] Ibid., p. 3.   [256] Fea, Diary, 1 March 1810.   [257] Ibid., 22 March 1810.

prisoners also had to pay for their lodging along the way.[258] Fea bounced between prisons, stables, poorhouses, and barracks, and was also at times billeted at private houses. In April 1810, he decided to treat himself to a proper room: 'Marched to Belgard & was had to a miserable [Cachot] but had leave to lodge at an Inn & paid very dear for our indulgence & 12 livres to the Gend[m].'[259] Every day, Fea consigned to paper a record of the pay he was owed.

These journeys were exhausting. During the Napoleonic Wars, people stayed in prison for longer. Some of the men who marched to Auxonne, noted Mulvey, an Irish surgeon who was detained in the very same places as Peter Fea and at the same time, 'had been prisoners upwards of six years'. Bodies were weakened by this long captivity, and the repetition of these forced journeys took their toll:

> I have seen them at different times, to the amount of some hundreds, arrive in a state of comparative nakedness; many under the influence of fever as well as other dangerous complaints; some with very serious accidents. Here was an abundant source of illness and tedious convalescence. They arrived at all times of the year from the wide extended coasts of the French empire, being *en route* for weeks, often for months, their usual lodging a jail, perhaps the cachot, sometimes a donjon.[260]

In March 1811, the prisoners were informed they would be marched to Longwy, in Lorraine, 'in rotation as Number'd on prison books'.[261] This sequential displacement took place over the following days, as small groups departed in bunches. Fea began his own journey, with 65 other men, on 16 April 1811. On 24 April, Fea and his companions left Toul, and 'marched 24 miles thro a hilly Country'. He added: 'One James died on his way to Longwy.' Finally, after twelve days of march, and about 207 miles, Fea reached Longwy on 27 April 1811. He would stay there for almost three years. In December 1813, an epidemic of typhus brought by sick troops of soldiers passing through Longwy struck the prison depot. At the same time, the steady stream of retreating and wounded French soldiers from the Rhine brought the news that the Cossacks had crossed the river.[262] In panic, the prisoners packed a few items and prepared to leave the city. Fea wrote in his diary:

> Wednesday 5 [*January 1814*] begins with a sense of Confusion Not knowing what to do, gave away all my Cooking utensils & took a few things in my Bag & left my Trunk to be forwarded if opportunity. At 10 left Longwy with my Bag on

[258] Ibid., 25 April 1811; Mulvey, *Sketches*, p. 3.   [259] Fea, *Diary*, 9 April 1810.
[260] Mulvey, *Sketches*, pp. 2, 4, 21. The title of this subsection comes from *Sketches*, p. 76.
[261] Fea, *Diary*, 21 March 1811.   [262] Mulvey, *Sketches*, p. 58.

my Back with about 100 in Company & Marcht 4 Legs to Longuion through a hoped Road [*indecipherable word*] up every step at 4 arrived at Longuin & slept on straw.

Orders were given to march to Beauvais, north of Paris, almost 300 km to the west of Longwy. The sick men who had been left behind were the first casualties. The ditches lining up these frozen back country roads turned into graves: 'heard one Man was found dead on the road' (6 January 1814), 'Mr. Tho.ˢ Walker died on the road' (7 January 1814). As pointed out by anthropologists, 'roads can disconnect as effectively as they forge connection'.[263] The winter weather, particularly in this part of France, can be particularly severe, and progression was impaired by 'hard frost with some snow' (8 January 1814). Fea reached Beauvais on 15 January, which he had to leave six days later, for Guise, 132 km to the north-east. On 23 January, his cartwheel broke, which meant spending an extra day in accommodation. At the beginning of February, the prisoners had to turn back again, following the news that the Cossacks were advancing towards them. They now had to walk 450 km to the south-west, to Châtellerault, in the Loire region, which took twenty days. Prisoners on the move used their financial allowance to travel, for some stages of the journey, in carts, but recalcitrant roads and carters often decided otherwise. On 11 February 1814, Fea 'march'd 2 legs thro the forest & Snow thro a very bad traversed road'. Disorder ruled, reflecting the state of the country's political decomposition, as Mulvey put it:

> Hundreds, on arriving at their gite, perhaps after a journey of some months, were suddenly ordered for the night to some other place; or often, owing to the confusion which prevailed at this period, to retrace their steps without being able to find a place where they might halt or repose.[264]

The lack of accommodation in Châtellerault forced Fea to be transferred yet again, to Le Blanc in Indre, along a rough road: '7 March 1814. 7 legs in a Valley by the side of the River Brenne along hilly Rocky precipies & much barren Ground.'

The roads on which the prisoners paced up and down were well trodden. Passing groups of prisoners relayed news about the front and the war to one another. In April 1814, it was by talking to another detachment of prisoners, who were returning from Issoudun, that Fea learnt that Paris had been taken five days earlier.[265] On their journeys, British prisoners conversed with their French counterparts: at Château-Renault Fea 'met a Gentⁿ on the Road who had just been releas'd from 11 years Captivity in England'.[266] It was now time for Fea to begin the long march back to England.

---

[263] Dalakoglou and Harvey, 'Roads', p. 460.   [264] Mulvey, *Sketches*, p. 77.
[265] Fea, *Diary*, 4 April 1814.   [266] Ibid., 2 May 1814.

In Boulogne, where he arrived on 15 May 1814, reproducing with delight a centuries-old cliché, Fea contemplated 'the white Cliffs of Albion . . . which caused a most pleasant sensation'. The wait was not immediately over. In Calais, he wrote: '16 May 1814. No Cartel nor any Vessels appointed to carry us over. Could not get away to day.' He finally touched ground at Dover on 17 May 1814:

> I fell on my knees & kisst the happy Ground I was once more upon, & thought it once of the happiest Moments of my Life, Captain Lamy who had brought me over would take nothing for my Passage, a Gentleman Passengers generously gave the 10£ amongst Us & we received from Messrs Fector & Minnit one Guinea per Man from the Fund.[267]

This level of details reflects, as we have seen, the pecuniary obsession of the prisoners. The journey from southern England to Fea's hometown reads like a tale of resurrection:

> 20 May 1814. . . . At 8 arrived safe by the blessing of God at Hull, where I was received with joy by a numerous concourse of people who seemed to rejoice to see a poor captive liberated and returning amongst them again, and was escorted home to my house by a great number of people.

The journey home presents a reverse image of the ordeal suffered abroad. Remembering his agonizingly slow progression on the French roads, Fea glided home, without encountering a single obstacle.

V. Conclusion

In this chapter, the driving question has been why and how prisoners of war moved, and what this tells us about their conditions and the state. The eighteenth-century imperial state should not be understood as a rational, well-oiled, and all-powerful machine, controlling myriads of employees and sprawling over huge distances. If one wants to use this metaphor, then the machine is better understood as structurally faulty, and often broken because the people who operated it did not agree on the best way to make it work. I have emphasized the human 'thickness' of the state. By focusing on forced migrations, the autonomy of local administrators has been shown, in the colonies as well as in the metropolis. Within the state, colonial governors wrangled with admirals, while army commanders bickered with Agents for Prisoners. Prisoners were often the victims of this internal strife. Linked to this were the central state's

---

[267] On the Fector & Minet packet-boats, see Morieux, *Channel*, pp. 289–96.

attempts (which often failed) to devolve the duty of maintaining prisoners to civilians and local populations. Once again, prisoners were at the receiving end of these tensions, coerced into moving because no one wanted to pay the price of their detention. The imprisonment and exchanges of prisoners of war thus reveals something about the structure of Empires: war captivity acted like a wedge between central governments, colonial and maritime administrations, and local actors.

As historians working on the 'contractor-state' have recently shown, the fiscal-military state was very much a private-public partnership. It is certainly true for the war at sea.[268] The flags of truce system is an example of the inventiveness brought about by war, and of the key role that was played by the circulations of prisoners in allowing the continuation of international trade. The incessant journeys of prisoners depended on the contributions of a large number of intermediaries, carriers, ship captains, or city guards. These people could enable the fluidity of circulations, slow them down, or block them. In the middle of the Atlantic Ocean, central states had little control over what ship captains would do with their prisoners. But even an *exempt de Maréchaussée* had extensive discretionary powers over the fate of the prisoners whom he shepherded. To a certain extent, considered from below, the state faced similar challenges and worked in comparable ways in Jamaica, Kent, and Brittany.[269]

Despite these continuing contingencies, for Britain at least, the Seven Years' War constituted a turning point in the West Indies, which were increasingly dependent on the metropolis because of the unabating French and Spanish naval and military threat in the region.[270] From this period onwards, a form of centralization of the administration of prisoners of war took place, first in the hand of governors, and then, after the American War of Independence, in the hands of admirals and military men. However, the state remained dependent on the help of private actors to feed or carry the prisoners. The succession of demographic crisis in the West Indies, where prisoners were dying in large numbers in chaotic conditions of detention, led to the exploration of more permanent solutions. The transfer of the prisoners to Europe, and the construction of purpose-built facilities, were considered more durable solutions. These debates were not specific to prisoners of war, as the same period also saw a wide-ranging discussion about penal imprisonment and penal transportation in Britain. These were part of the same problem, as we will see in the next chapter.

The routes followed by the prisoners, on land or at sea, were not abstract lines drawn on maps: winds, storms, snow, and frost could upset the best-laid itineraries. Bringing circulation and imprisonment together thus leads us to question

---

[268] On the hiring of ships from local contractors, see Graham, 'British fiscal-military states', pp. 18–20; Bowen, 'Contractor state'; Knight, *Britain*.
[269] As argued by Newman, *New World*.   [270] O'Shaughnessy, *Empire*, pp. 31–2.

the idea that a circulation is necessarily a continuous and dynamic movement, a force integrating spaces separated by long distances. Circulations are often limited and restrained. The same people could be classified differently depending on the moment and on the stages of their journeys. Because of the constant strains on manpower at sea, prisoners were a valuable resource, and they were often put to work on board privateers or transport ships. This issue, once again, was not specific to this group: slaves, hostages or convicts could also be relabelled by their captors to the same end. This reversibility of categories could give the captives the possibility to disappear altogether. When they did not need extra hands on board, the captains of privateers sometimes preferred to dump the prisoners on longboats or on random shores, even though legislation forbade it.[271] State bureaucracy created the fiction of oversight, but the archives of the Marine and of the Admiralty overflow with cases of impostors and impersonators—and even of prisoners 'invented' by local administrators.

---

[271] Zabin, *Dangerous Economies*, pp. 116–17.

4

The Anatomy of the War Prison

I. Introduction

In *Lazarettos* (1791), the prison reformer John Howard evoked the convoluted history of Shrewsbury poor-house, which had been 'originally designed for a foundling hospital, and afterwards occupied by Dutch prisoners of war [and] is now purchased for a work-house'.[1] This example is typical of the sheer diversity of compounds, which could be, at one time or another, requisitioned to accommodate prisoners of war. Tellingly, no single name existed in the eighteenth century to designate the buildings used to detain prisoners of war.[2] According to the architectural historian Thomas Markus, 'if a form has no constructional or functional purpose, there is no unambiguous word for it'. Conversely, the name attributed to a type of building 'affects the choice of designer, how the building is financed, its location, and the precedents used'.[3] As Robin Evans has noted, this applies to prison buildings more generally: 'the prison took patterns of so varied a character yet of such fundamental ordinariness that it could not be said to constitute a specific building at all.'[4]

This chapter focuses on the physical layout of detention; it argues that war prisons were locales of great material and social uncertainty.[5] Michel Foucault writes in *Madness and Civilisation* that 'the same walls could contain those sentenced by common law, young men who disturbed their families' peace or who squandered their goods, people without profession, and the insane'.[6] Historians have not yet considered that prisoners of war should also be analysed in the same framework: that of a 'continuity of confinement'.[7] This is not to say that prisoners of war were randomly confused with other inmates. Increasing reflection took place, as the eighteenth century wore on, upon the specificity of the

---

[1] Howard, *Lazarettos*, p. 175.

[2] The first term used to designate them, in the early nineteenth century, was 'prisons of war'. It was for instance applied to Dartmoor: Risdon, *Chorographical Description*, p. xxix.

[3] Markus, *Buildings*, p. 12.

[4] Evans, *Fabrication*, p. 14. An increasing number of purpose-built county gaols were constructed in Britain in the eighteenth century, but until Newgate was rebuilt, in the 1770s, these places did not have a prison-specific character: McGowen, 'Well-ordered prison'.

[5] The title of this chapter is borrowed from one of Jeremy Bentham's chapters, in *Panopticon*, entitled 'anatomy of the prison': *Works*, vol. IV, p. 92.

[6] Foucault, *Madness*, p. 56. The same logic was at work in English prisons until the last quarter of the eighteenth century: Ignatieff, *Just Measure*.

[7] Harcourt, 'From the asylum', p. 1752.

The Society of Prisoners: Anglo-French Wars and Incarceration in the Eighteenth Century. Renaud Morieux, Oxford University Press (2019). © Renaud Morieux. DOI: 10.1093/oso/9780198723585.001.0001

buildings required for accommodating prisoners of war, by comparison with army barracks, hospitals, or county jails.[8] This function of buildings, as 'classifying devices', is central from our perspective.[9]

In a prison, power is, in an explicit way, enacted spatially. The French Marxist geographer and philosopher Henri Lefebvre, in his *Production of Space*, talks about 'social space'. His approach is 'to analyse not things in space but space itself, with a view to uncovering the social relationships embedded in it'. In other words, one might start with space in order to understand society. There is an entanglement between the layout of space, and the social relations negotiated in the prison as they are mediated through space. Space, here, is not just a theatre where social interactions take place, but also the material means by which these interactions unfold. Therefore we must pay attention to the specificity of prisons as buildings, and to how prisoners, guards, and others relate to and interact with the buildings themselves, in their materiality and concreteness. What is the 'lived' or 'experienced' space of the prisoner of war?[10]

Before proceeding further, and while this is going to be specifically dealt with in subsequent chapters, the complexity of the government of war prison in the eighteenth century must be alluded to. While the central state was the ordering party, deciding where and how prisoners were to be detained, it was by no means the only protagonist. Local authorities and private landlords also played a considerable part in this business, since they held facilities that could be borrowed or rented out by the state.

Purpose-building is always in tension with possible changes in demand, and the length of war is highly unpredictable. As the first section will show, until the 1780s at least in Britain, and throughout the period in France, the places of detention used for prisoners of war were multipurpose and catch-all institutions, which were not purpose-built. The reason for this change and difference must be explained. As the following two sections will demonstrate, the processes of establishing the categories of detainees and identifying their places of detention were not necessarily correlated. Even when specialization won the day in Britain, and 'reformed prisons' started to be built, implementing the separation between prisoners of war and other detainees was often problematic. Detaining prisoners of war in reformed prisons raised many issues, practical as well as theoretical ones,[11] not least because the occupants and users of buildings never passively abide by the architects' intentions. The fourth section analyses the relationship between prisoners and their spatial environment, in terms of the constraints that the latter exerted on the former, but also in terms of the prisoners' ability to reconfigure the spaces they (temporarily) inhabited, against the will of prison authorities.

[8] On comparison and the history of incarceration, see Jones, 'Construction'.
[9] Markus, *Buildings*, p. 4.   [10] Lefebvre, *Production*, pp. 89, 362.
[11] Markus, *Buildings*, ch. 2.

II. Emergency Buildings (Late Seventeenth Century–American War of Independence)

Throughout the eighteenth century, the British and the French states faced the same challenge in wartime: how to find suitable and sufficient accommodation for their prisoners of war, while public resources were scarce and already needed elsewhere. We have seen how determinedly the central state tried to deflect on to local communities the cost of detaining and transporting prisoners of war in the West Indies.[12] The same phenomenon was at work in Europe, on an even bigger scale. These economic constraints dictated the type and shape of buildings selected for war imprisonment. Before the last quarter of the eighteenth century, they were primarily pre-existing buildings hastily repurposed to host their new populations.[13] The diversity of modes of confinement for prisoners is striking. Derelict churches, stables, barns, fortified castles, aristocratic mansions, barracks, and former hospitals, could all, at one point or another, be employed for the accommodation of prisoners of war. They each raised problems of their own. But regardless of their typology, the state had to choose whether it was worth paying to adapt these buildings to their new function, or if it would be less costly simply to build anew on their site. During this period, there were more similitudes than differences in the way the two countries addressed these questions.

A. A Question of Time

Early modern states struggled to cope with emergency situations. Even though the economic and military challenges they faced remained stable, and while the institutions in charge of prisoners of war were largely unchanged, no real attempt was made by state administrations before the 1780s to plan for their needs. The main preoccupation was trying to address and solve current crises. Any war puts pressure on governments to take decisions quickly, without much time for reflection.[14] But in the eighteenth century, people, news, and goods still circulated slowly. While military historians love to dwell on the speed with which marching armies crossed Europe—a speed which accelerated between the time of Louis XIV and Napoleon—prisoners of war, just like civilians, were not easily moved. In the last decades of the eighteenth century, state administrators started to think again about the best way to adapt stocks of buildings to flows of population:[15] what we could call the premises of prison planning.

---

[12] Ch. 3.
[13] On the administrative logistics of landing, detention and transfer during the Anglo-Dutch wars, see Rommelse and Downing, 'State formation', pp. 162–4.
[14] Rosa, *Social Acceleration*, ch. 8.
[15] On the history of town planning, see Daunton, 'Experts'.

The carceral capacity of a state was always stretched at the beginning of a conflict, when prison infrastructure was not yet ready. Planning how much building space would be necessary for the incarceration of prisoners of war was contingent to international relations, a factor that was specific to this type of detainee. But knowing when hostilities would begin, and when and how prisoners would be brought in, was a shot in the dark. Nor did it make sense to maintain empty detention buildings without knowing when they would be needed.[16] States were usually caught by surprise when the first waves of prisoners of war washed upon their shores. When France declared war on Britain in March 1744, the ports could only accommodate around 6,400 prisoners, with the three main detention places, Portsmouth (1,800), Plymouth (1,200), and Kinsale (1,000), accounting for more than half of this number.[17] These figures steadily increased in the following years.[18]

Lack of preparation was a structural problem. When Captain John Hamilton, who was carrying out investigations into the condition of the French and Spanish prisoners held at Plymouth and Kinsale for the Admiralty, visited the New Hospital at Plymouth on 28 January 1744, he was not impressed by what he saw. He noted in his report that the ceiling consisted of 'planks not well laid', and that the frame let in dust and wet. In answer to his queries, the agent for the contractor reported that

> a number of sick fell down so suddenly, he had not time to [furnish] this hospital for their reception so compleatly as he would have wished, but that to obviate the inconvenience as much as the shortness of the time, and the urgency of the necessity would permit, he had laid other boards access over those.[19]

This impression of haste was confirmed in the following days, when Captain Hamilton visited the 'New Prison', which had only been completed the day before. There he found 'the mortar quite wet', but did not think that the place would be 'safely habitable till the greatest part of the summer's sun has gon over it'. The sense of urgency left no other choice but to confine prisoners in places known to be unhealthy, as in Saltrum Prison, where Spanish prisoners were detained: 'upon

---

[16] The commissioner at Plymouth asked whether it was worth repairing the house at Ware, purchased in 1694, that had been used as a prison for French prisoners and then as a hospital, as it was in 'a ruinous Condition': Kendrick Edisbury to S&W, 8 October 1733, The National Archives, Kew (TNA), ADM106/851, fo. 115.

[17] S&W to LCA, 12 March 1744, ADM98/2, fo. 108v.

[18] In 1746, 2,300 prisoners could be accommodated in Plymouth prisons: S&W to LCA, 10 November 1746, ADM98/4, fo. 26v. 1,600 prisoners were detained in Kinsale in 1747: same to same, 8 December 1747, fo. 183v.

[19] John Hamilton, 'Diary of my visitation of...the hospitals and prisons, appointed for the reception of the French and Spanish Prisoners at...Plymouth', 30 January 1744, National Maritime Museum, Greenwich (NMM), ADM/M/390, no. 46, p. 1.

the whole it has much the appearance of a dungeon, and I would recommend it to be used no more as a prison when the prisoners now in it are discharged.'[20] The statement of a militia commanding officer in 1744 with reference to Kinsale Prison could easily be generalized to most war prisons at the time:

> So unlike is it to a Prison, That a Sheep fold in England I am very well persuaded is a Place of greater Security, by reason that many other Houses are adjoined to it, and all the Walls are so thin and so ill built, That a Child of five years old may easily break through any of them.[21]

The same problem repeated itself in the following wars, and it would become more acute when the scale of the conflict widened and newly arrived prisoners of war competed for space with other detainees.

Some places were even less prepared for the sudden arrival of prisoners of war. For instance, prisoners were often landed in small ports by their captors, who then washed their hands of them. In 1745, the Agent at Weymouth was left to deal with 200 French prisoners who had just arrived in England. The lack of facilities to keep these men made the situation 'very dangerous', and amounted to 'a monstrous Expence'.[22] He therefore decided, without waiting for instructions from the Sick & Wounded Board, to send away seventy-eight of these prisoners to Portchester Castle, explaining his reasons:

> I could hire no other Place for their Reception than a Barn, which was no Way secure for such a Number of People, nor big enough to hold them, so that some were obliged to stand while others did lay down; and I could give them no sort of Liberty, because this Place is quite defenceless, for We have no Forts of Consequence, nor any armed Men, but what I procured out of the Inhabitants and was advised by Captain Griffin and the principle Inhabitants of this Place to send half of them away as soon as possible, or they would soon break out of that Place, and take Our Shipping to convey them over to France again.[23]

In the end, the Board suggested that in the future, prisoners should 'never' be disembarked in places where they could not be secured.[24] This remained wishful thinking, and the problem of finding temporary detention sites resurfaced during each war.[25]

---

[20] Ibid., p. 22.
[21] Copy of George Lucy, commanding officer, to James Belcher Esq., secretary to the Lords Justice of Ireland, Kinsale, 3 February 1744, NMM, ADM/M/390, no. 3.
[22] Copy of Agent at Weymouth to S&W, 28 May 1745, TNA, ADM98/2, fo. 140v.
[23] Extract of Agent to S&W, 29 May 1745, ibid., fo. 154v.
[24] S&W to LCA, 30 May 1745, ibid., fo. 140.
[25] Agent at Penzance to S&W, 30 May 1781, ADM98/13, fo. 179.

Besides the big prisons that were built to last in places where the arrival of prisoners of war was, if not predictable, then at least expected, there was the issue of accommodating those prisoners who were already on the territory, when their relocation was a matter of urgency. Invasion threats led to contingency plans, involving massive transfers of prisoners and a trickle-down effect on a large scale.[26] Thus, in June 1759, the Lords of the Admiralty requested to know where the prisoners detained in southern England could be moved in case of an invasion. The Board replied that the problem was also one of numbers: adding up the prisoners detained in Portsmouth, Winchester, Plymouth, Exeter, Bideford, and Penryn, there were more than 13,000 prisoners to remove and accommodate. Marching all these people, with the enemy at the gates, could become an 'extreem hazard'.[27] Once again, finding suitable places to detain them on their way would not be straightforward, and would require 'a Military Force, as shall be thought sufficient to guard them, and quell any Spirit of Mutiny which is likely to arise among them from Time to Time'. Preparing castles to accommodate such a large number of men would take a long time, and very few of them were adapted for such a purpose, such as York, Lancaster, Chester, or Carlisle castles, which were already serving as gaols. The scheme was simply impossible to implement, and in the end much more modest displacements took place, as in the late summer and early autumn of 1759, when prisoners from Dover, Dundee, and Sissinghurst were removed to the interior.[28] The same issues were raised in the summer of 1779, with the fear of a Franco-Spanish landing.[29]

Situations of emergency often conditioned a pragmatic choice of buildings, because they were available, and not because they corresponded to their projected use—a mode of thinking that was late in coming. This problem was not specific to Britain: in Normandy, the prisons of Le Havre, Dieppe, Fécamp, Cherbourg, and Granville had a limited capacity, with room for thirty prisoners at most.[30] Raoul, the *commissaire de la Marine* in Le Havre pointed this out in 1758: 'because they only stay in the prisons of this *département* momentarily in order to be transferred to Dinan where the general depot is, they were until now only given straw as beds.' However, he noted that they were detained 'sometimes for a long period' in these prisons, and thus advised that prisoners be given proper beds with blankets.[31] Using non-specialized, ad-hoc places of detention for prisoners in transit was a stopgap strategy, whose success was contingent on a quick turnover to avoid conditions of detention becoming

---

[26]   Taziolli and Garelli, 'Containment', p. 9.
[27]   S&W to LCA, 23 June 1759, NMM, ADM/F/19.
[28]   S&W to LCA, 31 August, 28 September, 11 October 1759, TNA, ADM98/8, fos. 16, 27, 35v.
[29]   S&W to LCA, 26 July, 6 August 1779, ADM98/12, fos. 56–7v, 63–v.
[30]   Raoul to SSM, 28 November 1758, Archives Nationales, Paris (AN), MAR/B3/538, fo. 182.
[31]   Ibid., fos. 180v–181.

unbearable. When a 'duck-and-go site' became a permanent detention space, new problems arose.[32]

B. Islands and Towers

The detention of prisoners in transit entailed a variety of problems. Besides the economics of location, other variables, such as the fear of epidemics or security, also needed to be addressed. Some sites were precisely selected as prisons because of their physical characteristics or their isolation, which made them easier to control. An examination of the schemes imagined in St Malo in the late seventeenth and early eighteenth centuries provides a case in point.

St Malo was one of the main military ports in France, where swarms of privateers brought the prisoners of war they had captured at sea.[33] It was also the main port of exchange for the transport ships conveying prisoners across the Channel. The Breton port was poorly equipped with prison facilities: it was above all a transhipment port, where prisoners were supposed to stay temporarily, before being redistributed inland or exchanged. The small town of Dinan, situated on the banks of the river Rance, 25 km upstream from St Malo, was the main collecting point for prisoners of war in eighteenth-century France. Problems occurred when weather conditions prevented the ships moving up the river. Despite the amplitude of the Rance's tides—among the biggest in the world— there were times where tidal flows did not rise all the way up to Dinan. At other times, the winds turned, which had the same consequences. Large numbers of prisoners could be stranded in St Malo for weeks.[34]

Solutions had to be invented to hold these people in transit, and St Malo became a laboratory for creative architectural and urban projects. Siméon Garangeau, 'chief engineer and director in chief of the fortifications in St Malo', to credit his full job title, was the architect and engineer who supervised the fortifications of northern Brittany in this period. He also built hospitals, churches and canals,[35] and this versatility might explain how he came up with new forms of detention buildings at St Malo. The Tour du Solidor, situated in St Servan, a St Malo suburb, seemed ideal for the purpose of imprisonment.

Built in the fourteenth century to watch over the entrance to the river Rance, this tower was refortified by Garangeau in the 1690s. In 1704, Monsieur de St Sulpice, *commissaire de la Marine* at St Malo, was therefore able to argue that the Tour de Solidor could be used for holding the prisoners of war *'par entrepost'* until the traffic could resume.[36] The same plans were again considered during the

[32] Tazzioli and Garelli, 'Containment', p. 9.   [33] Bromley, *Corsairs*, ch. 13.
[34] SSM to Guillot, 27 November 1744, MAR/B2/323, fo. 234.
[35] 'Garangeau (alias Garengeau)', in Blanchard, *Dictionnaire*, pp. 312–13.
[36] St Sulpice to SSM, 13 October 1704, AN, MAR/B3/123, fos. 582–v. Quotation on fo. 582.

following war, as shown on a 1744 cross-section (Fig. 4.1).[37] The use of great towers to hold people apart was nothing new—the Bishop of Durham was the first prisoner detained in the Tower of London, and the first to escape from there, in 1100.[38]

One form of prison which was considered time and again was the island-type. It is easy to understand why their isolation made them attractive sites for prisons. But this could also be their main flaw. The more isolated the prison was, the more difficult it would be to supply. The 'Tallar' sanatorium was long considered an attractive alternative to both St Malo and Dinan Castle. Monsieur de Gastines, the French *commissaire de la Marine*, described in 1693 'a place... situated out of town and very proper to detain prisoners of war in whatever quantity, this place is called tallar and within a gunshot of the town, almost remote and surrounded with good walls and in a good state'. Located on marshy shores, the Tallar was, for six hours a day, at high tide, completely isolated from the coast. Secluded, and at the same time within walking distance from St Malo, it presented many advantages compared to Dinan, which the French naval administrator described as 'a badly shut town from where they escape whenever they please'. By contrast, in the Tallar, which could 'comfortably accommodate a thousand men... we will be the masters of them as if they were detained in a room'.[39] The spatial analogy illustrates a dream of absolute domination over the captives, whose freedom of movement would be contained solely by being settled on a tidal island. This project did not materialize, but, during the following war, *Marine* administrators once again toyed with the idea.[40] It was probably due to the legal complexity of the scheme that it did not go further.[41]

'Proper' islands were another option. The *commissaire de la Marine* at Brest proposed to send English prisoners to the isle of Tréhéron, off Brest, where they would be put in the lazaret built in 1720 for quarantining sailors returned from the tropics or weakened by long voyages. In Versailles, the secretary of state for the *Marine* was sceptical as to the viability of the scheme, which was not pursued.[42] Islands continued to be used as prisons throughout our period and beyond.[43]

The choice of the lazaret was not coincidental: as noted by Thomas Markus, 'these naval bases became experimental models for public health and hygiene since a body of powerless individuals—whether military or sick—were ideal subjects of study'.[44] The same remark applies to prisoners of war. Technologies

---

[37] Frézier, 'Plan... du château de Solidor' to accommodate '350 ou 400' prisoners of war, 27 November 1744: AN, Map G/210.
[38] Nevell, 'Castles', p. 205.   [39] Gastines to SSM, 18 March 1693, AN, MAR/B3/75, fo. 240v.
[40] Siméon Garangeau's estimation: 3 December 1702, MAR/B3/117, fos. 339–41.
[41] St Sulpice's memorandum to Comte de Pontchartrain, 10 January 1703, MAR/B3/120, fos. 467–9v.
[42] SSM to Bigot de la Mothe, 27 November 1744, MAR/B2/323, fos. 228v–229.
[43] See, for instance, Cuthbertson, *Melville Prison*.
[44] Markus, *Buildings*, p. 114. See also Bashford, *Quarantine*.

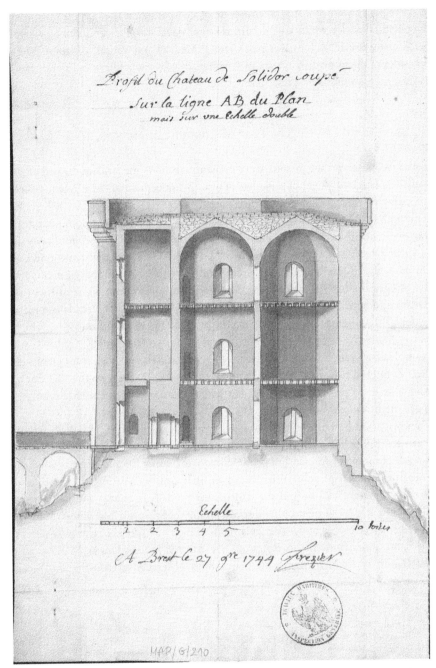

Fig. 4.1. Frézier, *Plan et profil du château de Solidor...*, *que l'on propose de rendre habitable pour y loger des prisonniers de guerre, dont il en pourra contenir 350 ou 400*, Brest, 27 November 1744. Archives Nationales (Paris), MARINE MAP/G//210/10.

of surveillance were transferred from one place to another: the lazaretto inspired the pavilion model, which was in turn used for naval hospitals and 'military-style penal institutions', such as Norman Cross.[45] Medical and 'moral contagion' were two sides of the same discourse, and prisoners of war—as soldiers and sailors, and as foreigners—embodied these many dangers.[46]

C. The Fear of Contamination

It was well known that prisons were breeding grounds for epidemics, and since there was a high turnover of prisoners of war, the movement of these people risked spreading diseases to the surrounding country.

In both France and Britain, there was a consensus among prison administrators that overcrowding endangered the health of prisoners. In 1695, the *commissaire de la Marine* in St Malo thus noted of the prison where Englishmen were detained, at Dunkirk, that it was 'so exiguous, and there is such a large number of prisoners, that they will all die if we do not take the precaution to send some of them to Berghe and neighbouring cities,... to prevent the infection that already begins to be felt'.[47] Increasing distance was a very ancient prophylactic measure, which was still used in our period when an epidemic was looming.[48] In 1778, for example, the French secretary of state for *Guerre* contemplated transferring all the 140 English prisoners detained in the Tower of La Rochelle to the Château of Angoulême, 'to prevent contagious diseases that a long stay in such a cramped space might cause'.[49]

In Britain, the terrible outbreak of 'jail fever' that struck the Old Bailey in 1750 increased public knowledge about the problem, after epidemics of typhus killed not just common criminals, but gentlefolk too, including JPs and mayors. Medical practitioners such as John Pringle proved that 'jail fever', 'hospital fever', and 'army fever' were 'all one and the same disease; a disease caused not by a type of institution, nor by some peculiar elective affinity between sin and illness, but by a linked chain of events under particular conditions'.[50] Prisoners of war were part of the same discussion. In his *Essay on the Most Effectual Means of Preserving the Health of Seamen*, physician James Lind observed that during the Seven Years' War he had seen the same infection attacking the sick at Haslar hospital,

---

[45] Markus, *Buildings*, pp. 114–18. Quotation on p. 118.

[46] Ibid., p. 120; Evans, *Fabrication*, pp. 94–117.

[47] To SSM, 5 May 1695, AN, MAR/B3/88, fos. 52–v. See also Lempereur to SSM, 8 July 1708, MAR/B3/157, fo. 202v.

[48] Markus, *Buildings*, p. 113. See, for example, S&W to Sunderland, 1 April 1709, British Library, London (BL), Add MS61693, fo. 44.

[49] Montbarey to SSM, 20 September 1778, AN, MAR/B3/659, fo. 68. The suggestion was not implemented: 3 October 1778, ibid., fo. 74.

[50] Evans, *Fabrication*, p. 95. See also Delacy, *Contagionism*, pp. 55–88.

the poor-house at Gosport, and 'French and Spanish prisoners, in their ships, in their prisons, and in their hospitals'.[51] At least since the 1740s, the Admiralty had been closely monitoring the diffusion of epidemics among prisoners of war, as shown by the example of Plymouth. In 1744, the commanding officer of an army regiment quartered in this town wrote to his superior regarding a 'feaver ... almost as infectious of the Plague', which was spreading among the 1,500 French and Spanish prisoners detained there.[52] The soldiers and the prisoners they were watching over often shared the same fate when a disease struck. Nor did prison walls stop the disease from reaching nearby cities, to the great alarm of their inhabitants. The mayor and principle inhabitants of Plymouth described how sick prisoners were interspersed with local populations:

> For want of Space in their Prisons the poor unfortunate sicken there in numbers dayly, and when sick, we having no Hospital for them, they are crouded into Houses at several ends of the Town, where for want also of convenient space and other necessaries many die daily of an ill natured Fever, which alarms many of the Inhabitants with Fear of it being disseminated through the Town.[53]

None of the solutions proposed was satisfactory. Preserving the prisoners' health could run counter to the imperative of keeping them secure, and it was near impossible to reconcile these contradictory aims.[54] Besides exchanging as many prisoners as possible and sending them back to France, the Board hence considered moving them, in health or not, to Trematon Castle, a Norman building situated nine km from Plymouth, across the River Tamar. But the remedy might be as bad as the disease: by displacing them 'higher into the Country', the epidemic might spread like wildfire. Furthermore, 'the County would undoubtedly be very much alarmed and offended at it'.[55] Prisoners of war presented additional challenges in comparison to normal inmates. Their mere presence, in their thousands, in wartime, aggravated economic and political tensions, and raised specific issues in terms of security. Conversely, the opposite solution—attempting to contain the disease behind prison walls—could end up sentencing the groups who inhabited the prison to death, while exposing its surroundings to the same risks.

In the second half of the eighteenth century, the prevention of epidemics focused above all on the control of air flows. The creation of vast airing yards in prisons, from the 1740s onwards, manifested the scientific obsession with

---

[51] Lind, *Essay* (1773), p. 307.

[52] To General Wentworth, copied in LCA to S&W, 18 January 1744, NMM, ADM/M/390, no. 26.

[53] Extract of petition to LCA, 22 January 1744, ibid., no. 31/1. The LCA ordered that the density of prisoners be reduced: 24 November 1744, ibid., no. 30.

[54] As noted by Evans, *Fabrication*, pp. 142–3, 181.

[55] S&W to LCA, 26 January 1744, TNA, ADM98/2, fo. 99.

ventilation in this period, which was also observable in hospital ships and slave ships.[56] Once again, and just like in normal prisons, designing recreation yards to preserve the health of prisoners would be costly, and could get in the way of the imperative of security, by increasing the space to be fenced in and monitored by sentries.[57]

D. The Castle-type

Since the twelfth century, in France as in England, castles, including royal castles, had been used as gaols.[58] Most of them were not purpose-built for holding captives. In the eighteenth century, this remained so: prisoners of war were put in Newgate, the Tower of London, or the keep at Portchester Castle. These structures were 'continually reworked over the centuries'.[59] In the eighteenth century, as war became costlier than ever, castles were constant works-in-progress, structurally unfinished due to lack of money.

Dinan provides us with a good example of this phenomenon. In the Breton town, the fortified fourteenth-century castle was turned into a detention centre for prisoners of war in the 1690s. Its dilapidation was a hazard for the safety of prisoners and guards alike. In June 1702, the drawbridge collapsed, as forty-nine prisoners arriving from Brest and Morlaix were passing over it; sixteen fell in the moat and three died, while three soldiers were severely hurt by dismantled parts of the broken bridge.[60] Shortness of cash delayed building works, and once these had been commissioned, the army, under whose remit castles and fortifications fell, dragged its feet to avoid paying for them.[61] In November 1702, St Sulpice remarked that the 443 English and Dutch prisoners detained in the two towers were exposed to the 'inclemency of the air' and to the cold, which infiltrated broken doors and windows.[62] A month later, he complained that the repairs to the castle were at a standstill because the entrepreneur had spent his allowance in fixing the drawbridge.[63] Holes in the vaulted roofs let the rain flow in, while large open windows allowed the prisoners to flow out.[64] In March 1712, half of the castle walls collapsed.[65]

---

[56] Evans, *Fabrication*, pp. 96–117; Markus, *Buildings*, p. 113.

[57] As in the discussion about Portchester Castle: S&W to LCA, 19 January 1745, TNA, ADM98/2, fo. 100; LCA to S&W, 31 January 1744, NMM, ADM/M/390, no. 42. Architects faced the same conundrum regarding the rebuilding of Newgate, following the jail fever of 1750: Evans, *Fabrication*, pp. 104–5.

[58] Nevell, 'Castles'.   [59] Ibid., p. 209.

[60] St Sulpice to SSM, 2 July 1702, AN, MAR/B3/117, fos. 187–8.

[61] Ibid., 18 August 1702, fo. 242.   [62] Ibid., 5 November 1702, fo. 312.

[63] Ibid., 1 December 1702, fo. 330v.

[64] Ibid., 3 December 1702, fo. 335; same to same, 29 April 1703, AN, MAR/B3/120, fos. 477v–478.

[65] SSM to Desmaretz, 12 March 1712, MAR/B2/226, fo. 894.

Castles were ancient structures, which were by definition both costly and slow to repair, and time and money were precisely the luxuries that the administrations in charge of prisoners of war did not possess. When France declared war on Britain, in March 1744, Guillot, the *commissaire de la Marine* in St Malo, knew where the difficulties lay ahead. St Malo would become the main hub and depot for all the prisoners sent from abroad. The burden would fall on Dinan, where, in the past, 1,000–1,200 prisoners had been admitted at once. But thirty years had elapsed since the War of the Spanish Succession, and the castle was in a derelict state: besides detention rooms, two guardrooms, one kitchen, and sentry boxes had to be built.[66] It was only in the middle of the summer that the Comte d'Argenson, secretary of state for *Guerre*, ordered the works to be carried out. In the meantime, prisoners of war were piling up in Brest and St Malo, where they were 'in a bad state', or placed in civilian prisons in Dinan, which could only hold up to forty men.[67] In September 1744, these prisoners were moved to the castle, which was not ready to receive them.[68] It only took a couple of days for the first escapes to happen.[69] In the following year, the number of prisoners swelled, while the works in the castle, the towers, and the hospital went on.[70] As soon as the rhythm of exchanges slowed down in St Malo, its repercussions were felt in Dinan.[71]

Across the Channel, Dover Castle had been used as a prison for centuries. King Henry II had begun building this impressive stone structure in the 1180s, and a great tower and defensive walls were added into the first half of the thirteenth century. While its fortifications were formidable, it was not adequate for the detention of prisoners of war. In April 1744, the Lords of the Admiralty proposed to detain prisoners of war in Dover Castle, as had been the case during the 'War of Queen Ann'.[72] The lack of planning is, once again, conspicuous. Barracks and sheds were to be appended to the castle in order 'to provide immediately for three or four hundred men', rather than 'putting the old building into a condition for that service'.[73] As the number of prisoners increased, new buildings were needed for their custodians, namely a guardroom for officers and another for private soldiers, as well as general facilities such as 'a cook-room, a store-room and a place for coals'.[74] In September 1744, the Board proposed to add new compounds to the castle, where 450 prisoners of war were already detained. New barracks for

---

[66] Guillot to SSM, 23 May 1744, MAR/B3/422, fos. 365–6.
[67] Ibid., 29 July, 2 August 1744, fos. 395, 399–v.
[68] SSM to Marquis de Coetmen, 6 September 1744, MAR/B2/323, fo. 82v.
[69] SSM to Thirat de Fiegalet, 18 September 1744, ibid., fo. 101.
[70] Guillot to SSM, 27 May 1745, MAR/B2/325, fo. 253v.
[71] All these reasons converged to make the prisoners' sojourn in Dinan particularly uncomfortable, a fact that the French authorities did not deny: Guillot to SSM, 15 September 1745, MAR/B2/326, fo. 121. It was still used during the following wars: Agent at Portsmouth to S&W, 10 August 1757, TNA, ADM98/6, fo. 211v.
[72] LCA to S&W, 3 April 1744, NMM, ADM/M/387, nos. 11–12.
[73] Corbett to S&W, 12 May 1744, ibid., no. 36.
[74] LCA to S&W, 26 July 1744, NMM, ADM/M/388, no. 128.

prisoners, new rooms for officers, and 'bog houses' were to be erected.[75] In addition, the Board proposed that the 'Old Church', first built by the Romans, be fitted out for detaining another 400 prisoners.[76] This plan, which was never realized, is an illustration of the two types of strategies that could be combined for accommodating prisoners of war. First, ancient, even antique, buildings, originally devoted to the service of god or to military defence, would imprison bodies and souls. At the same time, new compounds were hastily built on the site, wherever space was available. The impression is of an absence of coherence.[77]

Converting old buildings into prisons involved political challenges, as well as technical and financial ones. The coveted buildings were often in private hands. Carisbrooke Castle on the Isle of Wight provides a good example. In 1744, the Sick & Wounded Board suggested that, following a precedent set during the Civil War, when it had been used to detain Charles I and two of his children, the castle could accommodate the prisoners of war brought into Spithead. However, when the request was put to Carisbrooke Castle's owner, the powerful Harry Powlett, Fourth Duke of Bolton, MP for Hampshire since 1722 and former Lord of the Admiralty, he was far from convinced, claiming, explained the Lords of the Admiralty,

> that it would be of great inconvenience to him for the following reasons vizt. That it is the only Place of Residence he has when he is in the Island, and is furnish'd for that purpose, & therefore a very improper Place; neither is it any ways strong enough for securing such Prisoners as may be taken from the Enemy, during the present War, there being no Barracks, or any other conveniency, but what is made use of by his servants that are actually there in taking care of his house.[78]

The Board was duly rebuked for not doing its homework. As this example shows, state administrators walked on eggshells because these were sensitive issues: expropriating a powerful landed grandee was plainly impossible. At the same time, this illustrates a broader phenomenon that we have encountered before: the state had to rely on 'private' interests in order to fulfil its missions. By contrast, royal palaces and residences could be 'borrowed' with less fuss, and these huge buildings served, throughout the eighteenth century, as detention facilities for prisoners of war. This was the case with the King's House at Winchester, a royal palace designed by Christopher Wren for Charles II, which was fitted out for 1,200

---

[75] S&W to LCA, 4 September 1744, TNA, ADM98/2, fos. 11v–12; LCA to S&W, 5 September 1744, NMM, ADM/M/388, no. 190.

[76] S&W to LCA, 4 September 1744, TNA, ADM98/2, fo. 11v.

[77] Another example is Portchester Castle, originally built by the Romans, which served as a war prison throughout the eighteenth century.

[78] LCA to S&W, 30 April 1744, NMM, ADM/M/387, no. 23.

prisoners of war during the American War of Independence.[79] Likewise, Edinburgh Castle, a royal residence since the twelfth century, which had served as a military barrack since the 1660s, held prisoners of war from the Seven Years' War until the end of the Napoleonic Wars.[80] The same principle held in France, where prisoners of war were put in medieval castles and towers, in Angoulême, Fougères, Limoges, La Rochelle, Niort, or Dinan.[81]

Generic spaces of detention were continuously reconfigured to accommodate the sick, the poor, criminals, soldiers, or prisoners. For most of the eighteenth century, the exceptional status of prisoners of war in the law of nations did not translate into specific material conditions of detention. The chief criteria for selecting these places were a combination of pragmatic and geographical rationales. Facilities had to be available, easy to adapt, and worth renovating, and closed off without being too remote. Islands and fortified towers embodied this fantasy of an ideal prison, which could be open and shut at will; where prisoners could be brought in and carried away by sea; sites where the danger of contamination, real and metaphorical, would be limited. This was a feature of eighteenth-century prisons more generally, Robin Evans observes: 'At best, the building was only a partial and indistinct reflection of the character of prison life and,...buildings were colonized as more or less passive receptacles for the purpose of confinement.'[82] Wherever we look, the impression that prevails throughout the period is that of the failure of prisons to address the basic needs of their occupants. Across generations of prisoners, the same complaints reverberated within the walls of prison-castles. But, despite these criticisms, castles remained very influential buildings in the long term. The shape of country houses and castles, in 'U', 'E', or 'H' form, as described by Thomas Markus, 'became the dominant eighteenth-century British institutional plan'. Continuing the tradition of palaces, with their 'enclosed courts', this shape 'made growth by accretion easier, especially when older buildings were being converted, and was adaptable to any size or site, whereas the radial or pavilion plans were virtually fixed'.[83] This explains why the castle-type did not disappear with the appearance of reformed prisons in the last quarter of the eighteenth century.

III. Prisoners of War in 'Reformed Prisons': The British Case

From the mid-1770s onwards, it seems that the detention of prisoners of war in France and Britain followed distinct trajectories, which explained our focus on the

[79] LCA to S&W, 22 July 1778, NMM, ADM/M/406; S&W to LCA, 16 September 1778, TNA, ADM98/11, fos. 266–7. It had been used for the same purpose during the Seven Years' War.
[80] S&W to LCA, 14 October 1778, ADM98/11, fo. 289. See Tabraham, *Edinburgh Castle*, pp. 25–35, 59–63.
[81] Montbarey to SSM, September–November 1778, AN, MAR/B3/659, fos. 51, 65, 70–2, 74–6, 86.
[82] Evans, *Fabrication*, p. 32.   [83] Markus, *Buildings*, pp. 101, 108.

latter. In France, the same buildings were used as in the previous wars, such as castles and citadels.[84] In Britain, the so-called 'age of prison reform' designates the massive rebuilding of prisons that took place between 1775 and 1795, and the rise of new ideas about the aims and modes of incarceration.[85] The two major explanations for this, it has been convincingly argued, were jail fever and the American War of Independence. While this is all well known, the role played by the detention of prisoners of war in this process has been overlooked. For example, the fear of jail fever meant that the installation of a prison facility near a city often elicited a hostile response from the local population. In Bristol, the search for a convenient detention place for 2,000 prisoners in 1778 was hindered by local opposition. The Sick & Wounded Board observed that 'the Magistrates and Inhabitants of Bristol, object to having a Prison within the City'.[86] This 'logic of distancing', according to which the prison must be physically rejected and hidden, and the prisoners segregated, to avoid the symbolic contamination of the free world, has been analysed by sociologist Philippe Combessie.[87] The Bristol civic elite settled their choice on Knowle, which had been used in the previous war, because it was conveniently 'situated about a mile from the City'. However, adapting the site to this purpose would be too costly and too slow, and it was instead decided to build a new prison, for the specific aim of detaining prisoners of war.[88] Stapleton Prison received its first prisoners of war in June 1780.[89]

Innovative structures, illustrating Howardian and later Benthamite principles, thus began to be designed specifically for prisoners and prisoners of war in this period. The idea of adapting buildings to their occupants or even inventing buildings specifically for them was new in the 1770s. These notions were also linked to a growing reflection on the conceptual and practical differences between the detention of prisoners of war and that of other inmates. Moreover, these discussions took place at a time of social and political turmoil for Britain.

A. New Challenges, New Solutions: The American War of Independence

The intensity of the challenges that state administrators had to overcome at that time exacerbated the structural tensions that had always been a feature of the

---

[84] See, for instance, Prince de Montbarey to *Intendant* Calonne, 21 June 1779, Archives Départementales du Nord, Lille, C4624/2.

[85] While similar debates took place in France during these two decades, the link with the question of prisoners of war appears less obvious. See, for example, Petit, *Peines obscures*, pp. 17–31.

[86] S&W to LCA, 16 September 1778, TNA, ADM98/11, fos. 262–3; LCA to S&W, 30 September 1778, NMM, ADM/M/406.

[87] Combessie, 'Marking', pp. 545–6.

[88] S&W to LCA, 7 December 1778, TNA, ADM98/11, fos. 361–3.

[89] S&W to LCA, 5 June 1780, ADM98/12, fo. 236v.

imprisonment of prisoners of war. The problems encountered, and the solutions imagined, provided a template for the following war.

Yet the links between changes in modes of war incarceration and penal imprisonment during the 1780s remain largely unexplored. In this period, the rapid rise in prison population meant that prisoners of war competed with other categories of detainees for the same spaces of incarceration. The blockade of the Atlantic Ocean made it impossible to transport convicted criminals to America, as had been the custom since the seventeenth century. About 1,000 new convicts per year now had to be accommodated in Britain. This clogged the prison system in the metropolis, opening major discussions about the best way to detain defendants awaiting their trial, in addition to managing convicts already within the system.[90] Taking into account the prisoners exchanged in British and French ports only, and excluding those who died in prison, as well as those exchanged in America, the West Indies, and in neutral ports, more than 30,000 French prisoners spent time in a British prison between 1778 and 1783.[91] This is without even counting the tens of thousands of North American, Dutch, and Spanish prisoners detained in Britain.[92]

By comparison with previous wars, even more diverse places of incarceration were used during this period, such as temporary buildings for prisoners in transit, prison-ships, and civilian jails, as well as newly built prisons. Although time pressure was relentless, for possibly the first time state administrators started to plan for their needs instead of simply managing a crisis. More broadly, in the 1770s the rising population and crime rates drove the rebuilding of many prisons, which was made possible by increasing financial resources and new ideas about architecture.[93] In many ways, the challenges remained similar, but they were more acute than ever. Fifteen years had elapsed since the Seven Years' War, and some facilities had deteriorated and needed to be fitted out and repaired, while others were no longer available. The search for new buildings became frantic towards the end of the summer of 1778, as the first wave of French prisoners arrived across the Channel. Throughout the country, vacant houses were converted to new purposes. A brewhouse, for 1,000 prisoners in Barnstaple, North Devon, was hired,[94] as was a 'Brick Building' for 350 prisoners near Liverpool.[95] Even when convenient buildings had been found, they promptly filled up, whatever their size.[96]

---

[90] Evans, *Fabrication*, pp. 119–20. See also Frost, *Convicts*, ch. 1.

[91] S&W to LCA, TNA, ADM98/14, 13 March 1783, fo. 162v.

[92] Perhaps 30,000 Americans were detained in British jails, either in America or in the metropole: Burrows, *Forgotten Patriots*, p. 11.

[93] Chalklin, *English Counties*, ch. 9; Evans, *Fabrication*, ch. 3.

[94] S&W to LCA, 16 September 1778, TNA, ADM98/11, fos. 129v–130; LCA to S&W, 30 September 1778, NMM, ADM/M/406.

[95] S&W to LCA, 13 October 1778, TNA, ADM98/11, fos. 139v–140. The same trend would continue throughout the war, and houses were rented out in Weymouth, Dublin, or Exeter: 2 January 1781, ADM98/13, fo. 167; 27 March, 25 June 1782, ADM98/14, fos. 68, 101v.

[96] As in Penryn in Cornwall: S&W to LCA, 4 November 1778, 15 January 1779, TNA, ADM98/11, fos. 153, 203v–204.

The ebb and flow of prisoners was a consequence of geopolitical and military dynamics on both sides of the Atlantic. As the war unfolded, the tide of prisoners in need of urgent accommodation in Southern England rose. Due to the lack of prison facilities in the region, small towns like Deal in Kent (comprised of maybe 4,000 inhabitants in the 1770s) bore the brunt of new arrivals.[97] On 18 May 1779, there were already eighty-six French prisoners of war in the prison, which was only ever 'intended as a Place of temporary confinement'. Less than a month later, there were 256.[98] The new prison that was built in July, 'for the temporary accommodation' of the prisoners who had been brought into the Downs, had a capacity of 150.[99] When Spain entered the coalition against Britain, this applied further pressure on Deal's prison, and the situation worsened when the United Provinces entered the war in December 1780.[100] The problem was systemic. Deal remained the main outlet for the south-east of England throughout the war.[101] Similar pressures built up around England's coastline at entry points.[102]

The situation was not much better further to the west, despite the building of new prisons. The prison that was set up in Forton, near Portsmouth, amalgamated pre-existing buildings, piled up against each other, whose location was determined by pragmatic considerations rather than according to any coherent plan. Forton had first been a hospital, built in 1713 for sailors, and was then converted into a war prison during the Seven Years' War.[103] It was modernized and reopened as a prison for American 'rebels' in June 1777. Including the new hospital erected on the site,[104] more than 2,000 French prisoners and 600 American prisoners could be detained at Forton.[105] But when this number reached 1,500, in May 1779, according to a contemporary report this already felt like overcrowding.[106]

When the news came in July 1779 that a combined Franco-Spanish invasion was on the cards, the strain on the prison system reached new heights. Those prisoners detained near the coasts, especially near the great shipyards of Portsmouth and Plymouth, were a danger for home security and had to be relocated inland. The Admiralty required that a plan for relocating these men inland be prepared, but the Board remarked on 'the very great difficulty of finding Places even for much smaller Numbers'. It came up with four options.[107] The first was to rent out 'Houses or Buildings as may be procured in the interiour part of the Kingdom'.[108] An advertisement was consequently inserted in newspapers, but the

[97] S&W to LCA, 3, 14 October 1778, ibid., fos. 136–7v, 141.
[98] S&W to LCA, 18 May, 11 June 1779, ADM98/12, fos. 11–v, 25v–26.
[99] S&W to LCA, 27 July 1779, ibid., fos. 57v–58.
[100] S&W to LCA, 3 January 1781, ADM98/13, fos. 88v–89.
[101] S&W to LCA, 22 November 1780, ibid., fo. 71v.
[102] As in Penryn: S&W to LCA, 14 May 1781, ibid., fo. 172.
[103] Cohen, *Yankee Sailors*, p. 32.   [104] Alexander, 'Forton Prison', p. 370.
[105] S&W to LCA, 10 July 1778, TNA, ADM98/11, fos. 216–17.
[106] Colonel Archibald McNable to Lord Armherst, Portsmouth, 31 May 1779, NMM, ADM/M/407.
[107] S&W to LCA, 26 July 1779, TNA, ADM98/12, fos. 56–7v.
[108] Ibid., fo. 57.

success of this initiative in such a short time was doubtful.[109] The second option was modelled on the techniques used by travelling armies: prisoners could be encamped 'within a Ditch Trench and Bastions...till the present alarm is passed'.[110] It possessed the advantage of necessitating fewer guards. As a third option, the 4,000 French and Spanish prisoners detained at Plymouth and Forton might also be transferred to Winchester.[111] But this would put pressure on a prison that was already congested. The final option, which we will investigate below, was to put the prisoners of war in one of the kingdom's forty county jails.[112]

In my brief presentation of the morphology of carceral spaces, I have not yet mentioned the most idiosyncratic of all, exemplifying the culture of 'recycling' which was a feature of eighteenth-century modes of incarceration. There was more than a quip in Samuel Johnson's famous sentiment that 'being in a ship is being in a jail, with the chance of being drowned'.[113] Indeed, old ships were used throughout the eighteenth century, in Europe as in the colonies, to detain convicts, prisoners of war or the sick on shores adjacent to ports. The masts, rigging, and sails had been removed from these retired warships, while superstructures were erected for the accommodation of prisoners, staff, and stores. These prisons were cut off from the outside by water, sand, and rocks. While British hulks have attracted considerable scholarly attention, the fact that this mode of confinement was not specific to Britain or Europe is often ignored. Some were used in Spain, Portugal, and France.[114] In May 1778, when John Paul Jones, the foremost naval commander of the American insurgents' 'navy', brought the crew of HMS *Drake*, a British prize, to Brest, these 200 sailors were detained in a French ship that was moored in the harbour for several months.[115] In general, the French never regarded hulks highly. When asked what he thought about grounding a prison-ship in the Rance river, mid-way between Dinan and St Malo, Commissaire Guillot replied that although this had been 'a long-established practice in England', such a 'floating prison' would be expensive and 'give occasion to a quantity of troubles of all kinds'.[116] By contrast, in Britain and in the British colonies across the Atlantic, hulks were used on a much grander scale to detain prisoners of war from the 1770s onwards.[117] First envisaged as a 'temporary expedient' to incarcerate criminals

---

[109] Ibid., fos. 56v–57.   [110] Ibid., fo. 56.   [111] Ibid., fo. 56v.

[112] The authors of the project did not specify whether Wales was included or not.

[113] 31 August 1773, in Boswell, *Tour to the Hebrides*, p. 137.

[114] 'Floating prisons' were moored in Brest and St Malo during the War of the League of Augsburg, and loaded with English prisoners of war captured by Jacobite privateers serving James II: Gastines to SSM, 7 September, 11 December 1695, AN, MAR/B3/89, fos. 181, 334. See Bromley, *Corsairs*, p. 156.

[115] Callo, *John Paul Jones*, pp. 58–9; Jones to French commissioners, 9 May 1778, in de Koven, *Life*, vol. I, p. 333; Hector, 'Notte concernant les prisonniers faits par M. Jonne', 2 December 1778, AN, MAR/F2/82.

[116] Guillot to unknown, 11 November 1778, MAR/F2/82.

[117] Crowhurst, *French War*, pp. 177–8. Prison ships had been used during the Seven Years' War, in Plymouth and Chatham: S&W to LCA, 12 February, 13 July 1757, TNA, ADM98/6, fos. 88, 88v–89, 190v.

awaiting transportation, in the winter of 1775/6, they became permanent when transporting penal prisoners to North American colonies was no longer possible.[118]

The conversion of generic spaces of detention worked both ways, and in 1782 the Board had to fend off the covetousness of the army, who tried to use prison buildings as barracks. This led the Admiralty to define the function of these prisons in some detail, and explain the purpose of keeping them empty. When army generals enquired whether some room might be made at Forton Prison and the hospital at Haslar for accommodating the troops on duty there, stressing that these buildings appeared to be vacant, the Board replied that the five buildings holding prisoners of war were not appropriate for soldiers:

> [They] are capable by computation of containing 665 Prisoners, but we think they would be too much crouded by this number, and as Prisoners are very often suddenly thrown in, in great Numbers, there is an obvious necessity for such an entrepot, where they may be lodged 'till they can conveniently be marched to Winchester or embarked at Warsash, nor do we see how the service could be carried on without it, and We think that an entrepot for about 600 Men, is by means too large, a line of Battle Ship of the Enemy, or two Frigates taken would at once fill it.[119]

This was not an overstatement: great ships of the line, such as the seventy-four-gun ships that were launched by the French navy during the 1740s, were operated by crews that could tally up to 700 men. The commissioners rightly underlined the problems caused by 'a general Battle or an Epidemic Disease in the Fleet'.[120] A growing sense of the specific challenge posed by the timing of prisoners' arrival unfolded in this period. At Forton Prison, there were in October 1782 two two-storeyed buildings, each one capable of hosting 650 prisoners, even though only 130 prisoners were accommodated in Forton at the time. The Board explained, however: 'how soon the Prison may be filled it is impossible to say.'[121] Instead of giving in to the contingency pressure of the army, and filling all the available beds with soldiers, the commissioners refused to make a decision based on emergency criteria only. Prison planning was a new phenomenon, which was just emerging in the 1780s, and the Board's decision to keep a certain number of beds available expressed their preoccupation with future needs, anticipating chronic congestion.[122]

The commissioners linked this to another argument, which, again, illustrates similarities with contemporary reflections on penal imprisonment: conditions of detention should depend on the category of inmates. Thus, 'owing to the very

---

[118] Ignatieff, *Just Measure*, pp. 80–2. The *Security* ship was thus fitted for French prisoners of war in Gillingham Reach (Medway): Lieutenant Francis Nott to Navy Board, 7 May 1779, TNA, ADM106/1248, fo. 283.
[119] S&W to LCA, 28 October 1782, ADM98/14, fo. 136.   [120] Ibid., fo. 263.
[121] Ibid., fo. 264.   [122] Wolff, 'Sens de l'urgence'.

different mode of accommodating Soldiers and Prisoners', the former occupied much more space than the latter. In a prison ward, prisoners lay in hammocks slung 'sometimes four over one another, according to the height of the Ceiling, and each Hammock takes up a space of only two feet and an inch in Breadth from one Hook to another', whereas in barracks and hospitals, men lay in cradles, leaving 'the whole space over their Heads ... void and unoccupied'. Space occupation was rationalized and more economical when accommodating prisoners. Placing troops at Forton meant that 100 men 'would take up the whole of the Prison'. And mixing heterogeneous groups could only end in confusion—a notion that was anathema for prison reformers:

> The consequences of Soldiers, Patients, and Prisoners, the Agent with his Clerks, Turnkeys and Laborers, the Surgeon with his Assistants all living within the same narrow Precincts, the distinct and separate authoritys perpetually clashing would produce endless Divisions and constant complaints.[123]

At the end of the war, the question of what was to be done with the prisons that had been converted to accommodate prisoners of war was not straightforward. Should these buildings be turned into barracks or hospitals? Rented out? Torn down, while their materials would be sold? Or carefully maintained until the next war? For the first time, the Sick & Wounded Board engaged in long-term reflection, illustrating their concern for the financial consequences of a massive prison-building programme, and a new attention to accountability. Clearly, lessons had been learnt from the recent past. The Board pointed out that considerable sums had been invested 'in filling up the Mill Prison at Plymouth and Forton Prison near Gosport, and erecting additional Buildings' for the detention of prisoners of war.[124] Similarly, the commissioners pointed out that it would be ill-advised to pull down Stapleton Prison, which had been so costly to build and could contain '1,500 Prisoners with a Suitable Hospital and various Offices'. Destroying this massive stone structure to sell its material would not be worth the effort. These premises, which enclosed a 'spacious Airing Ground', could instead be rented out, to set up a manufacture, or, better, leased to the Ordnance or War Offices, 'on condition of their paying the General Rent, and keeping the Buildings in Repair, and delivering them up to Us whenever the Service shall require'.[125] These hopes were disappointed, however, as the army was not interested in any of the three big vacant prisons. Along with Deal and Winchester Prisons, they would have to be rented out or maintained during peacetime.[126]

---

[123] S&W to LCA, 28 October 1782, TNA, ADM98/14, fos. 264–6.
[124] Ibid., 16 April 1783, fo. 176.   [125] Ibid., 2 May 1783, fos. 178v.
[126] Ibid., 11 July 1783, fo. 187. On Deal: ibid., 22 April 1783, 5 November 1784, fos. 228, 452. On Winchester: ibid., 17 May 1784, fo. 216v.

These almost new and unoccupied prisons are examples of what architect Mélanie Van der Hoorn calls 'undesired architecture', a category in which she includes 'unbuilt projects, because their existence was questioned and rejected before they could even be realized', as well as 'buildings that were destroyed, damaged or abandoned to progressive dilapidation, transformed, removed or hidden by other constructions'.[127] Who should inhabit these prisons once the war was no more?

B. The First War Prisons: The Revolutionary and Napoleonic Wars

In France, during the French Wars, building new prisons was not a priority, and prisoners were detained in a variety of non-dedicated buildings. In January 1797, following the wreck of HMS *Amazon*, a thirty-six-gun frigate, in Audierne Bay (Brittany), one of the sailors began a diary documenting the crew's captivity until their exchange in March 1798. During their journey across Brittany, the prisoners were put in all sorts of buildings, such as common jails, stables, or military camps. The diarist reached 'Doirlene' [*Doirnenez?*] on 16 January. Echoing, twenty years later, Gibbon's meditations on the ruins of the Roman Empire, the prisoner contemplated the derelict church in which he had been housed for the night:

> In the Morning to Took a View of our Ruinous Habitation and Moralizing a little on the Antiquity of the Building Servd us for a Breakfast.... Whilst we were thus Ruminating amongst our Selves and Talking of the Ruinous Situation of France for her Once Magnificent and Respected Churches were now Polluted and made use off for Magazones for Millitary Stores and for the Reception of Prisoners of Warr.[128]

By the time of the French Revolution, a side effect of the nationalization of church property had been to make these buildings available for purposes other than the worship of God. More than 3,000 British prisoners were detained in the repurposed convent of the Ursulines in Dunkirk in 1793–4.[129] The biggest prison depots used in France during the French Wars were the military citadels built by Vauban in the late seventeenth century to defend the north and north-eastern borders, such as Lille, Valenciennes, Arras, Givet, Longwy, Sarrelibre, Bitche, Auxonne, and Briançon.[130] They were emptied depending on the need to leave

---

[127] Van der Hoorn, *Eyesores*, p. 15.
[128] An account of the wreck of HMS *Amazon*, NMM, REC/57, pp. 17–18.
[129] Le Prat, 'Faire face', p. 213.
[130] Chamberlain, *Hell*, ch. 8; Lewis, *Napoleon*, pp. 57, 84, 265; Marquis, 'La Convention', pp. 68, 70.

room for soldiers on the move, but they were well suited to the detention of prisoners, as Courtenay Ilbert, a young army officer incarcerated in Lille Citadel, wrote to his mother in August 1798: 'As the place is not very full our men have almost as good barracks as in England and much better than some that I have seen. We have our parades morning and evening just the same as in England.'[131] These depots were smaller than the biggest war prisons built in Britain in these years, and none of them had a capacity exceeding 3,000.

In Britain, 'old' places of detention were still in use, too, as in Winchester or Portchester Castles. The use of prison hulks was also revived. Indeed, by 1794 land prisons were insufficient to accommodate the considerable number of prisoners arriving from France and elsewhere. Their pattern of arrival followed the rhythm of British victories. The number of hulks began to increase, after the Battle of the Nile in 1798. In 1805, after Trafalgar, four new hulks were opened. The Continental Blockade made it necessary to open three further hulks in 1806. In total, across the period fifty-five prison-ships were used in Britain to detain French, Danish, Dutch, American, German, Italian, and Spanish prisoners of war.[132] The same phenomenon happened in the West Indies. In November 1803, after Rochambeau—the planter backed by Napoleon who ruled St Domingue—had been defeated by Dessalines, Toussaint-Louverture's successor, the British squadron captured three French frigates and twenty smaller vessels. Thousands of prisoners were thus brought to Jamaica. Seven thousand of them were detained in the prison-ships anchored in Kingston Harbour.[133]

The denunciation of British hulks became a *passage obligé* of French propaganda during this period. One captivity narrative was published in 1815 by René-Martin Pillet, a *maréchal-de-camp* and former prisoner of war on board the *Brunswick* hulk. Hulks were not just an unfortunate outcome of terrible war conditions, claimed Pillet: their very architecture displayed an intent to effect the 'destruction of prisoners'. Gun ports were left half-open, letting in freezing air in the winter, which caused pneumonia, and unbearable heat in the summer, causing death by suffocation. Pillet called these holes *meurtrières*—a standard medieval fortification term describing the narrow vertical slits through which an archer could launch arrows. The guards were accused of shooting through them on the prisoners at will.[134] Overcrowding was the main problem, noted by every observer: the largest hulks were three-deck ships with a carceral capacity of 1,200 men. According to Pillet, this was no coincidence: 'everywhere this congestion is the fruit of a dreadful reflexion, of a bloodthirsty calculation.'[135] His description,

---

[131] 5 August 1798, Devon Record Office, Exeter, 316M/4/F/2/3. He was released six months later: 12 January 1799, 316/M/4/F/2/6.
[132] Chamberlain, *Hell*, pp. 58–60.   [133] *Lady Nugent's Journal*, introduction, p. xxiv.
[134] Pillet, *Angleterre*, pp. 372, 376, 373.   [135] Ibid., p. 378.

although the comparison was not made explicit, evoked slave ships, a connection that would not have been lost on his readers.[136]

The real innovation, during this period, was the construction of the first purpose-built war prisons. In the 1790s, it was decided to 'reduce [the] unnecessary Establishments in Towns upon the Coast' which had been used for the reception of prisoners, because they were too expensive to maintain and presented security risks.[137] Instead, prisoners were concentrated 'in fewer (if larger) depots'. Immediate demand and 'economical' preoccupations were the overriding factor in the decision to invest in prisoner of war buildings. The first war prison was Norman Cross in Cambridgeshire.[138] This large wooden prison was erected in 1797 on cheap agricultural land. Norman Cross's inland location was chosen carefully, to be secured from an enemy invasion, but sufficiently close to the sea to receive the thousands of prisoners captured in the North Sea from the French and their new satellite the Batavian Republic.[139] Norman Cross, which could accommodate 7,000 prisoners,[140] was well connected to the south-east of the country. It borrowed traditional designs; this war prison embodied the 'older tradition of cruciform blocks and courts', divided by a central axis.[141] Dartmoor prison opened in 1809, and followed a much more ambitious programme. Like all war prisons at the time, however, it quickly exceeded its capacity. The covered galleries that allowed prisoners to promenade in bad weather were consequently converted into sleeping wards.[142] But from an architectural perspective, Dartmoor really marked a turning point, as shown on a 1810 map (Fig. 4.2).

This new prison was far from being a complete failure. It was built in this deprived region thanks to the lobbying of Thomas Tyrwhitt, secretary to the Duchy of Cornwall and MP for Plymouth. In Tyrwhitt's mind, the prison would be the engine of regional development. An anonymous article published in 1810 in the *Repository of Arts* hinted that Tyrwhitt was directly interested in the scheme: that gentleman, whose seat 'lies within a mile and half of the barracks... is constantly pursuing and extending his agricultural improvements on the moor, in which he has expended a considerable sum of money'.[143] He had it in mind to use the cheap labour force provided by prisoners of war for developing the neighbouring town of Princetown.[144] The building of Dartmoor prison is an illustration of the link in this period between agricultural innovation, moral reform, patriotism, and economic profit.[145] The plan to convert Dartmoor into a

---

[136] Wood, *Blind Memory*, pp. 16–40.
[137] *Ninth Report* (1809), referring to changes in the mid-1790s, p. 22.
[138] On land prison depots during the French Wars, see Chamberlain, *Hell*, pp. 80–113.
[139] Crowhurst, *French War*, p. 179.   [140] Ibid., pp. 91–3; Walker, *Depot*.
[141] Markus, *Buildings*, p. 122.
[142] Andrew Baird, former inspector of His Majesty's hospitals and prison hospitals, 15 April 1818, *Report from the Committee on the Prisons* (1818), pp. 175–6.
[143] 'Plate 19. Description of the new prison of war, Dartmoor, Devon', in *Repository of Arts*, (September 1810), p. 163.
[144] Richardson, 'Architect', p. 78.   [145] Bayly, *Imperial Meridian*.

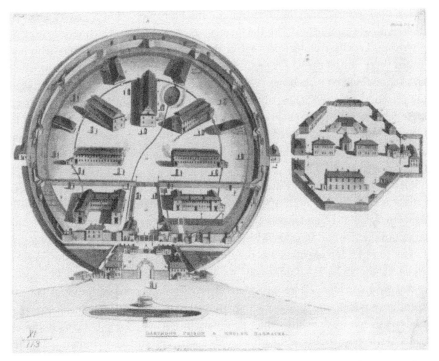

Fig. 4.2. *Dartmoor Prison & English Barracks* (1810). © The British Library Board, K Top XI 113.

depot for convicts, which fits into the same logic, was present from the very beginning. Such a level of planning was clearly unprecedented. The *Repository* article mentioned that

> at the termination of the war, when the present occupants of the prison are restored to their families and countries, it is said to be in contemplation to convert this vast, and then useless building, into a receptacle for convicts, whose labours on the moor will prove highly important and beneficial to the nation, and an incredible saving in the enormous expense incurred both at home and in transportation.[146]

A prison need not be a financial disaster. On the contrary, the men who imagined Dartmoor thought of it as a shrewd economic investment. Tyrwhitt's dreams were fulfilled after the Napoleonic Wars. A Committee on the Prisons was set up in the House of Commons in 1818, to discuss what this huge establishment should become. This was part of a wider reflection on the penal system post-bellum: the committee also examined the state of Newgate and other London prisons,

---

[146] *Repository of Arts*, p. 163.

following reports about the dreadful conditions of detention there. A series of interviews was conducted, with the former superintendent of Dartmoor Prison, its physician, and its architect, as well as those guards and army officers who had served there during the war. The Commons' committee wanted to know whether Dartmoor could be turned into a 'prison for convicts', without forestalling its use for prisoners of war, 'at any future period'.[147] A plan, which had already been considered as soon as the prison had been cleared of its prisoners of war in February 1815, was to collect the convicts at Dartmoor, before embarking them at Plymouth for New South Wales, instead of shipping them down the Channel from London in the winter season.[148]

Dartmoor presented advantages for confining convicts, not least its sheer capacity. Constructed for 7,500 prisoners, it was subsequently enlarged,[149] and between April 1812 and April 1814, it held on average 7,831 prisoners.[150] The largest of the five buildings could hold 1,200 men, divided in three large rooms of 175 by 33 feet, each of which was occupied by 400 men. According to the prison's architect, these rooms could 'easily' be divided into individual chambers, partitioned by a corridor. There, prisoners of war were detained in the same way as 'common soldiers' and 'sailors', with hammocks and paillasses filled with straw.[151] And the prison was healthier than a military barracks.[152] Despite being purpose-built, Dartmoor could be filled with different categories of inmates. In this conception, the occupational needs of prisoners of war were not fundamentally different. This did not mean, however, that they should be detained alongside other inmates.

IV. Coexistence or Separation?

It was one thing to reuse empty buildings and to house new populations, and another to have prisoners of war rub shoulders with criminals and debtors. We know that by the middle of the eighteenth century, there was a clearer definition of the legal status of prisoners of war, while some separation principles were already well established by the end of the seventeenth century: criminals and debtors, petty and serious criminals, men and women, began to be kept apart. These principles became a staple of the discourse of prison reformers, which started to be systematized from the 1780s onwards. But what do we see if we enter the

---

[147] 8 May 1818, *Report*, p. 9.
[148] Captain James Bowen (one of the commissioners of the Transport Board (TB)), 15 April 1818, *Report*, p. 173; copy of TB to Lord Viscount Sidmouth, 18 February 1815, *Report*, Appendix 33, p. 238.
[149] Daniel Alexander, architect, 15 April 1818, *Report*, p. 180.
[150] Transport Account Office, 6 May 1818, *Report*, p. 236.
[151] Daniel Alexander, 15 April 1818, *Report*, pp. 178, 179, 172.
[152] Captain James Bowen, ibid., p. 173.

prison? In the following section, we will question whether distinctions that existed before captivity, such as those between prisoner of war and criminal, or those of class or nation, follow the same chronology, and whether they continued to operate behind prison walls. We will pay attention to the experience of incarceration of prisoners of war, in order to understand what they shared with other inmates, what set them apart, and what changed over time. The competition for the use of the so-called 'reformed' prisons to detain prisoners of war will provide us with a case in point.

A. Prisoners of War and Criminals

There was universal agreement with the idea that prisoners of war should normally be removed from other inmates, for reasons to do with international law, morality, or security. But in practice, even in the age of 'reformed' prisons, this was very complicated to implement. Robin Evans has noted with respect to normal prisons, 'prison society was by no means always a reflection of recognized relationships of degree'.[153] Throughout the century, many prisoners of war were detained alongside and in the same manner as civilians. In this period, war imprisonment was not always different to 'normal' imprisonment: prisons were private enterprises, run by keepers who made money out of the detention business, usually by directly raising fees on the prisoners or selling food and drinks to them.[154]

Detaining those of a contested status together with common prisoners could be a deliberate decision on the part of their captors. In 1708, Captain Edmund Fitzgerald, an Irish Jacobite who was imprisoned at Newgate for high treason alongside the rest of the crew of the *Salisbury*, wrote a long petition detailing their conditions of detention. He remonstrated that they were handled 'like ye most infamous of common malefactors', instead of being treated as prisoners of war.[155] Fitzgerald and his companions were first thrown into 'ye condemned hole', where they were put on irons and remained for ten days. Thereafter they were moved to the common side of the prison, which he described as 'a nauseous room subject to all ye inconveniencies yt ye neighbourhood of a publick vault can bring along with it'. They stayed there for forty-seven days, sleeping on 'bare boards'. They were finally moved to the 'Master's side' of Newgate—joining those prisoners who

---

[153] Evans, *Fabrication*, p. 31.
[154] Watson, 'Commission'. French jailors and food contractors often complained that prisoners of war were not a profitable business, because the state reluctantly reimbursed them: Du Guay to SSM, 29 July 1711, AN, MAR/B3/191, fos. 404v–405v.
[155] Fitzgerald to [Sunderland], 25 August 1708, BL, Add MS61595, fo. 52v. An anonymous writer ('Anglicus') similarly complained about the mishandling of French prisoners at Bristol by the sword-bearer, who treated 'them in such a manner as the jaylor of Newgate would blush at': copy, 10 October 1747, NMM, ADM/M/399, no. 318/1.

could afford to pay for their own food and accommodation—where the sixteen of them lived among themselves, sharing two rooms and sleeping two to a bed.[156] Fitzgerald emphasized the spartan conditions which they had to put up with, and the large sums they had to pay to the keeper of the prison:

> We have neither courtines to our beds nor shutters to our windows: we have no other place to dress our meat in, notwithstanding which we find ye cold as excessive now, as ye heat was in summer, to say nothing of ye wildness of ye place continually infected with weezels and such like vermin.[157]

The keeper of Newgate, William Pitt, replied that Fitzgerald and his fellow officers had no grounds for complaint. They benefited from a privileged treatment compared to normal criminals, since they had chosen to live in an apartment, bought 'their own meat and drink', and had a cook to prepare it 'after their own manner'. Even the sick among them had 'better places and freer of it is allowed ym yt is usual to other prisoners', and they had obtained to be moved to the 'presse-yard'—the area reserved for special prisoners.[158] Pitt notoriously extracted a lot of money from his Jacobite prisoners, and in February 1709, the Sick & Wounded Board stated that the sums demanded by the keeper 'for their lodging and bedding to this day', which amounted to more than £103, was 'a very extravagant & unreasonable demand'.[159] What matters in this discussion is the choice of comparison: compared to those who Pitt called 'all criminals', there was nothing anomalous in the situation of the Jacobite prisoners. Putting 'so great a number of lusty men' on irons was nothing abnormal, he argued.[160] But Fitzgerald and his companions precisely resented being imprisoned alongside detainees whose infamy symbolically rubbed off on them.

It was this same feeling of being tainted by association that drove the complaints of Abbé Saujon, a French Catholic chaplain, who wrote in November 1707 to the Bishop of Quebec, his superior, also detained in England: 'I have been put, despite being a prisoner of war, in a prison for criminals.'[161] The Bishop of Quebec supported Saujon's protest. While he admitted that Saujon had broken his parole, it was no justification for putting him in a 'bridouel' [*bridewell*]: 'this prison in such an infamous place, will be regarded in France as an insult not only to the

---

[156] Fitzgerald to [Sunderland], 25 August 1708, BL, Add MS61595, fo. 52. On Newgate's wards, see Evans, *Fabrication*, pp. 34–40. While bed-sharing was a common practice in the eighteenth century, it was not the case for men belonging to the elite.
[157] Fitzgerald to [Sunderland], 25 August 1708, BL, Add MS61595, fo. 52.
[158] Unsigned and undated, ibid., fo. 54.
[159] S&W to Sunderland, 12 February 1708–9, BL, Add MS61593, fo. 17. See McConville, *History*, p. 70.
[160] And rightly so: see Beattie, *Crime*, pp. 297–8.
[161] Saujon to Bishop of Quebec, 27 November 1707, BL, Add MS61594, fo. 62.

nation, but also to our religion.'[162] Three months later, Saujon was still in the same place, and his 'sad tale' took on more dramatic overtones.[163] As a letter from March 1708 testifies, the identity of his fellow prisoners added insult to injury: 'I am here among the most prostituted whores, but God is my support, pray for me.'[164] The Agent for Prisoners at Southampton explained in March 1708 why Saujon had been committed to the bridewell. Not only had he transgressed the terms of his parole by venturing far beyond the 'walls of the town' of Southampton, but in Winchester, according to the JPs, he had apparently engaged in 'scandalous and dangerous behavior', inciting the local people, 'in a riotous manner' to support James II Stuart, to whom he had publicly drunk a toast. The judicial officers added the dubious claim that Saujon appeared to be 'an Irishman born'. His fate was sealed, and when the Agent for Prisoners at Southampton 'made a demand of him as a Prisoner of War',[165] the JPs refused: he had now been recategorized as an enemy of the state, who faced the death penalty, and putting forward his 'qualité de François' was not going to help him.[166]

Arguably, these examples seem exceptional, since these were people whose political and religious affiliations were suspect, and it was precisely for that reason that the privileged status of prisoner of war was ultimately denied to them.[167] But even in the middle of the eighteenth century, it still happened regularly that prisoners of war were detained alongside felons in town gaols.[168] By the American War of Independence, the necessity to insulate prisoners of war from criminals, at least in Britain, had become widely accepted. John Howard, in the report he wrote to the Board in 1779, contrasted the confusion he observed in Calais prison with Britain. In the French town, 127 prisoners were in jail, 'Crowded in the Prison, and mixed with English prisoners for debt, and some soldiers, 7 or 8'. In contrast, Howard remarked with a sense of national pride that in Britain prisoners of war had long been removed from other types of detainees:

No prisoners for debt of felons were ever suffered to be mixed with French prisoners of war there, or had any communication whatever with them, nor has any thing like it in the present hostilities taken place, except it may be called so,

---

[162] Bishop of Quebec to unknown, [November 1707], ibid., fos. 64v–65. Bridewells were prisons for petty offenders, such as prostitutes, vagrants or beggars. Conditions of detention in bridewells emphasized punishment, work, and obedience: Evans, *Fabrication*, pp. 47–56.

[163] Goffman, *Asylums*, p. 66.

[164] Copy of navy chaplain to Bishop of Quebec, 11 March 1708, BL, Add MS61594, fo. 66.

[165] Roger Clutterbuck to S&W, in S&W to Sunderland, 27 March 1708, Add MS61592, fo. 53. Clutterbuck appears as the Agent for Prisoners at Southampton in 1708: 'Declared Accounts: Navy', in *Calendar of Treasury Books*, vol. 24, 1710, ed. William A Shaw (London, 1952), pp. clxx–clxxxix.

[166] Copy of navy chaplain to Bishop of Quebec, 11 March 1708, BL, Add MS61594, fo. 66.

[167] Ch. 1.

[168] See Yarmouth town clerk to LCA, 2 May 1744, NMM, ADM/M/387, no. 26. British prisoners in France were also sometimes confined 'in the common gaol with felons, some of whom were condemned to die', as in Vannes: *London Chronicle*, 475 (10–12 January 1760).

they having permitted the French when sick, to be taken care of in the same hospitals with the Americans . . . and when all receive exactly the same treatment as the seamen of His Majesty's Navy.[169]

Howard absolutely refused to confuse prisoners of war with criminals or debtors. He was not alone in holding these views, and the same ideas were prevalent in the Admiralty. Detaining prisoners of war in county or city jails raised concrete problems. Prison keepers were reluctant to look after these men, who were less profitable than 'normal' inmates. In December 1778, six French prisoners of war were thus confined in Yarmouth town gaol, but the jailor was 'unwilling to subsist them at the rate of sixpence p Day', which was the amount granted by the Admiralty throughout the war, and they were shipped to other prisons.[170] There was also the problem of space. In June 1780, there were 180 French prisoners in Yarmouth Gaol, which 'is very small and incapable of accommodating so large a Number': the Sick & Wounded Board decided to transport them back to France without delay.[171] When the rumours of a Franco-Spanish invasion became real in 1779, one of the options considered in Britain was to move the prisoners of war from the south coast further inland, and to detain these men in common jails. The suggestion was not adopted because so many guards would be needed to escort the prisoners. Moreover, these men would have to be secluded from 'Felons, with whom it is presumed it would not be thought right to intermix the Prisoners of War'.[172]

The new prisons built from the late 1770s onwards were organized around the separation principle, and they were purpose-built with the notion that each category of inmates needed a different type of prison. But the war presented a real challenge to these new ideas, as spaces of detention were sparse and coveted by many. The example of Bodmin's gaol and house of correction presents us with a case in point. In September 1779, the 'Corporation, Gentlemen and Inhabitants' of this Cornish town wrote a petition to the Lords of the Admiralty, expressing their 'Dread & Anxiety' after 350 prisoners of war had been relocated there from Falmouth since the beginning of August, following the invasion scare:

They now remain at Bodmin without a single Person being left by the Commissary to Guard them & that the whole Guard over them consist of about 18

---

[169] John Howard, memorandum on British prisoners of war in France, TNA, ADM98/11, 15 January 1779, fo. 213.
[170] S&W to LCA, 25 December 1778, ibid., fo. 189v; S&W to LCA, 31 July 1782, ADM98/14, fo. 114v.
[171] S&W to LCA, 22 June 1780, ADM98/12, fos. 242–v. Likewise, at Harwich prisoners were put in the town gaol: S&W to LCA, 31 October 1780, ADM98/13, fo. 64v. And in Carlisle, the French were kept 'in a County Gaol', which 'is not proper': S&W to LCA, 24 February 1779, ADM98/11, fo. 234.
[172] S&W to LCA, 26 July 1779, ADM98/12, fo. 56.

Persons of the Town of Bodmin most of them are old infirm and badly armed that of this Number six only do Duty.

Should the prisoners escape, the petitioners feared the worst: 'the whole strength of the town of Bodmin is not sufficient to oppose them', and they would certainly destroy it.[173] Sixty-nine men signed the petition. The petitioners were not far off the truth: after all, Bodmin was a small town, inhabited by fewer than 2,000 people at the time.[174] If we deduct women and children, and account for the fact that many of the local men would have been mobilized for the war effort, there were probably more prisoners of war than British men in Bodmin. But there were other reasons behind such a strong opposition. Bodmin's county jail had only opened in June 1779, just two months before the first prisoners of war arrived. Besides the jail for criminals, a prison for debtors and a house of correction had also been erected at Bodmin following a 1778 Act of Parliament.[175] The key principle guiding the conception of the building was that of separation 'between the different kinds of Criminals'[176] advocated by Howard. The reformer's influence was explicit. An engraved plan of the Bodmin jail, drawn by its engineer, the gentleman farmer and JP John Call, was also published and dedicated to Howard.[177] It is therefore not surprising that Howard commended the new jail in the third edition of his State of the Prisons, published in 1784.[178]

William Masterman, a powerful London attorney with West Country roots, who would be elected MP for Bodmin in 1780, wrote to the Admiralty, to express his support for his 'Friends and Neighbours at Bodmin'. Incarcerating prisoners of war 'in the common Jail for Debtors and Felons', he wrote, gave rise to the fear of distemper among men 'being kept together closely confined'.[179] A month later, the JPs assembled in Quarter Session, in their role as county jail trustees, also wrote to the Admiralty, and demanded the removal of the prisoners of war from the county gaol. They went further and denounced the confusion between different types of inmates. The JPs' arguments underline the competition for the use of the same spaces of incarceration by different categories of inmates. The judicial officers reminded the Admiralty that they had only consented to the loan of the county jail until the 'immediate Danger' of invasion was cleared. The county jail of Cornwall, they argued, had been built with the aim of 'securing the Health and amending the

---

[173] Petition to LCA, 10 September 1779, NMM, ADM/M/408.
[174] According to the figures collected and shared with me by Peter Langton, Bodmin had a population of 790 in the late seventeenth century, and 1,951 in 1801.
[175] 'An act for building an additional jail', 18 Geo. 3, c17 (1778).
[176] Key of the Plan, Elevation and Section, of the Gaol, Bridewell, and Sherriff's Ward, lately built at Bodmin. For Howard's suggestions for prison buildings, see State of the Prisons (1777), pp. 40–8.
[177] Plan, Elevation ... built at Bodmin. See Evans, Fabrication, pp. 134, 169.
[178] Howard, State, pp. 394–7. James Neild, who visited the prison a few years later, was as laudatory as Howard: Neild, State (1812), pp. 51–6.
[179] Masterman to LCA, 7 September 1779, NMM, ADM/M/409.

Morals of the Prisoners',[180] and this purpose would be defeated by the detention of so large a number of prisoners therein. For the same reason, the prison, which was designed for a hundred inmates, had already suffered 'considerable Damage' by the confinement of more than three times this number of men.[181] The final straw was the request by the Sick & Wounded Board to make 'Alterations' to the jail 'for the better Accommodation of the said Prisoners on the Approach of Winter', which would essentially amount to making permanent a situation that had originally been presented as temporary. The JPs obtained that the jail be cleared of its prisoners of war.[182] The prisoners were marched to Winchester Prison.[183] This example shows the tension between the central state administration, which defended the reversible use of these spaces, and local authorities, who pushed for specialization. By the end of the 1770s, separation principles started to prevail.

Just like Bodmin's county jails, the bridewells, houses of correction and common jails built by Gloucestershire County in the 1790s were amongst the paradigmatic prisons of the 'new age' of prison building, model-prisons which were 'by far the most highly praised and the most widely known' at the time.[184] The main force behind this project was George Onesiphorus Paul, a magistrate converted to Howardian ideals of reform, who brought in William Blackburn, the most important architect of the era.[185] Gloucestershire prisons were typical of the first phase of reformed prison building, which was engineered by local authorities, steered by the central state.[186] The French Wars, once again, put local prisons under pressure, and Gloucestershire prisons soon attracted the interest of the Transport Board. On 19 November 1803, the secretary of state for War, Charles Yorke, wrote to the lord lieutenant of the county of Gloucestershire, to advise him that 'it would be very desirable to appropriate to the reception of Prisoners of War under a Military Guard some of the newly built Gaols of the Kingdom', and asked him to consult with the magistrates of Gloucestershire about using the 'spacious and well constructed prisons of the County'.[187]

G.O. Paul replied to the Transport Board on 2 December. He did not mince his words, and raised the question of equity between English counties. While the inhabitants of Gloucestershire were ready to pay their share of the 'common

---

[180] This expression was an explicit reference to the Penitentiary Act of 1779 (19 Geo. 3, c74), which had been drafted by Howard and William Blackstone. See Devereaux, 'Making'.

[181] According to a report published in 1815 by a London committee that visited the prison in July 1814, the average number of prisoners at Bodmin was then forty-two (adding up the jail and the bridewell): Johnson, History, p. 91.

[182] 7 October 1779, in LCA to S&W, 15 October 1779, NMM, ADM/M/409.

[183] S&W to LCA, 19 October 1779, TNA, ADM98/12, fos. 112v–113.

[184] Evans, Fabrication, pp. 139–42.

[185] See Whiting, Prison Reform and Moir, 'Sir George Onesiphorus Paul'. Neither mentions the episode analysed here.

[186] Evans, Fabrication, pp. 139, 185.

[187] Yorke to Earl of Berkeley, lord lieutenant of Gloucestershire, Gloucestershire Record Office, Gloucester (GRO), QS SO12, pp. 563–4.

Burtherns & Inconveniences' hitting Britain at the time, the specific demands placed upon them amounted to a 'punishment' for having so successfully engaged in the 'Reform of prison Establishment & Regulation'.[188] In a letter to Yorke, he denounced the 'impolicy and injustice of Government', who chose to claim such a large 'sacrifice' from a county which had been 'exemplary' in reforming its prisons, implementing the wishes of parliament. He also referred to the precedent of the previous war, by which 'state prisoners' had been provided for and maintained 'for years at the Cost of the County', while the demands to be even partially reimbursed had been met 'almost with insult'.[189]

The lack of national coordination, and the continuing state practice of dumping prisoners of war onto localities, created competition between regions, in the same way as Jamaican parishes rejected prisoners in the same period.[190] It was the corporation of the city of Bristol that had suggested that 'the Houses of Correction unoccupied in the County of Gloucestershire' should be used to detain prisoners of war, instead of the large Stapleton Prison.[191] G.O. Paul condemned this 'intestine War' which was going on between fellow Britons to avoid having to carry the burden of looking after prisoners of war.[192]

The prison reformer also pointed out that while Gloucestershire had massively invested in the reconstruction of its prisons, their size had not increased. These establishments, he argued, had been built 'on the Howardean System', with an emphasis on individual confinement.[193] These new prisons could not easily be converted for new users, in such large numbers: they would have to be completely rebuilt. G.O. Paul also explained why it was vital to keep some prison places available. The four bridewells of Gloucestershire, which contained at most 322 prison places, were near their full capacity. They filled up and were emptied depending on the judicial calendar.[194] Symbolic deterrence had been, from the outset, the thinking behind the scheme in Gloucestershire: the prisons' effectiveness relied on their emptiness, the voids always available to be occupied by criminals.[195] As Napoleon's armies were massed in Boulogne, invasion fantasies were publicly discussed in Britain.[196] G.O. Paul imagined a nightmare scenario, in which a large number of criminals would plunder the country, while the enemy had landed. Would it not be wise, he asked, to leave some cells unoccupied, which could be used for the 'confinement, of those Plunderers, Marauders, Deserters, Spies, & others disaffected' who would no doubt try to benefit from the ensuing

---

[188] G.O. Paul to TB, 2 December 1803, ibid., pp. 564–5.
[189] G.O. Paul to Yorke, 4 December 1803, ibid., p. 575.   [190] Ch. 3.
[191] TB to G.O. Paul, 3 December 1803, GRO, QS SO12, p. 573. The quotation is from an undated letter from the magistrates of Bristol, p. 574.
[192] G.O. Paul to Yorke, 4 December 1803, ibid., p. 577.
[193] G.O. Paul to TB, 2 December 1803, ibid., pp. 565–6. On Paul's conceptions, see Evans, *Fabrication*, pp. 169–70.
[194] G.O. Paul to TB, 2 December 1803, GRO, QS SO12, pp. 566–8.
[195] As argued by Evans, *Fabrication*, pp. 141–2.   [196] Philp, *Resisting*.

confusion and distress?[197] In this new mode of thinking, keeping the prisons empty was a shrewd policy, which would be beneficial in the long term, if not in the short term. In the end, the secretary of state for War conceded that these grievances were justified: the prisons of Gloucestershire were unfit for the confinement of prisoners of war.[198] But the debate was not over, and throughout the Napoleonic Wars, prisoners of war were still detained in 'civilian' facilities, as in Tothill Fields Bridewell, where sixty-seven prisoners were brought by the Transport Office in 1813 and 1814, and where they would stay alongside felons, vagrants, enemy aliens, and debtors.[199]

A brief (and tentative) comparison with France is useful to understand the specificity of the British situation. In France, the mixing of prisoners of war with normal prisoners seemed even more common. In 1695, the French *commissaire de la Marine* in Dunkirk prided himself on the way in which English prisoners were handled by the staff in the Flemish prison, where they had been put together with four French Huguenots recaptured after emigrating to England: 'Apart from the beds, they are not required to pay for anything that the subjects of the King are not asked to pay.'[200] Just as in England, prisoners of war were detained 'privately', like other prisoners, and Lempereur saw nothing wrong with that. But, in contrast with Britain, this physical coexistence continued throughout our period. The lack of alternatives was probably the main reason for this, as in Isle de France (today's Mauritius) in 1794, where two French soldiers were incarcerated in a French 'floating prison', presumably for misbehaving. They were put together with a motley crew of detainees, composed of two black slaves, twenty-one English and Dutch officers, eighty 'English, Dutch, American, Danish, Swedish, Irish, German, Russian, as well as Spanish' sailors, thirteen sailors from Manilla in the Philippines, and ten black servants of the British officers.[201] In metropolitan France, the testimony of Peter Fea, an English merchant who was detained during the Napoleonic Wars, is irreplaceable.[202] Fea was marched from St Malo in Brittany to Lorraine, and, during his journey, he was put in makeshift places of detention. From Verneuil in Normandy, he wrote on 14 March 1810: 'rested & was left alone My Mate & Crew Marcht off for Cambray & I left in Much distress of mind not knowing what was to be done with me & no person to speak to.' Lack of sociability was propitious to self-absorption and dark thoughts, fuelling his sense of abandonment. But being detained with Frenchmen, and common criminals at that, was not felt to be an improvement. In

---

[197] G.O. Paul to TB, 2 December 1803, GRO, QS SO12, p. 567.

[198] Yorke to Berkeley, 5 December 1803, ibid., p. 578.

[199] *Report on the State of the Police* (1816), p. 386. See also the example of the Liverpool borough gaol, built according to Howardian principles in 1786, and used for French prisoners in the 1790s: Chamberlain, *Hell*, pp. 84–5.

[200] Lempereur, 'Etat des prisons de Dunkerque', 15 December 1695, AN, MAR/B3/88, fos. 129v–130.

[201] LaBassière, 'Notte des Marins Qui Sont à Bord de Là prison flotante', 16 July 1794, National Archives of Mauritius, A104/3.

[202] Ch. 3.

Chartres, his morale reached a low ebb. He wrote on 22 March 1810: 'Very Unhappy a Condemned Criminal in Next Cell in heavy Irons waiting Execution.' The following day, his mood had not lightened: 'Still here in the Greatest dejection of Mind placed with the most abject of Mankind in Close prison & none to converse with.' The feeling that he was confined with the lowest of the low, with whom he could not converse, would not dissipate, and his isolation reached its peak on 26 March: 'None to speak to nor Understand the Miserable Objects round me.' Just as, a century earlier, Abbé Saujon had despised being detained in an English bridewell, Fea's mood swung with the identity of the people with whom he was forced to coexist, and as soon as he encountered countrymen, his spirits lightened.[203]

While putting prisoners of war in the same jails as common criminals was probably not the result of a political design, but of financial pressures, the psychological consequences were immense. Prisoners of war, in Napoleonic France, were often made to feel that their status was a meaningless label.

B. Hell is Other Prisoners of War

Did the experience of captivity foster solidarity between all prisoners of war, whatever their social, religious, or national origins? Throughout our period, incidents opposed prisoners along 'national' lines. Spanish and French prisoners, for example, coexisted with difficulty within the same walls, even when their sovereigns were allies. In 1744, in Portchester, the French prisoners petitioned the Duke of Newcastle, the Prime Minister, to complain that their unscrupulous custodians were triggering 'mortal antipathy' between themselves and Spanish prisoners. The surgeon of Fareham hospital, they wrote, 'is everyday encouraging the Divorce between the two Nations without predicting the fatal Consequences', for instance, by giving meat to the Spaniards but not to the French.[204] In Portsmouth and Plymouth, where many more Frenchmen were detained than Spaniards, the latter were always at risk of being tormented by the former. To prevent these troubles, the Admiralty wrote that it was vital to 'keep such a strong & effectual separation between the French & Spanish Prisoners, that they may not possibly have any communication together'.[205] These were no fantasies. In Bristol prison, following a fray between these two communities, a Frenchman was murdered by a Spaniard.[206]

The problem of the physical coexistence of these groups of militaries, sleeping in the same buildings or sharing the same recreation yards, became more acute

---

[203] Fea, *Diary*, 6 April 1810.   [204] 17 March 1744, NMM, ADM/M/390, no. 96.
[205] LCA to S&W, 17 May 1744, ADM/M/387, no. 43.
[206] S&W to LCA, 28 March 1748, TNA, ADM98/4, fos. 206–v. He was sentenced to death at the assizes for the crime: 5 September 1748, fo. 245v.

during the American War of Independence, because prisoners serving multiple sovereigns were detained on British soil. At Deal, in July 1779, the local Agent cried for help when he faced the daily arrival of a great number of French and Spanish prisoners who, he argued, had to be kept apart in the prison.[207] At Winchester, the Lieutenant Colonel of the Surrey Militia complained that these two national groups could not be kept apart, and that the French abused the Spaniards.[208] Despite being 'confined in separate Appartments', noted the Board, they still had 'a large airing ground in common', where too many disputes occurred.[209] While the risk posed by such cohabitation was well known, the lack of available facilities often left no other choice.

While prisoners of war were increasingly set apart from criminals and, if possible, from other national groups, an internal principle of separation was respected throughout the period: that between the common people and the elite. Not all officers were detained on parole, and many could end up incarcerated together with their subordinates. But upholding military hierarchies remained as crucial in prison as on the battlefield. On board ships, common sailors and officers had been physically segregated, with the decks laying out social and spatial boundaries between the officer class and the rank and file. Negating these pre-existing distinctions, in the context of the prison, could cause disorder. The internal pecking order thus required that officers and the common men should be incarcerated separately. This was the manifestation, for prisoners of war, of the 'grading of accommodation', which was one of the few domains, in the unre-formed prison, where social relations were moulded 'from bricks and mortar'.[210] In the prison that opened in Plymouth in 1695, French Commissaire Gastines noted approvingly, 'there will be rooms for officers'.[211] But the same man also regretted that, by contrast with Dinan, where 'those of the least distinction', including merchants and passengers, benefited from the parole system, in England French officers were put in prison with 'common sailors and soldiers'.[212] Exter-nally valid hierarchies should remain in place within the prison.[213]

Prison administrators were conscious of the risks of not separating officers from their subordinates, as demonstrated by the long diary of John Hamilton, an envoy from the Admiralty who was sent in 1744 to investigate Plymouth prisons. In the newly built 'New Prison', which could accommodate a thousand men, common men complained whenever officers were given privileges; as when the

---

[207] S&W to LCA, 27 July 1779, ADM98/12, fos. 113–14.
[208] Extract of lieutenant-colonel Wilkinson to secretary of state for War, 30 January 1780, NMM, ADM/M/410.
[209] S&W to LCA, 11 February 1780, TNA, ADM98/12, fo. 182v.
[210] Evans, *Fabrication*, p. 32.
[211] Gastines to SSM, 9 October 1694, AN, MAR/B3/82, fo. 229.
[212] Gastines, 'Mémoire des principales plaintes des prisonniers de guerre françois étant à Plymouth', 4 July 1696, MAR/B4/17, fo. 434.
[213] Ch. 5.

food contractor, as a gesture of gratification to the officers, had 'made an alteration in their allowance of one specie for another which occasioned such a grudging among the common prisoners, as broke out into an open mutiny and he was obliged immediately to desist from'.[214] While on the outside no one would have even entertained the thought of questioning the military hierarchy, any semblance of favour, in the prison context, was bound to create jealousies on the part of the rank and file, just as the failure to obtain such favours was seen as degrading for the officers. The physical layout of the prison facilitated these incidents:

> It consists of three stories, but has no apartment in it (or adjoining to it) to separate the officers, and other prisoners of better degree from the common crew, which they prompted me to observe by a petition they delivered in setting forth the insults and outrages they daily suffer from the sailors, and comparing it with the different provision made for English prisoners of the same degree in France, who are divided from the inferior sort, lodged in a better air; and gratified with better accommodations.[215]

As this excerpt reveals, separation was a social as well as a spatial imperative. One should not breathe the same air as the lesser sort. In Cockside Prison, the contrast between the conditions of detention of common prisoners and officers could not be starker. While two rooms were fitted out for holding 'very conveniently from 20 to 25 the present number' of officers, the rank and file were crammed in the main body of the building, often more than 900 at a time, 'lying all down upon the Floor in Bulk', and trampling 'promiscuously'.[216] Breathing space reflected social status, and Hamilton recommended emulating the good practices in place on the other side of the Channel, by ordering 'a separate prison for such among the officers, and better sort of prisoners, as are not enlarged upon parole as also a separate apartment in the hospitals, it being a courtesy and indulgence frequently exercised by our enemies towards us'.[217] While they (rightly) doubted that British prisoners in France always benefited from such kindness, the Board agreed with the need to apply social-spatial segregation in prison.[218] These imperatives were implemented in the following decades, whenever possible. During the American War of Independence, Forton Prison consisted of two main buildings that could

---

[214] John Hamilton, 'Diary', 30 January 1744, NMM, ADM/M/390, no. 46, p. 16.

[215] Hamilton, 'Diary', 28 January 1744, ibid., pp. 12–13. The French officers at Portchester made similar complaints, and the Admiralty decided 'to cause a distinct place to be built for them accordingly': LCA to S&W, 16 July 1745, ADM/M/392, no. 198.

[216] Hamilton, 'Diary', 30 January 1744, NMM, ADM/M/390, pp. 17, 19.

[217] Hamilton' proposal, 4 February 1744, TNA, ADM98/2, fos. 103–v.

[218] Observations of the S&W on Hamilton's proposal, 13 February 1744, ibid., fos. 103–v. British prisoners in France petitioned the LCA to complain that at La Rochelle, 'the captain & officers are put into the prison without any distinction, among a crowd of common men': 16 July 1779, NMM, ADM/M/408.

host up to 2,000 prisoners, one destined for officers of a higher rank, and the other for common soldiers and sailors and lower officers.[219]

To avoid displaying these inequalities of treatment, it made sense to dissociate the two groups physically. This was implemented in the early nineteenth century in Dartmoor, where 'the petty officers had a separate prison to themselves, a whole building'; within it, they socialized in the manner they preferred: 'old shipmates messed together, and officers of acquaintance selected themselves and messed together.' The spatial boundary between officers and the common prisoners was clear: communication between them did not go further than speaking 'to one another from their windows; there was no mixture'.[220] In the same way, prisoners from different 'nations' were detained in different buildings. Dartmoor, one of the very first war prisons ever constructed, applied the techniques designed by Blackburn, the prison architect, to delimit 'ward territories'. Subdivision and compartmentalization would 'make intercommunication between classes [of prisoners] more difficult'.[221] Like other 'classifying devices', prison buildings aimed at governing the social interactions that took place within it.[222]

V. Violent Buildings

To understand fully what goes on behind prison walls, one must keep in mind the forms and functions of the buildings we are looking at. As Bruno Latour argues, all objects come with a script.[223] Applied to prisons, this means that prisoners can only move according to the plan, and that all movements are charted and predetermined, according to the axiom of sequestration. Historian of architecture Thomas Markus similarly writes: 'Time and space are joined in rules which govern the opening times of specific spaces. In short the building and its management determine who does what, where, with whom, when and observed by whom.'[224]

Prison rules, in the eighteenth century as in the present, define the moments when it is legitimate or obligatory to gather in the courtyard; which parts of the prisons are communal spaces and which are segregated, for hygiene, sleep, or work; and which are no-man's-lands.[225] There is no doubt that prisons are explicitly built to constrain their occupants to behave in certain ways. But in the eighteenth century, as we saw, most detention places were not built *as* prisons. Some of the physical and material elements of these buildings, when they were used as churches or stables, became significant and constraining when their function changed. But even purpose-built prisons, like all buildings, were

[219] *Memoirs of... Captain Nathaniel Fanning*, p. 9.
[220] Captain James Bowen, 15 April 1818, *Report* (1818), p. 172.   [221] Evans, *Fabrication*, p. 174.
[222] Markus, *Buildings*, p. 20.   [223] Latour, 'On technical'.   [224] Markus, *Buildings*, p. 97.
[225] Goffman, *Asylums*, pp. 203–12.

constantly changing, imperceptibly or dramatically, because of their very physical nature or because of external events.[226] They were dynamic material and social objects. One reason for this was the alterations made by their occupants.

In this section, I am interested in testing the idea that the occupants of buildings always follow a predetermined script, what Michel de Certeau describes as the tension between the strategies of town planners and the tactics of walkers.[227] Can the arrangement or assemblage itself open the possibility of transgressing the script?[228] The spatial layout of the prison building must be placed at the centre. While the prison is a place where power is exercised through space, it is also a place where power is resisted through space. The architect Bernard Tschumi writes that attention should be paid to 'the use and misuse of the architectural space'. In any relationship between individuals and spaces, he writes, violence is implied. The violence inflicted by architectural spaces on the bodies of those who inhabit or move through them, forcing them to follow certain paths and not others, go through certain corridors and exit through certain doors.[229] And the violence that bodies inflict on spaces 'by their very presence, by their intrusion into the controlled order of architecture'.[230] In Britain as in France, as we will now see, the prison was a space of contestation and ordering, of constraint and resistance, all at the same time.

A. Holes

Prisons were divided into multiples spaces of confinement. Prison sociologist Gresham Sykes coined the notion of 'deprivation of liberty' to describe the system by which prisoners are first confined 'to the institution', and then confined 'within the institution', with restrictions to their freedom of movement.[231] At the bottom of this hierarchy of unfreedom was the 'Dungeon' or black hole, a prison within the prison and a place of maximum isolation.[232] The term was already in use at the beginning of the eighteenth century, to designate a punishment cell in a prison or barrack.[233] In the black hole, the walls were close and the ceiling low. This is where, perhaps more than any other prison space, Tschumi's 'spatial torture' finds its clearest expression.[234] The hole was sometimes described as a synecdoche for the prison. In 1694, depicting conditions of detention in Portsmouth, French

---

[226] Markus, *Buildings*, p. 6.   [227] De Certeau, *Practice*, ch. 7.
[228] On Foucault's and Latour's concept of the *dispositif*, see Pottage, 'Materiality'.
[229] Tschumi, *Architecture*, pp. 122 (quotation), 123–4.
[230] Ibid., p. 123. On these perspectives, see also Moran and Jewkes, 'Linking the carceral', pp. 165–6; Jewkes, 'On carceral space'; Blundell Jones, 'Primacy'.
[231] Sykes, *Society*, p. 65.
[232] 'Rules to be observed by all Prisoners of war in the Kingdom of France' (1758), article 5.
[233] *OED*, 'black hole', with a first reference in 1707. See Howard, *State* (1784), pp. 446–7.
[234] Tschumi, *Architecture*, p. 124.

Commissaire Gastines wrote about 'the very vice of prisons that are in reality loathsome and cramped cachots, with nasty vaults ... which leak continuously on those who are locked up inside'.[235] Gastines used a moral vocabulary and anthropomorphized the place: the prison itself was perverse and 'vile', not the jailors, though by a metonymic relationship the latter were contaminated as well.[236] The absence of natural light and the dampness of the hole made it a hellish space, imperilling the prisoners' health and safety.[237]

An extra mark of cruelty was to physically restrain and tie up prisoners who were already powerless in the hole, as was the case in Brest in 1744, when a prisoner who was 'out of his sences' died from this maltreatment.[238] Prisoners were put in the hole for misbehaviour, but its impropriety for detaining prisoners of war was often noted. Thus, in 1744 the French monarchy was informed that French prisoners were 'kept in the cachot in Ghent, fed with bread and water like criminals'.[239] The same representations, of the cachot as a repugnant space, persisted throughout the period and beyond. During the French Wars, the reference to the black hole was a *topos* in the rhetoric of propaganda denouncing the enemy's inhumanity, a synonym for dungeon.[240] In Britain, it became the normal practice to handcuff prisoners who had been put in the cachot, as the Transport Office reminded the Agent of Dartmoor in 1810.[241]

In his diary, an American prisoner, Timothy Connor, described the cachot in the following terms in 1777: 'The Black Hole is a place where you are by yourselves, and not allowed to come out, or even to speak to us.'[242] However, the extent to which prisoners were actually incarcerated individually in the hole is unclear. Even this confined and supposedly impregnable locale was not sealed off from the outside. In Forton, prisoners managed to dig their way out of the hole and make their escape in 1778:

Last night there was a breach made among our officers through the Black Hole, by undermining, about thirty-five feet under ground, out into the public road. Thirteen French and two Americans ... that were confined in the Black Hole, and forty-five officers from above stairs, all made their escape.[243]

[235] Gastines to SSM, 24 February 1694, AN, MAR/B3/82, fo. 21v.
[236] Gastines to SSM, 11 August 1693, MAR/B3/75, fo. 394v.
[237] De Béhague, commandant in Belle-Isle, to Montbarey, 27 August 1778, MAR/B3/659, fos. 47–8.
[238] Affidavit sworn by the English master of a merchant ship brought into Brest, 15 November 1744, NMM, ADM/M/390, no. 48.
[239] In Givry to SSM, 19 August 1744, AN, MAR/B3/421, fo. 298.
[240] Subprefect of Dieppe, in Normandy, to prefect of *département* of Seine-Inférieure, 24 Ventôse an 9 (15 March 1801), Archives Départementales de Seine Maritime, Rouen (ADSM), 1M209.
[241] Transport Office (TO) to Cotgrave, 9 August 1810, TNA, ADM98/226, fo. 10.
[242] 23 June 1777, in Connor, 'A Yankee privateersman', 30 (July 1876), pp. 344–5.
[243] 8 August 1778, in ibid., 32 (January 1878), p. 73.

Prisoners of war were not incarcerated in individual cells. This does not mean that they did not try to assert a 'private claim on space'.[244] One evening of 1761, in Sissinghurst Castle, French prisoners were quietly reading and writing in their ward, between 6 and 7 pm, by candlelight, when an officer of the militia barged in and created havoc, striking the prisoners left and right with his naked sword. The prisoners were put 'into the Cachot' for two nights and one day, and on half allowance for seven days, 'for having light at that time'.[245] They had unknowingly transgressed the curfew. Disobeying the rules could have dramatic consequences, as when, again in Sissinghurst, a French prisoner, Jean Loffe, was shot in his ward by a sentry who believed he had not snuffed out his candle.[246] The poor state of the building also led the prisoners to obscure the windows for their own safety, in the absence of shutters. In Ward 24, where the above incident had happened, the turnkey noted that 'some part of the Window is done up with Brick & dirt to keep the Cold out & part with Blankets'.[247] This was a problem in this prison more generally, but the commissioner sent by the Sick & Wounded Board preferred to blame the prisoners for the failings of the administration:

> I attentively visited every Ward of the P.^{n} & found the Wards called the Stable Wards very close & bad smells in them for want of air & holes made in the Walls by the P.^{rs} which might be remedied by I impute to the P.^{rs} improperly stopping up the Windows w.^{h} dirt & other things in order to keep themselves warmer.[248]

Prisoners daily struggled to carve a space beyond the reach of custodians.[249] These practices were also common in 'reformed' prisons, where prisoners blocked the air holes in winter or removed wooden shutters in the summer, to regulate the temperature inside.[250]

B. Walls

Focusing on the spatial boundaries between spaces of incarceration and spaces of recreation, as well as on the interstitial spaces between the inside and the outside of the prison, provides a way to understand the spatial economy of the prison, and the social dynamics of the relationships between inmates and custodians. Regimes of surveillance are not evenly distributed in or through space. The defining elements of prisons, as buildings, are their walls. Walls simultaneously enclose,

---

[244] Goffman, *Asylums*, p. 216.
[245] Jean Charles Maison's interrogation, 1 December 1761, TNA, ADM105/42, fo. 108v.
[246] Agent Cooke's interrogation, 8 December 1761, ibid., fo. 16.
[247] Joseph Punnell's interrogation, 1 December 1761, ibid., fos. 112v–113.
[248] Maxwell's inquiry on the state of the prison, undated, ibid., fo. 183v.
[249] Wener, *Environmental Psychology*, pp. 137–60.   [250] Evans, *Fabrication*, p. 162.

protect, and filter. The height, width, and texture of prison walls varied, but their function was everywhere the same: to erect symbolic and material barriers to the circulation of prisoners and to impede their movements. Walls can be studied from a phenomenological perspective: that of the specific effect they had (or were supposed to have) on the prisoner.

The internal walls delimiting prison units were not necessarily very high, because their role was principally a dissuasive one. In Dover Castle, in 1744, the Board proposed creating an airing ground between two residential barracks, enclosing this space to prevent escapes 'with Pales 5 Feet 6 Inch high'.[251] The paling would be sufficiently high for this purpose, the Board explained, 'especially with tenturing the Points, since it is not easy to conceive that any Prisoner would be hardy enough to attempt to get over them in day Light, in the Face of the Centinels and therefore at the Hazard of his Life'.[252] At Portchester Castle, a project was also devised in 1744 for enclosing the airing field with a palisade fence, which would be 'pointed sharp on the top, with Tanter Hooks [*tenterhooks*] on Each Top'.[253] As these two examples indicate, prison surveillance implied predicting the conduct of prisoners, and more specifically preventing them from behaving in a certain way by erecting physical obstacles to their actions, and defeating what was seen as their driving motive, namely escaping.

While most architectural designs aim to make the lives of their occupants practical, convenient, and 'easy', the function of a prison is to incapacitate and to impair the movements of its occupants, by devising forms of 'hostile architecture'.[254] The 'script' of the prison fence, like its walls, it to exert a form of agency on its occupants, in a Latourian sense. The building itself 'forces' the inmates to conform to the architects' intentions, at the risk of being hurt, or, to return to the examples we just mentioned, of losing their life.[255] As Robin Evans demonstrates, 'reformed' prisons were buildings reconciling conflicting priorities—those of security, health, and reformation.[256] The prison plans drawn by William Blackburn exemplified the function of architecture in his mind, which consisted in 'keeping people apart', through a 'nesting sequence of containers, the perimeter walls enclosing the ward boundaries, in turn enclosing the cells'.[257]

The meaning and use of these spatial boundaries could be subverted by the prisoners, intentionally or not. In Sissinghurst, during the Seven Years' War,

---

[251] S&W to LCA, 30 October 1744, TNA, ADM98/2, fo. 32v.

[252] S&W to LCA, 2 November 1744, ibid., fo. 35v.

[253] Same to same, 30 January 1744, ibid., fo. 100. The project was accepted by the LCA the following day: LCA to S&W, 31 January 1744, NMM, ADM/M/390, no. 42.

[254] The term has been used to designate the attempts to prevent some of the inhabitants of modern cities, such as homeless people, to use such public spaces in a way that was not intended by their owners or inventors.

[255] On the agency of things, see Latour, *Reassembling*, pp. 71–2; Van der Hoorn, *Eyesores*, pp. 206–9.

[256] Evans, *Fabrication*, p. 143.   [257] Ibid., pp. 170–1.

several serious incidents between guards and prisoners took place over the policing of spatial thresholds. Some prisoners were, for instance, beaten for having dried their laundry on a fence, a form of spatial appropriation that was seen as a challenge to the authority of the custodians, whereas the prisoners saw this as an unjustified overreaction.[258] A sentry knocked out a prisoner who was trying to pass a 'pair of shoes and a tin colander' through a fence, suspecting him of illicit communication with the outside.[259] The mere fact of standing too close to one of these delineating spaces could be dangerous. On 11 July 1761, at nine in the morning, an incident took place in the garden of the prison, next to the outside wall known as the 'Barrier'. As three prisoners of war, who had just been recaptured after attempting their escape, were brought back to the prison, and were walking across the field towards the prison, John Branston, a sentry, fired his musket in the direction of a small group of prisoners who had been attracted to the scene by mere 'curiosity'.[260] Two of these men, who were standing twenty feet away from the 'Barrier', on the other side of a large flooded moat which divided the garden from the outside, were caught in the line of fire and fatally wounded.[261] In any prison, the control of circulation patterns is a vital component of maintaining authority, and thresholds played a key role in this, both symbolically and materially. The prisoners' defiance of the official meaning of a prison building, as it was understood by custodians, was sufficient to justify the sentries who shot them. Such actions were not necessarily the result of deliberate strategies: prisoners often pleaded their ignorance or misunderstanding. Part of the problem was also the plurality of meanings that could be attributed to the same spaces.

Dartmoor Prison embodied principles that had existed for half a century at least. Five detached blocks, for policing as well as health purposes, were arranged radially around a central market square. They were surrounded by three strata of 'boundary walls' and a patrol path, just as in Blackburn's prisons.[262] The walls were lined with thick wood filled with nails.[263] The external boundary wall was ten feet high. It was divided from the fourteen-feet-high internal boundary wall by a space called 'the Military way', thirty feet large, which was patrolled by sentries. Finally, an eight-foot-high palisade made up the third layer. The space between the internal boundary wall and the palisades was dug up, and called 'No-man's land'.[264] The analogy with poliorcetics—the art of conducting and resisting sieges—went beyond the use of a military lexicon: Dartmoor resembled a military fortress turned inside-out. The enemy was expected to come not from outside, but from within: Andrew Baird, the former inspector of prison hospitals, who was

---

[258] On this phenomenon, see Sparks, Bottoms, and Hay, *Prisons*, p. 192.
[259] Interrogation of William Flower, 4 December 1761, TNA, ADM105/42, fo. 157v.
[260] Interview of Cooke, agent, 12 December 1761, ibid., fo. 140.
[261] Ibid., fos. 139–v.   [262] Evans, *Fabrication*, pp. 145–6.
[263] TO to Cotgrave, 24 September 1811, TNA, ADM98/226, fo. 101v.
[264] Andrew Baird, 15 April 1818, in *Report* (1818), p. 179.

interviewed by a House of Commons committee after the Napoleonic Wars, remarked in 1818 that 'the walls were constructed with points resembling bastions, so as that the centinels could flank themselves every way, and guard the prison in proportion with a fewer number of men'.[265] In other words, sieges were brought inwards, in a period which saw the decline of siege warfare, while the walls of fortresses were brought down ('defortification') in France and Europe.[266] This reasoning was not new. In fact, the formal resemblance between prisons, castles, and military fortifications had been explicit since the seventeenth century at least, and we saw that in France, Napoleon also turned fortresses into war prisons.[267] This certainly owed to the fact that castles had been used as prisons since the Middle Ages, and to the fact that the same engineers and architects designed all these buildings. In France, military engineers influenced and trained by Vauban were involved in building fortifications and adapting them for the purpose of imprisoning people, as was the case with Garangeau in St Malo.

Dartmoor was a variation of the panopticon. Jeremy Bentham's prison, which was designed in the aftermath of the 1780 Gordon Riots, was supposed, as he wrote in 1786, to detract 'enterprises from within' as well as 'clandestine enterprises from without', relying on a 'military guard'.[268] But he was aware that soldiers alone were not sufficient, as had been shown by 'French and other prisoners of war [who] have,...too often, and in too great numbers, contrived to make their escape'.[269] The panopticon was all about the physical layout of the building itself, which allowed the guards to keep a constant watch on the prisoners. At Dartmoor, platforms were erected at the top of the internal boundary walls, patrolled by sentries. Prisoners were forbidden to access the 'no-man's land', at the risk of being confined to the hole, with the exception of those prisoners who were planting or collecting potatoes.[270] It was not enough to avoid the sentries' gaze. These walls were multisensorial boundaries. Booby-traps were triggered by the prisoners' movements: Colonel Wood, who commanded the East Middlesex Militia stationed at Dartmoor in October–November 1815, mentioned in 1818 that 'bells are suspended at different parts of the walls, connected all round the top with wires, which would be rung by any person getting over the wall in a very dark and blowing night, when the sentry might not otherwise discover him'.[271]

Altogether, the system put in place at Dartmoor seemed to present a formidable obstacle to prisoners who dreamed of escaping. Daniel Alexander, the architect of the prison, recalled in 1818 an instance when prisoners had dug twelve feet deep

[265] Ibid. Sykes used a similar language to describe the massive prison walls, which give the prison the appearance of 'a fort to keep the enemy within rather than without': *Society*, p. 3.
[266] See, for example, Mintzker, *Defortification*, ch. 3.   [267] Markus, *Buildings*, p. 95.
[268] Bentham, *Works*, vol. IV, pp. 105, 107. On the reference to the Gordon Riots, see Linebaugh, *London Hanged*, 372n2.
[269] Bentham to Committee of the Laws relating to Penitentiary Houses, 6 May 1811, in Bentham, *Works*, Part XXI, *Appendix*, p. 154.
[270] Baird, *Report* (1818) , p. 179.   [271] Wood, 22 April 1818, ibid., p. 187.

under the walls, and had only been caught after the sentry noticed that the ground was gradually sinking, 'as sand does in an hour-glass'.[272] Whether it was intentional or not at Dartmoor, this collapse of the ground chimed with the building techniques recommended by William Blackburne to defeat the purpose of prisoners trying to escape. Jeremy Bentham cited a conversation with his predecessor:

> To prevent [a man] getting through, I make [the wall] of stone, and of stones too massy to be displaced, as bricks may be, by picking. To prevent his getting under, I make a drain. As he undermines, no sooner is he got within the arch, than out flows the water and spoils his mine.[273]

By the time he was commissioned to work on Dartmoor, Daniel Alexander had already enjoyed an illustrious career. In 1800, he was appointed surveyor to the London Dock Company, where he built docks and warehouses until 1831.[274] Besides working on churches, lighthouses, and bridges, he was employed by the navy, adding colonnades to the Royal Naval Asylum at Greenwich. His work at Dartmoor won him a contract for building the Maidstone County Gaol (1810–17).[275] This variety of commissions illustrates the transfer of architectural concepts and skills between the navy and other institutions, which is even more apparent in the contribution played by Samuel Bentham, Jeremy's brother. Samuel Bentham was the Inspector-General of Naval Works from 1796 onwards, and as such he wrote regulations that applied to all naval buildings during the Napoleonic Wars, including prisons and hulks.[276] It is also Samuel, not Jeremy, who was the true inventor of the idea of the panopticon, which he realized in Russia from the late 1780s onwards and tried to incorporate in England.[277] In January 1797, the Admiralty consulted Samuel's opinion regarding a plan it was considering for a prison for 10,000 prisoners of war. He proposed to erect a guard-house at the centre, 'so that, on the principle of the Panopticon, the prisoners might at all times be under central observation and control'. With this scheme, which was not implemented, he argued that instead of 1,200 men to guard the prisoners, only a hundred would be needed.[278]

It should not surprise us, therefore, that Dartmoor's architect used in 1818 the language of prison reform to describe the prison he had designed: 'the whole

---

[272] Alexander, ibid., p. 181.
[273] Bentham, *Works*, vol. IV, p. 108, cited and discussed by Evans, *Fabrication*, p. 146.
[274] Richardson, 'Architect', pp. 77–8; Colvin, *Biographical Dictionary*, p. 66.
[275] Richardson, 'Architect', p. 79.
[276] See Samuel Bentham, 'Regulations relative to the Preservation and Repairs of... several Naval Establishments', 18 January 1804, in *Instructions to Dispensers*, Appendix No. 40.
[277] Morriss, *Science*; Steadman, 'Samuel Bentham's panopticon'; Cooper, 'The Portsmouth system', p. 193.
[278] Bentham, *Life*, pp. 121–2.

scheme is comprised in a circular plot of ground, containing about twenty-two acres, which is subdivided into rays, in which rays the buildings are placed, so as to afford complete separation and ventilation to the whole.' When asked by the Committee on the Prisons whether 'any principle of general inspection' could be established in Dartmoor, Alexander replied: 'the prison was designed to meet that especial end, by the concentrality of its principle.' But Dartmoor departed in some important ways from the ideal of the panopticon. The house of the prison keeper was not placed at the centre of the war prison:

> Is there any place in the arrangement of the building where the governor...
> might be enabled to inspect all the different yards in which the prisoners were
> out taking their exercise?—The governor's house, as it is now placed, the building
> having been designed as a prison of war, was purposely placed outside the
> boundary-wall, because it was manifest he could not live in the midst of enemies;
> but if it was applied to any civil purpose, it would be obvious that the governor or
> keeper's house might be placed in the centre, for which there is ample space.[279]

The nature of the prisoner of war implied a physical separation with the governor. The house of the prison keeper was placed at the boundary between the inside and the outside, just as in unreformed prisons.[280] In addition to its construction, because of the prison's location, the challenges facing an escaped prisoner of war were formidable, as noted by Colonel Wood: 'A French prisoner... after having effected his escape from the prison,... had afterwards to work his way out of the country; whereas a convict would only have to effect his escape out of the prison, and would then find himself in his own country.'[281] There, Wood was highlighting a central feature of war imprisonment: the double curtain, cultural as well as physical, which secluded the prisoner of war. Nicholas Bull, an adjutant of the Middlesex Militia who had also served at Dartmoor, considered that an escapee would have to take the main roads in order to get off the moor, making it easy to apprehend him.[282]

A dedicated environmental history of Dartmoor prison remains to be written. Such a study would underline the use of peat and local stones, the ambitious drainage scheme, and agricultural innovations. Suffice it to say here that the swampy terrain in the middle of which Dartmoor is located was itself hostile to human occupation. At least this was a shared belief at the time. In a long speech before the House of Commons, on 14 June 1811, Lord Cochrane described his attempts to investigate the truth of the complaints emanating from France about the

---

[279] Alexander, 15 April 1818, *Report* (1818), pp. 178, 179, 180. The central question of the location of prison government was a clear point of departure between Bentham and his predecessors, including Howard: *Works*, vol. IV, pp. 106–7.
[280] Evans, *Fabrication*, p. 30.   [281] Wood, 22 April 1818, *Report*, p. 187.
[282] Nicholas Bull, 24 April 1818, *Report*, p. 201.

treatment of French prisoners in Britain.[283] He went to Dartmoor, and described the 'climate of the prison', where the prisoners' health was debilitated. He gave a sense of the desolate and dramatic landscape in which the prison was implanted:

> It is exposed on the summit of the highest and most bleak range of mountains in Devonshire, where the winter winds pierce with all the keenness possible, increased by constant fogs and sleet, and rain; it is situated in the midst of a barren moor, on which no vegetable grows, I was told that the prison wall had only been seen nine times from the Agent's house during the whole winter, although it is as near to it as from your chair, Sir, to that door, and in such a state of obscurity was Dartmoor involved, by fog and rain, that when I was there I had a guide each time to conduct me.[284]

A spot where neither 'broom, whins, heath, briers, or thistles grew' was not propitious for the installation of men, and Cochrane derided the main proponent of the scheme, Tyrwhitt, who had managed to attract public money for a project at the end of the world.[285] He concluded that the prisoners' complaints were justified. The physical layout of the buildings meant that a third of the prisoners, about 2,000 per day, were constantly exposed to the violence of the elements, having to wait for their breakfast and dinner standing 'in an open space for several hours'.[286] Erecting a prison there might have been a very bad choice in the first place.[287]

C. Fire

In 1708, Commissaire Lempereur in St Malo remarked, in a disheartened tone, that the English prisoners at Fougères (Brittany) could simply not be restrained: 'despite all the precautions that we take and all the punishments we enact, we cannot prevent them from breaking and wreaking everywhere they go.'[288] While there is always a dynamic, often a creative relationship between a building and its users, in the case of the prison there is a conflict between the built environment and its occupants. These 'patterns of "misuse"'[289] of the prisons by their occupants took various forms, but the regularity and scale of the damages inflicted by prisoners of war to their temporary places of abode is striking.

---

[283] Lord Cochrane, 14 June 1811, *HCH*, vol. 20, cols. 634–8. This was part of Cochrane's campaign against corruption.
[284] Ibid., col. 635.   [285] Ibid., cols. 636–7.   [286] Ibid., col. 636.
[287] Baird, 15 April 1818, *Report*, p. 176.
[288] Lempereur to SSM, 8 January 1708, AN, MAR/B3/157, fo. 48v.
[289] Tschumi, *Architecture*, p. 6.

The structural inadequacies of the places of incarceration were often success-fully taken advantage of by the prisoners. At Fougères Castle, in 1703, twelve English prisoners managed to escape during the night, breaking down doors and metal gates in the towers in which they were detained. The official investigation identified 'a gap of about fourteen or fifteen inches deep, underneath the door above the guardroom, through which the Prisoners apparently went out'. Tools were used to dig in 'a petrified earth'. In the 'Tour des Bourgeois', the window railings were completely broken open, the 'dressed stones of the said window weakened and half displaced, so that by pushing the said railings by hand there was enough room for a man to get through and come down the tower with a rope', sixty feet below.[290] In 1746, Commissaire Guillot morosely listed the damage that prisoners caused to the castle:

> They have furiously degraded the castle from where they have removed stones similar to those with which tombs are made, filed down and cut several gates, and pierced through several places. We are working flat out to fix those damages, and to make a new double door, repair and bound the wickets about with iron work.[291]

Prison buildings were constant works-in-progress—in this sense, the prisoners contributed indirectly to creating the prison, forcing engineers and architects to adapt these spaces to their actions. The problems remained the same in more recent prisons, such as Forton, where prisoners climbed 'over the pales', dug under or through the walls, broke open the doors or the prison gates, escaped from the kitchen, the storeroom, the 'privy-house', the 'necessaries', the Black Hole, or the hospital.[292] Prisoners accelerated the deterioration of their temporary 'homes', deconstructing them, exposing their structures.[293]

Damaging buildings was usually the means, not an end in itself, for prisoners trying to escape. But vandalism could also be interpreted as a continuation of war by other means and as an assertion of the prisoners' autonomy of action. Michel Foucault argues, a propos the riots of the 1970s, that these movements 'have been all about the body and material things', in the sense that 'what was at issue was not whether the prison environment was too harsh or too aseptic, too primitive or too efficient, but its very materiality as an instrument and vector of power'.[294] Destroying prison property with fire and breaking through the walls might have

---

[290] Report by the *conseiller du roi* and his *seneschal* in Fougères, 6 July 1703, AN, MAR/B3/120, fos. 535–v.

[291] Guillot to SSM, 17 September 1746, MAR/B3/445, fo. 208.

[292] 13, 31 October, 19 November, 2, 11 December 1777, 15 January 1778, 27 May 1778, 5 August 1778, in Connor, 'A Yankee privateersman', vol. 30, pp. 346–8, vol. 31, pp. 19, 32, 40, 70–1; Fanning, *Memoirs*, p. 15; 'Diary of George Thompson', 29, 30 January 1779, p. 225.

[293] Van der Hoorn, *Eyesores*, p. 213.   [294] Foucault, *Discipline*, p. 30.

been goals in themselves, while the outcome of such actions was secondary.[295] In his account of the destructions at Nantes, *commissaire des guerres* Monsieur de Lusançay tried to make sense of the prisoners' actions in June 1711:

> We do not know what to do with our English prisoners detained in the castle, they are enraged and cannot be controlled, several have set the door of their prison on fire and four have escaped, they refused to comply as previously, maybe because we do not feed them in the castle, or possibly because they are tired of being detained for so long, some of them have been there for eight or ten months.[296]

This incident seemed to have been triggered by a sense of injustice on the part of the prisoners, which built up their resentment and eventually resulted in their open revolt against the prison authorities. Their expectations had been hampered, and they took revenge by destroying the prison itself. The large-scale devastation that took place in Sissinghurst, an Elizabethan mansion used as a prison since the 1740s, is well documented thanks to the frequent investigations conducted there by the Sick & Wounded Board. In 1761, the Agent for the Prisoners, Cooke, stated that 'the p.[rs] had frequently committed great Damages & breaches in the Prison especially in a Ward called the Black dog by destroying the Hammock posts & pulling up and making away with the Board of the floor'.[297] An 'estimate of the damage don by the Prisoners and [militia] forces at Sissinghurst', compiled in 1763 by the individual who had purchased it from the Admiralty, shows the extent of the destruction sustained by the building during the war:

1. To 2092 foot of Glass destroyed and gon wih great damge to the winder frames by many jams & Iron Barrs being gon & winders and many Parts & winders stoped up with Bricks Morter or Mud. 100:0:0.

2. To the Chapel by Destroying the Pulpett Pewes Pertition Carve work Table floor ceiling and all the timber of the ceeling Floor. 40:0:0.

...

6. To the East House by four Oasts being pulled down & gon & by Cutting out the Principal Beams. 40:0:0.

...

9. To Palesade fence to Kitchen Garden with Other Fences & Gates Destroyed & Gon. 10:0:0.

Total: 361:10:0.

---

[295] Goffman, *Asylums*, p. 166.

[296] Lusançay to SSM, 9 June 1711, AN, MAR/B3/196, fo. 157. These 145 English prisoners were transferred to Dinan: ibid., 21 July 1711, fo. 208.

[297] Interview of Cooke, 18 December 1761, TNA, ADM105/42, fo. 174.

The 'best garden by the Wall front' had been ravaged: all the trees had been cut down 'and not even the [stump] of a shurb nor Tree left'.[298] By the end of the war, Sissinghurst Castle was a wreck: it had been effectively dismantled by its prisoners, who made sure that it would never again be used as a prison.[299] Prisoners had reduced the prison to its constituent parts, which they used to make fires. Such an example, however extreme, was not exceptional. In 1800, the author of a regional history of Kent wrote that the keep of Dover Castle 'had been much damaged by the French prisoners, who, to the number of fifteen hundred, were in the late wars with France kept here, who within the space of a twelvemonth carried off most of the timbers and floors, disabling it even for that use in future'.[300] Norman Cross was wrecked in the same way, as shown by the report written by Mr Fearnall, the surveyor sent there in 1813.[301] Barely seventeen years after its construction, this prison had not aged well. Partly, this was due to a lack of maintenance, as in the surgeon's house, which has not been painted since it was built, 'about eight years since'. The boundary wall itself could not be expected to stand, due to its poor construction, and threatened to fall into the ditch at any moment.[302] But prisoners contributed to making it even worse. Fearnall noted that the 'innumerable holes cut through all parts of the buildings by the prisoners for the admission of light have caused them to be extremely weak, by the braces being cut through and destroyed in many parts'. In Prison No. 1, 'the story posts, that support the roof and floor, are so much damaged by being cut by the prisoners, and in parts decayed, as to require to be new in many places'.[303]

This destructive behaviour was so common that prison rules explicitly mentioned wilful damages to the buildings and the punishments incurred for it. These regulations defined a kind of symbiotic relationship between the prisoner and the prison, according to which the prisoner paid for the cost of his misbehaviour with pain inflicted on his body, the confiscation of part of his food, or his confinement in the hole. This was the ultimate form of the government and disciplining of incarcerated bodies. In January 1748, the Board drafted a list of prohibited acts for the 2,450 prisoners detained at Portchester Castle.[304] Vandalism was punished: 'Whoever will at any time knock down, burn or destroy any of the staircases leading to the different lodgings' would expose all the inmates to retributions. Mere imprudence, by 'pretending to make fire' indoor, was also condemned.[305] The cost of repairing the buildings would be deducted from the prisoners'

---

[298] 'Estimate', 1763, sent by the landlord to the Admiralty to claim compensation: document reproduced in Nicolson, *Sissinghurst*, p. 232, without source reference.
[299] S&W to LCA, 13 July 1778, TNA, ADM98/11, fo. 107.
[300] *The History... of the County of Kent*, p. 25.
[301] 'A report of the survey of the depot for prisoners of war at Norman Cross, 31st May 1813', in Walker, *Depot*, Appendix A, pp. 259–64.
[302] Ibid., pp. 262, 263–4.   [303] Ibid., pp. 259–60.
[304] The figure is given in S&W to LCA, 21 May 1747, TNA, ADM98/4, fo. 105v.
[305] S&W, 1 January 1747/8, ADM97/125.

provisions. In the following wars, similar prison regulations were adopted nationally.[306] Attempting to set a prison on fire was also a felony and a crime of arson, and the culprits could be prosecuted in common law.[307]

Another type of regulation asserted the prisoner's duty to look after their new place of abode, almost to care for it, for moral as well as disciplinary reasons. The prison had to be kept in a state of cleanliness by the prisoners themselves, at the cost of being deprived of their food allowance, as described in the 1758 French rules: 'The Prisons shall be kept clean and neat by the sailors, every man in his turn as shall be regulated, and whatever sailor shall refuse this service in his turn, his food shall be whit-held from him 'till he submit to it.'[308] The use of the term 'sailors' instead of 'prisoners' shows that this article might have originated in naval regulations—just as the crew's duty lay in sweeping the decks of their ship, imprisoned sailors had to do the same on land. This type of exchange is not surprising, since prisons were administrated by a branch of the Admiralty. The 1807 British 'Règles' (in French) made this even clearer, and this article blurred the lines between life at sea and in prison:

> The Prisons and Hulks will be swept, scrubbed, and washed, by the Prisoners, in turn...; One Prisoner in six will be employed, every day, for this duty; and during the Time that the Prisons or Hulks will be cleaned, all the Prisoners, except for those who will be on *Corveé*, will leave the Prison Rooms or Cells (article 4).

This article illustrates the blend of hygienism and moralism that coloured the official view on the government of prisons, war prisons included. There too, the choice of vocabulary was not coincidental: 'corvée' means a meaningless, repetitive, and arduous task, often performed as a punishment; in eighteenth-century France, it also referred to forced and unpaid labour, which was a form of taxation paid by the non-privileged part of the population to the monarchy and the *seigneurs*, which was universally hated and abolished in 1789. Besides its utilitarian connotations, the task served a wider purpose: that of turning the prisoners into custodians of their new life space. The imperative of cleanliness, both of the bodies of the prisoners and of the prison itself, was increasingly asserted in British

---

[306] S&W, 'Regles que tous les Prisonniers de Guerre, dans la Grande Bretagne, & l'Irlande, doivent observer', [1757], article 4, TNA, SP42/136. The same provisions were repeated in the 1780 regulations, article 4 (in Howard, *State*, p. 473), and in the 1807 'Règles', article 5. French rules were similar: *Rules* (1758), article 4.

[307] In 1748, Nicholas Butain, a French prisoner, 'willfully set Fire' to the Glasshouse Prison near Exeter: S&W to LCA, 12 December 1748, TNA, ADM98/5, fo. 6. Citing 9 Geo. 1, c22, the Attorney General considered that 'it will be proper to Indict him for both' a felony and a crime of arson at common law: Dr Ryder, 9 December 1748, fo. 6v.

[308] *Rules*, article 7. The 1746 British rules used the term 'private Men': 'Regulation', article 7, [11 January 1746], TNA, SP42/30, fo. 12.

prisons as the eighteenth century wore on, expressing an ideology of moral, social, and political order.[309] The 1807 regulations contained several articles about the prisoners' personal hygiene, and they condemned drunkenness, intemperance, debauchery, thievery, or dupery. Even though the detention of prisoners of war did not serve the purpose of 'reforming' them, during their captivity they were subjected to the same type of discipline as the 'undesirables' and 'marginals' studied by Foucault. A crucial component of this disciplinarization of the body was the obligation to look after and mend the prison, that great organism of which the prisoners formed a part.

This is not simply a story of coercion. In the eighteenth century as in con-temporary prisons, prisoners actively sought work, as a means to re-establish a semblance of normality and reconnect 'with the whole lost world'.[310] The Spanish Prisoners on board the Prince George prison-ship at Spithead attracted their jailors' goodwill by working:

> The behavior of the Spanish Prisoners has been so remarkable...they deserve every attention that can be shewed them, and as I believe they all request to be separated from the French Prisoners...they have assisted chearfully in working both their own ships and the Kings Ships that have been short of Hands, and even offered to assist in manning the Resolution's Guns against the Prothée.[311]

We are not talking only about forced labour here. Rose-tinted or not, this excerpt indicates the perception that work is inherently virtuous, a conception which constituted a central tenet of confinement in early modern Europe, and was also part of the mental universe of the authorities who were looking after prisoners of war.[312] As Dartmoor was being constructed, its first prisoners of war could volunteer to be employed by contractors to carry materials inside the prison.[313] Nurses, cooks, and laundrymen in the hospital were also chosen from amongst the prisoners, who were paid six pence per man per day, in cash, for their duties.[314] Prisoners were also remunerated to whitewash the prison walls, pave the prison yard, or keep the slating in repair[315]—like the sailors who were constantly at work

---

[309] 'A sufficient Number of the Prisoner Barbers be employed to shave their Countrymen, and be paid...for that Service': Captain Hamilton's Proposals, 4 February, and Observations of the S&W, 13 February 1744, TNA, ADM98/2, fo. 104v. The 1779 Penitentiary Act contained similar provisions: Ignatieff, *Just Measure*, pp. 93–4.

[310] Goffman, *Asylums*, p. 52.

[311] Copy of R. Digby, Prince George, Spithead, 6 March 1780, NMM, ADM/M/410.

[312] Foucault, *Madness*, pp. 50–75.

[313] TB to Captain Cotgrave, 31 May 1809, TNA, ADM98/225.

[314] TO to Cotgrave, 12 March 1810, ibid.; 'Instructions for Agents' (1807), article 11. In Stapleton prison, French prisoners were employed 'at the pomp', as assistant surgeons or as blacksmiths: TO to Crawley, 27 July, 26 August 1808, 13 January 1810, ADM98/269, fos. 10v, 12v, 68.

[315] TO to Cotgrave, 26 May 1810, TNA, ADM98/225; 20 July, 1 October 1811, ADM98/226, fos. 82v, 102v.

on their vessels, adding or replacing pieces of wood to the fragile structures that were navy ships.[316] Others were even employed to build a church or to repair 'the Boundary of the Prison Ground'.[317] This cheap labour force was widely coveted, and Thomas Tyrwhitt appointed prisoners to work 'on the Moor', while others were privately employed to work on the roads.[318] This once again shows that the boundaries between statuses were more flexible than is often assumed: while prisoners of war were not detained as a punishment, they were sometimes put to work alongside convicts and criminals.[319] Here as well, during the Revolutionary and Napoleonic Wars successive French governments went further than Britain in eroding the protections traditionally granted to prisoners of war, forcefully putting them to work, in mines, on the roads, in manufactures or in the fields.[320]

Nowhere was this interdependence between the prison and its occupants more obvious than in the discussion about the future of Dartmoor after the Napoleonic Wars. The former physician of the prison asserted that, left empty, the building would deteriorate:

> In your opinion, supposing the prison to be occupied by prisoners now, would it not be better fitted to send prisoners to hereafter; ... – Certainly. It must be a ruin, unless strict attention is paid to it; if occupied, of course it would not be suffered to go into decay.
>
> You think that the prison would be extremely injured, if it be suffered to remain unoccupied?—I do think so.[321]

In this interview with a doctor, the vocabulary of ailing and healing was used to qualify not the health of the inmates, but that of the buildings they inhabited.

VI. Conclusion

As this chapter has shown, how, where, and with whom the prisoners of war were detained changed over time. In principle, by the middle of the eighteenth century, both the French and the British believed that prisoners of war needed to be detained separately. However, in France, the recourse to non-specialized buildings

[316] Dening, *Bligh's Bad Language*.
[317] TO to Cotgrave, 10 January, 10 June 1812, TNA, ADM98/227, fos. 3–4, 39.
[318] TO to Cotgrave, 15 June 1812, 13 May 1813, ibid., fos. 44v, 99v. This presented opportunities to escape, which prisoners sometimes seized: ibid., 17 December 1812, fo. 75v.
[319] On prisoners of war as a workforce, see Rommelse and Downing, 'State formation', p. 157; Tycko, 'The legality'; Childs, 'Surrender'.
[320] Marquis, 'Convention', pp. 74–6. See, for instance, 'Extrait du registre des arrêtés du Comité de Salut Public', 17 July 1794 (29 Messidor an 2), articles 24, 31, ADSM, L4556.
[321] Dr George Maggrath, 5 May 1818, *Report* (1818), p. 202.

remained the rule throughout the period. In Britain, by contrast, new reforming ideas about imprisonment started to trickle down to the level of practice from the 1770s onwards. While the historiography has linked this movement of so-called prison reform to debates about the law, humanitarianism, and religion, it also overlapped with discussions about the rightful treatment of prisoners of war. The repeated attempts by the Sick & Wounded Board to place prisoners of war in renovated prisons exemplify the tension between different conceptions of captivity. For prison reformers, the goals of the new prisons built from the 1780s onwards were threefold: 'security, salubrity, and reformation'.[322] Incarcerating prisoners of war in these buildings, and putting them alongside other detainees, risked nullifying these aims. State administrators, on the other hand, had different priorities: demographic pressure and the near-constant situation of emergency forced them to compromise their principles. The frantic search for available spaces of detention led these administrations to compete with other users. This ambiguity towards the different purposes of war imprisonment still existed at the end of our period. The building of dedicated war prisons in Britain, such as Norman Cross and Dartmoor, has to be understood as part of a broader issue, namely the search for long-term solutions for accommodating convicted criminals. It is no coincidence that the main proponent behind the Dartmoor scheme was Sir Thomas Tyrwhitt, who saw prisoners of war in the same light as convicts, as potential labourers who could be contracted out by private enterprises and used to colonize and develop his region. In this sense, the economic function of prisoners of war and that of convicts in New South Wales are two sides of the same coin. This also tells us something important about the continuing involvement of private actors in the fate of prisoners of war.

A focus on the functions of buildings is clearly insufficient if we want to understand what went on behind their walls. Prison spaces can be differentiated in terms of the levels of freedom and restriction they delineate, as well as the varying degrees of surveillance that are exerted within them. While mobility within the prison was monitored, there was more freedom in the wards and the recreation yard than at the prison market, and at the same time there were places of absolute deprivation of freedom, such as the black hole. Walls or gates materialize the boundaries between the prison and the outside, and they concentrate surveillance. Paying attention to what prisoners of war did to their buildings is another way to look at detention as a social and spatial experience. Prisoners did not sit patiently, waiting for the time of their exchange. They resisted the conditions of their detention, by targeting the buildings themselves. In the most extreme cases, they turned them into empty carcasses. More commonly, through their repeated attempts to pierce the walls or dig under them, they reinvented the

---

[322] Evans, *Fabrication*, p. 181.

prison and forced prison architects constantly to adapt these spaces to their fractious occupants.

Prisoners could also reconfigure the space of the prison through their material culture or sociability. Despite the rise of separation principles, diverse groups of people interacted in prison. Being detained in the same facilities created new opportunities for encounters, peaceful or not, between common criminals and military men, officers and rank-and-file, guards and inmates, Frenchmen and Spaniards. The question thus needs to be asked, in the following chapters, whether life within prison walls and more broadly in captivity zones, mimicked the outside society or whether an alternative society developed.

5

The Reinvention of Society?

I. Introduction

How far did war captivity challenge the social hierarchies that existed on the outside? How much did captivity 'reshuffle' the 'social distinctions already established in the environing society', such as those of rank, gender, or race?[1]

In part, such questions echo the work of historians of war captivity in America, who favour a history of cultural and religious exchanges between Indians captors and their European captives, from an anthropological or literary point of view.[2] The methodology chosen here is different. Envisaged as a category of practice rather than a normative category, the status of the prisoner of war is unstable, contingent, and constantly renegotiated. I focus here on social interactions, on processes of 'mutual evaluations'[3], to bring to the fore the role of 'social estimation' and the 'language of self-description', i.e. how people place themselves and others on the social ladder.[4] As Alexandra Shepard has powerfully demonstrated, people in early modern England 'were acutely status conscious and heavily invested in finely graded differentiation throughout the social scale'.[5] But the large numbers of outsiders who were brought from abroad and detained in France and Britain could not always be easily cast in familiar categories. Local populations, state administrators, and prisoners of war themselves discussed at length the rightful placing of foreign captives within existing social hierarchies.

This chapter argues that war captivity was a form of 'trial' or 'testing' of society. Focusing on situated social interactions, pragmatic sociologists define a trial (*épreuve*) as a 'moment in collective life when individuals, their respective statuses, their mutual relations and the social order itself end up profoundly transformed'.[6] This approach, focusing on controversies and disputes, is particularly fruitful for us, as a point of entry into how the prisoner of war society worked. In captivity zones and prison camps, pre-existing social categories might not be seen as relevant or did not operate in the same way as outside the prison, and different

---

[1] Goffman, *Asylums*, p. 113. See also Agier, 'Between war'; Pollak, *L'expérience*.
[2] See, for instance, Steele, 'Surrendering rites'.   [3] Speier, 'Honour', p. 92.
[4] Shepard, *Accounting*, p. 1. Shepard assesses the importance of wealth and material possessions in 'social reckoning' (ibid.). I place honour at the heart of my analysis, because this is the key variable in the language used by the actors I am studying.
[5] Ibid., p. 27.
[6] Lemieux, 'De la théorie', p. 186. On this approach, see Boltanski and Thévenot, *On Justification*.

The Society of Prisoners: Anglo-French Wars and Incarceration in the Eighteenth Century. Renaud Morieux, Oxford University Press (2019). © Renaud Morieux. DOI: 10.1093/oso/9780198723585.001.0001

conceptions of the social order could clash. This is not to say, however, that durable social differences did not exist, and that war captivity permitted a free-flowing and constant reinvention of society. There were limits to the redefinition of social categories, which need to be examined more closely. At the same time, these encounters did not take place in a vacuum: in France and even more so in Britain, status distinctions were already imperilled by other developments, which have been depicted as the rise of a bourgeois or commercial society.

The prisoners' social status was actualized, made visible, in specific contexts. The first section is concerned with the parole system, which in many ways created the most obvious challenge to existing conceptions of the social. Prisoners on parole were socially and spatially privileged vis-à-vis their compatriots. But these privileges were not taken for granted and were often contested, by other prisoners as well by the host population. In this sense, the parole zone can be described as what Norbert Elias calls a social configuration, i.e. 'a fluctuating, tensile equilibrium, a balance of power moving to and fro'.[7] By narrowing the social distance between prisoners and local populations, the parole system created the condition for multiple conflicts between different conceptions of the social hierarchy. The chances for such disputes were increased by the reduction of the spatial distance between these prisoners and locals: their prison was enclosed not by walls, but by symbolic limits. The legal rules of the parole of honour thus brought together the French and the English, combatants and civilians, aristocrats and plebeians, urban people and country people. In this constrained framework, new forms of social relations were invented, which had not been anticipated by the legislation. While the parole system was not restricted to Europe, this section only concerns itself with the metropoles.[8]

The social estimation of the prisoners' worth is the focus of the second section of this chapter. Social classification was at the heart of the job of state officials in charge of exchanging prisoners of war. These administrators engaged in lengthy discussions over the rightful 'placing' of particular people in the exchange system. These negotiations provide us with another perspective on social hierarchies, where state officials tried to construct spaces of equivalence that made sense across national borders. The question raised here is how easily social hierarchies could be translated, and how much social categories made sense outside of their context of origin. By considering the case of black sailors captured in the West Indies, whose claims to be treated as prisoners of war was always subject to qualifications, the chapter finally tries to define the limits

---

[7] Elias, *What is Sociology?*, p. 131.

[8] See, for example, the case of French prisoners allowed to go to Mauritius on their parole: Lord Clive, governor at Fort St George, to governor general in India, 6 January 1801, British Library (BL), MS IOR/F/4/95/1921, fos. 235–8. See also Kingston vestry minutes, 29 March 1798: 'there are an extraordinary number of prisoners of war and strangers of various descriptions at large in the town of Kingston', Jamaican Archives (JA), 2/6/7, fo. 81v.

of the possible: social hierarchies, in the context of captivity, could not be perpetually reinvented.

II. The Parole Zones

Unlike rank-and-file captives, a small proportion of prisoners were paroled, living under fairly minimal restrictions. Overall and consistent figures for prisoners on parole are generally lacking. According to a list from May 1758, at that date there were 16,329 prisoners in England, of whom 2,261 (14 per cent) were on parole.[9] A return from June 1812 gave a total figure of 3,231 French prisoners on parole in Britain, including 2,369 army and naval officers, 211 masters and mates of merchant vessels, 176 captains of privateers, 211 passengers 'and other Persons of respectability', 149 servants to officers, and 115 women and children.[10]

At the heart of social estimation lies the question of the social worth of people and groups.[11] For prisoners on parole, this issue was framed in the language of honour. The parole of honour was rooted in the idea that some prisoners were worthier than others. More specifically, these prisoners were morally superior to others because they were socially superior. But these claims often conflicted with the reality of their position: they often found themselves at the mercy of the surrounding population, who refused to grant their claims to moral superiority by bestowing honour on them.[12] The normative expectations of the prisoners on parole, who expected the parole system to be blindly obeyed by local populations, were often disappointed.[13] Thus, the disputes between prisoners on parole and the host population shed light on the normative and moral resources that were used by eighteenth-century Englishmen and Frenchmen to legitimize themselves in situations of conflict.[14] More broadly, they tell us something important about the uncertain place occupied by prisoners of war in social hierarchies.

A. The Parole System

Requiring an oral as well as well as a written bond, the parole of honour belonged to the category of promissory oaths, 'committing the swearer to a future action'.[15]

---

[9] 1 May 1758, National Maritime Museum, Greenwich (NMM), ADM/F/17. As war against Spain was only declared in January 1762, only French prisoners are listed.

[10] Transport Office (TO), 26 June 1812, 'Return of the Prisoners of War at present in the United Kingdom', PP, no. 331.

[11] Muldrew, Economy.   [12] Speier, 'Honour', pp. 75–8.

[13] Shepard, Accounting, pp. 28–9.

[14] A dispute can be defined as a confrontation and negotiation about accepted norms of behaviour in a given situation: Thireau and Wang, 'Introduction', in Disputes, p. 18. See also Roberts, 'The study of dispute'.

[15] Spurr, 'A profane history', p. 38.

As usual, seventeenth- and eighteenth-century legal writers were more interested in describing how the system ought to work than in its actual mechanics.[16] The parole was a form of contract, which, argued Réal, suspended the state of war between the swearer and his captor.[17] While the prisoners who were incarcerated were perfectly justified to attempt their escape, those who had given their parole were bound by it: all these authors agreed that the oath was meaningful.

The procedures of life for prisoners on parole evolved throughout the eighteenth century, but a basic structure persisted, in both countries. Originally, the notion of 'freedom on parole' meant the authorization given to a prisoner of specified rank to return to his own country, provided he gave his word of honour not to fight against his captors until another prisoner of similar rank was exchanged for him. The system was a survival from the Middle Ages, when mounted knights were too valuable to be slaughtered on the battlefield and could be ransomed against their oath of honour.[18] In the eighteenth century, reflecting a more fluid society, the system had become more flexible, allowing a wider range of groups to benefit from the privilege. Depending on the period, besides naval officers, officers on board merchant ships, as well as the captains of privateers, and even passengers, army surgeons, and servants, could thus be exchanged. Having personal connections certainly helped.[19] But whatever the social remit of the privilege, naval and army officers always benefitted from it. The way in which the French secretary of state for the *Marine* justified the parole privilege is typical of the state officials' view:

> It is a mitigation that the goodness and humanity of the two Sovereigns have procured to Officers whose long detention can only cause considerable disorder in their personal business. In the Exchanges Officers of both Kingdoms will always have the preference and this usage is too just not to be reciprocally established.[20]

In principle, should the exchange fail to be completed within a specified period, these prisoners had to come back to their captors. The system was still in place during the Napoleonic Wars, when the oath of honour was also used at sea:

---

[16] Grotius, *Laws of War*, pp. 459, 468–9; Vattel, *Law of Nations*, book II, ch. 16, par. 246, book III, ch. 8, par. 150–1; Martens, *Précis*, vol. II, book VIII, ch. 3, par. 275.

[17] Réal, ch. 2, section VIII, par VIII, p. 513. See Stacey, 'Age of chivalry', pp. 36–7; Keen, *Laws of War*, pp. 156–85.

[18] Ambühl, *Prisoners*.

[19] See, for example, letters requesting aid by or on behalf of French prisoners of war, addressed to William Mildmay and Earl Fitzwalter, 1757–61, Essex Record Office, D/DM/O1/23.

[20] Copy of Berryer to Lords Commissioners of the Admiralty (LCA), 12 January 1759, NMM, ADM/F/19.

'treatises of exchange' were directly concluded between the captains of captured ships and the captains of privateers.[21]

Those prisoners who were not sent back to their country were called 'prisoners on parole' and were given the freedom of a town or village. On signing their parole certificate, prisoners received a certificate of protection and travelled, on their own, to an allotted parole town. During their time in Britain, they were given subsistence money proportional to their rank, which was distributed to them by parole agents.[22] On reaching their destination, they were free to circulate within a variable perimeter, provided they gave their word not to abscond. The rank-and-file, on the other hand, were crammed into prisons.

The very existence of the parole must be understood in the context of an honour-based society. Once sworn, an oath modified the social relations between those involved and created both obligations and solidarities. Giving a word of honour bound the swearer three times over: firstly, it was given at the risk of losing one's honour; secondly, it was a legal and moral engagement to the monarch, which risked discrediting him, while also putting at risk fellow prisoners, as potential victims of reprisals;[23] finally, it was a bond of trust with the individual to whom the parole was sworn, sometimes against money. But this commitment was balanced by a highly rated prize: the preservation of privileged status (as well as some freedom). Indeed, the oath recognized a social superiority, based on the claim to pride embodied in the parole of honour itself. The parole delineated social frontiers between those who benefited and those who were excluded from it. While the rank-and-file were imprisoned, officers of a certain rank would be paroled if they chose to because they were gentlemen—often noblemen—and as such deemed to be worthy of this mark of trust. The links between personal esteem and military honour were intimate.[24]

Getting parole was a privilege, in the sense that it strictly conformed to the social hierarchies of the time. But these hierarchies were not carved in stone. This is illustrated by the question asked by Antoine Casamajor, *Intendant de la Marine* in Rochefort, who wondered in 1778: 'who are those of the crews who will be put in prison, and those who will be left free?'[25] While administrative procedures institutionalized the social pre-eminence of parole prisoners of war, they also reflected a finely grained sense of dynamic internal rankings. All prisoners on parole were not equal in status, and regulations mirrored this. Indeed, the

---

[21] 'Cartel of exchange' signed by Captain James Blackstone of the ship Sidbury, captured by a French privateer, 13 January 1812: Service Historique de la Défense, Vincennes (SHD), FF2/20, no. 219.

[22] Anderson, 'Treatment', pp. 74–5. The financial workings of the system have not been studied by historians, and would be worth investigating further.

[23] Barbara Donagan argues that besides this 'wider moral world', keeping one's word was also 'a powerful agent in the enforcement of the rules of war': *War*, p. 167.

[24] Rodger, 'Honour', pp. 425–47.

[25] Casamajor, 29 August 1778, Archives Nationales, Paris (AN), MAR/F2/82.

question of where to draw the line between honourable officers and the others was the subject of heated debate.

Spatial freedom thus reflected a social hierarchy that ultimately relied on the notion of honour. In a passage expanding on Hobbes' definition of liberty as 'the absence of impediments to motion', Pufendorf argued that the degrees of liberty granted to a captive reflect both the trust of their captors, and the moral obligation of his captives, which is 'built on his Exemption from Chains and Imprisonment'.[26] A 'Slave of War' who is granted 'corporal Liberty' is bound morally to his master, who has put an end to 'the State of War' between them. Two categories of captives thus need to be distinguished:

> There is a great Difference between those Slaves who are secur'd in Prisons, Work-houses, and the like, and those who are tied by Convenant to their Master.... For to hold a Person in Chains, or Durance, is a Sign, that we do not think him sufficiently ensured to us by any Obligation, or moral Restraint.[27]

This analysis also applies to the difference between the prisoner who is restrained within prison walls, and the prisoner on parole, who is deemed sufficiently trustworthy to give his oath of honour he would not escape, and walk around almost freely, bound by his consciousness and not by any physical barrier. But even among prisoners on parole, there was an even subtler gradation. There again, Pufendorf's language is helpful: 'things are said to be more or less *free*, as they have more or less space to move in; as a Man in a wide Prison is more at liberty, than another under close Confinement.'[28] Depending on their status, prisoners had more or less spatial freedom. In 1706, Lempereur, the French commissaire at St Malo, thus wrote about three English prisoners, two captains and one diplomat: 'I will send them tomorrow without fail to Dinan, where they prefer to go rather than Rennes.'[29]

Prisoners of a high social status, like these men, were sometimes given the choice of their place of detention. The more eminent the prisoners were, the more extensive the boundaries of their parole zone could be. Thus, the Lords of the Admiralty agreed in 1744 with their French counterparts that parole limits should vary 'according to different Ranks or Qualities, as Five miles to Commissioned Officers, and Two or Three to others'.[30] The Board even proposed that a Spanish lieutenant, lately arrived from Jamaica, who 'is represented to us to be a man of rank in Spain', should be given 'the liberty of London upon his parole'.[31] These limits, which could be marked by trees or large stones, were extended to

---

[26] See Skinner, *Hobbes*.   [27] Pufendorf, *Of the Law*, book VI, ch. III, par. 6, p. 617.
[28] Ibid., p. 620.
[29] Lempereur to secretary of state for the *Marine* (SSM), 28 February 1706, AN, MAR/B3/135, fo. 81v.
[30] LCA to Sick & Wounded Board (S&W), 4 July 1744, NMM, ADM/M/388, no. 98.
[31] LCA to S&W, 9 July 1744, ibid., no. 103.

244 THE SOCIETY OF PRISONERS

five and eight miles in 1778 for the ranks above surgeons on ships of war, as well as volunteers 'if Gentlemen of Family' and captains and 'Passengers of Rank' on board merchant ships.[32] By contrast, 'some of the inferior Ranks formerly admitted to parole', who were suspected of betraying their oath, were now excluded from it.[33] This shows that depending on the context, not all officers were entitled to this privilege. Parole limits could also have a temporal component as well as a spatial one. Just as the prisoners could be freed on their parole to return home, short-term leaves within the host country could be granted. For instance, French prisoners in England, for a while, obtained a month's leave to go to London or to Bath upon their parole, for health, business, or pleasure.[34] In 1760, a Monsieur Duval asked for an authorization to go '5 miles of Faringdon [Oxfordshire]...to go to teach some Ladies to Dance in the Neighbourhood'.[35] Similar indulgences continued during the Napoleonic Wars. Lieutenant Tucket wrote from Verdun in May 1806:

> With respect to indulgence we have no reason to complain, we have six miles in every direction round the town to walk and ride in, provided we are in town for the shutting of the gates at 9 o'clock. The Captains are obliged to sign their names every five days, Lieutenants once a day, and all the other prisoners twice a day. These are all the restrictions we are under, and we may lodge where we please, and as we like.[36]

Larger walking limits were, above all, reflections of the prisoners' rank. They were the condition for continuing to cultivate a lifestyle proper to their station. For instance, in 1706, despite the opposition of the town's military governor, English prisoners on parole at Dinan were allowed to go to Rennes in order to visit the tailor, while Mr Hamilton, thanks to his acquaintance with the Comtesse de Gramont, was allowed to go to Paris.[37] Six captains detained in Sodbury requested in 1757 to be allocated a zone of '3 miles...for our promenade and dissipate our boredom'.[38] Social esteem is based on constant comparisons with others, and 'preferences' given to other prisoners were interpreted as personal slights on their honour.[39] In July 1758 for example, the Sick & Wounded Board explained the

---

[32] S&W to LCA, 17 August 1778, The National Archives, Kew (TNA), ADM98/11, fo. 115; LCA to S&W, 5 September 1778, NMM, ADM/M/406. On the materiality of these limits, see TO's circular to Agents, 27 May 1808, TNA, ADM98/170, fo. 4.

[33] S&W to LCA, 17 August 1778, TNA, ADM98/11, fo. 115.

[34] LCA to S&W, 21 May 1744, NMM, ADM/M/387, no. 47. From August 1744 onwards, London was forbidden, owing to fear of espionage: LCA to S&W, 10 August 1744, ADM/M/388, no. 153.

[35] S&W to LCA, 3 March 1760, ADM/F/20.

[36] From Lieutenant Tucket, of HMS Calcutta, Verdun, 10 May 1806, quoted in Cox, Captain Daniel Woodriff, p. 113. Degrees of freedom of movement varied from depot to depot, and nationality to nationality: Mulvey, Sketches, p. 89.

[37] Lempereur to SSM, 3 January 1706, AN, MAR/B3/135, fo. 7v.

[38] Petition to S&W, 23 April 1757, TNA, ADM97/121.

[39] Duguay to SSM, 24 July 1709, AN, MAR/B3/165, fo. 327.

discontent of the French prisoners on parole at Alresford, who had not been permitted to venture too far from the town:

> The circumstances which they mention of desiring to go to a House within Musket Shot of Alresford is misrepresented, as it appears to be in a Village three miles distant from that place and upon the whole it seems to us that their Complaints have arisen from the uneasiness they are under at hearing that some French Officers at other places have greater Liberties than they themselves enjoy.[40]

Having a larger roaming zone also meant that the prisoners were able to observe their faith. As the Spanish prisoners on parole at Bandon in Ireland remarked in 1745, 'the Liberty of walking round the Town' gave them 'an Opportunity of hearing Mass... on Feast Days.'[41] Many other internal distinctions underscored the parole system, such as money allowance, which was lower for 'inferior French Prisoners of War on Parole', food rations, or the right to keep servants.[42] Because honour is inherently comparative, it could be diluted when it was bestowed on too many people: hence the constant striving to extend these privileges.[43]

To prove he was trustworthy, the prisoner signed a written oath. A British certificate from 1747 is quite typical of the procedure. The prisoner allowed to remain in Britain on his parole would be allowed to live in a certain place, and gave his parole of honour 'neither to withdraw myself from the bounds prescribed me there, without leave for that purpose' from the Board. He also swore that he would behave 'decently, and with due regard to the Laws of the Kingdom', and would not hold any correspondence 'either with France or with Spain, during my continuing a prisoner of war'. Finally, he recognized that he was placed under the supervision of the Agent for the Prisoners.[44] There were some variations, for instance regarding the manner in which the oath had to be sworn. The mechanics of oath-taking were not formalized at the beginning of the War of the Austrian Succession, and on 28 May 1744 the Lords of the Admiralty asked to be informed 'when officers taken prisoners, and suffered to return home upon their parole of honour, to whom they gave that parole of honour?'.[45] Similarly in France, Monsieur de Casamajor, *Intendant de la Marine* in Rochefort, inquired in 1778 whether the governor of the province was the only person empowered to witness the oath and receive the parole certificate.[46] The forms of these certificates and the

---

[40] S&W to LCA, 12 July 1758, NMM, ADM/F/18.
[41] Petition in English to the LCA, 30 January 1745, ADM/M/394, no. 38/1.
[42] TO's circular to parole agents, 11 September 1809, TNA, ADM98/170, fo. 27; LCA to S&W, 7 September 1744, NMM, ADM/M/388, no. 194; French translation of S&W to Guillot, 29 July 1745, AN, MAR/B3/432, fo. 229.
[43] Speier, 'Honour', pp. 89–90.   [44] NMM, ADM/M/398, no. 157/1.
[45] LCA to S&W, ADM/M/387, no. 52/1.
[46] Casamajor to unknown, 29 August 1778, AN, MAR/F2/82.

nature of the oath fluctuated considerably, and this remained the case during the Napoleonic Wars, a period of bureaucratic invention.[47] During the 1810s, some of the pre-printed forms delivered by the French minister of *Marine du Commerce* blended the religious compromise defended by Napoleon and the practice of oath-taking popularized by the Revolution. One of these forms thus stated that the captain of the captured ship would engage himself 'as well by oath on the Byble, as by my word of honour, to cause [*name of the prisoner handwritten*] now prisoner of war in [*to be filled*] prison, to be set at liberty'.[48]

When they were not exchanged, the prisoners could be given the right to reside in a specific town. In this case, state administrations usually asked these men to obtain 'good behaviour bonds', which were financially guaranteed by merchants.[49] Relying on commitment and trust, the logic of this measure fell within the moral economy of the parole system, but with a supplementary requirement, since a pecuniary as well as a moral contract was involved. Crucially, the security was given by a private individual, who was financially interested in the fulfilment of the prisoner's pledge. In 1695, the English prisoners at Dinan thus wrote to the Sick & Wounded Board that they were allowed to lodge in 'private houses', and were given the 'freedom of a town' if they paid 'a security not to escape'. This privilege was granted to all the prisoners 'who can afford to pay for their lodging', and not just officers.[50] The system was attractive for bourgeois lodgers, who would collect the rents paid by the prisoners during their stay.[51] This policy was considered to be too liberal, and to facilitate escapes; in the following years, the French naval administration tried to monitor the delivery of bails by private hosts.[52] The same system remained in place in both countries in later wars.[53]

Accommodation in private houses was not always the prisoners' preferred option. Given the choice to be detained in urban forts and citadels or to be allowed to live on their parole in small villages, prisoners often preferred the former, as those officers of English privateers and merchant ships in Bayonne and Dieppe.[54]

---

[47] 'Instructions for Agents' (1807), article 4, p. 3. A blank form of parole was annexed, in Appendix No. 5.

[48] On board of the French privateer the *Furet* of St Malo, 6 November 1812, filled by the two captains, in French and in English: SHD, FF2/20.

[49] This system was in place at least since the late seventeenth century, and continued throughout the eighteenth century: LCA to S&W, 4 July 1744, NMM, ADM/M/388, no. 88; S&W to LCA, 26 February 1759, ADM/F/19; 'Règlement concernant les prisonniers ennemis détenus en France', undated, article 10, in 'Circulaire aux intendants', 14 December 1778, AN, MAR/F2/82.

[50] Copy of letter to S&W, 13 October 1695, AN, MAR/B3/89, fos. 215–v.

[51] Gastines to SSM, 10 November 1694, MAR/B3/82, fo. 268v; St Sulpice to SSM, 16 January 1704, AN, MAR/B3/123, fo. 427.

[52] St Sulpice to SSM, 1 December 1702, MAR/B3/117, fos. 331–2. A detailed register containing the names of all the prisoners accommodated in town and of all the bourgeois who gave security for them was kept and updated in Dinan from 1708: Lempereur, 18 March 1708, MAR/B3/157, fos. 108–v.

[53] See, for example, S&W to LCA, 26 August 1757, TNA, ADM98/6, fos. 223–v.

[54] SSM to S&W, 17 February 1747, AN, MAR/B2/331, fo. 544v.

Living in town was costly, and some officers preferred to spend the night in prison, and wander freely during the day, as in Portchester Castle, where half of them were 'permitted to Air and refresh themselves in the Village of Portchester on Mornings, and the other half, Afternoons, provided they have a Soldier to attend, and see them again into the Castle'.[55] When French officials expressed their disbelief at this arrangement, the prisoners wrote a petition explaining that this had been their own choice. Even though they had the right to be on their parole in Alresford, they had 'preferred staying in prison' and taking their turns to stroll in Portchester Castle, because 'having no money and the half-shilling that the King gives for bails is not sufficient'.[56]

Parole transgressions were not rare. In 1745, an English lieutenant's command of a navy sloop was cancelled when the Admiralty realized that he was a 'prisoner on his parole of honour'.[57] Perjury was taken very seriously by state administrations, not least because military men were expected to be less casual than civilians about making promises that involved the safety of their comrades-in-arms.[58] If apprehended on his return home, the prisoner was often sent back to his captors. Guillot, *commissaire de la Marine* in St Malo, wrote in 1745 that he would return two French officers on parole, who had escaped from Jersey, emphasizing his wish, 'with this example of justice and usage, to accustom these men, if possible, to keep their parole inviolably'.[59] The French secretary of state for the *Marine* explained in 1758 that these were sacrosanct principles:

> The King disapproves much of the behaviour of those of his Subjects who thus violate their Promises. I have given orders following those of His Majesty to search for these escapees, so that if they arrive in any Port of this Kingdom, they will be arrested, and sent back to England.[60]

When the prisoners tried to walk beyond their parole limits, they were normally punished. The French officers on parole in Oakhampton, who had been recaptured while venturing more than five miles beyond their parole zone, disguised and provided with a false certificate allowing them to circulate freely, were hence 'committed to prison' in 1778.[61] The prisoners on parole who were recaptured gave up their claims to being treated differently from the rank-and-file, and their fate was often to be confined with them,[62] or even to be put in common

---

[55] LCA to S&W, 18 July 1745, NMM, ADM/M/392, no. 199.
[56] Petition signed by twenty prisoners, 14 October 1745, AN, MAR/B3/432, fo. 300.
[57] LCA to S&W, 17 July 1745, NMM, ADM/M/392, no. 198.
[58] Langford, *Public Life*, p. 105.   [59] Guillot to SSM, 25 June 1745, AN, MAR/B3/432, fo. 185.
[60] Copy of Marquis de Massiac to Paris de Montmartel, member of the *Conseil d'Etat*, 10 July 1758, NMM, ADM/F/18.
[61] S&W to LCA, 21 August 1778, TNA, ADM98/11, fo. 116v. See also ibid., 13 October 1778, fo. 140.
[62] St Sulpice to SSM, 17 September 1702, AN, MAR/B3/117, fo. 274v; S&W to LCA, 13 November 1756, 11 June 1757, TNA, ADM98/6, fos. 9–10v, 170v.

jails—which caused fears of collusion with debtors and criminals.[63] During the Napoleonic Wars, the Transport Office was adamant that 'the men who absconded from parole and were retaken [were] not to be put with the petty officers, but with the Common Prisoners as Men devoid of Honor'.[64] This was not always considered sufficient, and retaken escapees were sometimes put in the cachot on half-allowance.[65]

Principles were thus one thing, and practice another. For one thing, it was not always possible to ascertain what the status of escapees had been during their captivity, as Monsieur Malo, commissaire in Calais, represented in 1748: 'those who have appeared here have been careful, by fear of being sent back, to inform me of their circumstances, despite my [attention] to question them.'[66] Besides, for this administrator, escapees deserved some indulgence for having given the slip to their jailors, and they had 'have done well to make use of the negligence of their guards'.[67] This man embodies the contradictory values that could operate simultaneously in the mind of administrators. On the one hand, in his opinion the significance of an oath of honour should not be overemphasized, and escapees could even be rewarded for playing the system and tricking the enemy. On the other, he could not endorse such actions without paying lip-service to state regulations, and he also kept a strict register of those who had transgressed their parole, so that they could be sent back if necessary.[68] These men were often not returned, and were instead credited to the balance of exchanges.[69] In accordance with the horizon of reciprocity that structured war captivity, the rules of the parole were never applied blindly. During the War of the Spanish Succession, the French thus complained that the English officers they had released with a promise to return after two months if their exchange was unsuccessful never carried out their oath: 'since the English are not sensible to our honest manners, in the future we must not have any indulgence for them,' wrote the French Commissaire Lempereur.[70]

Oaths or not, in the eighteenth century, prisoners' escapes were thus more common than is often asserted and were not an invention of the French Revolutionary Wars. Many escapes of paroled prisoners in Britain were reported during each war. In 1759, the Board remarked that 'Desertions have lately been very frequent among the French Prisoners of War, who are permitted to reside on

[63] S&W to LCA, 8, 9 November 1759, NMM, ADM/F/20; S&W to LCA, 25 September 1778, TNA, ADM98/11, fo. 134. The Agents for Prisoners of War were informed that parole-breakers would 'be sent to the common Prison, and lose their Turn of Exchange': 'Instructions for Agents' (1807), article 4, p. 4.
[64] Transport Office (TO) to Cotgrave, 24 September 1811, TNA, ADM98/226, fo. 102.
[65] TO to Cotgrave, 11 March 1812, ADM98/227, fo. 22v.
[66] Malo to SSM, 27 September 1748, AN, MAR/B3/463, fos. 194.
[67] Ibid., fos. 194–v.   [68] Ibid., fo. 194v.
[69] Copy of Lempereur to de la Croix, commissary for the exchanges in Kinsale, 10 February 1706, MAR/B3/135, fos. 65–6.
[70] Lempereur to SSM, 29 January, 25 March 1708, MAR/B3/157, fos. 65v–66, 119v. See also anonymous, 14 August 1779, MAR/F2/95.

Parole in this Kingdom'.[71] These figures remained high during the American War of Independence. A 'List of French Prisoners who broke their Parole, between 13 June 1778 and 30 June 1780' compiled by the Board in April 1781 contained 265 names, including ninety-three captains and 144 officers.[72] While escapees were found in all social ranks, state officials tended to explain the problem by the growing social inclusion of the parole privileges.

The discussion, during the 1740s, regarding which ranks should be entitled to benefit from the freedom of a town on their parole, is a good illustration of this. In July 1744, the Admiralty decided that the masters or commanders of merchant ships, passengers, and the commanders of privateers could reside upon parole 'at Inland Places, a Convenient distance from any Sea Port of the Kingdom, they ... giving one hundred Pounds a Man security for their good behavior'.[73] High-ranking officers were exempted from the measure. In July 1745, the obligation to give security was also waved for the officers of merchant ships and privateers, whose oath of honour was now considered to be sufficient. But the French officials made a U-turn the following year, expressing their suspicion towards officers from the lower decks and privateers:

> One should not count on the parole of this sort of unrefined and ill-mannered people, who feel so little the obligations of a parole of honour, that a great number has deserted, and many have tried to do so. . . . I believe My Lords . . . that this sort of people should not be left at large.[74]

Both sides agreed that such individuals should thereafter only be granted their parole if their captains vouched for them.[75] In 1759, 'good behaviour bonds' were again required for the captains of merchant ships and privateers, for whom swearing an oath of honour was judged insufficient. Those who failed to procure such bonds were put in prison.[76] Commissioned officers were exempted.[77] Similar measures were in place in France.[78]

In 1778, the Lords of the Admiralty wrote that desertions, which had been so numerous during the Seven Years' War, 'were chiefly to be ascribed to the too great extension of the parole List'. The commander in chief of the King's ships at Portsmouth was of the opinion that only officers 'of the superior Ranks' and

---

[71] S&W to LCA, 26 February 1759, NMM, ADM/F/19.
[72] 16 April 1781, AN, MAR/F2/98.
[73] LCA to S&W, 4 July 1744, NMM, ADM/M/388, no. 98.
[74] Guillot to S&W, 22 April 1746, TNA, ADM97/103, fo. 83v.
[75] S&W to SSM, 30 May 1746, AN, MAR/B3/445, fo. 138. See also *A true and authentick narrative* (1745), p. 11.
[76] S&W to LCA, 26 February, 21, 23 March, 1 May 1759, NMM, ADM/F/19.
[77] S&W to LCA, 26 February 1759, ibid.
[78] 'Mémoire au sujet de la détention . . . à la Rochelle' (1778), describing the system in place for all the categories of British prisoners during the Seven Years' War, AN, MAR/F2/95; 'Règlement concernant les prisonniers ennemis' (1778), articles 9–10, AN, MAR/F2/82.

'Gentlemen of Family' should be given their parole, while 'those of inferior Rank did not appear to him Persons whose honor was to be trusted to'.[79] The Cartel of 1780 stated that 'none of the officers inferior to ensigns will have, in the future, permission to give their parole not to serve until they have been exchanged'.[80] This social closure reflected the belief, on the part of state officials, that honour was an embodied ethos that only the social elite valued and understood. The only true honour was that of the well-born.[81] This felt need to assert what had hitherto been self-evident manifested a broader phenomenon, which was at work in both countries in the last decades of the eighteenth century, namely the closing of the ranks of a traditional elite criticized for its immorality, its lack of patriotism, or its effeminacy.[82] This was a defensive manoeuvre, aimed at shoring up some status distinctions that were being increasingly challenged.

But reality was always murkier. 'Escapes' were a code word for less avowable practices on the part of the captor states. Commissaire Lempereur noted in 1709 that all the French captains of privateers who lived in Plymouth on their parole had escaped in a few days:

> It would not have happened if the English had not wanted it, these prisoners have embarked at noon-day with their clothes either in neutral [ships] or in ships, and they had boasted to the commissaries themselves that they would escape, i.e. in good French that, because the English did not want us to believe that they had been forced to return them, they were pleased to let them go.[83]

Whoever was involved in facilitating these escapes, the local inhabitants who had given security for them had to pay the consequences. For example, in 1702 three English captains on their parole in Saint-Malo escaped from the Breton town, stealing a ship in the process. The 'hosts' of the fugitives had to defray the ship-owners for the damage.[84] In 1707, after several prisoners on parole had escaped from Dinan, the French commissaire at St Malo received the order from the secretary of state for the *Marine* in Versailles to put in prison

> The securities of the prisoners who escaped until they have paid the six hundred livres they have committed to pay for each of them in order to oblige them, either

---

[79] LCA to S&W, 22 July 1778, NMM, ADM/M/406. From October, the parole list was accordingly reduced: Anderson, 'Treatment', p. 74.
[80] Article 20, in *CTS*, vol. 47.   [81] Andrew, *Aristocratic Vice*, pp. 15–42.
[82] Colley, *Britons*, pp. 155–207; Langford, *Public Life*, pp. 510, 565–6.
[83] Lempereur to SSM, 7 July 1709, AN, MAR/B3/169, fos. 210–v. The same practices were secretly encouraged in France towards British and Irish Catholic prisoners who disappeared as they were about to embark on board packet boats or left their prisons without hindrance: SSM to Lempereur, 30 January 1709, MAR/B2/214, fo. 327; SSM to M. de Belamy, 9 July 1745, MAR/B2/326, fo. 325v.
[84] St Sulpice to SSM, 31 December 1702, MAR/B3/117, fo. 363.

not to be bound so easily in the future, or to watch the prisoners they bail, one hopes this will make them more careful in the future.[85]

In the same way, when French prisoners escaped from Kinsale, the chaplain for the Catholics in the town, who had given security for them, was jailed.[86] The bond system presented significant risks for bondsmen if the prisoners forfeited their pledge. In 1757, the English captain of a privateer, Henry Brooker, absconded from his parole in Bergues in the French Flanders and flew to England. The merchant who had given security for him, a Mr Ghovane from Dunkirk, asked the British government that Brooker be sent back to France. The Admiralty replied that it was not in its power 'to oblige one of His Majesty's subjects to return into captivity, ... and ... the present case seems to be of the nature of a private contract at the risque of Mons.[r] Ghovane, if he gave bond without taking a counter security'.[87] The French *ministre de la Marine*, the Marquis of Massiac, also contended that these merchants would not be indemnified from their loss: 'it is not possible for the King to be tied by Obligations that can only be regarded as the particular business of the Merchant who bails with the Prisoner who is bailed.'[88] Just like the hostages could rot in prison after the war, finding themselves outside the reach of the states, prisoners of war who were given private bonds inhabited a legal grey zone.

While the French Wars did not put an end to the parole system (see Fig. 5.1), it was severely damaged. For instance, in France, the detention of merchant officers together with common men became more frequent.[89] Freedom on parole, on the French side, also became increasingly rare. But the most important bone of contention was the treatment of Captain Sidney Smith by the French Directory. Smith had served in the British fleet fighting alongside the French royalists to defend Toulon in 1793. Captured off Le Havre in April 1796, he was held in the Temple Prison in Paris for two years, because the French government refused to exchange or to grant parole to a man they described as an 'arsonist' and a criminal rather than as a prisoner of war.[90] In November, Henry Swinburne, the British envoy in Paris, proposed a compromise that would preserve 'the Point of Honour on both Sides'. Smith would be returned his sword, and granted the permission to reside on his parole of honour, in some place assigned him, 'either the City of Paris, a Section, a Street, a Garden, a Court, &c. no Matter which; so that he may

[85] Pontchartrain to Ferrand, 6 July 1707, MAR/B2/198, fo. 85.
[86] Copy of Thomas [Mulshenoga], priest in Kinsale, to Lempereur, MAR/B3/145, 19 August 1707, fo. 318.
[87] 'Report upon ... Henry Brooker', 19 July 1758, NMM, ADM/F/18.
[88] Copy of Massiac to Montmartel, 10 July 1758, ibid.
[89] TO to Swinburne, 18 February 1797, in *Report* (1798), pp. 97–8.
[90] Barrow, *Life*, p. 200. See also Extract of letter from Captain Cotes to Transport Board, 12 December 1797, in *Report* (1798), p. 127.

Fig. 5.1. Thomas Rowlandson, *French prisoners of war on parole at Bodmin*, Cornwall (1795). Yale Centre for British Art.

be a Prisoner on *Parole* the English Government will be satisfied'.[91] This attempt to maintain the fiction of the parole of honour failed, as did the repeated demands to release the captive. After numerous threats, in November 1797, Britain finally retaliated by incarcerating all French prisoners on parole, contributing to eroding further a principle it was claiming to defend.[92] Despite these limitations, exchanges on parole did not stop completely during the Napoleonic Wars.[93]

Historians agree that escapes of French officers on parole surged during the French Wars, usually without quantifying the phenomenon.[94] This has been attributed, following contemporary opinions, to the rise of new republican and egalitarian principles, and to the mutation of the concept of honour in an army of plebeians and citizens. In other words, the parole was rejected as an embodiment of Ancien Regime aristocratic conceptions of honour.[95] More traditional

[91] Swinburne to the Minister of Marine and Colonies, 18 November 1796, in *Report* (1798), Appendix, p. 84.

[92] They were still confined in March 1798: TO, 'A statement of the general treatment of prisoners of war in health, since the 1st of January 1796', 19 March 1798, in *Report* (1798), p. 37.

[93] See, for instance, the case of an English lieutenant belonging to an East Indiaman, 7 November 1807, Devon Record Office, Exeter (DRO), 6105 M/O/1/25.

[94] Compare Chamberlain, *Hell*, pp. 114–37; Lewis, Napoleon, pp. 44–5, 61–5; Bennett, 'French prisoners'. A dedicated study would be needed in order to ascertain whether escapes massively increased during this period. For 1810–12, the figure is 682, of whom 464 were commissioned officers: *Account of the Number* (1812).

[95] For example Best, *Humanity*, pp. 112–21; Daly, 'Lost legions', pp. 370–1.

explanations were also invoked at the time. Just like in the eighteenth century, at the end of 1796 the 'general Misconduct of the Officers' of privateers led the Transport Office to restrict the privilege to commissioned officers in the French army and navy.[96] In 1812, Viscount Sidmouth, the Home Secretary, remarked that these escapees 'could not have done so without the assistance of others who were subjects of this country'.[97] To understand the continuing prevalence of these practices, one must therefore underline the strength of the ties binding prisoners and local communities: escapees always built on the support of local populations, who openly defied state regulations.[98]

B. Disputes of Honour

The preservation of social hierarchies was at the root of the parole system, which was supposed to reproduce military ranks and privileges. The parole, in principle, also delineated a boundary between the French and the British populations, which was not physical, like the walls of a prison, but psychological, relying on the acceptance of the social norms and beliefs that justified the privilege. In practice, these distinctions were frequently unsettled.

Between 1744 and 1780, forty-three English towns received prisoners on parole; the same places were generally reused in successive wars. The majority were south of a line from Bristol and London, mainly in Kent, Hampshire, and Devon: it was easier and less costly to accommodate them in the hinterland of the main Channel ports of Dover, Portsmouth, and Plymouth, where prisoners would be landed and exchanged. Concern for security probably also explains why prisoners on parole were sent to small market towns and villages rather than spas and provincial towns. In France, for reasons of accessibility, most of the parole towns were situated in the Northern and Western part of the country, in Brittany (Dinan, Rennes), the Loire region (Tours, Saumur, Niort), and the North (Boulogne, Dunkirk). A list sent to the Lords of the Admiralty in May 1758 gives a snapshot of the ratio between these prisoners and the English population in different towns. Prisoners on parole, for instance, accounted for about 13 per cent of the populations of Wye (Kent, ninety-two prisoners for 690 inhabitants) and Callington (Cornwall, 107/830), and 15 per cent of the population of Petersfield (Hampshire, 156/1049).[99]

---

[96] TO, 19 March 1798, in *Report* (1798), p. 37.
[97] 23 July 1812, *House of Lords Hansard*, vol. 23, col. 1193–4.
[98] On the role of smugglers in transporting escapees, see Daly, 'Lost legions', p. 378.
[99] 'A list shewing the several places in England', 1 May 1758, NMM, ADM/F/17. Jack Langton kindly allowed me to use his town estimates for the late seventeenth century and the 1801 census. The ratio was smaller in bigger towns, such as Crediton in Hampshire (57/2250, 2 per cent), or Launceston in Cornwall (103/1503, 7 per cent).

The arrival of dozens of foreign prisoners unsettled the demographic balance and worried local authorities. In 1744, the mayor of Bristol, alarmed by the presence of 'near six hundred French Prisoners in and near this City', wrote to the Duke of Newcastle, the secretary of state for the Southern Department. Not only were the prisoners detained in Bedminster Bridewell riotous, he observed, but those on parole made 'an ill use of the Liberty they have had': some of them had been seen contemplating 'the shipping of the Quay, and the River, and making observations, and others lurking near the Magazine of powder'. The mayor doubled the city watch, and ordered all French men found at large in the city to be secured.[100] Four companies of infantry were also marched to the city.[101] After the 1745 rebellion broke up, the fear of illicit correspondence with Irish papists also led to their confinement in Kinsale,[102] while the roaming space of the prisoners who had the freedom of towns was curtailed throughout the country in December 1745.[103] The following year, in Penrith, French officers going to the theatre were assaulted by a 'mob', and riots against the prisoners continued in other Cumberland towns in 1747.[104]

French mayors feared that the prisoners would act as spies, as in Morlaix or Bayonne,[105] or that they would create disorder with local populations, as in Dinan.[106] Some French cities adopted regulations to police the prisoners on parole. The rules adopted in Tours in 1779 are exemplary, and were copied in other cities.[107] The regulations, explained the town council, 'reassured the citizens already anxious to see that no sort of discipline was imposed on such a large number of prisoners who roamed in the city... at any hour of the day or night, armed with canes weapons of all kinds and sticks'.[108] These articles mapped out the spectrum of possible relations between the prisoners and local populations. French inhabitants were warned against attempting to help the prisoners to escape (article II), but were also rewarded financially if they helped catching escapees (article III). Furthermore, the parole not only reinforced social hierarchies among the prisoners; it also underlined the distance that separated officers from the

<hr/>

[100] John Berrow, mayor, to Duke of Newcastle, 8 September 1744, NMM, ADM/M/389, no. 207.
[101] Holles Newcastle to LCA, 13 September 1744, ibid.
[102] LCA to S&W, 12 November 1745, ADM/M/393, no. 318.
[103] Their 'liberty' was restrained 'to the circumference of the towns' in which the agents had placed them: ibid., 2 December 1745, no. 336.
[104] 'The Riot's Theatre, etc. 1746–7', Cumbria Archive Centre, D/HUD 8/19/1. See also D/HUD 8/19/1–3.
[105] David, mayor of Morlaix, to SSM, 30 May 1746, AN, MAR/B3/451, fo. 193; Chamber of Commerce of Bayonne to unknown, 2 January 1745, MAR/B4/57, fos. 368–9v.
[106] Lempereur to SSM, 21 May 1706, MAR/B3/135, fo. 136.
[107] Règlement of Tours, 29 July 1779, MAR/F2/82. Prisoners on parole were forbidden to 'wander beyond one mile from the gates [barriers] of this town' (article II), and were under curfew from 9 pm (article V). They were only allowed to live within the city boundaries and the inner faubourgs (article VIII). See also 'Règlement' of Angers for prisoners on parole, 3 August 1779, in Code des prises, vol. II, pp. 743–4.
[108] 'Mémoire pour les maires... de... Tours' on the English prisoners (1779), MAR/F2/82 (1779).

THE REINVENTION OF SOCIETY? 255

surrounding population. For example, officers were authorized to keep their swords (article VII), a symbol of social superiority that was tolerated in both countries throughout our period of study, and caused bloody conflicts between the prisoners, their guards, and the local population.[109] Such misunderstandings were legion and illustrate the inherent tension in the status of the officer on parole as a captive with privileges. Potential disputes were mentioned in the Tours regulations: '[The prisoners] are forbidden to abuse or insult any of the inhabitants of the city, just as the said inhabitants are forbidden to insult them, subject to punishments' (article VI). It is to these disputes that I now turn.

Disputes are forms of social interaction, involving much more than a simple social or political confrontation between two well-defined groups.[110] Rather than starting with pre-established definitions of the groups that were involved in these interactions, it is the activity of 'group delineation' by the actors themselves which can be the focus of enquiry.[111] Placing the emphasis on 'groupness as event' leads us to address new questions.[112] The disputes opposing prisoners of war and host populations can be interpreted as clashes about what Julian Pitt-Rivers called the 'hierarchy of honour'.[113] The prisoners' honour was jeopardized through social challenges, which threatened their status and transgressed the protection that the parole system granted them. In the military and aristocratic worlds, the preservation of social etiquette was of paramount importance, as in the court society studied by Norbert Elias.[114] Dishonour happened precisely when there was a contradiction between an individual's self-image and the image which society attributed to him.[115] The prisoners faced such a situation when their social pre-eminence, evident at home, was denied abroad. Consequently, these quarrels bring to light conflictual conceptions of honour. Honour as a quality based on inherited social pre-eminence had a specific significance for noblemen, but not all officers, and not all prisoners on parole, were nobles. Honour was also a reputation, linked to the esteem that a given society could attribute to an individual. In this second sense, the officers' honour could be effectively challenged by local populations. The discrepancy between the officers' pretension to social superiority and their helplessness was exposed in several ways.

What follows is primarily based on the actors' own ways of interpreting these incidents, through an analysis of a hundred-odd letters of complaint sent by French prisoners of war, either as individuals or in the form of collective petitions, to 'Messieurs' the Lords Commissioners of the Admiralty and to the Commissioners

---

[109] For the example of a deadly duel between an Englishman and an Irishman in Dinan: Pontchartrain to Earl of Dartmouth, 30 July 1710, TNA, SP78/157, fo. 216v. Prisoners on parole could still keep their swords during the Napoleonic Wars: circular to parole agents, 28 December 1811, ADM98/170, fo. 121.
[110] Gulliver, *Disputes*.   [111] Latour, *Reassembling*, p. 32.
[112] Brubaker, 'Ethnicity', p. 168.   [113] Pitt-Rivers, 'Honour', p. 24.
[114] Elias, *Court Society*.   [115] Pitt-Rivers, 'Honour', pp. 21, 24, 72.

for the Sick & Wounded Seamen. These complaints, written in French and dating from 1745 to 1779, detailed the incidents which opposed the Frenchmen to English-men and women in the localities. Most of these letters were written by sea-officers, who were particularly sensitive to matters of rank and status:[116] this certainly influenced the way in which they reacted to insults—real or imaginary—offered by the host community.

First of all, incidents typically happened in public places, on the streets and roads, or thresholds between the private and the public, like the doorsteps of hotels. Private spaces were not completely safe either, as illustrated by an incident that happened in Chipping Sodbury in Gloucestershire in January 1758. Between ten and eleven o'clock in the evening, several Englishmen attacked the house occupied by four Frenchmen, banging at the doors and windows. One of the assailants then entered their room, and 'started to look at them and Count them as a Mockery'. Mister Boquet, a lieutenant, was violently assaulted the same night, while standing 'at the door of his boarding house,' and severely hurt. When the word was passed on that the wounded had been brought to a neighbouring house in order to be bandaged, the assailants 'broke the windows of the lodging' with stones.[117] This pattern of violence conformed to a well-established ritual of crowd behaviour in eighteenth-century Britain.[118] These deeds aimed at preventing the prisoners from fully enjoying the privileges of their parole by contesting their freedom of movement in the public space. A prisoner's complaint from 1757 illustrates the point:

> We have not been safe from being insulted even inside our own houses, where six weeks ago a troop of young people came to break our windows and snap the trees in the gardens. ... The authors of these disorders do not merely insult us in town, and not content with heaping abuse on us when they meet us in the countryside, rain stones on us.[119]

This hostile conduct openly challenged the officers' cultural and social hegemony, something which, they claimed, would never have happened in France. While it is possible to wonder about a tendency of the emigrants to exaggerate the contrast between their homeland and their place of exile, these public encounters forced the prisoners to recognize their inferior status, by submitting to the Englishmen's precedence.[120] A Frenchman in Tenterden (Kent), for example, stated that he was 'very nearly thrown in the mud' while walking on a public path, although he

---

[116] See Morieux, 'French prisoners', 60–1n25.
[117] Twenty-one prisoners to LCA, 7 January 1758, TNA, ADM97/122.
[118] Rudé, Hanoverian London, pp. 225–6.
[119] Belingant to 'Messieurs', Basingstoke, 12 July 1757, TNA, ADM97/121.
[120] These officers were idealizing the rigidity of the society they were coming from: instances of anti-military riots were commonplace in France. See Nicolas, La rébellion française, pp. 607–15.

'intended to give way'.[121] This officer's efforts to respect a code of polite public etiquette were to no avail. This incident may confirm that it was more usual for a newcomer to receive abuse while walking the streets of small towns than in Paris, London, and provincial towns, where norms of politeness were spreading.[122] It seems, however, that the French were specifically targeted, and similar encounters happened regularly. Because we have not found comparable sources about English prisoners of war in France, it is difficult to know whether they faced similar attitudes as their counterparts in England, but one might expect it to be the case.

Stones, bundles of sticks, mud, dogs, knives, fists, cudgels, and pelted guns were used as assaulting weapons, and some of these encounters would occasionally result in very bad injuries.[123] More importantly for our argument, these were attacks both on the body and on the honour of the French 'prisoners'. To be beaten with a stick was socially degrading for men who fought with swords: as Montesquieu remarked in *The Spirit of the Laws*, 'the baston was looked upon as the instrument of insults and affronts, because to strike a man with it was treating him like a villain.'[124]

Some gestures were clearly intended as social challenges. A French prisoner related an incident that had happened in Goudhurst, Kent, in May 1758, between the second captain of a French privateer and an English servant: 'the Englishman hit him twice in the face, which has left him terribly scarred these are the facts as if you had witnessed it with your own eyes.'[125] The attacker was a servant, and the officer almost literally risked losing face. These actions diminished and lowered the victim below the social rank to which they aspired.

Verbal insults were also commonly used. In early-modern societies, appearance remained a key element of social belonging and status, and what made the insult especially humiliating was its public character. The incident took place in front of a crowd of witnesses, not only of foreigners, but of equals.[126] Provided their meaning was understood, the most humiliating words mixed a social, a moral, and a national connotation, as in Torrington in Devon in 1757:

One of them told us in good French that all the Frenchmen are Villains, an injurious term which Conveys all the conceivable vices, and which was a

---

[121] D'Helincourt to 'Messieurs', 4 October 1757, TNA, ADM97/121.

[122] Shoemaker, 'The decline', p. 118.

[123] See, for example, prisoners at Sodbury to S&W, 3 January 1748, TNA, ADM97/115; French officers at Crediton to S&W, 22 July 1758, ADM97/122. A surgeon's certificate was attached to the letter addressed by a prisoner at Ashford to the S&W, to prove the veracity of his claims: 26 July 1758, ADM97/119.

[124] Montesquieu, *Spirit of Laws*, vol. II, book XXVII.

[125] Beche Reneaux to 'Messieurs', 28 May 1758, TNA, ADM97/119.

[126] D'Helincourt to S&W, 30 March 1758, ADM97/121.

Thousand times more painful to Us than all the losses We suffered when we have
been taken, through the fortunes of war.[127]

This language was not only xenophobic, but also socially derogative, since 'villain',
a French social-economic category dating back to the feudal times, meant both
rascal and peasant—the very antitype to 'nobleman'. The prisoners' attitude
towards local women could also be perceived as offensive by local communities.[128] In 1757, in Basingstoke, a French officer tried 'as a joke' to kiss a girl who
apparently did not object; a young Englishman who had witnessed the scene
angrily reacted by abusing and punching the prisoner, who protested that
'it wasn't proper to use bad terms towards an officer who was not insulting
anybody'.[129] Coming from an outsider to the parish, this was perceived as
provocation, which led to rituals of collective violence, such as hullabaloos and
'rough music'.[130] By so acting, the Frenchman was tainting the woman's sexual
purity and forcing (the) local men to protect her and defend their virility.[131] In
such matters involving women, the question of collective honour was at stake—
not to mention that the child of this union was a French bastard. It is less the lack
of understanding of the parole rules by local populations than their refusal to
acknowledge the alleged superiority of these Frenchmen that seems to account for
such behaviour.

These were indirect speeches, made more readable for the needs of the com-
plainants: they should not be interpreted as exact descriptions of the interactions,
as they happened. What matters for us is the fact that shaming gestures or words
were described as effective by the French officers: these skirmishes became the
yardstick by which honour was measured. This put the prisoners in an uncomfortable situation: if the parole of honour had been respected, their superiority of
status would have been recognized by all; but since these rules were openly and
publicly scorned, they had to find a way to react which preserved their social
standing. From the perspective of the prisoner, captivity operated as an inversion
of the usual norms of sexual relations. Whereas the military institution traditionally arbitrates questions of masculinity, the prisoner found himself at the mercy of
women, who could even provoke him and yet be defended by the local community. These officers were exposed to company that they would not normally have
to deal with at home. Seeking redress was in itself an admission of weakness.

In the vast majority of cases, the prisoners did not fight back. At first glance, this
was surprising from military men. Honour was associated with courage, and could
not bear the slightest mark of contempt. An officer who had, for example, refused

---

[127] Sixteen prisoners at Torrington to the 'general commissary in London', 21 October 1757,
ADM97/122.
[128] Foyster, *Manhood*, pp. 177–8, 198.
[129] Belingant to 'Messieurs', 12 July 1757, TNA, ADM97/121.
[130] Thompson, *Customs*, pp. 467–531.   [131] Pitt-Rivers, 'Honour', pp. 41–6.

a challenge, could be 'subject to peer group ostracism' and even court-martialled 'for conduct unbecoming an officer and a gentleman'.[132] Male honour relied on a capacity to defend oneself physically in the face of insults.[133] Even more than other men, soldiers and sailors, imbued with a culture of physical violence, were expected to follow the military code of honour.

However, in the context of captivity, refusing to fight back could also be interpreted as honourable behaviour. As prisoners on parole, the Frenchmen had to leave the affront unpunished, since they knew they would be prosecuted for breaching their oath. The French navy lieutenant Maupin complained in 1759, from Rumsey, that his hands were tied:

> Prisoners of War . . . rigidly observe what they have engaged to do by their Parole of honor, of abandoning every vocation that might render them useful to their Country, and would be, by this douceur less punished as military men, than they are by the frequent affronts to which they are exposed, for want of meeting with esteem in a Foreign Kingdom. It is sufficient that in bloody Engagement we preserve our honor as long as our lives, but it is too much not to be able to avoid the injurious treatment which we are obliged to bear in silence. . . . Here we are sometimes beat, but we must as the Gospel says turn the other cheek.[134]

Although obeying the law was demanded by the authorities, it was not the most honourable solution, since it amounted to cowardice.[135] Other issues further complicated the situation. On the one hand, it was unbearable to be insulted by social inferiors; on the other, in such cases, refusing to fight was usually not considered dishonourable.[136] Looking for redress through a duel, for example, was inappropriate since it would have put the protagonists on an equal footing. By the same token, from the attackers' point of view, challenging the officers, and daring them to retaliate, was a way to deny that there was any hierarchy in their status.[137] For all of these reasons, the French prisoners were torn between conflicting loyalties: either comply with their oath of honour, or respect the ethics of their group and defend themselves. This resulted from the parole system itself, which was supposed to shield the prisoners' honour, but actually put it in jeopardy by forcing them to assert it, whereas it was a given in their home country.

---

[132] Gilbert, 'Law and honour', pp. 77, 80. See also Rodger, *Wooden World*, pp. 244–9; Rodger, 'Honour', pp. 435–6.

[133] Shoemaker, 'Male honour', pp. 193–5.

[134] Maupin to S&W, 21 January 1759, NMM, ADM/F/19.

[135] Gilbert, 'Law and honour', p. 81.   [136] Bourdieu, 'The sentiment', p. 200.

[137] The literature on duelling is large. See, for example, Andrew, *Aristocratic Vice*; Starkey, *War*, pp. 69–103; Brioist, Drévillon, and Serna, *Croiser le fer*.

To escape this double bind, prisoners were left with no alternative but to ask for external redress, which allowed for a collective management of the crisis.[138] Several judicial and political courses of action were indeed available for solving such dissensions.[139] As a result, the social interactions that developed in the parole zone were not simply face-to-face encounters between French prisoners and English villagers. Locally, the prisoners were 'under the care' of the Agents for the Prisoners of War,[140] who were supposed to watch over them and prevent strife with their English neighbours, playing the part of 'official mediators' between the conflicting parties.[141] However, the French almost always contested this arbitration. From Goudhurst, some prisoners denounced 'the little support they found (not to say more) in the administrators of the laws in charge of executing your orders'. In this case, the Agent, it was alleged, 'although he has been appointed to keep order in the area of this county, has declared he does not want to get involved'.[142] This mirrored, on the outside, a relational pattern which was also at play inside the prisons.[143]

The prisoners emphasized that their Agents, whom they also called their 'commissaires', were much below their own social standing, and resented a 'partial justice': 'The commissaries of this country, sometimes a shoemaker, sometimes a tailor, sometimes lastly an apothecary, wouldn't dare to quell [the populace revolting against us]; for fear of losing their customers, they prefer to sacrifice us to the people's whim.'[144] A plebeian, governed by individual motives, could not be the judge of conflicts of honour, as Chevalier de Tarade argued from Tavistock in 1779:

> We probably would not have to complain if your intentions were followed, but, to fulfil private interests, the positions of commissaries, instead of being occupied by people of a decent profession, happen to be shared between three ordinary people.... [None of us] would stop behaving according to the feelings of honour which every soldier must be imbued with, but these feelings themselves demand that we depend on someone who can value them, and not from a craftsman.[145]

The key word here was the French verb *apprécier*, which can be translated as either 'to value' or 'to estimate', blending the psychological and economic meanings. Honour was a commodity which could only be acquired through the judgement of others, but in this case the Agent was not honourable enough to partake in this market in reputation. He was unworthy of settling the argument, because he could

[138] Boltanski, *Love*, pp. 253–8.   [139] Hindle, 'The keeping'.
[140] According to the wordings of the parole certificates. See, for example, NMM, ADM/M/398, 157/1, undated and left blank.
[141] Thireau and Hansheng, *Disputes*, p. 33.
[142] Prisoners at Goodhurst to the LCA, 9 November 1757, TNA, ADM97/119.
[143] Ch. 6.
[144] The chaplain of count of Gramont to 'Monsieur', Ashburton, 29 November 1757, TNA, ADM97/122.
[145] 9 April 1779, NMM, ADM/M/407.

not be trusted: his low social standing implied the lack of a personal sense of morality. Such a man would only defend his community's interest, instead of acting as an impartial arbitrator. The language of credit and trust permeated the description of early modern economic relations, while this vocabulary would also be used to qualify the morality and worthiness of a person.[146] A man of credit was deemed to be trustworthy, because he would pay back his debts: as we saw, the parole of honour was rooted in similar social conceptions. Resorting to the help of a 'man without any credit nor power in this town', as prisoners in Crediton in Devon put it in 1758, would downgrade their own reputation—dishonour them— without earning the respect of the rest of the population.[147]

In the same year, the prisoners on parole in Alresford cheekily defied their Agent. If invited by 'any of the Gentlemen in the Neighborhood' to any place more distant than four miles from Alresford, the prisoners had been ordered to apply for leave for that purpose: in consequence of which, noted the Board, 'whenever they go further, they send the Agent word where they are going and think that sufficient'.[148] When lacking real means to implement his orders, and confronted by men who refused to obey the regulations, the Agent was also caught in the crossfire of the local gentry, as in Chippenham in Wiltshire: 'Our Agent adds, that the Gentlemen of the Neighbourhood have censured him for not allowing the Prisoners Liberties which he is not Warranted to do by his Instructions.'[149]

When the Agent's mediation failed, other solutions existed locally: mayors, for example, were frequently called to conciliate the different sides. Most of the time, these officials would take innocuous decisions—for example, reading proclamations or sticking posters on the walls of the town forbidding insult of the French prisoners. These measures were usually ineffective, as in Tenterden in 1757: 'the poster has been torn down the same day another one has been put.'[150] The authorities were sometimes openly parodied, as in Sodbury in 1748:

> Yesterday at five pm, a character of this town has gathered, at the sound of bells, some of the people who live there, and then said aloud that it was enjoined, following the King's order, not to accommodate the French prisoners past next Sunday, that those who after this period will admit them at their place will be punished according to the laws, and moreover that their houses will be set on fire in order to burn them with the prisoners.[151]

---

[146] Muldrew, *Economy*, pp. 121–96.   [147] To S&W, 22 July 1758, TNA, ADM97/122.
[148] S&W to LCA, 30 October 1758, NMM, ADM/F/18.
[149] S&W to LCA, 9 January 1759, ADM/F/19.
[150] D'Helincourt to S&W, 4 October 1757, TNA, ADM97/121.
[151] Copy of two complaints addressed to the Sodbury JP, in LCA to S&W, 25 June 1748, NMM, ADM/M/402, no. 183/1. Such rituals of political defiance were common in the eighteenth century: see Brewer, *Party Ideology*, ch. 9.

Again, the prisoners exposed a biased treatment, as in Basingstoke, where offenders were 'assured of the lack of justice we will find in all those who form the corporation of this market town'.[152] It was such accusations of local partiality which ultimately motivated the decision to call for help at a higher level.

In an aristocratic society where honour was the dominant value, having recourse to external justice—even to noblemen—was an admission of helplessness which could be interpreted as dishonourable. It was therefore necessary to use a rhetoric legitimizing the call for help. The prisoners wrote to the Admiralty or the Board as a sort of tribunal of honour, who had the power to re-establish their social pre-eminence and their sense of distinction from the populace. In a petition written from Whitchurch, sixty prisoners thus declared in 1779 that 'enemies without weapons are human beings, the character of a prisoner is respectable and sacred, we are under your safeguarding'.[153] Here were blended the language of the just war, of the law of nations in its 'Enlightened' version, and references to specific wartime codes of conduct.[154]

What was the reaction of the local authorities to these pleas? In practice, solving altercations which opposed protagonists from different social and national universes proved to be complex, not least because the parole agreements did not describe the *modus operandi*. Rather than making a painful choice between the two parties, local mediators sometimes preferred a more informal process.[155] For example, in August 1778, five French officers on parole in the village of Kimpson, Hampshire, complained to the justice of the peace, Captain John Luttrell. At 6pm on Saturday 25 July, on the road from Alresford to the neighbouring village of Ovington, three men had struck them 'several times both with fist and cudgel'. A few hours later, the assailants came back with six other men 'armed with clubs, sticks and stones', and grabbed them again.[156] They were apparently robbed of their money because they had walked beyond the parole limits, and the villagers had taken it upon their hands to administer what they saw as justice. The magistrate, stating that he was also an army officer, wrote to the Lords of the Admiralty to express his fear of disorder if such a situation was allowed to create a precedent. But according to the instructions to the Agents, 'the Persons seizing & bringing' those prisoners who had walked beyond one mile from home should receive a reward of ten shillings.[157] This created a legal imbroglio:

[152] Belingant to LCA, 12 July 1757, TNA, ADM97/121.
[153] To S&W, 15 August 1779, ADM97/124.
[154] See also prisoners in Goudhurst to LCA, [9 May 1758], ADM97/119.
[155] For an example of an assault against a prisoner on parole leading to a prosecution: DRO, QS/4/1757/Epiphany/RE/55 and QS/4/1757 Epiphany RE/37.
[156] 'The information of Alexander Tonssins de Kerger ensign' taken before John Luttrell and Harry Harmood, two JPs for the County of Southampton, 4 August 1778, NMM, ADM/M/406.
[157] See ch. 6 on these rewards.

An idea has gone forth amongst the peasants, that to collar, strike & rob them comes within the limits of these instructions. What the extent of them really are, I confess myself at a loss to discover, for I can find no statute which gives such authority, and I think I may venture to say that it is against the common law of this land for one man to lay his hand upon another, therefore I do not at present see how a justice can admit as a plea to justify assault, that the party was out of distance from the place of his parole.

The judicial status of the prisoners on parole thus remained uncertain. John Luttrell suggested explicitly giving a magistrate the power to grant a warrant to apprehend such offenders, in order to remedy 'this evil', which pitted the country people and the French officers against each other at every opportunity. From the point of view of the assailants, these attacks were lawful, but the magistrate feared that 'infinite mischiefs might attend the execution of the rigour of the law'. Condemning the Englishmen for assault could only raise a feeling of injustice among the locals, however.[158] Appealing to a third party might cause further violence and private retaliation by publicizing the disagreement, as had happened in Torrington in 1757, where the prisoners managed to get their antagonists legally prosecuted: 'We have today As Enemies not only the rabble,' the prisoners wrote, 'but Also Some of the main people in the Town, who looked at Us with a Matchless Wrath, blaming us because We had resolved to implore Your Highness.'[159] The Frenchmen were guilty of breaching the local consensus and culture of conciliation and negotiation.

In order to express his solidarity with the prisoners, John Luttrell took to receive them at his table, 'as a proof to the common people of the civility I consider them entitled to'. Rather than following the letter of the law, he thus resorted to a form of 'clientele friendship', to publicize that these officers were his protégés.[160] Such a practice displayed the social cohesion between the elites of two enemy countries. These demonstrations of solidarity emphasized that, despite the context of war and the crossing of international borders, the station of a noble officer, captive or not, remained above that of plebeians and civilians. Conversely, the officers of privateers were not entitled to the same empathy.[161]

The preceding explanatory framework has been built upon the actors' own categories of understanding. The fact that complaints clustered in particular periods indicates that general 'external' factors might also have been at work. Economic stress was always a consequence of war, and prisoners might be

---

[158] John Luttrell to LCA, 6 August 1778, NMM, ADM/M/406.
[159] 21 October 1757, TNA, ADM97/122, no. 16. On this phenomenon, see Hindle, 'Keeping', p. 214.
[160] Briquet, 'Des amitiés'.
[161] The steward of the duke of Bedford criticized their 'impudent and audacious' behaviour, calling them 'the very dreggs of the people, of desperate fortunes': copy of letter from J. Wynne, 23 October 1747, NMM, ADM/M/399, no. 339.

held responsible for this. Forty-four out of fifty-three letters written during the Seven Years' War were from 1757 to 1758, in the wake of the most violent food riots England had ever known, caused by a succession of bad harvests.[162] In Goudhurst, the galloping inflation was attributed to the prisoners: 'Every day the inhabitants blame us and say we are the cause of the high prices of their foodstuffs.'[163] Those same years saw a surge of military, anti-aristocratic, and anti-French patriotic tropes, which came together during the militia riots of 1757.[164]

The question of how these disputes unfolded can only be answered by adopting a local perspective. As in the French Mediterranean villages studied by Julian Pitt-Rivers, there was no 'general agreement . . . as to who was superior socially to whom' in these English localities.[165] Between a French officer prisoner and an English shopkeeper, the pecking order was not obvious. The French officers often chose to explain the violence against them in reference to a general lack of respect to the social order. Antoine Voizard thus wrote from Okehampton, Devon, in 1758:

> M^r l'Ecuyer Luxemore . . . was also insulted for trying to establish the peace, and also said, like other Messrs from here, that I was lucky not to have been killed given that the populace was angry with me and that these people do not respect nor fear, the influential people of this town, on the contrary they threaten them.[166]

However, in a given town, the choice of one side over the other did not automatically follow social status. Attitudes towards the French could vary significantly depending on the local balance of power. Again, this vulnerability introduced an element of uncertainty which French nobles were not used to in their own country. Vertical solidarities were sometimes at play, and gentlemen could be found cheering on the demotic assailants.[167] Patronage also played a part.[168] While the conflict often started between two individuals, they were frequently joined by supporters. Servants would defend their master's honour, a ship's boy his captain, or a husband his wife.[169] By contrast, because these incidents could be seen as endangering hierarchies of rank, local elites sometimes sent warnings to the French officers, as on 14 June 1748: 'the observations which the most notable [sic] of the town of Sodbury daily make to

---

[162] Rogers, *Crowds*, pp. 58–75; Ashton, *Economic Fluctuations*, pp. 36, 46.
[163] Prisoners at Gourhurst to LCA, [9 May 1758], TNA, ADM97/119. Prisoners also complained of the high cost of food and rent: four officers on parole at Wye to S&W, 20 May 1757, ADM97/121.
[164] Wilson, *The Sense*, pp. 190–6; McCormack, 'New militia'.
[165] Pitt-Rivers, 'Social class'.
[166] Voizard to S&W, Okehampton, 1758, TNA, ADM97/120. He was referring to 'Esquire' Luxmoore, a member of a wealthy family of notables.
[167] Thirty-eight prisoners on parole at Goudhurst to S&W, undated, ADM97/119.
[168] Pitt-Rivers, 'Honour', pp. 36, 52–3.
[169] Beche Reneaux to 'Messieurs', Goudhurst, 28 May 1758, TNA, ADM97/119; prisoners' petition to S&W, Petersfield, Hampshire, 22 December 1757, ADM97/121; prisoners to S&W, Sodbury, 3 January 1748, ADM97/115.

us ... on the risk we run, night and day, to be murdered.'[170] Cross-national alliances were not restricted to the social elites, however, as a petition signed by nine, including a tailor and an innkeeper, demonstrates. These men expressed their sympathy with the French by delegitimizing their aggressors in strong moral and social terms:

> We the Inhabitants of the Parish of Goudhurst certifie that we never was Insulted in any Respects by the French Gentlemen nor to our Knowledge have they caused any Riot except when they have been drawn in by a Parcel of Drunken ignorant scandalous men sake of a little Money.[171]

While disputes challenged relative social positions, local norms of acceptable conduct, in religious, sexual, or economic matters, were more difficult to destabilize. Many Englishmen and women were reluctant to accept the premises of the parole system itself, which was imposed upon them and was disconnected from their own concepts of honour and justice.[172] The French officers were assaulted because they transgressed a set of customs and traditions, embodied in the notion of 'neighbourliness', from which none—even rich and privileged foreigners—could free himself.[173] Blowing hunting horns and oboes could seem like an innocent pastime—but when the performance was held in an enclosed pasture, property rights were at stake, and this roused the landlord's ire.[174] In these cases, the French officers' lack of compliance to local norms underlined their condition of 'extraneousness'.[175] Their actions singled them out as outsiders to the parish, which, as Keith Wrightson has described, was a dynamic 'unit of identity and belonging', which was 'perennially defined and redefined by processes of inclusion and exclusion'.[176] A strong sense of place and loyalty to the parish lasted at least until the end of the nineteenth century in England, and sometimes resulted in attitudes of 'local xenophobia' directed against outsiders coming from neighbouring parishes, which were 'shared across local social hierarchies'.[177] The Frenchmen's language, their Catholicism, their status of enemy, and their distant geographical origins were all variables which, in a conflictual context, could flag their imperfect blending in the local social fabric. It is therefore difficult to reconstruct the specific part which national hostility played in these incidents. It is certainly not coincidental that in the letters, all the references to discourses of national xenophobia dated from the late 1750s, when chauvinism and 'formalized

---

[170] Eighteen prisoners to 'Monsieur', Sodbury, 14 June 1758, ADM97/117.
[171] 9 November 1757, ADM97/119.
[172] This interpretation is inferred from Wrightson, 'Two concepts'.
[173] Wrightson, 'Politics', p. 18.
[174] Prisoners at Goudhurst to LCA, [9 May 1758], TNA, ADM97/119.
[175] Cerutti, *Etrangers*, p. 11.   [176] Wrightson, 'Politics', pp. 11–12.
[177] Snell, *Parish and Belonging*, p. 73.

anti-gallicanism' reached an unprecedented scale in England.[178] However, since these complaints had the specific function of delegitimizing the attackers, they should not be taken as literal and neutral descriptions.

Just like the English, the French prisoners were split over many issues which cut across national solidarity. Many presented themselves as spokesmen for the whole group, 'in the name of all the officers of the French royal navy and of all the other Frenchmen detained here', 'in the name of all these Frenchmen we are beseeching you'.[179] But this discourse of unanimity hid internal divisions. From the prisons, low-rank officers such as boatswains or privateer captains protested about being mixed up with those they described as their social inferiors. A second *lieutenant de frégate*, imprisoned at Plymouth, complained:

> To be confined in a prison among people of all sorts, and of all Kinds, and seeing myself Equal to them, a thing which I cannot Bear,...which had made me fall ill....Whereas I see petty officers, people who are below me in France, go to Tavistock, where they have their liberty.[180]

A French privateer detained in Tynemouth in 1779, who described himself as a gentleman, asked to be freed from his prison on his parole of honour. He complained of being mixed 'with people who are worse than brute and savage animals....I would prefer to be incarcerated in the darkest dungeon than remain with such people....I believe there is no slave who suffers as much as I do.'[181] Outside the prisons, paroled officers also craved for further social distinctions from each other.[182] Chevalier Prince de Rohan, on parole in Hampshire, asked in 1758 to be 'indulged with more extensive limits than the ordinary Prisoners of War'; he justified his demands by reference to the superiority of the French navy officers, who being titled gentlemen should not suffer 'any comparison with the merchants and privateers'.[183] Subtle national differences—imperceptible in the eyes of the captors—could also come to the fore in captivity. In 1708, Mr de Lundin, a Scottish colonel prisoner of war at Rennes, wrote several letters to the French administration because he could not 'get used to the air nor the company of the other Englishmen', and asked to be transferred to Nantes.[184]

[178] Wilson, *Sense*, p. 190. For example: 'explaining in precise terms that they wanted to kill the French': twenty-one prisoners to the 'commissioners of the admiralty in London', Sodbury, 7 January 1758, TNA, ADM97/122, no. 30.
[179] Chevalier Goupillon de Bélisal, Alresford, 6 July 1779, TNA, ADM97/123/9; 'The French officers at Pontefract' to 'Messieurs', 16 October 1779, ADM97/124.
[180] Louis François Faure to LCA, 17 July 1748, NMM, ADM/M/402, no. 196/1.
[181] De Thierry, 28 April 1779, TNA, ADM97/124.
[182] LCA to S&W, 4 July 1744, NMM, ADM/M/388, no. 598.
[183] S&W to LCA, 24 May 1758, NMM, ADM/F/17; same to same, 5 July 1758, ADM/F/18; Rohan to the Agent for Prisoners, Rumsey, 4 July 1758, TNA, ADM97/119.
[184] Lempereur to SSM, 1 April 1708, AN, MAR/B3/157, fos. 127–v.

The social coordinates of captivity zones were fuzzy, a situation which encouraged the prisoners who wanted to rid themselves of the domination of their patrons. In 1709, an English servant imprisoned in Dinan accused his master and captain, Mr Percy, of mistreating him, and he left him. The servant, who remains unnamed in the archives, then converted to Catholicism and asked to be allowed to remain in France. Lempereur, the French commissaire, was ambivalent. On the one hand, he was inclined to support the servant's claims, and he reprimanded the master. On the other, there would be international consequences. Allowing the servant to stay in France would prompt the British government to encourage French prisoners in England to convert to Anglicanism.[185] There were two sets of related issues here. The first one regarded the ability of the captor state to rearrange social hierarchies, by emancipating a servant from his master; the second one was about encouraging prisoners to renounce their faith. To complicate things further, Percy was not a model prisoner: a few weeks later, this 'quite extraordinary man' was embroiled in an incident, drawing his sword against the *milice bourgeoise* in Dinan while wandering in town after hours, an action which Lempereur thought not 'worthy of a prisoner [on parole]'.[186] But in the end, the French authorities recoiled, fearing that Percy would make too much fuss if his servant was taken away from him: the servant was returned to his master.[187] Social deference had to be preserved at all costs. In the same way, in 1779, the Marquis de Ransanne, on parole in Alresford, described the inappropriate conduct of his former secretary on board the frigate *Las Pallas* who, 'for the third time...said impertinent remarks to me'. The Marquis explained 'how essential it was to make an example which would keep the others within the rules of subordination so necessary among soldiers'.[188]

But spatial promiscuity created multiple opportunities to destabilize the social hierarchies that pre-existed captivity. Feuds could take a new turn in this context, and bold individuals would seize their chance to rewrite the past and settle their accounts. In 1747, the first lieutenant of a privateer, Audebert, who had been caught stealing red-handed by Monsieur Lory, his captain, tried to enact his revenge by tarnishing Lory's reputation once they were both prisoners in England. Audebert publicly accused his captain of having willingly let an English prize sink with several sailors on board. According to Commissaire Guillot, this accusation of 'inhumanity' had caused 'a big stir in Tavistock' where both men were detained, 'and might have regrettable consequences' for the captain.[189]

---

[185] SSM to Lempereur, 31 July 1709, MAR/B2/216, fos. 614–15.
[186] SSM to Lempereur, 21 August 1709, ibid., fo. 989; same to same, 25 August 1709, ibid., fo. 1102.
[187] Same to same, 14 August 1709, ibid., fo. 884.
[188] Ransanne to the LCA, 12 August 1779, NMM, ADM/M/407.
[189] SSM to Guillot, 15 May 1747, AN, MAR/B2/331, fo. 218. The French official came to Lory's rescue, painting him as an 'honest man' who would never behave with 'so much inhumanity': fos. 218–v. For a similar example in Dartmoor during the Napoleonic Wars, see Bolster, *Black Jacks*, p. 105.

III. The Worth of the Prisoners

As we have seen, the status of the prisoners of war was understood to be situational by locals, even when the authorities and the prisoners themselves had a clear idea of their station. Captivity zones were social laboratories, spaces where people's social ranks were never taken for granted but constantly adjusted. One key variable, to decide how to place individual vis-à-vis each other, was to assess their comparative worth. The views of state administrators and prisoners were often at odds with each other.

A. The Search for Equivalences

The French and British commissioners for the exchange of prisoners adopted analogies and equivalences that helped to make the labels they assigned to them 'stick', in spite of a constantly changing social landscape. The social categories that would provide the basis for individual or general exchanges (the so-called 'exchange cartels') were the result of years of correspondence across the Channel. Intellectual and political spaces of equivalence were produced through discussions on the comparability of French and British social statuses. These men had to find a common ground, a terrain of mutual understanding, in order to achieve the repatriation of as many of their compatriots as possible without weakening the war effort by striking an inequitable deal. In specific transactions, how did protagonists who belonged to different societies, with different histories and sometimes conflicting aims, manage to iron out their differences and invent working equivalences? Conversely, when was it that a comparison did not work or failed to convince, and why? Was it simply a problem of misunderstanding or mistranslation?

The commissioners for exchange of prisoners had to grapple with the knotty problem of the worth of prisoners and of how to assess it. Worth should not be conceived of solely in objectively measurable terms, determined by the market and by fixed monetary prices. Different 'standards of valuation' could coexist and compete among themselves.[190] Many principles could justify the evaluation of the prisoners' worth in the context of transactions about their exchange. Individual prisoners could be converted into monetary equivalents, but also commodified and turned into goods, or 'converted from one condition to another'.[191] In 1708, the French secretary of state for the *Marine* asked his British counterpart that the Marquis de Levy, prisoner of war in England, be sent back to France on his parole:

---

[190] Guyer, *Marginal Gains*.
[191] Barber, 'When People', p. 114. The notion of the prisoner as a commodity is inspired by Appadurai, 'Introduction'.

'We do not have in France any prisoner of his rank taken at sea, but we could, if you think it fit, give you an equivalent in other prisoners... let me know what you consider this equivalent might be.'[192] Eighteenth-century states were hard at work to commodify people.[193] This conversion of military officers into a precise number of rank-and-file soldiers and sailors became standardized. In the cartel of exchange for prisoners of war taken in the Indian Ocean, signed between France and Britain in 1805, the unit of measure was that of 'simple sailors'; for instance a *capitaine de frégate* was the equivalent of a 'master and commander', or eight men, and so on.[194] The process of commodification did not stop here and, if needed, one common sailor could be converted into one monetary unit.[195] These conventions ensured commensurability between classes of people who did not have an exact equivalent. Such exchanges also revealed conceptions of society in which only people of a certain rank or class were worthy of being exchanged as individuals; surgeons, merchants, and officers of privateers were interchangeable and were only 'considered... with regard to their number'.[196]

How a particular equivalence could be achieved depended on the local context of negotiation as well as on general principles. Even apparently unproblematic equivalences proved to be complicated to agree on in practice. Could a *commissaire des guerres* be exchanged for a *capitaine de vaisseau*? Was a *capitaine d'infanterie* worth less or more than either?[197] And how many subcategories should be introduced?[198] The laws of supply and demand could also determine the attribution of value to prisoners. When prisoners were sick or old, their value was depreciated and they were liberated 'for free'. In 1704, the French Commissaire Monsieur de St Sulpice thus complained that his English counterparts only sent him back 'the oldest ones the youngest ones and the puny ones', instead of these who had been imprisoned the longest, which was unfair; he followed the same usage to retaliate.[199]

And what should be the criteria for assessing the prisoners' place on the social ladder? The Board, for example, proposed in 1746 that king's officers captured on board privateers should be exchanged against king's officers serving in men-of-war. Guillot, their French counterpart, agreed in principle, but he added that the

[192] Pontchartrain to Sunderland, 16 May 1708, BL, Add MS61594, fo. 27v.
[193] On the standardization, classification, and codification of social categories by modern states, see Desrosières, *Politics of Large Numbers*.
[194] Cartel of exchange for the prisoners of war taken in the Indian Ocean, signed by the French and the British commanders, 18 July 1805, article 1, National Archives of Mauritius, Coromandel, GB 10G/1.
[195] Convention with Spain for a general exchange of all prisoners taken at sea, 25 June 1782, in S&W to LCA, 28 November 1783, TNA, ADM98/14, fo. 206.
[196] Guillot to SSM, 28 November 1746, AN, MAR/B2/329, fo. 250; SSM to Guillot, 29 May 1747, MAR/B2/331, fo. 233.
[197] See the exchange between Lempereur and the S&W, 22 August, 2 September 1708, MAR/B3/157, fos. 266v, 276v.
[198] S&W to Givry, 20 November 1744, with Givry's marginal comments, MAR/B3/421, fo. 415v.
[199] St Sulpice to SSM, 24 August 1704, MAR/B3/123, fo. 568v.

two states still needed to agree on the quality of these men, since 'most of them, on both sides, describe themselves as king's officers whereas they are not'.[200] The British commissioners returned to the subject a year later, asking that their French correspondents 'propose some method to distinguish the officers of the French marine who serve on board privateers', to which Guillot commented: 'Nice proposition! Is it feasible? And are there other ways than mutually to rely on what we will say about it?'[201] Mutual trust was hard to build. While this establishment of commensurability was not theorized but was largely implicit, it reveals the existence of a shared conception of society, which these exchanges contributed to solidify.

One problem for the state officials in charge of exchanges regarded what to do with those cases for which they could find no equivalent across the Channel. These exceptions, exemptions, and anomalies can help the historian to delineate, by induction, the spaces of comparability that were thinkable at a given time. I will develop one example to illustrate this argument. St Vallier, the bishop of Quebec, was imprisoned in England during the War of the Spanish Succession; his exchange dragged on for six years between 1704 and 1709, and demonstrates how the assessment of an individual's value was highly contextual.[202] Should this clergyman, captured at sea in 1704, be exchanged against Parker, the English governor of St John's in Newfoundland, as the French government offered?[203] Or should he be bartered against the 'governor of Sumatra' and his wife, who had been arrested in France as reprisals, suggested the French government in December 1706?[204] The French Commissaire Lempereur answered that there was no equivalence with the latter, since 'this governor was not a man of quality, but a simple director on the Company's wages'.[205] Maybe the Grand Dean of Liège, another cleric, who had been arrested for treason by the elector of Cologne, an ally of Louis XIV, was a better comparison, argued the British in 1707.[206] But their French counterparts underlined 'the different conditions of those two Ecclesiastics', as one was a prisoner of war, the other a prisoner of state. 'There can be no resemblance between them,' [he] added, as one had been captured at sea, the other on land.[207] In this case, arguments seem to be endlessly reversible.

The exchange value of a prisoner often changed during their captivity, and did not depend only on their military worth. Nobody embodied this better than a bishop. The French commissioners proposed in January 1707 to exchange the

---

[200] Translation of S&W to Guillot, with Guillot's observations, 15 October 1746, MAR/B3/445, fo. 254.
[201] Ibid., 14 July 1747, MAR/B3/453, fo. 80v.   [202] See Thomas, 'Quebec's Bishop'.
[203] St Sulpice to S&W, 28 September 1704, AN, MAR/B3/123, fo. 594.
[204] Lempereur to SSM, 19 December 1706, MAR/B3/135, fos. 329–v.
[205] Ibid., 26 December 1706, fos. 332v–333.
[206] See Morieux, 'Indigenous comparisons', p. 70.
[207] Extract of translation of Lempereur to S&W, 25 January 1707, BL, Add MS61591, fo. 103.

bishop and his retinue against army officers, consenting to an asymmetrical exchange that would be more beneficial to England:

I know Gent.^m very well at what value among men so respectful for Religion as we are, the Ecclesiasticall state ought to be rated, but you will confess again on your parts, that one days service of an officer of war is of more value to the politicall state, than one hundred years service of the most zealous devotee can be to the ecclesiasticall one, wherefore all the disproportion that can be in the exchange I propose to you, falls on our side, because you will have that service of your officers that we cannot expect of our ecclesiaticks.[208]

In other words, in the spiritual and civil world a bishop was highly ranked. In wartime, his value was contested and subject to fluctuations.[209] While this exchange could be interpreted as a sign that the state of war profoundly unsettled traditional conceptions of social hierarchy and social worth, in fact it is possible to argue the very opposite. Whatever military imperatives might have been, clergy-men remained at the apex of the French social pyramid: choosing whom to exchange them against was a reflection of the esteem they were entitled to. This was the reason for trading English officers against French clerics, Lempereur explained in April 1707:

You know, Messieurs, that in exchanging them against sailors, I could obtain the release of more than 100 [sailors] who could be employed by the King, and this is only because of the particular consideration that I have for their persons and the respect that is owed to their character, that I ... renew my demands for their release.[210]

St Vallier was actively involved in this discussion about his worth, and he gave his opinion about what equivalence he saw as honourable. He was for instance repelled by the proposition to trade him for a French Protestant priest who had been sent to the galleys. As he wrote to the French government in 1708, in itself, being so placed 'en concurrence with a galley-slave' was humiliating.[211] The bishop of Quebec was eventually exchanged in August 1709 against the dean of Liège, who had died in the meantime.[212] The status of clergymen as prisoners of war remained uncertain throughout the eighteenth century.[213]

---

[208] Extract of Lempereur to S&W, 25 January 1707, ibid., fo. 104.
[209] See Foucault, Order of Things, pp. 180–232; Kopytoff, 'Cultural biography'.
[210] Lempereur to SSM, 4 April 1707, AN, MAR/B3/145, fo. 112.
[211] Copy of S&W to Lempereur [marginal note by Lempereur], 22 June 1708, MAR/B3/157, fo. 228v.
[212] SSM to Lempereur, 21 August, 4 September 1709, MAR/B2/216, fos. 987, 1219.
[213] S&W to LCA, 24 December 1746, TNA, ADM98/4, fo. 43.

As this example demonstrates, prisoners of war participated in this process of attribution of worth by trying to resist their commodification or by claiming other labels than those ascribed to them.[214] For some people, being a prisoner of war opened new futures. Just like patients in mental hospitals, prisoners might present themselves by choosing 'an optimistic definition of [their] occupational status', or even a fictional one.[215] Real-life Barry Lyndons haunt the archives. In 1707, one Colin Campbell, a prisoner on parole in Rennes who claimed to be the English commissioner at 'Isle St Jean' (Prince Edward Island), was accused by the French authorities of being a 'rascal who counterfeited a man of quality', and had conned 'an infinity' of French people who had loaned him money.[216] His creditors put pressure on the French commissioner in St Malo for jailing him to prevent his escape.[217] This was unsuccessful, and he remained at large. Two years later, against fierce local opposition, Campbell even obtained from the French government his freedom on parole to negotiate his exchange with Monsieur de Segent, a French *commissaire de guerre* prisoner in England.[218] In February 1709, Lempereur thus reported that Campbell's creditors were all writing to him 'begging me to ask you to arrest him'.[219] This was not the only difficulty: in Britain, this exchange was not accepted by the Sick & Wounded Board, which did not surprise the French Commissaire Lempereur, 'this alleged English commissioner having neither character, nor birth, nor any personal qualities that could entitle him to such a comparison'.[220] Campbell certainly kept the French official on his toes. It soon appeared that the adventurer had converted to Catholicism and secretly married a well-born French woman in Rennes.[221] Because he had some property in England, he had to return there to claim it without betraying his new situation,[222] while his wife (understandably) feared that he would vanish in the air once across the Channel.[223]

This story raises a wider issue, i.e. the criteria for verifying and ascertaining people's social standing. How much trust should be placed in the prisoners' self-assessments was open for discussion. In December 1746, the Board wrote to Guillot in St Malo, admitting that 'there are vain people, who, in some occasions, give themselves titles to which they have no right', but, they argued, this was probably due to mistranslation rather than bad faith: 'maybe some purser, who gave himself the title of *commissaire de la marine*, did it in ignorance of the French

[214] Becker, *Outsiders*; Goffman, *Stigma*. On how labelling modifies value, see Berry, 'Marginal Gains', p. 60.
[215] Goffman, *Asylums*, p. 142.
[216] SSM to Lempereur, 13 July 1707, AN, MAR/B2/198, fos. 199–v.
[217] Copy of Plumptre to S&W, 3 August 1707, MAR/B3/145, fos. 386–v.
[218] Lempereur to SSM, 20 January 1709, MAR/B3/169, fo. 26.
[219] Lempereur to SSM, 3 February 1709, ibid., fo. 41v.
[220] Lempereur to SSM, 24 February 1709, ibid., fo. 61v.
[221] Lempereur to SSM, 10 March 1709, ibid., fo. 76v.
[222] Lempereur to SSM, 21 March 1709, ibid., fo. 94.
[223] Lempereur to SSM, 26 May 1709, ibid., fo. 154.

language, believing that *commissaire des vivres* and *commissaire de la marine* were similar things although very different.' The British officials believed in their capacity to separate the wheat from the chaff: 'it is easy to discover the truth of these things by inquiring about their character from the people captured with them.' Guillot was less optimistic. He commented in the margin: 'It is not in this way that their character will be discovered, one is often deceived.'[224] Instead of relying on the prisoners' self-accounts, state officials in the ports could have recourse to a grammar of interpretation based on verbal and non-verbal evidence. In 1706, the twenty-year-old 'Jean Hamilton from Londonderry', who had been captured in a ship returning from Antigua, arrived in Dinan. He claimed to be the son of a sheriff, which left the French official La Fon unmoved. A sheriff, explained La Fon, would be equivalent to 'a man above a mayor in France', whereas 'the said Jean Hamilton does not look like an *homme de connaissance*, but rather like a merchant'.[225]

The prisoners themselves had their own views about this. They might even reject the very classification of 'prisoner'. In the summer of 1778, when the Agent at Gosport showed the form of the parole form to the French officers on parole there, who had been captured before Britain declared war on France in March, their reaction was unexpected:

> They objected to the word Prisoners, and Mr Bell upon reasoning with them found they were one and all resolute never to sign any Parole in which they were so termed alledging that no War was declared, and that they knew several of their Countrymen who had acknowledged themselves Prisoners in the Hostilities before the declaration of the last War, who had been injured in their preferment by having done so.[226]

The Frenchmen were referring to the capture of thousands of their compatriots by Admiral Boscawen before the declaration of war in 1755, who had remained in captivity for years because the French monarchy had refused to consider them as legitimate prisoners of war.[227] Bell—one of the Commissioners for the Sick & Wounded Board—failed to make the prisoners budge, but he consented to let them add to the parole form 'any explanation from themselves, that should appear unexceptionable'. The Board suggested that to avoid similar difficulties in the future, 'the Word Prisoners in both the Parole and Certificate' could be left out,

---

[224] Translation of S&W to Guillot, with Guillot's observations, 4 December 1746, AN, MAR/B3/453, fo. 13.
[225] Memorandum of La Fon following Hamilton's questioning, 11 December 1706, MAR/B3/135, fo. 335.
[226] S&W to LCA, 8 July 1778, TNA, ADM98/11, fo. 104v.
[227] Copy of duc d'Aiguillon to maréchal de Belleisle, 22 September 1758, AN, MAR/B4/97, fos. 165–v. See Pradier-Fodéré, *Traité*, pp. 620–1; Baugh, *Global Seven Years War*, p. 144.

replacing it with 'French Officers on Parole'. The prisoners thus added the following words [*in French*]: 'we...promise to obey all the abovementioned articles except that we do not recognize ourselves as prisoners (since the war has not been declared) but as detainees for the moment.'[228] Official documents thus acknowledged the prisoners' accounts of themselves as legitimate.

B. Crossing Racial Boundaries: The Case of the Atlantic Ocean

Social categorization was not simply a question of recognizing claims to precedence: the choice of one label over another could determine one's fate. Did everyone have the capacity to contest their classification, though? Some boundaries of status were more difficult to cross than others, as can be shown by looking, somehow tentatively, at the extreme case of black prisoners of war. In the eighteenth century, the constant European need for manpower meant that black sailors, soldiers, and militiamen were frequently employed to wage war.[229] They were serving on board French, British, Spanish, or Dutch men-of-war and privateers.[230] In most Caribbean islands, these sailors could be free blacks, as well as slaves. In Bermuda, probably the British island where the proportion of slaves on board ships was the highest, these men represented maybe 25 per cent of the sailors in the 1740s, and 45 per cent in the 1770s.[231] But how robust was this legal difference in practice, when these men were captured by enemy ships? Were they automatically granted the status of prisoners of war? As historians of slavery have demonstrated, freedom and unfreedom should not be understood as absolute statuses; rather, there existed a wide variety of situations: people could be more or less free.[232] It is in this context that one might understand the debate over the categorization of 'black' sailors and soldiers as prisoners of war.

For a small minority of black slaves, military service could be a stage on the path to freedom. Army and navy commanders did not care about the provenance and status of their recruits, many of whom were impressed or runaway slaves.[233] Once on board a ship, these men could hope 'to refashion themselves as free men in distant ports', or simply disappear from view once they had enlisted.[234] Moreover, and while this was far from being the norm, slaves could sometimes count on the support of their captains and commanders against the demands of their owners, while some of them would be emancipated for their services.[235] For the sailors who

---

[228] S&W to LCA, 8 July 1778, TNA, ADM98/11, fos. 104v–105.
[229] Although not necessarily in a fighting role. For British examples, see Bollettino, 'Slavery', pp. 63, 69.
[230] Voelz, *Slave*; Brown and Morgan, *Arming Slaves*; Bollettino, 'Slavery'; Bolster, *Black Jacks*; Jarvis, 'Maritime masters'; Scott, 'Crisscrossing empires', pp. 132–41.
[231] Jarvis, 'Maritime masters'. For other islands, see Foy, 'Unkle Sommerset, p. 24; Foy, 'Prize negroes', pp. 380–1; Bollettino, 'Slavery', p. 16.
[232] Drescher, *Abolition*, pp. 20–1.   [233] Bollettino, 'Slavery', pp. 26–7, 76.
[234] Ibid., pp. 27, 135–6.   [235] Ibid., 'Slavery', pp. 84–7, 138, 165, 167–8. See also Voelz, *Slave*.

were born free or emancipated, being captured by the enemy could mean just the opposite, i.e. being reclassified as slaves.[236] Knowing the risks they faced, some of these men were reluctant to enlist in European navies. In 1762, the free blacks in Jamaica refused to take part in the expedition against Havana.[237]

Skin colour was often the key factor, albeit not the only one, for the decision to categorize them as prisoners of war or not.[238] This also depended on where they had been captured, by whom, and where they landed, which determined which jurisdictions were involved in settling their case, and how much the prisoners themselves managed to get heard. The cartel concluded in 1705 between the Leeward Islands and Martinique hence stated that the 'mulatoes and negroes that are free' were to be 'delivered as other freemen'.[239] Certain mixed-race groups were thus seen as vulnerable to enslavement too. Spatial context often determined legal status, because sovereignty and subjecthood were rooted in geography.[240] The principle of the 'native free soil' contended that while slavery persisted in the colonies, it had been abolished in North-Western Europe since the sixteenth century.[241] This belief informed the instruction given to privateers from St Malo by French officials in 1708, telling them that by default, black men serving in British ships 'can only be regarded as slaves if taken at sea, and must be reckoned merchandize belonging to the captors', but as soon as they landed in a French port, 'they become free... and they can freely choose whether they want to stay in France or return to England'. If these men chose to return to England, they should be exchanged 'as prisoners of war'.[242] In reality, the situation was often more complicated. In Britain in particular, slavery was still legal in the eighteenth century, even after Somerset's Case.[243] Somerset's Case was a common-law case, whereas captured seamen were dealt with as prizes (admiralty law) or as prisoners of war (subject to ad-hoc international regulations). French naval captains imprisoned in Britain were allowed to keep their slaves with them. In 1744, one Captain Roullier thus obtained a return to France, taking with him 'a negro slave a favorit of his wife, that was given him by Cap.ⁿ Reed who took his ship'.[244]

In order to be exchanged as prisoners of war, the key question was to decide whether these men were 'Free Negroes', a question which was itself bound up with that of subjecthood.[245] But freedom and slavery were not fixed statuses. The legal

---

[236] Rogers, *Press Gang*, pp. 81–2, 92–5.   [237] Voelz, *Slave*, p. 441; Pares, *War*, pp. 256–7.
[238] Voelz, *Slave*, pp. 441–50.
[239] Copy of an agreement made with M. de Machault, *Intendant* of the French Islands in America, 6 February 1705, article 4, *Calendar of State Papers*, vol. 22, p. 373.
[240] Gould, 'Zones of law'; Benton, *Search*; Halliday, 'Law's histories'.
[241] Peabody and Grinberg, 'Free soil'; Weiss, *Captives*; Drescher, *Abolition*, pp. 22–4.
[242] SSM to Lempereur, AN, MAR/B2/207, fos. 360, 361. By the same logic, black servants were normally treated as prisoners of war in France. They were detained alongside English soldiers in Nantes in 1707: SSM to Lusançay, 5 October 1707, MAR/B2/99, fo. 73.
[243] Foy, 'Unkle Somerset', pp. 27–31. See also Gould, 'Zones of law', pp. 503–6.
[244] John James Porter to [S&W], 8 August 1744, TNA, ADM97/116/2.
[245] LCA to S&W, 19 September 1744, NMM, ADM/M/389, no. 209.

distinction between slaves and freedmen was often insignificant when a black man serving on board a privateer was captured by the British navies or privateers.[246] 'When free blacks were captured at sea,' writes Jane Landers, 'the British presumed them by their colour to be slaves, thus eligible for sale.'[247] More than any other captives of war, black soldiers and sailors were thus subjected to the whim of their captors.

The tribulations of two sailors born in Havana and Porto Bello illustrate this. In 1745, an English captain wrote to the Lords of the Admiralty to complain that 'two Negroes' had been taken out of his ship, the *Matthew*, upon arrival in London, by the orders of the Sick & Wounded Board, 'as Spanish Prisoners'.[248] The captain testified before a JP that these two men had been sold 'at publick sale at Antigua' as booty, and bought by the *Matthew*'s owner 'to help to Navigate her to England'. The captain added that 'Insurance was made on them for the Run home and that they were never looked on or deem.^d Prisoners of War'.[249] Here we see the tension between two conceptions: West Indian slave owners and captains labelled these men, by default, as slaves; central state administrators, by contrast, assumed that they were prisoners of war. The two captives, Francisco Xavier Gonzalez and Desiderio Joseph, told their own story. They had originally served on board a Spanish man-of-war. After wrecking on the coast of Cumana in Venezuela, they had ended up in Martinique, where the French governor had forced them to serve on board a French privateer. Between St Vincent and St Lucia, the privateer had been taken by an English privateer; the two men had then been recruited as sailors on the English ship, and 'after they been 4 or 5 Months on a Cruise with S.^d Brig.^{ne}', they were carried to Antigua. They were subsequently transferred on board another ship, the *Matthew*, which had carried them to England. These men's experience was typical of the travails of Afro-American sailors, who served multiple sovereigns, were transferred from one ship to another, and whose freedom was always put in doubt. When they were asked 'Whether ever put up at Publick Sale at Antigua or elsewhere', Francisco and Desiderio replied 'Never to their knowledge, for they were but one day a shore at Antigua'. Most importantly, they insisted that they were not slaves but free men, and 'born so'.[250]

It is impossible to know who was speaking the truth. As pointed out by Lauren Benton, ship-owners and captains knew that when they captured a ship, the possibility of legal adjudication was very real. Consequently, 'they actively engaged in imaginative legal posturing, rehearsing stories that might serve to establish actions as legal in judicial forums'.[251] In the same way, it is safe to assume that the

---

[246] Rodger, *Wooden World*, pp. 159–60; Bollettino, 'Slavery', p. 167.
[247] Landers, *Black Society*, p. 44.
[248] LCA to S&W, 25 May 1745, NMM, ADM/M/391, no. 161.
[249] Nathaniel Warner, sworn before JP, Tower London, 28 May 1745, ibid.
[250] Ibid., no. 161/2. On the slaves' rhetorical strategies, see Rupert, '"Seeking"', pp. 211–12.
[251] Benton, *Search*, p. 113.

'black' sailors who had been captured in the Caribbean and brought to Britain or France used similar strategies to obtain recognition of their freedom. Having to decide between two contradictory accounts, neither of which was backed up with documents, the Lords of the Admiralty decided to trust the white owner and captain and reversed the Board's decision to categorize these men as prisoners of war; his 'property' was restored to the owner.[252] For these two sailors, the initial 'moment of imposition of status'[253] influenced their later fortune, and they struggled to shake off the labels which constrained them.

Even when he had documents asserting his freedom, any black man captured by the British was likely to be sold as a slave. Historians have emphasized that British officials were more punctilious that their French or Spanish enemies, and often rebuffed the documents presented by men who claimed to be free, always asking for more.[254] By contrast with the Spanish prize system, the British colonial prize system was heavily tilted in favour of the captors, and 'the pervasive presumption' of vice-admiralty courts was that the black seamen who appeared before them 'were in fact slaves'.[255] In 1746, even when British and Spanish colonial governors agreed to respect these men's freedom and to exchange them as prisoners of war, British colonial courts did their best to prevent this from happening, refusing to acknowledge the certificates of freedom granted by enemy governors.[256] Until the Seven Years' War, black sailors captured on board Spanish and French ships struggled to convince British vice-admiralty courts that they were free men. It sometimes took many years before they could escape the grasp of their captors.[257] A strategic explanation has also been proposed: British navy captains knew the greater reliance of the French and Spanish navies on free men: treating these men as slaves, and not as prisoners of war, intended to scare them off serving on these ships.[258]

But the opposition between British and other European colonial prize courts must not be overstated. All these courts were at times 'driven by local interests', not by metropolitan directives, and obtaining the release of a prize frequently involved a long legal dispute.[259] At the same time, it might be argued that the treatment of prized 'black' sailors by vice-admiralty courts was part of the same general context of imperial competition and legal entanglement in the West Indies.[260] Thus, the treatment of captured black seamen by British colonial prize courts informed how their European rivals approached the same issue. On 30 September 1747, seven men wrote a petition from a Granville jail to the Lords

---

[252] LCA to S&W, 25 May 1745, NMM, ADM/M/391, no. 161.
[253] Scott, 'Paper thin', p. 1064.
[254] Pares, 'Manning', pp. 32–3; Landers, *Black Society*, pp. 43–5; Foy, 'Prize negroes', pp. 383–4. Gould, 'Entangled histories', pp. 765–6.
[255] Foy, 'Prize negroes', pp. 381–2.
[256] Pares, 'Manning', 32–3n1.   [257] Zabin, *Dangerous*, pp. 106–31.
[258] Pares, 'Manning', p. 31; Landers, *Black Society*, p. 45.   [259] Benton, *Search*, p. 153.
[260] Gould, 'Entangled histories'.

of the Admiralty. They represented that they were free born blacks from Bermuda, whose sloop had been taken by a French privateer. These black sailors had been 'condemned as goods and merchandize' and had been detained for three months when they put pen to paper. The petition stated that they had been told 'several times that [they] should be cleared as prisoners of war', a promise which was never fulfilled. They had documents attesting to their freedom:

> We are black men its very certain, but, we are all free born, & got our Passes for such, from the Governour of the Island of Bermudas, & sealed wth his Majesties seal, to which they take no regard, but still keep us here as Slaves.[261]

The Lords of the Admiralty supported their claims and demanded their exchange as prisoners of war.[262] Following this, the Board wrote to Commissaire Guillot in St Malo, requesting their release, on the ground that they were free men.[263] The French official refused to comply, 'because, as he says, the English in the West Indies make no Distinction between free Blacks & others, but confiscate all'. The question was not one of principle, but one of reciprocal administrative policy. Guillot thus proposed to admit 'free Negroes on both sides to y.[e] Priviledges of Prisoners of War, when at any Time taken by the Enemy for the future'. The Board found the idea of such a convention appealing:

> As the People who have concerned themselves about the Release of the Blacks abovementioned, have affirmed, that a great part of our Trade in America is carried on by means of free Negroes, & that it would suffer very much if these, when at any time taken by the Enemy, were to be considered as Slaves, not Prisoners of War.[264]

But the Lords of the Admiralty let the matter lie dormant and they did not reply to the French proposal. In the meantime, the Bermudian sailors were still detained in France in May 1748.[265] This diplomatic exchange illustrates a process analysed by Lauren Benton, which started in the late seventeenth century and was completed by the middle of the eighteenth century. Through the 'interimperial negotiation' of the cases adjudicated by Atlantic prize courts, imperial states such as Britain, France, the United Provinces, and Spain 'fashioned prize law into a loose international regulatory framework'. This framework, adds Benton, 'did not guarantee

---

[261] Petition to the Admiralty, 30 September 1747, NMM, ADM/M/399, no. 328/1.
[262] LCA to S&W, 24 October 1747, ibid., no. 328.
[263] Copy of S&W to Guillot, 7 October 1747, TNA, ADM98/4, fos. 164v-5. The S&W also sent a certificate signed by the master and the supercargo of the sloop testifying that these men were free blacks: 22 September 1747, AN, MAR/B3/453, fos. 105-6.
[264] S&W to LCA, 2 December 1747, TNA, ADM98/4, fos. 181-v.
[265] S&W to LCA, 20 May 1748, ibid., fos. 221v-222.

or even encourage peaceful relations, but it did rely on an assumption of a certain degree of institutional continuity across empires'.[266] Just like pirates, privateers, and fugitive slaves, incarcerated black sailors appealed to several jurisdictions, and their actions contributed to this legal dialogue between imperial states.[267] In the last years of King George's War, the pressure by the French and Spanish governments increased on the British central and colonial authorities to stop enslaving free men and instead treat them as prisoners of war.[268] According to Serena Zabin, at least in New York, this campaign was successful, and during the Seven Years' War, the enslavement of French and Spanish black mariners by the vice-admiralty prize court became very rare.[269]

However, practices continued to vary considerably, as illustrated by the contrasting fate granted to slaves by the British armed forces in Guadeloupe and Martinique during the Seven Years' War.[270] After the British conquest of Guadeloupe, the capitulation signed in 1759 between the French inhabitants of the island and the British military and naval commanders stated that the 'Free Mulattoes & Negroes who had been taken shall be treated as Prisoners of War, and not treated as Slaves'.[271] By contrast, in 1762, when the neighbouring island of Martinique capitulated, British commanders refused to differentiate between free blacks and slaves, despite French requests that 'the free Negroes and Mulattos, taken Prisoners of War, will be treated as such, and be Released like other prisoners to continue enjoying their freedom'. The British negotiators commented that instead 'all Negroes taken in Arms are deemed Slaves'.[272] British officials did not speak with one voice concerning the men captured at sea either. For instance, in 1757, in order to prevent freedmen from being exchanged, Admiral Thomas Frankland came up with a scheme to sell 'all Mulattoes & Negroes indiscriminately' captured on board French privateers.[273] Fearing reprisals on British prisoners captured by the French, the governor of Antigua George Thomas rejected the plan, but Frankland ordered the navy to implement it nonetheless.[274] The constant predicament that European navies had to confront in the eighteenth century—the need for manpower—led many naval commanders to employ black men who had been condemned as prizes to man their crews.[275]

[266] Benton, *Search*, pp. 158, 160.   [267] Ibid., p. 159; Rupert, '"Seeking"'.
[268] Landers, *Black Society*, pp. 44–5; Zabin, *Dangerous*, p. 128.
[269] Zabin, *Dangerous*, pp. 128–30.
[270] This paragraph is based on Bollettino, 'Slavery', pp. 110, 169–70. See also Pares, *War*, p. 257.
[271] Capitulation of Guadeloupe, 2 May 1759, article 9, TNA, CO110/1, fos. 160v, reference cited in Bollettino, 'Slavery', p. 110.
[272] Capitulation of Martinique, 13 February 1762, article 9, enclosed in Monckton to Pitt, 27 February 1762, TNA, CO166/2, fo. 58v, reference cited in Bollettino, 'Slaves', p. 113.
[273] Bollettino, 'Slaves', pp. 110, 169–70.
[274] Ibid., p. 169. As pointed out by Bollettino, Frankland's racial prejudices played a large part in this decision: ibid., p. 170.
[275] Rodger, *Wooden World*, pp. 159–60.

The condition of free people of colour was further complicated during the American War of Independence, which prompted an increasing number of slaves to run away from American plantations, believing the promises they received that they would obtain their freedom if they served in the British military forces.[276] To discourage the fugitives, the Insurgents' courts of admiralty continued to assume that all the black sailors they captured were prize goods, not prisoners of war.[277] Once again, European generals and admirals lacked consistency in the treatment of their black captives. After taking Grenada in 1779, the French army sold all the English blacks they had taken in arms there, whereas in St Kitts and Nevis in 1782, combatants of colour were released and allowed to go home.[278]

During the French Wars, the allocation of the prisoner of war status to black sailors and soldiers varied considerably. The French forces which fought against the British in the Caribbean were composed, in their majority, of black men, following the abolition of slavery on 4 February 1794 (16 Pluviôse Year II).[279] All these men were now free, and as such entitled in principle to be categorized as prisoners of war. But the treatment of armed former slaves was a bone of contention between the Republicans and the British.[280] In fact, the treatment of black captives by European powers continued to vary a great deal throughout the 1790s.[281] During the Napoleonic Wars, however, guaranteeing the status of prisoners of war to free blacks serving in European armies and navies seems to have become more straightforward.[282] In 1809, the Kingston assembly thus represented to Admiral Bartholomew Rowley, commander-in-chief at the Jamaican Station, that

> various prisoners of war of a dangerous description, being persons of colour and negroes who have been soldiers in the French service are now confined in the Bath prison under the charge of Black troops belonging to the West India Regiments, by which the safety of this island may be endangered from the intercourse which will probably take place from their being so guarded.[283]

---

[276] Foy, 'Unkle Somerset', pp. 21–36.
[277] Foy, 'Prize negroes', pp. 385–7.
[278] 'Projet de capitulation de l'Ile de la Grenade' [1779], article 10, AN, MAR/B/4/163, fo. 148; 'Articles of Capitulation for the Islands of St Christophers and Nevis', 12 February 1782, article 2, TNA, CO318/9, fo. 126.
[279] Popkin, 'Facing racial revolution', p. 523.   [280] Geggus, Slavery, pp. 265, 364–5.
[281] In 1794–6, black soldiers from St Domingue were seized as prisoners of war by the Spanish and the British: Yingling, 'Maroons', p. 39. The French commissaire in Britain complained that the same happened to black men serving in the defence of the French colonies: Charretié to TO, 4 April 1796, in Report (1798), p. 63.
[282] Fabel, 'Self-help'.
[283] 24 July 1809, Jamaica Archives, Spanish Town (JA), 2/6/8 (Kingston).

The issue, two years after the British abolition of the slave trade, was not the right of these men to be categorized as prisoners of war, but the fear of illicit communication with their guards and the civilian population more broadly; the assumption was not that these men should have been treated like slaves, but that their common blackness would trump their patriotism.[284] Jeffrey Bolster uses the case of Dartmoor, where hundreds of black sailors were imprisoned in 1812–14, to argue that 'boundaries of race' took a new significance in the context of captivity. Being categorized as prisoners of war thus gave these black men opportunities to carve out some spaces of autonomy from white oppression, which they did not have on the outside. There were certainly multiple cases of 'interracial fraternization' in prison 'between equals', on the stage, at church, on the boxing ring or against the prison authorities, but Bolster contends that race remained 'the primary relationship' between these groups.[285] While more comparative work would be required to be more conclusive, the hypothesis that war prisons might have been spaces where black men were paradoxically freer than in the outside world is worth considering seriously.

In the eighteenth century, subjecthood allowed access to the legal protection granted by the sovereign.[286] For black sailors and soldiers, claiming the status of a prisoner of war was another way to say that they were free men and subjects, and as such worthy of the protection of the Crown against enslavement. The Commissioners for the Sick & Wounded Seamen put it clearly in 1746: they asked that a man of colour detained in France be exchanged, because he was a 'free man', and as such 'a subject of His Majesty'.[287] There is an apparent paradox here: these men claimed to be prisoners of war in order to gain their freedom. But this makes sense if one understands that freedom 'existed along a continuum from the slave...to the independent property owner, and during a lifetime an individual might well occupy more than one place on this spectrum'.[288] While the status of the prisoner of war was transitory, for a black man who was so categorized, it implied the state recognition of his freedom.[289] In New York, 'at least one third' of enslaved sailors managed to be released by obtaining their reclassification as prisoners of war.[290] But the status of the prisoner of war was like a revolving door between freedom and slavery, which colonial actors could use in unexpected ways. In wartime, Bermudian masters gave certificates of freedom to the slaves who manned their ships. When these ships were captured by the enemy, they hoped that presenting

---

[284] In 1803, the rumour of a conspiracy bringing together French prisoners on parole, Irish convicts placed to guard the King's House, the free blacks and the slaves spread in Spanish Town: 13–15 December 1803, *Lady Nugent's Journal*, pp. 241–3. There were many black men among the French prisoners on parole who had been brought to Jamaica from St Domingue, a scary fact for the Kingston assembly: 14 December 1803, JA, 2/6/7 (Kingston).

[285] Bolster, *Black Jacks*, pp. 130, 127, 129–30.   [286] Halliday, 'Law's histories', pp. 270–1.

[287] S&W to Guillot, 15 October 1746, AN, MAR/B3/445, vo. 253.

[288] Eric Foner, *The Story of American Freedom* (1998), p. 10, quoted in Zabin, *Dangerous*, p. 120.

[289] Zabin, *Dangerous*, p. 107.   [290] Ibid., p. 123.

these documents would allow their 'property' to be exchanged as prisoners of war and return to Bermuda. Even more surprisingly, these captured sailors usually chose to return home, instead of escaping and facing the risk of being enslaved elsewhere.[291]

Whereas most eighteenth-century legal writers agreed that the statuses of slave and that of the prisoner of war were starkly different, this distinction did not always apply to the black men serving in European military and naval forces. The question of granting black men the status of prisoners of war remained contentious well into the nineteenth century: during the American Civil War, the South consistently refused 'to entitle black captives to the privileges of prisoners of war' and treated them like criminals.[292] For captives of colour, to borrow Rebecca Scott's expression, the decks could be reshuffled as individuals moved from one place to another.[293] But it could be argued that social fluidity was inherent to the state of war captivity, to one degree or another. In a way, the struggles of officers on parole to safeguard their privileges and the travails of free blacks to protect their freedom are two sides of the same coin.

IV. Conclusion

The presence of prisoners of war had a major impact on local societies. The mere presence of these foreigners destabilized or, to use the language of pragmatic sociologists, 'tested' social hierarchies. Prisoners of war, by definition, were abstracted from their milieu of origin. Consequently, there was no simple answer to the question of knowing or, more accurately, *deciding* who was socially superior to whom. The parole system turned enemies into neighbours. These prisoners lived alongside host populations, in the same villages or towns, went to the same inns for a drink, and had to share the same public space. This made the social differentiation between the prisoners and the host population more important, since they were not segregated spatially. War had local repercussions, caused by these points of contacts with prisoners, in the depths of the host countries. Knowing whether these interactions had any lasting consequences is more difficult to assess.

As a configuration characterized by shifting social relations, the parole zone brought together local, national, and international issues, intertwined primarily in the language of honour. This language not only described these interactions, but also constituted them, revealing a struggle for classifying and defining the very terms of group relations.[294] On the one hand, the shift of the social balance of power, where aristocrats were at the people's mercy, was made possible because

---

[291] Jarvis, 'Maritime masters', pp. 614–17.   [292] Witt, *Lincoln's Code*, p. 256.
[293] Scott, 'Paper thin', p. 1087.   [294] Bourdieu, 'Social space', pp. 22–3.

of the international context. English attackers often got away without serious punishment, because these Frenchmen were official enemies of their own sovereign. But local authorities and gentility were ambivalent and divided: while encouraging rioting could be dangerous, defending French enemies was never an easy choice. On the other hand, it might be argued that the onslaught on the prisoners on parole was just another example of the extensive toleration of violence in eighteenth-century English society, which persisted well into the following century. This level of violence was not specific to the attitude towards foreigners, but was rather typical of everyday relations in a non-metropolitan and market-town context. The culture of civility had not spread to all the English localities in the eighteenth century.

As the study of disputes between prisoners and local populations has shown, a whole range of attitudes could be observed at the local level. These quarrels could help to strengthen the ties of local communities behind the defence of neighbourliness. But interactions with outsiders could also be divisive and accentuate local tensions. The prisoners' complaints evidence both their failure to impose their preferred representation of the social world onto the host society and their own internal divisions. There was no systematic alignment of class and national discourses and actions, while the precise standing of prisoners on parole on the social ladder was constantly challenged and debated. The resulting quarrels therefore show a series of social inversions: dominant groups at home, in terms of social prestige and power, were in many respects dominated once in captivity. Rather than being a mere reflection of pre-existing social hierarchies, such micro-incidents reinvented them, albeit in the limited time and space of the captivity.

At the same time, the category of the prisoner of war was not a purely linguistic construction. The label did stick, and the social inventiveness we have analysed took place within bounds. While the privileges of prisoners on parole were contested, their rights to be treated as prisoners of war were a given. By contrast, black captives were, by default, assumed to be slaves, not prisoners of war. The case of these black sailors who were treated as booty, even when they were legally free men, and as such entitled to the status of the prisoner of war, underscores the importance of considering legal geographies. To be categorized and treated as a prisoner of war did not mean the same thing in Jamaica, St Domingue, or New York. The legal spaces of captivity, and the meaning of the category of the prisoner of war, differed on both sides of the Atlantic. They also differed in France and in Britain, and they changed over time. For the most privileged of the prisoners as for the weakest ones, war captivity shook social hierarchies, forcing the captives to justify and argue their rights, trying to fix a picture of the social world which would not make them worse off.

We saw how often prisoners on parole challenged the regulations and the officials in charge of applying them. Did similar attitudes take place within the prison?

6

War Captivity and Social Interactions

I. Introduction

This chapter focuses on the issue of order in prison, both in a social and in a political sense. I want to analyse whether there existed a structure of social order inside the war prison: forms of social relations and conflict regulation that did not simply replicate what went on outside but were 'indigenous' to the carceral world. The practical conditions of detention of prisoners of war, as has been shown in previous chapters, were a legal grey zone: while they were not completely irrelevant, the legal norms of the law of nations applied indirectly behind prison walls, when prisoners chose to appeal to their sovereign. In everyday interactions, however, what mattered was a different set of norms—which were not always explicitly defined, but which were part of a set of shared expectations, on the part of guards as well as prisoners, regarding the types of behaviour that were acceptable, and those that were seen as illegitimate.

Historians have paid some attention to everyday life encounters that took place in prison, especially debtors' prisons.[1] Sociologists can also provide us with frameworks in which to analyse them. Almost since its inception, the field of penal sociology has been divided between the 'prisonization' and the 'importation' schools of thought.[2] The first school of penologists, influenced by Donald Clemmer's concept of 'prisonization' and Gresham Sykes's concept of 'deprivation', has argued that the prisoners' culture is the result of what goes in within the prison.[3] According to these scholars, the prison world and the outside world are antithetical. Presenting the story of war imprisonment in these terms inevitably evokes Erving Goffman's classic study of 'total institutions'. In *Asylums*, Goffman defined a 'total institution' as

a place of residence and work where a large number of like-situated individuals cut off from the wider society for an appreciable period of time together lead an enclosed, formally administered round of life. Prisons serve as a clear example, providing we appreciate that what is prison-like about prisons is found in institutions whose members have broken no laws.

---

[1] Sheehan, 'Finding solace'; Innes, 'Prisons'; Innes, 'King's Bench'; Finn, *Character*; White, *Mansions*; Foucault, *Discipline*; O'Brien, *Promise*; Petit, *Peines*; Castan, Zysberg, and Petit, *Histoire*.

[2] See Western, 'introduction', in Sykes, *Society*, pp. xiv–xv; Crewe, 'Sociology'.

[3] Clemmer, *Prison Community*; Sykes, *Society*, pp. 138–43. See also McManimon, 'Deprivation'; Dobbs and Waid, 'Prison culture'; Austin, 'Prisonisation'.

The Society of Prisoners: Anglo-French Wars and Incarceration in the Eighteenth Century. Renaud Morieux, Oxford University Press (2019). © Renaud Morieux. DOI: 10.1093/oso/9780198723585.001.0001

For Goffman, the key feature of the total institution is its 'binary character', i.e. the 'social distance' between those representing the authority, and those who are incarcerated. Ultimately, and most contentiously perhaps, Goffman argued that in the total institution, 'two different social and cultural worlds develop, jogging alongside each other with points of official contact but little mutual penetration'.[4] This model has been criticized, not least because it artificially constructs coherent groups, with the prisoners on one hand and the staff on the other, who were themselves riven by internal differences.[5]

The second school, whose main proponents are John Irwin and David Cressey, is grouped under the notion of an 'importation' or 'negative selection' model. These scholars contend that what goes on inside the prison is the result of the importation of a culture that pre-existed outside. For instance, the culture and values of street gangs are imported into and enforced within the space of the prison. Yet this model, in turn, has been criticized for focusing on violence and confrontational behaviour, and for ignoring consent and peaceful interactions.[6] More recent studies have side-stepped this opposition, arguing that

> At one level prisoners and staff are clearly in opposition. And yet prisoners and staff also have what Christie calls 'thick' social relations. They share the same physical and social space. They cannot sustain a state of submerged warfare all the time. They develop familiarities. They banter. There are acts of concern and kindness. It is a situation marked by contradictions.[7]

This is the perspective I take in this chapter. The idea of an 'autonomous' prison subculture is problematic, partly because of the extent of the prisoners' interactions with outside cultures. And if there was such a thing as a prisoner culture, how far was it the fruit of conditions that pre-existed their incarceration? In some ways, it could be argued that life inside the prison was not that different from life on board ships or in an army regiment, where discipline and long periods of separation from one's folks structured social relations. But how far can we push this analogy? It was one thing to comply with a captain's orders, and another to accept the dictates of a foreign jailor. Besides, prisoners of war were usually incarcerated with men of the same origins, with whom they shared a language and a religion: these were important cultural differences with their jailors. On the other hand, as we saw, there were also multiple sources of tensions between prisoners of war themselves.[8]

---

[4] Goffman, *Asylums*, 18n2, pp. 19–20.
[5] See Davies, 'Goffman's concept'; Rostaing, 'Pertinence'; Faure, 'Les historiens'.
[6] Thomas and McManimon, Jr, 'Importation'.   [7] Sparks, Bottoms, and Hay, *Prisons*, p. 196.
[8] Ch. 4, 5.

A focus on the social relations which existed behind the walls of war prisons will allow us to interrogate how closed off these institutions really were. In *The Society of Captives*, the sociologist Gresham Sykes argued that, far from holding total power over the inmates, prison staff cannot simply *impose* order, but must negotiate and compromise with them.[9] While the work of Michel Foucault remains fundamental, it is often noted that his account of power, in *Discipline and Punish* at least, does not leave enough room for the ability of prisoners to resist their captors.[10] The analysis that follows builds on this debate.

It is first necessary to underline what might be called the laws of the war prison, in contrast to 'normal' prisons—this framework had effects on social relations behind prison walls. In the following two sections, I will analyse riots and corruption. While these two modes of interaction appear to be fundamentally opposed, I argue, following Goffman, that they are better understood on a continuum, as two complementary ways of maintaining order behind prison walls.[11] As the fourth section will explain, the prison should be considered as a synapse between the inside and the outside world.

II. A Multi-layered Surveillance System

A. Who Guarded the Prisoners of War?

In both France and Britain, three groups principally were involved in guarding prisoners of war. First of all, civilians could be asked to look after the prisoners, especially when they were passing through a town or village, or briefly detained in a stable or a church. In France, the *milice* or *garde bourgeoise* could fulfil this duty, but it was not always considered to be a satisfactory option in terms of security. Civilians could be useful, but only as an adjunct force.[12] The recourse to them had little to do with considerations of security: the driving factor was financial, since *milices bourgeoises* were equipped by town governors, unlike *invalides*, who were paid by the *Marine*.[13] Using civilians to guard prisoners of war blurred the distinction between civilians and soldiers. Thus, in 1744, Dinan's inhabitants were lent guns by the town and military authorities.[14] In Britain during the

---

[9] Sykes, *Society*.
[10] Sparks, Bottoms, and Hay, *Prisons*, p. 67. See also Garland, *Punishment*, p. 173; Ignatieff, 'State'; Rhodes, 'Towards an anthropology', p. 71; Megill, 'Reception'. It should, however, be pointed out that Foucault, in *Dits et Ecrits*, mentions resistances to *disciplinarization*.
[11] Goffman, *Asylums*, p. 180.
[12] 'Mémoire... au sujet des prisonniers anglois [in] dinan', 25 July 1744, Archives Nationales, Paris (AN), MAR/F2/72.
[13] See *Secrétaire d'Etat de la Marine* (SSM) to Guillot, 12, 18 October 1744, MAR/B2/323, fos. 46, 159.
[14] Guillot to SSM, 23 May 1744, MAR/B3/422, fo. 366.

American War of Independence, civilians patrolled around Forton and Portchester prisons to apprehend escaped prisoners.

Secondly, behind prison walls, professional guards watched over the prisoners. These turnkeys or *tourne-clefs* were civilians too, who were in the pay of the prison keeper, and, increasingly as the century wore on, of the central state administration. Left on their own, these unarmed men struggled to cope with prisoners' unrest. For instance, on 23 April 1757, the Board informed the Lords of the Admiralty that after the escape of three prisoners from Liverpool prison, the others had taunted the turnkeys: they 'had behaved very insolently; and even derided the Men who are set over them as a Guard, knowing they have no Authority upon any Occasion to proceed to Extremities with them, which His Majesty's Troops would be warranted in'. Consequently, the Board required that a 'Military Guard' be placed over the prisoners, as 'we fear without it, the Agent can in no wise be answerable for their Security', since the men under his command were unable to fire on the prisoners.[15] The cat had been set among the pigeons. As the eighteenth century wore on—and this was a peculiarity of war prisons— military personnel became heavily and systemically involved in prison surveillance. In Britain as in France, militiamen, invalids, and soldiers were tasked with patrolling the prisons and their surroundings.[16]

The consequences of this layered surveillance system were twofold. First, while the official role of military sentries was to deter escapes, they also helped jailors and turnkeys to maintain order inside the prison. The sharing out of their duties was far from obvious, and this jurisdictional uncertainty created multiple conflicts of prerogatives, which complicated the maintenance of order in prisons. Second, the army and militia's civil duty was always a catch-22. Tasked with preventing public disorder, these men often struggled to control crowds and made the situation worse, as was dramatically shown during the Gordon Riots in 1780.[17] Watching over disarmed enemies while respecting their rights was a real conundrum, and it was risky to entrust soldiers with solving it.

The imbalance of forces also affected the nature of social relationships in prison. The problem was particularly acute in the larger prisons, which will be the focus of the analysis that follows. In Dinan, for instance, the Castle was insufficiently defended against mutinous prisoners, but Commissaire Guillot's requests for the hundred-men garrison to be reinforced by fifty invalids were not granted by the government: the need to defend Brittany against an invasion was seen as more pressing than the surveillance of prisoners of war.[18] In Sissinghurst Castle, 1,996 prisoners of war were detained in May 1758 (of about 19,000

---

[15] Sick & Wounded Board (S&W) to Lords Commissioners of the Admiralty (LCA), 23 April 1757, The National Archives, Kew (TNA), ADM98/6, fo. 140.

[16] S&W to Guillot, 31 January 1745, AN, MAR/B3/432, 261v; S&W to LCA, 28 February 1757, TNA, ADM98/6, fos. 103–v. On the French Wars: Chamberlain, *Hell*, pp. 45–52.

[17] Hayter, *Army*, p. 28.   [18] SSM to Guillot, 11 October 1746, AN, MAR/B2/329, fo. 166.

prisoners in Britain at the time).[19] Between seven and twelve sentries watched over the prison walls. They were recruited in a regiment of armed militia posted next to the prison.[20] A civilian personnel of fourteen men, under the orders of the Agent for the Prisoners, was also working in the prison. Only three of them, the turnkeys, were tasked with maintaining order; the others were clerks, cooks, or medics.[21] The sentry duty was taxing. Dartmoor Prison was under the watch of forty sentries, a large number explained by the necessity 'to surround one of the walls entirely with sentries', as noted by Colonel Wood in 1818.[22] This required an extreme level of 'vigilance' and 'alertness' from these men, whose attention, he added, 'wears off' after two nights on duty, making it necessary to relieve them frequently.[23]

This explains the siege mentality of some of the guards and sentries. Thus, on 23 June 1759, the *Whitehall Evening Post* published the following report:

> Falmouth, June 21. This Morning, about One o'Clock, there was an Alarm of 700 French Prisoners attempting to make their Escape; they had undermin'd the Walls, so that four Men might go out abreast, but were prevented by a timely Discovery. The whole Town was under Arms all Night. There were but fifty Soldiers left in the Town; all the rest went from Falmouth and Penryn the 19th Instant, which made them take that Opportunity.

This occasioned a demand for explanation by the Lords of the Admiralty.[24] The Agent at Penryn explained what had really happened: the crisis was to be attributed solely to 'the pusilanimousness of the Serjeant' of the guard, who had received information from one of the sentries that the prisoners were undermining the walls to make their escape. Without ascertaining the truth of the matter in person, the military officer had panicked, and sent a messenger for reinforcements. By the time this faint-hearted man reached the town, 'he conceited the Guard was attacked & overcome, and accordingly reported it to be so'.[25] The description of this incident is one of the many examples of the petty 'war-within-a-war' that the civilians and militaries in charge of watching over prisoners of war were waging against one another.

---

[19] 'A list shewing the several places', 1 May 1758, National Maritime Museum, Greenwich (NMM), ADM/F/17. The figure for Britain in 1758 comes from Le Goff, 'Problèmes', p. 231.
[20] S&W to LCA, 3 August 1757, TNA, ADM98/6, fos. 204v–205; interview of a turnkey (name missing), 9 December 1761, ADM105/42, fo. 192. This disproportion was worse than at Newgate Prison in the same period, where the ratio between turnkeys and inmates was about one to a hundred: Ignatieff, *Just Measure*, p. 38.
[21] 'List of salaries and allowances', 10 August 1763, TNA, ADM98/9, fos. 207v–208.
[22] Colonel Wood, 22 April 1818, 'Report' (1818), p. 187. These people came from the garrison of Plymouth, which numbered 'between 550 and 600 men'.
[23] Ibid.   [24] S&W to LCA, 29 June, 7 July 1759, NMM, ADM/F/19.
[25] Extract from Richard Lloyd to S&W, 2 July 1759, ibid.

The Agents oversaw the civilian hierarchy in prison. Until the end of the eighteenth century, they were recruited on an ad-hoc basis, and discharged at the end of the war.[26] In this period, Agents usually combined this job with another one, as in this case from 1745:

> The business of agent … was made a branch of the Duty of the Surgeon, at that port [Kinsale], and has continued so ever since, and is now in the Hands of Mr Charles Newman, a Man of a very good Character in his Profession, who also takes care of, and victuals the Prisoners of War at four pence a Man a day, and … he keeps and transmits to the Office all his Account in a very regular Manner.[27]

While Joseph Crew, who served as an Agent in Exeter for seven years, started his career as a customs officer, the professional training of many Agents often bore little relation to either the Admiralty or the sea.[28] At Kinsale, a Mr Howe, who had fulfilled this function in 1777, explained that the 'usual salary of £100' was insufficient to defray his costs. He wrote to the Sick & Wounded Board that he

> did not live at Kinsale at the Time …, he removed thither with his Family …, leaving his Harvest and other concerns in the Management of an Agent, by which he suffered much, and that he thought what We offered him was not an adequate compensation for his Service, and proposed his being paid thirty Guineas.[29]

While Agents were not fully professionalized during the American War of Independence, this began to change in the 1790s, as part of the broader movement of state bureaucratization of the prisoner of war service in this period. These men were increasingly recruited from the navy.[30] The trajectory of Daniel Woodriff is a good example of this. A former sailor, he was appointed Agent at Norman Cross between 1799 and 1802. He joined the navy again and, in an extraordinary reversal of fate, was captured in September 1805, and detained as a prisoner of war, first in a French ship, then in La Rochelle and finally Verdun, until his release in June 1807.[31] He afterwards became the captain of a transport ship for convicts, before re-joining the prison administration business, as the Agent at Forton Prison (1809–13).[32] This professional trajectory might explain the circulation of

---

[26] Petition of Agent at Kinsale between 1711 and 1713 to be reappointed: William Bowles to S&W, 11 February 1744/5, NMM, ADM/M/390, no. 45.

[27] S&W to LCA, 11 February 1745, TNA, ADM98/2, fos. 101–v.

[28] Petition of Joseph Crew to Henry Pelham, 20 February 1748, British Library (BL), Landsdowne 820/7, fos. 132–3.

[29] S&W to LCA, 23 February 1780, TNA, ADM98/12, fo. 187.

[30] All prison hulks were commanded by naval officers: Chamberlain, Hell, pp. 32–3.

[31] On his stay in Verdun, see Duché, Passage, pp. 143, 287–8.

[32] Walker, Depot, pp. 265–7; Cox, Captain Daniel Woodriff, pp. 102–17, 119.

disciplinary practices across different carceral institutions, from land prisons to sailing ones, and the other way around. By the early nineteenth century, the Agent's role was well defined, as shown by the very detailed 'Instructions for Agents' adopted in 1807. As these stated, with respect to the superintendence of the prison and hospital departments, 'although the various Duties... be divided among several Officers..., we shall consider you, and you are to consider yourself, as being responsible for the general Economy, Discipline, and good Order of the whole'.[33]

While the conditions of living of the soldiers and of the prisoners were not necessarily that different, and while soldiers were always a small minority monitoring a large number of prisoners, there was a clear 'disparity in power between prisoners and custodians'.[34]

B. Rules, Punishments, and Rewards

The framework of the relations between prisoners and guards was defined in a set of prescriptions called the prison rules, which had been adopted for prisoners of war in both countries by the 1740s.[35] These texts acted as a 'blueprint for behaviour within the prison'.[36] Prison rules followed what Foucault calls an 'infra-penality'—in the sense that their application was beyond the remit of a judge—which is at the heart of all 'disciplinary systems'.[37] While prison rules were not specific to war prisons, their very existence and application to prisoners of war are significant in themselves. Punishing prisoners of war seems, in theory, to violate the idea that these people deserved to be protected and shielded from violence, and this justified the language in which prisoners of war phrased their complaints to their respective governments.[38] Although the purpose of the detention of prisoners of war was not their reformation, prison administrators nonetheless chose their punishments within a pre-existing repertoire. In addition to these were specific punishments and rewards designed for this population, based on the prison administrators' perception of prisoners of war: of their ethos, psychology, and motives. Before prison rules were designed, during the 1740s, prison administrators and guards often raised their concerns about the best means of maintaining order when facing the unruliness of prisoners of war.

In the first decades of the eighteenth century, prison officials already felt the need to justify themselves when they punished prisoners. The marshal for prisoners of war at Plymouth wrote in 1706: 'I am doing everything possible to treat

---

[33] 'Instructions for Agents' (1807), article 26, p. 18.

[34] Sparks, Bottoms, and Hay, *Prisons*, pp. 49–50.

[35] They might have appeared much earlier, locally, as in Dunkirk: Du Guay to SSM, 25 August 1707, AN, MAR/B3/142, fos. 392v–393.

[36] Sykes, *Society*, p. 13.   [37] Foucault, *Discipline*, p. 178.   [38] Ch. 2.

the prisoners with the utmost civility, but when they break the prison ... and cause disorders, I must punish them in some way, otherwise I could not survive.'[39] This quotation highlights that, at the time, punishment was a last recourse. In the absence of agreed rules, however, guards themselves were unsure what they were authorized to do. This was linked to contemporary perceptions of what prisoners of war were, and how they ought to be treated. Punishing them for trying to escape was, for a long time, judged to be unnecessarily cruel. Thus in 1696 Gastines, *commissaire de la Marine* at St Malo, criticized the jailors in Plymouth for putting escaped prisoners in irons, a treatment which he contrasted to his much more lenient way of dealing with such cases:

> I have often caught some Englishmen who had escaped from our prisons, I have never punished them for that..., I contented myself to give them up to their comrades and to have them better watched over. In the whole world, it is allowed and natural for a poor prisoner to look for his freedom.[40]

Gastines was putting his finger on a fundamental dimension of incarceration: in the same way that, since the Middle Ages, noblemen were decapitated while peasants were hanged, the choice of a given punishment expressed the institution's conception of the inmate's 'nature'. The perception that the prisoner was naturally driven to try his escape meant that he should not be blamed, and much less punished for it. In the same spirit, in 1709, the secretary of state for the *Marine* wrote to French Commissaire Lempereur, that the English practice of fining a French sailor who had escaped from Dover Castle was 'against the rules, being natural for a prisoner to look for his freedom, and that it had to be an enterprise on the part of their jailor to ransom the sailors'.[41] The term 'rules', in this excerpt, referred to the customary and unwritten norms which still guided the reciprocal treatment of prisoners of war in this period. The notion that escaping from prison was not to be harshly punished continued to be widely shared, even after formal rules had been accepted, as in this 1757 letter by Moras, the French secretary of state for the *Marine*: 'it seemed [to us] that this fault should be regarded as a natural act, which can be excused by the love that all human beings have for freedom.'[42]

Some punishments were chosen because they were infamous. Thus, while restraining prisoners who presented a danger to their captors was allowed by the law of nations, in practice the use of irons was reserved for specific groups,

---

[39] Copy of Slaughter to Lempereur [*in French*], 13 November 1706, AN, MAR/B3/135, fo. 340.
[40] Gastines, memorandum, 4 July 1696, MAR/B4/17, fos. 434-6.
[41] SSM to Lempereur, 4 December 1709, MAR/B2/217, fos. 954v-955.
[42] Moras to S&W, 13 September 1757, TNA, ADM97/106, fo. 116v.

such as buccaneers, or Jacobite 'rebels' who had opted to serve the French monarchy.[43] Prisoners suspected of spying, of engaging in rioting, and of trying to escape were often treated in the same way.[44] In 1757, Moras described the caning of fractious prisoners as 'a barbarian punishment'.[45] Prison reformers would also single out such practices as typical of the primitive age with which they wanted to break.[46]

In the middle of the century, in both countries, there still was no consensus regarding which punishments could legitimately be imposed on prisoners of war. The example of the roll call, or muster, illustrates this. This practice was not yet part of the disciplinary apparatus at work in normal prisons. Imported from the military, it was generally used in war prisons in the second half of the century. While the roll call would become a staple of all prison rules, a debate took place in Britain in 1744 to decide whether it should be adopted, and what the punishment for refusing to comply should be. Article 3 of the draft regulations submitted by the Board stated: 'If any prisoner refuse to answer to his call at the musters, he shall be punished for the contempt, by the forfeiture of his subsistance till he do submit.'[47] The term 'contempt' underlines the perception that refusing to answer one's name was a challenge to prison discipline as a whole. However, the Lords of the Admiralty wrote back to state their disapproval 'of mulcting or lessening the Allowance of Provisions to the Prisoners upon any Account', fearing that it would provide a pretext for the French to generalize this punishment to all British prisoners.[48] The question raised here was to find a punishment that would be appropriate for controlling prisoners of war, which would be fair rather than cruel, and would not expose one's own prisoners abroad to retaliation. The Commissioners for the Sick & Wounded Seamen respectfully disagreed and pointed out 'that experience has convinced not only our officers, but the military ones who have had the guard of them, that mulcts of this kind are things too easy to keep them in tolerable decorum'. Deprived of these means of pressure, the Agents would lose their grip over the prisoners: 'It will destroy the obligation which the Prisoners are now under to answer to their Call and Musters, and to keep clean their Prisons by Turns; . . . without Mustering it will be impossible for the Agents to know when they have or have not all the Prisoners put into their Custody.'[49]

---

[43] Extract of Lempereur to S&W, 1 April 1707, BL, Add MS61591, fo. 113v; ibid., 18 April 1708, Add MS61592, fo. 58v; Ponchartrain to Dartmouth, 9 March 1712, AN, MAR/B2/230, fo. 444; LCA to S&W, 27 December 1745, NMM, ADM/M/393, no. 368. During the Civil Wars, Irish prisoners, including women, were the most harshly treated: Donagan, *War*, pp. 206–10.

[44] De la Reinterie, commander of Brest, to SSM, 22 October 1708, AN, MAR/B3/163, fos. 341v–342; SSM to Thirat de Fiegadet, 18 October 1744, MAR/B2/323, fo. 159.

[45] Moras to S&W, 13 September 1757, TNA, ADM97/106, fo. 115v.

[46] Howard, *State* (1784), pp. 13–15.

[47] 'Regulations to be observed by all Prisoners of War in Great Britain and Ireland', article 3, S&W to LCA, 1 November 1744, TNA, ADM98/2, fo. 34. See also *Rules to be observed . . . in France* (1758), article 3.

[48] LCA to S&W, 5 November 1744, TNA, ADM98/2, fo. 38v.   [49] Ibid., fo. 39.

This argument was successful, and the original wording was kept in the final version of the rules.[50]

Although Commissaire Guillot extolled how 'reasonable' these rules generally were, he thought the treatment of recaptured prisoners too harsh: 'it would be better to content ourselves to restrain them a little more; such a punishment seems to be sufficient and more suitable than diminishing the subsistence of prisoners, which is not very substantial as it is.'[51] The exercise of disciplinary violence in prison was formally regulated from the 1740s onwards. Prison rules were first adopted in local prisons, and then harmonized nationally under the aegis of the Admiralty and the *Marine*. During the Seven Years' War, Britain and France adopted the same regulations.[52]

These rules delineated an absolute boundary between custodians and inmates. According to Goffman, 'these diffuse rulings occur in an authority system of the *echelon* kind: *any* member of the staff class has certain rights to discipline *any* member of the inmate class', which increases the probability of sanction.[53] Thus, the 1746 regulations to be observed by all prisoners in Britain and Ireland began with an article forbidding the prisoners to 'molest or obstruct [the Agent] or the Turnkey', to 'use any ill or threatning Language to, much less strike, or in any other Manner maletreat either of them, or any Person employed about the Prison'.[54]

Prison rules generally forbade prisoners, as in 1746, to quarrel among themselves or to 'make any Disturbance in the Prisons',[55] or, as outlined in greater detail in 1758, 'to fight, quarrel or make any riot in the Prisons or places where the Prisoners are allowed to take the air'.[56] The degree and type of punishment were left at the discretion of the Board, who delegated this power to the Agent in the prisons. Some of these punishments were designed specifically for prisoners of war, such as the loss of their 'turn of being exchanged'.[57] This 'withdrawal of privilege' amounted to increasing the duration of imprisonment.[58] This punishment was resorted to in both countries early on, before it was introduced in the prison rules.[59] Thus, in 1704 the English commissioners justified their decision

[50] S&W to Guillot, 28 December 1744, AN, MAR/B3/432, fos. 76–7. See 'Regles qui se doivent observer...dans la Grande Bretagne et l'Irlande' [1745], MAR/A/5/6.

[51] Guillot, in margin of S&W's letter, 28 December 1744, MAR/B3/432, fo. 74; SSM to Guillot, 5 February 1745, MAR/B2/325, fo. 71. The S&W preferred food deprivation to corporal punishment: S&W to Guillot, 28 December 1744, MAR/B3/432, fos. 75–v.

[52] 'Regulations for...French Prisoners in Great Britain' [1757], TNA, SP42/136; *Rules...Prisoners of War in...France* (1758).

[53] Goffman, *Asylums*, p. 46.

[54] 'Regulation', article 1, TNA, SP42/30. Similar articles were adopted in subsequent wars: *Rules* (1758), article 1; 'Règles' (1807), article 1.

[55] 'Regulation' (1746), article 6, TNA, SP42/30.

[56] *Rules* (1758), article 6. The same prohibition was repeated in 1807: 'Règles', article 2.

[57] *Rules* (1758), article 1.   [58] Goffman, *Asylums*, p. 53.

[59] See, for instance, St Sulpice to SSM, 10 May 1704, AN, MAR/B3/123, fos. 507–v. This was still the case in 1807: 'Instructions for Agents', article 39.

not to release French prisoners who had tried to escape, and suggested to their French counterparts that they should act similarly with their English prisoners: 'We will hold them back to scare them, to prevent them from causing such disorders in the future, we will not disapprove it if you hold back ours for the same reason.'[60] During the American War of Independence, according to the American sailor Fanning, detained in Forton in 1778–9, escapees were punished with confinement in the so-called 'black hole' for 'forty days and forty nights', to be fed on bread and water only, and to lose their turn of exchange, which meant staying in prison for 'three or four years'.[61] The psychological consequences of this long retention could be dire. Being left in total darkness about their future drove some prisoners to a deep melancholia.

Other punishments were tailored for specific groups. The 1758 French rules targeted the sense of social distinction of the officers who had tried to escape: 'A Sea-officer, thus contravening shall from that moment be looked upon and treated as a common sailor.'[62] Collective punishments, such as the putting of all the prisoners on half-allowance, were an integral part of the repressive arsenal. This method was used to force Spanish prisoners to give up the name of one of their compatriots in Portsmouth who had killed another in 1744, and to compel American prisoners to denounce an escapee who had broken through the walls at Forton in 1778.[63]

While jailors could justify the infliction of violence on seditious prisoners in the name of order, foreign diplomats had different views. In 1745, for example, the French Commissaire Guillot defended two Frenchmen who had been put in Portchester Castle 'under the pretext of an alleged rebellion in which they have been implicated'. Guillot did not care about the reasons the guards had for detaining them, and he rejected their threat 'of retaining them until the peace' was signed. The commissaire deprived the guards of the leverage provided by the rewards/punishment system: 'they have been in prison for more than a year, they seem punished enough.'[64]

To elicit compliance from the prisoners, prison authorities relied on a retributive justice system, based on discretionary punishments. Favours and incentives belonged to the custodians' arsenal, as noted by Goffman.[65] Rewards mirrored the punishments described above. Thus, while bad behaviour meant moving down in the pecking order, to be released later and see one's freedom of movement restrained by spending time in the hole, good conduct led to being exchanged

---

[60] S&W to SSM, 24 August 1704, AN, MAR/B3/123, fo. 591v.   [61] Fanning, *Memoirs*, p. 13.
[62] *Rules* (1758), article 5.
[63] LCA to S&W, 28 November 1744, TNA, ADM98/2, fo. 48v; Connor, 'Yankee privateersman', 31 (30 May 1778), p. 19. See also 'Copy of the Instructions' to Agents by S&W, article IV, in *Report* (1798), Appendix, p. 29.
[64] Guillot to S&W, 27 July 1745, TNA, ADM97/103, fos. 36–7.   [65] Goffman, *Asylums*, p. 163.

before one's turn.[66] For instance, in 1746, a project to escape from Dinan Castle was thwarted by the betrayal of two English prisoners, who were promptly rewarded and sent home early; the escapees were put in the town hole.[67] In 1809, all prisoners in British depots were instructed that whoever informed the Agent of any attempt 'to introduce or manufacture offensive Weapons calculated for Murder or Insurrection, or any Plot for undermining or breaking down the Boundaries of the Prison for the Purpose of Escape or Mischief', would be entitled to their 'Liberty, and also Conveyance to the Continent', while their name would be 'carefully concealed' from the others. Conversely, culprits of such offences would be restrained in the black hole and would not be exchanged 'till the End of the War'.[68] The prisoners' own attitude, during the time of their captivity or before, could also influence their fate. For instance, a French prisoner in Dover, who had shown good behaviour in Havana towards English captives, was released in 1744, as a reward for his past generosity.[69] Likewise, in 1810, Peter Fea wrote in his diary from Auxonne Depot that 'Nineteen Men who had been active in extinguishing a fire in Town in dec.^r rec.^d passports to go home'.[70]

While prison rules mostly listed the obligations of prisoners, a few articles listed their rights. In October 1757, to obviate the abuses of food contractors and 'to give notice to the Prisoners of what they have the right to call upon', British commissioners asked the French that 'in each prison be posted up copies of the orders for their treatment, and that prisoners be able to know who to have recourse to in case of a contravention'.[71] This article became a stalemate in all subsequent prison rules.[72] In 1807, for instance, the Agents were instructed to hang up 'in the most conspicuous Parts of the Prisons, or Prison-Ships, Hospitals or Hospital-Ships, the printed Regulations..., translated in the several Languages of the Prisoners... respecting the Behaviour of the Prisoners, and the Rations of Provisions allowed them'.[73] Food rations had already been detailed in an article in 1746, and a table of victualling was annexed to the rules thereafter, listing the daily allowances of beer, bread, beef, butter, cheese, and peas to which the prisoners were entitled. A procedure was also established by which the prisoners could appoint either

---

[66] See Schneider, 'Good time credit'.

[67] Guillot to SSM, 11 September 1746, AN, MAR/B3/445, fo. 201v; SSM to Guillot, 21 September 1746, MAR/B2/329, fo. 141.

[68] Transport Office (TO)'s circular to Agents, 28 September 1809, TNA, ADM98/170, fos. 29–30.

[69] LCA to S&W, 19 September 1744, NMM, ADM/M/389, no. 210. See also S&W to LCA, 16 February 1757, TNA, ADM98/6, fo. 91.

[70] Peter Fea's diary, 18 May 1810, Devon Record Office, Exeter (DRO), 1317M/F/1.

[71] 'Memoire', November 1758, AN, MAR/B4/97, fo. 179v. The French complied: Raoul, commissaire in Le Havre, to SSM, 28 November 1758, MAR/B3/538, fos. 180–2. Prison rules, translated in French and in Spanish, were already 'hung up in every Prison for the Perusal of the Prisoners' in the 1740s: 'Regulation', [11 January 1746], TNA, SP42/30.

[72] This had been a practice in the Fleet's debtor's prison since at least 1729: Howard, *State* (1777), pp. 161–3.

[73] 'Instructions for agents' (1807), article 30, p. 20.

three or five representatives to witness the weighing of bread and meat rations, to ensure that they were not cheated on quantity or quality. They could voice their complaints to the Agent, and, if he failed to pay heed to them, to his superiors, 'who will not fail of doing them justice in the matter'.[74] In this sense, prison rules were 'a government of law'.[75]

The 1807 prison rules were more extensive (eighteen articles in total) than previous ones. The punitive regime was more detailed than ever, with thirteen articles out of eighteen mentioning punishments for various infractions, including new ones, such as stealing prison property, trying to buy or sell food rations, or attempting to send letters outside without obtaining the Agent's agreement.[76] The prisoner who had disposed of the clothes issued by the Transport Office would also be kept on short allowance and put in the black hole.[77] Although these bans could be seen as a hardening of repression, it could be argued that these regulations limited the arbitrariness of the jailors. The instructions to the Agents, which came together with these rules, thus introduced checks to prevent the jailors' punishments from getting out of hand:

> The Prisoners are not to be struck with the Hand, Stick, Whip, or any Weapon whatever, but are, on all Occasions, to be treated with Humanity. Their just Complaints are to be attended to, and their real Grievances redressed. . . . As no Punishments are to be inflicted without our Knowledge, you are, weekly, to transmit to us . . . a List of all the Prisoners who have been confined in the Black-Hole in the Course of the preceding Week.[78]

This symmetry between the rights and duties of guards and prisoners, who were all subjected to a more thorough and systematic regime of surveillance, also aimed at breaking the informal solidarities and corruption which brought these groups together.[79] Some of these principles were implemented, as illustrated by the frequent sending of inspectors to prisons by the Sick & Wounded Board. But the prisoners who tried to activate these rights faced a number of challenges. When the Agent failed to redress their complaints, we saw that prisoners often appealed outside, to the Admiralty, or to their own government.[80] In Sissinghurst Prison, the prisoners' complaints to London and Versailles led to an extensive investigation in 1761. Their main object of discontent was the failure to apply the rules by Cooke, the Agent, who went so far as to punish the prisoners who appealed to him.[81] When, in accordance with article 9 of the 1758 prison rules, a prisoner unhappy about the quantity and quality of his food

---

[74] 'Regulation' (1746), article 9; *Rules* (1758), article 9; 'Règles' (1807), article 8.
[75] McCleery, 'Governmental process', p. 161.   [76] 'Règles' (1807) , articles 10, 11, 13.
[77] Ibid., article 10.   [78] 'Instructions for Agents' (1807), article 36.
[79] Ignatieff, *Just Measure*, pp. 77–8.   [80] Ch. 2.
[81] Interrogation of Jean Berrurier, 25 November 1761, TNA, ADM105/42, fo. 48v.

complained to the clerk in charge of distributing food, he was called a 'son of a Bitch & dog'.[82] In the words of one of the prisoners, Cooke was 'not zealous enough for the good of the P.ʳˢ'.[83] The enforcement of prison rules was problematic when the individual in charge of their implementation was dragging his feet. The impact of these regulations on everyday practices should therefore not be overemphasized. The existence of rules does not mean that they were known or executed.

At the end of our period, the rights of prisoners were increasingly blended with their obligations. The 1807 prison rules emphasized the internal organization of the inmates, who were explicitly regimented as on navy decks. The distribution of food would be supervised by a prisoner who would be in charge of the 'ration for six men': 'each Mess will nominate a Leader, responsible for the *Gamelle* [*wooden bowl*],...for the Can, for the *Pot*, and for the Spoons delivered to the said Mess, who will also have to be present when the Rations of the Mess will be delivered, as soon as the Distribution begins.'[84] These messes were the basic unit of 'regimentation'.[85] If an escapee was not denounced by other mess members, their own rations would be diminished by one-third for ten days (article 16). The (apparent) delegation of authority to prisoners became a way to maintain order. Thus, the Agent would appoint some prisoners as 'Inspectors of the conduct of the Prisoners' to maintain '*le bon ordre*' in the prisons, ensure that the prison rules were respected by the prisoners, and report the names of the offenders to the Agent (article 17).[86] These men, appointed at the rate of two prisoners per floor of a prison building, or per deck of a prison ship, were paid three pence per day. Asking the prisoners to implement regulations devised by their captors was an effective, if cynical, way to divide the prison community—yet, from another perspective, this could be interpreted as an acknowledgment of the prisoners' agency.

John Howard saw in prison rules a way to legitimize the custodians' authority, to limit the arbitrariness of punishment, and to protect the prisoners against the frauds of contractors and gaolers.[87] They would ultimately 'prevent mutiny in prisons and attempts to escape'.[88] In particular, the prison reformer professed his admiration for the rules adopted during the American War of Independence by France and Britain. A passage about convicts, in *Lazarettos*, cites as a model the 1780 prison rules: 'there should also be a table of rules and orders, similar to that

---

[82] Interrogation of Jean Pierre Joseph Bruère, 28 November 1761, ibid., fo. 90v. In English in the original.
[83] Interrogation of Maugendre, 18 November 1761, ibid., fo. 221v.
[84] 'Règles' (1807), article 15.
[85] Goffman, *Asylums*, p. 46. Prisoners used the same language to describe their sociability in private lodgings and fortress depots in France: Duché, 'Passage', p. 60.
[86] 'Règles' (1807), articles 16–17.   [87] Ignatieff, *Just Measure*, pp. 72–3.
[88] Howard, *Lazarettos*, p. 222, quoted in Ignatieff, *Just Measure*, p. 73.

for prisoners of war.'[89] As we saw, this reasoning was part of Howard's quest for good practices, which entailed adopting a comparative framework.[90]

As a juridical instrument for regulating social relations in prison, prison rules were, however, imperfect for many reasons. As pointed out by Erving Goffman, the objects of the staff's attention were not 'inanimate objects', passively abiding by the rules. The extent to which prisoners of war conformed to the 'forced deference pattern' we just underlined remains to be seen.[91] These different tools of management were based on the assumption that the fear of deprivations and the attractions of gifts would be effective in controlling the prisoners' behaviour. The efficiency of a system of government by rules relies on the prisoners' belief in their fair implementation, and on the custodians' ability to apply it appropriately and with moderation.[92] Failing this, these rules could have the opposite effect.

III. Prison Riots

Prison riots before the twentieth century have been almost completely overlooked by historians, which is surprising given the rich historiography on food and urban riots in early modern Britain and France.[93] In contrast, prison sociologists have long been interested in the topic. What do we mean by 'prison riots'? Bert Useem and Michael Reisig differentiate four types of inmate collective action: riot, disturbance, non-violent protest, and threats of violence.[94] Ideally, one needs to include a larger set of phenomena than narrowly defined riots, in order to account for a richer picture of social interactions in prison. Prison riots reveal something fundamental about the structure of authority in prison; about the nature of the social bonds linking inmates, on the one hand, and the custodial staff on the other; about the levels of violence tolerated towards prisoners, and the factors mitigating it; and, finally, about the prisoners' ability to resist the power of their captors.

Let us start with a voyage to Plymouth, in an evening of May 1706. In a legal statement sworn in front of the mayor of the city, Lawrence Darcy, a soldier posted at Plymouth prison, described a riot that had begun around 9 pm and climaxed at 11 pm. French prisoners had refused to obey the sentinels' orders to return to their lodgings, and threw stones at them. The sentinel on duty, William Hellstone, asked the prison underkeeper, named Ellis, 'how to behave himself'; Ellis replied 'that it was not his duty to advise the centinells, but that they should use their own discretion or observe the orders they had received from their office.'[rs']. One of the prisoners then 'came by ... Hellstone, & seized the muzzle

---

[89]   Howard, *Lazarettos*, pp. 218–19.   [90]   Ch. 2.   [91]   Goffman, *Asylums*, pp. 78–9, 31.
[92]   Cressey, 'Contradictory directives', p. 8.
[93]   See, however, Ignatieff, *Just Measure*; Innes, 'King's Bench'.
[94]   Useem and Reisig, 'Collective action', p. 744.

of his musquett & spit in his face, & called him English booger, & said that he would sacrifice him or words to that effect'. Closing his report, Darcy justified Hellstone's action: 'The Prisoners being assembled in a Tumultuous Manner, & the Centinell not knowing what the Consequences of it might be', he 'did fire his musquett att the Door of the said Prison Yard, and ... one of the Prisoners was wounded thereby & that he dyed of the s.^{d} Wound'.[95] Other soldiers, also on duty that night, as well as a turnkey and a prison servant, confirmed this version of events.

This pattern was replicated in numerous cases. But what does the death of one prisoner signify, in the grand scale of things? In reality, the killing of an inmate by a guard was an extremely rare occurrence in eighteenth-century prisons. It was far more common for military sentries to kill prisoners of war in similar situations. This difference must be explained. Moreover, the significance of the death of a prisoner of war at the hands of a member of the custodial staff was not a trifling matter: it engaged two states, in a context of war, and opened the possibility of retaliations. The Plymouth affair we just described also reveals the institutional structure of authority in the prison. The sentry was left on his own, without support from his military hierarchy. His request for advice from the civil authorities of the prison was ignored. This institutional tension had left the sentry in the dark as to the best course of action to follow.

This riot sheds light on three elements that were usually present in such incidents, which we will analyse in succession. First, the incident was often triggered by communication issues, such as the use of the wrong language or gesture, which were felt to be humiliating. Although there are some formal analogies with the disputes involving prisoners on parole and civilians analysed before, the consequences of these quarrels for the prisoners were vastly different. Second, the sentry felt justified to act upon what he had perceived to be threatening and unruly behaviour; we need to unpack the rationale behind his actions and ex-post facto justifications. Third, the author of the report tried to clear the sentry of any wrongdoing. He presented his narrative in a way that would maximize the chances of acquitting the soldier. Applying the right legal qualification to these unfortunate events was all the more necessary because they had led to the death of a foreigner, protected by the laws of war. This leads us, in turn, to consider the legal repercussions of such incidents.

A. The Power of Insults

While the consequences of the prisoners' misbehaviour might be minor, all depended on the sentry's ability to restrain himself to avoid the incident escalating

---

[95] Sworn deposition of Lawrence Darcy before the mayor of Plymouth, 13 May 1706, BL, Add MS61591, fos. 22–v.

into a full riot. Take the following incident, which occurred in Dover in November 1744. According to a report from the major of a regiment stationed at the prison, unruly French prisoners began to make 'a great Blaze of fire from their Chimney, in order to make their Escape. . . . About 5 a Clock they began to abuse, and spit in the Centry's Face through their Shed, and gave them many opprobrious Words, upon which he often told'em to be quiet'.[96] Further details were communicated by the Lords of the Admiralty to the French *commissaire de la Marine* at Dunkirk, Givry: prisoners in Dover were 'Extremely mutinous and disorderly, to the point of even Insulting the Sentries, throwing Sticks and Stones at them, hitting one of them, spitting in the Face of another and hurling abuse at them'.[97] According to Goffman, 'collective teasing', in the form of 'brief gestures of anonymous or mass defiance', such as booing, are common 'secondary adjustments' on the part of prisoners.[98] Rejecting the staff and fraternizing among prisoners are two sides of the same coin.[99] These gestures and words, in all their variety, aimed at a similar thing: dishonouring the sentries and provoking them. While prisoners resorted to a rich repertoire of insults, spitting in someone's face was a recurrent behaviour, which symbolically defaced one's antagonist—an action, as we saw, that was also very common to humiliate officers on parole.[100] Unfortunately for the prisoners, it worked only too well; the sergeant of the guard at Dover fired his piece and killed one of them.

Let us travel forward another sixteen years, and 120 miles to the north-east, to Knowle Prison near Bristol. In June 1760, several prisoners, trying to climb up a palisade gate, were ordered by a soldier to keep down, 'which they refused, and laughed and made game of him toutering [*taunting*] and swearing in their own language'.[101] Other guards witnessed the scene. Prison riots, just like popular 'emotions', have an carnival-like dimension: humour, wordplay and role inversion allow the weak to challenge the authority of the powerful, in a festive and 'hedonistic' atmosphere.[102] One of the prisoners 'greatly insulted the centinel, by spitting at him, and having a short stick in his hand and pushing the said at the centinel crying pugh, pugh, pugh, and giving him ill language by calling him bougre the chien and other names'.[103] At this point, Johnson fired his musket and killed the prisoner. Insults could amalgamate several meanings, as we saw already: 'bougre the chien' blended a religious and sexual insult ('bougre' meaning heretic

[96] 'Extracts of a letter from Major Bell, of Lieutenant General Harrison's Regiment', Dover, 14 November 1744, TNA, ADM98/2, fo. 41v.
[97] Translation of LCA to Givry, 20 November 1744, AN, MAR/B3/421, fo. 417.
[98] Goffman, *Asylums*, p. 59. On insults in prison, see Collins, *Violence*, pp. 169–70.
[99] Goffman, *Asylums*, p. 59. [100] Ch. 5.
[101] Ensign Armstrong Frank, 16 June 1760, BL, Add MS38848, fo. 190.
[102] Sparks, Bottoms, and Hay, *Prisons*, p. 82. On early-modern riots see, for example, Zemon Davis, 'Rites'; Rogers, *Crowds*; Nicolas, *Rebellion*.
[103] Ensign Armstrong Frank, 16 June 1760, BL, Add MS38848, fo. 190v.

and sodomite[104]) with the animalization of the antagonist, who was doubly impure. In war prisons as in the parole zones, the linguistic boundary between custodians and inmates adds another variable to the social interactions taking place: the limited understanding of the foreign language meant that the exact nature of the verbal insult was not always grasped. Whether these words were uttered or not is not important here: they were used as justifications for the sentry's subsequent actions. Insults could go both ways. In 1779, a French assistant surgeon complained to the Board about the conduct of Gordon, the prison surgeon, in terms that conveyed his belief that his social rank had been disregarded. Gordon had treated him

> the most rudely, taking him by the arm and pushing him from behind with punches and kicks, uttering insults unworthy of a gentleman and which decency does not allow me to repeat … It is almost impossible sirs to believe that I have been treated in this way by a civilized man except an intoxicated one.[105]

In such situations, the soldiers might fall back on deeply held prejudices about the nature of the rioters, as bad subjects and criminals. The act of rioting revealed the putative meanness and debauchery of the prisoners. Let us go back to Plymouth in 1706. The marshal for prisoners of war there, William Slaughter, wrote to his French counterpart in 1706 to defend the attitude of the underkeeper, Ellis, who had severely punished French inmates; these men were 'very troublesome and mutinous and caused many disorders, threatening to kill the servants'.[106] The use of moral language aimed at vilifying the prisoners' complaints: 'the said … were the leaders of all this mischiefs, and excited the others to do the same, and I have never seen and I do not believe I will ever see such evil and turbulent people.'[107] Such an attribution of moral depravation to the prisoners of war confused the notion, prevalent in the law of nations, that they fundamentally differed from common criminals. This register was commonly used by custodians. In 1708, unruly English prisoners at Dinan were called 'worse than demons' and 'damned scoundrels', and in 1746, those who 'conspired' to escape from the Castle and set the town of fire were described as 'wretched men' and 'naughtier and naughtier' by the French commissaire.[108] The same vocabulary was again used in Saumur in 1779 to describe riotous English prisoners: 'most of them bad subjects, genuinely mutinous, seditious, who have even had a hand in the Dinan riots.'[109] The

---

[104] Garrioch, 'Verbal insults', p. 110.
[105] E. Laffont to S&W, 28 August 1779, TNA, ADM97/124, no. 23.
[106] Copy of 'Guillaume Slaughter' to Lempereur, 13 November 1706, AN, MAR/B3/135, fo. 339.
[107] Ibid., fo. 340.
[108] Lempereur to SSM, 1, 29 April 1708, MAR/B3/157, fos. 127, 163v; Guillot to SSM, 17 September 1746, 1 January 1746, MAR/B3/445, fos. 208, 213.
[109] Fayolle to unnamed, 25 July 1779, MAR/F2/82.

implication was that, on entering the prison, prisoners of war did not shed the label of enemy; worse, they took on a new role, that of criminal. This interpretation chimes with Goffman's argument that the values of any organization include 'a thoroughly embracing conception of the member—and not merely a conception of him *qua* member, but behind this a conception of him *qua* human being'.[110] Every action on the part of the prisoners could be interpreted in this light, and this would explain why sentries underlined that they were merely doing their duty by shooting men who should know better than to challenge them.[111] Behind prison walls, custodians did not necessarily see the laws of war as sacrosanct principles. Conversely, the prisoners of war did not always comply with the injunctions of turnkeys and sentries. In both cases, what mattered was not outside norms, rather the custodians' ability to convince the prisoners of the legitimacy of their authority.

B. Legitimate and Illegitimate Violence

In an influential study, the political theorist David Beetham noted that power cannot maintain itself by coercion only: the key element is its legitimacy in the eyes of those on whom it weighs.[112] Beetham's analysis has been applied to the carceral world by sociologists.[113] How much violence did prison sentries feel justified to display in order to subdue prisoners of war? Here, it is important to remember that soldiers were not bound by formal prison rules, but by customary rules, rooted in their traditions; what has been called 'their "ethos" or "way"'.[114]

Let us take the example of Sissinghurst Castle during the Seven Years' War as a case in point. In principle, the instructions given to military sentries were clear. On 5 December 1761, Lieutenant Mortimer, from the Leicestershire Militia, testified in front of Dr Maxwell, the commissioner sent by the Sick & Wounded Board who was carrying out an investigation in the prison: 'I frequently heard Capt Burlton give it out in verbal orders that the men should not treat the P.^rs ill.'[115] But what did this officer mean by 'ill treatments'? Lieutenant Mortimer described the procedure for leading the prisoners from their wards to the main courtyard, to do the roll-call, or to bring them back to their wards at dusk. He detailed an incident he had witnessed:

The Off.^rs Orders are for the men to look well into the Sheds to see that none of them stay behind ... & likewise to examine the Sheds & Staircases ... &

---

[110] Goffman, *Asylums*, p. 164.

[111] Such an interpretation of staff-inmates relations has been nuanced: Shapira and Navon, 'Staff-inmates cooperation'.

[112] Beetham, *Legitimation*.   [113] Sparks and Bottoms, 'Legitimacy'.

[114] Sparks, Bottoms, and Hay, *Prisons*, p. 80.

[115] Interrogation of Lieutenant Mortimer, 5 December 1761, TNA, ADM105/42, fo. 149.

if they found any to drive them down & send them into the upperCourt to Muster.... About 5 weeks ago as I was stand.^{g} at the Window in the Off.^{s} G.^{d} Room I saw one of the P.^{rs} at a great distance behind the rest & seemingly unwilling to go to his Ward. I heard one of the Sold.^{rs} call to him desiring him to join the rest which he did not obey. The soldier went back to him & gave him a blow with the flat of his Hangers between the shoulders upon which he immed.^{y} joined the other P.^{rs} & thinking the Soldier did no more than his duty I said nothing to him for striking the P.^{r}.

Invited to specify what he meant by 'driving the prisoners'—a term used for describing the act of forcefully conducting men or cattle—Mortimer explained himself: 'My mean.^{g} is to follow them rather than drive them, but if any P.^{r} loiter behind & do not obey orders We then allow the Soldiers to drive them on.' Likewise, to clear a crowd of prisoners who would not obey their orders, sentries would customarily hit them with the flat of their swords.[116] Informal norms authorized and even encouraged physical violence, as a legitimate tactic of control of the prisoners.[117] Discretionary practices were recognized as acceptable by militia officers when they aimed at maintaining order through the 'smooth running of routine', i.e. 'the organization of activity in its proper times and places'.[118] Conversely, a prisoner's infraction of the routine, by refusing to be counted or being late in his ward at night, could be seen as an act of resistance to the authority, justifying coercion. However, norms of tolerance to violence changed over time and place. The distinction between legitimate violence, defined in terms of discipline, and maltreatment, which supposed cruel, illegal, and extreme violence, varied considerably.[119] Some categories of prisoners could expect more lenient treatment than others. In the 1770s, at Forton Prison, the sentries turned a blind eye on the daily escapes of Americans. The reluctance of the commanding officers to authorize firing on people who were still seen as compatriots certainly played a part in this.[120]

Equally, the prisoners' horizons of expectation influenced how they interpreted the actions of their guards. For instance, 'the sense of being hurried along' several times a day to be counted, which the staff justified in terms of security, was often viewed as an unnecessary 'control over [the prisoners'] environment'.[121] For military men, being subjected to the authority of foreigners was difficult to swallow, and the prison routine multiplied potential slights of honour. While

---

[116] Ibid., fos. 149–50, 150v.
[117] Marquart, 'Prison guards', pp. 359–60.   [118] Sparks, Bottoms, and Hay, *Prisons*, pp. 81–2.
[119] Neither 'mistreatment' nor 'maltreatment' appear in Samuel Johnson's *Dictionary of the English Language* (1755 and 1785 ed.).
[120] According to Commissioner Bell, sent by the S&W to Forton, the commanding officer 'had no orders for the Guards Loading and Firing in any Case of necessity': 30 June 1777, TNA, ADM98/11, fo. 55.
[121] Sparks, Bottoms, and Hay, *Prisons*, p. 190.

most prisoners of war came from a world in which hierarchy, physical coercion, and obedience were omnipresent, one should not underestimate the obligation of answering one's name when called by a foreign soldier or prison official. The roll-call was particularly resented by officers and gentlemen, as indicated by this letter addressed by a British army captain detained in France to Colonel Bertrand, commanding the Auxonne depot for prisoners of war in 1810: 'I have the honour to inform you that, in my quality of captain of infantry, I have never been subjected to roll-call in any of the depots I have been.' At Auxonne the muster took place twice daily, and sometimes three times a day.[122] Likewise, while staff discretion was legitimate and necessary in the eyes of the prison authorities, the line between discretion and arbitrariness was a fine one from the prisoners' viewpoint.[123] The prisoners' expectation to be treated fairly, respectfully, and consistently is key in explaining why they obeyed rules in prison.[124]

The length of detention was a constant bone of contention. Tensions always ran high at the time of release from prison, and when the prisoners' hopes were hampered, it became near-impossible to quiet them down. In 1707, a cartel vessel landed in Dover, ready to embark more than 190 French prisoners detained in the Castle. As they were marching towards the ship, the winds turned and the captain decided that it was too dangerous to come out of the port. Told to return to their compounds, the prisoners started a 'sedition'.[125] They 'insulted the guard', from whom they 'snatched with violence two Muskets'. As the rioters were throwing 'big rocks and hurt some soldiers', order was given to fire on them: two were killed.[126] In 1745, the Agent for the Spanish prisoners at Portchester, William Rickman, faced the French prisoners' 'insolence and insurrections' because of a rumour (apparently ungrounded) that he had preferred to put Spaniards instead of Frenchmen on board a cartel transport ship intended for French prisoners returning home.[127] Likewise, the Agent at Yarmouth requested in 1756 that a military guard be sent to the prison, fearing 'a Rising amongst the Prisoners daily, for they...are a set of stout Desperate Fellows; no ship is come for them though the Wind is fair'.[128] While stopping short of excusing the prisoners, his final words betrayed the Agent's acknowledgment that the prisoners' behaviour was far from irrational.

The prisoners' sense of injustice revolved around the idea that they were not treated as well as they should. Some riots were thus set off by the prisoners' perception that they had been treated unfairly by comparison with other French prisoners, in another prison.[129] What happened in Plymouth in 1756 is a good

[122] Anonymous to Colonel Bertrand, [November] 1810, Appendix No. IX, *Sketches* (1818), pp. 92–3.
[123] Sparks, Bottoms, and Hay, *Prisons*, p. 167.   [124] Ibid., pp. 87–9.
[125] Chasteauneuf to SSM, Calais, 1 July 1707, AN, MAR/B3/143, fo. 48v.
[126] Report by the S&W, 16 June 1707, ibid., fo. 52v.
[127] Extract of Vice Admiral Stewart to Corbett, 14 May 1745, NMM, ADM/M/391.
[128] Extract of Colby to S&W, 25 September 1756, TNA, ADM98/5, fo. 220.
[129] Sparks, Bottoms, and Hay, *Prisons*, p. 80.

example of this. The immediate cause of the riot was the distribution of the French King's bounty. The prisoners at Plymouth had received a letter from their comrades at Portsmouth informing them that their bounty was inferior to what was paid in that port, and they started to become agitated.[130] The Agent 'ordered them all in Yard to Muster', and 'cautioned them to behave well, as those should be punished who were noisy or disorderly', and to express their demands 'in a mild manner'. Attempting to exonerate himself, he explained that the decision was entirely in the hands of the French King's representatives, but failed to convince the prisoners, who claimed that he had cheated them. Things then unravelled quickly:

> One said he wou'd cut my Ears off; I took hold of him that said it, and was bringing him to the Officer of the Guard, who was near, when they pushed upon me in a Mutinous Noisy Manner, and rescued him from me, swearing they would not be mustered.

It was only when military reinforcements entered the prison that the prisoners surrendered. The 'ringleaders' were punished and the 'mutiny' was suppressed.[131]

There seemed to exist a prisoner of war 'culture', in the sense of shared knowledge and expectations about material conditions of detention, which travelled from one war prison to another. This complicates the binary opposition often drawn between the inside and the outside of a prison. There are many examples of this common knowledge, which was gained by accretion, as waves of prisoners came and left one prison to go to another. At Sissinghurst in Kent, some of the French prisoners of war interrogated in December 1761 by Commissioner Maxwell mentioned their experiences in other prisons. Prisoner Masson expected, because of his previous detention in Portchester, that the Agent at Sissinghurst would listen to his demands regarding the quality of beef and bread.[132] Jean Pierre Joseph Bruère complained that the prisoners were served meat of inferior quality. He based his judgement not on the conformity to prison rules, but on an equality of treatment between French prisoners in Britain and British prisoners in France: 'He has no other reason but it is not just to serve the necks & shanks as in other P.[ns] it is not done.... Because English P.[rs] have told him, that it is not done in France, & he has seen it served himself at Calais.' Jean Berurier explained that he had seen the prison rules put up at Kinsale in Ireland and Berwick-upon-Tweed in Northumberland, but not at Sissinghurst. Pierre Teinot signed the collective memorandum to the French authorities because it aimed to 'do them Justice as it should', because 'they are not treated as in the other P.[ns]'.[133] In this reasoning,

[130] Agent at Plymouth to S&W, 27 July 1756, TNA, ADM98/5, fos. 185v–186.
[131] Ibid., fos. 186, 186v.
[132] Masson's cross-examination, 21 November 1761, TNA, ADM105/42, fo. 8.
[133] Bruère, 28 November 1761, ibid., vo. 88; Berurier, 28 November 1761, fo. 85; Teinot, 25 November 1761, fo. 64.

direct observation in the prison where they were detained, the testimonies of other prisoners elsewhere, and external norms such as the laws of war, helped to determine whether one's treatment was fair.

So far, I have assumed that prisoners of war knew the rules of the game, and that they only ever disobeyed the guards and the sentries because they had chosen to do so. In fact, getting used to captivity was never straightforward, and it always took time to understand what the custodians expected. It was even more complicated for civilians, such as the merchant seamen detained in the French depots during the Napoleonic Wars. In his prison narrative, Farrell Mulvey, an Irish surgeon, described this uncertainty:

> When first a man is made prisoner, he has to encounter a new mode of life. In whatever depot he may be placed, he is necessarily under control, and his ignorance of the language, and of forms and manners different from his own, make him fall into many errors, that may be injurious to him, and render his captivity more rigorous. In some depots, the slightest misconception of a written or verbal order,...would...lead to the Souterreins of Bitche.[134]

For merchant mariners, who 'had never been accustomed to such discipline', the lack of obedience to prison orders was not always the sign of outright hostility, but of their ignorance of the tacit rules governing prison society.[135] By contrast, military men were better prepared for their sojourn in prison. Obeying institutional rules was not an alien experience for soldiers and sailors, not least because some of the rules adopted in war prisons were inspired by military or naval regulations. In sum, the process of acculturation was much easier for some prisoners.

C. Legal Consequences

Whenever jailors and sentries were accused of abusing their position of power, they tended to deny everything outright. They could count on the *esprit de corps* of the army, which closed ranks. The version of the accused was normally backed with explanations post facto. At Sissinghurst prison, Lieutenant Thomas Cooper was accused of beating up, robbing and insulting the prisoners; his colleagues vouched for him. Another lieutenant, Deacon, considered that 'they w.^{d} not have used the P.^{rs} ill here if they had not deserved it'.[136] The ethos of the

---

[134] Mulvey, *Sketches*, pp. 15–16. Bitche was a military fortress where the most recalcitrant of prisoners were sent: Lewis, *Napoleon*, pp. 142–8.
[135] Mulvey, *Sketches*, p. 37.   [136] Deacon, 4 December 1761, TNA, ADM105/42, fo. 155v.

group provided a show of solidarity to the outside world, in order to void the procedure.[137]

The soldiers could also rely on the passivity of the Agent, who often closed his eyes instead of arbitrating the disputes between prisoners and soldiers. When he was asked why the prisoners did not use their right to call the Agent for help, prisoner Charles Maquet replied: 'We have complained a hundred times… but never were heard anymore than if We were nothing.' The Agent's diffidence gave sentries a free hand. Maquet also described his conversation with a soldier who had beaten him black and blue: 'I asked them why did he beat me in that manner, & told him that I would make my Complaint. He said that I might go & complain to the Devil & then drove me down Stairs.'[138] The contestation of the Agent's authority rebounded on his subordinates, clerks, turnkeys, or surgeons.[139] These problems were not specific to Sissinghurst: they were structural to the government of the prisons. The attributions of the Agent were never clarified and agreed to by all sides.[140]

It was one thing to hit a prisoner who insulted you; another to kill him. The actions of soldiers were partly determined by the penalties they incurred, and partly by the jurisdiction on which they depended. They could thus hesitate between several options. And, as shown by their depositions after such incidents, they understood how justice worked. In October 1747, the following orders were read to the regiment guarding Kinsale Prison in Ireland, where 1,346 French and Spanish prisoners were kept at the time: 'The first centry who suffers any prisoner to escape near his post, shall be court martialled and severely punished for neglect of duty.'[141] The common punishment for this was a certain number of lashes. The commanding officer of the regiment even 'gave a hint, that if any prisoner was kill'd endeavouring to make his escape, [he] should be glad of it'.[142] But if the sentinel shot a prisoner trying to escape, he was to be judged by a civil court, and he risked hanging for murder.[143] Even in such cases, soldiers did their utmost to be examined by courts martial, knowing (rightly) that verdicts would be more lenient.[144]

Murder, like robbery, forgery, or theft, was not categorized as a military crime because it was 'non-threatening to the army in particular'.[145] By contrast,

---

[137] Marquart, 'Prison guards', p. 355.

[138] Interrogation of Maquet, 1 December 1761, TNA, ADM105/42, fos. 104–v, 106v.

[139] The soldiers put the prisoners in the black hole 'at their pleasure', without consulting with the Agent as was their duty: interrogation of Atkins, turnkey, 4 December 1761, ibid., fo. 138v.

[140] Anderson, 'Treatment', p. 81. See ch. 5.

[141] 'An Extract from the Adjutant's [sic] Book, of the Orders given by Major Monro, Commanding Lieu.ᵗ Gen.ˡ Otway's Regiment in Kinsale', in Major Monro to Lord Lieutenant of Ireland, 30 October 1747, NMM, ADM/M/400, no. 365/5. This was adopted following the escape of seventeen prisoners: S&W to LCA, 7 October 1747, TNA, ADM98/4, fos. 156v–157.

[142] Monro to Lord Lieutenant, 30 October 1747, NMM, ADM/M/400, no. 365/1.

[143] Gilbert, 'Military', p. 46.   [144] Steppler, 'British military law'.

[145] Gilbert, 'Military', p. 46.

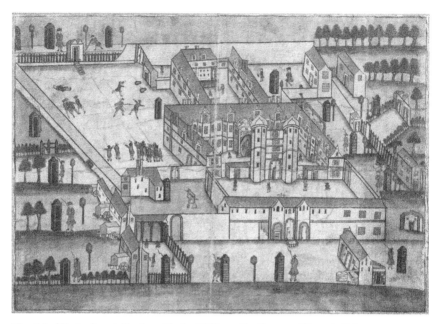

Fig. 6.1. 'Sissinghurst Castle with the Killing of a Group of French Prisoners at Sissinghurst Castle Garden, Kent' [1761]. National Trust.

deserting, arguing with your officer or falling asleep while on sentry duty were prosecuted by courts martial. Criminal law itself was ambiguous in this regard. Sir Matthew Hale, Chief Justice, thus wrote in his classic treatise, which was regularly republished until the nineteenth century, that 'if a man kills an alien enemy within this kingdom, yet it is felony, unless it be in the heat of war, and in the actual exercise thereof'. But, he added, this time with reference to criminals, 'if the prisoners in gaol assault the gaoler, and he in his defense kills any of them, this is no felony, nor makes any forfeiture'.[146] Although Hale was not talking about soldiers or prisoners of war specifically, they fell under his definition. In reality, there was a grey area, which was particularly apparent with regard to the 'civil duty' of army sentinels who were in charge of guarding prisoners of war.[147]

Sissinghurst Prison is again a good observatory of these practices, because, between 1758 and 1761, four incidents led to the death of prisoners killed by sentries.[148] This violence was depicted in a contemporary drawing by an anonymous prisoner (Fig. 6.1). In no instance were the killers condemned. The first victim was Fernandino Gratez, from Dunkirk, killed one morning in November 1758 for hanging out his laundry on a fence. The Sick & Wounded Board, once informed,

[146] Hale, *Historia*, vol. I, ch. 33, p. 433.   [147] Tytler, *Essay*, pp. 127–8, 207.
[148] See Morieux, 'Dilemme'.

let justice follow its course; a court martial acquitted the sentry.[149] In July 1761, the sentry John Branston fired his musket in the direction of a prisoner, missing his target and fatally wounding two others who were watching. The prisoners who had witnessed the scene declared that Branston had fired without warning.[150] A coroner (a civil magistrate), was sent to Sissinghurst to certify the death of the two prisoners: he ordered an investigation and convened a jury to determine whether Branston should be tried in the assizes.[151] The jury 'acquitted the Soldier as doing no more than his Duty according to the General Orders at the Castle'.[152] This was always the reason invoked for acquittal.[153] In most cases, sentries were cleared before a judicial process was even conducted. In Stapleton Prison (Bristol) for instance, a Spanish prisoner was shot and killed by a sentinel in 1780; his body was buried before the Agent or the coroner could see it.[154] Similar offenses led to the same verdicts during the Napoleonic Wars.[155]

Acquittals were so common that French authorities were under no illusion that they would obtain justice in such instances. In 1744, the Commissioners for the Sick & Wounded Seamen informed Givry, their counterpart in Dunkirk, that a Frenchman detained at Dover Castle had been 'unfortunately killed' by a sentry on 15 November while taking part in a mutiny. They left no room for ambiguity as to the reasons why this had occurred. The sentry, who, unsurprisingly, had done 'his duty' and behaved 'like a soldier', had been provoked by prisoners who had only themselves to blame. In the British version of events, the prisoners appeared to have made trouble for the sake of it. The commissioners preferred to pass over the cause of this discontent: the prisoners had retaliated after a sentry had killed one of them a few days before.[156] The entire responsibility for the riots was put on the prisoners, and the Board even suggested that it was the French government's responsibility to keep its men on a tighter leash, which might 'prevent... in part similar accidents in the future'.[157] In the margin of this letter, Givry commented that there was no point asking for redress, since the British army was both judge and jury.[158] The French commissaire preferred a structural explanation for the

---

[149] Interrogation of Cooke, 8 December 1761, TNA, ADM105/42, fo. 163v.

[150] Interrogations of prisoners Bazire, Caillou, Allardine de Maisonneuve, 2 December 1761, ibid., fos. 120–6.

[151] Interrogation of Cooke, 4 December 1761, ibid., fos. 140–v.

[152] 'Heads of Mr. Cooke's Informations to the B.d of P.rs of War at Sissinghurst being shot by the Centry', ibid.

[153] Copy of Guillaume Slaughter, Plymouth, to Lempereur, 13 November 1706, AN, MAR/B3/135, fo. 339v.

[154] 19 September 1780, TNA, ADM98/13, fos. 41v–42.

[155] Walker, Depot, pp. 150–1, 159.

[156] 'Extracts of a letter from Major Bell, of Lieutenant General Harrison's Regiment', Dover, 14 November 1744, TNA, ADM98/2, fo. 41v.

[157] S&W to Givry, 20 November 1744, AN, MAR/B3/421, fo. 417v.

[158] Ibid. In 1746, the S&W noted that French officials had never written to them to complain about such incidents; the British government should do the same: S&W to LCA, 18 November 1746, TNA, ADM98/4, fo. 29v. See also 'Mémoire touchant les prisonniers français en Angleterre',

riots: if prisoners of war were treated in the same way in Dover as in France, English sentries 'would not be reduced to the necessity of shooting them'.[159]

The systematic exculpation of the sentries by their superiors and their government also had the effect of diminishing the protections that prisoners were entitled to as per international law. In the spring of 1708, when an English prisoner who was trying to escape from Dinan Castle was killed by a sentry, and another almost died while breaking his legs falling over the high walls, Commissaire Lempereur wrote to the French secretary of state for the *Marine* that he would order reports to be drawn up, adding:

> However, this precaution does not seem necessary to me, especially since they do not make such a fuss and since last year, following my complaints that one of their sentries had killed one of our prisoners in Plymouth, they were satisfied to reply that they had inquired about it and that it was proven that the sentry had done his duty.[160]

This sense of impunity gave the sentries a feeling of omnipotence. To return to Sissinghurst: the sentry John Branston, who had shot and killed two prisoners in 1761, did not keep a low profile. Three days later, as he was held on custody in the guardroom, he found himself next to prisoners recaptured after attempting their escape. One of them, Captain Macquet, narrated his conversation with Branston:

> I asked him why he killed the two man, he answered that if he had killed more it would not have given him any uneasiness. I asked if he was P.ʳ in France if he would like to be treated in that manner, [*comment in margin:* spoke in English] he sayd he would not have anymore Pity on us that if We were dogs.[161]

Through these degrading comparisons, Branston openly proclaimed his contempt for the status of prisoner of war: for him, Frenchmen remained worthless enemies. Ten days after the tragic incident, he was back at his post, and he 'threatened if he heard the least noise or walking in the Wards he would kill more than 10 of the P.ʳˢ'. A month later, Branston was seen parading, a bayonet in one hand and a stick in the other, and 'sayd he had killed 2 P.ʳˢ already & he would kill more before he went away'.[162] It took many more provocations before he was finally

London, February 1763, Archives du Ministère des Affaires Etrangères, La Courneuve (AMAE), CPA449, fo. 339.

---

[159] Givry, margin of S&W's letter, 20 November 1744, AN, MAR/B3/421, fo. 417.
[160] Lempereur to SSM, 13 May 1708, MAR/B3/157, fos. 172v–173.
[161] Interrogation of Capitaine Macquet, 3 December 1761, TNA, ADM105/42, fos. 129v–130.
[162] Interrogation of Pierre Jean Cousan and Million de Villeroy, 4 December 1761, ibid., fos. 135v–136.

relieved of his duties.[163] From this, we might conclude that the power of the custodians was boundless. In fact, Branston had gone too far. His erratic actions alienated him from other British soldiers: local norms of behaviour aimed to prevent escapes, but they did not endorse murder. After Branston's acquittal, the officers on duty in Sissinghurst conveyed their uneasiness to the Agent.[164] His fellow soldiers also broke ranks with him, and decided to warn the Frenchmen: 'the other soldiers of that Regim.^t told the P.^rs to be carefull of that Soldier for he was resolved to kill them all.'[165] The sentry had crossed a line: killing prisoners in cold blood was an assassination, not an act of war or self-defence. As we can see from this example, the soldiers expressed their dissatisfaction with a legal verdict which condoned the wrongful behaviour of one of their comrades. They preferred to cross the normative boundary with the French prisoners, in order to maintain order in the prison.

Prisoners did not necessarily blame carceral violence on sentries only. In his prison narrative, Farrell Mulvey, who was detained at Auxonne and Longwy during the Napoleonic Wars, lamented the recourse to collective punishments, but he chose to absolve individual sentries: 'the French soldiery, though in general very civil, both in speech and manners, are sometimes forced to commit acts, for which they are by no means so blameable as those who give the orders.' Mulvey did not pass over the fate of many prisoners who had been wounded or killed 'on trivial pretences of misconduct', or false accusations by soldiers. But in the end, such displays of violence on the ground were only possible because the bad example had been set from above: 'power, which is not easily borne even by the most self-controlled, becomes galling in the extreme, when in the hands of incapacity and meanness.'[166] An alternative to violence existed.

IV. Crossing the Boundary

Gresham Sykes and Erving Goffman have described the 'vicious circle' or 'looping effect', by which the prison guard has to punish misbehaviours that originate in his own attempt to apply the law indiscriminately, unleashing a spiral of violence.[167] The attempt to avoid this situation by bending the rules or ignoring them altogether explains that the bargain to 'keep the peace' is endemic to the prison structure.[168] While such practices take place in every institution of confinement, some of them were specific to the situation of war imprisonment.

[163] Interrogation of François Bazire, 2 December 1761, ibid., fos. 121v–122.
[164] 'Heads of Mr. Cooke's Informations to the Board', ibid.
[165] Pierre Jean Cousan, 4 December 1761, ibid., fos. 135v–136.
[166] Mulvey, Sketches, pp. 17, 86, 18, 34.   [167] Sykes, Society, p. 22; Goffman, Asylums, p. 41.
[168] Sykes, Society, pp. 47, 257–62. Cressey talks about 'unofficial arrangements': 'Introduction', The Prison, p. 3. See more recently Crewe, 'Soft power'.

A. 'The Corruption of Authority'

The 'structural weakness' of the government of prisons lies in the need to obtain the prisoners' cooperation to maintain internal order—what Sykes describes as the 'corruption of authority'.[169] In some situations, prison officials deliberately transgressed the officer's and the inmate's codes, i.e. the unwritten attitudes and rules of behaviour that dictated that group members should stick together and not fraternize with the 'other side'.[170]

The balance between coercion and corruption was fragile, as illustrated by the attitude of the governor of the Saumur prison during the American War of Independence. In Saumur (in the Loire region) the prison warden, Dupetit Thouard, was accused by Fayolle, one of his subordinates, of betraying his duty by lending a sympathetic ear to the pleas of the prisoners. In the hospital, he would, for instance, support sick prisoners against the medical staff: 'he brings himself food to the sick, helps and provokes their complaints and supports them in all their requests to the extent that they throw the allowance ordered by the physician to the face of nurses who they often mistreat.' After a drunken man had assaulted a male nurse, he was put in jail and on bread and broth, but Dupetit Thouard overruled this order and released him. The prison governor's preference for compromise over coercion caused more serious disorders:

> He has been forced 8 days ago to yield to a little rumour that had arisen after he tried to have a mutineer arrested who was not punished and [he] contented himself to make representations the following day, in writing [and with] plenty of indulgences for the prisoners. Such a lack of firmness can be very dangerous, Monseigneur, with men who ceaselessly threaten to bring down the castle.[171]

Rioting tarnished the prison governor by association. More worryingly, he was reluctant to police the prisoners, despite the availability of a large number of soldiers in Saumur. Since the Seven Years' War, the brigade of the royal corps of *carabiniers* was garrisoned in this town. As many as 1,200 men and officers lived in the barracks erected in 1768, and this number increased in the following years.[172] But only twelve *carabiniers* 'and half a dozen of old Invalids who are not worth a punch' were mobilized to watch over the 800 prisoners detained at Saumur Castle.[173] Although their commander at Saumur, the Chevalier de Montaigu, was willing to double the number of soldiers, Dupetit Thouard considered that he had enough guards at his disposal. This imbalance naturally led to what Goffman calls practices of 'crossing the line'.[174] Soldiers socialized with the

[169] Sykes, *Society*, pp. 61, 127.   [170] Kauffman, 'Officer code'.

[171] 25 July 1779, AN, MAR/F2/82.   [172] Bodin, *Recherches historiques*, vol. II, pp. 367–8, 375.

[173] 25 July 1779, AN, MAR/F2/82.   [174] Goffman, *Asylums*, p. 90.

prisoners, and often left the guardroom empty: 'the *carabiniers* walk about or drink at the canteen with the prisoners, while weapons are at the disposal of those who are in the yards.'

A day after writing his report, the author of these recriminations against the governor hastily put his pen at the end of the document, narrating how the situation had unravelled. The governor's inaction was once again at fault. The fire had been sparked, as often in such cases, by a trifling incident, after a prisoner had stolen a turkey at the canteen. When the guards tried to punish him, 'his comrades have resisted, have forced the guard, snatched the culprit from their hands and even collared some *carabiniers*'. This 'very considerable riot' was only appeased after the governor was forced to go and reason in person with the 'mutineers', in his night dress.[175]

The last sentence seems to contradict all the preceding remarks, about the governor's responsibility in the troubles. After all, it could be argued that the riot was only tamed in the end thanks to the direct intervention of Dupetit Thouard and his negotiation with the prisoners, not because of his passivity. Of course, these interpretations are not mutually exclusive, and explanations for collective disorders in prison continue to divide sociologists.[176] The so-called inmate-balance theory developed by Sykes and others in the late 1950s posits that prison officials are guilty of disrupting the fragile 'social equilibrium' reigning in prison, which depends upon the informal delegation of authority to the inmates. By tightening security measures and cracking down on illegal activities, custodians are the primary cause of riots. In the 1980s, as the prison population boomed in the United States, an alternative interpretation, called the administrative-control theory, was advanced. It argues that riots, far from being caused by over-zealous discipline, are the by-product of the weakness of prison authorities. In this second model, the guards are guilty of not exercising fully their power of 'administrative sanction' over the prisoners. The problem is compounded by a lessening sense of *esprit de corps* among custodians, and this administrative breakdown weakens the legitimacy of the guards, in the eyes of the prisoners, which renders the occurrence of riots more likely. While the discussion clearly had a contemporary political and ideological component,[177] its implications are pertinent for this study: as our analysis of eighteenth-century war prisons riots demonstrates, riot and corruption must be placed on a continuum.

B. Extortion and Corruption

Prison staff commonly engaged in illicit economic exchanges with the prisoners. Although the practices of prison officials lower down the hierarchy of

---

[175] 25 July 1779, AN, MAR/F2/82.
[176] This paragraph is based on Carrabine, 'Riots'; Useem and Reisig, 'Collective action'.
[177] See Thompson, *Blood.*

employment, those in direct contacts with the inmates, are the focus here, it is worth remembering that wars were always a great opportunity to make money. In 1744, the words used by the *commissaire de la Marine* in St Malo Guillot, in a letter to the secretary of state for the *Marine*, give an idea of the scale of corruption:

> I can only be very grateful to the efforts you have made to prevent the abuses proceeding from different usages, which during previous wars benefited the governor, the staff-officers, the *commis aux classes* of Dinan and even the *commissaire de la Marine* of St Malo.[178]

Purchasing foodstuffs and everyday items of clothing was not easy for prisoners of war. Most of their income usually came from allowances received from their own state; this money was transferred to Agents in the prisons, who in turn distributed it to them.[179] But prisoners of war had to buy goods from local contractors, who had a monopoly on the prison trade, and over whom the central state had little control. While the state's scrutiny increased with time, abuses were continual—not least because turnkeys were legally entitled to make money out of the prisoners.[180] Among their privileges was the 'tap', i.e. the permission to sell small beer to the prisoners and keep the profit.[181] Such practices were normal, and accepted in eighteenth-century prisons. But prisoners of war depended on Agents and turnkeys in more than one way: the men in charge of distributing their allowances also fixed the price of the commodities they bought.

In 1696, following complaints from French prisoners at Plymouth, Monsieur de Gastines, the commissaire in St Malo, compared the conditions of captivity in Plymouth and Dinan.[182] French prisoners in Plymouth were forced to buy 'Provisions commodities or refreshments only from the hands of the Jailor or from prisoners who had paid him large fees so that everything they buy costs them three times what it costs which is an evident Concussion and absolutely contrary to the laws and Freedom of England'.[183] Butter, cheese, tobacco, and even well water were sold for an extortionate price. Prisoners who wanted to be released also had to pay for their exchange.[184] These wrongdoings did not happen in Dinan, wrote Gastines, because the prisoners were given sufficient allowances and were

---

[178] Guillot to SSM, 25 September 1744, AN, MAR/B2/323, fos. 119–v.
[179] S&W to LCA, 24 January 1744, TNA, ADM98/2, fo. 97v. The only exceptions were Dover, Portsmouth, and Plymouth, which were visited by a member of the S&W Board two or three times a year, and Falmouth and Bristol, which had been visited once.
[180] This was legal in British prisons until 1775: Beattie, *Crime*, pp. 289–91; Finn, *Character*, pp. 116–7, 134–8.
[181] During the American War of Independence, John Stacey was a turnkey at Portchester Castle as well as the proprietor of a public house, in town: Chamberlain, *Hell*, p. 36.
[182] Gastines, 'Mémoire', 4 July 1696, AN, MAR/B4/17, fos. 434–6.   [183] Ibid., fo. 434.
[184] Ibid., fos. 435–6.

released without haggling. Monsieur Brilac similarly wrote from Dinan, in 1705, that the scarcity of the rations forced the prisoners at Plymouth to buy them at any price from the gaoler, despite their meagre revenues.[185] In reality, these practices continued throughout the period on both sides of the Channel. Bribing jailors remained a very common way to move forward one's turn to be exchanged.[186] This shows how decentralized the administration of war captivity really was: choosing which prisoners would remain in detention and which would be freed depended not so much on decisions taken at the central level, but on the preferences of individual jailors.

This was common knowledge on the part of the officials in charge of the exchange of prisoners of war. As Du Guay, the commissaire at Dunkirk, put it candidly in November 1744, 'there is no advantage, for either power, to keep their prisoners, only jailors and sutlers profit from this, and subjects mutually suffer.'[187] The French administrator had a point. Because jailors were often also contractors, corruption was rife.[188] In 1745, Commissaire Roux wrote from Morlaix that a new contract for feeding prisoners of war had been passed 'to remedy the striking abuses' which 'the whole town' was aware of,[189] while the following year Guillot described the contractors at Dinan as 'beggars and untrustworthy in every respect'.[190] Many men no doubt abused their privileged position as intermediaries between these foreigners and the prison administration. At Bayonne, British prisoners complained that they had to pay twenty-two sols per month for food and lodging; they 'imputed this monopoly' to an English merchant settled in the French port, 'who writes for the Jailor and occupies the function of inter-preter'.[191] Tellingly, in 1782 an edict was passed by the Parliament of Rennes to forbid the selling of food, drinks, and goods to prisoners of war at prohibitive prices.[192] While these practices were common in every prison, prisoners of war, who could not count on the support of their families, were even more dependent than others. However, as we saw, prisoners of war were not power-less, and their appeals outside the prison against such monopolies were often successful.[193]

---

[185] SSM to Brilac, 24 June 1705, AN, MAR/B2/181, fos. 792v–793.

[186] Gastines to SSM, 11 July 1694, MAR/B3/82, fo. 153v; copy of Lempereur to S&W, 9 February 1706, MAR/B3/135, fo. 71; Lempereur to S&W, 16 October 1709, MAR/B3/169, fo. 324v; S&W to LCA, 16 September 1748, TNA, ADM98/4, fos. 247–8v.

[187] Du Guay to SSM, 11 November 1744, AN, MAR/B3/421, fo. 380.

[188] SSM to Lempereur, 4 March 1711, MAR/B2/226, fo. 740v.

[189] Roux to SSM, 12 March 1745, MAR/B3/432, fo. 404.

[190] Guillot to SSM, 7 January 1746, MAR/B3/445, fo. 13.

[191] SSM to De la Courtaudière, 22 April 1746, MAR/B2/328, fo. 460.

[192] Edict of Parliament of Rennes, 26 January 1782, in Guichard, Code, p. 224. See also 'Regulations for the management of French Prisoners in Great Britain' [1757], article 8, TNA, SP42/136.

[193] The turnkey at Dover Castle was dismissed for monopolizing 'the Suttling to himself': Investi-gation following Givry [commissaire at Dunkirk]'s complaints about conditions at Dover Castle, 7 December 1744, ADM98/2, fos. 54–v.

Exeter Prison, which was fitted for 800 prisoners, is a good example of how deeply entrenched corruption was.[194] In November 1747, the Admiralty began an enquiry into the conduct of the Agent, Joseph Crew, suspected of having committed multiple frauds in his management of the prison and the hospital.[195] Crew faced thirty-three charges of misconduct.[196] He expertly monetized the most menial of the 'services' he rendered the prisoners. He pocketed the fines he charged them with for misbehaving, or put them on half-allowance without entering it in his books, claiming the difference.[197] He granted parole to people 'who were not entitled to it, on their paying money; and others, who were entitled to it, have been refused till such time as they have paid for it'.[198] The Agent vehemently denied all these accusations, blaming his subordinates, adding that 'no class of gentlemen acting in any publick capacity whatsoever, could have a greater abhorrence, or detestation, of being prompted to do any thing for the sake of any reward, gratuity, or any mercenary views whatsoever'. If he had done wrong, his 'humane compassion' was to blame.[199] Crew developed with the prisoners a patron–client relationship,[200] using his position of contractor, alongside that of Agent, to keep sick prisoners in the hospital for weeks after they had been cured, and in the meantime employed them in grinding malt for his profit, for one penny a man a day.[201] He was dismissed in October 1748.[202] Despite having so many of these dubious achievements to his name, Crew managed to delay the final verdict for years, but he was deposed and bankrupted as a result of his embezzlements.[203] However shocking Crew's behaviour might seem, he was only partly to blame: Crew was not paid any salary, and the Sick & Wounded Board had noted with approval, back in 1746, that he 'is Satisfied, and we believe may very well be so, with the Profits arising from [his] Victualling of the Prisoners', an arrangement which saved expenses to the crown.[204]

In October 1779, the Agent for Liverpool, Oliphant, was accused of 'irregularities of conduct' by the prisoners, who believed that they were cheated on the

[194] The figure is given in S&W to LCA, 27 October 1747, ADM98/4, fo. 166.

[195] S&W, 'Report of proceedings upon informations against Mr. Joseph Crew', 27 January 1748, BL, Lansdowne 820/7, fo. 89. Also S&W to LCA, 3 November 1747, TNA, ADM98/4, fos. 169–70.

[196] 'A. Copy of the Articles of Charge against Mr. Joseph Crew' and 'B. Copy of Mr. Crew's answers to the articles of his charge', in S&W to Henry Pelham Esq., 30 January 1748, BL, Lansdowne 820/7, fos. 95–122.

[197] 'C. Copy of the Boards' Resolutions upon the articles of charge against Mr. Crew', 27 January 1748, ibid., fo. 128.

[198] 'A. Copy of the Articles', ibid., fo. 100v.

[199] 'B. Copy of Mr. Crew's answers', ibid., fos. 120–v, 121–v.

[200] See Goffman, Asylums, pp. 252–8.

[201] 'C. Copy of the Boards' Resolutions', BL, Landsdowne 820/7, fos. 126–v.

[202] S&W to LCA, 13 October 1748, TNA, ADM98/4, fo. 251.

[203] In 1750, Crew was still contesting the verdict of the Admiralty: S&W to LCA, 1 May 1750, ADM98/5, fos. 52–3. His accounts were finally adjusted and the claims of his creditors settled thirteen years later: S&W to LCA, 22 July 1763, ADM98/9, fos. 200–1v.

[204] S&W to LCA, 10 November 1746, ADM98/4, fo. 26.

weight and quality of their meat allowance. He explained that 'he considered their provisions as a perquisite of office'. He had 'falsely charged' the government, with the contractor's help, for meat he never provided to the prisoners, but for which he had been paid.[205] Oliphant was discharged, and a hefty sum (£20) was distributed among the Frenchmen still in prison, for their troubles.[206] While it is difficult to quantify changes in levels of corruption over time, the American War of Independence certainly multiplied the opportunities for all those involved in the prisoners of war business to enrich themselves, in Europe as in the colonies. In the British West Indian islands, victualling, caring for, and housing the prisoners remained the responsibility of colonial governors, who often used this prerogative as a means of enriching themselves. Governor Burt in Antigua colluded with local contractors to overcharge the subsistence, medicine, and gaol fees of French and American prisoners 'confined in the common prison' in this island and St Christopher's, and then billed the Treasury for their reimbursement.[207] Agents in the West Indies were also suspected of overcharging their disbursements for prisoners of war.[208]

The scale of the turnkeys' corruption might be explained by their low allowances. In Britain, during the War of the Austrian Succession, the head turnkey at Kinsale was paid £25 a year, and the other turnkeys between 13 p and 16 p a day.[209] During the Seven Years' War, turnkeys in English war prisons earned a salary of £30 per annum.[210] While £30 would be enough to live on, it was not enough to deliver anyone from temptation. The allowances of turnkeys slightly increased during the following war. In Deal, Winchester, or Kinsale, they were paid £40 a year, while in Jamaica, when the system was not abused, they were normally paid £60.[211] In France, the income of prison keepers was often insufficient, despite the extra money they made by contracting food for the prisoners of war. Their main difficulty was to get the state to reimburse them, which could take months. In the meantime, they had to repay their creditors; those who did not have deep enough pockets would be bankrupt before the state machine got moving.[212]

---

[205] S&W to LCA, 19 October 1779, ADM98/12, fos. 113v, 114.   [206] Ibid., fos. 115v–116.
[207] LCA to S&W, 11 August 1780, NMM, ADM/M/410; S&W to LCA, 29 January, 21 August 1781, TNA, ADM98/13, fos. 109v, 223–4.
[208] As in Jamaica: S&W to LCA, 23 April, 5 May, 18 July 1783, TNA, ADM98/14, fos. 177v, 179v, 187v.
[209] LCA to S&W, 10 July 1744, NMM, ADM/M/388, no. 104; S&W, 'List, shewing the Number of Officers and others, . . . and their Salaries or Allowances', 6 June 1748, TNA, ADM98/4, fos. 225v–226.
[210] 'List of salaries and allowances', 10 August 1763, TNA, ADM98/9, fos. 207v–211. On turnkeys, see McConville, *History*, pp. 72–3, 77. £40 might be considered a borderline middle-class income: Langford, *Public Life*, p. 235.
[211] S&W to LCA, 23 February 1779, TNA, ADM98/11, fo. 232v; S&W to LCA, 'Particular showing the Expences . . . for . . . Prisoners of War', 29 October 1783, ADM98/14, fo. 200; S&W to LCA, 28 March 1783, ibid., fo. 171v.
[212] Du Guay to SSM, 24 April 1709, AN, MAR/B3/165, fo. 207v.

In Britain, the allowances of the Agents were much higher than those of turnkeys.[213] But this did not immunize them against the lure of easy money. Although enriching oneself on the job was seen as problematic by the middle of the century, this had not always been the case, and the idea of the agency as a sinecure endured for decades. Many prison officials did not have a sense that they were doing anything wrong, not least because the modern concept of corruption, as a crime against the state, was just beginning to be defined and addressed in our period. Abuses on such a large scale were only possible because, in prisons, so much power lay in the hands of so few individuals.[214] By the end of the eighteenth century, in Britain at least, the state's sensitivity to corruption at every level induced an increased scrutiny. This culminated in the *Instructions for Dispensers... for the Care and Custody of Prisoners of War at Home* (1808), which established bureaucratic practices that aimed to put an end to such illicit dealings.[215]

These affairs illustrate the tension, which ran within the state, between two conceptions of order that should be maintained in prison. Inside the prison, turnkeys and Agents saw no contradiction between their duty of overseeing prisoners of war and treating them like cash cows. This conception probably owed a great deal to the fact that these men had in mind how normal prisons were run as business ventures. Outside the prison, the Sick & Wounded Board, just like their French counterparts, objected to these abuses; they were preoccupied with the well-being of prisoners of war. While the historiography has focused on the 'humanitarianism' of these administrators, praising their aversion to human suffering, there were other reasons for their concern. The fear of retaliation against one's own prisoners, the danger of epidemics, and military and financial concerns, all converged: prisoners of war were just too valuable a resource for the state to be wasted.

In the complex world of the war prison, social and political divisions could run through both sides of the boundary between guards and inmates.

C. The Prisoners' Dilemma

Prisoners knew when to close ranks. Retaliating against a prisoner who had betrayed comrades was common practice. In January 1744, a prisoner in Plymouth, Raymond Kewe, informed on some of his escaped comrades, in exchange

---

[213] They ranged between £50 and £200 per annum, depending on the type of prison (temporary or permanent detention) and their occupation rate from the American War of Independence onwards: S&W to LCA, 23 February 1779, TNA, ADM98/11, fos. 232v–233; LCA to S&W, 21 April 1781, NMM, ADM/M/405.

[214] Cressey, 'Introduction', *The Prison*, pp. 8–9.

[215] See, for example, 'FORM of an OATH, to be taken and subscribed by all Officers and Clerks at the Depôts for Prisoners of War', *Instructions for Dispensers*, Appendix 41. See also 'Instructions for Agents' (1807), article 50, p. 30.

for which he was rewarded with the liberty of the town on parole. He lived there happily for eight months, and even married an English woman. But 'upon some false information' given against him by other prisoners, he was incarcerated again.[216] This was the price he paid for having crossed the line between prisoner and custodian. Prison officials were well aware of the risk, and time and again tried to rescue the prisoners who were 'in danger of ill treatment' for having snitched on their comrades' illegal activities.[217] There were many means by which the prisoners could punish traitors among them. The mimicking of official sentences was part of the prison counter-theatre, which resembled popular politics more generally.[218] Thus, American prisoner George Thompson, detained in Forton, wrote in his diary in January 1779 how an informer had been lashed and publicly shamed:

> Jan. 24 Sunday ... in the afternoon 7 of the prisners was put in to the blak hole fore passing the Sentens on one Rodgers an Informer his Centens was 100 Strips after that thay was put in the Rest of thay prisners went and took the Informer out of the Cook Roum and husseld him over the Yard.[219]

The prison was a violent environment, and not just because of the guards. Ratting on one's companions in captivity was risky, and the ultimate punishment could be death.[220] By the same logic, prisoners could also choose to stand up to 'bad' jailors, refusing to abide by the logic of the punishment and reward system, as in Dinan in 1704: 'The English prisoners in Dinan in the Tour des Sillons have shut up with them a man named Macarty jailor who was doing his visit and walloped him.'[221] Instead of appealing to the prison hierarchy or writing to their government, these prisoners chose to take the matter into their own hands, squaring accounts with their tormentors. While such actions inevitably led to further punishments, they reasserted the boundaries with the guards.

However, most situations were muddier than this. A petition against a prison keeper, signed by dozens of prisoners of war, could be read in many ways. Prisoners could find themselves embroiled in internecine quarrels between Agents, contractors, and town officials, but they could also fall victim to arm-twisting by other prisoners. In the autumn of 1744, French prisoners in Falmouth (Cornwall) wrote two petitions to the Admiralty, accusing their Agent, named

---

[216] LCA to S&W, 10 January 1744, NMM, ADM/M/387, no. 1.
[217] TO's circular to agents, 11 June 1812, TNA, ADM98/170, fo. 138. See also TO to Cotgrave, 19 November 1810, ADM98/226, fo. 27v; 5 December 1812, ADM98/227, fo. 73v.
[218] See, for example, Shoemaker, *London Mob*, p. 275.
[219] Thompson, 'Diary', p. 225.
[220] Although we do not always know the causes for the murders of prisoners of war by other inmates, they happened on a regular basis, as in Dinan: St Sulpice to SSM, 30 January 1703, AN, MAR/B3/120, fo. 473; or in Portchester: Agent at Portsmouth to S&W, 19 June 1748, TNA, ADM98/4, fo. 227v.
[221] St Sulpice to SSM, 9 July 1704, AN, MAR/B3/123, fos. 544–v.

Pendar, of numerous misbehaviours. He had withheld half of their allowance of provisions, and threatened one prisoner that he would 'perish, either by length of imprisonment, or otherwise' for having dared to complaint of their bad treatment. The matter was taken seriously in London, and the Board prepared a heavy dossier, allowing the Lords of the Admiralty to reach an informed judgment of this case.[222] The evidence was presented in two tables, outlining the depositions for and against Pindar, under a dozen headings, ranging from the quantity and quality of food to the prisoners' 'treatment in general'.

The prisoners at Falmouth seemed to be completely divided over the matter. Twenty-five of them testified against the Agent. They did not mince their words. The dressing, according to four sailors, consisted of 'Beef blood raw Peases thin as Water, nasty & full of Grease being boiled with the [skewing] of the Pot the day before'.[223] All the deponents reported cases of cruelty. One prisoner had been so badly beaten by Pendar's servant that he died shortly after, as his wounds were left unattended by the surgeons. A sick man was 'neglected though [he] applied for assistance and died for want of it, having drank his own urine'.[224] One of the prisoners, named Beriet, was particularly angry at Pendar, who had first allowed him and others 'to walk the streets at large', paying them hand-somely over the king's allowance, before changing his mind and extorting money from them.[225]

But another seventeen prisoners gave depositions in favour of Pendar. The collective portrait of the Agent that emerges from the second table was the negative of the first one. Far from the squalid concoction described before, the pease was 'Every other day thick and well boild with Beef or Pork out into it, and more allowed than they could eat'.[226] All these prisoners insisted that they were well treated by Pindar and his staff. Crucially, this second group of deponents accused one character, the prisoner Beriet, of having forced their hands in signing the petitions, obliging them 'to sign [the] Complaint to live easy'. Joseph Gautier and James Chauwitt thus stated that they had 'no cause of Complaint though they signed the Petition', and decided to make this declaration 'to clear their Con-sciences'. A goldsmith by the name of Millon declared that 'Several of the Prisoners who complained acknowledged it to be without Reason and that they were threatned with ill treatment if they did not do it'.[227] The conclusions of the Board were almost unilaterally in favour of their Agent, dismissing all the com-plaints about food, accommodation, or staff violence.[228] Mr Beriet was blamed for starting a personal vendetta against the Agent, perjuring himself, and convincing

[222] S&W to LCA, 11 December 1744, TNA, ADM98/2, fos. 56v, 57v.
[223] Table 1, 'Abstract of the Affidavits to the Truth of the Prisoners Complaints against Mr. Thomas Pendar', ibid., fo. 58v.
[224] Ibid., fo. 59.   [225] Ibid., fos. 59v–60.
[226] 'Table 3. Abstract of Depositions in Evidence for Mr. Thomas Pindar', ibid., fos. 60v–61.
[227] Ibid., fos. 59v–62.   [228] S&W to LCA, 11 December 1744, ibid., fos. 57v–58.

other prisoners to sign the petition by using 'violent means'.[229] This quarrel sheds light on the reasons motivating a prisoner to put his name at the end of a collective text: either to transgress the dividing line with the prison staff, or, on the contrary, to reassert it by siding with his compatriots.

Trying to disentangle the immediate and long-term causes of the troubles, the commissioners realized that the Agent himself was partly to blame. Problems had begun as soon as a group of French officers had arrived in the prison. These men had proceeded to treat the Agent 'in a very indecent manner'.[230] Instead of applying the prison rules, and of treating the prisoners evenly, Pendar had tried to buy peace by giving undue privileges to the troublemakers, inviting them to eat in his house or giving them free passes to spend time in town.[231] Distributing favours to some prisoners but not to others, then withdrawing these privileges on a whim, Pendar had fuelled the social tensions which were always latent within the prison. Worse, the Agent had got on the wrong side of 'some angry and designing people of Falmouth', especially the mayor, by preventing the prisoners from honouring their invitations.[232]

In this case, as in a myriad of others, the border between 'inmates' and 'custodians' was blurred. The social and economic dynamics at play in the prison were partly a combination of outside factors and internal logics. Class was a factor of tension, inside as well as outside. Disagreements over money illustrate this clearly. Most prisoners preferred to be paid in cash rather than in kind, out of fear of being defrauded by food contractors.[233] There were other reasons why having cash in prison was convenient. Money could buy you a bed, instead of sleeping on the floor, or food extras.[234] As the French commissaire in Le Havre explained in 1758, English prisoners preferred to be paid ten sols per day rather than being given the food ration, 'which they were unable to save or position themselves to use to obtain other means of help'.[235] As highlighted by prison sociologists, having cash in hand gives a sense of freedom and autonomy; by contrast, being paid in goods is often perceived as humiliating and infantilizing.[236] This was exactly the reasoning behind the refusal of prison officials to entrust prisoners with money. According to this logic, common sailors and soldiers were not temperate enough to restrain themselves from spending all their money on liquors and luxuries. In 1745, Commissaire Roux wrote from Morlaix that he would reluctantly comply with the government's instructions to pay daily the prisoners in cash for their

---

[229] Ibid., fo. 58.   [230] Richard Kingston, surgeon, ibid., fos. 61v–62.

[231] 'Abstract of depositions', ibid., fos. 62v–63. This was a perversion of the household—traditionally seen as the model for a well-governed prison: Spierenburg, *Prison Experience*, ch. 6.

[232] S&W to LCA, 11 December 1744, TNA, ADM98/2, fo. 58.

[233] Such as in Plymouth: St Sulpice to SSM, 24 August 1703, AN, MAR/B3/123, fo. 566v.

[234] Lempereur, 'État des prisons de Dunkerque', 15 December 1695, MAR/B3/88, fos. 129–v.

[235] Raoul to SSM, 28 November 1758, MAR/B3/538, fo. 180v.

[236] Sykes, *Society*, pp. 23, 75–6.

food, adding that 'it will undoubtedly follow, despite all my care, that this money will be converted into drinks'.[237]

These perceptions were not just entertained by prison officials: they were shared by the prisoners' own officers. It was in these terms that Captain Traboulet de Korgan, former commander of the *Astrée* frigate and Commissary for the French Prisoners in Britain—a function which temporarily disappeared after 1759, after the French monarchy had ceased to send money for the subsistence of its prisoners—explained why he preferred to pay prisoners in kind 'rather than in cash, which they do not always use to alleviate themselves'. The sick in Fareham hospital, he elaborated, 'corrupted sentries and nurses' so that they would buy them 'everything that is liable to make them fall ill again', such as raw fruits, smoked herring, or gingerbread.[238] These eternal minors needed the protection of guardians to look after their health. Moral and physical health were thus closely related, and the prisoners' passion for gaming exemplified this connection. Traboulet thus required a ban on gambling from British prison administrators: 'I have endeavoured to establish some order as far as possible in Portchester Castle, by praying the commissary to remove public gaming tables, and to authorize me to put in the dungeons those who would gamble their pay or sell their clothes.' Traboulet used the same infantilizing discourse towards his own men as the custodians. Just as prison guards crossed the boundary with the prisoners when it served their purpose, officer-class prisoners also knew how much they shared with the gentry and high officials: a form of social elitism. As exemplified in their discourse on money, class was a key distinction to maintain, which sometimes entailed making cross-national alliances with the guards. Strikingly, Traboulet insisted that he, not the custodians, should punish the prisoners who misbehaved. While this might indicate a form of self-regulation among the inmates, it also signals the sharing of some principles with prison officials with respect to the noxiousness of gaming, which we must explain.

Gambling seems to have spread among prisoners of war during the French Wars.[239] The surgeon Farrell Mulvey explained in his captivity narrative why some addictions were so popular among his companions of captivity in France. Excess of alcohol consumption, he wrote, was 'one of the dire effects of the species of exile we suffered in France', while gambling was 'inseparable from a long-protracted captivity.[240] Games, like all 'secondary adaptations' to incarceration, allowed the prisoners to forget the dreariness of their everyday lives and avoid thinking about the distant future. But prison administrators saw gambling as a social evil which had to be eradicated. The historiography on the topic, and more

---

[237] Roux to SSM, 12 March 1745, AN, MAR/B3/432, fo. 404.
[238] Copy of Traboulet de Korgan's letter, 14 March 1756, AN, MAR/F2/83.
[239] See Abell, *Prisoners*.   [240] Mulvey, *Sketches*, pp. 26–7.

generally on games in prison, is rather slim.[241] What follows is a brief and limited exploration of a problem that would deserve a dedicated study. The specific context for this was the long-standing dispute with France regarding the vast number of Frenchmen dying in the British depots. The French government attributed the problem to the lack of care given to their prisoners in Britain and specifically the British insistence that each government should clothe their own prisoners. Replying to these accusations, British prison administrators blamed the prisoners themselves for their sorry state. On 9 September 1800, the Agent for the Prisoners at Norman Cross confessed to the Transport Board his failure 'to prevent the Prisoners from selling their ration of Provisions for Days to come, and their Bedding'.[242] As a consequence of this behaviour, he argued, these men were prone to catching diseases, as winter was approaching. The cause of their distress had nothing to do with the 'Smallness of their Rations' in Britain, as the French government alleged, but, according to the Transport Board, 'to their depriving themselves of it by Gaming'.[243] 'This pernicious Practise', continued the British commissioners, 'had become so prevalent in the Prisons' that the Agent's prohibitions were to no avail: 'an invincible Spirit of Gaming' led these men to 'sport away' their provisions, clothing, and bedding.[244] Over the following years, prison officials took innumerable measures to stop this illicit traffic. In Norman Cross, Stapleton, Liverpool and Dartmoor, the prisoners who were selling their clothing, blankets, or food rations were closely confined or put on short allowance, just like those who were found in possession of those items, while the soldiers involved in these transactions were court-martialled.[245] But the repetition of the bans indicates their failure.

The virulence of these denunciations has to be explained by the social effects of gambling. Games of fortune had been viewed with suspicion by governments and urban authorities since the sixteenth century, as they challenged principles of social, political, and moral stability guaranteed by God and the monarchy.[246] In France, twelve ordinances against gambling were adopted between 1717 and 1781. In Britain, in the 1740s only four laws were voted to curtail the problem.

---

[241] See, however, Walker, *Depot*, pp. 95–6, 107–23; Abell, *Prisoners*, pp. 19–20; Chamberlain, *Hell*, pp. 104–5. Neither Walker nor Abell reference primary sources. See also Bolster, *Black Jacks*, pp. 126–7.

[242] Letter reproduced in full in Walker, *Depot*, p. 276.

[243] Transport Board (TB) to Evan Nepean, 18 October 1800, TNA, ADM1/3740, fo. 185v.

[244] TB to Otto, Commissary for the French Prisoners of War in Britain, 1 November 1800, ibid., fos. 229v–230. On these diplomatic exchanges, see Abell, *Prisoners*, pp. 10–20.

[245] Extract of Captain Woodriff to TO, 23 January 1801, TNA, ADM1/3740, fos. 378–v; TO to Evan Nepean, 26 January 1801, ibid., fos. 393–v; Agent at Liverpool to Commissioner Serle, 28 January 1801, ibid., fos. 396–v; TB to Cotgrave, 3 July 1808, 18 July 1809, 14 December 1810, TNA, ADM98/225; same to same, 4 February, 20 June 1811, ADM98/226, fos. 47v, 76. Prison regulations forbade purchasing or selling prison property: 'Instructions for Agents' (1807), article 39, p. 26. Article 11 of the 'Règles' for the prisoners of war (1807) referred to gaming specifically.

[246] Freundlich, *Monde*, p. 10.

As is often the case, the multiplicity of laws probably signals the failure to eradicate the phenomenon.[247] Moralists denounced games because they prevented people from fulfilling their moral, familial, or professional obligations, fuelling disputes and disorder.[248] During the 1780s and 1790s, fear of gambling reached a climax in Britain.[249] John Howard was a staunch opponent of gaming in prison, whether cards, dice, or skittles, because of the disorder it created: 'I am not an enemy to diverting exercise: yet the riot, brawling, and profaneness, that are the usual consequences of their play.'[250] Howard admired the prison rules adopted in Genoa, Bern, Ghent, and Bodmin, which prohibited gaming.[251] And the exemplary rules that he proposed to establish in reformed prisons treated gaming and drinking as a sin.[252] These discourses no doubt informed and structured the way in which prison officials saw gambling by prisoners of war.

Gambling revealed the putative moral deviances generated by a long incarceration. By selling their clothes and food, gamblers not only put their own health at stake, but also exposed the whole prison to the risk of disease. And what could be more selfish than selling goods which had been generously bestowed on them by the public? Gambling led to insolvency, more borrowing, begging, and more debts. The impact of credit dealings on social relations and spiralling debts was a common topic of discussion in Georgian Britain. Debtors' prisons were a popular literary theme from the 1740s onwards, which contributed to raising public awareness of the problem.[253] Unlike debtors, who were imprisoned for debts contracted outside, prisoners of war contracted debts *inside* the prison. Thus, gamblers were not the only ones to blame for their sorry fate. At the beginning of 1800, Captain Woodriff, the Agent at Norman Cross, wrote the following letter to Otto, the Commissary for the French Prisoners in Britain, describing how usury worked:

There are in those prisons some men, if they deserve that name, who possess money, with which they purchase of some unfortunate and unthinking Fellow-prisoner, his Rations of Bread for several days together, and frequently *both Bread and Beef for a month*, which he, the merchant, seizes upon daily, and sells it out again to some other unfortunate being, on the same usurious terms; allowing the former one halfpennyworth of potatoes daily to keep him alive; not contended with this more than savage barbarity he purchases next his clothes, and bedding, and sees the miserable man lie naked on the planks, unless he will

---

[247] Crump, 'Perils', pp. 9–10.
[248] Favier, 'Jouer', pp. 70, 78.   [249] Crump, 'Perils', p. 21.
[250] Howard, *State of the Prisons* (1784) , p. 13 (quotation).
[251] Ibid., pp. 119, 126, 147, 396.   [252] 'Table 1', ibid., p. 471.
[253] Finn, *Character*, pp. 51–62.

consent to allow him one halfpenny a night to lie in his own hammock, and which he makes him pay by a further Deprivation of his rations when his original debt is paid.[254]

The use of the term 'deprivation' is striking for the reader of Sykes, since he made this concept the cornerstone of his theory. Usurers exploited the psychological weakness of their compatriots, entangling them in ever-tighter webs of debts and obligations. Just as prison officials refused to tolerate the abuses committed by jailors, they refused to condone the robbing of prisoners by their comrades. This form of extortion was even more shocking on the part of fellow soldiers. Ultimately, this social vice dissolved the spirit of community among prisoners of war. This idea was brought about through the language of disease: the Transport Board blamed the 'incurable spirit of Gaming' which induced all sorts of disorder.[255] Gambling was considered through a moral lens: it was a 'Vice', and those who fell victims to it were 'weak or wicked'.[256] This language strikingly resembled the rhetoric of the moralists, who also used the disease metaphor to characterize the upper classes' addiction to gambling, which corrupted society as a whole, ruining the gentility and leading to moral despair.[257]

The sociological effects of the passion that consummated gamblers, i.e. the redistribution of wealth and the reshuffling of social hierarchy, were particularly worrying in a carceral context. The microsocieties of gamblers, with their rules and rituals, became the object of fascination as well as repulsion for prison officials. In 1818, a Committee on the Prisons met in London. It interviewed a surgeon, William Dyker, who had served at Dartmoor for five years. The interview, which started with a discussion about the general state of the prisoners' health, focused on the men 'who called themselves Romanists'. Dyker estimated their number to be around 700. 'Entirely naked' because they had sold all their clothing, 'frequently without any food at all, except perhaps a few raw potatoes', 'they lay in the upper part of the prison in fifties and hundreds, upon one another's laps'.[258] In 1812–13, Dartmoor's governor took drastic measures. The prisoners who purchased their provisions and clothes were put in close confinement on short allowance for months.[259] Billiard tables were also banned, due to the 'Impropriety and Danger' they presented.[260] The 'Romans' were confined separately from other inmates.[261]

---

[254] Extract from TB to Otto, early 1800, in Walker, *Depot*, pp. 107–8. Otto concurred with his British counterparts: those prisoners who 'deal in Provisions' must be severely punished: Otto to TO, 4 November 1800, in ibid., p. 285.

[255] TB to Otto, early 1800, in Walker, *Depot*, p. 281.

[256] Extract of Commissioner Serle's report to TB, 25 July 1800, TNA, ADM1/3740, fos. 233–v.

[257] Crump, 'Perils', pp. 13–15.

[258] 24 April 1818, *Report* (1818), p. 195.

[259] TO to Cotgrave, 18 April 1812, 10 July 1813, TNA, ADM98/227, fos. 31, 83.

[260] Ibid., 20 October 1812, fo. 63.   [261] Ibid., 16 February 1813, fo. 84v.

The Romans' name came from the place of their residence, 'from living in the capitol, or in other words, at the top of the prison'. This counter-society, physically segregated, was organized entirely around gaming: 'I have known them frequently to gamble away their provisions for six weeks in advance; and when every implement of gambling was taken away from them, they would gamble at push pin.' Begging a few pennies from the country people who came to the prison market, they could barely afford to survive in the winter. Their absolute social equality threatened the pillars of a society built on the principles of hierarchy. 'Extremely filthy', dressed in rags, or naked, sleeping collectively—which might have hinted at another type of disorder often linked to gambling, that of sexual deviancy—these wretches were incapable of thinking beyond tomorrow.[262] They had given up on their humanity. This description of the Dartmoor gamblers was not mere hyperbole: in many ways, their behaviour was typical, albeit in an extreme way, of the thrills that all gamblers crave. As pointed out by Gerda Reith, 'the apex of the gambling experience is the moment when excitement peaks and gamblers are gripped by the fever of play, playing on and on, oblivious to their surroundings, to their losses, to the passage of time and even to themselves.' Gambling is a form of psychological escape, allowing the player to forget the pains of imprisonment, dissolving the past and the future, and melting them into 'the time of the eternal present'.[263] During the game, the players experience a form of psychological dissociation, leaving behind their sense of self.[264] For prisoners of war, trapped for months or years in a foreign land, ignorant of when they might be released, the temptation to forget everything, and engage in what Goffman calls 'removal activities', could be a powerful one.[265] Gambling provided an antidote to boredom, of which so many prisoners complained. It could also, as in Dartmoor, create an alternative world, where money, social norms, and even one's own survival were devalued as meaningless.

As we saw in chapter 5, war captivity generated upwards or downwards social mobility, which governments attempted to discourage, because it threatened their conceptions of social hierarchy. An extreme variant of this happened in prison, where criminal enterprise led some men to rise above their position in society and others to tumble down the ladder. Furthermore, gambling undercut the idea of the war prison as a shelter from the violence outside its walls. Captivity exposed the prisoners to systematic moral corruption. Social rank, self-respect, dignity, and frugality were all challenged by the gamers, who followed their own rules, and in so doing betrayed their obligations to their brothers in arms, and threatened the fabric of society more generally. Eventually, these men were removed to prison ships.[266] Prison administrators failed to grasp the meaning

---

[262] Ibid., 24 April 1818, p. 195.   [263] Reith, *Age of Chance*, pp. 129, 131, 140.
[264] Ibid., p. 133.
[265] Goffman, *Asylums*, p. 271.   [266] *Report* (1818), p. 195.

of gambling for the prisoners themselves, which was precisely to forget about their surroundings, leaving the prison society altogether to invent other forms of social relations.

In 1818, former employees of Dartmoor Prison were called in by a select committee of the House of Commons to share their knowledge about potential improvements to the facilities, at a time when its reconversion into a prison for convicts was being discussed. The committee discussed the causes of an epidemic that had raged in 1808–9. For Andrew Baird, former inspector of the King's hospitals and prison hospitals, the sickness had been 'generated' *in situ*, by 'the bad regulations of the prison'.[267] George Maggrath, who had been surgeon at Dartmoor ('medical superintendent') between September 1814 and February 1816, preferred another interpretation: diseases had 'moral causes': American prisoners, in particular, were 'exceedingly prone to dissipation' and indulged in the consumption of spirits. In the same way, he attributed outbreaks of pneumonia, measles, and smallpox, which all hit Dartmoor in this period, to outside influences, arguing that they had been 'imported to the depôt by the market people holding intercourse with the prisoners'.[268]

The perception that diseases found a fertile ground in prisons was not unfounded. Constant flows of people indeed connected war prisons to their surroundings.

V. The Prison as Synapse

To describe his approach to the study of space, Henri Lefebvre employed the powerful metaphor of a house: instead of a static building, one should strip the house imaginatively of its walls. The house 'would emerge as permeated from every direction by streams of energy which run in and out of it by every imaginable route.... Its image of immobility would then be replaced by an image of a complex of mobilities, a nexus of in and out conduits.'[269] If we imagine the war prison in the same way, it is not so much the dichotomy between the inside and the outside as the flows connecting the prison's occupants with their host societies that must be emphasized. The permeability of prison walls was a feature of eighteenth-century debtors' prisons and houses of correction.[270] This fact continued to characterize 'reformed' prisons.

First, I will show that the social and spatial organization of detention places, as well as the structural exchanges between war prisons and surrounding societies,

---

[267] Baird, 15 April 1818, *Report* (1818) , p. 177.
[268] George Maggrath, 5 May 1818, ibid., p. 202.   [269] Lefebvre, *Production*, p. 93.
[270] Evans, *Fabrication*, p. 27; Ignatieff, *Just Measure*, p. 34; Innes, 'King's Bench', pp. 233–4; Finn, *Character*, p. 115 sq; Paton, *No Bond*, pp. 42, 46.

facilitated the schemes of prisoners who planned to escape. Secondly, the separation from the outside was not absolute; other economic transactions were encouraged, within certain limits. Prison markets were legal and spatial enclaves, designed with the intention of focusing social and economic exchanges and preventing illicit trade between prisoners and local populations.

A. Escapes

Escapes were common in eighteenth-century war prisons. In both countries, two main kinds of explanation were invoked by prison officials. The first related to the materiality of prison buildings. The deficiencies of prisons were often identified as an aggravating factor for the haemorrhage of prisoners.[271] The second explanation was a human one: escapes were caused by collusions between inmates, custodians, and local populations. In this sense, prison outbreaks were the product of social, cultural, and institutional factors. In this respect, too, there is no apparent difference between the two countries. The example of an escape from Dinan is typical of the techniques used by the fugitives; it also reveals the mindset of the state administrators who tried to find culprits. In March 1708, at dusk, twenty English sailors escaped from the Castle, by making an opening in the toilets on the ground floor of the great tower. The sentry witnessed them without reacting, and he only sounded the alarm once they had vanished into the night.[272] Once they were outside, the fugitives took hold of a docked ship, whose 'rudder sails and oars' had not been removed, against official regulations.[273] State officials did not believe in fortune, however, and they punished those who had, by their negligence or designs, facilitated this endeavour. The sentry was put in the black hole for failing to do his duty, and the ship master was put in prison, because he was suspected, on principle, of having colluded with the prisoners.[274] Similar incidents were punished in the same way across the Channel.[275] Just as inmates were supposed to obey prison rules, guards might face the wrath of the disciplinary regime they were tasked with maintaining.[276] The prisoners' and the guards' fates were intertwined, which Rowlandson's undated drawing (Fig. 6.2) represents admirably. In a mirror effect of the prison rules, jailors were forced to

---

[271] Du Guay to SSM, 10 January 1690, AN, MAR/B3/60, fo. 187; copy of Deal magistrates to LCA, 24 April 1744, NMM, ADM/M/387, no. 22/1.

[272] Lafon to SSM, 10 March 1708, AN, MAR/B3/157, fos. 104–v.

[273] SSM to Pontbriand, 28 March 1708, MAR/B2/206, fo. 1039v.

[274] Maux and Pontbriand's letters to SSM, 28 March 1708, MAR/B2/206, fos. 1039–v. See also Lempereur to SSM, 12 July 1711, MAR/B3/195, fo. 188.

[275] S&W to LCA, 8 October 1744, TNA, ADM98/2, fo. 51v. Jailors were similarly held responsible for escapes from houses of correction: Beattie, *Crime*, p. 297.

[276] St Sulpice to SSM, 15 June 1704, AN, MAR/B3/123, fo. 524; SSM to Lempereur, 18 February, 11 March 1711, MAR/B2/226, fos. 568, 854.

Fig. 6.2. Thomas Rowlandson, *Escape of French Prisoners* (undated). The Cleveland Museum of Art.

reimburse the costs of retaking, convoying, and feeding the prisoners they had failed to guard.[277]

These sanctions did not prevent such problems from repeating themselves, time and time again.[278] This type of affair is typical of how the state, in both countries, dealt with dysfunctions of the prison system, by blaming a small number of individuals and expecting that local populations would take their share of responsibilities. For the same reasons, the French secretary of state for the *Marine* rapped the knuckles of the prison governor: 'His Majesty has been very surprised of the lack of precautions you take to guard them, he wants you to oblige the inhabitants to guard them themselves . . . and you must tell them that if they don't they will be made responsible for these escapes.'[279]

---

[277] SSM to Marquis de Coetemen, 29 September 1744, MAR/B2/323, fo. 129. Similar penalties were adopted in Britain: LCA to S&W, 19 October 1744, NMM, ADM/M/389, no. 239.
[278] SSM to Barentin, La Rochelle, 29 August 1746, AN, MAR/B2/329, fos. 385–v.
[279] SSM to Maux, 28 March 1708, MAR/B2/206, fo. 1039.

330 THE SOCIETY OF PRISONERS

Amateurs, who were commonly used in France at the beginning of the eighteenth century, were rarely up to the task of watching over prisoners of war, as illustrated by the case of Dinan. In 1702, Lempereur observed that in the Breton town, soldiers were more apt to secure the castle than 'the guard... composed of wretches and boys who have already let some prisoners escape'.[280] The *garde bourgeoise* was also notoriously unreliable, because the bourgeois were reluctant to take on what they saw as a chore.[281] In 1704, Monsieur de St Sulpice thus attributed the 'frequent escape of prisoners' from Dinan Castle to the 'careless way in which the inhabitants guard these prisoners when they wander around the towers to take the air'.[282]

The corruption of the jailors was also attributed to their lack of financial means. When, in July 1711, seven prisoners escaped from Dinan, Lempereur wrote that 'as the jailor is poor and he has not been paid for almost three years, it would not be surprising if he is tempted by money'.[283]

In Britain, the two main explanations for the escapes—that they were caused either by material or by human failures—were favoured respectively by the army and by the Admiralty. In other words, while the army defended the military sentries and blamed the buildings, the Admiralty took the exact opposite stance. The discussion, as it unfolded during the American War of Independence, raised important political and economic concerns, as illustrated by the example of Forton Prison.[284] Until 1778, while the Thirteen Colonies were officially alone in their fight against Britain, the inmate population at Forton consisted of American insurgents. Thereafter, French and later Spanish prisoners joined them.[285] As soon as Forton opened, escapes became a problem that never went away. Barely a week after the prison had opened, on 20 June 1777, eleven prisoners broke through the walls, 'notwithstanding a Centinel had been placed in the Prison Day & Night'.[286] John Bell, one of the Commissioners for the Sick & Wounded Seamen, was sent to Forton to examine the prison and improve its security.[287] He concluded that the building itself was faulty. New technologies of surveillance were emerging in these years, in war prisons as in other prisons. Reducing the circumference of the outside walls, Bell thought, would make it harder for the prisoners to evade the custodians' gaze. This change would 'admit of the Centries properly communicating with each other, to go round the whole of

[280] Lempereur to SSM, 5 November 1702, MAR/B3/117, vo. 312.
[281] Gastines to SSM, 29 October 1695, MAR/B3/89, fo. 259.
[282] St Sulpice to SSM, 15 June 1704, MAR/B3/123, fo. 524.
[283] Lempereur to SSM, 29 July 1711, MAR/B3/195, fo. 206.
[284] See Anderson, 'American escapes'.
[285] Between 1777 and 1779 there were on average 200–250 American prisoners; from 1779 on, they averaged 350: Alexander, 'Forton Prison', p. 369. By October 1778, 554 French prisoners were detained there: Connor, 30 October 1778, 'Yankee privateersman', 32, p. 281.
[286] S&W to LCA, 21 June 1777, TNA, ADM98/11, fo. 54.
[287] Bell to S&W, 30 June 1777, ibid., fos. 55–v.

it with ease'. But architectural improvements could only be stopgaps. The real problem was a human one: 'No Security against attempts to escape can be derived from any strength of these buildings, but...the prevention...must entirely depend...upon the proper disposition and vigilance of the Guard.'[288] As the summer unfolded, the Board was increasingly convinced that the complicity of sentries was the real problem.[289] In November 1777, Commissioner Bell did not mince his words when assessing the guards' skills:

> Such a Corps, from various Infirmities, natural Inabilities, & even an incorrigible propensity to Drunkenness, cannot be fit in any respect for the duty & trust of such a Guard, over a N.° of Men confined under the circumstance of those Pris.[rs] from whom every attempt, however desperate to gain their liberty, may be expected.[290]

Following their enquiry in August 1778, the commissioners blamed the sentries' negligence, corruption, or desertions.[291] The numbers of the prisoners escaping were, in truth, staggeringly high. On the night of 6–7 September 1778, forty-nine Americans and seven French prisoners escaped; the colonel of the regiment on duty exonerated the sentry, which the Board found hard to swallow.[292] In their view, the guards were the weak link in the chain of surveillance. Besides physical impairments, psychological and moral explanations proved their flawed character. 'Considering the real nature of the Guard', Commissioner Bell wrote, more escapes should be expected.[293] The air of the prison was morally corrupting, not just for the prisoners but also for custodians. Beyond this indictment lay a justified criticism: in both countries, the use of invalids was a sign that the guarding of prisoners of war was not the priority for the army, who preferred to commit able troops to the battlefield.

These continuous escapes became a moot point between the army and the Admiralty. In the autumn of 1778, Lieutenant General Monckton, governor of Portsmouth and MP for the town, attributed the escapes to 'the badness of the Prison'; the Sick & Wounded Board countered that for this very reason, 'the vigilance of the Guard [was] the principal security'.[294] Whatever the explanation, the prison continued to leak escapees. An American prisoner, Timothy Connor, listed the names of 112 escaped prisoners, out of the 415 who were detained at Forton while he was there, between 14 June 1777 and 13 June 1779.[295]

---

[288] Ibid.   [289] S&W to LCA, 14 July 1777, ibid., fos. 56v–57.
[290] 12 November 1777, ibid., fo. 67.   [291] 5 August 1778, ibid., fos. 113–v.
[292] 9 September 1778, ibid., fo. 124v.   [293] 12 November 1777, ibid., fo. 67.
[294] 6 November 1778, ibid., fo. 156. The respective positions had stiffened by May–June 1779: S&W to LCA, 14 June 1779, TNA, ADM 98/12, fos. 27v–28; Archibald McNable to Lord Armherst, Portsmouth, 31 May 1779, NMM, ADM/M/407.
[295] 'Roll appended to journal of a Forton prisoner', in Connor, 'Yankee privateersman', 33, pp. 36–9. Calculation by Alexander, 'Forton Prison', p. 382.

In November 1780, the Sick & Wounded Board noted that 229 Americans had escaped from Forton and Mill prisons (in which French and Spanish prisoners were also detained) in two years, and 118 since January 1780 only.[296] This was the last straw, and a thorough investigation was carried out in November 1780 to get to the bottom of the matter. The Board admitted that the confinement of prisoners of war, by comparison with other categories of inmates, raised specific challenges. The compounds where prisoners were detained were not 'originally designed like County Gaols, for the confinement of Prisoners without the aid of a Guard, and the Prisoners not being secured in Irons',[297] unlike common criminals, their mobility could not be restrained as efficiently.

This placed the main responsibility of monitoring the prisoners on military sentries. But posting a large number of sentinels on the walls, locking them up in the wards with the prisoners at night, or keeping close watch over them in the airing grounds made no difference.[298] Prisoners evaporated like morning dew. The Commissioners for the Sick & Wounded Seamen finally made their criticism of the army explicit: 'to prevent the Corruption or Connivance of the Centries', they wrote in the same report, they should be subjected to 'a true Military Discipline'. In this context, using the word 'discipline', which was reiterated three times in this letter, was not anodyne. If the disciplinarization of the sentries failed, then prisoners of war would have to be confined 'in the standing Jails of the Kingdom, calculated as before observed for the security of Prisoners without the aid of a Military Guard'.[299] Implicitly, the message was the army's inability to prevent escapes, a task to which turnkeys were much more attuned.

Eventually, the Admiralty came up with architectural solutions, by inventing building forms that would allow for a filtering and channelling of human flows and restrict opportunities of interactions between prisoners and sentries. The Board proposed 'to prevent' or 'preclude' all 'communication' between guards and prisoners, which meant that the spatial economy of the whole prison and the relationship between its compounds had to be rethought. Between the officers' houses, the hospital, and the airing ground, new walls would be erected, palisade fences would be closed up, and people forced to walk through passages and doorways.[300] The sentries' contacts with prisoners would also be limited by digging a 'Fossé...within the Boundary Wall with a view to prevent all the inconveniencies of a communication between the Centries when within that Wall and the said Patients'. In this way, it was hoped that bribing and 'agreements' between the sentries and prisoners would cease.[301] The problem was partly an

[296] S&W to LCA, 22 November 1780, TNA, ADM98/13, fo. 141. From the spring of 1780, following the failure to conclude a cartel of exchange with Britain, Benjamin Franklin actively encouraged these escapes: Prelinger, 'Franklin', pp. 282–5.
[297] S&W to LCA, 22 November 1780, TNA, ADM98/13, fo. 72.   [298] Ibid., fo. 72v.
[299] Ibid., fos. 72, 73v, 74.   [300] S&W to LCA, 6 January 1781, ibid., fos. 91–2v.
[301] Ibid., fos. 91v, 92v.

institutional one, as both the army and the Admiralty—in the guise of the sentries and the Agents—claimed the prerogative of controlling the threshold between the inside and the outside of the prison. A symbolic struggle over the ownership of, or responsibility over, the keys of the prison gates, lasted for decades in British war prisons. This was really about who held the real power: that of deciding who could come in and out through the prison gates.[302]

Besides adapting prison buildings to direct the behaviour of guards and inmates, local populations, who were also involved in escapes, could be kept in line by linking them, positively as well as negatively, to the fate of the prisoners. The following announcement was published in the *Gazette* during the Seven Years' War:

Office for Sick & Wounded Seamen and for Exchanging Prisoners of War, Oct. 24, 1757. Whereas Escapes of Prisoner of War in this Kingdom...have of late been very frequent...; the Commissioners...will prosecute, to the utmost Rigour of the Law, all such Persons who shall be aiding and assisting to His Majesty's Enemies, by helping Prisoners of War to escape, or who shall harbour or conceal them, or be in any wise instrumental to their leaving the Places of their Confinement, or those where they may be permitted to reside upon Parole, or who shall facilitate their leaving the Kingdom.

After the stick came the carrot. The commissioners offered to 'gratify any Person or Persons who shall inform them of [the Offenders'] Names and Places of Abode, and the Circumstances necessary to found a Prosecution upon'. All persons helping to apprehend the escapees would also be rewarded.[303] It is plausible that the idea of using such incentives for prisoners of war was inspired by the reward of informers for the apprehension of army and navy deserters, a practice that came into being in the first decade of the eighteenth century.[304] More broadly, rewards had become 'an established element in the system of criminal administration' in the 1690s.[305] The promise of 'a reasonable Reward' for information on the escaped prisoners of war was well established from the War of the Austrian Succession at least.[306] Comparable means were used in France. In March 1779, two English sailors who had escaped from Fougères Castle were captured by a *paysan* who brought them before the mayor of Pontorson; 'in order to sustain surveillance

---

[302] The same phenomenon was at work in private houses, castles, or at city gates: Jütte, *Strait Gate*, pp. 81–133. See also Linebaugh, *London Hanged*, pp. 365–7.

[303] *Gazette*, 9735 (29 October 1757).   [304] Scouller, *Armies*, p. 296.

[305] Beattie, *Crime*, p. 51.

[306] See the 'established Gratuity to encourage the Country People' to help apprehend escaped parolees: S&W to LCA, 1 July 1748, TNA, ADM98/4, fo. 231v. Advertisements were frequently placed in the papers offering rewards: S&W to LCA, 7 December 1756, ADM98/6, fos. 20–v. See, for example, *Gazette*, 9955 (8 December 1759).

among country folk', he was rewarded with a gratification of twenty-four sols, a sum 'similar to that granted to those who kill a wolf'.[307]

But these solutions could backfire, and escapes could be encouraged by the very means introduced by the prison authorities to prevent them from happening. The system stimulated illicit trading relations between local populations, guards, and prisoners.[308] In theory, the scheme was well conceived. At Forton, as early as June 1777, the Admiralty offered £5 rewards for the recapture of American prisoners.[309] Nathaniel Fanning, an American prisoner who was detained there in 1778–9, described in his diary the countrymen patrolling around the prison walls, 'followed by their great dogs, and armed with great clubs'. As soon as an escape was reported, he wrote, 'I could see sometimes seventy or eighty in a few minutes in search of their booty, beating the bushes, running to and fro, from ditch to ditch'.[310] For their labour, these civilians were rewarded by the Agent with five pounds sterling for an American, and half a guinea for a Frenchman, i.e. a tenth of the first sum.[311] Presumably, this difference in the value of these prisoners was due to the existence of an American, who could legally be pressed into the navy, unlike a Frenchman, who had to be exchanged.

According to the JPs at Fareham, who granted warrants for apprehending American prisoners of war who had eloped from Forton, these rewards had been 'greatly abused'. Hence, they wrote in September 1779, once at large prisoners 'have often suddenly surrendered to those who are suspected to be their Friends, in order to give them an undue Claim to the Bounty, which ... has been by this means improperly paid and divided, and the Publick greatly injured'.[312] Prisoners were thus willingly commodified. This traffic brought much-needed extra resources to everyone involved. These economic exchanges depended on the circulation of the bodies of the prisoners across prison walls, just as prisoners were the conditions for the continuation of trade between North America and the Caribbean.[313] In both cases, state policies were subverted by crossing the boundary between captors and captives.

The army and the Admiralty blamed the failures of the reward system on each other. In the autumn of 1781, Captain Fitzwilliam of the Surrey Regiment of militia encamped near Gosport and on guard at Forton Prison, was adamant he had identified the roots of the problem. The reward for capturing the American prisoners who had escaped, he wrote to the Earl of Sandwich, First Lord of the Admiralty, was

---

[307] [Esmangart], *Intendant* of Caen, to Meslé, subdelegate in Avranches, 21 March 1779, Archives Départementales du Calvados, Caen (ADC), C4155.

[308] TB to Agents, TNA, ADM98/226, fo. 23.

[309] S&W to LCA, 25 June 1777, ADM98/11, fos. 54–v.   [310] Fanning, *Memoirs*, p. 10.

[311] £5 was equivalent to 100 shilling; half a guinea to 10.5 shilling.

[312] JPs at Fareham to LCA, 29 September 1779, NMM, ADM/M/404.   [313] Ch. 3.

A Temptation, that few Persons in a lower class can, or that few do withstand; and in my own mind (I may be wrong, perhaps) I am persuaded that the Clerks and Turnkeys of this Prison, are frequently induced to let the American Prisoners escape, in order to retake them, and then to claim the reward.[314]

He pointed out the lifestyle of a prison clerk named Robinson, 'whose salary is fifty or sixty pounds a year' and 'lives like a Gentleman and keeps his horse'.[315] Citing the depositions of two carpenters who worked in Forton Prison, Fitzwilliam thought he had uncovered 'a confedracy of the Clerks and Turnkeys of Forton Prison being in a league to let the American Prisoners out of the Prison in order to retake them and then to claim the reward'.[316] An enquiry was carried out, and Fitzwilliam's claims were refuted.[317] Such accusations were not totally far-fetched,[318] but more sincere observers admitted that the success of this traffic could only be explained by the diversity of the people involved. In November 1780, the Board thus referred to a 'collusion between the Prisoners and Centinels and perhaps Turnkeys, to share the large Reward of £5 for each recapture'.[319] In February 1782, Major General Smith, commanding the army forces at Portsmouth, expressed this frustration at the false escapes that he observed at Forton:

I can no longer refrain from complaining of the insufficiency of that Prison, as well as the Traffic which is carried on there, scarce any Prisoners ever get entirely away. They get out, they give themselves up into the hands of particular Inhabitants near, who bring them back, & the rewards as regularly divided between the Inhabitants and Prisoners, who get out, as any Prize Money whatever, those Centries who are open to Bribery for coniving get some small share, the Turnkeys have likewise been strongly suspected. The Centries are sometimes convicted of Neglect of Duty, and in consequence very severely punished, but this does not stop it.[320]

The term 'Prize Money' explicitly referred to the distribution of spoils under prize law, by which the crew of a ship divided the product of the sale of a captured ship and cargo. This was a powerful analogy to describe the collusions that linked so many people across prison walls. Local populations were key stakeholders in this

---

[314] Fitzwilliam to Earl of Sandwich, 28 September 1781, NMM, ADM/M/405.   [315] Ibid.
[316] Fitzwilliam to Earl of Sandwich, 3 October 1781, ADM/M/405.
[317] LCA to S&W, 17 October 1781, ibid.; Corbett to S&W, Royal Hospital at Haslar, 3 November 1781, ibid.; S&W to LCA, 12 November 1781, TNA, ADM98/13, fos. 255–v.
[318] Three turnkeys who had released prisoners from Forton without authorization were simply dismissed: LCA to S&W, 28 July 1781, NMM, ADM/M/405. Upon petitioning the Lords of the Admiralty, they were soon reappointed: S&W to LCA, 13 August 1781, TNA, ADM98/13, fos. 216v–217.
[319] S&W to LCA, 22 November 1780, TNA, ADM98/13, fo. 73v.
[320] Copy of Mayor General Smith to War Secretary, Portsmouth, 14 February 1782, NMM, ADM/M/405.

fraud, but it worked so well because it had relays inside as well as outside the prison, while the gatekeepers, both turnkeys and soldiers, were closing and opening their eyes upon request. As underlined by Major-General Smith, the prisoners did not really try to leave the prison: the whole point was to return, then leave again, in a cyclical and profitable journey. One Thomas Kinsey was a specialist in fake escapes—or he was just very clumsy. Either way, he was 'retaken for the fifteenth time' in February 1782. In a downbeat letter, the Lords of the Admiralty asked that he should be watched with 'more care' in the future.[321]

How could this traffic be discontinued? In July 1779, Fareham JPs highlighted the danger that the Americans represented, which was greater than any other prisoners of war: they were 'a more dangerous Enemy than either the French or Spaniards'. Here we touch on the special status of a prisoner of war during a civil war. These escapees blurred the boundary between friend and enemy, between Britons and foreigners:

> Many of them know the Country about Portsmouth, better than the Inhabitants of it; that when they Escape from Prison, they are not to be distinguished from Englishmen, and are known to have many Friends in the Neighbourhood, who take every occasion of giving them Protection & Assistance.[322]

The circulation of these prisoners fed the fear of political and moral contagion. While increasing the amount of the rewards for American prisoners had been the favoured option in the past,[323] the JPs looked at the problem the other way round, through the eyes of the offender. Cutting down the financial incentive would presumably lower the temptation to transgress the law. They suggested suppressing or greatly lowering the rewards given for retaking American prisoners of war. This solution was again brought up in November 1780 by the Board, which proposed decreasing the 'value' of American prisoners of war and aligning the reward with that given for the retaking of French and Spanish prisoners:

> The said Reward has operated contrary to the intention of it, whether it may not be eligible to reduce it to 10s the sum which is always paid for the recapture of French or Spanish Prisoners who escape, and which has been found a sufficient inducement to Persons meeting with them to secure and deliver them to Our Agents,... escapes are seldom attempted by these Prisoners with any view to share the reward.[324]

---

[321] LCA to S&W, 16 February 1782, ibid.
[322] JPs at Fareham to LCA, 29 September 1779, NMM, ADM/M/404.
[323] S&W to LCA, 5 February 1779, TNA, ADM98/11, fo. 224v.
[324] S&W to LCA, 22 November 1780, ADM98/13, fo. 73v.

By the end of the war, it was obvious to everyone that Forton's walls had more holes than Swiss cheese. Although the problem had first been identified almost three years before, it was only in April 1782, when the war was almost over, that the Admiralty finally decided to reduce the reward for apprehending American prisoners of war from five pounds to ten shillings to prevent collusion.[325]

We saw previously that the escape of prisoners on parole probably increased during the French Wars.[326] The British state tried to address this problem in the same way for all escapees.[327] Thus, when French and two Dutch prisoners of war ran away from the hospital for prisoners of war and the Castle at Edinburgh in 1798, announcements were published in the press, paying a reward of one guinea for each prisoner, whose descriptions were also given.[328] Once again, despite introducing a series of safeguards to try to prevent abuses, escapes did not stop in this period.[329] While the rewards were not the only explanation, it is clear that civilian populations kept aiding prisoners to escape. Hundreds of British people were prosecuted at the assizes for this crime.[330] Hardening the penalties for this offence did not succeed either: neither transportation nor the pillory seemed to discourage people from taking the risk,[331] despite the passing of 'the French prisoners of war Escape Bill' in July 1812, which punished people aiding prisoners of war to escape with transportation.[332] Instead of solving the problem of escapes, the reward system helped perpetuate it.[333]

Prisoners, guards and locals all benefitted from the respective parts they played in the traffic in rewards. However, these transactions were often a fool's game. In their journals, American sailors detained at Forton described how they bribed sentries.[334] But just as escapes could be faked, bribing could be an oblique way to squeeze money out of the prisoners, who had nowhere to complain. In 1779, George Thompson wrote in his diary: 'Jan. 19. Tuesday in the Morning Tow of the prissoners Thrid to Maeck thire Escapes and Gave the Sentry £1-ˢ7 as soon as the Sayd Sentry Gote the Monny from the prisners he that Instant Informed on them and Gote them put in black hole.'[335]

---

[325] LCA to S&W, 29 April 1782, NMM, ADM/M/405.   [326] Ch. 5.

[327] See Copy of S&W's Instructions to Agents, in *Report* (1798), art. 25, p. 32. See also Chamberlain, *Hell*, pp. 172–6.

[328] Agent for Prisoners of War's Office, Edinburgh, 13 August 1798, *Caledonian Mercury*, 11999 (16 August 1798). In 1811, a reward of £1, 1 s was paid by the Agent at Selkirk to recapture French prisoners on parole: *Caledonian Mercury*, 13990 (19 August 1811).

[329] In 1807, a reward of one guinea was paid for retaking and bringing back escaped prisoners, but neither guards nor turnkeys were to be paid for this: 'Instructions for Agents', article 35. See also TO to Cotgrave (Dartmoor), 17 December 1812, TNA, ADM98/227, fo. 75v.

[330] See *Royal Cornwall Gazette*, 403 (16 March 1811). See also *Commitments*.

[331] *The Scots Magazine* (1 August 1815).

[332] *An Act for the more effectual Punishment*, 29 July 1812 (52 Geo. 3, c156).

[333] See 'Fraud on the Transport Board', *Morning Post*, 10168 (11 April 1801).

[334] Alexander, 'Forton Prison', p. 383.

[335] Thompson, 'Diary', p. 224. See also Connor, 4 November 1778, 'Yankee privateersman', 32, p. 281.

B. The Prison Market

The prison market was an 'interface between the prison and the external world', a 'mediational' space, which occupied a unique function in the political economy of the prison.[336] In this space, economic transactions between prisoners and the local populations were legal and even encouraged by state authorities. The market was an economic middle ground, which extended the spatial logic of the begging grate to a whole courtyard, while encouraging commerce in both directions.[337] At the market, prisoners were allowed to buy goods from local peasants and merchants; prisoners were also allowed to sell objects they had made with materials they had acquired legally, purchased from said civilians, or illegally (for instance, by recycling the straw of their mattresses). Prison markets were in this sense a space of validation of the economic transactions, legal or not, that took place in the prison. They were created to protect the prisoners against the abuses of their jailors, by allowing them to purchase goods elsewhere. But the presence of this cheap workforce could also, it was hoped, be profitable—a point which more generally is related to the economic importance of prisoners of war for the host country.

The painting in Fig. 6.3 of the market of Norman Cross shows the entanglement of the different functions of a prison of war.[338] The presence of sentries

Fig. 6.3. Arthur Claude Cooke, *French Plait Merchants Trading with French Prisoners of War at Norman Cross or Yaxley Camp, Cambridgeshire, 1806–1815* (1906). Wardown Park Museum, Luton.

---

[336] Lefebvre, *Production*, p. 366; Combessie, 'Marking', p. 536. See Chamberlain, *Hell*, pp. 141–8.
[337] On the grate, see Evans, *Fabrication*, pp. 27–8; Finn, *Character*, pp. 129–32.
[338] Walker points out the many inaccuracies and anachronisms of this painting: *Depot*, pp. 135–6.

reminds us that the chief purpose of prisons was to prevent escapes; but the prison was also a space of production, like the manufacture or the workhouse; and a place of economic exchanges involving a variety of actors, coming from within and from without. In this sense, the prison can be approached as a connecting space: a synapse, where goods, people, and ideas flowed in multiple directions. One might draw an analogy between the market space and the port in the mercantilist economy: there, prisoners, like merchants, were allowed to exchange goods, as long as this did not hurt the national economy or defy other state policies. The market materializes the tension between the contradictory functions of war prisons, and illustrates the constant interplay between closure and opening. We have previously described the variety of economic transactions that took place within a prisoner of war camp; these were predicated on exchanges with the outside world.

To understand the specificity of the market space vis-à-vis the rest of the prison, one must remember that a stark spatial frontier was delimited between the inside and the outside by the administration. The 1807 instructions to the Agents stipulated that entering a prison, a military hospital, or a prison ship was strictly prohibited for outsiders. The only permissible way to communicate with prisoners was via letters, which had previously been checked and forwarded on by the Agents. By the same logic, 'any intercourse' between prison staff and prisoners was to be kept to a minimum.[339] At Dartmoor, which was the closest thing to a total institution in our period,

> Strangers, accompanied by a military officer, are allowed to walk round the military way; but, except the agent, officers on duty, surgeon, and turnkeys, no person, however high his rank, can procure admittance within the second iron gates, unless provided with a pass or special order from the Transport Board.[340]

How did prison markets work exactly? It seems that they first appeared during the Seven Years' War. The 1758 French rules stated:

> It shall be allowed to tradesmen or sellers of ware (except such as deal in thing that are not fit to be sold to Prisoners) to wait at the great gate of the Prisons from 10 o'clock in the morning 'till 3 in the afternoon, in order to sell their ware to such Prisoners as have where withal to pay for them on the spot (article 10).[341]

A small group of prisoners at a time could attend the market and purchase food or clothing for the whole prison. They would then sell these commodities to their

---

[339] 'Instructions for Agents' (1807), article 38.
[340] 'Plate 19. Description of the new prison of war, Dartmoor, Devon', in *Repository* (1810), pp. 162–3.
[341] *Rules to be observed... in... France* (1758).

companions. This explains the coexistence of two markets. The first one, which is the main concern of this chapter, was the market outside the walls, 'where there is a free access of the Country People with all sorts of Provisions Beer and Produce, which they are not allowed to sell but at the fair Market Price'.[342] What was actually sold there was difficult to control, as the Board noted in 1779 at an unspecified prison:

> There is a Sutler at the Guard House, who constantly sells Strong Beer, Bread, Fruit, and other Articles, are likewise sold near the Gate upon the Crown Land beyond the Precincts of the Hospital, neither of which Practices they have been able to suppress.[343]

At Dartmoor, this market was located between the first and the second iron gates. 'Outside the Entrance to the Prison', a 'thatched Cart Lodge' was erected 'for the Market People to leave their Cattle under during the Market Hours'.[344] Only a few prisoners at a time were presumably allowed to attend the market held at the prison gate, taking orders from their comrades and bringing back goods, which they would then sell inside.[345] The second market was 'a kind of Market within the walls', where prisoners had 'stalls' and made transactions with one another, in particular selling and buying the goods bought at the external market.[346] At Norman Cross, there was one such inner market in each quadrangle.[347] The importance of this institution for the prisoners is highlighted by the introduction of a new type of collective punishment during the Napoleonic Wars: the market was shut down to force prisoners to give up the names of their comrades who had made and sold daggers or forged bank notes and counterfeited coins.[348]

The alleged reason for creating these zones of legal trade was the desire to protect prisoners from the extortion of the turnkeys and contractors.[349] The Commissioners for the Sick & Wounded Seamen explained to the Lords of the Admiralty, in January 1757, that the

> sole Motive for making the Regulation was to prevent all kind of Monopoly, by increasing as much as possible the number of Persons to offer Things to sell, and thereby lowering the Prices of them; and shew the Prisoners that it was Our

[342] Extract of report by Commissioner Serle to TB, 25 July 1800, TNA, ADM1/3740, fo. 233v.
[343] S&W to LCA, 13 October 1779, TNA, ADM98/12, fos. 110v–111.
[344] 'Order additions and alterations to be made to Dartmoor Prison, following report of Commissioner [Serle]', 19 September 1809, ADM98/225.
[345] Walker, Depot, p. 98; Lloyd, Arts, p. 19.
[346] Extract of Serle's report to TB, 25 July 1800, TNA, ADM1/3740, fo. 233v.
[347] Walker, Depot, p. 98.
[348] TO to Cotgrave at Dartmoor, 11 August, 3 October 1809, TNA, ADM98/225; 28 December 1810, ADM98/226, fo. 39; 12 January, 18 February 1812, ADM98/227, fos. 7, 14–v. See also Bolster, Black Jacks, p. 128; Lloyd, Arts, p. 28; Chamberlain, Hell, pp. 152–7.
[349] 'Rules to be observed at the Market, at [name to be inserted] Prison', articles 1, 2, 4.

design to hinder their being awed into buying of the Officers or others who had any Concerns with the Prisons at advanced Rates.[350]

The absence of such a prison market was precisely the object of John Howard's criticism of Calais Prison in 1779: 'a regulation and scheme of diet was affixed in the prison, but no open market was allowed, and everything was oblidged to be brought from the gouler. No regulations were affixed at Calais till after mr howard had visited the prison.'[351] By contrast, Howard noted that in Britain, 'the open market in certain hours, under certain restrictions at the prisons was an article introduced in the last war, very essentially of the benefit of the prisoners'. The idea that the market was introduced for the prisoners' own good remained prevalent at the end of our period. The prison market at Dartmoor was thus lauded in *The Repository of Arts, Literature, Commerce, Manufactures, Fashions, and Politics*, an illustrated fashion magazine. Published by Rudolph Ackermann, a successful entrepreneur and picture dealer, the periodical aimed, among other things, at promoting British manufactures. In its September 1810 issue, the *Repository* described the market in the following terms:

A well-supplied daily market is held in the agent's square, where provisions of every kind are sold at a moderate price. For one hour the market people are admitted within the first iron gates for the prisoners' benefit, who, by their own ingenuity and industry, are thus enabled to indulge in many trifling luxuries. Captain Cotgrave [*the Agent for Prisoners of War at Dartmoor*] is indefatigable in discountenancing exorbitant prices and extortion.—Whoever sells articles of inferior quality, or charges excessively, is foerever excluded [from] the market.[352]

In this rather idealistic description, prisoners are the captive cousins of the metropolitan customers who shopped in Ackermann's boutique on the Strand. This perception of the market as a positive and innocuous mode of exchange between prisoners and the local populations was part of a wider discourse presenting Dartmoor as a humane and modern prison. But one also notes that these transactions were unequally 'beneficial': only the prisoners seemed to profit from the market. In reality, prisoners of war were a welcome source of income for local populations in times of scarcity.[353] They were a captive market, in the literal sense, and their purchases from local merchants were structurally skewed and unequal.

---

[350] S&W to LCA, 1 January 1757, TNA, ADM98/6, fo. 37v.
[351] Howard, Memorandum on British prisoners of war in France, 15 January 1779, ADM98/11, fo. 214.
[352] 'Plate 19', in *Repository* (1810), p. 162.
[353] On this phenomenon in contemporary prisons, see Combessie, 'Marking', p. 542; Piacentini, *Surviving*.

In practice, the market at Dartmoor did not succeed completely in shielding the prisoners from economic abuses. In 1811, the Transport Board asked Captain Cotgrave, the Agent, whether it was true that a French prisoner had 'the peculiar Privilege of selling Potatoes at Dartmoor Prison', and, if so, 'why the Market is not an open one'.[354] Some of the prisoners who were delegates at the external market abused their position of wholesalers to connive with local merchants.[355] After receiving confirmation that this was the case in Dartmoor, the Board stressed the economic principles that guided the prison regulations, explaining that prison markets had been created precisely to prevent 'this Monopoly':

> We see no Reason whatever for not having an open Market at Dartmoor Prison, as well as at all the other Depôts, and we therefore desire, that our Orders on the Subject may be immediately executed. It is your Duty to take Care that the Prisoners be not imposed on at the Market (as mentioned in Article 31 of your Instructions) which is to be kept open from 9 o'Clock until 12 in the Forenoon; and neither Potatoes, Bread, or any other Articles is to be sold by any Prisoner or other Person exclusively.[356]

Prisoners also sold their wares to civilians. The Transport Board contended in 1800 that some of the prisoners who were granted this 'Privilege' had been known 'to earn and to carry off upon their Release, more than an Hundred Guineas each'.[357] Britain's museums are filled with the artefacts made by French prisoners during the Napoleonic Wars.[358] Using the bones of mutton and beef rescued from their plates, human hair, and wood, they made ship models, chessboards, jewellery boxes, or commodes. While it is not usually possible to identify the names of those who made or bought these objects, a few proofs of purchase survive.[359] Thus, the ship model of HMS *St George*, made by French prisoners and on display at Edinburgh Castle, was sold to the Duke of Atholl for a total of £5, 4 s, 6 d, including the cost of the box to carry it, the 'oyl cloath to keep it dry to the Carriage of it to Dunkeld'.[360] Like the selling of prison or hospital clothes and sheets to gamble, these practices illustrate the prevalence of 'make-do's' in social institutions: the use of objects in a manner that was not intended by the institution authorities.[361] This economy of scavenging, recuperation, and recycling of 'waste' characterizes scarce economies, and the phenomenon was exacerbated in prison.

---

[354] 6 February 1811, TNA, ADM98/226, fo. 49.   [355] Lloyd, *Arts*, p. 24.

[356] 16, 19 February 1811, TNA, ADM98/226, fos. 51, 52v.

[357] TO to Otto, 1 November 1800, ADM1/3740, fo. 230v.   [358] Lloyd, *Arts*.

[359] Out of the 500 artefacts made by French prisoners and kept in the Peterborough Museum, only the names of six artists are known: Walker, *Depot*, p. 97.

[360] 'Receipt dated 7 March 1760', on loan from The Blair Charitable Trust, Edinburgh Castle.

[361] Goffman, *Asylums*, pp. 187–9.

While prison authorities hoped to open new horizons of mutual enriching for the prisoners and the locals, they were also aware that markets heightened the risks of illicit exchanges or escapes. This is the reason why trade was limited in time and space.[362] In a scheme set forth in 1779 for regulating the prisons, Lieutenant General Monckton, governor of Portsmouth, proposed that the number of the members of the public allowed to attend the market should be 'in proportion to the Prisoners'. A turnkey and a sergeant of the guard were also to attend the market, 'to prevent the Introduction of Spirituous Liquors, and all prohibited Articles', while the officer of the guard was to do his utmost 'to prevent any Communication between Prisoners and Strangers'.[363] The 1807 'Instructions for Agents' stated that the market would take place daily, in a segment of the prison's inner circle, every day apart from Sunday.[364] Anyone attending was searched at the gate. No one was allowed 'to go beyond the Limits allotted for that Purpose: and, on no Pretence, to be admitted within the Pailing, or suffered to have any private Communication with the Prisoners'. Once the market was over, these people were 'immediately to leave the Prison'.[365] These regulations were printed out and posted around the prisons and in their neighbourhood for the information of British subjects, but they were routinely ignored.[366] In September 1810, the Transport Board even wrote to the Agent at Dartmoor, Captain Cotgrave, to inquire 'whether the Market-People [should] be not separated from the Prisoners by an Iron Railing'.[367]

Not all goods could be legally traded, and the list of forbidden items changed over time. The 1757 regulations thus forbade the use of the market to sell 'Things that it is not proper to sell to Prisoners' (art. 10), and the smuggling of liquors or the traffic of letters was similarly prohibited (art. 11).[368] In 1807–8, the regulations added 'Newspapers or political Publications' and also 'Knives, or Weapons of any Kind' to the list of prohibited goods, under punishment of being confined to the black hole on half-allowance.[369] The prisoners were not totally free to make and sell whatever they wanted either.

In a letter written to Louis-Guillaume Otto, the French commissioner for the exchange of prisoners of war, the Transport Board thus stated in 1800 that the prisoners of war in all the British depots were 'at full Liberty to exercise their Industry, within the Prisons in manufacturing and selling any Articles they may

---

[362] 'Regulations for . . . French Prisoners' [1757], TNA, SP42/136.

[363] Monckton, 'Standing Orders for the Guards at the Prisons', in LCA to S&W, 13 September 1779, NMM, ADM/M/408.

[364] 'Instructions for Agents', article 31.

[365] 'Rules to be observed at the Market', articles 1 and 2.

[366] TO's circular, 12 October 1809, TNA, ADM98/170, fo. 33.

[367] TO to Cotgrave, 10 September 1810, ADM98/226, fo. 15v.

[368] 'Regulations for the management of French Prisoners in Great Britain' [1757], TNA, SP42/136.

[369] 'Instructions for Agents', article 31, and 'Règles', article 7, in *Thirteenth Report*. The procedures for examining and censoring letters were very detailed: 'Instructions for Agents', article 37.

think proper, excepting Hats, which would affect the Revenue in opposition to the Laws', as well as 'obscene Toys and Drawings', and articles 'made either from their Clothing or the Prison Stores'.[370] Article 5 of the 1808 market rules stated that:

> Every Person is to be permitted to purchase from the Prisoners any Article of their own Manufacturing, with the Exception of Woollen Mittens or Gloves,— Straw Hats, Caps or Bonnets,—obscene Pictures, Images, or Toys,—and Articles made from Prison Stores, which are strictly prohibited.[371]

The prisoners guilty of making, selling, or owning forbidden objects, would be put in the black hole and lose a third of their food allowance for three days.[372] What was the reason behind the prohibition of these particular items? With regard to manufactures, the fact that the prison economy was 'bound in with the local free economy' is the main explanation.[373] The work of prisoners of war had generated dissent in Warwickshire during the American War of Independence, when the weavers of Coventry turned against the nine Spanish prisoners in the town, fearing that these men might be 'endeavouring to learn the Country Manufactures'.[374] At Penryn, local inhabitants managed to prevent the production of pastry and confectionery by the French prisoners.[375] But the controversy over the work of prisoners of war was particularly intense regarding straw plait objects manufactured in prison. For more than a decade, packets of straw were secretly brought into the prisons by soldiers and manufactured into plait hats or bonnets by prisoners; the soldiers brought the items in the other direction and handed them over to merchants. Many other individuals were involved in this trade, such as prisoners on parole and English civilians.[376]

The example of Stapleton Prison (Bristol) provides us with a case in point, since it appears to have been a particularly active production centre during the Napoleonic Wars. For the proponents of this prison manufacture, such as General Yorke, in charge of the militia, this work kept the prisoners 'from misery and idleness', while allowing for a backward integration to the local children who prepared the straw.[377] The industry already existed in Britain, but imports had continued to be important.[378] Wartime provided an opportunity to try to expand import-substitution. But in Bristol, local cottagers had since 1799 successfully opposed what they saw as an unfair competition by the cheap labour of prisoners

[370] TO to Otto, 1 November 1800, TNA, ADM1/3740, fo. 230v. The hat tax or hat duty was introduced in 1784 to raise revenue.
[371] 'Rules to be observed at the Market', article 5.
[372] Ibid., articles 1 and 2; 'Règles' (1807), article 8.   [373] Goffman, Asylums, 241n34.
[374] LCA to S&W, 15 July 1780, NMM, ADM/M/410.
[375] Walker, Depot, p. 96. See also Lloyd, Arts, p. 22.
[376] On the straw plait controversy in Norman Cross, see Walker, Depot, pp. 134–45.
[377] Cited in Vinter, 'Prisoners of war', p. 163.   [378] Inwards, Straw Hats.

of war detained at Stapleton Prison to their manufacture of straw hats and bonnets.[379] A similar debate had been waged when workhouses had first been opened in England in the early seventeenth century: giving work to the confined was a means to occupy virtuously the vagabonds, but local authorities objected to a competition that drove down the prices and increased poverty.[380] In any case, despite the prohibition, the smuggling of plaited items outside Stapleton Prison continued unabated.[381] In May 1808, a letter from a prisoner at Stapleton to a prisoner on parole at Montgomery on the English–Welsh border was intercepted by the Transport Board: it contained three samples of straw plait that he proposed to sell. The Board instructed their Agent to do his best 'in order to prevent a Traffic so prejudicial to our own poor Manufacturers whose dependence is on their Labour, while the French Prisoners are amply fed and well clothed and lodged at the Expense of this Government'.[382] The prisoner of war was here cast not just as a military enemy, but as the traditional economic rival, who defrauded the revenue.

Local manufacturers stepped into the breach to eliminate all productions emanating from Stapleton. In September 1808, the Bristol journeymen boot and shoe makers wrote to Lord Hawkesbury, 'complaining of their being out of Employ from the Circumstances of the Prisoners of War at Stapleton Prison being permitted to manufacture Boots & Shoes'. The Transport Board consequently ordered their Agent to take 'especial Care that no Cause of Complaint, of the Prisoners being suffered to manufacture Straw Hats, Clothes, or Shoes, or any other Article whatever, interfering with the Employment of the labouring Poor of Great Britain, be given in future'.[383] These instructions confused the Agent at Stapleton, who wondered what articles exactly the prisoners were now allowed to make and sell. In October 1809, the Board wrote back to their Agent, to clarify the matter: 'If the Manufacture of Plait could be effectually prevented, it is not our Wish to prohibit the Prisoners from making Baskets, Boxes, or such other Articles of Straw.'[384] Depending on the moment, new items were thus added to the list of prohibitions, always with the aim of protecting local producers. By the end of 1810, it looked like the Board had had enough with the all-round production going on at Stapleton. In October, it was ordered to put a stop to the manufacture of cabinet carried on from there, 'and as well as to every other Manufacture, not expressly authorized by us'.[385] In 1813, the manufacture of lace by prisoners of war

[379] Vinter, 'Prisoners', pp. 163–4.
[380] Foucault, Madness, p. 63.　　[381] Vinter, 'Prisoners', pp. 163–4.
[382] TB to Captain Crawley, 28 May 1808, TNA, ADM98/269, fo. 4.
[383] TO to Crawley, 24 September 1808, ibid., fo. 15. The same order was subsequently circulated to all Agents: Circular, 26 September 1808, ADM98/170, fo. 9.
[384] TO to Crawley, 21 October 1809, ADM98/269, fo. 55v.
[385] TO to Captain Evans, Stapleton, 24 October 1810, ibid., fos. 100–v.

all over the country was targeted, because it was carried out 'to the serious Detriment of a numerous Class of industrious British Subjects'.[386]

But to return to straw plait, this trade was still a national problem in 1812. In a letter to Henry Addington, Viscount Sidmouth and Home Office minister, the Transport Board explored ways to legalize a traffic that was mutually beneficial to the prisoners and the soldiers who guarded them. The troops who guarded the prisons should not be punished for being exposed 'to a temptation that we know they cannot resist'. Since the prisoners were successfully bribing soldiers to smuggle the straw plait objects out of the prison, it was better to lay a small duty 'on the manufactured bundles of straw upon their being received into the Prisons'. The duty so collected would be used for the prisoners' 'comfort and relief'. Crucially, it was argued that 'the detail of the regulations' could 'only be settled on the spot with the Prisoners'.[387] This is just one example of the economic conventions agreed on the ground between custodians and inmates.

But the prisoners did not limit themselves to making and selling straw hats and straw plaits. The 1808 market rules mentioned above referred to 'obscene' objects. The story begins in London in 1802, with the founding of the Society for the Suppression of Vice, also known (ironically) as the 'Vice Society'.[388] Moral reform had been simmering in England since the mid-1780s, when a sense of 'moral crisis' among economic, judicial, and political elites led to the formation of organizations wishing to enforce existing laws against drunkenness, irreligion, gaming, or licentious behaviour.[389] This background explains the setting up in 1787–8 of the Proclamation Society.[390] The fear of moral corruption heightened during the long wars of the 1790s and 1800s.[391] The 'Vice Society' was the translation of the volunteer movement into the moral sphere: it aimed to fight the war for virtue and order on the domestic front. It was also distinctly orthodox in its religious viewpoint, and was socially more inclusive than other associations, recruiting among the London middling sorts as well as small traders and artisans.[392]

Religious and sexual licence, which paved the way to political and social disorder, figured high on the priorities of the 'Vice Society'. It was also a prosecuting society which, centrally for our concerns, conducted investigations to eradicate the trade in obscene books and prints.[393] In 1808, such an inquiry uncovered the intricate ramifications of a criminal conspiracy which extended nationally. Called to appear as a witness in front of a parliamentary committee on the Metropolitan Police in 1817, the Society's secretary, George Pritchard, presented some of the evidence from the Society's files dating back to 1808. Pritchard

---

[386] TO's circular, 30 August 1813, ADM98/170, fo. 163.
[387] George to Viscount Sidmouth, 6 August 1812, DRO, 152M/C/1812/OH/78.
[388] Roberts, *English Morals*, p. 61.   [389] Ibid., p. 24.   [390] Ibid., pp. 33–5, 45–6.
[391] Ibid., pp. 59–95.   [392] Ibid., pp. 65–71, 73–5; Roberts, 'Society'.
[393] Roberts, *English Morals*, pp. 67, 87–9.

blamed the trade on an immoral congregation of social, sexual, and geographical outsiders. This wicked coalition was said to be led by 'several foreigners... of apparent respectability, and considerable property' based in London, who carried on 'an extensive traffic in obscene books, prints, drawings, toys, &c'. About thirty Italians, 'under the assumed character of itinerant hawkers', were the 'agents' who disseminated this material to the whole country with their infamous trade.[394] As noted by Michael Roberts, in wartime, attributing all moral vices to a foreign enemy was not particularly original, but the fact that there was a market in England for these pernicious objects made such a rhetorical strategy risky.[395] The total number of those involved was large: 'at least six hundred' people took part in this traffic. They introduced their dirty material in schools, chiefly 'ladies boarding schools', by way of 'servants' and women. In addition to these usual suspects, merchants of all sorts, from 'opulent tradesmen of fair reputation' to 'keepers of ballad stalls' and 'booksellers', also participated.[396] This trade had already attracted the attention of the Transport Office by 1798.[397] The Peace of Amiens facilitated the import of these lascivious items from the Continent, and with the return of the war, in 1803, they were back in circulation. Indeed, an indigenous production had been set up in the prison depots where Frenchmen were detained.

An investigation to ascertain the truth of the rumours was carried out in Stapleton Prison by the secretary of the local branch of the 'Vice Society', John Birtill.[398] At the prison market, this Bristol merchant purchased 'a variety of devices in bone, and indeed of the most obscene kind, particularly those representing (sodomy), a crime which ought not be named among Christians, which they termed "*the new fashion*"'. Traditional perceptions of French immorality were revived by this whole affair. Following an official complaint to the mayor, and the sending of some of these obscene objects and drawings to the Duke of Portland, the Prime Minister (who was also the Lord High Stewart for Bristol), and finally to Lord Hawkesbury, a stop was put to the 'abominable practice'.[399] The Transport Office wrote to Captain Edmund Crawley, the Agent at Stapleton Prison, worrying that this trade 'must tend to the subversion of all Decency and Order, and to Vitiate the Minds of the Rising Generation particularly', and ordered that the prison market immediately be closed down, for the following reasons:

---

[394] *Second Report... State of the Police* (1817), p. 479.   [395] Roberts, *English Morals*, p. 61.
[396] *Second Report*, pp. 479, 479–80, 483, 480.
[397] Lloyd, *Arts*, p. 23 (no source reference given).
[398] *Society for the Suppression of Vice* (1810), p. 2.
[399] John Birtill to George Pritchard, Bristol, 6 December 1808, in *Second Report*, pp. 480–1.

It is a Strong Measure, and the innocent may suffer with the guilty, but if they connive at such scandalous Proceedings, they can no longer be thought free from Blame, and the Punishment will be justly merited. But if the Body of the Prisoners shall give up the Persons who actually made or Sold the obscene Drawings and Toys, the Market shall again be opened, under such Restrictions, as may prevent a Recurrence of this infamous Traffick.[400]

Given the small size of the market, which was held at the turnkey's door for two hours every day, it seemed clear to Birtill that the prison staff was aware of this traffic, and possibly complicit.[401] Someone had to pay the price for 'this Evil', and the Duke of Portland proposed to remove the guards under whose care the prisoners were placed, 'for neglecting their Duty'.[402] It did not take long before the culprits were identified. Agents for prisoners of war at Bristol, Norman Cross, Dartmoor, Chatham, Yarmouth, Forton, and Edinburgh were ordered to punish the prisoners who manufactured these 'obscene and blasphemous Drawings and Toys'.[403] The prisoners' attempts to clear themselves by blaming the customers and their own 'great want' were unsuccessful. At Stapleton Prison, seventeen of them were found guilty and put in the black hole on short allowance, before being marched to prison-ships at Portsmouth.[404] The objects were apparently destroyed, except for a couple of specimens, which were safely kept in a triply locked tin box.[405] The market at Stapleton Prison was reopened in a matter of days, but the Agent was instructed to avoid a recurrence of the problem:

The Market may be again opened, after you shall have publickly admonished the Prisoners as to their future Conduct, in Conferring themselves to the Manufacture and Sale of such Articles only, as are allowed by us to be made & sold. It is particularly desireable that you should endeavour to discover the Persons who have been concerned in purchasing the Articles abovementioned, in order that they may be prohibited from having any Intercourse, whatever with the Prisoners in future.[406]

It was the danger of corruption from within, at the hands of enemies living at the heart of the motherland, which made this trade so threatening. Far from isolating the French prisoners, the prisons were the forward operating bases from which the

[400] TO to Crawley, 12 December 1808, TNA, ADM98/269, fo. 22.
[401] Second Report, p. 480.
[402] TO to Crawley, 12 December 1808, TNA, ADM98/269, fo. 22v.
[403] Second Report, p. 481.
[404] TO to Crawley, 17 December 1808, TNA, ADM98/269, fo. 23. The same treatment awaited the prisoners at Norman Cross who were guilty of the same crime: Society for the Suppression of Vice, (pp. 2–3).
[405] Second Report, p. 484.
[406] TO to Crawley, 17 December 1808, TNA, ADM98/269, fo. 23.

French could launch an attack against British morale. As the committee of the 'Vice Society' put it in a letter to the Duke of Portland, 'continued and unremitting vigilance will be necessary to put down a practice which renders our natural enemies more dangerous to us in the character of prisoners, than they could possibly be in the open field.'[407] The conspicuous location of Stapleton Prison, as the secretary of the Bristol branch highlighted, increased the danger for the innocent: 'The prison is a pleasant walk of three miles, and is the promenade for the youth of both sexes of this city in fine weather, as well as the resort of strangers, so that the mischief is incalculable.'[408] The prison depot was a place of sociability, and the central node in a process of acculturation of the British family by French prisoners, whose immoral values slowly percolated in Britain, via the traffic of snuff-boxes, drawings, and toys.

Interacting with prisoners of war provided civilians with the opportunity to gaze at their enemies without risking their lives, and gave the prisoners a chance to hear news from the outside world. Captivity narratives or prison journals often referred to this.[409] On Sunday 23 August 1778, the American sailor Timothy Connor wrote in his diary: 'Clear weather. Great numbers of the inhabitants came up here to see the American and French prisoners.'[410] These visits were still going on at the end of our period, even in a prison like Dartmoor, where the infrastructure of surveillance was particularly refined. In December 1811, a 'Market Girl' was apprehended in possession of letters written by and addressed to prisoners; guards were instructed to search civilians in the future.[411] It remained extremely arduous to prevent the exchange of illicit goods and information.

VI. Conclusion

The administration of the surveillance and guarding of prisoners of war does not correspond to what Max Weber called a 'rational bureaucracy'.[412] As demonstrated by Gresham Sykes, the prison guard's job was 'a complicated compound of policeman and foreman, of cadi, counsellor, and boss all rolled into one'.[413] The guard must, at the same time, prevent prisoners' escapes without provoking riots; punish rioters while respecting their 'humanity'; and refuse to tolerate traffics, without being too pernickety about rules.[414] Those staff members who were at the bottom of the prison and military hierarchies had to implement prison

---

[407] *Society for the Suppression of Vice*, p. 4.
[408] John Birtill to George Pritchard, 6 December 1808, reproduced in *Second Report*, p. 481.
[409] Fanning, *Memoirs*, p. 11.   [410] Connor, 'Yankee privateersman' (1878), p. 71.
[411] TO to Cotgrave, 5, 13 December 1811, TNA, ADM98/226, fos. 116v–117, 118.
[412] Bosworth, *Encyclopedia*, p. 3; King, 'Governance'.   [413] Sykes, *Society*, p. 54.
[414] Sykes, *Society*, pp. 53–4, 124; Cressey, 'Contradictory directives', pp. 2, 4; Sparks, Bottoms, and Hay, *Prisons*, pp. 150–6.

regulations. Their low social status, added to their subordinate position in the chain of command, meant that they were often disrespected by all sides. Prison guards were on the front line, and they took the blunt of the prisoners' anger. Ultimately, they had to decide on the spot whether it was better to coerce the prisoners or to compromise with them. At worst, they ended up being caught between the discontent of prison and government authorities, those of a foreign government, and that of the prisoners.

Riots were the most obvious means by which prisoners resisted their incarceration. But trading insults, gambling, engaging in forbidden exchanges with the staff, or escaping were 'messing up activities'—ways to test the rigidity of the legal boundaries established in prison rules.[415] Inside the prison, the fear of punishment was not always sufficient to dictate obedience to the rules. The law had to be accepted and internalized, by guards as well as prisoners. These groups could tacitly decide to ignore the law when its implementation was too risky.[416]

I am not arguing that the war prison was an irenic space. In fact, prisoners of war were exposed to more direct violence than 'normal' prisoners. For the military sentries, the protected status of the prisoner of war in the law of nations was somehow irrelevant. These soldiers justified their actions according to a different set of legal norms, which one could call 'the law of the prison': the fragile equilibrium that aimed at maintaining order behind prison walls.

For an institution to be 'total', in Goffman's sense, all inmates must be treated in the same way. Furthermore, formal regulations dictate the form of social interactions with the custodians. We saw in this chapter that social relations in war prisons departed markedly from the first two principles. Finally, total institutions are characterized by spatial enclosure. In these 'segregated establishments', Goffman argues, there are physical barriers 'to social intercourse with the outside and to departure', such as 'locked doors, high walls, barbed wire, cliffs, water, forests, or moors'.[417] As the examples of escapes and markets showed, however, war prisons could be considered as a gateway for the circulation of people, money, and objects.

---

[415] Goffman, *Asylums*, pp. 55–6.   [416] Innes, 'King's Bench'; Chauvenet, 'Guerre et paix'.
[417] Goffman, *Asylums*, pp. 137, 15. See Davies, 'Goffman', p. 91.

Conclusion

In this book, I have highlighted the creative tension between the state imperative of military conflict, on the one hand, and the emergence of powerful moral and legal norms that emphasized the need to wage civilized and humane wars, on the other. For most of the time, this tension between the growth of violence and the preservation of life was productive. For example, the differentiation between civilians and combatants, and the exceptional status of women and children, were acknowledged by legal writers. These principles were implemented in administrative regulations and international agreements from the beginning of the eighteenth century. These exemptions could always be revoked, and practices were highly contingent throughout the period. But in the eighteenth century, the customary laws of war, the law of nations, and humanitarian patriotism encouraged the states to try to get the upper hand on the moral front and treat their prisoners better than their enemies did theirs. In itself, this account contrasts with the Francophobic and Anglophobic perspectives explored by other historians.

But there were moments when there was a contradiction between policy and ethics. In France, during the French Wars, the 'humanitarian' discourse took on a new meaning, producing an opposition between civilization and barbarism that authorized forms of violence towards the prisoners.[1] As the war became more radical and extreme in the 1790s, the protections guaranteed to prisoners were severely limited. British and French conceptions of prisoners of war began to bifurcate. But because the treatment of prisoners of war was normally based on principles of reciprocity, this also had consequences across the Channel. The French detention of Captain Sidney Smith in 1796–8 provides a case in point. The British government was incensed by the exceptional treatment awarded to this officer, who as such should have been detained on his parole of honour in France. According to the Duke of Portland, the Prime Minister, there was no 'justifiable Ground of Distinction between' his case 'and that of any other Officer captured in His Majesty's Service', 'the Rights and Advantages of which he cannot be deprived without a Violation of Justice, and of the Laws of Nation'.[2] The French government replied that Smith's behaviour exempted him from the protection of

---

[1] Bell, *First Total War*.
[2] Copy of Duke of Portland to Lords of the Admiralty, 23 June 1796, *Report* (1798), Appendix, p. 71.

The Society of Prisoners: Anglo-French Wars and Incarceration in the Eighteenth Century. Renaud Morieux, Oxford University Press (2019). © Renaud Morieux. DOI: 10.1093/oso/9780198723585.001.0001

the category of the prisoner of war: he could only be considered as such 'from Indulgence and Humanity'.[3] The British discourse was based on the traditional respect of international legal customary norms, while France was now waging war in the name of mankind, reason, and justice.[4] In this case, prisoners on both sides paid the price for the inability of their governments to reach a mutual understanding. The French limitations of the rights of Sidney Smith were echoed in Britain, which implemented reprisals: all French prisoners on parole were jailed for a time. The French minister of the *Marine* characteristically condemned this measure, which was authorized by the law of nations although it had been used more rarely in the eighteenth century, 'as contrary to Justice and Humanity'.[5] Under Napoleon, French and British policies towards prisoners of war continued to go their separate ways, as highlighted by the incarceration of British civilians in France, with the famous decree of 1803. The victims of wrecks, who had always been exempted from war imprisonment in the eighteenth century, were now treated like other enemies. Napoleon's behaviour towards Ottoman prisoners in Jaffa was also widely publicized and condemned at the time, and he was widely perceived as a transgressor of *jus in bello*.

This book also argues that the focus on prisoners of war allows us to approach the history of international law from an original perspective. The category of the prisoner of war in the eighteenth century was not shaped by changing political, legal, and moral norms only. Nor was it produced by legal theorists alone. It was also an administrative category, the implementation of which was left to the discretion of state officials of various standings. The international exchange of prisoners of war was premised on their commensurability, but sometimes it was impossible to work out equivalences: for example, there was no exchange value for the Bishop of Quebec, who remained trapped in England for many years. Hence, captor states stretched and restricted the category of prisoner of war, making it possible to detain or release them depending on their needs. Furthermore, the distinction between public and private wars is not totally satisfactory. Captured in wartime, but kept in private hands and detained long after the war had ended, hostages experienced a reality that seems very different from that of prisoners of war. But the multiple attempts to 'convert' the hostages into prisoners of war, and prisoners of war into hostages, as well as the many comparisons drawn between these types of captivity, contradicts the notion that the invention of the prisoner of war meant the end of ancient modes of war captivity. Instead of the succession of different stages of war imprisonment—the slave giving way to the hostage, who, in turn, was replaced by the prisoner of war—it seems apposite to think in terms of a

---

[3] Extract of letter from Captain Cotes to Commissioners from Transport Board, 12 December 1797: *Report* 1798, Appendix, p. 127.

[4] See Best, *Humanity*; Edelstein, 'War'; Frey and Frey, '"The Reign"'.

[5] Extract of Captain Cotes to Transport Service, 11 January 1798, *Report* (1798), Appendix, p. 139.

gradation of overlapping categories. It is the existence of flexible boundaries between statuses that explains why prisoners of war could be paid to work in the prisons or manned the ships transporting them home.

Prisoners were also actors of their own destinies, and many resorted to legal arguments in order to improve their situations and obtain their release. The black freedmen who were enslaved and the Jacobite sailors imprisoned in Newgate as traitors fought for their reclassification as prisoners of war, contesting the labels that had been assigned to them by the state. These people could use a rich variety of rhetorical strategies to back up their claims. By contrast with normal prisoners, prisoners of war could draw from the language of the law of nations as a repertoire of arguments. This was often successful, as illustrated by their capacity to 'censor' their prison guards by soliciting the help of their own state. In the second half of the eighteenth century, governments increasingly had to answer publicly accusations of maltreatment of disarmed enemies, in the press but also through the launching of official investigations. This is not to say that this process of publicization of the complaint was imposed on states by non-state actors: principles of morality and transparency, implemented in the prison rules that were formalized from the 1740s onwards, encouraged the prisoners to voice their concerns. It is only when these procedures failed to satisfy the prisoners' demands that they called for help from outside.

War captivity is also—and this is the third argument I put forward—a privileged observatory of wider changes in society as well as in the structure of the state. Economic and technological structures underscored this institution, which mirrored more broadly the modern state's ability to wage war on a large scale. In turn, this provides us with a different perspective on the history of the category itself. In both countries, by the time of the War of the Austrian Succession, a consensus had been reached that prisoners of war should be detained separately from other inmates. But while France continued to resort to generic buildings all the way through the Napoleonic Wars, Britain began to address the challenges presented by war imprisonment differently from the 1770s onwards. These contrasting answers tell us something about the differing nature of the relations between the military, state, and society in both countries. In Britain, economic and military constraints applied to penal and military imprisonment at the same juncture, forcing the administration in charge of prisoners of war to explore alternative solutions. While prison hulks were still used massively, they were very expensive to fit out as prisons and to maintain, and the real innovation was elsewhere. The erection of purpose-built prisons, during the French Wars, was the outcome of a reflexion that had begun two decades earlier about the reform of the British state. While it would be too much to say that policies towards prisoners of war helped to lay the ground for 'prison reform', as the example of prison-building shows, the potential hybridization between different models of imprisonment, which was always there, became particularly apparent during the second half of the eighteenth century. Humanitarian campaigns often involved people active in the prison reform, and the prison rules shared similar principles.

War prisons were social microcosms, with some defining features. War imprisonment brought together people from much broader social, national, and ethnic backgrounds than normal prisons. To force some prisoners to socialize with people they resented or felt alienated from could be a means used by the captor states to punish recalcitrant captives or as a measure of retaliation against their state. Abbé Saujon, the Catholic priest detained in a bridewell with prostitutes, or the captains of privateers who resented being mixed with common sailors, believed that the identity of their companions of captivity was a social stigma, which degraded their self-worth. Reshuffling tendencies characterize all carceral societies, but they took a specific shape in captivity zones. The meanings of honour and pride, of national belonging and rank took a different connotation inside and outside, opening up a world of possibilities. The social superiority of a foreign officer on parole could not be taken for granted and was not always recognized by the civilians with whom he crossed paths. Behind prison walls, the solidarity of the battlefield could quickly crumble, as the rank-and-file could contest their officers' claims to precedence.

The temporal and spatial coordinates of war imprisonment were, to some extent, specific too. All prisons suspend time and create spatial hiatuses, but this phenomenon was exacerbated for prisoners of war, whose imprisonment essentially depended on the ebbs and flows of fickle international relations. The term of their detention was structurally indefinite, and many of them remained trapped in limbo for many years, not knowing when their detention would end. The prison staff's capacity to affect the length of imprisonment is key to understanding the nature of the relations they negotiated with the prisoners. The prisoners' hope to be released was built up in prison regulations, which rewarded good behaviour and punished misbehaviour, before or during captivity, by shortening or extending the duration of imprisonment. Considerable discretion was left to the interpretation of the custodial staff. Unscrupulous prison keepers, turnkeys, and sentries knew how to exploit the prisoners' craving for freedom, bartering with them in order to move forward their turn to be exchanged. Notions of moral legitimacy and reciprocal normative expectations played a major role in explaining the nature of the relations negotiated in prison between prisoners and guards. But many compromises were worked out on the ground between these groups, who knew how to break down the social, national, and linguistic boundaries between them. The traffic in rewards, which relied on a tight collaboration between prisoners, guards, and civilians to pocket the money granted by the state to recapture escapees, illustrates the success of these strategies. Power was also enacted spatially over prisoners of war, and different types of institutionalized spatial coercion were at work. The movements of prisoners on parole were merely contained, whereas the deprivation of the freedom of movement could, in its most extreme form, consist in being detained in the 'black hole' with shackles. But even a prisoner apparently at the mercy of his captors retained some agency to negotiate the conditions of his incarceration, not least thanks to the various forms of contacts that were developed with civilians during their transfers.

By comprehending the prison in society, we get to perceive the distance that often separated the violence of discourses of propaganda from the reality of everyday interactions between prisoners and host societies. The statement of Commissioner Serle, who was sent by the Transport Board to report on the mood of the 125 prisoners on parole in Bodmin in 1797, captures in an exemplary way the rich tapestry of these social relations, and how they could change over time: 'At first they had been very unruly and troublesome, actuated with all the Fervour of the Revolutionary Spirit of their Countrymen, and zealous to proselyte others, and especially the lower Sort, to their Opinions. But this Heat is much abated, and their Conduct has become more temperate and ordered.'[6] These relations often shifted as new forms of transactions were negotiated between captors and captives. While parole zones were 'open' prisons, even prisons with stone walls were permeable to the outside world. Prison-ships or purpose-built prisons such as Dartmoor embodied the same fantasy of absolute separation between subjects and enemies. But no prisons—even so-called 'supermax' prisons in the twenty-first century—are ever completely shut off from surrounding societies, however hard their governors try to insulate them.[7] Merchants from neighbouring towns flowed to the prison markets to sell food and returned with ship models and lewd drawings, while hopeful Methodist missionaries saw the prisoners as lost souls to convert. By inventing new forms of social relations, captivity maintained the connections between countries divided by war.

---

[6] 'Extracts from the Report of Commissioner Serle, on the State of the Prisons and Prisoners...on Parole at Bodmin, Callington...', 7 July 1797, in *Report* (1798), Appendix, p. 43. Similar peaceful interactions are documented in France: Duché, 'Passage'.

[7] Sykes, *Society*, p. 8.

Epilogue: Napoleon the Prisoner of Peace

It is somehow paradoxical to end a book entitled *The Society of Prisoners* with a focus on an individual, and a very illustrious one at that. But Napoleon's case is an exception that reveals the theoretical and practical issues that underpinned the category of the prisoner of war in the long eighteenth century, and arguably beyond that period.

Between Napoleon's escape from the Isle of Elba in February 1815, his ultimate defeat at Waterloo on 18 June, and his eventual surrender at sea on 15 July, the question of what should be done with him, once secured, agitated European generals, diplomats, jurists, and journalists.[1] In wartime, in the name of the preservation of their sovereignty and their interests, European states commonly introduced qualifications to the principles of the laws of nations. The labelling of Napoleon as a perpetual prisoner of war, and the decision to send him to St Helena, is, however, a liminal case in the history of international law, which presents us with a series of puzzles, if we are to understand the history of the category of prisoner of war in the long eighteenth century. The first question is to decide whether the post-1815 situation is paradigmatic of a new regime of war imprisonment, or whether the case of Napoleon reveals and actualizes a structural characteristic of war captivity, which was already discernible before.

In other ways, the trajectory of Napoleon Bonaparte from triumphant emperor to exile in St Helena exemplifies and exacerbates the possibilities inherent in the category of the prisoner of war. St Helena is a nexus connecting the different threads we have explored in the book. It is by moving from France to Elba, from Rochefort to Portsmouth, and ultimately to his final place of abode in the Atlantic Ocean, that the emperor's legal status changed, and he was turned into a prisoner of war. Napoleon was simultaneously deported and imprisoned—like a convict. He was not just detained in the metropole, but brought to a territory whose legal status was undetermined. This was not coincidental: legal uncertainty was key to the choice of St Helena.

The categorization of Napoleon was not just a matter of state discussion; the lawfulness of detaining an enemy as a prisoner of war once the war had ended was publicly debated in Europe for years. In practical terms, how was the fallen sovereign to be detained? In a proper prison, as a punishment for his crimes, or

---

[1] See, however, Hale Bellot, 'Detention'; Melikan, 'Caging'; Semmel, *Napoleon*, ch. 5, considers the public debates in the press and in Parliament.

The Society of Prisoners: Anglo-French Wars and Incarceration in the Eighteenth Century. Renaud Morieux, Oxford University Press (2019). © Renaud Morieux. DOI: 10.1093/oso/9780198723585.001.0001

on parole, like the general he remained? To what kind of surveillance should this exceptional prisoner be subjected? Would he retain some rights? The fact that Napoleon contested his label as a prisoner of war until his death also explains the features of the society of prisoners that took shape in St Helena after 1815.

I. Napoleon as a Prisoner of War

One of the main challenges facing diplomats and jurists after Waterloo was to find a way to deal with Napoleon that would ensure the security of Europe, while respecting some legal principles that had been seriously challenged during the French Wars. The Allied powers faced a dilemma when they heard that Napoleon had escaped from Elba: as his reception in France seemed to prove, their despicable enemy remained hugely popular; how could a new war against Napoleon be justified? One legal solution was to try to detach him from the French: war was to be waged not against a state or a collectivity, but against an individual, with whom Europe could never be at peace. It was he who should be punished, not those he had duped. At first glance, the so-called Declaration of Outlawry, adopted at Vienna on 13 March 1815, and signed by Britain, Austria, Russia, Prussia, and others, seemed to promise the worse for Napoleon:

> By thus violating the Convention which had established him in the Island of Elba [*the Convention of 11 April 1814, concluded between Austria, Prussia, Russia and Napoleon*], Buonaparté destroys the only legal title on which his existence depended; by appearing again in France with projects of confusion and disorder, he has deprived himself of the protection of the law, and has manifested to the universe that there can be neither truce nor peace with him.
>
> The Powers consequently declare, that Napoleon Buonaparté has placed himself without the pale of civil and social relations, and that as an enemy and a disturber of the tranquillity of the world, he has rendered himself liable to public vengeance.[2]

In what many saw as a thinly veiled call for assassination, the Declaration asserted that the fallen Emperor had 'rendered himself liable to public vengeance'. France was urged to make the right choice and support 'its legitimate sovereign', the Bourbon Louis XVIII, instead of this 'enemy and disturber of the tranquility of the world', animated by a 'criminal and impotent delirium'. Failing to support its true king, the French nation would face, once again, a military coalition of European powers.

This text placed the onus for the legal consequences to follow on Napoleon Bonaparte's actions. This connected to the claim that he had foregone his French

---

[2] *CTS*, vol. 63.

citizenship and made himself the subject of his own sovereignty, which had ceased to exist through his own actions. A more drastic solution than exiling him far away was considered: the Prussian Field-Marshal Gebhard Leberecht von Blücher did not concern himself with the law of nations when he communicated to the Duke of Wellington his intention to shoot Napoleon 'whenever he caught him'.[3] Blücher justified himself by quoting the Declaration of Outlawry. A warrant for Napoleon's arrest, addressed to the German nation, was circulated on 30 April 1815; it propagated to the German public the view that Napoleon was a 'delinquent', an 'outlaw', an 'outcast of humanity', and as such could lawfully be captured 'alive or dead'.[4]

Wellington protested against this interpretation, adding that European opinion as well as posterity would tarnish the reputation of those who would be guilty of such an action.[5] In theory, the British diplomatic stance was simple: since Napoleon was a French subject, he should be delivered to the French King Louis XVIII. In the words of Lord Liverpool, the British Prime Minister: 'we should have a right to consider him as a French prisoner, and as such to give him up to the French Government.'[6] Ideally, he should then be tried by the restored French monarchy as a traitor and rebel, and duly executed.[7] But the main problem with this plan was the French monarchy's own reluctance to have anything to do with Napoleon, who remained immensely popular.[8] By so doing, France shifted onto the rest of Europe the responsibility to deal with the fallen dictator, blurring the distinction between national and international law.

Such heated exchanges illustrate that there was no unanimity in Europe at the twilight of the Napoleonic Wars with regard to the treatment of defeated enemies, and specifically vanquished heads of state. On the one hand, the decision to confine Napoleon at St Helena, which was the result of an international deliberation led by Britain, seems to illustrate the beginnings of a legal collaboration between the executives of several European powers, which paralleled the signing of treaties of alliance. On the other hand, the legal justifications for sending him to the tiny south Atlantic island were very shaky, and seem to illustrate the triumph of a principle of necessity in the law of nations. One wonders why European sovereigns broke so radically, in 1815, with the usual eighteenth-century practice, which was 'to grant amnesty to the subjects of the warring states for their actions in the conflict'.[9] Sovereigns were entitled to a special regime vis-à-vis common prisoners of war according to *jus gentium*. For Schmalz, for instance, because

[3] Von Müffling, *Passages*, p. 252.
[4] See http://www.100days.eu/items/show/76#. Translated from the German by Katherine Hambridge.
[5] Von Müffling, *Passages*, p. 253.
[6] Liverpool to Castlereagh, 7 July 1815, quoted in Thornton, *Napoleon*, p. 57.
[7] Castlereagh to Liverpool, 12 July 1815, quoted in Hale Bellot, 'Detention', p. 174.
[8] Hale Bellot, 'Detention', p. 182.   [9] Witt, *Lincoln's Code*, p. 286.

sovereigns fight against one another not 'in order to settle a private dispute, but to defend the cause and rights of their people', they must not be a target in wartime; if captured, they must be treated not as prisoners of war but 'with all the consideration due to their rank'.[10] In order to deny Napoleon the customary rights that the laws of war accorded sovereigns, he had to be labelled differently.

The British government was adamant that the law of nations should be respected, and it never claimed to be suspending the legal order. This is fundamental to understanding the decision to categorize Napoleon as a prisoner of war. On 15 July 1815, Lord Liverpool wrote to Castlereagh, the Foreign Secretary, that, if 'the King of France does not feel sufficiently strong to bring him to justice as a rebel, we are ready to take upon ourselves the custody of his person, on the part of Allied Powers'.[11] On 28 July, Castlereagh presented his government's proposals: only Britain would decide the place where Napoleon would be detained as well as of 'the details of his surveillance'; the British ministry would bear this important 'responsibility' in the name of a 'common and solidary interest'. The allied governments would send commissioners to the place of detention, to 'officially certify from time to time the existence or non-existence of Bonaparte and the reality of his detention in the place that will be assigned for it'.[12] By the Convention of 2 August 1815, this decision was agreed on: Russia, Austria, and Prussia would send commissioners to the place where Napoleon was to be detained. While Britain was in practice solely in charge of Napoleon's detention, he was, in the words of the Austrian commissioner, Baron Stürmer, the 'prisoner of Europe'.[13]

On 15 July 1815, Napoleon left Rochefort, the French Atlantic port where he had taken refuge after Waterloo, and surrendered to Captain Frederick Lewis Maitland of the seventy-four-gun frigate HMS *Bellerophon*, a British ship-of-war. The vessel then sailed to Britain. It anchored off Brixham and Torbay (Devon) on 24 July and reached Plymouth on 26 July. The exact terms by which he was received on board the *Bellerophon*, and the exact nature of his conversation with the British captain, remain uncertain to this day, but they are crucial for our story. Indeed, while Napoleon argued that he had voluntarily come on board the ship in the belief that he was going to be offered political asylum in Britain by Maitland, Maitland would always claim that he answered that he 'did not know what was the intention of the British government'.[14]

[10] Schmalz, *Droit des gens*, book VI, ch. III, p. 237, quoted in Mattei, 715n516. Schmalz does not mention Napoleon.
[11] 15 July 1815, quoted in Hale Bellot, 'Detention', p. 178.
[12] 'Extrait du Protocole de la Conférence ministérielle', 28 July 1815, Archives du Ministère des Affaires Etrangères, La Courneuve, 53MD/1803, fos.7v–8, fos. 8v–9. France was subsequently invited to do the same, at the session of 3 August: ibid., fo. 9v.
[13] Stürmer, 13 December 1816, in Stürmer, *Napoleon*, p. 38. The text of the Convention of 2 August is reproduced in: 2 February 1816, HCH, vol. 32, cols. 235–6.
[14] Letter to Admiral Keith, 8 August 1815, in Maitland, *Narrative*, appendix, p. 239.

From that moment until the end of his life, Napoleon vigorously protested against the decision to treat him as a prisoner of war. On 31 July, when Admiral Lord Keith informed him that he would be sent to St Helena, Napoleon refused, and demanded instead to be granted the right of asylum in Britain. There are several versions of this conversation. Reporting Napoleon's speech, Admiral Keith's undersecretary gives a sense of the nature of Napoleon's objections:

'I am come here voluntarily,' said he; 'me placer sous les foyers [*at the hearth*] de votre nation, and to claim the rights of hospitality. I am not even a prisoner of war. If I were a prisoner of war, you would be bound to treat me selon le droit des gens; but I am come to this country a passenger on board one of your ships of war, after a previous negotiation with the commander. If he had told me I was to be a prisoner I should not have come.... In coming on board a British ship of war, I confided myself to the hospitality of the British nation as much as if I had entered one of their towns—une vaisseau, une village, tout cela m'est égal. Quant à l'isle de St Helena, c'est l'arrêt de ma mort. I protest against being sent thither, and I protest against being imprisoned in a fortress in this country.'[15]

The 'rights of hospitality' was another term for the right of asylum, which remained a fraught question between the two states at the time. Despite the absence of a treaty of extradition between Britain and France, religious refugees, criminals on the run, and eloped daughters were commonly granted hospitality across the Channel throughout the eighteenth century. During the French Wars, tens of thousands of émigrés benefited from asylum in Britain, and Napoleon had repeatedly complained about the leniency of the British laws with respect to those he described as criminals.[16] In 1815, however, he was content to praise the liberality of these same laws.

One problem raised by Napoleon's hovering along the English shores was the geographical reach of the law, upon which, as we have seen, the categorization of a prisoner of war depends. At what point in space exactly had Napoleon become subjected to British laws? According to the laws of nations and British law at the time, a British ship fell under the jurisdiction of the British crown.[17] In accordance with this principle, Napoleon apparently asserted: 'as soon as I had set foot on the *Bellérophon*, I was in the *foyer* of the British people.'[18] As his British partisans would also argue, simply by entering Plymouth harbour on board the frigate, Napoleon was entitled to the protection of habeas corpus and to trial by jury.[19]

[15] Allardyce, *Memoir*, p. 376. The quote is from Sir Henry G. Bunbury, the undersecretary.
[16] Morieux, *The Channel*, pp. 321–2.
[17] Halliday, *Habeas Corpus*, p. 147; Heller-Roazen, *Enemy of All*, pp. 126–7.
[18] 4 August 1815, in Montholon, *Histoire*, tome I, p. 89. The phrase reads as badly in French as in English.
[19] Semmel, *Napoleon*, pp. 204–5.

Since the late seventeenth century, as Paul Halliday has shown, writs of habeas corpus were used by the King's Bench to oversee any detention, including military prisoners and prisoners of war.[20] By granting habeas corpus to Napoleon, his supporters hoped that the justification of his confinement would be investigated; if it could be proven that he had been wrongly labelled as a prisoner of war, his release might have been ordered. The ministers' fear of such an outcome partly explains the decision to prevent the ship from landing in Britain.[21] Napoleon himself asked to be brought before a British court of justice—a right he possessed, he claimed, just like any other individual present on the British soil.[22] Napoleon's legal argument, here, seems to fit with Paul Halliday's analysis of 'local subject-hood': the idea of a contextual allegiance, which grants the King's protection even to foreigners or alien enemies.[23] From his capture to his death, Napoleon's status was the object of controversy. In St Helena, he would continue ruminating against the Convention of 2 August 1815.[24] The Convention was void, he wrote, because neither Austria nor Russia or Prussia had any rights on his person, in fact as in theory: it had been signed while he 'was in England' (i.e. on board HMS *Bellerophon*).[25]

How can we explain Napoleon's reluctance to be categorized as a prisoner of war? He might have feared that, as such, he would not be entitled to habeas corpus. This might also be explained by his (well-founded) intuition that the status of a prisoner of war was in fact very flexible, and that this would allow his captor considerable room for manoeuvre to decide upon his future. Thus, at the last minute he decided not to go on with his plan to escape Rochefort on board a Danish sloop, fearing British capture would jeopardize the good treatment he was hoping to get if he surrendered voluntarily: 'There is always danger in confiding oneself to enemies, but it is better to take the risk of confiding in their honour than to fall into their hands as a prisoner according to law.'[26]

If he did not want to be granted the *status* of a prisoner of war, he demanded the same rights as prisoners on parole as a gesture of courtesy and tribute to his rank, if he was allowed to reside on British soil:

Let me be put in a country-house in the centre of the island, thirty leagues from the sea. Place a commissioner about me to examine my correspondence and to report my actions; and if the Prince Regent should require my parole, perhaps I would give it. There I might have a certain degree of personal liberty.[27]

---

[20] Halliday, *Habeas Corpus*, pp. 165–74. For a different interpretation, see Hamburger, 'Protection'.
[21] Melikan, 'Caging', 352n12.   [22] Las Cases, *Mémorial*, pp. 1156–7.
[23] Halliday, *Habeas Corpus*, pp. 202–7.
[24] Napoleon Bonaparte's memorandum, 23 August 1816, in Montchenu, *La captivité*, p. 71.
[25] Ibid., p. 72.   [26] 13 July 1815, quoted in Hale Bellot, 'Detention', p. 182.
[27] Allardyce, *Memoir*, p. 376. Napoleon is quoted by H.G. Bunbury.

This kind of intellectual bricolage shows Napoleon's awareness that categorization mattered. He offered to 'live in England as a private citizen', and would give his 'word of honour' not to hold any correspondence with France nor to engage 'in any political affairs whatever'.[28] Napoleon was right to fear that his label as a prisoner of war would give his captors legal rights over his person.

II. A New Definition of War: The Lawyers' Debates

The British government tried to ground legally its decision to imprison Napoleon, a subject of France, in peacetime, and for this it asked for the advice of senior judges. Legal difficulties were indeed raised by this unprecedented situation. Lord Eldon, the Lord Chancellor of Great Britain, wondered what the legal grounds were for labelling Napoleon as a prisoner of war after his surrender.[29]

One of the key obstacles was Napoleon's subjecthood. As a French subject, could he be imprisoned by Britain once the war was over? Was it Britain's right to decide what to do with him? Sir William Grant, Master of the Rolls, believed that 'Bonaparte' could be considered either as a French subject, or as 'a captain of freebooters or banditti, which would place him out of the pale of protection of nations'.[30] The final expression was borrowed from the Allies' Declaration of Outlawry of March 1815. By categorizing him as a pirate or a brigand, Grant was trying to justify his exemption from the law of nations, and to give some legal content to the notion of 'outlawry' used in the Decree.[31] The declaration of outlawry, in English common law, was used literally to put someone outside the protection of the law. But labelling Napoleon as an outlaw gave rise to new legal problems, as Eldon complained: Britain could not have been at war with someone who was defined by the law of nations as being outside the rules of war![32]

The central question remained to know 'in *which* character...he [did] make war on the King of France, our ally', after his escape from Elba.[33] One solution was to consider that Napoleon was not a French subject anymore, and not a sovereign. This claim was, in truth, flimsy, since the Treaty of Fontainebleau of 11 April 1814, which had granted him the Isle of Elba, had made it clear that he was to be a sovereign in full right. In any case, once deprived of his French subjecthood, Napoleon could be relabelled. In the words of Lord Eldon: 'he has no character at all, and headed his expedition as an outlaw and outcast; *Hostes humani generis.*'[34]

---

[28] Ibid., pp. 376–7, 382.
[29] Eldon to Sir W. Scott, undated, reprinted in Twiss, *Public and Private Life*, vol. II, 273–80.
[30] Grant was quoted in Lord Eldon to Sir William Scott, 1 October 1815, in ibid., vol. I, p. 536–7.
[31] Grant's case rested on the notion that Napoleon, by escaping Elba, had forfeited his sovereignty: Melikan, 'Caging', p. 355.
[32] This point is made by Melikan, ibid.
[33] Liverpool to Eldon, 1 October 1815, in Twiss, *Public*, vol. I, p. 536.
[34] Liverpool to Eldon, 1 October 1815, p. 536.

The use of this term has a long genealogy.[35] Different incarnations of the figure of the enemy overlapped across the centuries. In the eighteenth century, Dan Edelstein argues, these types 'acquired sounder legal footing in works that dealt with international law'.[36] Violators of natural rights such as savages, brigands or pirates were *hostis humani generis* who should be placed outside the rule of law.[37] William Blackstone, in his *Commentaries on the Laws of England* (1765–8), thus considered that because the pirate 'has reduced himself afresh to the savage state of nature, by declaring war against all mankind, all mankind must declare war against him'.[38] According to Vattel, 'the enemy of the human race', by transgressing the law of nations, stripped himself of its protection.[39] By applying this language to Napoleon, British lawyers were saying that he was not entitled to any legal protection; but the practical consequences of such a labelling remained open.

For the British government, it mattered to respect, as much as possible, the law of nations, while accommodating for a situation of emergency—the danger of a renewal of war if Napoleon remained at large or was detained in Europe. The problem hinged upon the exceptionality of this case with respect to the law of nations. Some jurists were of the opinion that no significant change to the legal rules should be implemented, even in time of crisis; others advocated the adoption of some 'extra-legal measures'.[40] The discussion between William Scott, Lord Stowell, eminent judge of the High Court of Admiralty, who took the former stance, and his brother Lord Eldon, who took the latter, exemplifies this tension. The only surviving evidence of this correspondence are the letters written from the former to the latter, in September–October 1815. Lord Stowell, a specialist of maritime law, considered that the law of nations should always supersede municipal law, with no exception. In many instances during his rich career, Stowell chose to apply supranational principles, even when British interests at sea were involved. In the words of one of his biographers, 'the law of nations remained the unshakeable bedrock of his legal convictions'.[41] His correspondence with his brother on the case of Napoleon illustrates the same view: as a French subject, Napoleon should be delivered to the French sovereign, Louis XVIII.[42] The political and military context of emergency did not matter: the rule of law must be respected. For political rather than legal considerations, Lord Eldon disagreed with his brother. The Allies, he wrote, would not consent to Napoleon being delivered up to France, after his escape from Elba. 'The safety of nations' required that Napoleon be put in custody. As he proved throughout his career, Eldon was prepared to support a certain level of what he called 'necessary tyranny', such as

---

[35] This paragraph is based on Edelstein, *Terror*, pp. 26–42.   [36] Ibid., p. 26.
[37] Ibid., pp. 29–30.   [38] Quoted in Edelstein, *Terror*, p. 35.
[39] Vattel, *Law of Nations*, Book III, chap. 8, par. 155.   [40] See Gross and Ni Aolain, *Law*.
[41] Bourguignon, *Sir William Scott*, p. 265.
[42] According to Eldon to Scott, 4 October 1815, in Twiss, *Public*, vol. I, p. 536.

the suspension of the Habeas Corpus Act or checks on the freedom of the press, in order to further a more fundamental aim: the protection of the British constitution against the dangers of a radical upheaval.[43] Likewise, the justification for imprisoning Napoleon after war with France was over could not be grounded in the law of nations as it existed: 'is it not a strange thing that the law of nations does not admit a case of exception?'[44] Eldon thus proposed to introduce 'a *casus exceptionis or omissus* within the law of nations, founded upon necessity'.[45] The 'within' is key: the government should maintain its adherence to the law of nations, while temporarily introducing a caveat that would not endanger the rule of law.[46] Eldon was looking for a way to justify a decision already taken, i.e. the incarceration of Napoleon overseas.

This discussion about the characterization of Napoleon raised a broader issue about the very definition of war. During the French Wars, defining who was a legitimate enemy and who was entitled to be treated according to the laws of war became even more complicated than before. For instance, the unprecedented participation of volunteers to the conflicts, in the Vendée, Spain, or Italy, had led to a redefinition of the status of those who were hitherto treated as brigands or unlawful combatants. The central question, for us, revolves around the separation between an individual and his state in times of war. While Vattel considered that an individual's fate was tied to his state when war was declared, we have seen throughout this book that there existed multiple exceptions to these principles, illustrated for example by the case of hostages.[47] More importantly, the clear connection of an individual to a single state was still a novelty in the early nineteenth century.[48] Practices around subjecthood and citizenship were still in flux in 1815.[49]

The case of Napoleon is a liminal one, because the issue was not to exempt him from the devastations of war, like women or civilians, but to *maintain* him in a state of war while the rest of his compatriots were at peace. But the same logic was at stake, i.e. the disentanglement in the law of nations of the state and the individuals who constitute it. According to the Lord Chief Justice, Edward Law, First Lord Ellenborough, it might be argued that Britain remained at war with Napoleon, as an individual: 'We may either include him in the aggregate of the French nation, . . . , or we may specially exclude him, in which case the state of war will subsist as to him, and so far only as a specific treaty with him shall qualify that state of war.'[50] This interpretation opened the door to a new conception of war: it

[43] Eldon to Scott, [29 September] 1819, in ibid., p. 346; Melikan, *John Scott*, p. 162.
[44] Eldon to Scott, 4 October 1815, in Twiss, *Public*, vol. I, p. 536.
[45] Eldon to Scott, 6 October 1815, quoted in Bourguignon, *Sir William Scott*, p. 57.
[46] On this 'political realist' argument, see Gross and Ni Aolain, *Law*, p. 111.
[47] Vattel, *Law of Nations*, book III, ch. 3, par. 70.   [48] See, for instance, Hall, *Treatise*, p. 68.
[49] This situation might have been familiar throughout the late medieval and early modern periods. See Kim, *Aliens*.
[50] Quoted in Eldon to Scott, [October–November 1815], in Twiss, *Public*, vol. I, p. 537.

did not necessarily pit states against state; it could also pit individuals against states. The situation was unprecedented, Ellenborough wrote, because Napoleon had waged war on his own, as it were:

> The question is new in specie, and can only be properly decided by considering what rights result upon principle from a state of war, as against all the *individuals of the belligerent nation*. Those rights are seldom, if ever, enforced against individuals; because individuals hardly ever make war but as part of an aggregate mass. But I think the case of B. is sufficiently distinguished from all other cases to warrant the application of a more rigorous principle.[51]

An obvious parallel can be made here with the reasoning used in 1793 in France to put Louis XVI on trial for treason and murder, as an 'outlaw' and an 'enemy of humanity' who had violated natural right and waged war against his own subjects, just like Charles I.[52] Understandably, such precedents were too embarrassing to invoke in Britain. Such a definition of war also begs the question of knowing how and if it could ever formally end. No wonder that Ellenborough could not find any precedent in the legal literature on this: 'nothing in Vattel, &c., upon this sort of case.'[53] Moreover, argued Eldon, the war between Britain and France, 'whatever be its character as to B.', was still ongoing, since no peace treaty had yet been signed. Britain thus retained 'a right to treat him as a prisoner of war, as we have to treat any person taken at Waterloo or surrendering there as a prisoner of war'. It was certainly consistent 'with justice or the law of nations' to continue to regard him as such until a peace was signed with him or his sovereign. However, if Napoleon was still considered as a French subject, once the peace was signed with France the same difficulties of finding legal grounds for imprisoning him after the peace would resurface. Therefore, like Lord Ellenborough, Lord Eldon supported the idea of excluding him from the benefits of a peace treaty with France, 'continuing him, as far as we think fit so to do, an *individual enemy*'.[54] In order to do so, the nature of the war which had taken place after Napoleon's escape from Elba had to be interrogated. This war had been declared 'against Bonaparte and his adherents, and not against France generally, by G.B.... Has there been war with *France* as FRANCE? I think not.' By becoming the Emperor of Elba, and by abdicating his claims to the sovereignty of France, Napoleon had by the same logic given up 'his character of subject to France'—since dual allegiance was impossible.[55] Thus, he would be

---

[51] Quoted in Eldon to Scott, undated, in ibid., p. 538. The specificity of Napoleon's case, compared to any other sovereign who had waged war in defiance of a treaty, was not obvious, and many English radicals contested the 'Declaration of Outlawry' on those grounds.

[52] Edelstein, 'War', pp. 250, 255, 257.

[53] Eldon to Scott, undated, in Twiss, *Public*, vol. I, p. 538.

[54] Ibid., pp. 539–40, 538. Emphasis in the original.   [55] Ibid., pp. 540, 541.

considered neither as a French subject nor as a rebel to France, and he could not be tried in France either.

Because Napoleon had showed numerous times that he could not be trusted, a peace with him would never do: 'In this war with him, he has become a *prisoner of war*, with whom *we can make no peace*, because *we can* have no safety but *in his imprisonment*—no peace with him, or which includes him.'[56] As an exception to the law of nations, at war against humanity as a whole, Napoleon presented a danger that could never disappear while he lived; he would have to remain a permanent prisoner of war, because this was a perpetual war. *In fine*, the whole case revolved around the possibility of depriving him of his subjecthood:

> If Bonaparte can be separated from France, and can be considered neither as a subject of France nor a French rebel, then he has been subdued in legitimate war against *him*—and if so, I presume that we have a right to consider him as and to treat him as a prisoner of war...as long as we please.[57]

Even if he was subjected to Britain's sovereignty, Napoleon was not a subject of any sovereignty. This countered Napoleon's claims on behalf of his own (local) subjecthood, and thus his clever use of British law. In another undated and posterior letter to the Prime Minister Lord Liverpool, Eldon summarized the case for imprisoning Napoleon for life, and gave his support to the British ratification of the Convention of 2 August 1815. Despite the mental gymnastics described above, Napoleon's captivity could not be justified by the law of nations, and the case ultimately rested upon the security of Europe. As Eldon put it, his imprisonment 'is of absolute necessity to the future internal peace & welfare of ourselves & of our Allies'. But the decision to make Bonaparte a 'distinct, substantive Enemy, independent of any relation to the Sovereign of France' was heavily loaded. The protection of the law of nations, to a captured and stateless enemy, became conditional and subordinated to the interest of the state: 'a conquered Enemy indeed, with whom, according to the Law of Nations, we should deal as mercifully as our Security would admit after he was conquered.'[58]

Lord Eldon, who elaborated the rationale behind the British government's stance, seemed to have a legal theory to justify a unique category designation for Napoleon Bonaparte. It is significant that Eldon did try very hard to ground this position in law, beyond simply asserting government fiat. This would fit in with Paul Schroeder's interpretation, according to which the new pragmatic spirit revealed at the Congress of Vienna did not preclude the respect of law in international affairs, which was a clear break with the French Wars.[59] Even when dealing with an outlaw, it remained of paramount importance to stick to

[56] Ibid., p. 541.   [57] Ibid.
[58] Eldon to Liverpool, Private, 1815, in Stewart, 'Imprisonment', pp. 574, 576.
[59] Schroeder, *Transformation*, pp. 581–2.

some legal principles, and to use pre-existing legal material to justify Napoleon's detention. Eldon was aware that his legal claims were effectively political ones. He was explicitly seeking a legal rationale for what amounted to a policy choice. He was also very clear that the problem before him was legally indeterminate; at the same time, he knew that politics was not simply juxtaposed to law. Eldon's idea of necessity did not push his government into an extra-legal zone, though it may lead into a zone of novelty. In other words, Eldon appreciated that a perpetual prisoner of war was new, but he argued that such a designation was legal. In dressing up Napoleon as the prisoner of a permanent war, a status which was sufficiently malleable and ill-defined, the British government hoped to have it both ways, apparently conforming to the rule of law while keeping a considerable flexibility as to the concrete treatment of the captive.

In the summer of 1815, the opposition, and particularly Lord Holland, focused its criticism of the government on the fact that Napoleon was to be transported to St Helena without even a trial. This threatened the rights of every Englishman, setting an uneasy precedent.[60] In order to avoid being tarred with the brush of authoritarianism and address the criticisms of the opposition, the British government decided to obtain Parliament's sanction retrospectively to legalize its decision to deport Napoleon to St Helena. Two statutes were thus voted in 1816, to suspend habeas corpus and to indemnify the ministers and state agents who were taking part in Napoleon's confinement.[61] The focus of Lord Holland's attack against the government's policy rightly identified its main innovation: the assumption that the fate of an individual, in international law, could be separated from the actions of his state. Holland asked: 'Whether any person could be considered as an alien enemy, who was not the subject of any state with which were at war? ... Could any person be held as a prisoner of war, who was not the subject of any known State? Could any man be so detained who was the subject of a state with whom we were not a war?'[62]

It is crucial to note that the British—unlike the Prussians, for instance—never argued for a suspension of the legal order. Instead of simply defining Napoleon as an outlaw, a *hostis humani generis*, a compromise was chosen, and the British government tried very hard to maintain the fiction that the prisoner was treated in accordance with the laws of nations, as an exception *within* the said laws. In order to do so, Napoleon was fitted under the umbrella of the category of a prisoner of war. The concept of the prisoner of war was thus considerably stretched: it was now possible to be detained *sine die* and in time of peace, without any hope of a future exchange or liberation.

[60] Semmel, *Napoleon*, pp. 205–6.
[61] *An Act...Napoleon Bonaparte* (56 Geo. 3, c22), and *An Act... Saint Helena* (56 Geo. 3, c23). See Hale Bellot, 'Detention', pp. 183–7; Melikan, 'Caging', pp. 357–62.
[62] 8 April 1816, *Cobbett's Political Register*, vol. XXX, p. 471.

III. St Helena, the Island-prison

In July 1815, the Allies (Britain, France, Russia, Prussia, and Austria) agreed that Britain should be given the custody of Napoleon, and that he should be incarcerated in a place where he would not present a danger to European peace any more.[63] At first, the project was to send him not overseas, but to Scotland, as an international prisoner of the allied powers: 'According to an arrangement made between the Powers he will be sent as a prisoner to Fort George, in the North of Scotland, and placed under the surveillance of Austrian, Russian, French, and Prussian commissioners.'[64] Fort George was a military fortress situated 20 km north-east of Inverness, built in 1748–69 to control the Highlands, and later used in 1798 to detain Irish rebels.[65]

Castlereagh shared the view that Scotland would be a perfect place of detention, for symbolic as well as material reasons:

> You must make up your mind to be his gaolers. The French Government will not try him as a traitor, and there is nowhere a place so suitable for his confinement as in Fort St George [sic] under a joint surveillance.

> The Emperor of Russia approves this plan, so does Austria, so does France and so no doubt will Prussia. He will be less exposed in England to any sudden change in European politics, and after fighting him for twenty years, as a trophy, he seems to belong to us.[66]

The war against Napoleonic France had been couched as a just war, and this final sentence seemed to express a return to a medieval conception of the prisoner, as the fruit of the plunders of war and as the property of the victor. There were further reasons why Britain should be the sole custodian of Napoleon, even though the other European powers would be more than willing 'to shut him up in one of their fortresses': he had escaped once, and 'in no other [hands] could he safely for our own interests be placed'.[67] However, Lord Liverpool flagged the 'very nice legal questions' that would certainly arise from a detention in Britain or Europe, as well as the danger of providing radicals with a rallying cry.[68] Exiling him in Europe had previously ended in a shambles. The choice was made to deport him far away.

The terms of the arrangement that made of Napoleon a prisoner of the international community were truly innovative. In truth, Lord Liverpool would

---

[63] Hale Bellot, 'Detention', p. 174.
[64] Metternich to the Empress Marie Louise, Paris, July 1815, in Metternich, *Memoirs*, vol. II, p. 613.
[65] Kelly, 'Official list'.
[66] Castlereagh to Liverpool, 17 July 1815, quoted in Hale Bellot p. 179.
[67] Castlereagh to Liverpool, 24 August 1815, in Webster, *British Diplomacy*, p. 370.
[68] Liverpool to Castlereagh, 21 July 1815, quoted in Hale Bellot, 'Detention', p. 179.

have preferred that 'the discretion should be vested entirely in ourselves', i.e. without the presence of European commissioners on site, and he listed potential places of confinement whose selection should, following the same logic, be decided solely by Britain: 'Either in Great Britain, or at Gibraltar, Malta, St Helena, the Cape of Good Hope, or any other colony we might think most secure. We incline at present strongly to the opinion that the best place of custody would be at a distance from Europe.'[69] These locations shared certain characteristics. Their main asset, as places of detention, was their geographic isolation and natural protections, which should prevent Napoleon from escaping as easily as from the island of Elba. They had all been used as prisons across the centuries, and therefore were equipped with facilities for detaining the illustrious prisoner. Moreover, these territories, in 1815, remained in a situation of 'legal anomaly' within the British Empire: their legal status was sufficiently undefined, and their legal apparatus sufficiently light, to provide the British government with room for manoeuvre, just like the penal colonies for convicts set up between 1780 and the 1850s.[70] Gibraltar had been used as a Royal Navy base throughout the war, and was essentially a military fortress: its governors were military men appointed in London. Malta had recently been conquered by Britain, in 1800, and only then did the island become part of the British Empire. The Cape of Good Hope, a Dutch colony, had been occupied by the British between 1795 and 1802, then again in 1806, and it was only in 1814 that the Dutch government formally ceded sovereignty over the Cape to the British. It is possible that what Liverpool had in mind was Robben Island, off the Cape colony, which had been used by the Dutch as a prison for political prisoners since the seventeenth century.[71] Other places were mentioned in the public papers, such as St Lucia in the Windward Islands, a former French colony which was only secured by the British in 1814. Finally, St Helena had been governed, colonized, and garrisoned by the East India Company since the 1650s.[72]

Lord Liverpool made the case for St Helena on 21 July:

[St Helena is] the place in the world the best calculated for the confinement of such a person. There is a very fine citadel there, in which he might reside; the situation is particularly healthy; there is only one place in the circuit of the island where ships can anchor, and we have the power of excluding neutral vessels altogether if we should think it necessary. At such a distance and in such a place all intrigues would be impossible; and being withdrawn so far from the European world, he would very soon be forgotten.... We wish that the King of France would hang or shoot Bonaparte as the best termination of the business; but if this is

---

[69] Liverpool to Castlereagh, 15 July 1815, in Webster, *British Diplomacy*, p. 345.
[70] Benton, *Search*, pp. 162–216.   [71] Ward, *Networks*, pp. 139–40, 150.
[72] Graham, 'Napoleon's naval gaolers'; Young, *Napoleon*, vol. I, pp. 102–3.

impracticable, and the Allies are desirous that we should have the custody of him, it is not unreasonable that we should be allowed to judge of the means by which that custody can be made effectual.[73]

The Convention of 2 August 1815 implemented these principles.

All of the places considered for Napoleon's prison had been quite recently added to the British Empire, and their legal status with respect to the metropole was still uncertain in 1815. By setting foot in these new dominions, a prisoner like Napoleon might be deprived, in practice rather than in law, of the rights he would be granted if he landed in Britain. In this, the British government returned to a practice common in the seventeenth century: during the Interregnum, sending political prisoners to insular places in order to keep them beyond the reach of the writ of habeas corpus had been common; Cromwell's council deported several royalists to Jersey and the Isles of Scilly, even though they had not been charged or tried.[74]

Like hundreds of thousands of prisoners of war in the eighteenth century, Napoleon was hence subjected to forced mobility: together with the fifty-eight companions who would share his fate, a number that included women and servants, he was transferred on 7 August to HMS *Northumberland* and brought to an isolated island, which he reached on 15 October 1815, after sixty-four days of navigation.[75] The journey and the exile were supervised by Vice-Admiral Sir George Cockburn, commander in chief of the Cape of Good Hope. The conditions of captivity on board were very comfortable, but not much more so than any captured officer: Napoleon ate at the captain's table, as was customary.

Napoleon's sojourn in St Helena has been much written about. What I want to suggest, in these final pages, is that this captivity, however exceptional it was, also followed some of the defining features of war imprisonment that I have analysed in this book. While the forms of social interactions that developed on the island were partly a consequence of the unique status of the prisoner, and of his unusual character in international law, they did not radically depart from the experience of many prisoners in the preceding period.

Since the early eighteenth century, thanks to its strategic location 'at the crossroads of oceanic trading systems', St Helena had been a stopping point for European ships, who replenished there on their return voyages from the Indian Ocean.[76] During the six years that Napoleon would stay there, the function of the island changed, as it was turned into a prison. The governor who arrived in April 1816 specifically to look after Napoleon, Hudson Lowe, was a soldier, just like his predecessor, Colonel Wilks. These officials were given very broad powers, which resembled the practice in British penal colonies, where convicts were placed under

[73] Liverpool to Castlereagh, 21 July 1815, in Wellington, *Supplementary Dispatches*, vol. XI, p. 47.
[74] Halliday, *Habeas Corpus*, pp. 227–41.   [75] Dwyer, *Napoleon*, p. 18.
[76] McAleer, 'Looking east'.

military authority—a confusion between judicial and military jurisdictions that often gave rise to criticisms of arbitrary power.[77] The island's coastal waters were patrolled by armed ships, to defeat any attempt at sending a rescuing party, and avoid a repetition of the Elba disaster, when Napoleon had vanished right under his captors' noses.[78] Any ship that obtained permission to anchor in St Helena was closely monitored, with guards placed on them. The island was impregnable, thanks to the fortifications erected by the East India Company during the wars against the Dutch in the 1790s. Jamestown fortress' batteries defended the harbour on the north side, and all strategic approaches were protected by heavy guns.[79]

The exceptional status of the prisoner was reflected in the balance between the number of custodians and that of prisoners of war. On the eve of Napoleon's arrival, St Helena's population numbered 2,871 souls, excluding the 1,000 soldiers posted on the island. The number of soldiers was doubled, to reach almost 2,000 men, and a naval squadron was harboured permanently in St Helena.[80] A battalion of the fifty-third regiment, which had served in the Peninsular War, was encamped at Deadwood, 1.6 km from Longwood—Napoleon's residence from December 1815 onwards, pictured in Fig. 7.1.[81]

THE GIFT OF A GREAT PRINCE TO A LITTLE EMPEROR.

Fig. 7.1. W. Fry, after H.J. Phelps, *The Gift of a Great Prince to a Little Emperor* (London: J. Jenkins, 20 September 1817). Cambridge University Library, RCMS 190/36.

[77] Benton, *Search*, pp. 185, 189–90.   [78] Jackson, *Notes*, pp. 156–7.
[79] Young, *Napoleon*, vol. I, p. 179.   [80] Ibid., p. 108.
[81] Lutyens, *Letters*, p. 9.

These 550 men had been shipped from Europe specifically to watch over Napoleon. Other regiments were subsequently brought from Britain and India. Sentries and pickets were scattered around the island, and, thanks to telegraphs posts placed on the main heights, no ship could hope to approach without being noticed.[82] Like Dartmoor, St Helena was conceived as a prison which could resist attacks both from within and from without. But whereas prison guards were always heavily outnumbered by prisoners of war, the opposite was true in St Helena. This did not mean that Napoleon and his companions were powerless.

The regime of Napoleon's captivity in St Helena was a form of detention on parole, which was tailored to the danger represented by these prisoners. The island was divided into zones, in which the prisoners' freedom of movement varied. Within the Longwood domain, which had a perimeter of four miles, there was no restriction. By day, sixteen men guarded the Longwood gate, and another four were placed around the Longwood domain. After dusk, the surveillance was tightened, and after 9 pm, forty-two men were placed at the gate, while sixteen other men were placed around the house. Within a circuit of twelve miles around Longwood, reduced to eight miles for a time by Hudson Lowe, the former Emperor could wander on his own. This plateau was bounded by deep precipices and eighty-two guards.[83] On the rest of the island, Napoleon was allowed to go everywhere, provided he gave notice to the governor and was accompanied by a British officer, who would prevent him from 'engaging into conversation with the persons he may meet'.[84] Jamestown, the main urban centre, presented risks, explained Hudson Lowe in a letter to Henry Bathurst, the Secretary for War and the Colonies:

> It is in the Town, where all the Commercial and Tradespeople, and in fact all the Inhabitants except a few Land Holders, constantly reside. It is there alone where Strangers or Seafaring Persons are to be met with, and it is one of the Port Regulations therefore, that no Passenger or any other Person, although landing from the ships can pass into the interior of the Island without permission.[85]

The prisoners found this regime unbearable, and they tried, like all prisoners on parole, to obtain an 'enlargement' of these limits.[86] But despite multiple propositions of compromise on the part of the British authorities, this remained a bone of contention.[87] There as well, there was nothing particularly unique about the prisoners of St Helena.

[82] Young, *Napoleon*, vol. I, pp. 178–9, 222–3.
[83] Ibid., pp. 163–4, 305–6, 324, 326–7.   [84] Ibid., pp. 308–9.
[85] 1 November 1819, British Library, London (BL), Add MS20128, fos. 351v–352.
[86] 'Notes of Conversation between Lowe and O'Meara', 24 July 1817, BL, Add MS20119, fo. 152.
[87] Young, *Napoleon*, vol. I, p. 325.

If one only considers St Helena from the perspective of Napoleon, it is easy to forget that he was not the only captive on the island. In addition to thousands of soldiers, the island's population was diverse. In September 1815, on the eve of Napoleon's arrival, 2,871 individuals resided there: 776 whites, 1,353 slaves, 447 free blacks, 280 Chinese, fifteen Lascars.[88] This hierarchy of colour, where the number of forced labourers vastly exceeded that of white settlers, was typical of a colonial situation. The interactions between the prisoners of war and these people showed how much their situations differed.[89] Napoleon frequently encountered black slaves and freedmen during his rides. Captain Poppleton, the ordinance officer, thus mentioned that Napoleon had 'given some black people money, for some trifling services rendered him on the Road, such as opening Gates, answering perhaps to his questions about the road, clear the road for him, which they did at one time by pulling down a Wall which lay in his direction'. He also gave two Napoleons—the Napoleon was a twenty- or forty-franc gold coin—to a slave who had brought him 'a pocket telescope he had lost'.[90] While Napoleon complained about his deprivation of freedom, he was daily confronted by people who were born in captivity—a fact that did not prevent him from making disturbing analogies between their fate and his, carefully avoiding any reference to his re-establishment of slavery in 1802.[91] For these people, St Helena was a prison too.

The whole island was put under surveillance due to the presence of Napoleon and his companions. Colonel Wilks, the governor, issued a proclamation on 17 October 1815, forbidding to 'pass in any part of the island (excepting in the immediate precincts of the town) between the hours of nine at night and daylight in the morning, without having the parole of the night'.[92] The town's drawbridge was raised at sunset, and fishing was prohibited until early morning. This transformation of the island into a military prison had major economic repercussions. The large naval squadron and the soldiers were supplied by a regular traffic of store ships, and the demand for local products grew. While some historians argue that this was a period of great prosperity for the island's economy, the majority of the population probably suffered from the dramatic increase in the price of commodities.[93] Instead of focusing on Napoleon alone, the perspective can be broadened precisely to observe the social consequences of the militarisation and

---

[88] Ibid., p. 108. Slavery was abolished in 1818: Ibid., p. 109.

[89] The Chinese labourers had been 'imported' by Governor Beatson in 1808 and his successor Colonel Mark Wilks in 1813: ibid., pp. 107–8. These indentured servants employed by the East India Company were barracked not far away from Longwood, and Napoleon regularly employed them to work at his residence: ibid., p. 159. See Po-Ching, 'Chinese seamen'.

[90] Questions put to Poppleton by Lowe, 21 July 1817, BL, Add MS20119, fos. 135–v.

[91] 29–30 November 1815, Las Cases, *Memorial*, vol. I, pp. 241–6.

[92] Quoted in Young, *Napoleon*, vol. I, p. 118.

[93] Ibid.; Grove, 'St Helena', pp. 266–7. The prisoners complained about these 'privations' and the lack of paper, oil, or coffee: 1 February 1816, Las Cases, *Memorial*, vol. I, pp. 347–8.

carceralisation of the small South Atlantic island. Here, we can observe a society of prisoners at the scale of an island.

Exchanges between the prisoners, custodians, and local populations were almost impossible to prevent. Four years after the captives' arrival, the governor was still eager to prevent 'any of the lower class of the Inhabitants' to come 'across Fisher's Valley at the back of the House to sell anything to the Servants or Communicate with them', but there were several instances of transgressions of his orders.[94] This failure to control the exchange of information between Longwood and St Helena was manifested on a larger scale: St Helena became a node in a global system of political communications. A steady flow of visitors, including the commissioners sent to St Helena to implement the Convention of 2 August 1815, brought news, packets, letters, and gifts to the former emperor.[95] Napoleon used the captains of the ships that stopped in St Helena on their way from India to Europe, requesting they convey his recriminations to European opinions.[96] Hudson Lowe tightened up the surveillance of the correspondence between Longwood, St Helena, and the rest of the world, and some of Napoleon's companions were expelled from the island for transgressing these orders, but communication continued. As soon as they had been expelled from the island, the captives hastened to publish their souvenirs.[97] Numerous tracts and newspaper articles describing allegations of the harsh treatments imposed on the captives of St Helena were published in Europe and elsewhere, forcing the Allied governments to respond to these accusations, and even to convene a conference to address their critics.[98] The masterpiece, in this enterprise of propaganda, was of course Las Cases' *Mémorial de Sainte-Hélène*, a maudlin and sycophantic piece of *martyrologie*. Not only did Napoleon and his followers display their mastery at playing for European audiences, they also used these publications to destabilize the British authorities on the island.[99]

Napoleon's relationships with his guards were shaped by his unabated refusal to admit the lawfulness of his treatment, from the day he had been categorized as a prisoner of war. The symbolic battle over the justice of his deportation and captivity was fought principally on the home ground of his residence at Longwood. The captive treated this house as the last remaining parcel of his sovereignty. If St Helena was the regional theatre of the dispute, Longwood must be considered as a local piece in the global game of chess that Napoleon played with

---

[94] Questions put to Poppleton by Lowe, 21 July 1817, BL, Add MS20119, fo. 137.
[95] Young, *Napoleon*, vol. I, pp. 280–6.
[96] 21 April 1816, Las Cases, *Memorial*, vol. II, pp. 87–8.
[97] See, for example, O'Meara, *A Voice from St. Helena* (1822).
[98] Hale Bellot, 'Detention', pp. 190–2.
[99] See the petition from the officers of the 66th Regiment defending Captain Henry Blakeney, the orderly officer, against the assertions in the *Courier* of 29 October 1818: St Helena, 20 March 1819, BL, Add MS20125, fos. 442–v.

his jailors. He tried, and often succeeded, to dictate the rhythm, the style, and the content of his interactions with them.

The most striking feature of Napoleon's sojourn in St Helena was his decision to live in a self-imposed 'system of seclusion', in order to reassert his control over his daily life.[100] If he could not be the sovereign of Europe, he could at least remain the emperor of his own house. This strange configuration was only possible because, as his captors themselves recognized, he was not a 'normal' prisoner of war. Due to the sensitivity of the issue in Europe, he needed to be treated well. A delicate balance had to be struck between security, and the captives' privacy and comfort. Napoleon and his followers remained ever more sensitive to the respect of their status. There too, the phenomenon was not fundamentally different to what we observed with regard to eighteenth-century prisoners of war on parole, but this took a more extreme form in St Helena. Napoleon wrote to Hudson Lowe, on 30 April 1816: 'I have not forgotten my first condition.'[101] One of the problems was the British authorities' refusal to call Napoleon an 'emperor', which led to endless discussions.[102] Comte Montholon also complained about the 'constant want of respect evinced for our rank and our sufferings'.[103] By the same token, Napoleon downgraded his captors. Hudson Lowe was for instance called a 'chief of jailors', a 'keeper of galley slaves', who treated the Frenchmen like 'felons'.[104] He did 'not know how to behave towards men of honour', and the post he had accepted in St Helena was that of 'a hangman', not that of a gentleman.[105] Similar epithets were used against Admiral Cockburn.[106] What was at stake behind these power struggles—just like the squabbles between officers on parole and their Agents—was the recognition of Napoleon's rank, which captivity could not stain.

Napoleon 'reorganized his Imperial Court', retaining his 'Grand Marshall of the Palace', a 'Lord Chamberlain', a 'Master of Horse', 'Dames d'honneur', and several valets and maids.[107] In total, in March 1816 this micro-society counted twenty-eight individuals, the majority of whom had been part of the Imperial household in Paris, in addition to which were twenty-four British officers and sailors and servants from St Helena, who worked in the stables, kitchen and garden, or as attendants to Napoleon and companions.[108] If, according to Napoleon, life in Longwood was miserable by comparison with his *train de vie* before St Helena, it was very comfortable, if not lavish, both according to his captors and by comparison with any prisoner of war.[109] He had a proper library, and had access

---

[100]   Earl Bathurst to Hudson Lowe, 6 October 1818, ibid., fo. 479v.
[101]   Young, *Napoleon*, vol. I, p. 244.   [102]   Ibid., p. 121, 317–24.
[103]   21 December 1815, in ibid., p. 182.   [104]   Young, *Napoleon*, vol. I, pp. 201, 250, 251.
[105]   Ibid., p. 292.   [106]   Las Cases, *Memorial*, vol. II, 17 April 1816, pp. 76–9.
[107]   Young, *Napoleon*, vol. I, p. 154.   [108]   Ibid., pp. 157–9.
[109]   See the list of expenses in ibid., pp. 160–3, including 'fresh roses for the table of His Majesty'.

to recent newspapers and books, including those that attacked the British government.[110] Just like prisoners on parole, the captives were invited to mix with the local gentry.[111]

But the most extraordinary privileges conceded to Napoleon and his retinue regarded the house itself. The captive was allowed, as it were, to design his own prison and shape its surroundings. Napoleon was an extreme case of a prisoner exerting agency on his living space.[112] A new, spacious, and very comfortable house, with marble chimney-pieces, large windows, and fireplaces, was built for Napoleon near his residence at Longwood. Although he was consulted throughout about his preferences, he never occupied it, objecting to the iron rails that surrounded it, at a distance of 127 feet.[113] Captain Engelbert Lutyens, an ordinance officer, thus wrote, citing Comte Montholon's conversation with him:

> The only thing the General disapproved of was the iron-rails, which formed a perfect iron-cage, and he always said, and says, he will not inhabit the house until they are done away with.... That if the railing is put up for the security of his person, they disgust him; if for ornament, it does not accord with his taste; and, if there is occasion for a fence, a wooden-rail would answer.[114]

The most revealing example of these micro-struggles over space was the tragicomic war that Napoleon declared against his guards at Longwood. Within the Longwood domain, Napoleon was granted extensive privileges.[115] However, he found impossible to obey the obligation to make himself visible to his captors. Despite being given the 'discretion' to 'fix the time' he would prefer the orderly officer to make him a visit, he found the very idea insufferable.[116] For the same reason, he could not stand the obligation to be accompanied by a British officer during his promenades outside Longwood.[117] Las Cases explained this misunderstanding: this captain considered that his presence should not be an affront for Napoleon, as 'he would be with us, as if he were not present. He seemed... unable to comprehend that the mere sight of him could be offensive to the Emperor.'[118] Napoleon maintained that he was still an emperor; he was everyone's focal point, but like an absolutist monarch, only he should decide when he could be gazed at. One can understand his resentment at being regularly reminded of his fall from

---

[110] Ibid., pp. 166–8.   [111] Young, *Napoleon*, vol. I, pp. 123–4.   [112] See ch. 4.
[113] Young, *Napoleon*, vol. I, p. 142.
[114] Lutyens to Major Gorrequer, Longwood, 26 March 1820, *Letters*, p. 29. Part of the iron railing was accordingly dismantled and replaced by a wooden railing, but Napoleon still refused to move in: Lutyens to Gorrequer, 23 November 1820, *Letters*, p. 69.
[115] He was allowed to receive the visitors he wanted, as long as they had a pass, and between October 1815 and 1817, he received more than a hundred English visits: Young, *Napoleon*, vol. I, p. 170.
[116] Extract of Bathurst to Hudson Lowe, enclosed with Lowe to Bonaparte, 21 March 1819, BL, Add MS20125, fos. 448–v.
[117] Questions put to Poppleton by Lowe, 21 July 1817, Add MS20119, fos. 136–v.
[118] Las Cases, *Memoirs*, vol. I, 9 January 1816, p. 312.

grace, and Hudson Lowe's insistence on a strict application of his order rubbed salt in his wounds. On 3 May 1816, following Napoleon's self-confinement for several days in a row, the governor reasserted 'the necessity of General Bonaparte showing himself twice a day, morning and evening, or giving by some other means certain indications of his actual presence in the house'.[119]

The orderly officer posted next to his house had a single job to do: to report daily that he had caught sight of Napoleon. The guards suffered from piercing solitude, and the task proved to be more challenging than it sounds. Captain George Nicholls regularly complained to his superiors about what would nowadays be called work-related stress. On 15 May 1819 he wrote to Major Gorrequer, his superior, that he had had to be 'upon [his] feet upwards of *ten hours*, endeavouring to procure a sight of Napoleon Bonaparte', and on 21 July he complained that the bad weather and the necessity to walk for hours around the house in the execution of this duty made him fear for his health. This duty was also psychologically draining. In a reversal of roles, the sentry was the object of everyone's gaze and sarcasm: 'during the whole of this time I was exposed to the observations and remarks of not only the French servants, but also to gardeners and other persons employed about Longwood House.'[120] Napoleon played cruel tricks on the guard, hiding as soon as he approached, while observing him through holes he had cut out in the shutters.[121] While the captive refused to be monitored, he spent hours witnessing the movement of the barracked British soldiers with his telescope.[122]

Captain Nicholls, who was ordnance officer at Longwood for 421 days in total, failed to see Napoleon for 134 days.[123] In September 1819, Nicholls demanded admission to the residence. He was handed a message, which stated that

> The Emperor ... hereby declares that no such admission shall be granted, except it be obtained by force.... The Emperor acknowledges that he is a Prisoner, and as such the Nation into whose hands he has fallen, can kill him if they please; but he does not conceive, that they ought so grossly to Insult him, as to cause the six small rooms allotted to him, to be entered without his permission.[124]

Napoleon was goading his jailors, hoping that they would resort to violence, thus confirming that he was a victim. He was also asserting that his consent was nécessary to enter his house. No other prisoner of war would have been conceded the right to be the sovereign in their own residence, or to be allowed to put locks

[119] Quoted in Young, *Napoleon*, vol. I, p. 245.
[120] Nicholls to Gorrequer, 15 May, 21 July 1819, in ibid., vol. II, pp. 161–3.
[121] Ibid., p. 163. On this cat-and-mouse game, see ibid., pp. 161–4.
[122] Luytens, *Letters*, p. 29.   [123] Young, *Napoleon*, vol. II, p. 164.
[124] Related by Lieutenant Frederick St Croad (who accompanied Nicholls) to Major Gorrequer, 4 September 1819, BL, Add MS20128, fo. 25.

and bolts on the *inside* of doors.[125] At the same time, we saw that the power of custodians was often a negotiated form of coercion.[126] Despite the instruction to do their duty forcefully if necessary, the orderly officers dragged their feet.[127]

A few days later, Nicholls gave his resignation (which was turned down), explaining that after being 'employed in this arduous duty twelve months', he wished to join his regiment.[128] On 13 September 1819, Nicholls wrote to his superior, Major Gorrequer:

I have not seen General Bonaparte today—At this moment there is a person sitting in the Generals Billiard room with a cocked Hat on—I however can only see the Hat moving about. If the French are accustomed to sit at Dinner with their Hats on probably this is Napoleon Bonaparte at his dinner.[129]

Gorrequer did not appreciate the comedy of situation and replied matter-of-factly that, if the orderly officer had any doubt as to the identity of the person so observed, he should try to glance through the windows 'to ascertain by closer personal observation, whether it is really him or not. Your principal duty is to see him.'[130] Remarking that it was 'impossible' to obtain 'a view of General Bonaparte by candlelight' unless one was 'actually peeping in at, the windows', Captain Engelbert Lutyens (the ordnance officer between February 1820 and April 1821) wrote in December 1820 that resorting to such an impolite behaviour would hurt his 'own feelings'.[131] This pusillanimity was scowled at by Lutyens's superior, Sir Thomas Reade, who wrote to Hudson Lowe: 'I really think he is afraid of affronting them [*the French prisoners*].'[132] A singular relationship was certainly developing between the guards and their famous prisoner.

Napoleon went further than merely hiding behind curtains and shutters. At the end of 1819, he was overcome by a gardening frenzy, which was not as innocent as it looked. Hudson Lowe thus quoted a letter from Comte Montholon to an English correspondent:

Nothing can exceed the bustle and activity, which has been recently displayed by General Bonaparte, in giving directions about his flower garden, and superintending the workmen employed at it. He is hemming it in all round, with as many bushy trees and shrubs, as he can get transplanted, and with sod walls, so as to screen himself as far as possible, from external observation.[133]

[125] As in the residence he temporarily occupied, the Briars: Young, *Napoleon*, vol. I, p. 112.
[126] Ch. 6.
[127] Hudson Lowe, 'Note for the information of Napoleon Bonaparte', 25 March 1819, BL, Add MS20125, fos. 478–9.
[128] Nicholls to Gorrequer, 8 September 1819, Add MS20128, fo. 70.
[129] Ibid., 13 September 1819, fo. 154.
[130] Gorrequer to Nicholls, 14 September 1819, ibid., fo. 158v.
[131] Lutyens to Gorrequer, 10 December 1820, *Letters*, p. 76.   [132] Ibid., 76n1.
[133] Lowe to Bathurst, 1 December 1819, BL, Add MS20128, fo. 430.

In February 1820, the captive then undertook to shield himself further, planting rows of peach trees around the railings, which would, in the words of Hudson Lowe, 'obstruct the walk and the view of the sentries round the house and railing at night'.[134] This scheme was interrupted. The situation was complicated by the extravagant privileges granted to the prisoners. As a sign of conciliation, and in accordance with eighteenth-century practices towards officers on parole, Napoleon's hunting guns had been brought back to him in January 1816.[135] He shot goats, bullocks, rabbits, and fowls with his fowling-pieces, loaded with ball, as the animals were wandering in his garden, alarming the governor.[136]

Napoleon's exile in St Helena reveals, in a microscopic way, how the society of prisoners was structured not only through the opposition between the captives and their guards, but also through their multiple exchanges across the boundary. On the one hand, Napoleon's companions were not a unified group. Their constant bickering was heightened by their awareness that, besides their personal fidelity to the emperor, their 'connexion was purely *fortuitous*, and not the result of any natural affinity'.[137] Boredom, jealousy, gossips, and duels quickly set in, atomizing the group in mini-cliques. On the other hand, there were multiple instances of transgressions of the boundary between Napoleon and his guards, from mere sympathy to corruption and collusions. The fascination of the guards for the famous captive had started before their arrival in St Helena.[138] Las Cases thus wrote that on board the *Northumberland*, midshipmen demonstrated a 'marked respect and attention' to the emperor.[139] On the island, the sailors from the *Northumberland* called Napoleon their 'shipmate',[140] while captains and even admirals went out of their way to visit him.[141] Las Cases attributed such behaviour to Napoleon's 'renown throughout the world'.[142] A common sailor told Las Cases that, after having 'twice braved the obstacle of sentinels and all the dangers of severe prohibition, to get a close view of the Emperor', he 'should die content'.[143] Despite Napoleon's continual jeremiads, he was paid as much respect as his situation allowed. On leaving the island, the officers of the fifty-third Regiment visited Longwood to take their leave of him.[144] Small gifts were often exchanged

---

[134] Lowe, 'Note to Extract from Orderly-Officer's Report', sent to Bathurst, [February 1820], Lutyens, *Letters*, p. 12.

[135] Las Cases, 1–3 January 1816, *Memorial*, vol. I, p. 304.

[136] Lutyens, 16 February 1820, *Letters*, pp. 11, 13; Young, *Napoleon*, vol. II, p. 183–4.

[137] Las Cases, 15–16 December 1815, *Memorial*, vol. I, p. 267.

[138] Even at the time of his supremacy, the perception of Napoleon was not all negative in Britain and among British soldiers: Semmel, *Napoleon*; Daly, 'British soldiers'.

[139] 27–31 August 1815, *Memorial*, vol. I, p. 72.   [140] 4–8 January 1816, ibid., p. 310.

[141] See, for example, ibid., 11 January, 4 March 1816, pp. 316, 377–8.

[142] 23–6 March 1816, *Memorial*, vol. II, p. 32.

[143] 4–8 January 1816, *Memorial*, vol. I, p. 309.

[144] Hudson Lowe to General Sir H. Torrent, 22 July 1817, BL, Add MS20119, fos. 139v–140.

between Captain Lutyens, the ordinary officer, and the prisoners.[145] Many soldiers also defied their orders to exchange a few words with the 'great captive' and 'the great man'.[146]

The mere presence of the famous prisoner had reverberated on all those living in his vicinity. On 6 May 1821, Ensign Duncan Darroch wrote a letter to his mother, informing her of the death of the man he called 'Old Nap'. The soldier described the emotions that seized him as he was standing in the death chamber, predictably meditating on the vanity of human affairs. He also described how the society of prisoners would dissolve now that the object of everyone's attention was no more:

> What a change the thread of his existence being severed has caused in this island! People who have laid in stock to serve the troops will have it now lying useless on their hands. Horses that were this day week worth £70 will not bring £10. Our huts that we have been obliged to build to put our servants in, and which have cost from £6 to £10 each, are now useless, for this part of the island will be uninhabited after we leave it; so that, we shall all more or less feel the effects of his death.[147]

This book is rooted in the belief that it is problematic to consider the eighteenth-century prisoner of war simply as a precursor to the legal world we have inherited from the Geneva Conventions. But I am not arguing for a complete discontinuity between the eighteenth century and the present either. It is indeed possible to take the problem by the other end, to think about 1815 as a precedent. Unusual episodes, such as Napoleon's exile, are, perhaps more than others, reinterpreted or reframed over time as doctrines develop and new questions or categories emerge within the legal discourse. Much ink has for example been spilled on the fact that the former French emperor was not tried but dealt with by the executive power. Gary Jonathan Bass thus considers that 'to this day, "the Napoleonic precedent" means the use of extralegal means to get rid of an enemy'.[148] We saw that Napoleon's deportation was dressed with the clothes of legality, as far as possible, and the label prisoner of war served this purpose.

In the twentieth century, with the notion that wars of aggression were crimes against the law of nations, Napoleon's banishment was considered in a new light. In 1919, article 227 of the Treaty of Versailles stated that the emperor Wilhelm II of Hohenzollern, who had found refuge in the Netherlands, was made personally liable to the jurisdiction of the Allied courts for his alleged crimes during the First World War. Another option would have been to banish him to some remote

---

[145] See, for example, Lutyens's gift of flower seeds to Comte Montholon: Lutyens to Reade, 17 March 1820, *Letters*, p. 27.
[146] Jackson, *Notes and Reminiscences*, pp. 132, 145.
[147] Darroch to his mother, 6 May 1821, *Letters*, p. 190. See also his letter of 7 May 1821, pp. 191–6.
[148] Bass, *Stay the Hand*, pp. 38–9.

island, such as the Falklands or Devil's Island, reflecting on the procedures followed in 1815.[149] Either way, the Netherlands refused to extradite him as a war criminal. In the vexed discussion that ensued for two years between the Allies, one notes that the British government was the most vociferous, while the French were apathetic. The Foreign Office described Wilhelm as an 'enemy of the human race', and Lord Hardinge, permanent undersecretary at the Foreign Office, tried to obtain that he would be interned under Allied control 'in some spot or island where he will be rendered incapable of again molesting the peace of the world'.[150] The shadow of Napoleon is everywhere present in this language. In the end, the Dutch clung on and Wilhelm was not extradited. In 1946, an American federal judge, Charles E. Wyzanski, argued that the Nuremberg trial was 'a potential danger to law everywhere', pointing out that it would have been preferable if the accused were dealt with by the executive, instead of imperilling due process.[151] On the contrary, he continued, there were precedents for empowering the executive in such a way: 'The example of Napoleon shows that our consciences would have no reason to be disturbed about the removal from society and the permanent detention of irresponsible men who are a threat to the peace of the world.'[152]

While we must remain cautious when making historical analogies, one is also struck by the similarity of the discussions which occurred in 1815 with early twenty-first-century legal debates about the treatment of fallen sovereigns by the international community, the tension between the protection of human rights and the need to guarantee state security, the relation between municipal law, the laws of war and international law, and the problem of fighting wars against enemies whose legal status is uncertain. Let us return to St Helena. From the seventeenth century on, many slaves and convicts passed through this island, and prisoners of war would again be detained there during the Boer War.[153] Islands have been used and reused as spaces of incarceration over the centuries.[154] A combination of geographical isolation and legal anomaly seem to have predisposed such locales for the function of confining enemies.[155] The choice of St Helena was premised on the desire to remove Napoleon from the reach of habeas corpus. This touches on the issue of the extension of the legal domain of the sovereign: a question raised, more recently, by George W. Bush's 'War against Terror'. In Kandahar, in Abu Ghraib or in Guantanamo, the Bush administration has systematically unsettled the norms of international law, by refusing to grant the status of prisoners of war to their enemies, categorizing them instead as 'unlawful enemy combatants'.[156]

---

[149] Marks, '"My name"'. This paragraph is based on this article. For a legal view, see Wright, 'Legal liability', pp. 127–8.

[150] Quoted in Marks, 'My name', p. 153.   [151] Wyzanski, 'Nuremberg'.

[152] Ibid. See Glueck, 'Nuremberg Trial', 115n147; Goodhart, 'Legality', p. 637.

[153] Royle, 'St Helena'.   [154] Ch. 4; Benton, Search, p. 163.

[155] Mountz, 'Enforcement archipelago'.

[156] Steyn, 'Guantanamo Bay'; Kaplan, 'Where is Guantanamo?'; Gregory, 'Black flag'; Press, 'Sovereignty'; Tyler, Habeas Corpus.

Instead of considering these situations as exceptions to a long-term narrative of progress, it might be argued that they are a possibility intrinsic to the laws of war and to the very category of the prisoner of war. Just like Napoleon was described as a *hostis humani generis*, a prisoner who deserved an exceptional treatment because he had fought a war without rules, the same notion has been applied after 9/11 to captives who were deemed not worthy of the Hague and Geneva Conventions.[157] In St Helena as in Guantanamo, sovereignty was uncertain, time 'indeterminate', and legal norms 'suspended'.[158] But even 8,000 km from Europe, Napoleon was not powerless. Relentlessly repeating that he was not a prisoner of war, while emphasizing that he was denied the rights of prisoners of war, Napoleon managed to publicize his cause, prefiguring nineteenth-century political prisoners who began to use their internment as a political weapon.[159] Legal vacuums can also become echo chambers.

Sources

I. Archives

As a rule, the stamped foliation is given in the footnotes. If it is not, the registers are unfoliated.

A. Britain

British Library, London (BL)
Add Ch76691
Add MS20119, 20125, 20128, 28559, 32772, 32804, 32815, 32819, 37877, 38217, 38338, 38848, 61281, 61591–61595, 61614, 70195
Egerton MS2135
Kings MS61
Landsdowne 820/7
MS IOR/F/4/95/1921

Bute Archives at Mount Stuart, Rothesay (Scotland)
BU/98/6/355

Cambridge University Library (CUL)
BSA/D1/5/3–7. British and Foreign Bible Society

Cumbria Archive Centre, Carlisle (CAC)
D HUD 8/19/1
D HUD 18/9/1
D HUD 18/9/3
DRC/7/3. Transcript of marriage bonds, 1753–1762

Devon Record Office, Exeter (DRO)
M/O/1/25
QS/4/1757/Epiphany/RE/55
QS/4/1757/Epiphany RE/37
DEX/7/b/1808/70
6105M/O/1/25
Z19/46/4
152M/C1795/OM/9–10
152M/C/1812/OH/78
316M/4/F/2. Courtenay Ilbert's letters as a prisoner of war from the French, 1798–9
1317M/F/1. Journal of Peter Fea, seaman, 1810–14

Essex Record Office, Chelmsford (ERO)
D/DM/O1/23
Q/SBb 353 (1793)

Gloucestershire Record Office, Gloucester (GRO)
Correspondence between G.O. Paul, the Secretary at War and the Earl of Berkeley, Lord Lieutenant of Gloucestershire, Easter Sessions, 44th year of King George III, Q SO12 Order Book, pp. 563–78

National Maritime Museum, Greenwich (NMM)
ADM/E/20
ADM/F17 to 20
ADM/M/387 to 410, 414. These are not foliated, but the documents are sometimes numbered. When this is the case I have indicated it in the footnotes.
JOD/202. John Robertson, 'Journal', 1806–1811
REC/57. An account of the wreck of HMS Amazon . . . off the coast of France on 14 Jan 1797. With a detailed description of events while the crew were prisoners of war in France and their eventual release in March 1798 (1 January 1797–31 Dec. 1798)

Public Record Office of Northern Ireland, Belfast (PRONI)
T3019/1024. Petition by French prisoners in Kinsale, thanking the Viceroy and Governor Folliott for distributing clothes to them, 29 April 1748–[10 May 1748]

Royal Society of Arts (RSA)
AD/MA/100/10/400 A4/16. Peter Templeman to the Honourable Committee appointed to manage the Contributions for cloathing French Prisoners of War, Strand, 28 August 1760

The National Archives, Kew (TNA)
ADM1/3740
ADM1/5125
ADM7/298, 341
ADM97/102 to 107, 114/2, 115 to 125, 126/3, 127/1
ADM98/1 to 14, 103, 104, 120, 122 to 124, 127/1, 170, 185, 189, 225 to 227, 269 to 271, 284
ADM103/601
ADM105/42
ADM106/504, 851, 1248
CO110/1, 166/2, 137/80, 318/9
HCA30/239, 32/196, 32/313
SP34/3, 4
SP42/30, 42, 64, 119, 136
SP78/153, 154, 156–8, 230, 261
SP89/87

B. France
Archives Départementales de Seine-Maritime, Rouen (ADSM)
1M208, 1M209
C773
L4456

Archives Départementales d'Ille-et-Villaine, Rennes (ADIV)
C90, 154, 1090, 1091, 1174

Archives Départementales du Calvados, Caen (ADC)
C4155

Archives Départementales du Nord, Lille (ADN)
C4609, 4624/1, 4624/2
L13162

Archives du Ministère des Affaires Etrangères, La Courneuve (AMAE)
CPA449
MDA48
53MD1803, 53MD1804

Archives Nationales, Paris (AN)
Map G/210: Frézier, 'Plan ... du château de Solidor'
MAR/A1/47, 93
MAR/A5/6
MAR/B2/82, 99, 135, 165, 168, 181, 198, 199, 206, 207, 214 to 217, 223, 226, 228, 230, 322, 323, 325, 326, 328, 329, 331
MAR/B3/60, 64, 75, 82, 88, 89, 95, 117, 120, 123, 128, 135, 142, 143, 145, 155, 157, 165, 166, 169, 178, 180, 191, 195, 196, 206, 211, 421, 422, 428, 429, 432, 440, 445, 451, 453, 463, 464, 465, 538, 659, 716
MAR/B4/17, B4/57, 97, 151, 163
MAR/F2/71 to 76, 78, 82 to 95, 97 to 101

Service Historique de la Défense, Paris (SHD)
A1/3123
FF2/18, FF2/20

C. Jamaica
Jamaica Archives and Records Department, Spanish Town (JA)
Jamaican Assembly.
Kingston: 2/6/6 (1782), 2/6/7 (1798, 1803), 2/6/8 (1807–9)
St Ann: 2/9/1 (1797)
St Catherine: 2/6/2 (1804)
St Thomas in the East: 2/1/1 (1800)

D. Mauritius
National Archives of Mauritius (Petite Rivière—Coromandel)
A104/3. List of the names of sailors detained in a 'floating prison' (1794)
GB106/1. Franco-British cartel for the exchange of prisoners of war in the Indian Ocean (1805)

E. Spain
General Archives of the Indias, Seville
Estado 1, no. 66 (1)

F. United States
Houghton Library, Harvard University
MS Eng 1191. Thomas Hollis's diary, 1759 Apr. 14–1770 July 3, vol. 1

Stanford University Library
Special Collections, M1368/2/2

II. Printed primary sources

Abbreviations

CSP   *Calendar of State Papers. Colonial Series, America and West Indies (His Majesty's Stationary Service)*

CTS   Clive Parry (ed.), *The Consolidated Treaties Series* (Dobbs Ferry, New York)

HCH   *House of Commons Hansard*

HLH   *House of Lords Hansard*

JAJ   *Journals of the Assembly of Jamaica*

JBTP   *Journals of the Board of Trade and Plantations*

PP   *Parliamentary Papers*

The places of publication are London and Paris unless otherwise stated.

A. Official documents

'American Treaty...concluded at Madrid, 8 July 1670', *A Complete Collection of all the Marine Treaties* (D. Steel, 1779).

An Act for the better encouragement of seamen in His Majesty's service, and Privateers to annoy the Enemy (17 Geo. 2, c34) (1744).

An Act for the better supply of mariners and seamen to serve in His Majesty's ships of war, and on board merchant ships, and other trading ships, and privateers (13 Geo. 2, c3) (1740).

An Account of the Number of all French Commissioned Officers Prisoners of War on Parole, in Great Britain [1801, 1811, 1812] (Transport Office, 25 June 1812), *PP*, IX (293).

An Act for building an additional jail, and also a prison and house of correction, within the county of Cornwall (18 Geo. 3, c17) (1778).

An act for enforcing the instructions given to all captains...having letters of marque and reprisal against the enemy, and for other purposes (41 Geo. 3, c19), 1801), in *The Laws of Jamaica: Comprehending All the Acts in Force...[1799–1803]*, 2nd ed., vol. IV (Jamaica: Alexander Aikman, 1812).

An Act for the more effectually detaining in custody Napoleon Bonaparte (56 Geo. 3, c22) (1816).

An Act for the more effectual Punishment of Persons aiding Prisoners of War to escape from His Majesty's Dominions (52 Geo. 3, c156) (1812).

An Act for regulating the intercourse with the island of Saint Helena, during the time Napoleon Buonaparte shall be detained there (56 Geo. 3, c23) (1816).

[The Barham Papers] Sir John Knox Laughton (ed.), *Letters and Papers of Charles, Lord Barham, Admiral of the Red Squadron 1758–1813*, vol. I (The Navy Records Society, 1907).

Boumediene v Bush, 553 U.S. 723 (2008).

Calendar of Home Office Papers (George III): 1760–5, ed. Joseph Redington (Public Record Office, 1878).

'Cartel for the Exchange of Prisoners Taken at Sea between France and Great Britain, signed at Versailles/London, 12/28 March 1780', *CTS*, vol. 47, pp. 287–307.

Cobbett's Political Register, vol. 30, January–July 1816 (G. Houston, 1816).

Code des prises ou Recueil des Edits... sur la Course & l'Administration des Prises, depuis 1400 jusqu'à présent, Première Partie (Imprimerie Royale, 1784), 2 vols.

Commitments, trials, convictions, &c. England and Wales: 1813–14, PP, XI (170) (1814–15).

Corps Législatif, Conseil des Anciens, *Rapport fait par Jean-Barthélemy Lecouteulx, Député du département de la Seine. Sur la résolution qui établit une taxe d'humanité* (Imprimerie Nationale, Pluviôse an VI).

Corps Législatif, Conseil des Cinq-Cents, *Rapport fait par Riou,... sur les souffrances des Français prisonniers en Angleterre, et sur les moyens de subvenir à leurs besoins,* (Imprimerie Nationale, Pluviôse an VI).

'Correspondence with the French government relative to Prisoners of war', *A Collection of State Papers, relative to the War against France*, vol. XI (John Stockdale, 1802) pp. 1–53.

CSP, Cecil Headlam ed., vols. 20, 21, 22, 26, 27.

'Declaration of the Powers who signed the Treaty of Paris, assembled at the Congress of Vienna, on the escape of Bonaparte' (1815), *CTS*, vol. 63.

Eighteenth Report from the Select Committee on Finance..., Transport Office, XII (1797).

[Lord Eldon], John Hall Stewart, 'The imprisonment of Napoleon: a legal opinion by Lord Eldon', *American Journal of International Law*, 45 (1951), pp. 571–7.

Gazette Nationale, ou le Moniteur Universel, 47 (7 November 1794), 102 (1795), 264 (12 June 1797).

HCH, Geo. III, 1st series, vols. 20, 32.

HCJ, vols. 15 (1705–8), 53 (1798).

HLH, Geo. 3, 1st series, vol. 23.

Instructions for Agents under the Commissioners for conducting his Majesty's Transport-Service, and for the Care and Custody of Prisoners of War, respecting the management of prisoners of war abroad, [n.l.] (Philanthropic Society, 1803).

'Instructions for Agents for Prisoners of War at Home', in *Thirteenth Report of the Commissioners for Revising and Digesting the Civil Affair of His Majesty's Navy*, 22 December 1807, VI (128) (1809), pp. 103–10.

JAJ, vol. VII (1777–83).

JBTP, K.H. Ledward ed., vols. 1 (April 1704–January 1709 (1920)), 2 (February 1709–March 1715 (1925)), 8 (January 1742–December 1749 (1931)), 9 (January 1750–December 1753 (1932)), 10 (January 1754–December 1758 (1933)).

Marsden, Richard, *Documents Relating to Laws and Customs of the Sea* (Navy Records Society, 1916), vol. II.

Ninth Report of the Commissioners for Revising and Digesting the Civil Affairs of His Majesty's Navy, 25 July 1807, PP (1809), VI (124).

Papers relating to the Negotiation for a General Exchange of Prisoners of War (1811), PP, X (252).

'Règles que tous les Prisonniers de Guerre seront tenus d'observer', in *Thirteenth Report of the Commissioners for Revising and Digesting the Civil Affair of His Majesty's Navy*, 22 December 1807, VI (128) (1809), Appendix 36, pp. 126–7.

Report from the Committee on the State of the Police of the Metropolis, PP, V (510) (1816).

Report on Treatment of Prisoners of War (1798), House of Commons Sessional Papers (Sheila Lambert ed.), vol. 118.

Report from the Committee on the Prisons within the City of London and Borough of Southward. 1. Newgate &c, 8 May 1818, PP, VIII (392) (1818).

A return of the Prisoners of War at present in the United Kingdom, Transport Office, 26 June 1812, PP, IX (301) (1812).

Rodney, *Letter-Books and Order-Book of George, Lord Rodney, Admiral of the White Squadron, 1780–1782*, vol. 1 (New York Historical Society, 1932).

Rules to be observed by all Prisoners of War in the Kingdom of France (Imprimerie Royale, 1758).

'Rules to be observed at the Market', in *Instructions for Dispensers under the Commissioners for conducting His Majesty's Transport Service ... established by His Majesty's Order in Council, dated the 14th of September, 1808* (Philanthropic Society, 1809), Appendix 37.

Second Report from the Committee on the State of the Police of the Metropolis, 1817, PP, VII (484) (1817).

Seventh Report of the Commissioners of Naval Enquiry (Sick and Hurt Office), 1804, PP, VII (309) (1809).

Stürmer, Baron, 13 December 1816, *Napoléon à Sainte-Hélène: Rapports officiels du Baron Stürmer* (Librairie Illustrée, n.d.).

Transport Office: Estimates of the Money that will be wanted for the several services of this office, for the year 1814, PP, XI (110) (1814).

Treaty of Limerick (3 October 1691), 'Military articles', in Thomas Dunbar Ingram, *Two Chapters in Irish History* (Macmillan, 1888), pp. 149–54.

Webster Charles, *British Diplomacy, 1813–15: Select Documents Dealing with the Reconstruction of Europe* (G. Bell, 1921).

B. Maps

Key of the Plan, Elevation and Section, of the Gaol, Bridewell, and Sherriff's Ward, lately built at Bodmin [BL, Maps K.Top.9.32.1].

C. Newspapers

Caledonian Mercury, 11999 (16 August 1798), 13990 (19 August 1811).
Gazette, 9735 (29 October 1757), 9955 (8 December 1759).
Gazette des Pays-Bas (11 March 1760).
Gazette d'Utrecht, 105 (31 December 1759).
Gazette de Leyde, 104 (24 December 1759).
Gentleman's Magazine, 29 (12 December 1759), 30 (1760).
London Chronicle (LC), 460 (8–11 December 1759), 467 (25 December 1759), 475 (10–12 January 1760), 483 (29–31 January 1760), 6073 (1 February 1798).
Lloyd's Evening Post, 5025 (17–19 January 1760), 6309 (31 January 1798).
Morning Post 10168 (11 April 1801).
Public Ledger or the Daily Register of Commerce and Intelligence (March 1760).
Read's Weekly Journal or British Gazetteer, 4014 (20 January 1759).
Royal Cornwall Gazette, 403 (16 March 1811).
The Scots Magazine (1 August 1815).
Sun, 1671 (31 January 1798).
True Briton, 1685 (22 January 1798).
Whitehall Evening Post, 2102 (6 September 1759).

D. Books and pamphlets

Adolphus, John, *Footsteps of Blood; or, the march of the republicans* (J. Hatchard, 1803).
Allardyce, Alexander, *Memoir of the Hon. George Keith* (Edinburgh and London, Blackwood, 1882).

Apologie du Capitaine Thurot, Extraite de différents Journaux de ses Navigations sur les Côtes d'Irlande & d'Ecosse, pendant les années 1757 & 1759, Contre l'Auteur anonyme d'un Journal, au sujet de ce brave Marin (Michel Lambert, 1778).

A True and Authentick Narrative of the Action between the Northumberland and Three French Men of War.... Also a Relation of the Usage the English Prisoners Met in France... By an Eye-witness (W. Payne, 1745).

Barrow, John, *The Life and Correspondence of Admiral Sir William Sidney Smith*, 2 vols. (Richard Bentley, 1848).

Bentham, Jeremy, *The Works of Jeremy Bentham, published under the Superintendence of his Executor, John Bowring* (Edinburgh: William Tait, 1838–43). 11 vols., vol. IV. 11/7/2017. http://oll.libertyfund.org/titles/1925.

Bentham, Jeremy, *The Works of Jeremy Bentham*, Part XXI (Edinburgh: William Tait, 1842).

Bentham, M.S., *The Life of Brigadier-General Sir Samuel Bentham* (Longman, 1862).

Blackstone, William, *Reports of Cases determined in the Several Courts of Westminster from 1746 to 1779*, vol. II, 2nd ed. (S. Sweet, 1828).

Bodin, Jean-François, *Recherches historiques sur la ville de Saumur*, 2 vols. (S. Degouy Qîné, 1814).

The Bordeaux-Dublin Letters, 1757: Correspondence of an Irish Community Abroad, L.M. Cullen, John Shovlin and Thomas M. Truxes (eds.) (Oxford UP, 2013).

Boswell, James, *The Tour to the Hebrides*, in *Life of Johnson*, vol. V: *The Life (1709–1765)*, Birkbeck Norman Hill and L.F. Powell (eds.), 2nd ed. (Oxford UP, 2014).

Burlamaqui, Jean-Jacques, *The Principles of Natural Law and the Principles of Political Law* (1748), trans. Thomas Nugent (1752) (Cambridge UP, 1807).

Canton, William, *A History of the British and Foreign Bible Society*, vol. I (John Murray, 1904).

Chardon, Daniel Marc Antoine, *Code des Prises: ou Recueil des édits,... sur la course*, 2 vols. (Imprimerie Royale, 1784).

Connor, Timothy, 'A Yankee privateersman in prison in England, 1777–1779', *The New England Historical and Genealogical Register (1874–1905)*, 30 (July 1876), 31 (January 1877), 32 (January 1878).

Considerations on the Exchange of Seamen, Prisoners of War (J. Noon, 1758).

de Koven, Reginald, *The Life and Letters of John Paul Jones*, 2 vols., vol. I (Werner Laurie, 1913).

Devon Notes and Queries: A Quarterly Journal devoted to the Local History Biography and Antiquities of the County of Devon, 1 (1901), pp. 197–8.

'Diary of George Thompson at Newburyport kept at Forton Prison, England, 1777–1781', *Essex Institute Historical Collections*, 76 (July 1940), pp. 221–42.

Dictionnaire de l'Académie française, Coignard, 1st ed. (1694), 5th ed. (1798).

[Drake, Peter], *The Memoirs of Capt. Peter Drake* (1755), republished as *Amiable Renegade: The Memoirs of Capt. Peter Drake, 1671–1753*, ed. S. Burrell (Stanford UP, 1960).

Durand, Rev. John Francis, *Genuine and curious Memoirs of the famous Capt. Thurot* (Dublin, W. Whitestone: 1760).

Emerigon, Balthazard-Marie, *Traité des Assurances et des Contrats à la Grosse* (Marseille: Chez Jean Mossy, 1783).

Falconer, William, *Remarks on the Influence of Climate, Situation, ... on the Disposition and Temper... of Mankind* (C. Dilly, 1781).

[Fanning, Nathaniel], *Memoirs of the Life of Captain Nathaniel Fanning, an American Naval Officer who served during part of the American Revolution* (New York: s.n., 1808).

Foster, Sir Michael, *Discourse on High Treason, in a Report of Some Proceedings on the Commission of Oyer and Terminer* (1762) (Dublin, 1767).

Gibbon, Edward, *The Letters of Edward Gibbon*, ed. by J.E. Norton, vol. I: 1750–73 (Cassell and Company, 1956).

Gibbon, Edward, *Miscellaneous Works of Edward Gibbon, Esquire, with Memoirs of his Life and Writings*, vol. I (Basil: J.J. Tourneisen, 1796).

Goldsmith, Oliver, *The Citizen of the World or Letters from a Chinese Philosopher residing in London, to his Friends in the Country* (1762), vol. I (Glasgow: J. Steven, 1809).

[Grotius, Hugo] *Hugo Grotius on the Law of War and Peace*, ed. Stephen Neff (Cambridge UP, 2012).

Guichard, Augustin Charles, *Code des prises maritimes et des armemens en course* (Garnery, an VII [1798-9]).

Guyot, Joseph-Nicolas, *Répertoire universel et raisonné de jurisprudence*, vol. 48 (Paris: Pancoucke, 1781).

Hale, Sir Matthew, *Historia Placitorum Coronae: The History of the Pleas of the Crown* (E. Rider, 1736).

Hall, William Edward, *A Treatise on International Law*, 3rd ed. (Oxford, Clarendon: 1890).

Hasted, Edward, *The History and Topographical Survey of the County of Kent*, vol. IX (Canterbury: W. Bristow, 1800).

Hey, Richard, *Dissertation on the Pernicious Effects of Gaming* (Cambridge: J. & J. Merrill, 1783).

Home, Henry, Lord Kames, *Essays on the Principles of Morality and Natural Religion*, 3rd ed. [1779], edited and with an Introduction by Mary Catherine Moran (Indianapolis: Liberty Fund, 2005).

Home, Henry, Lord Kames, *Sketches of the History of Man* (1774), 3rd ed. (Dublin: James Williams, 1779), vol. I.

Howard, John, *State of the Prisons*, 1st ed. (1777), 3rd ed. (Warrington: William Eyres, 1784).

Howard, John, *An Account of the Principal Lazarettos in Europe*, 2nd ed. (J. Johnson, 1791).

Hume, David, *Further Letters of David Hume*, Felix Waldmann ed. (Edinburgh Bibliographical Society, 2014).

Jackson, Basil, *Notes and Reminiscences of a Staff Officer. Chiefly Relating to the Waterloo Campaign and to St. Helena Matters During the Captivity of Napoleon* (New York: E.P. Dutton & Co., John Murray, 1903).

Johnson, Samuel, 'Introduction', republished in Oxford English Classics, *Dr Johnson's Works. Reviews, Political Tracts, and Lives of Eminent Persons. The Works of Samuel Johnson*, vol. VI (W. Pickering, 1825), pp. 147-9.

Keppel, Thomas, *Life of Augustus Viscount Keppel, Admiral of the White, and First Lord of the Admiralty in 1782-3* (Henry Colburn, 1842).

Kurnaz, Murat, *Five Years of My Life: An Innocent Man in Guantanamo*, trans. Jefferson Chase (New York: Palgrave Macmillan, 2008).

Lady Nugent's Journal, Cambridge UP (2010).

Las Cases, Count de, *Memoirs of the Life and Conversations of the Emperor Napoleon*, 4 vols. (Henry Colburn, 1826).

Lebertre, Colonel, *Apercu du traitement qu'éprouvent les prisonniers de guerre français en Angleterre* (J.G. Dentu, 1813).

Lind, James, *An Essay on the Most Effectual Means of Preserving the Health of Seamen in the Royal Navy... Together with observations on the Jail Distemper*, new ed. (D. Wilson, 1774).

Lutyens, Captain, *Letters of Captain Engelbert Lutyens*, ed. Sir Lees Knowles Bar.t (New York: John Lane Company, 1915).

Maitland, Captain F.L., *Narrative of the Surrender of Buonaparte and of his Residence on Board H.M.S. Bellerophon*, 2nd ed. (London: Henry Colburn, 1826).

Martens, G.F. de, *Précis du Droit des Gens moderne de l'Europe*, 2nd ed. (1789), vol. II (Guillaumin, 1864).

Merlin, Comte, *Répertoire Universel et Raisonné de Jurisprudence*, 4st ed., vol. IX (Garnery, 1813).

Metternich, Prince Richard (ed.), *Memoirs of Prince Metternich 1773–1815*, vol. II (New York: Charles Scribner's sons, 1880).

Molloy, Charles, *De Jure Maritimo it Navale: or, a Treatise of Affaires Maritime and of Commerce* (Printed for John Bellinger, 1682).

[Montchenu], *La captivité de Saint-Hélène. D'après les rapports inédits du Marquis de Montchenu, commissaire du gouvernemnt du roi Louis XVIII dans l'île*, par Georges Firmin-Didot, secrétaire d'ambassade (Firmin-Didot, 1894).

Montholon, Général, *Histoire de la captivité de Ste-Hélène* (La Haye: Chez les Héritiers Doorman, 1846).

Mulvey, Farrell, *Sketches of the Character, Conduct, and Treatment of the Prisoners of War at Auxonne, Longwy &c from the Year 1810 to 1814* (Longman, 1818).

Neild, James, *State of the Prisons in England, Scotland, and Wales* (John Nichols, 1812).

Ninth Report of the British and Foreign Bible Society (J. Tilling, 1813).

Owen, John, *The History of the Origin and First Ten Years of the British and Foreign Bible Society*, 2 vols. (Tilling and Hugues, 1816).

Pillet, René Martin, *L'Angleterre vue.à Londres et dans ses provinces, pendant un séjour de dix années, dont six comme prisonniers de guerre* (Eymery, 1815).

Proceedings of the Committee appointed to manage the contributions begun at London Dec. XVIII MDCCLVIIII for cloathing French prisoners of war (Printed by order of the Committee, 1760).

Pufendorf, Samuel von, *Of the Law of Nature and Nations: Eight Books*, 4th ed. (J. Walthoe et al., 1729).

Réal de Curban, Gaspard, *La Science du Gouvernement*, vol. V (Libraires Associés, 1764).

The Remenbrancer; or, Impartial Repository of Public Events. For the Year 1783, Part I (J. Debrett, 1783).

Reports of the British and Foreign Bible Society, with Extracts of Correspondence and Lists of Subscribers and Benefactors, vols. I, II (Stanhope & Tilling, 1808, 1813).

Repository of Arts, Literature, Commerce, Manufactures, Fashions, and Politics, vol. IV, No. XIX (September 1810).

Risdon, Tristram, *The Chorographical Description ... of Devon* (Rees and Curtis: 1811).

Schmalz, M., *Le droit des gens européen*, trans. Leopold de Bohm (chez Maze, 1823).

Second Report of the British and Foreign Bible Society (Stanhope & Tilling, 1806).

Secondat, Charles de, Baron de Montesquieu, *The Spirit of Laws* (1748), trans. Thomas Nugent, 2 vols. (1752).

Summary Account of the Proceedings of the British and Foreign Bible Society (Tilling and Hugues, 1816).

Society for the Suppression of Vice. Occasional Reports, No. V (1810), Bodleian Library.

Toase, William, *The Wesleyan Mission in France: with an account of the Labours of Wesleyan Ministers among the French Prisoners, during the Late War* (John Mason, 1835).

Twiss, Horace, *The Public and Private Life of Lord Chancellor Eldon*, 3rd ed., 2 vols. (John Murray, 1846).

Tytler, Alexander Fraser *Essay on Military Law, and the Practice of Courts Martial* (Edinburgh, Printed by Murray & Cochrane: 1800).

Valin, René-Josué, *Nouveau Commentaire sur l'Ordonnance de la Marine, du mois d'août 1681*, vol. II (La Rochelle: Jerôme Légier, 1766).

Valin, R.-J., *Traité des Prises, ou Principes de la Jurisprudence françoise concernant les Prises qui se font sur mer*, vol. I (La Rochelle: Jerôme Legier, 1763).

Vattel, Emer de, *The Law of Nations, Or, Principles of the Law of Nature*, edited and with an Introduction by Béla Kapossy and Richard Whitmore (Indianapolis: Liberty Fund, 2008). <http://oll.libertyfund.org/titles/2246>.

Von Müffling, Baron, *Passages from my Life*, 2nd ed., revised (Richard Bentley, 1853).

Ward, Robert, *An Enquiry into the Foundation and History of the Law of Nations in Europe*, 2 vols. (A. Strahan and W. Woodfall, 1795).

Wellington, Arthur, Duke of, *Supplementary Despatches, Correspondence, and Memoranda*, vol. XI (John Murray, 1864).

Wesley, John, *Minutes of the Methodist Conferences, from the First, held in London, by the late Rev. John Wesley, A.M., in the year 1744*, vol. VI (John Mason, 1833).

Wolff, Christian, *Principes du droit de la nature et des gens* (Amsterdam: Chez Marc Michel Rey, 1758).

Wyzanski, Charles E., 'Nuremberg: a fair trial? A dangerous precedent', *The Atlantic*, 66 (1946).

Young, Arthur, *Arthur Young's Travels During the Years 1787, 1788, and 1789*, ed. Matilda Betham-Edwards (Cambridge UP, 2012).

Bibliography

Abbreviations

AHR *American Historical Review*
APSR *American Political Science Review*
EHR *English Historical Review*
HC *History Compass*
HES *Histoire, Economie et Société*
HJ *Historical Journal*
ICLQ *International and Comparative Law Quarterly*
JBS *Journal of British Studies*
JICH *Journal of Imperial and Commonwealth History*
JMH *Journal of Modern History*
JMiH *Journal of Military History*
MM *Mariner's Mirror*
P&P *Past & Present*
RH *Revue Historique*
RHMC *Revue d'Histoire Moderne et Contemporaine*
SH *Social History*
WMQ *William & Mary Quarterly*

Abbott, John Lawrence, 'General notes', *Journal of the Royal Society of Arts*, 119 (1971), pp. 711–15, 801–7, 874–8.
Abell, Francis, *Prisoners of War in Britain 1756 to 1815: A Record of their Lives, their Romance and their Sufferings* (Oxford UP, 1914).
About, Ilsen, and Vincent Denis, *Histoire de l'identification des personnes* (La Découverte, 2010).
Abruzzo, Margaret, *Polemical Pain: Slavery, Cruelty, and the Rise of Humanitarianism* (John's Hopkins UP, 2011).
Acerra, Martine, and André Zysberg, *L'essor des marines de guerres européennes (vers 1680-vers 1790)* (SEDES, 1997).
Agier, Michel, 'Between war and city: towards an urban anthropology of refugee camps', *Ethnography*, 3 (2002), 317–41.
Alexander, J.K., 'Forton Prison during the American Revolution', *Essex Institute Historical Collections*, 103 (1967), 365–89.
Alger, John Goldworth, *Napoléon's British Visitors and Captives 1801–1815* (Archibald Constable, 1904).
Allan, D.G.C., 'Laudable Association of Antigallicans', *Journal of the Royal Society of Arts*, 137 (1989), 623–8.
Ambühl, Rémy, *Prisoners of War in the Hundred Years War: Ransom Culture in the Late Middle Ages* (Cambridge UP, 2013).

Anderson Clare, Niklas Frykman, Lex Heerma van Voss, and Marcus Rediker (eds.), *Mutiny and Maritime Radicalism in the Age of Revolution: A Global Survey, International Review of Social History supplements* (Cambridge UP, 2014).

Anderson, Gary M., and Adam Gifford, Jr, 'Privateering and the private production of naval power', *Cato Journal*, 11 (1991), 99–122.

Anderson, Olive, 'American escapes from British naval prisons during the War of Independence', *MM*, 51 (1955).

Anderson, Olive, 'The treatment of prisoners of war in Britain during the American War of Independence', *Bulletin of the Institute of Historical Research*, 28 (1955), 63–83.

Anderson, Olive, 'The impact on the fleet of the disposal of prisoners of war in distant waters, 1689–1783', *MM*, 45 (1959), 243–9.

Anderson, Olive, 'The establishment of British supremacy at sea and the exchange of naval prisoners of war, 1689–1783', *EHR*, 75, 1960, p. 77–89.

Andrew, Donna T., *Philanthropy and Police: London Charity in the Eighteenth Century* (Princeton UP, 1989).

Andrew, Donna T., *Aristocratic Vice: The Attack on Duelling, Suicide, Adultery, and Gambling in Eighteenth-Century England* (Yale UP, 2013).

Anheim, Étienne, Jean-Yves Grenier, and Antoine Lilti, 'Repenser les statuts sociaux', *Annales HSS* 4 (2013), 949–53.

Appadurai, Arjun, 'Introduction: commodities and the politics of value', in Id. (ed.), *The Social Life of Things: Commodities in Cultural Perspective* (Cambridge UP, 1986), 3–63.

Arnold, Catherine, 'Affairs of humanity: Arguments for humanitarian intervention in England and Europe, 1698–1715', *EHR*, 141 (2018), 835–65.

Asch, R.G., 'War and state-building', in Frank Tallett and D. J. B. Trim (eds.), *European Warfare 1350–1750* (Cambridge UP, 2010), 322–37.

Ashton, *Economic Fluctuations in England,1700–1800* (Oxford UP, 1959).

Atkins, Gareth, 'Christian heroes, providence and patriotism in wartime Britain, 1793–1815', *HJ*, 58 (2015), 393–414.

Austin, Andrew, 'Prisonisation', in Bosworth, *Encyclopedia of Prisons & Correctional facilities* (Sage Publications, 2005), 765–7.

Axtell, James, 'The white Indians of colonial America', *WMQ*, 32 (1975), 55–88.

Barber, Karin, 'When people cross thresholds', *African Studies Review* 50 (2007), 111–23.

Bashford, Alison (ed.), *Quarantine: Local and Global Histories* (Palgrave, 2016).

Bass, Gary Jonathan, *Stay the Hand of Vengeance: The Politics of War Crimes Tribunals* (Princeton UP, 2000).

Bassi, Ernesto, 'Beyond compartmentalized Atlantics: a case for embracing the Atlantic from Spanish American shores', *HC*, 12 (2014), 704–16.

Baugh, D.A., *The British Naval Administration in the Age of Walpole* (Princeton UP, 1965).

Baugh, D.A., *The Global Seven Years' War 1754–1763: Britain and France in a Great Power Contest* (Routledge, 2011).

Bayly, C.A., *Imperial Meridian: The British Empire and the World 1780–1830* (Routledge, 1989).

Beattie, J.M., *Crime and the Courts in England 1660–1800* (Princeton UP), 1986.

Becker, Annette, *Oubliés de la Grande Guerre. Humanitaire et culture de guerre: populations occupées, déportés civils et prisonniers de guerre* (Noêsis, 1998).

Becker, Howard, *Outsiders* (Free Press, 1963).

Beetham, David, *The Legitimation of Power* (Palgrave Macmillan, 1991).

Bélissa, Marc, and Sophie Wahnich, 'Les crimes des Anglais: trahir le droit', *AHRF*, 300 (1995), 233–48.

Bell, David, *The Cult of the Nation in France: Inventing Nationalism, 1680–1800* (Harvard UP, 2001).

Bell, David, *The First Total War: Napoleon's Europe and the Birth of Warfare as We Know It* (Bloomsbury, 2008).

Ben-Amos, Ilana Krausman, *The Culture of Giving: Informal Support and Gift-Exchange in Early Modern England* (Cambridge UP, 2008).

Bennett, Roy, 'French prisoners of war on parole in Britain, 1803–1814', PhD, University of London, 1964.

Benthall, Jonathan, 'Charity', in Didier Fassin (ed.), *A Companion to Moral Anthropology* (John Wiley & Sons, 2012), 360–5.

Benton, Lauren, *A Search for Sovereignty: Law and Geography in European Empires, 1400–1900* (Cambridge UP, 2009).

Benton, Lauren, and Richard J. Ross, 'Empires and legal pluralism: jurisdiction, sovereignty, and political imagination in the early modern world', in Id. (eds.), *Legal Pluralism and Empires, 1500–1850* (NYU Press, 2013), 1–17.

Benvenisti, Eyal, and Amichai Cohen, 'War is governance: explaining the logic of the laws of war from a principal-agent perspective', *Michigan Law Review*, 112 (2014), 1363–415.

Berry, Sara, 'Marginal gains, market values, and history', *African Studies Review*, 50 (2007), 57–70.

Best, Geoffrey, *Humanity in Warfare* (Columbia UP, 1980).

Biloghi, Dominique, *Logistique et Ancien Régime: De l'étape royale à l'étape languedocienne* (PULM, 1998).

Black, Jeremy, *Natural and Necessary Enemies: Anglo-French Relations in the Eighteenth Century* (Gerald Duckworth, 1986).

Blanchard, Anne, *Dictionnaire des ingénieurs militaires 1691–1791* (Montpellier, Université Paul Valéry, 1981).

Blundell Jones, Peter, 'The primacy of bodily experience', in Id. and Mark Meagher (eds.), *Architecture and Movement: The Dynamic Experience of Buidings and Landscape* (Routledge, 2015), ch. 13.

Bollettino, Maria Alessandra, 'Slavery, War, and Britain's Atlantic Empire: Black Soldiers, Sailors, and Rebels in the Seven Years' War', PhD University of Texas (Austin), 2009.

Bolster, Jeffrey W., *Black Jacks: African American Sailors in the Age of Sail* (Harvard UP, 1997).

Boltanski, Luc, *Distant Suffering: Morality, Medias and Politics* (1993), trans. Graham Burdell (Cambridge UP, 1999).

Boltanski, Luc, *Love and Justice as Competences* (1990), trans. Catherine Porter (Polity Press, 2012).

Boltanski, Luc, and Laurent Thévenot, *On Justification: The Economies of Worth (1992)*, trans. Catherine Porter (Princeton UP, 2006).

Bosworth, Mary (ed.), *Encyclopedia of Prisons & Correctional facilities* (Sage Publications, 2005).

Bosworth, Mary, *Inside Immigration Detention* (Oxford UP, 2014).

Bourdieu, Pierre, 'The sentiment of honour in Kabyle society', in Jean G. Peristiany (ed.), *Honour and Shame: The Values of Mediterranean Society* (University of Chicago Press, 1966), 191–241.

Bourdieu, Pierre, 'Social space and symbolic power', *Sociological Theory*, 7 (1989), 14–25.

Bourguignon, Henry J., *Sir William Scott, Lord Stowell* (Cambridge UP, 1987).

Bowen, H.V., 'The contractor state, c. 1650–1815', *International Journal of Maritime History*, 25 (2013), 239–74.

Bowen, H.V., E. Mancke, and John G. Reid, *Britain's Oceanic Empire: Atlantic and Indian Ocean Worlds, c. 1550–1850* (Cambridge UP, 2012).

Branch-Johnson, W., *The English Prison Hulks* (Johnson, 1957).

Brewer, John, *Party Ideology and Popular Politics at the Accession of George III* (Cambridge UP, 1976).

Brewer, John, *The Sinews of Power: War, Money and the English State, 1688–1783* (Harvard UP, 1990).

Brioist, Pascal, Hervé Drévillon, and Pierre Serna, *Croiser le fer: Violence et culture de l'épée dans la France moderne, XVIe–XVIIIe siècles* (Champ Vallon, 2002).

Brion Davis, David, *The Problem of Slavery in Western Culture* (Oxford UP, 1966).

Briquet, Jean-Louis, 'Des amitiés paradoxales: échanges intéressés et morale du désintéressement dans les relations de clientèle', *Politix*, 12 (1999), 7–20.

Bromley, J.S., *Corsairs and Navies 1660–1760* (The Hambledon Press, 1987).

Brown, Christopher Leslie, *Moral Capital: Foundations of British Abolitionism* (University of North Carolina Press, 2006).

Brown, Christopher Leslie, and Philip D. Morgan (eds.), *Arming Slaves from Classical Times to the Modern Age* (Yale UP, 2006).

Brubaker, Rogers, 'Ethnicity without groups', *European Journal of Sociology*, 43 (2002), 163–89.

Bruijn, Jaap R., 'States and their navies from the late sixteenth to the end of the eighteenth centuries', in Philippe Contamine (ed.), *War and Competition between States* (Oxford UP, 2000), 69–98.

Burgess Jr, Douglas R., 'Hostis Humani Generi: Piracy, Terrorism and a New International Law', *University of Miami International & Comparative Law Review*, 13 (2006), 293–342.

Burns, Alan, *History of the British West Indies* (George Allan and Unwin/Macmillan Company, 1954).

Burrows, Edwin, *Forgotten Patriots: The Untold Story of American Prisoners during the Revolutionary War* (Basic Books, 2008).

Cabantous, Alain, 'Gens de mer, guerre et prison: la captivité des gens de mer au XVIIIe siècle », *RHMC*, 28 (1981), 246–67.

Cabantous, Alain, *Dix mille marins face à l'Océan* (Publisud, 1991).

Cabantous, Alain, *Les côtes barbares: Pilleurs d'épaves et sociétés littorales en France (1680–1830)* (Fayard, 1993).

Callo, Joseph F., *John Paul Jones: America's First Sea Sailor* (Naval Institute Press, 2006).

Calloway, Colin G., 'Indian captivities on the Upper Connecticut River', *Journal of American Studies*, 17 (1983), 189–210.

Cameron, Iain R., 'The police of eighteenth-century France', *European Studies Review*, 7 (1977), 47–75.

Campbell, Charles, *The Intolerable Hulks: British Shipboard Confinement 1776–1857* (Heritage Books, 1994).

Canny, Nicholas (ed.), *Europeans on the Move: Studies in European Migration 1500–1800* (Oxford UP, 1994).

Caputo, Sara, 'Alien seamen in the British navy, British law, and the British state, c. 1793–c. 1815', *HJ* (2018), 1–23.

Carrabine, Eamon, 'Riots', in Bosworth, *Encyclopedia*, 853–8.

Carrington, Selwyn H.H., *The British West Indies during the American Revolution* (Foris Publications, 1988).

Castan, Nicole, André Zysberg, and Jacques-Guy Petit (eds.), *Histoire des galères, bagnes et prisons, XIIIe–XXe siècles* (Privat, 1991).

de Certeau, Michel, *The Practice of Everyday Life* (1980), trans. Steven Rendall (University of California Press, 1984).

Cerutti, Simona, *Etrangers: Etude d'une condition d'incertitude dans une société d'Ancien Régime* (Bayard, 2012).

Chadwick, Owen, 'The religion of Samuel Johnson', *Yale University Library Gazette*, 60 (April 1986), 119–36.

Chalklin, Christopher, *English Counties and Public Building, 1650–1830* (Hambledon Press, 1998).

Chamayou, Grégoire, *Les chasses à l'homme* (La Fabrique: 2010).

Chamberlain, Paul, *Hell upon Water: Prisoners of War in Britain 1793–1815* (The History Press, 2008).

Chandler, D., *The Art of Warfare in the Age of Marlborough* (Staplehurst, 1990).

Chanzy, Clémence, 'Projet de débarquement en Angleterre et offrandes volontaires: le don patriotique à travers la souscription, 1797–1798', Master 2 Histoire, University Paris-Panthéon-Sorbonne (2018).

Charli Carpenter R., *'Innocent Women and Children': Gender, Norms and the Protection of Civilians* (Ashgate, 2006).

Charters, Erica, 'The administration of war and French prisoners of war in Britain, 1756–1763', in Erica Charters, Eve Rosenhaf, and Hannah Smith (eds.), *Civilians and War in Europe, 1618–1815* (Liverpool UP, 2012), 87–99.

Charters, Erica, *Disease, War and the Imperial State: The Welfare of the British Armed Forces during the Seven Years' War* (University of Chicago Press, 2014).

Chauvenet, Antoinette, 'Guerre et paix en prison', *Les cahiers de la sécurité intérieure*, 31 (1998), 91–100.

Childs, John, 'Surrender and the laws of war in Western Europe, c. 1660–1783', in Holger Afflerbach and Hew Strachan (eds.), *How Fighting Ends: A History of Surrender* (Oxford UP, 2012), 153–68.

Christopher, Emma, Cassandra Pybus, and Markus Rediker (eds.), *Many Middle Passages: Forced Migration and the Making of the Modern World* (University of California Press, 2007).

Clemmer, Donald, *The Prison Community* (Christopher Publishing House, 1940).

Cochet, François, *Soldats sans armes. La captivité de guerre: une approche culturelle* (Bruylant-LGDJ, 1998).

Cochin, Augustin, 'Patriotisme humanitaire', *Revue Universelle* (1920), republished in *Les sociétés de pensée et la démocratie moderne* (1921).

Cohen, *Yankee Sailors in British Gaols: Prisoners of War at Forton and Mill, 1777–1783* (University of Delaware Press, 1995).

Colley, Linda, *Britons: Forging the Nation 1707–1837* (Vintage, 1996).

Colley, Linda, *Captives. Britain, Empire and the World 1600–1850* (Pimlico, 2003).

Collins, Randall, *Violence: A Microsociological Theory* (Princeton UP, 2008).

Colvin, Howard M., *A Biographical Dictionary of British Architects, 1600–1840*, 4th ed. (Yale UP, 2008).

Combessie, Philippe, 'Marking the carceral boundary: penal stigma in the long shadow of the prison', *Ethnography*, 2 (2002), 535–55.

Combessie, Philippe, *Sociologie de la prison* (La Découverte, 2004).

Condon, M. E., 'The establishment of the Transport Board: a subdivision of the Admiralty, 4 July 1794', *MM*, 58 (1972), 69–84.

Contamine, Philippe, 'The growth of state control: practices of war, 1300–1800: ransom and booty', in Contamine (ed.), *War and Competition*, 163–93.

Conway, Stephen, *War, State and Society in Mid-Eighteenth-Century Britain and Ireland* (Oxford UP, 2006).

Conway, Stephen, 'Christians, Catholics, Protestants: the religious links of Britain and Ireland with Continental Europe, c.1689–1800', *EHR*, 74 (2009), 833–62.

Conway, Stephen, *Britain, Ireland and Continental Europe in the Eighteenth Century* (Oxford UP, 2011).

Conway, Stephen, *Britannia's Auxiliaries: Continental Europeans and the British Empire, 1740–1800* (Oxford UP, 2017).

Cooper, Carolyn, 'The Portsmouth system of manufacture', *Technology and Culture*, 25 (1984), 182–225.

Cox, Margaret E., *Captain Daniel Woodriff R.N. C.B. of His Majesty's Ship Calcutta: 1756–1842* (Fast Books: 1993).

Cressey, Donald R., 'Contradictory directives in complex organizations: the case of the prison', *Administrative Science Quarterly*, 4 (1959), 1–19.

Cressey (ed.), Donald R., *The Prison: Studies in Institutional Organization and Change* (Holt, Rinehart and Winston, 1961).

Crewe, Ben, 'The sociology of imprisonment', in Yvonne Jewkes (ed.), *Handbook on Prisons* (Willan Publishing: 2007), 123–51.

Crewe, Ben, 'Soft power in prison: implications for staff-prisoners relationships, liberty and legitimacy', *European Journal of Criminology* 8 (2011), 455–68.

Crewe Ben, J. Warr, P. Bennett, and A. Smith, 'The emotional geography of prison life', *Theoretical Criminology*, 18 (2013), 56–74.

Crimmin, Patricia K., 'French prisoners of War on parole, 1793–1815: the Welsh border towns », in n.a., *Guerres et Paix 1660–1815* (Service historique de la Marine, 1987).

Crimmin, Patricia K., 'Prisoners of war and British port communities, 1793–1815', *The Northern Mariner/Le marin du nord*, 6 (1996), 17–27.

Cromwell, Jesse, 'More than slaves and sugar: recent historiography of the trans-imperial Caribbean and its sinew populations', *HC*, 12 (2014), 770–83.

Crowhurst, Patrick, *The French War on Trade: Privateering, 1793–1815* (Scolar Press, 1985).

Crump, Justine, 'The perils of play: eighteenth-century ideas about gambling', Centre for History and Economics Papers, University of Cambridge. April 2004. <http://www-histecon.kings.cam.ac.uk/docs/crump_perils.pdf>.

Cullen, L.M., 'The Irish diaspora of the seventeenth and eighteenth centuries', in Canny, *Europeans*, 113–50.

Cunningham, Hugh, and Joanna Innes, *Charity, Philanthropy and Reform: From the 1690s to 1850* (Palgrave Macmillan, 1996).

Cuthbertson, Brian, *Melville Prison and Deadman's Island: American and French Prisoners of War in Halifax 1794–1816* (Formac-Lorimer, 2011).

Dalakoglou, Dimitris, and Penny Harvey, 'Roads and anthropology: ethnographic perspectives on space, time and (im)mobility', *Mobilities*, 7 (2012), 459–65.

Daly, Gavin, 'Napoleon's lost legions: French prisoners of war in Britain, 1803–1814', *History*, 89 (2004), 361–80.

Daly, Gavin, 'British soldiers and the legend of Napoleon', *HJ*, 61 (2018), 131–53.

Daunton, Martin, 'Experts and the environment: approaches to planning history', *Journal of Urban History*, 9 (1983), 233–50.

Davies, Christie, 'Goffman's concept of the total institution: criticisms and revisions', *Human Studies*, 12 (1989), 77–95.

Delacy, Margaret, *Contagionism Catches On: Medical Ideology in Britain, 1730–1800* (Palgrave Macmillan, 2017).

Deluermoz, Quentin, *Policiers dans la ville: La construction d'un ordre public à Paris (1854–1914)* (Publications de la Sorbonne, 2012).

Dening, Greg, *Mr Bligh's Bad Language: Passion, Power and Theater on the Bounty* (Cambridge UP, 2010).

Denis, Vincent, *Une histoire de l'identité: France, 1715–1815* (Champ Vallon, 2008).

Desrosières, Alain, *The Politics of Large Numbers: A History of Statistical Reasoning (1993)*, trans. Camille Naish (Harvard UP, 2002).

Devereaux, Simon, 'The making of the Penitentiary Act, 1775–1779', *HJ*, 42 (1999), 405–33.

Dobbs, Rhonda D. and Courtney A. Waid, 'Prison culture', in Bosworth, *Encyclopedia*, 719–22.

Donagan, Barbara, 'Codes and conduct in the English civil war', *P&P*, 118 (1988), 65–95.

Donagan, Barbara, *War in England, 1642–1649* (Oxford UP, 2010).

Douglas, Mary, *How Institutions Think* (Syracuse UP, 1986).

Downing, Roger, and Gijs Rommelse, 'State formation and the private economy: Dutch prisoners of war in England, 1652–1674', *MM*, 104 (2018), 153–71.

Doyle, Robert C., *The Enemy in Our Hands: America's Treatment of Prisoners of War from the Revolution to the War on Terror* (University Press of Kentucky, 2010).

Drescher, Seymour, *Abolition: A History of Slavery and Antislavery* (Cambridge UP, 2009).

Dubost, Jean-François, and Peter Sahlins, *Et si on faisait payer les étrangers? Louis XIV, les immigrés, et quelques autres* (Flammarion, 2000).

Duchhardt, Heinz, 'War and international law in Europe, sixteenth to eighteenth centuries', in Contamine (ed.), *War and Competition*, 279–300.

Duché, Elodie, 'A Passage to Imprisonment: The British Prisoners of War in Verdun under the First French Empire', PhD dissertation, University of Warwick, 2014.

Duché, Elodie, 'Charitable connections: transnational financial networks and relief for British prisoners of war in Napoleonic France, 1803–1814', *Napoleonica*, 21 (2014), 74–117.

Duffy, Christopher, *The Military Experience in the Age of Reason* (Routledge, 1987).

Dull, Jonathan R., *The French Navy and American Independence: A Study of Arms and Diplomacy, 1774–1787* (Princeton UP: 1975).

Duprat, Catherine, *'Pour l'amour de l'humanité': Le temps des philanthropes: La philanthropie parisienne des Lumières à la Monarchie de Juillet* (CTHS, 1993).

Durand, Corentin, 'Construire sa légitimité à énoncer le droit: étude de doléances de prisonniers', *Droit et Société*, 87 (2014), 329–48.

Dwyer, Philip G., '"It still makes me shudder": memories of massacres and atrocities during the Revolutionary and Napoleonic Wars', *War in History*, 16 (2009), 381–405.

Dwyer, Philip G., 'Violence and the revolutionary and Napoleonic wars: massacre, conquest and the imperial enterprise', *Journal of Genocide Research*, 15 (2013), 117–31.

Dwyer, Philip G., *Napoleon: Passion, Death and Resurrection, 1815–1840* (Bloomsbury Publishing, 2018).

Dziembowski, Edmond, *Un nouveau patriotisme français, 1750–1770: La France face à la puissance anglaise à l'époque de la guerre de Sept Ans* (Voltaire Foundation, 1998).

Eastwood, David, '"Amplifying the province of the legislature": the flow of information and the English state in the early nineteenth century', *Historical Research*, 62 (1989), 276–91.

Edelstein, Dan, 'War and terror: the law of nations from Grotius to the French Revolution', *French Historical Studies*, 31 (2008), 229–62.

Edelstein, Dan, *The Terror of Natural Rights: Republicanism, the Cult of Nature, and the French Revolution* (The University of Chicago Press: 2009).

Elias, Norbert, *What is Sociology?* (1970), trans. Stephen Mennell and Grace Morrissey (Hutchinson, 1978).

Elias, Norbert, *The Court Society*, trans. Edmund Jephcott (Oxford: Blackwell, 1983).

Eltis, David, 'Free and coerced migrations from the Old World to the New', in Id. (ed.), *Coerced and Free Migrations: Global Perspectives* (Stanford UP, 2002), 33–74.

Emsley, Clive, *Gendarmes and the State in Nineteenth-Century Europe* (Oxford UP, 1999).

Fabel, Robin F.A., 'Self-help in Dartmoor: black and white prisoners in the War of 1812', *Journal of the Early Republic*, 9 (1989), 165–90.

Farcy, Jean-Claude, ' "Je désire quitté la france pour quitté les prisons": les requêtes de prisonniers pour obtenir leur exil (années 1870)', *Champ pénal/Penal field*, 2 (2005), http://champpenal.revues.org/418.

Fassin, Didier, 'L'ordre moral du monde: essai d'anthropologie de l'intolérable', in Fassin and Bourdelais (dir.), *Les constructions de l'intolérable: Études d'anthropologie et d'histoire sur les frontières de l'espace moral* (La Découverte, 2005), 17–50.

Fassin, Didier, and Patrice Bourdelais, 'Introduction: Les frontières de l'espace moral', in Fassin and Bourdelais (dir.), *Les constructions de l'intolérable*, 7–15.

Faure, Olivier, 'Les historiens face à l'institution totale', in Charles Amouroux and Alain Blanc (eds.), *Erving Goffman et les institutions totales* (L'Harmattan, 2002), 43–57.

Favier, René, 'Jouer dans les villes de province en France au XVIIIe siècle', *Histoire urbaine*, 1 (2000), 65–85.

Finn, Margot, ' "Frictions" d'empire: les réseaux de circulation des successions et des patrimoines dans la Bombay coloniale des années 1780', *Annales HSS*, 5 (2010), 1175–1204.

Finn, Margot, *The Character of Credit: Personal Debt in English Culture, 1740–1914* (Cambridge UP, 2003).

Finzch, Norbert, and Robert Jütte (eds.), *Institutions of Confinement: Hospitals, Asylums and Prison in Western Europe and North America (1500–1950)* (Cambridge UP, 1996).

Fischer, Nicolas, 'Un lieu d'exception? Retour sur le statut de la rétention administrative dans un contexte démocratique', *Politix*, 104 (2013), 181–201.

Fischer, Nicolas, 'The detention of foreigners in France: between discretionary control and the rule of law', *European Journal of Criminology*, 10 (2013), 692–708.

Fishman, Sarah, *We will wait: Wives of French prisoners of war, 1940–1945* (Yale UP, 1991).

Fontenay, Michel, 'Routes et modalités du commerce des esclaves dans la Méditerranée des temps modernes (XVIe, XVIIe et XVIIIe siècles)', *RH*, 640 (2006), 813–30.

Fontenay, Michel, 'Esclaves et/ou captifs: préciser les concepts', in Wolfgang Kaiser (ed.), *Le commerce des captifs: Les intermédiaires dans l'échange et le rachat des prisonniers en Méditerranée, XVe–XVIIIe siècle* (EFR, 2008), 15–24.

Forrest, Alan, *Conscripts and Deserters: The Army and French Society during the Revolution and Empire* (Oxford UP, 1989).

Fox, Richard Hingston, *Dr John Fothergill and his Friends: Chapters in Eighteenth Century Life* (Macmillan, 1919).

Foucault, Michel, *Dits et Ecrits*, vol. III (Gallimard, 1993).

Foucault, Michel, *Discipline and Punish: The Birth of the Prison* (1977), trans. Richard Howard (New York: Vintage, 1995).

Foucault, Michel, *Madness and Civilization: A History of Insanity in the Age of Reason* (1961), trans. Richard Howard (Vintage Books, 1988).

Foucault, Michel, *The Order of Things: An Archeology of the Human Sciences* (1966) (Routledge, 2002.

Foy, Charles R., 'Unkle Sommerset's freedom: liberty in England for black sailors', *Journal for Maritime Research*, 13 (2011), 21–36.

Foyster, Elisabeth A., *Manhood in Early Modern England: Honour, Sex and Marriage* (Routledge, 1999).

Freundlich, Francis, *Le monde du jeu à Paris (1715–1800)* (Albin Michel, 1995).

Frey, Linda, and Marsha Frey, ' "The reign of the charlatans is over": the French revolutionary attack on diplomatic practice', *JMH*, 65 (1993), 706–44.

Frost, Alan, *Convicts and Empire: A Naval Question, 1776–1811* (Oxford UP, 1980).

Gardiner, Robert (ed.), *Navies and the American Revolution, 1775–1783* (Chatham Publishing, 1997).

Garland, David, *Punishment and Modern Society* (Oxford UP: 1990).

Garrett, Aaron, and Ryan Hanley, 'Adam Smith: history and impartiality', in Aaron Garett and James A. Harris (eds.), *Scottish Philosophy in the Eighteenth Century, Volume I: Morals, Politics* (Oxford UP, 2015).

Garrioch, David, 'Verbal insults in eighteenth-century Paris', in Peter Burke and Roy Porter (eds.), The social history of language (Cambridge UP, 1987).

Geggus, David, *Slavery, War and Revolution: The British Occupation of Saint Domingue, 1793–1798* (Clarendon Press, 1982).

Genet-Rouffiac, Nathalie, *Le Grand Exil: Les Jacobites en France, 1688–1715* (Service Historique de la Défense, 2007).

Gilbert, Alan D., 'Methodism, dissent and political stability in early industrial England', *Journal of Religious History*, 10 (1979), 381–99.

Gilbert, Arthur N., 'Law and honour among eighteenth-century British army officers', *HJ*, 19 (1976), 75–87.

Gilbert, Arthur N., 'Military and civilian justice in eighteenth-century England: an assessment', *JBS*, 17 (1978), 41–65.

Gill, Nick, *Carceral Spaces: Mobility and Agency in Imprisonment and Migrant Detention* (Routledge, 2016).

Gill, Nick, Deirdre Conlon, and Dominique Moran, 'Carceral circuitry: new directions in carceral geography', *Progress in Human Geography*, 42 (2018), 183–204.

Glaisyer, Natasha, 'Networking, Trade and Exchange in the Eighteenth-Century British Empire », *HJ*, 42 (2004), p. 451–76.

Glueck, Sheldon, 'The Nuremberg Trial and aggressive war', in Guénaël Mettraux (ed.), *Perspectives on the Nuremberg Trial* (Oxford UP, 2008), 72–119.

Goffman, Erving, *Asylums: Essays on the Social Situation of Mental Patients and Other Inmates* (Penguin Books, 1991 (1961)).

Goffman, Stigma, *Notes on the Management of Spoiled Identity* (Prentice-Hall, 1963).

Goodhart, Arthur L., 'The legality of the Nuremberg trials', in Mettraux (ed.), *Perspectives*, 626–37.

Gould, Eliga H., 'Zones of law, zones of violence: the legal geography of the British Atlantic, circa 1772', *WMQ*, 60 (2003), 471–510.

Gould, Eliga H., 'Entangled histories, entangled worlds: the English-speaking Atlantic as a Spanish periphery', *AHR*, 112 (2007), 764–86.

Graham, Aaron, 'The British fiscal-military states, 1660–1830', in Aaron Graham and Patrick Walsh (eds.), *The British Fiscal-Military States, 1660–c. 1783* (Routledge, 2016).

Graham, Aaron, and Patrick Walsh (eds.), *The British Fiscal-Military States, 1660–c. 1783* (Routledge, 2016).

Graham, Gerald S., 'Napoleon's naval gaolers', *JICH*, 7 (1978), 3–17.

Greene, Jack P., *Negotiated Authorities: Essays in Colonial and Constitutional History* (University Presses of Virginia, 1994).

Greenwood, Christopher, 'The concept of war in modern international law', *ICLQ*, 36 (1987), 283–306.

Gregory, Derek, 'The black flag: Guantanamo Bay and the space of exception', *Geografiska Annaler*, 88 (2006), 405–27.

Gross, Oren, and Fionnuala Ni Aolain, *Law in Times of Crisis: Emergency Powers in Theory and Practice* (Cambridge UP, 2006).

Grove, A.T., 'St Helena as a microcosm of the EIC world', in Vinita Damdaran, Anna Winterbottom, and Alan Lester (eds.), *The East India Company and the Natural World* (Palgrave Macmillan, 2014), 249–69.

Gulliver, P.H., *Disputes and Negotiations: A Cross-Cultural Perspective* (Academic Press, 1979).

Gunn, Steven, 'War and the emergence of the state: Western Europe, 1350–1600', in Tallett and Trim (eds.), *European Warfare*, 50–73.

Guyer, Jane I., *Marginal Gains: Monetary Transactions in Atlantic Africa* (Chicago UP, 2004).

Hale Bellot, H., 'The detention of Napoleon Buonaparte', *Law Quarterly Review*, 39 (1923), 170–92.

Halliday, Paul, *Habeas Corpus: From England to Empire* (Harvard UP, 2010).

Halliday, Paul, 'Law's histories: pluralisms, pluralities, diversity', in Benton and Ross (eds.), *Legal Pluralism*, 261–77.

Halliday, Paul, 'Subjecthood made at sea: the case of the prisoner of war', unpublished paper, Centre for History and Economics, Cambridge (2013).

Halttunen, Karen, 'Humanitarianism and the pornography of pain in Anglo-American culture', *AHR*, 100 (1995), 203–334.

Hamburger, Philip, 'Beyond protection', *Columbia Law Review*, 109 (2009), 1823–2001.

Harcourt, Bernard, 'From the asylum to the prison: rethinking the incarceration revolution', *Texas Law Review*, 84 (2006), 1751–2135.

Harding, Richard, *Amphibious Warfare in the Eighteenth Century: The British Expedition to the West Indies 1740–1742* (RHS-Boydell Press, 1991).

Harling, Philip, and Peter Mandler, 'From "fiscal-military state" to laissez faire state, 1760–1850', *JBS*, 32 (1993).

Harling, Philip, *The Waning of 'Old Corruption': The Politics of Economical Reform in Britain, 1779–1846* (Cambridge UP, 1996).

Harris, James A., 'The early reception of Hume's theory of justice', in Ruth Savage (ed.), *Philosophy and Religion in Enlightenment Britain* (Oxford UP, 2012), 210–30.

Hayat, Samuel, and Lucie Tangy, 'Exception(s)', *Tracés. Revue de Sciences humaines*, 20 (2011), 5–27.

Hayter, Tony, *The Army and the Crowd in Mid-Georgian England* (Macmillan, 1978).

Heller-Roazen, Daniel, *The Enemy of All: Piracy and the Law of Nations* (Zone Books, 2009).

Hempton, David, *Methodism and Politics in English Society 1750–1850* (Routledge, 1984).

Hershenzon, Daniel, 'The political economy of ransom in the early modern Mediterranean', *P&P*, 231 (2016), 61–95.

Hershenzon, Daniel, *The Captive Sea: Slavery, Communication, and Commerce in Early Modern Spain and the Mediterranean* (University of Pennsylvania Press (2018).

Heullant-Donat, Isabelle, Julie Claustre, and Elisabeth Lusset (eds.), *Enfermements: Le cloître et la prison (VIe–XVIIIe siècle)* (Publications de la Sorbonne, 2011).

Hindle, Steve, 'The keeping of the public peace', in Paul Griffiths, Adam Fox, and Steve Hindle (eds.), *The Experience of Authority in Early Modern England* (Basingstoke, 1996), 213–48.

Hodson, Christopher, and Brett Rushforth, 'Absolutely Atlantic: colonialism and the early modern French state in recent historiography', *HC*, 8 (2010), 101–17.

Holdsworth, W.S., *A History of English Law*, vol. IX (Methuen, 1926).

Hole, Robert, *Pulpits, Politics and Public Order in England: 1760–1832* (Cambridge UP, 1989).

Hoock, Holger, 'Mangled bodies: atrocity in the American revolutionary war', *P&P*, 230 (2016), 123–59.

Hopkins, A.G., 'Back to the future: from national history to imperial history', *P&P*, 164 (1999), 198–243.

Hoppit, Julian, 'Compulsion, compensation and property rights in Britain, 1688–1833', *P&P*, 210 (2011), 93–128.

Hoppit, Julian, 'Compensating imperial loyalty, 1700–1800', unpublished (2015).

Houlding, J.A., *Fit for Service: The Training of the British Army, 1715–1795* (Clarendon Press, 1981).

Howard, Michael, 'Constraints on warfare', in Howard et al. (eds.), *Laws of War*, 1–11.

Howard, Michael, George J. Andropoulos, and Mark R. Shulman (eds.), *The Laws of War: Constraints in Warfare in the Western World* (Yale UP, 1994).

Howson, Gerald, *The Macaroni Parson: A Life of the Unfortunate Dr Dodd* (Hutchinson, 1973).

Hunt, Lynn, *Inventing Human Rights: A History* (WW. Norton & Company, 2007).

Ignatieff, Michael, *A Just Measure of Pain: The Penitentiary in the Industrial Revolution 1750–1850* (Penguin, 1978).

Ignatieff, Michael, 'State, civil society and total institutions: a critique of recent social histories of punishment', *Crime and Justice*, 3 (1981), 153–92.

Innes, Joanna, 'Prisons for the poor: English bridewells, 1555–1800', in Francis Snyder and Douglas Hay (eds.), *Labour, Law, and Crime: An Historical Perspective* (Tavistock Publications, 1987), 42–122.

Innes, Joanna, 'Legislation and public participation 1760–1830', in David Lemmings (ed.), *The British and their Laws in the Eighteenth Century* (The Boydell Press, 2005), 102–32.

Innes, Joanna, 'The King's Bench prison in the later eighteenth century: law, authority and order in a London debtor's prison', in *Inferior Politics: Social Problems and Social Politics in Eighteenth-Century Britain* (Oxford UP, 2009), 227–78.

Inwards, Harry, *Straw Hats: Their History and Manufacture* (University of California Libraries, 1922).

Iverson, John R., 'La gloire humanisée? Voltaire et son siècle', *HES*, 20 (2001), 211–8.

James, Trevor, *Prisoners of War at Dartmoor: American and French Soldiers and Sailors in an English Prison during the Napoleon Wars and the War of 1812* (McFarland, 2013).

Jarrousse, Frédéric, *Auvergnats malgré eux: Prisonniers de guerre et déserteurs étrangers dans le Puy-de-Dôme pendant la Révolution française, 1794–1796* (Presses Universitaires Blaise Pascal, 1998).

Jarvis, Michael, 'Maritime masters and seafaring slaves in Bermuda, 1680–1783', *WMQ*, 59 (2002), 585–622.

Jewkes, Yvonne, 'On carceral space and agency', in Dominique Moran, Nick Gill, and Deirdre Conlon (eds.), *Carceral Spaces: Mobility and Agency in Imprisonment and Migrant Detention* (Ashgate, 2013), 127–32.

Joannic-Séta, Frédérique, *Le Bagne de Brest: Naissance d'une institution carcérale au siècle des Lumières* (PUR, 2000).

Johnson, Bill, *The History of Bodmin Jail. Compiled, edited and arranged from Contemporary Sources* (Bodmin Town Museum, 2009).

Johnson, James T., *The Just War Tradition and the Restraint of War: A Moral and Historical Inquiry* (Princeton UP, 1984).

Jones, Colin, 'Some recent trends in the history of charity', in Martin Daunton (ed.), *Charity, Self-Interest and Welfare in the English Past* (UCL Press, 1996), 51–63.

Jones, Colin, 'The construction of the hospital patient in early modern France', in Norbert Fintzsche and Robert Jütte (eds.), *The Institutions of Confinement: Hospitals, Asylums and Prisons in Western Europe and North America, 1500–1950* (Cambridge UP, 1996), 55–76.

Jones, Colin and Simon Macdonald, 'Robespierre, the Duke of York, and Pisistratus during the French revolutionary terror', *HJ*, 61 (2017), 643–72.

Jones, Heather, *Violence Against Prisoners of War in the First World War: Britain, France and Germany, 1914–1920* (Cambridge UP, 2011).

Jütte, Daniel, *The Strait Gate: Thresholds and Power in Western History* (Yale UP, 2015).

Kaiser, Wolfgang (dir.), *Le commerce des captifs: Les intermédiaires dans l'échange et le rachat des prisonniers en Méditerranée, XVe–XVIIIe siècle* (EFR, 2008).

Kaplan, Amy, 'Where is Guantanamo?', *American Quarterly*, 57 (2005), 831–58.

Kauffman, Kelsey, 'Officer code', in Bosworth, *Encyclopedia*, 649–51.

Keen, Maurice, *The Laws of War in the Late Middle Ages* (Routledge, 1965).

Kelly, James, 'Official list of radical activists and suspected activists involved in Emmet's rebellion, 1803', *Analecta Hibernica*, 43 (2012), pp. 129–200.

Kenney, Padraic, *Dance in Chains: Political Imprisonment in the Modern World* (Oxford UP, 2017).

Kert, Faye M., *Privateering: Patriots and Profits in the War of 1812* (John's Hopkins UP, 2005).

Kiernan, V.G., 'Foreign mercenaries and absolute monarchy', *P&P*, 11 (1957), 66–86.

Kim, Keechang, *Aliens in Medieval Law: The Origins of Modern Citizenship* (Cambridge UP, 2001).

King, Ryan S., 'Governance', in Bosworth, *Encyclopedia*, 377–80.

Klein, Herbert S., Stanley L. Engerman, Robin Haines, and Ralph Shlomowitz, 'The slave trade in comparative perspective', *WMQ*, 58 (2001), 93–118.

Knight, Betsie, 'Prisoner exchange and parole in the American Revolution', *WMQ*, 48 (1994), 201–22.

Knight, Roger, *Britain against Napoleon: The Organization of Victory, 1793–1815* (Allen Lane, 2013).

Koot, Christian, *Empire at the Periphery: British Colonists, Anglo-Dutch Trade, and the Development of the British Atlantic, 1621–1713* (NYU Press, 2011).

Kopytoff, Igor, 'The cultural biography of things: commodification as process', in Arjun Appadurai (ed.), *The Social Life of Things: Commodities in Cultural Perspective* (Cambridge UP, 1986), 64–92.

Kretzmer, David, 'Civilian immunity: legal aspects', in Igor Primoratz (ed.), *Civilian Immunity in War*, 21–41.

Kroener, Bernhard R., 'The modern state and military society in the eighteenth century', in Contamine (ed.), *War and Competition*, 195–220.

Kverndal, Roald, *Seamen's Missions: Their Origins and Early Growth* (Wm. Carey Library, 1986).

Kverndal, Roald, 'Sowing by sea: empowering seafarers with the Gospel', in Stephen Batalden, Kathleen Cann, and John Dean (eds.), *Sowing the Word: The Cultural Impact of the British and Foreign Bible Society 1804–2004* (Sheffield Phoenix Press, 2004).

Lagadec, Yann, Youenn Le Prat, and Stéphane Perréon, 'Un aspect des relations trans-Manche: les échanges de prisonniers de guerre depuis la Bretagne pendant la Seconde guerre de Cent Ans (1689–1815)', *Mémoires de la Société d'histoire et d'archéologie de Bretagne*, 2013, 257–84.

Landers, Jane, *Black Society in Spanish Florida* (University of Illinois Press, 1999).

Langford, Paul, *Public Life and the Propertied Englishman, 1689–1798* (Oxford UP, 1991).

Latour, Bruno, 'On technical mediation: philosophy, sociology, genealogy', *Common Knowledge*, 3 (1994), 29–64.

Latour, Bruno, *Reassembling the Social: An Introduction to Actor-Network Theory* (Oxford UP, 2005).

Lauterpacht, Hersch, 'The problem of the revision of the law of war', *British Yearbook of International Law*, 29 (1952), 360–82.

Le Carvèse, Patrick,'Les prisonniers français en Grande-Bretagne de 1803 à 1814', *Napoleonica. La Revue*, 2 (2010), 3–29.

Lee, Wayne E., 'Peace chiefs and blood revenge: patterns of restraint in native American warfare, 1500–1800', *JMiH*, 71 (2007), 701–41.

Lee, Wayne E., *Barbarians and Brothers: Anglo-American Warfare, 1500–1865* (Oxford UP, 2011).

Lefebvre, Henri, *The Production of Space*, trans. Donald Nicholson-Smith (Oxford: Blackwell, 1991).

Leeson, Peter T., *Anarchy Unbound: Why Self-Governance Works Better Than You Think* (Cambridge UP, 2014).

Leeson, Peter T., and Alex Nowrasteh, 'Was privateering plunder efficient?', *Journal of Economic Behavior and Organization*, 79 (2011), 303–17.

Le Goff, T.J.A., 'L'impact des prises effectuées par les Anglais sur la capacité en hommes de la marine française au XVIIIᵉ siècle', in Martina Acerra and Jean Meyer (eds.), *Les marines de guerre européennes, XVIIe–XVIIIe siècles* (Presses de l'Université de Paris Sorbonne, 1985), 103–22.

Le Goff, T.J.A., 'Problèmes de recrutement de la marine française pendant la Guerre de Sept Ans', *RH*, 283 (1990), 205–33.

Lemieux, Cyril, 'De la thérie de l'habitus à la sociologie des épreuves: relire *L'Expérience concentrationnaire*', in Liora Israël and Daniel Voldman (eds.), *Michaël Pollak: De l'identité blessée à une sociologie des possibles* (Complexe, 2008), 179–205.

Le Prat, Youenn, 'Faire face à la détention: représentations et stratégies des prisonniers de guerre marins dans le Finistère (1794–1795)', in Laurent Jalabert (ed.), *Les prisonniers de guerre (XVe–XIXe siècles): Entre marginalisation et reconnaissance* (PUR, 2018), 213–32.

Leunig, Tim, Jelle van Lottum, and Bo Poulsen, 'Surprisingly gentle confinement: British treatment of Danish and Norwegian prisoners of war during the Napoleonic Wars', *Scandinavian Economic History Review*, 66 (2018), 282–97.

Lewis, Michael, *Napoleon and his British captives* (George Allen & Unwin, 1962).

Lewis, W.S. and R.M. Williams, *Private Charity in England* (Yale UP, 1938).

Liebling, Alison, 'Distinctions and distinctiveness in the work of prison officers: legitimacy and authority revisited', *European Journal of Criminology* 8 (2011), 484–99.

Lilti, Antoine, *Figures publiques: L'invention de la célébrité 1750-1850* (Fayard, 2014).

Lindegren, Jan, 'Men, money, and means', in Contamine (ed.), *War and Competition*, 129–62.

Linebaugh, Peter, *The London Hanged: Crime and Civil Society in the Eighteenth Century* (Allen Lane, 1991).

Linhardt, Dominique, and Cédric Moreau de Bellaing, 'Ni guerre, ni paix: dislocations de l'ordre politique et décantonnements de la guerre', *Politix*, 26 (2013), 9–23.

Lipkowitz, Elise, '"The sciences are never at war?": the republic of science in the era of the French Revolution, 1789-1815', PhD dissertation, Chicago, Northwestern University, 2009.

Lloyd, Clive L., *The Arts and Crafts of Napoleonic and American Prisoners of War 1756-1816* (Antique Collector's Club, 2007).

Lovegrove, Deryck, *Established Church, Sectarian People: Itinerancy and the Transformation of English Dissent, 1780-1830* (Cambridge UP, 2004).

Luban, David, 'Military necessity and the cultures of military law', *Leiden Journal of International Law*, 26 (2013), 315–49.

Lutz, Catherine, and Kathleen Millar, 'War', in Didier Fassin (ed.), *A Companion to Moral Anthropology* (John Wiley & Sons, 2012), 482–99.

MacKenzie, S.P., 'The treatment of prisoners of war in World War II', *JMH*, 66 (1994), 487–520.

MacKenzie, Norman, 'Napoleon: An extraordinary rendition', *History Today*, 60 (2010).

Malcomson, Thomas, *Order and Disorder in the British Navy, 1793-1815* (Boydell & Brewer, 2016).

Malešević, Siniša, *The Sociology of War and Violence* (Cambridge UP, 2010).

Marchal, Roland, 'Les frontières de la guerre', *Politix*, 15 (2002), 39–59.

Marks, Sally, '"My name is Ozymandias": the Kaiser in exile', *Central European History*, 16 (1983), 122–70.

Markus, Thomas, *Buildings and Power: Freedom and Control in the Origins of Modern Building Types* (Routledge, 1993).

Marquart, James W., 'Prison guards and the use of physical coercion as a means of prisoner control', *Criminology*, 24 (1986), 347–66.

Marquis, Hugues, 'La Convention et les prisonniers de guerre des armées étrangères', *HES*, 3 (2008), p. 65–81.

Masson, Philippe, *Les sépulcres flottants: Prisonniers français en Angleterre sous l'Empire* (Ouest France, 1987).

Mathiesen, Thomas, *The Defences of the Weak: A Sociological Study of a Norwegian Correctional Institution* (1965), 3rd ed. (Routledge, 2012).

Mattéi, Jean-Mathieu, *Histoire du droit de la guerre (1700-1819): Introduction à l'histoire du droit international* (Presses Universitaires d'Aix-Marseille, 2006).

Maurice, Sir John Frederick, *Hostilities without Declaration of War from 1700 to 1870 (1883)* (Kessinger Publishing, 2010).

McAleer, John, 'Looking east: St. Helena, the South Atlantic and Britain's Indian Ocean world', *Atlantic Studies*, 13 (2016), 78–98.

McCleery, Richard H., 'The governmental process and informal social control', in D.R. Cressey (ed.), *The Prison: Studies in Institutional Organization and Change* (Holt, Rinehart and Winston, 1961).

McConville, Sean, *A History of English Prison Administration: Volume I. 1750–1877* (Routledge & Kegan Paul, 1981).

McCormack, Matthew, 'The new militia: war, politics and gender in 1750s Britain', *Gender & History*, 19 (2007), 483–500.

McGowen, Randall, 'The body and punishment in eighteenth-century England', *JMH*, 59 (1987), 651–79.

McGowen, Randall, 'Civilizing punishment: the end of the public execution in England', *Journal of British Studies*, 33 (1994), 257–82.

McGowen, Randall, 'The well-ordered prison: England, 1780–1865', in Norval Morris and D. J. Rothman (eds.), *The Oxford History of the Prison: The Practice of Punishment in Western Society* (Oxford UP: 1997), 79–110.

McKeogh, Colm, 'Civilian immunity in war: from Augustine to Vattel', in Igor Primoratz (ed.), *Civilian Immunity*, 62–83.

McLeod, Emma, *A War of Ideas? British Attitudes towards the French Revolutionary Wars, 1792–1802* (Ashgate, 1998).

McManimon, Patrick F., 'Deprivation', in Bosworth, *Encyclopedia*, 225–6.

McNeill, John, *Mosquito Empires: Ecology and War in the Greater Caribbean, 1620–1914* (Cambridge UP: 2010).

Megill, Allan, 'The reception of Foucault by historians', *Journal of the History of Ideas*, 48 (1987), 117–41.

Mégret, Frédéric, 'From "savages" to "unlawful combatants": a postcolonial look at international humanitarian law's "other"', in Anne Orford (ed.), *International Law and its Others* (Cambridge UP, 2006), 265–317.

Melikan, R.A., 'Caging the Emperor: the legal basis for detaining Napoleon Bonaparte', *Tijdschrift voor Rechtsgeschiedenis*, 67 (1999), 349–62.

Melikan, Rose A., *John Scott, Lord Eldon, 1751–1838: The Duty of Loyalty* (Cambridge UP, 1999).

Mennell, Stephen, 'Les anthropologues et l'agonisticisme du développement', in Sophie Chevalier and Jean-Marie Privat (eds.), *Norbert Elias et l'Anthropologie* (CNRS Editions, 2004), 53–64.

Meyer, Jean, and Martine Acerra, *Histoire de la Marine française: des origines à nos jours* (Ouest-France, 1994).

Milhaud, Olivier, *Séparer et punir: Une géographie des prisons françaises* (CNRS, 2017).

Miller, Ken, *Dangerous Guests: Enemy Captives and Revolutionary Communities during the War for Independence* (Cornell UP, 2014).

Mintzker, Yair, *The Defortification of the German City, 1689–1866* (Cambridge UP, 2012).

Moir, Esther, 'Sir George Onesiphorus Paul', in H.P.R. Finberg (ed.), *Gloucestershire Studies* (Leicester UP, 1957), 195–225.

Moniz, Amanda B., *From Empire to Humanity: The American Revolution and the Origins of Humanitarianism* (Oxford UP, 2016).

Moore, Bob, and Barbara Hately-Broad (eds.), *Prisoners of War, Prisoners of Peace* (Bloomsbury, 2005).

Moran, Dominique, *Carceral Geography: Spaces and Practices of Incarceration* (Ashgate, 2015).

Moran, Dominique, and Yvonne Jewkes, 'Linking the carceral and the punitive state: a review', *Annales de Géographie*, 702–703 (2015), 163–84.

Morieux, Renaud, 'French prisoners of war, conflicts of honour and social inversions in England, 1744–1783', *HJ*, 56 (2013), 55–88.

Morieux Renaud, 'Patriotisme humanitaire et prisonniers de guerre en France et en Grande-Bretagne pendant la Révolution française et l'Empire', in Laurent Bourquin et al. (eds.), *La politique par les armes: Conflits internationaux et politisation, XVe-XIXe siècles* (PUR, 2014), 301–16.

Morieux, Renaud, 'Anglo-French fishing disputes and maritime boundaries in the North Atlantic (1700–1850)', in Peter Mancall and Carole Shammas (eds.), *Governing the Sea in the Early Modern Era* (Huntingdon Library Press, 2015), 41–75.

Morieux, Renaud, *The Channel: England, France, and the Construction of A Maritime Border* (Cambridge UP, 2016).

Morieux, Renaud, 'Indigenous comparisons', in John Arnold, Matthew Hilton and Jan Rüger (eds.), *History after Hobsbawm: Writing the Past for the Twenty-First Century* (Oxford UP, 2017), 50–75.

Morieux, Renaud, 'Le dilemme de la sentinelle: droit de la guerre et droits des prisonniers de guerre en Grande-Bretagne au dix-huitième siècle', *RHMC*, 64 (2017), 39–67.

Morriss, Roger, *Science, Utility, and Maritime Power: Samuel Bentham in Russia, 1779–91* (Ashgate, 2015).

Morriss, Roger, *The Foundations of British Maritime Ascendency: Resources, Logistics and the State, 1755–1815* (Cambridge UP, 2010).

Mountz, Alison, 'The enforcement archipelago: detention, haunting, and asylum on islands', *Political Geography*, 30 (2011), 118–28.

Mulcahy, Matthew, *Hurricanes and Society in the British Greater Caribbean, 1624–1783* (Johns Hopkins UP, 2008).

Mulcahy, Matthew, *Hubs of Empire: The Southeastern Lowcountry and the British Caribbean* (Johns Hopkins UP, 2014).

Muldrew, Craig, *The Economy of Obligation: The Culture of Credit and Social Relations in Early Modern England* (Basingstoke, 1998).

Neff, Stephen C., *War and the Law of Nations: A General History* (Cambridge UP, 2005).

Neff, Stephen C., 'Prisoners of war in international law: the nineteenth century', in Sibylle Scheipers (ed.), *Prisoners in War* (Oxford UP, 2010), 57–74.

Nevell, Richard, 'Castles as prisons', *The Castle Studies Group Journal*, 28 (2014–15), 203–24.

Newman, Simon, *A New World of Labor: The Development of Plantation Slavery in the British Atlantic* (University of Pennsylvania Press, 2013).

Nicolas, Jean, *La rébellion française: Mouvements populaires et conscience sociale 1661–1789*, 2nd ed. (Gallimard, 2008).

Nicolson, Adam, *Sissinghurst: An Unfinished History* (HarperPress, 2009).

Noiriel, Gérard, *Etat, nation et immigration: Vers une histoire du pouvoir* (Belin, 2001).

O'Brien, Patricia, *The Promise of Punishment: Prisons in Nineteenth-Century France* (Princeton UP, 1982).

O'Brien, Patrick, 'The nature and historical evolution of an exceptional fiscal state and its possible significance for the precocious commercialization and industrialization of the British economy from Cromwell to Nelson', *Economic History Review*, 64 (2011), 408–46.

O'Higgins, Paul, 'The treaty of Limerick 1691', in C.H. Alexandrowick (ed.), *Studies in the History of the Law of Nations*, Grotian Society Papers 1968 (Martinjus Nijhoff, 1970), 212–32.

Oldfield, J.R., *Popular Politics and British Anti-Slavery: The Mobilisation of Public Opinion against the Slave Trade, 1787–1807* (Routledge, 1998).

Oldham, James, *The Mansfield Manuscripts and the Growth of English Law in the Eighteenth Century* (University of Carolina Press, 1992).

Oldham, James, *English Common Law in the Age of Mansfield* (University of North Carolina Press, 2004).

Oliver, Vere Langford, *History of the Island of Antigua, One of the Leeward Caribbees in the West Indies*, vol. I (Mitchell and Hugues, 1894).

O'Malley, Gregory, *Final Passages: The Intercolonial Slave Trade of British America, 1619-1807* (University of North Carolina Press, 2016).

O'Shaughnessy, Andrew Jackson, *An Empire Divided: The American Revolution and the British Caribbean* (University of Pennsylvania Press, 2010).

Pares, Richard, *War and Trade in the West Indies, 1739-1763* (Oxford UP, 1936).

Pares, Richard, 'The manning of the navy in the West Indies, 1702-63', *Transactions of the RHS*, 20 (1937), 31-60.

Pares, Richard, 'Prisoners of war in the West Indies in the eighteenth century', *Journal of the Barbados Museum and Historical Society*, 5 (1937), 12-7.

Pares, Richard, *Yankees and Creoles: The Trade between North America and the West Indies before the American Revolution* (Harvard UP, 1956).

Parker, Geoffrey, *The Military Revolution, Military innovation and the rise of the West, 1500-1800* (Cambridge UP, 1988).

Parker, Geoffrey, 'Early modern Europe', in Howard et al., *Laws of War*, 40-58.

Parrott, David, 'From military enterprise to standing armies: war, state and society in western Europe', in Tallett and Trim (eds.), *European Warfare*, 74-95.

Paton, Diana, *No Bond but the Law: Punishment, Race, and Gender in Jamaican State Formation, 1780-1870* (Duke UP, 2004).

Peabody, Sue and Keila Grinberg, 'Free soil: the generation and circulation of an Atlantic legal principle', *Slavery & Abolition*, 32 (2011), 331-9.

Perl-Rosenthal, Nathan, *Citizen Sailors: Becoming American in the Age of Revolution* (Harvard UP, 2015).

Perréon, Stéphane, *L'armée en Bretagne au XVIIIe siècle: Institution militaire et société civile au temps de l'intendance et des États* (PUR, 2005).

Perrot, Michelle (dir.), *L'Impossible prison: Recherches sur le système pénitentiaire au XIXe siècle* (Seuil, 1980).

Petit, Jacques-Guy, *Ces peines obscures: La Prison pénale en France, 1780-1875* (Fayard, 1990).

Philp, Mark, *Resisting Napoleon: The British Response to the Threat of Invasion, 1797-1815* (Routledge, 2006).

Piacentini, Laura, *Surviving Russian Prisons: Punishment, Economics and Politics in Transition* (Willan, 2012).

Pitt-Rivers, Julian, 'Social class in a French village', *Anthropological Quarterly*, 33 (1960), 1-13.

Pitt-Rivers, Julian, 'Honour and social status', in Jean Peristiany (ed.), *The Values of Mediterranean Society* (Weidenfeld & Nicolson, 1965), 19-78.

Po-Ching, Yu, 'Chinese seamen in London and St Helena in the early nineteenth century', in Maria Fusaro et al. (eds.), *Law, Labour and Empire: Comparative Perspectives on Seafarers, c. 1500-1800* (Palgrave Macmillan, 2015), 287-303.

Pollak, Michael, *L'expérience concentrationnaire: Essai sur le maintien de l'identité sociale* (Métailié, 1990).

Popkin, Jeremy, 'Facing racial revolution: captivity narratives and identity in the Saint-Domingue insurrection', *Eighteenth-Century Studies*, 36 (2003), 511-33.

Pottage, Alain, 'The materiality of what?', *Journal of Law and Society*, 39 (2012), 167–83.

Pradier-Fodéré, Paul, *Traité de droit international public européen et américain*, 8 vols. (G. Pedone-Lauriel, 1885–1906).

Prelinger, Catherine M., 'Benjamin Franklin and the American prisoners of war in England during the American Revolution', *WMQ*, 32 (1975), 261–94.

Press, Steven, 'Sovereignty at Guantánamo: new evidence and a comparative historical interpretation', *JMH*, 85 (2013), 592–631.

Price, Jacob M., 'The last phase of the Virginia-London consignment trade: James Buchanan and Co., 1758–1768', *WMQ*, 43 (1986), 64–98.

Pritchard, James, *Louis XV's Navy, 1748–1762: A Study of Organization and Administration* (McGill-Queen's UP, 1987).

Rachamimov, Alon, *POWs and the Great War: Captivity on the Eastern Front* (Oxford, Berg: 2002).

Rappaport, Stéphane, *La chaîne des forçats : 1792–1836* (Aubier, 2006).

Reith, Gerda, *The Age of Chance: Gambling in Western Culture* (Routledge, 1999).

Rhodes, Lorna A., 'Towards an anthropology of prisons', *Annual Review of Anthropology*, 30 (2001), 65–83.

Richardson, A. E., 'The architect of Dartmoor', *Architectural Review*, 43 (1918), 77–80.

Richter, Daniel K., 'War and culture: the Iroquois experience', *WMQ*, 40 (1983), 528–59.

Shapira, Rina and David Navon, 'Staff-inmates cooperation in Israeli prisons: towards a non-functionalistic theory of total institutions', *International Review of Modern Sociology*, 15 (1985), 131–46.

Robbins, Caroline, 'The strenuous Whig: Thomas Hollis of Lincoln's Inn', *WMQ*, 7 (1950), 407–53.

Roberts, Adam, 'The civilian in modern war', in Hew Strachan and Sibylle Scheipers (eds.), *The Changing Character of War* (Oxford UP, 2011), 357–77.

Roberts, M.J.D., 'The Society for the Suppression of Vice and its early critics, 1802–1812', *HJ*, 26 (1983), 159–76.

Roberts, M.J.D., *Making English Morals: Voluntary Association and Moral Reform in England, 1787–1886* (Cambridge UP, 2004).

Roberts, Simon, 'The study of dispute: anthropological perspectives', in John Bossy (ed.), *Disputes and settlements: Law and Human Relations in the West* (Cambridge UP, 1983), 1–24.

Robertson, William Spence, *Francisco de Miranda and the Revolutionizing of Spanish America* (Government Printing Office, 1909).

Rodger, C.J. (ed.), *The Military Revolution: Readings on the Military Transformation in Early Modern Europe* (Oxford UP, 1995).

Rodger, N.A.M., *The Wooden World: An Anatomy of the Georgian Navy* (Fontana Press, 1988.

Rodger, N.A.M., 'Honour and duty at sea, 1660–1815', *Historical Research*, 75 (2002), 425–47.

Rodger, N.A.M., *The Command of the Ocean: A Naval History of Britain, 1649–1815* (Penguin, 2005).

Rogal, Samuel J., 'John Wesley on war and peace', in *Studies in Eighteenth-Century Culture*, vol. 7 (Roseanne Runte ed.) (University of Wisconsin Press, 1978), 329–44.

Rogers, Nicholas, *Crowds, Culture and Politics in Georgian Britain* (Oxford UP, 1998).

Rogers, Nicholas, *The Press Gang: Naval Impressment and Its Opponents in Georgian Britain* (Continuum, 2007).

Rommelse, Gijs A., 'An early modern naval revolution? The relationship between "economic reason of state" and maritime warfare', *Journal of Maritime Research*, 13 (2011), 138–50.

Rommelse, Gijs A., and Roger Downing, 'State formation, maritime conflict and prisoners of war: the case of Dutch captives during the Second Anglo-Dutch War (1665–1667), *Tijdschrift voor Sociale en Economische Geschiedenis*, 11 (2014), 29–56.

Rommelse Gijs A., and Roger Downing, 'State formation and the private economy: Dutch prisoners of war in England, 1652–1674', *MM*, 104 (2018), 153–71.

Rosa, Hartmurt, *Social Acceleration: A New Theory of Modernity*, trans. Jonathan Trejo-Mathys (Columbia UP, 2015).

Rosas, Allan, *The Legal Status of Prisoners of War: A Study in International Humanitarian Law Applicable in Armed Conflicts* (Suomalainen Tiedeakatemia, 1976).

Rosenfeld, Sofia, 'Citizens of nowhere in particular: cosmopolitanism, writing, and political engagement in eighteenth-century Europe', *National Identities*, 4 (2013), 25–43.

Rostaing, Corinne, 'Pertinence et actualité du concept d'institution totale', in Amouroux and Blanc, *Erving Goffman*, 137–53.

Rothenberg, Gunther, 'The age of Napoleon', in Howard et al., *Laws of War*, 86–97.

Rowlands, Guy, *An Army in Exile: Louis XIV and the Irish Forces of James II in France, 1691–1698* (Royal Stuart Society, 2001).

Royle, Stephen A., 'St Helena as a Boer prisoner of war camp, 1900–2', *Journal of Historical Geography*, 24 (1998), 53–68.

Rubin, Alfred P., *The Law of Piracy* (Naval War College Press, 1988).

Rubin, Ashley T., 'Resistance or friction: understanding the significance of prisoners' secondary adjustments', *Theoretical Criminology*, 19 (2015), 23–42.

Rudé, George, *Hanoverian London 1714–1808* (Secker and Warburg, 1971).

Rupert, Linda M., '"Seeking the water of baptism": fugitive slaves and Imperial jurisdiction in the early modern Caribbean', in Benton and Ross (eds.), *Legal Pluralism*, 199–231.

Rutherford, G., 'The king against Luke Ryan', *MM*, 43 (1957), 28–38.

Savory, Reginald, 'The Convention of Ecluse, 1759–1762', *Journal of the Society for Army Historical Research*, 42 (1964), 68–77.

Scarry, Elaine, *The Body in Pain: The Making and Unmaking of the World* (Oxford UP, 1985).

Schein, Edgard H., 'The Chinese indoctrination program for prisoners of war', *Psychiatry*, 19 (1956), 149–72.

Scheipers, Sibylle, 'The status and protection of prisoners of war and detainees', in Strachan and Scheipers (eds.), *Changing Character*, 394–407.

Schneider, Jennifer E., 'Good time credit', in Bosworth, *Encyclopedia*, 374–5.

Schroeder, Paul W., *The Transformation of European Politics 1763–1848* (Oxford UP, 1994).

Schwartz, Stuart, *Sea of Storms: A History of Hurricanes in the Greater Caribbean from Columbus to Katrina* (Princeton UP, 2015).

Scott, Rebecca J., 'Paper thin: freedom and re-enslavement in the diaspora of the Haitian revolution', *Law and History Review*, 29 (2011), 1061–87.

Scouller, R.E., *The Armies of Queen Anne* (Clarendon Press, 1966).

Selesky, Harold E., 'Colonial America', in Howard et al., *The Laws of War*, 59–85.

Semmel, Stuart, *Napoleon and the British* (Yale UP, 2004).

Senellart, Michel, 'La qualification de l'ennemi chez Emer de Vattel', *Astérion*, 2 (2004) (asterion.revues.org).

Senior, W., 'Ransom bills', *Law Quarterly Review*, 34 (1918), 49–62.

Shaw, J.J.S., 'The Commission of Sick and Wounded and Prisoners, 1664–1667', *MM*, 25 (1939), 306–27.

Sheehan, W.J., 'Finding solace in eighteenth-century Newgate', in J.S. Cockburn (ed.), *Crime in England, 1550–1800* (Princeton UP, 1977), 229–45.

Shepard, Alexandra, *Accounting for Oneself: Worth, Status, and the Social Order in Early Modern England* (Cambridge UP, 2015).

Shoemaker, Robert B., 'The decline of public insult in London, 1660–1800', *P&P*, 169 (2000), 97–131.

Shoemaker, Robert, 'Male honour and the decline of public violence in eighteenth-century London', *SH*, 26 (2001), 190–208.

Shoemaker, Robert B., *The London Mob: Violence and Disorder in Eighteenth-Century England* (Hambledon Continuum, 2004).

Sirota, Brent, *The Christian Monitors: The Church of England and the Age of Benevolence* (Yale UP, 2016).

Skinner, Quentin, *Hobbes and Republican Liberty* (Cambridge UP, 2008).

Smith, Denis, *The Prisoners of Cabrera: Napoleon's Forgotten Soldiers 1809–1814* (Da Capo Press, 2001).

Snell, K.D.M., *Parish and Belonging: Community, Identity and Welfare in England and Wales 1700–1950* (Cambridge UP, 2006).

Sparks J. R., and A.E. Bottoms, 'Legitimacy and order in prisons', *British Journal of Sociology*, 46 (1995), 45–62.

Sparks, Richard, Anthony Bottoms, and Will Hay, *Prisons and the Problem of Order* (Clarendon Press, 1996).

Spector, Robert D., *Samuel Johnson and the Essay* (Praeger, 1997).

Speier, Hans, 'Honour and social structure', *Social Research*, 2 (1935), 74–97.

Spierenburg, Pieter (ed.), *The Emergence of Carceral Institutions: Prisons, Galleys, and Lunatic Asylums, 1550–1900* (Rotterdam, 1984).

Spierenburg, Pieter, *The Prison Experience: Disciplinary Institutions and their Inmates in Early Modern Europe* (Rutgers UP, 1991).

Spurr, John, 'A profane history of early modern oaths', *Transactions of the RHS*, 11 (2001), 37–63.

Stacey, Robert C., 'The age of chivalry', in Howard et al., *The Laws of War*, 27–39.

Stafford Smith, Clive, *Bad Men: Guantanamo Bay and the Secret Prisons* (W&N, 2008).

Starkey, Armstrong, 'Paoli to Stony Point: military ethics and weaponry during the American Revolution', *JMiH*, 58 (1994), 7–27.

Starkey, Armstrong, *War in the Age of Enlightenment, 1700–1789* (Praeger, 2003).

Staub, Michael E., *Madness is Civilization: When the Diagnostic was Social, 1948–1980* (University of Chicago Press, 2011).

Steadman, Philip, 'Samuel Bentham's Panopticon', *Journal of Bentham Studies*, 14 (2012), 1–30.

Steele, Ian Kenneth, *The English Atlantic, 1675–1740: An Exploration of Communication and Community* (Oxford UP, 1986).

Steele, Ian K., 'Surrendering rites: prisoners on colonial North American frontiers', in Stephen Taylor et al. (eds.), *Hanoverian Britain and Empire: Essays in Memory of Philip Lawson* (Boydell Press, 1998), 137–57.

Steele, Ian K., *Betrayals: Fort William Henry and the "Massacre"* (Oxford UP, 1993).

Steinhoff, Uwe, 'Killing civilians', in Strachan and Scheipers (eds.), *Changing Character*, 381–91.

Steppler, G.A., 'British military law, discipline, and the conduct of regimental courts martial in the later eighteenth century', *EHR*, 102 (1987), 859–86.

Stern, Peter, 'The white Indians of the Borderlands', *Journal of the Southwest*, 33 (1991), 262–81.

Stern, Philip J., *The Company-State: Corporate Sovereignty and the Early Modern Foundations of the British Empire in India* (Oxford UP, 2011).

Steyn, Johan, 'Guantanamo Bay: the legal black hole', *ICLQ*, 53 (2004), 1–15.

Stone, Lawrence (ed.), *An Imperial State at War: Britain from 1689 to 1815* (Routledge, 1994).

Storrs, Christopher (ed.), *The Fiscal-Military State in Eighteenth Century Europe* (Ashgate, 1999).

Sutcliffe, *British Expeditionary Warfare and the Defeat of Napoleon, 1793–1815* (Boydell & Brewer, 2016).

Swanson, Carl E., *Predators and Prizes: American Privateering and Imperial Warfare, 1739–1748* (University of North Carolina Press, 1991).

Sykes, Gresham M., *The Society of Captives: A Study of a Maximum Security Prison* (Princeton UP, 1958).

Tabraham, Chris, *Edinburgh Castle: Prisons of War*, (Historic Scotland, 2004).

Tarruell, Cecilia, 'Prisoners of war, captives or slaves? The Christian prisoners of Tunis and La Goleta in 1574', in Christian G. De Vito and Anne Gerritsen (eds.), *Micro-Spatial Histories of Global Labour* (Palgrave, 2018), 95–122.

Tazzioli, Martina, and Glenda Garelli, 'Containment beyond detention: the hotspot system and disrupted migration movements across Europe', *Environment and Planning D: Society and Space* (0: 2018), 1–19.

Thireau, Isabelle, and Hansheng Wang (eds.), 'Introduction', in *Disputes au village chinois: formes du juste et recompositions locales des espaces normatifs* (Editions de la MSH, 2001).

Thomas, James H., 'Quebec's Bishop as Pawn: Saint-Vallier's Imprisonment in England, 1704–1709', *CCHA, Historical Studies* 64 (1998), 151–60.

Thomas, Jim, and Patrick F. McManimon, Jr, 'Importation', in Bosworth (ed.), *Encyclopedia*, 461–2.

Thompson, Edward P., *Customs in Common* (Penguin, 1991).

Thompson, Heather Ann, *Blood in the Water: The Attica Prison Uprising of 1971* (Pantheon Books, 2016).

Thornton, Michael John, *Napoleon after Waterloo: England and the St-Helena Decision* (Stanford UP, 1968).

Tilghman, Douglas Campbell, 'Woodriff, Daniel (1756–1842)', *Australian Dictionary of Biography*, vol. II (Melbourne University Publishing, 1967).

Towsey, Mark, 'Imprisoned reading: French prisoners of war at the Selkirk subscription library, 1811–1814', in Charters et al., *Civilians and War*, 241–61.

Trombik, Emily, 'The incarceration of German prisoners in France: perspectives and the limits to projects of reintegration', *Champ Pénal/Penal Field*, 4 (2007) http://champpenal.revues.org/7433.

Truxes, Thomas M., *Defying Empire: Trading with the Enemy in Colonial New York* (Yale UP, 2008).

Tschumi, Bernard, *Architecture and Disjunction* (MIT Press, 1996).

Tsing, Anna Lowenhaupt, *Friction: An Ethnography of Global Connection* (Princeton UP, 2005).

Tuck, Richard, 'Democracy and Terrorism', in Richard Bourke and Raymond Guess (eds.), *Political Judgement. Essays for John Dunn* (Cambridge UP, 2009), 313–32.

Tuck, Richard, *The Rights of War and Peace: Political Thought and the International Order* (Oxford UP, 2001).

Turley, David, *The Culture of English Antislavery, 1780–1860* (Routledge, 1991).

Tycko, Sonia, 'The legality of prisoner of war labour in England, 1648–1655', *P&P*, forthcoming.

Useem, Bert, and Michael D. Reisig, 'Collective action in prisons: protests, disturbances, and riots', *Criminology*, 37 (1999), 735–59.

Van der Hoorn, Melanie, *Indispensable Eyesores: An Anthropology of Undesired Buildings* (Berghahn, 2009).

Vaughan, Alden T., and Daniel K. Richter, 'Crossing the cultural divide: Indians and New Englanders, 1605–1763', *Proceedings of the American Antiquarian Society*, 90 (1980), 23–95.

Vinter, Dorothy, 'Prisoners of war in Stapleton jail near Bristol', *Transactions of the Bristol and Gloucestershire Archeological Society*, 75 (1956), 134–70.

Voelz, Peter M., *Slave and Soldier: The Military Impact of Blacks in the Colonial Americas* (Garland, 1993).

Vo-Ha, Paul, *Rendre les armes: Le sort des vaincus, XVIe–XVIIe siecles* (Champ Vallon, 2017).

Wacquant, Loïc, 'The curious eclipse of prison ethnography in the age of mass incarceration', *Ethnography*, 3 (2002).

Wahnich, Sophie, 'La Révolution française comme conflit d'intolérables: comment définir l'inhumanité en période révolutionnaire', in Fassin and Bourdelais (eds.), *Constructions* (La Découverte, 2005), 51–90.

Wahnich, Sophie, *L'impossible citoyen: L'étranger dans le discours de la Révolution française* (Albin Michel, 1997).

Wahrman, Dror, 'The English problem of identity during the American Revolution', *AHR*, 106 (2001), 1236–62.

Walker, Thomas James, *The Depot for Prisoners of War at Norman Cross Huntingtonshire, 1796 to 1816* (Constable & Company, 1913).

Walton, Charles, *Policing Public Opinion in the French Revolution: The Culture of Calumny and the Problem of Free Speech* (Oxford UP, 2011).

Walzer, Michael, 'Prisoners of war: does the fight continue after the battle?', *APSR*, 63 (1969), 777–86.

Ward, Kerry, *Networks of Empire: Forced Migration in the Dutch East India Company* (Cambridge UP, 2009).

Watson, P.K., 'The Commission for victualling the Navy, the Commission for sick and wounded seamen and prisoners of War and the Commission for Transport 1702–1714', PhD dissertation (University of London, 1965).

Weiss, Gillian, *Captives and Corsairs: France and Slavery in the Early Modern Mediterranean* (Stanford UP, 2011).

Wener, Richard E., *The Environmental Psychology of Prisons and jails* (Cambridge UP, 2012).

Western, Bruce, 'Introduction to the Princeton Classic edition', in Sykes, *Society*, ix–xxv.

White, Jerry, *Mansions of Misery: A Biography of the Marshalsea Debtors' Prison* (Bodley Head: 2016).

Whiting, J.R.S., *Prison Reform in Gloucestershire, 1776–1820: A Study of the Work of Sir George Onesiphorus Paul, Bart* (Phillimore: 1975).

Whitman, James Q., *The Verdict of Battle: The Law of Victory and the Making of Modern War* (Harvard UP, 2014).

Wilson, Kathleen, *The Sense of the People: Politics, Culture and Imperialism in England, 1715–1785* (Cambridge UP, 1994).

Wilson, Peter, 'Prisoners in early modern warfare', in Scheipers (ed.), *Prisoners*, 39–57.

Witt, John Fabian, *Lincoln's Code: The Laws of War in American History* (Free Press, 2013).

Wolff, Valérie, 'Le sens de l'urgence à l'hôpital', *Bioéthique Online*, 5/37 (2016).

Wood, Marcus, *Blind Memory: Visual Representations of Slavery in England and America, 1780–1865* (Manchester UP, 2000).

Wright, Quincy, 'The Legal liability of the Kaiser', *APSR*, 13 (1919), 120–8.

Wrightson, Keith, 'The politics of the parish in early modern England', in Griffiths, Fox, and Hindle (eds.), *Experience of Authority*, 10–46.

Yingling, Charlton W., 'The maroons of Santo Domingo in the age of revolutions: adaptation and evasion, 1783–1800', *HWJ*, 79 (2015), 25–51.

Young, Norman, *Napoleon in Exile: St Helena (1815–1821)*, 2 vols. (Stanley Paul, 1915).

Yonge, Charles Duke, *The Constitutional History of England From 1760 to 1860* (Harper & Brothers, 1882).

Zabin, Serena R., *Dangerous Economies: Status and Commerce in Imperial New York* (University of Pennsylvania Press, 2009).

Zahedieh, Nuala, 'The merchants of Port Royal, Jamaica, and the Spanish contraband trade, 1655–1692', *WMQ*, 43 (1986), 570–93.

Zahedieh, Nuala, 'A frugal, prudential and hopeful trade: privateering in Jamaica, 1655–89', *JICH*, 18 (1990), 145–68.

Zanetti, Véronique, 'Women, war, and international law', in Primoratz (ed.), *Civilian Immunity*, 217–38.

Zemon, Davis Natalie, 'Rites of violence: religious riots in sixteenth-century France', *P&P*, 59 (1973), 51–91.

Zurbuchen, Simone, 'Vattel's *law of nations* and just war theory', *History of European Ideas*, 35 (2009), 408–17.

Index

Printed and bound by CPI Group (UK) Ltd, Croydon, CR0 4YY